FIELD MARSHAL VISCOUNT ALANBROOKE
from an unfinished portrait by R. G. Eves, R.A., painted in
the summer of 1940 and reproduced by kind permission of
the Honourable Artillery Company

ARTHUR BRYANT

THE TURN
OF THE TIDE
1939-1943

*A Study based on the Diaries and
Autobiographical Notes of Field Marshal
The Viscount Alanbrooke*

K.G., O.M.

COLLINS
ST JAMES'S PLACE, LONDON
1957

PRINTED IN GREAT BRITAIN

COLLINS CLEAR-TYPE PRESS: LONDON AND GLASGOW

For
ALANBROOKE
whose war diaries are the jewel
for which this book is
the setting

FOREWORD

by Field Marshal Lord Alanbrooke

I AM grateful to Arthur Bryant for having written this book and for making known, while interest in the late War persists, both the story of what my colleagues of the Chiefs of Staff Committee and I tried to achieve in concert, and the lessons of our joint experience—lessons, I believe, of enduring value in the life of our nation. Naturally the book, based as it is on my personal diaries and auto-biographical notes, stresses my own viewpoint and experience rather than that of my colleagues whose part in shaping the strategy that led to victory was at least as great as mine. Inevitably, too, it revives old controversies —between ourselves, with our allies and, occasionally, with the political chiefs who were our comrades in adversity, struggle and, ultimately, triumph.

A diary is necessarily an impulsive and therefore somewhat unbalanced record of events. If in writing it I sometimes gave vent to criticisms of my colleagues and of the great man to whom, above all others, we owe our national survival, that criticism needs to be set, as Sir Arthur Bryant has set it, against the background of theirs and Churchill's titanic services to Britain and of my own admiration and affection for him. Such scattered expressions of irritation and impatience at the defects that arose out of his very greatness are insignificant when set against the magnitude of his achievement. My abiding impression of him remains that expressed by an entry in my diary made in the heat and stress of war: " He is quite the most wonderful man I have ever met, and it is a source of never-ending interest studying him and getting to realise that occasionally such human beings make their appearance on this earth—human beings who stand out head and shoulders above all others."

ALANBROOKE

Hartley Wintney,
December, 1956

CONTENTS

LIST OF MAPS

Prelude

A PARTNERSHIP IN GENIUS

My long experience in these matters had taught me that a Minister of Defence must work with and through responsible advisers—that is to say, war chiefs who can give effect to the decisions taken and are accountable for the results.

WINSTON CHURCHILL

O N THE September night that saw the completion of Hitler's conquest of Poland a British lieutenant-general, crossing from Southampton to Cherbourg, began to keep, for the wife to whom he had just bidden farewell, a private diary of his thoughts and experiences. Written in a succession of small leather lock-up pocket-books, bought at a Salisbury bookshop out of remaindered stock from the *Queen Mary*, and consigned, as each was completed, to his wife for safe keeping, " my evening talk with you on paper," as he called it, became an inseparable companion, a safety-valve for repressed irritation, anxiety and frustration, and a reflection of a self that few suspected in this most reticent of professional soldiers.

In that diary's early pages one can trace the hopes and fears of a senior officer of the British Army, embarking on the task that has confronted it at the outset of all its wars—of shouldering the burden of a nation's long neglect and standing in the breach while its people armed themselves for the responsibilities they had assumed. During those waiting months in France it mirrors a sense of impending disaster—a terrifying awareness of the moral rot that was sapping the courage of Britain's ally and of her own unpreparedness and lack of realism. Then, in

13

a slender volume that may take its place among the nation's military treasures, the soldier who covered the flank of the British Army in the most perilous retreat of its history tells the story of how he and his men fought their way from the Dyle to Dunkirk—a tale of courage and resource in disaster that rivals the Navy's achievement in transporting the Army back to England.

· · · · · · · ·

For eight months after Alan Brooke sailed in command of the II Corps to France the British Expeditionary Force was in deadly danger. On May 21st, 1940, the German armour, driving round its southern flank through the demoralised French armies, reached the sea near Abbeville and turned north to seize the Channel ports in its rear. Boulogne fell on the 23rd; on the 26th, after a heroic defence, the Rifles at Calais were overwhelmed, leaving only a single port, Dunkirk, intact. While the Commander-in-Chief, Lord Gort, struggled to improvise new defences and a striking-force to restore his severed communications, a still graver threat had developed on the left of the main British line, where the Belgian Army had begun to disintegrate. By the night of the 25th a thirty-mile gap lay wide open to the north of the British forces on the Franco-Belgian frontier, through which the Germans were about to pour in behind them. Nearly a quarter of a million troops—the core of the British Regular Army—lay between the closing pincers of a new Sedan.

Most of the Regular officers who were to train and lead Britain's future armies were fighting in those seven imperilled divisions, forty or fifty miles to the south-east of Dunkirk. Among them were Kenneth Anderson who was to command the First Army in Tunisia; Dempsey, who was to command the Second Army in Normandy; Ritchie, a future commander of the Eighth Army, and Stopford, who was to become Commander-in-Chief in Burma and South-East Asia; William Morgan, who was to end the war as Chief of Staff in the Mediterranean, and Franklyn, who was to be Commander-in-Chief, Home Forces; Lindsell, the great Quarter-Master-General who organised the two-thousand mile advance of the

Eighth Army across the deserts of North Africa, and Adam, who was to be Adjutant-General during the years when Britain was training her D-Day armies. The two who were to win most fame of all were Harold Alexander and Bernard Montgomery, commanding the 1st and 3rd Divisions, both of whom served during the retreat—the one for part of it and the other for the whole of it—under the orders of Lieutenant-General Alan Brooke, Commander of the II Corps. The first was to expel the Germans and Italians from Africa and conquer Italy; the second, the victor of Alamein, to force the re-entry to France and receive the German surrender on Lüneburg Heath.

At that moment, however, it looked as though all of them would spend the rest of the War in German prisons. The Expeditionary Force's communications had almost completely broken down, its Commander-in-Chief, at his headquarters near the coast, had no means of knowing whether his orders were reaching the battle-line on the Belgian frontier, and the encircling German armies on either side of Dunkirk were closing in fast. Without armour save for a few light and some slow, scattered infantry tanks, its channels of supply severed by the panzers and disrupted by the Luftwaffe, and the roads behind it congested with panic-stricken refugees, the British Army lay like a floundering fish, almost cut off from the sea on which it depended for life, in a long, sagging bag of which the ends were being rapidly closed and at whose foot, fifty miles inland, its finest divisions were fighting against apparently hopeless odds.

Speaking a week later, after the deliverance of Dunkirk, the Prime Minister, Winston Churchill, told the House that he had feared on that day that it would be his lot to announce " the greatest military disaster in our long history." " It seemed," he said, " that the whole of the British Expeditionary Force north of the Amiens-Abbeville gap would be broken up in the open field or else would have to capitulate for lack of food and ammunition. . . . The whole root and core and brain of the British Army, on which and around which we were to build, and are to build, the great British armies in the later years of the War, seemed about to perish upon the field or to be led into an ignominious and starving captivity. . . . It seemed impossible that any large number of Allied troops could reach the coast."

That they did so was due mainly to one man. During the four crucial days between the Belgian collapse and the beginning of the evacuation Alan Brooke, with the four divisions of his Corps, covered the long exposed flank opened by King Leopold's surrender, and took command of all the desperately pressed men fighting their way back down a narrowing corridor to the improvised evacuation lines which Lord Gort was throwing up in the marshes around Dunkirk. Though seventeen German divisions had been released by the Belgian capitulation, by his speed and foresight Brooke anticipated the attacker's every move and, in the words of the official historian, " directed operations with great skill on a plan which the enemy was not allowed seriously to upset."[1] He not only directed the movements of his own Corps but, travelling from one threatened point to another, co-ordinated those of the whole east wing of the retreating army. Many of his verbal orders of this time, recorded in individual war diaries, were given from twelve to twenty-four hours earlier than the identical written orders of G.H.Q. and H.Q. 1st Corps. " By almost universal testimony," wrote Sir James Grigg, then Permanent Head of the War Office, " it was due largely to his skill and resolution that, not only his own Corps, but the whole B.E.F. escaped destruction on the retreat."

" All this day of the 28th," Churchill has recorded, " the escape of the British Army hung in the balance. On the front from Comines to Ypres and thence to the sea, facing east and attempting to fill the Belgian gap, General Brooke and his II Corps fought a magnificent battle. . . . The German thrust between the British and Belgian armies was not to be prevented, but its fatal consequence, an inward turn across the Yser which would have brought the enemy on to the beaches behind our fighting troops, was foreseen and everywhere forestalled. . . . The Germans sustained a bloody repulse. . . . All the time, only about four miles behind Brooke's struggling front, vast masses of transport and troops poured back into the developing

[1] *The War in France and Flanders, 1939-1940.* (H.M.S.O.) 201.

bridgehead of Dunkirk and were fitted with skilful improvisation into its defences."[1]

Thus the miracle of the Navy's evacuation was preceded by an equal miracle—that of the Army's reaching the coast at all. Alan Brooke's achievement in bringing it through the closing defile of its enemies was one of the great feats of British military history. At the time he was within two months of his fifty-seventh birthday, an alert, youthful-looking man with a slightly stooping figure and dark aquiline features, always immaculately dressed, punctual, methodical and with the reputation in the Service of an almost machine-like proficiency. A cadet of a family of Northern Irish baronets—the " fighting Brookes " of Brookeborough—until he went to Woolwich at eighteen he had been brought up in France, whose language he spoke like a native. During the 1914-18 war—from which he emerged a brevet lieutenant-colonel with a D.S.O. and Bar, a Croix-de-Guerre and six Mentions in Despatches—he had distinguished himself by adapting and developing new French methods of controlling the great rolling barrages that in the closing stages of the war broke the resistance of the German Army. Thereafter, he had been a man marked for command, spending eight years as student and instructor at the Staff College, Camberley, and the new Imperial Defence College—founded to teach the science of Inter-Service co-operation and the higher direction of war—where he worked with most of the men who were to direct Britain's Forces in the Second World War. Keenly interested in novel technical devices, whose use he was always pressing on more conservative seniors, he had held in the 'thirties a succession of appointments in which he was responsible for developments affecting every branch of the Service—Commandant of the School of Artillery, commander of an Infantry brigade, Inspector of Artillery, Director of Military Training, commander of the first Mobile Division—forerunner of the Armoured Divisions to come—and, during the year after Munich, General Officer Commanding-in-Chief of the new Anti-Aircraft Command that gave Britain its earliest shield of ground-defence against air-attack. His diversity of experience was unrivalled in any of the Services.

[1] *Churchill*, II 84-5.

But for the unexpected promotion in 1937 of Lord Gort to be Chief of the Imperial General Staff over the head of Sir John Dill—Brooke's former teacher at the Staff College—Brooke, as Dill's favourite pupil, would probably have succeeded him as professional head of the Service. As it was, the outbreak of war found Dill commanding the First Corps at Aldershot and Brooke just appointed to Southern Command—a post he at once relinquished to follow Gort and Dill to France in command of the second of the two Corps comprising the original Expeditionary Force. During the winter he had transformed it from a very inadequately trained into a highly-efficient fighting formation. He was now only three years from the regulation retiring age, and, with the premium placed by War on youth, might have expected, for all his professional proficiency, to be relegated to the shelf. Fate, and his handling of the retreat, decided otherwise.

From that hour, until he laid down his office more than six years later, Brooke remained at the very summit of his profession. Within forty-eight hours of his return from Dunkirk he was appointed to command the 140,000 troops still left in France and to form with four fighting divisions—all that Britain could muster—the nucleus of a new Expeditionary Force. Sent back to the Continent to help save a dissolving France, by his quick grasp of the situation and the moral courage with which, at the risk of his career, he refused to sacrifice military to political considerations, he extricated his army in the nick of time and, in the teeth of conflicting instructions, brought it safely back to England. " He acquitted himself," wrote Churchill, " with singular firmness and dexterity, in circumstances of unimaginable difficulty and confusion."

A month later, with the unanimous approval of all who had served with him, Brooke was entrusted with command of the Forces preparing to repel invasion. He took over an army which had lost its entire equipment, with little armour, no provision for air support, a terrifying shortage of anti-tank weapons, ammunition and even rifles; and with scarcely enough artillery for two divisions. Within two months he had transformed the situation, reorganising the country's defences on an offensive basis and creating mobile reserves to throw the enemy back into the sea before he could consolidate. Thereafter, as the danger of invasion receded, he became the trainer of the new armies whose task it was to hold the ring of sea-power round the Axis and one day fight their way back to the Continent. During this time nearly all the chief commanders of the latter war years served under him. In his sixteen months as Commander-in-Chief, Home Forces, he inculcated throughout the higher ranks of the Army a common doctrine of command and battle training and laid the foundations on which a force capable of taking the field against the *Wermacht* could be built.

In 1941 Alan Brooke was summoned by the Prime Minister to succeed John Dill as Chief of the Imperial General Staff. As such he became operational head of the British Army in the greatest war of its history and the co-ordinator of all its campaigns. His concern was no longer with tactics but with grand strategy. He was called to the control of the Service at the moment that the war, hitherto confined to Europe and North Africa, became global with the entry of a fully armed and mobilised Japan and a still almost completely unarmed America. It was a time of dreadful disaster, when five of Britain's capital ships—a third of her battle fleet—were sunk within a fortnight, and when, following the catastrophe at Pearl Harbour, command of the western and south-west Pacific passed to the enemy. A terrible price had to be paid for the neglect and wishful thinking of years, as the British and Dutch Empires in south-east Asia fell, almost without resistance, to Japan. It was as though a string of pearls was disintegrating after the string, which was sea-power, had been cut. Meanwhile Britain's long-maturing plans for a North African offensive faltered, as reinforcements were deflected to the Far East and urgently-needed tanks and supplies were sent to fortify a Russia fighting for survival at the approaches to Moscow.

The beginning of Alan Brooke's tenure of office as Chief of the Imperial General Staff thus coincided, like Churchill's assumption of the Premiership, with the disappearance of nearly all the conditions on which his predecessors had depended. He and his two colleagues, the First Sea Lord and Chief of Air Staff, whose collective duty it was to advise the Prime Minister on the conduct of the war, had to cope with a situation which no British soldier, sailor or airman had ever had to face. A continuous attack was being made on every ocean against the tenuous sea communications which alone kept the scattered United Nations in being. One German offensive menaced Russia's oil supplies in the Caucasus, and, more remotely, Britain's in Persia and Iraq, and another, in North Africa, the Suez Canal. Gravest of all, a Japanese advance across Burma and the Indian Ocean imperilled India and the sea communications with the Middle East and threatened a link-up between the two halves of the Axis. Any major mistake by the Allies would have been fatal.

Three months after he became C.I.G.S., on the morrow of the fall of Singapore, Brooke was asked by the Prime Minister to take the place of the First Sea Lord as chairman of the Chiefs of Staff Committee—the executive triumvirate of the Heads of the Fighting Services entrusted with the military direction of the war. He thus became, in the words of the wartime Secretary for War, Sir James Grigg, " head of the central organisation by and through which the Minister of Defence and the Cabinet conducted the war as a whole," and the Government's principal strategic adviser. Henceforward until the end of the war he was in daily consultation with the Prime Minister, accompanied him on all his wartime journeys and to his conferences with Stalin and Roosevelt, and, as chief British spokesman on the Combined Chiefs of Staff of the United Kingdom and United States, played a leading part in inducing the American Service chiefs to adopt the concentric strategy that brought about during 1942 and 1943 the turn of the tide.

The British Chiefs of Staff Committee had been formed after the first war to co-ordinate the higher direction of the Fighting Services. It consisted of the professional heads of the three Services and in peacetime was responsible for giving strategic advice to the Committee of Imperial Defence. In wartime it fulfilled the same role under the War Cabinet and directed and co-ordinated the plans and operations of the Fighting Services. It was through its medium that the war, in all its complexity, was ordered from day to day and the Theatre Commanders controlled in the field. Ultimate responsibility rested, under the Constitution, with the Prime Minister as Minister of Defence and with the War Cabinet over which he presided and to which, as the joint repository of the confidence of Crown and Parliament, he was responsible. But it was an accepted administrative practice that the Defence Minister should not act in any purely military matter contrary to the corporate opinion of his official Service advisers. Churchill was particularly careful to make this clear to Parliament. " I do not conduct this war from day to day myself," he explained in a speech during the disastrous winter of 1941-42, while defending himself from charges of military incompetence and interference; " it is conducted from day to day, and in its future outlook, by the Chiefs of Staff Committee. . . . These officers sit together every day and often twice a day. They give executive directions and orders to the Commanders-in-Chief in the various theatres. They advise me, they advise the Defence Committee and the War Cabinet on large questions of war strategy and policy. . . . I do not think there has ever been a system in which the professional heads of the fighting Services have had a freer hand or a greater or more direct influence or have received more constant and harmonious support from the Prime Minister and the Cabinet under whom they serve."[1]

It was the existence of this Committee, as much as Churchill's dominating presence as Defence Minister, that distinguished the higher control of the second World War from that of the first. It prevented the fatal clash between political leaders and military experts—the " frocks " and " brass-hats "—that so nearly resulted in disaster in 1918. Though the members of this high Service triumvirate could be dismissed at will by the Prime Minister, and though they in their turn had their corporate and individual remedy of resignation, there is no case on record in which, after Brooke became their chairman, their considered advice on a major strategic issue was overruled. Despite the immense powers entrusted to him by Parliament, Churchill was too good a parliamentarian and too deeply rooted in English constitutional tradition to insist on any course

[1] *Cit.* Lt.-Gen. Sir R. Weeks, *Organisation and Equipment for War* 11.

of military action which he could not afterwards tell the House
of Commons had received the support of the Chiefs of Staff.
He might over-persuade them by his eloquence and persistence,
but, provided they were unanimous and stood firm, it was their
military judgment, not his, that prevailed.

It was Alan Brooke who gave to the Chiefs of Staff Committee
the full cohesion and power of which it was capable. He made
it what its creators had intended—an expert precision-
instrument for directing a vast, complex war machine. In his
hands it became that rarest but most potent of all military
weapons—a Council of War operating with the consistency
and speed of a single will. When agreement had been reached
between its members, it was his duty to acquaint the Defence
Minister and War Cabinet with the reasons for it. If he was
instructed that on political or economic grounds a different
course of action was necessary, he would co-operate wholeheartedly and loyally, but he always made certain beyond any
possibility of doubt that the military implications were understood. Once the Chiefs of Staff had decided on a purely
military issue, he was like rock.

Before Alan Brooke appeared on the strategic scene the
enemy, with his infinitely greater strength, had enjoyed the
initiative, and Britain had been saved, not only by her people's
courage, but because she had as leader a man whose instinct
was to fight back whatever the odds. Henceforward, by that
leader's side was one who not only hit back, but knew exactly
where to hit to hurt most. Within eight months of Brooke's
assumption of the chairmanship of the Chiefs of Staff Committee
Germany had ceased to call the tune to which Britain danced
and had begun to dance to hers. To Churchill's lightning
flashes of inspiration and the courage that refused to admit
defeat yet sometimes endangered victory by spurring him to
attack prematurely, Brooke brought what Wellington, who also
possessed it, saw in Marlborough—a cool, clear and steady
understanding.

The character of that partnership was illustrated by a
remark made at its beginning by a hostess of the Prime Minister
after the new C.I.G.S. had come to visit him at her country
house. " I don't know," she said, " how he is going to get on

with Winston, but he spent all the afternoon sitting on the sofa and seemed all the time to be saying, ' No, no, sir, you can't! ' "
Yet, though of all attitudes this was the one the Prime Minister most detested, their partnership remained unbroken until the day, three and a half years later, when in the hour of victory Churchill was repudiated by the country he had saved. Except during his occasional illnesses and Brooke's few brief spells of leave, hardly a day passed without their being together, in consultation, discussion and argument, in private conference or in committee with others.

No statesman save Alfred has done England such service as Churchill. In the summer of 1940 his courage made her the hope of the world. His whole career had been an essay in fighting back from disaster. " You ask," he said when the German armies were driving through the broken lines of France, " what is our aim? I can answer in one word: Victory —victory at all costs, victory in spite of all terrors, victory, however long and hard the road may be." His resolve to attack the colossus dominating Europe at any point within reach was then the only policy. So long as the Navy held the narrow seas and the R.A.F. the air above, the enemy, for all his immense strength, could bring Britain no lower than she already was. Every attack on her mighty adversary, however daring, could serve only to revive and rouse her people's courage and offensive spirit.

The Prime Minister's virtues as a war leader were immense. The higher the tide of trouble rose, the higher rose his courage. His nerves never failed, and the worst of disasters left his sleep and appetite unimpaired. He had the imagination to foresee dangers and opportunities that others would have missed and the drive to ensure that neither took the country unawares. He would never take No for an answer. For five years he was a spur in the flanks of every military and civil commander in the land.

He was an orator, a poet and a sage with a taste for splendour and good living, an aristocrat who possessed the common touch that the English like to see in their rulers. For all his eighteenth-century eloquence and Victorian imperialism, he was the ideal champion for a people whose favourite song was " The Lambeth

Walk " and whose pet hobby a daily flutter on a horse. They liked his cigar, his glass of brandy, his bulldog face and figure, the twinkle in his eye. They loved his humour, his way of pronouncing foreign names, his indomitable courage. Above all, he had the power to touch chords in men's hearts that transcended politics. His sense of history never failed. He believed in a Providence that worked through human instruments and, like Elizabeth and Cromwell, he made the people he led believe in it too. He bade them be " unyielding, persevering, indomitable, in the overthrow of another continental tyranny as in the olden times." A few weeks before the Japanese struck at Britain's rear, speaking to the boys of Harrow School who had sung a song in his honour containing the words "darker days," he declared: " These are not dark days; these are great days—the greatest days our country has ever lived."

His failings as a leader were impatience and impetuosity. The qualities that made him so great in adversity—the insistence on fighting back at all points, the obsession with attack, the tireless energy, the soaring imagination—sometimes made him essay enterprises which, had he not been dissuaded, would have ended in disaster. Nor, since he always threw the whole of his heart and head at the nearest fence, was he good at choosing between conflicting objectives—a choice which became increasingly important as Britain's resources and those of her allies began to offer a chance of wresting the initiative from the enemy. After 1941 any needless dispersal of force, any commitment that could drain away resources that might be needed at the decisive point at the decisive moment, might have deferred victory for a long time and, perhaps, for ever. Churchill's eloquence and persistence then became something of a problem to his military advisers. It was hard for them to concentrate and build up reserves and a striking-force for the future when he was always seeking, and with such intensity, to use them at once against the nearest foe.

It was in checking these tendencies that Alan Brooke proved the necessary counterpart to his leader. In contrast to the latter's sweeping Edwardian impatience for inconvenient details and ' method of suddenly arriving at some decision as it were by intuition, without any kind of logical examination of the problem,'[1] Brooke's whole career had been a training in adapting means to ends. He had the imagination to see what was possible and the practical knowledge to know how, when and where it could be made so. He saw the war steadily and never, whatever the pressure of the moment, lost sight of the global picture. He had the ability—the hallmark of the born strategist—to grasp all the essentials of a problem at once. " He was more qualified," wrote James Grigg, " than any other soldier, or possibly than any other sailor or airman, to look at the war as a whole."

In all their arguments and differences, though they sometimes failed to realise it, the Prime Minister and his C.I.G.S. were the complement to one another. Churchill had the iron nerves, the splendid good humour and robust resilience of perfect health; the inspired instinct for the right word and the power to simplify great issues so that others could see them in the same clear terms. In his first speech as Prime Minister he had declared that the policy of his Administration would be " to wage war, by sea, land and air, with all our might and with all the strength God can give us." It was a promise faithfully fulfilled. The root of the matter was in him. " War," he wrote, " is a constant struggle and must be waged from day to day." He never for one moment gave up doing so. And he did it with a flame of hope that communicated itself to the whole nation. He saw what was necessary, and, with his prescient imagination, often long before it was required, but his expectations outran what was achievable and caused him to seek what in the circumstances of the time was impossible. ' Planned strategy,' as Alan Brooke wrote, ' was not his strong card. He preferred to work by intuition and by impulse. . . . He was never good at looking at all the implications of any course he favoured. In fact, he frequently refused to look at them.'

To correlate the Prime Minister's prophetic vision to the realities of what was immediately practicable became Alan Brooke's most important task. For this he was far better suited than his predecessor, Dill, who for all his brilliant gifts and noble character, had allowed himself to be drawn into endless argument and had been worn down by these clashes. Like most

[1] *Notes on My Life*, VI. 466.

soldiers Brooke knew little of politics and instinctively distrusted those who practised them. But he had the gift which is at the root of all politics, as of all professions that concern the management of men: of distinguishing between what is practicable and impracticable, and because of it, was able to establish a successful *modus operandi* with his great, though mercurial, chief. Like him, he knew exactly what he wanted to achieve. He was no mere staff officer, putting the pros and cons of alternative courses of action and leaving the decision to others—an attitude which always irritated the Prime Minister—but a leader taking full responsibility for the advice he tendered. He had the good sense never to oppose or argue with him over unessentials, realising that a Minister so tireless and abounding in energy was like some great natural force that must often have its way. He refused, therefore, to allow himself to be irritated by the continual pin-prick minutes on matters of detail which were part of Churchill's technique for keeping his subordinates up to the mark. When his assistants wished to reply to the more provocative of these, he would stop them. " We mustn't argue with Winston on small things," he used to say, " but only on things that really matter."

Yet on essentials he never gave way. So long as he remained C.I.G.S. he was resolved that purely military decisions should only be taken by those who were officially and professionally responsible for them. The Prime Minister found in him a companion whose wit and flexible mind he enjoyed as much as Brooke did his. But he also found him immoveable and uncompromising on any matter in which his soldier's knowledge convinced him that he was arguing on insufficient premises. After each tremendous argument in War Cabinet or private session came the unvarying and outwardly imperturbable reply: " Sir, we will examine the point you have raised at the Chiefs of Staff committee in the morning and report on it immediately." No entreaties or abuse could move him, nor to whatever lengths the Prime Minister went could he circumvent this quick-minded, unyielding soldier. With his instinctive liking for a fighter he respected this quality in Brooke, even when it thwarted him. Though the two men had many a hammer-and-tongs argument, they resumed their friendship as soon as the storm had passed. Both were too magnanimous for it to be otherwise. On every essential point, in Sir James Grigg's words, they " argued themselves into agreement before final action was taken."

.   .   .   .

The wartime dictatorship entrusted by Parliament to Churchill was the answer for which Britain and the free world had been waiting. After the braggarts and appeasers had failed to stem the tide of tyranny, it met Hitler's resolve and daring with a resolve and daring as ruthless as his own. Yet all dictatorships carry the defects of their qualities, creating deserts around the wielder of power. And, as Napoleon's fate proved, no single man, whatever his genius, can wage war without sooner or later making fatal mistakes unless he submits himself to the correction of facts and of others who know facts which he cannot know himself. Perhaps the greatest of all Churchill's claims to the gratitude of his country is that, though he had the power to be a dictator in the day-by-day conduct of the war, he refused to be one. That a leader so interested in strategy and the most detailed military matters, should for four years have endured the restraint of an official adviser so often in disagreement with himself and whom he could have dismissed at any time he chose, and that he should never once have overruled him and the Chiefs of Staff in a major military decision, is a tribute not only to his magnanimity, but to the genius of the nation's parliamentary system and Churchill's profound respect for it. Throughout those years of strain and trial, he remained true to England's tradition of consultation and ordered freedom. He constantly helped to form military decisions yet never dictated them. Had Hitler, also a man of intuitive genius, shown the same restraint and wisdom, the war might have ended very differently.

.   .   .   .

The Chiefs of Staff Committee presented to Britain's allies the same unbroken front in military matters that it presented to the Prime Minister. During the spring and summer that followed Brooke's appointment to its chairmanship, military

co-operation between the Atlantic Powers first became a
practical issue. In the aftermath of Pearl Harbour, while he
was still learning the ropes at the War Office, the Prime
Minister, with his predecessor, Sir John Dill, and his Naval and
Air Force colleagues, were in Washington laying the foundations of Anglo-American strategic unity. The plans they made
there for dealing with the immediate situation in the Pacific
broke down almost at once under the impact of events. But
one outcome of the visit survived: the decision that the Chiefs
of Staff of the two nations should act together as a Combined
Chiefs of Staff to draw up, under the President's and Prime
Minister's political direction, all major strategic plans affecting
both.

Until the end of 1941 Britain could scarcely be said to have
had a strategy for winning the war except to fight back with
all she had and hold her European foes in a ring of salt water
and desert. Beyond that she could only, as Churchill had
taught her, hope for some change in the tide of world
affairs that might weaken her enemies. She lived by the
faith he gave her, and from hand-to-mouth, for she had no
other choice. Her seamen sought to keep open her trade
routes, her soldiers to guard the British Isles and Nile Delta,
her airmen to build up a force that, by subjecting the Reich
to growing air bombardment, might one day engulf it in
a pyre of flame and rubble. America's entry into the war, and
the unexpected toughness of Russia's resistance, offered new
vistas of opportunity if only the German and Japanese drives
could be held. With a victorious naval Power to fight in the
vast spaces of the Pacific, the American admirals naturally
wished to concentrate the United States' war potential against
Japan. Her soldiers, with the support of her President,
favoured the nearer and more easily attainable objective of
Germany first. But their experience of modern warfare was
very small, and they at first grossly underestimated the difficulties both of transporting troops and supplies to Europe and
of fighting inside Hitler's continental fortress. When General
Marshall declared his belief that the quickest way to end the
war was to invade France in 1942 or 1943, Brooke replied,
" Yes, but not the way we want to end it! "

Brooke's strategy, like that of all Britain's greatest commanders, depended on salt water. With his grasp of essentials, he saw that sea transport was the key to the offensive. Without it nothing could be done to take the pressure off Russia or deprive the enemy, with his central land position, of the initiative. In the early months of 1942 the Allies were losing vast quantities of shipping to the U-boats. There was only one way in which such losses could be made good and only one way to relieve the Red Army. That was not, as the Russians and Americans argued, by premature and inadequately supplied offensives against Hitler's Western Wall, but by striking at the Axis in the one theatre where, because of salt water and geography, logistics could enable the still comparatively minute land-forces of the United Nations to exert an influence out of all proportion to their size. By expelling the Germans and Italians from North Africa, Britain and America could re-open the Mediterranean and, shortening their supply route to India and the Middle East, release at least a million tons of shipping for immediate offensive operations. Then, by threatening the enemy across that sea and forcing him to man hundreds of miles of hitherto secure coastline, they could strike, through Sicily and Italy, at the point of his continental fortress where his communications were most strained. Having knocked Italy out of the war and made Germany deploy her reserves in the one area from which, owing to poor and mountainous communications, they would be hardest to extricate, they could thereafter assail Hitler's Western Wall across the Channel without having to face too powerful a counter-attack and maintain their thrust till it had reached her heart, while the Russians, similarly relieved from the threat of a central reserve using Germany's fast west-to-east communications—the cause of their defeat in 1914—could safely advance on the frontiers of the Reich from the opposite direction.

Such was the policy that, at Brooke's instance, Britain and America adopted and, in spite of many differences of opinion, systematically carried out until, first Italy, and then Germany were destroyed, and the whole weight of the United Nations could be turned against the surviving Axis partner in the Pacific. The agency which devised it and by which it was directed was the Combined Chiefs of Staff. At the early meetings of that body in 1942 and the first half of 1943, as the military spokesman of what was still the predominant and by far the more experienced of the Western Powers, Alan Brooke took the lead in proposing this joint strategy. This did not mean that he was either its sole originator, or that agreement on the lines he advocated was reached except after prolonged, and often heated argument, first between himself, his British colleagues and their political chief—who, though a strong protagonist of a Mediterranean strategy, championed so much else that was at the time logistically incompatible with it—and then between the British Chiefs of Staff and the American. In overcoming the latter's resistance, Brooke's colleague, Portal, and his predecessor, Dill—Head of the British Military Delegation at Washington—played an invaluable part, winning the profound respect and affection of their transatlantic comrades. Brooke was at first less successful with the Americans, who tended to be suspicious of his abrupt manner and quick speech, his refusal to compromise over essentials or to suffer fools gladly. His lack of small talk and continual concentration on the task in hand made them uneasy; they felt, not unjustly, that he was trying to " sell them something." They suspected that his resistance to their proposals for an immediate cross-Channel attack sprang from his experiences in the First World War and the *blitzkrieg*, and that his arguments, though seemingly unanswerable, were animated by a fear of casualties, with an afterthought for British imperialist interests in the Levant—a suspicion that was much aggravated by the vehemence and eloquence with which his political chief sought to win over theirs to what they regarded as a Mediterranean side-show.

Yet, little by little, by his persistence, patience and the unfolding logic of events, Brooke and his colleagues induced the Americans to accept a policy that led, first to the halting of the Axis tide and then to the counter-offensive which, with exquisite timing and balance, wrested the initiative from the enemy. In restraining them from adventures which could not have been sustained from the slender resources then available and which might have resulted in irretrievable disaster, and in persuading them to follow a gradually expanding strategy, founded, like Wellington's and MacArthur's, on sea-power, they brought to bear on the Axis in Europe a steady and continuously-growing pressure, first from the south and then from the west, that, more effectively than any premature bid to break Hitler's Western Wall, took the pressure off Russia and led to Italy's collapse and Germany's growing debility.

. . . .

Three times during their partnership Brooke was offered by the Prime Minister command in the field—in 1942 of the Eighth Army and of the Middle East, and, in the following year, of the Allied invasion of Europe. The first two he refused, feeling, for all his longing to accept, that at that critical period his place was at the Prime Minister's side. The offer of the third, to his bitter disappointment, was withdrawn because of the political need, which he was the first to recognise, for an American to be given the Supreme Command. He never, therefore, received the popular acclaim won by his lieutenants, Montgomery and Alexander, and by the American Supreme Commanders, Eisenhower and MacArthur. The honours showered on him by the State—greater than those bestowed on any British soldier save Marlborough, Wellington and Roberts —passed almost unnoticed: a Field Marshal's baton, the Garter, the Order of Merit, a peerage, the Grand Crosses of the Bath and Victorian Orders, the great honorary offices of Lord High Constable of England, Constable of the Tower, and Master Gunner. Even when it was turned on him Brooke avoided the limelight, shunning it deliberately lest it should impede his work or embarrass his relations with the Prime Minister. When his task was done, he retired to the gardener's cottage of his former home—which he was forced to sell to educate his children—and immersed himself in country pursuits and public duties. The man who saved the Army at Dunkirk and helped to chart the road to victory is best known to-day as a lecturer on bird films and ex-President of the Zoo.

Yet, if the palm for courage and constancy in the struggle against Hitler belongs to Churchill, that for far-sighted strategy may well be awarded by posterity to Alanbrooke. Field Marshal Montgomery—no mean judge—has described him as

" the greatest soldier—soldier, sailor or airman—produced by any country taking part in the last war." "Those on the inside of affairs would assess his contribution to victory as second only to Churchill," wrote the man who, first as Permanent Secretary and Secretary of State for War, was his colleague and official chief throughout the war years. As Montgomery's place in England's annals is with her great captains of the set battle—with the Black Prince, Henry V and Cromwell—so Alanbrooke's is with her overall strategic commanders, Marlborough and Wellington. Like them he understood the roots of her being: was Neptune's general.

On the eve of D-Day Montgomery wrote to his chief at Storey's Gate: " I cross over to France to-morrow night—if all goes well—and may not see you again. . . . My great desire throughout has been to justify your confidence in me, and not to let you down; and I hope I have been able to do this to your satisfaction." Six months later when France and Belgium had been cleared of the enemy, he wrote again, " We have been through difficult times together, and it may well be that some even more difficult times lie ahead. I would like to say that the credit for anything I may have been able to do lies wholly with you." And on the day that it was announced that he was to succeed him as C.I.G.S., he sent Lord Alanbrooke, as he had then become, the following letter.

" British Army of the Rhine
1/2/46

My dear Brookie,

Now that it has been announced that I am to succeed you, I must write and tell you how I feel about things.

During the late war you have given me many tasks to carry out; each one has been more difficult than the last, and each one has somehow been brought to a successful conclusion. But there have been moments when I have gone ' off the rails ": due to impetuosity, irritation, or some such reason. You always pulled me back on to the rails, and I started off down the course again. I know very well that when I used to go " off the rails," it increased your own work and anxieties 100 per cent. But you never complained. In the goodness of your heart you lent me a helping hand and asked nothing in return: not that I could have done anything for you.

I want to say two things.

First.—I am terribly grateful for all you have done for me.

Second.—I could never have achieved anything if you had not been there to help me; it has been your wise guidance, and your firm handling of a very difficult subordinate, that really did the business. I could have done nothing alone.

And now, when I succeed you as professional head of the Army, I shall need your wisdom and advice more than ever. I do hope that you will let me come to you with my problems and discuss them with you. I shall do my best, as you know. I don't think I have ever lacked confidence in my own ability to do any job you have given me to do. But past jobs have involved fighting the Germans and, given adequate resources, that was always relatively simple. This next job is very different, and I shall need you in the background more than ever.

Thank you so very much, Brookie. You have been a true friend at all times.

> Your very devoted admirer,
> MONTY.[1] "

. . . .

Lord Alanbrooke's diary is probably the most important of all contemporary first-hand personal records of the war. It is a reflection of an experience that grew more and more momentous until it became, on a high, lonely peak of decision, identical with that of Britain herself. It was written in longhand, usually last thing at night, but occasionally in some hurried interval of the day, to record, in brief outline, what he regarded as its chief events, military and personal. The entries are seldom long, and, as he had little rest or private life, the personal is mostly swallowed up in the military. Every now and then, however, he makes some reference to the beloved companion for whom he kept it, to the two small children of

[1] Lord Alanbrooke, *Personal Files.* By kind permission of Field Marshal Viscount Montgomery.

his second marriage, and to the country pursuits, particularly
of bird-watching and animal photography, that were his
refuge from the unceasing strain and responsibility of his work.
It was characteristic of Brooke's sense of duty that, though
quartered for the last five years of the war in London, he did
not live with the wife and family to whom he was so devoted,
but only saw them when they came up for an occasional meal
or on Sundays, which he usually contrived to spend with them
at his Hampshire home except when he was detained at the
War Office, summoned to Chequers or travelling with the Prime
Minister. What these Sundays meant to him can be seen from
an entry made in October, 1940, when the threat of invasion
was beginning to recede.

> " *October 19th*. Another day gone and thank God for
> it. Every day that passes must at least be one day less of
> the war. But there are times when the madness and the
> fallacy of war almost choke one. Why human beings must
> behave like children at this stage of the evolution of the
> human race is hard to understand. At any rate, it proves
> that we have still got to go a long way on the road that
> leads to perfect human beings. . . . Ultimately I suppose
> that human beings from much suffering will become wiser
> and will appreciate that greater happiness can be found
> in this world by preferring their neighbour to themselves.
> Meanwhile for all my philosophy, I am very tired of this
> war and long for peace. A peace that will allow us to spend
> the remaining years of our life quietly together in a small
> cottage with a garden to work in, some bees to look after
> and perhaps a stream close by where I can watch the fish
> even if I don't catch them! And above all, somewhere
> where I can bask in the sublime happiness of the sunshine
> of your company. But even if I can't be with you at
> present, I still thank God for having allowed me to know
> you and for the wonderful happiness of seeing you once a
> week."

> " I am now counting the hours till to-morrow when I
> hope to start for my Sunday with you."

Brooke possessed his political chief's capacity for both intense concentration and relaxation. During these Sundays at home he was able to put the war out of his mind, to sit motionless for hours with his cine-camera in the garden or some neighbouring spinney, photographing a nightingale's nest or a nesting wry-neck, or draw for his children nonsense-sketches of animals dressed as humans to illustrate the stories he invented for them.

" Spent peacefully at home recuperating from the last week and building a goat-cart with Pooks and Ti." . . . ' A complete rest, as I forgot all about the war, ' Bumper ' Exercise and Winston's mad Norwegian plans whilst work-ing with my children listening to their incessant chatter on every conceivable subject except those I wished to forget temporarily.'[1]

' My entry for April 12th is short, but there lay a world of happiness, love and recreation behind it. I wrote, " Sunday at home pruning roses and playing with darling Pooks." '

When, in 1946, Brooke's separation from his family ended, he ceased to keep a diary. But some years later, when the Royal Regiment of Artillery began to collect material for an official biography of its greatest son, he was induced to set down his recollections of his youth and military career. When he reached the beginning of the Second World War, he unlocked the diaries to refresh his memory. And, as he copied extracts from them for his future biographer, he added notes of comment and amplification. These, which are sometimes much fuller than the entries they elucidate, were written, unlike the diary, at leisure and with time for reflection. Often they correct some hasty or, as their writer considered, unfair judgment, or point out where he was wrong in his opinion of the hour. Thus on February 2nd, 1942, the diary reads:

". . . At 5 p.m. Cabinet Meeting. As usual, most un-pleasant remarks by various Ministers in connection with defeats of our forces. As we had retired into Singapore Island and lost Moulmein, besides being pushed back in Libya, I had a good deal to account for. I found it hard

[1] *Diary*, 5th October, 1941.

to keep my temper with some of the criticisms that were raised. . . ."

On this Brooke's subsequent comment is:

' I was being bombarded with unpleasant remarks, when Bevin suddenly asked me some question. I thought at the time that the remark was meant offensively, and my blood was up. I therefore turned on him and gave him a short and somewhat rude reply. He said nothing more at the time, but came up to me as we were going out and in a most charming manner explained that he had not been trying to get at me but was genuinely asking for information. A typical action on his part and nothing could have been nicer. I apologised for the rudeness of my reply, and asked him to dine quietly alone with me when he could ask me any questions he wished. This he did, and we had a most pleasant evening together. The more I saw of him in later years, the more I admired him. A very great man.'

These two documents—the diary and the comments written a decade later—constitute a historical record which so far as I know is unique. I can think of no other instance in which a leading actor in great events recorded them at the time and, without altering his contemporary account, later commented on and criticised it. The diary and autobiographical notes together run to nearly a million words. For a variety of reasons only a fraction of them can be used at present, and not till our generation has passed away will it be possible to publish them in their entirety. Apart from the magnitude and secrecy of the affairs he handled during the seven years covered by the diary, their author came into contact with almost every-one of any importance in the country's military and civil life, and, though little given to gossip, he was as frank and outspoken in his private judgments as in his official. Like most men, he had his *bêtes noires*, to whom, in the secrecy of his diary, he was probably unjust. " As he gets older," he wrote of one character, " his face discloses more and more to the world his crookedness; he is a repulsive creature." The diary was Brooke's only outlet, and he sometimes let himself go.

" Whilst taking my midday exercise in the Park," runs another entry, " I ran into ———, looking more greasy and objectionable than ever. He insisted on walking with me, which annoyed me, as I did not want to talk to him and wanted to look for the Scaup Duck on St. James's Lake."

Such expressions of passing irritation pepper the pages of any frank diary. To print it in its entirety without them and those more numerous passages which, though not derogatory, might wound sensitive feelings, would be to rob it of so much vitality as to present it and its writer in a false light. One has only to edit a page of Pepys's diary on the assumption that everyone mentioned in it is still alive to realise how emasculating such a process must be. Yet, though it has only been possible for this reason to use occasional complete entries, I have been able to print, almost in their entirety, a number of long passages from both the diary and autobiographical notes which convey some impression of their quality and interest. During his journeys with the Prime Minister to America, the Middle East and Russia, Brooke was not under the same pressure from miscellaneous callers as at home. The diary and notes enable one to watch the leaders of the two nations wrestling with one another until they had reached agreement on a blueprint for victory. All were big men engaged in mighty issues, and pettiness and self-interest were left far behind. Most of them have given their versions of the controversies in which they were engaged, either in their memoirs or in official biographies. Churchill, Harry Hopkins—and, through him, Roosevelt—King, Leahy, Arnold, Eisenhower and Andrew Cunningham have all spoken. Only Pound and Dill, who both died during the struggle, Marshall—now believed to be writing his memoirs—Portal and Alanbrooke have failed as yet to give their version of these momentous debates.

It is because Lord Alanbrooke's diaries and autobiographical notes contain so much that is indispensable to an understanding of the strategic direction of the war, and because they show how much, in the period between Dunkirk and the Italian surrender, this country contributed to victory, that after consultation with their author and the late Lt. Gen. Sir Otto Lund, then Colonel Commandant of the Royal Regiment of Artillery,

I decided to write this book and make the story they reveal known now instead of waiting till the official biography can be written and the diaries published in full. It is so easy, as happened in the case of Haig and the First World War, for a false legend to grow up while interest in contemporary events is still strong, and to be perpetuated for lack of some essential part of the evidence. Despite the spate of war books and the vast accumulation of material which the State is making available in its Official Histories, there seems some danger that the story of Britain's achievement in the Second World War may be transmitted to posterity without the figure of her greatest soldier. With the help of his diaries and autobiographical notes I have, therefore, tried to show what he achieved for Britain and the Allied cause in the early war-years of unpreparedness and disaster, and in particular in the crucial nineteen months between the fall of Singapore and the Italian surrender. This was the period in which this country's contribution to the Allied war-effort was relatively greatest, when the recovery of her fortunes was most marked and the foundations of victory were laid. My sequel, *The Triumph of the West*, will deal with a period in which, though checkered by disappointments, the burden had become easier for those who directed the nation's strategy. In this volume I have sought to show how, by putting first things first and seeking what was desirable in the light of what was immediately possible, Alanbrooke, with his political chief and his British and American colleagues, made a pattern for victory from which the Western Allies, despite superficial differences of opinion, never radically departed. Anyone reading the diary during these months cannot fail to be struck by the consistency of his vision and judgment. To watch his mind at work—so prophetic and accurate in every mechanical detail of military knowledge—is like watching the recordings of some delicate precision instrument.

.   .   .   .

Many famous men cross Lord Alanbrooke's pages. The greatest of all is the Prime Minister with whom he worked in daily association for three and a half years. The picture he paints of him is not that of a man always pedantically right.

It is the portrait of a leader, daring sometimes to the point of recklessness, who was often wrong in minor matters, who could be perverse, puckish, wayward and overbearing and make the lives of those who worked with him a burden, yet who won their love and admiration, never gave in, never despaired, never blurred the essential issues on which the survival and triumph of Britain depended. One sees in his pages this formidable, poetic, indomitable, humane and humorous being, pacing the hall at Chequers in the small hours of the morning, expounding plans for Hitler's destruction while demonstrating his skill with bayonet and bren-gun, dictating in bed in scarlet and green dragon dressing-gown with cigar in cheek and papers strewn around him, or in impassioned argument with Stalin and Roosevelt or his own military advisers. Though the latter had constantly to struggle with him, they depended on him completely and knew that without him all they were seeking would be in vain. He was irreplaceable and, therefore, indispensable. " P.M. very tired and complaining of a pain inside," ran one diary entry after he had been particularly difficult, " I hope to God there is nothing wrong with him." That Brooke was at times exasperated beyond endurance and at others reduced to laughter by his formidable, unpredictable master only adds to the stature of the titan who emerges. " I wonder if any historian of the future," he wrote, " will ever be able to paint Winston in his true colours. It is a wonderful character, the most marvellous qualities and superhuman genius mixed with an astonishing lack of vision at times, and an impetuosity which, if not guided, must inevitably bring him into trouble again and again. . . . He is quite the most difficult man to work with that I have ever struck, but I would not have missed the chance of working with him for anything on earth." " As I look back on those five years of close contact with the greatest war leader of modern times," he said after the war, " I carry away in my memory deeply engraved impressions of unbounded genius, unrelenting energy, dogged determination, a refusal to accept defeat in any shape or form, vast personal courage, a deep sense of humour, and an uncanny faculty of inspiring respect, admiration, loyalty and deep affection in the hearts of all those fortunate enough to work in close touch with him. With that memory as a background I shall to my dying day thank God for the great privilege of having been associated with him during those momentous years."[1]

. . . .

The portrait Alanbrooke paints of himself is, inevitably, less successful. Diaries can never show the whole of a man; as Pepys's monumental naval correspondence shows, even the most revealing of diaries is an incomplete picture of the public servant who kept it. To anyone who worked with Alanbrooke during the war, there seems an almost incredible contrast between the decisive, iron-willed Commander-in-Chief and C.I.G.S. the Army and Cabinet War Room knew and the sensitive, imaginative and often apprehensive being disclosed by the diary. In his work Alanbrooke was, above all, a man who kept his own council. In his diary he does not; it is this that makes it so valuable. Yet, with its unguarded expressions of exasperation and anxiety, it gives no indication of the tremendous patience and self-control he exercised in his dealings with others. To those around him he seemed a man of steel, never hurried or harassed, whose calm nothing could shake. He appeared to be even less moved by shocks and disasters than the Prime Minister—" a precision brain-machine," as one of his political chiefs called him, born without nerves. The impression was deliberate. ' I considered it essential,' he wrote, ' never to disclose outwardly what one felt inwardly. One might be torn with doubts, misgivings and despondency, but it was essential no vestige of the inward feelings should appear on the surface. If and when they did, they inevitably spread like wild fire and with snowball increase. It was of primary importance to maintain an outward appearance that radiated confidence. . . . My diary often acted as a safety valve, the only safety valve I had.'

To the Army, during the four war years in which Brooke controlled it from the C.I.G.S.'s room, he was an almost legendary figure, remote, stern and aloof—a dark, unsmiling

[1] Speech at the unveiling of Winston Churchill's portrait at the Junior Carlton Club, 19 Dec., 1950.

man, with an inscrutable poker face, who expected from everyone about him his own clockwork efficiency, industry and speed of thought and action. Even to those closest to him he seemed a man apart; Ian Jacob, who as a member of the War Cabinet Secretariat saw him almost every day for five years, never wholly lost his awe of him. Yet while he terrified those who did not understand his quick, abrupt, staccato way of speaking, and in any matter affecting the Service was outspoken and short to the point of rudeness, off duty he was remarkable for his courtesy and considerateness and for his apparently complete unconsciousness of his own rank and importance. " The extraordinary thing about Brookie," an associate said of him, " is that he always talks as if he were still a brigadier." Subalterns and unassuming regimental officers found him as easy to talk to as their own contemporaries. In his subaltern days in India he had been a notable big-game hunter and, though out of a dislike for killing the wild creatures of the jungle he had later substituted the camera for the rifle and become an expert on bird-photography, he was still passionately addicted to fishing and shooting and loved to talk of them with those who shared his enthusiasms. Though since his first wife's death by his side in a motor accident in the 'twenties he had withdrawn into himself and taken little part in the normal social round and banter of a soldier's life, to the few who knew him intimately he was the most delightful of companions, a close observer of nature with a genius for story-telling and a wicked Irish gift of mimicry. When he relaxed in their company, by the riverside with rod and camera, or at home with his wife and the two small children of his intensely happy second marriage, he put off every restraint and care.

Occasionally the emotional side of his nature broke through the mask of strict professional rectitude and iron control under which he kept his quick temper and highly-strung temperament, as when he handed over his apparently doomed corps to Montgomery on the La Panne beaches with tears streaming down his face. Like Wellington, whom in many ways he resembled, though he had hardened himself and was capable of great physical endurance, he was an extremely sensitive man to whom the horrors of war were more than usually painful.

Few who served under this austere soldier—" as regimental as a button-stick "—who threatened to have a French general at Dunkirk shot if he disobeyed his orders, would have guessed that he began his diary of the war with the words, " It is all too ghastly even to be a nightmare," and that, after attending Armistice Service on Vimy Ridge, he had written:

> " I felt throughout the ceremony as if I were in a dream. The white tall pillars of the monument standing out against the ashy-grey sky seemed entirely detached from this earth, whilst the two red wreaths of poppies looked like two small drops of blood on that vast monument. They seemed as a vivid reminder of the floods of blood that had already been spilt on the very ground we were standing on, and of the futility of again causing such bloodshed. I suppose that it is through such punishments that we shall eventually learn to ' love our neighbour as ourselves.' "[1]

" The first feelings of spring," he wrote in his diary a few weeks before the German offensive opened in the West, " a lovely mild day which makes it harder than ever to realise that humanity can be so mad as to be at war again. I went for a walk in the woods and wished I could wake up out of this nightmare of war and find myself by your side again with the world at peace."

. . . .

Nor does Alanbrooke's self-portrait sufficiently convey the sense of his own consistency. Like all diaries, it reflects the changing moods, hopes and fears of the day; not the sustained patience and resolution with which a great man carries out his purpose over the years. It reveals his aspirations, but gives only a partial indication of the means by which he achieved them. There is a passage in the diary of Eisenhower's aide-de-camp, Captain Butcher, recording a dictum of Churchill's—made at a dinner-party in Algiers in the summer of 1943—that " it was foolish to keep a day-by-day diary because it would simply reflect

[1] *Diary*, 11th November, 1939.

the change of opinion or decision of the writer, which, when and if published, makes one appear indecisive and foolish."[1] There is much truth in this, though to a historian a contemporary entry is far more valuable than any justification written afterwards. Yet, when it can be read in its entirety, I believe Alanbrooke's diary will stand this test far better than most. It will, however, always remain necessary to seek the man in his work and achievements. His claim to fame must rest in the last resort, not in what he wrote, but in his impress on the war.

One further *caveat* is necessary. Lord Alanbrooke's diary was not a conscious work of art. It is full, like all diaries, of repetitions. It was written in haste and under conditions of often intolerable strain, as its author's frequently untidy and harassed handwriting reveals, so different from his normal bold, slanting hand. So does the erratic spelling, the words missed out, the use of exclamation marks and underlinings to emphasise meaning. Its writer was not a literary man, but a professional soldier who, having been educated in France, had not even received the normal English literary schooling; until he went to Woolwich at eighteen, he had been brought up almost entirely in France. His writing is often stilted, pedestrian, marred by clichés and mixed metaphors, and totally unrevised and unpolished. Only when his imagination is aroused and his perceptions riveted by some striking scene of human drama, humour or natural beauty does his Muse take wings. Yet when it does, as in his wonderful account of Churchill listening to Montgomery's exposition of his plans on the beach at Alamein, or the description of the sardonic pig with the orangepeel mouth at the Kremlin banquet, it stands comparison with that of any professional writer. For all his faults of grammar and syntax, he can make a scene live as few can.

.   .   .   .

To distinguish between the Diary and the Autobiographical Notes I have used double quotation marks for the former and single quotation marks for the latter, which are also set in a slightly less deep inset than the diary extracts. Through the

[1] H. C. Butcher, *Three Years with Eisenhower*, 270. " For his part, the Prime Minister said, he would much prefer to wait until the war is over and then write impressions so that, if necessary, he could correct or bury his mistakes."

great generosity of Field Marshal Viscount Montgomery of Alamein, Lady Dill and Lieutenant-General Sir Ian Jacob, I have been able to include in the book extracts from unpublished letters of Field Marshals Montgomery and the late Sir John Dill and from Sir Ian Jacob's MS diaries. My many debts to others is set out at the end of this volume.

PART ONE

The Day when Heaven was Falling

Chapter One

DEFENCELESS ISLAND

Britannia needs no bulwarks!
T. CAMPBELL

WHEN ON September 3rd, 1939, Britain, carrying with her a deeply-divided and hesitant France, met Hitler's invasion of Poland by war, the bulk of her battle-fleet had been re-armed against air-attack and the first of the great ships laid down in 1936 was within a year of completion. And, having grown in four years from 500 to nearly 1500 first-line aircraft and from 30,000 to 120,000 men, her Metropolitan Air Force, though still only a third of the size of the Luftwaffe, offered, in its small but superlatively trained Fighter Command,[1] some answer to the trump card of unopposed bombing with which for the past eighteen months Hitler had blackmailed Europe. For the first time, too, as a result of the rapid build-up of Anti-Aircraft Command, London and the principal ports and factory towns had some rudimentary ground defence against day bombardment from the air.

Yet on land, in the light of the immense technical changes of the past decade, Britain was still almost in the position of a nineteenth-century Asiatic State challenging with the traditional arms of the past a European power armed with modern artillery and machine-guns. Her Regular Army, equipped only for colonial warfare, was far less ready for a Continental war than in 1914, when it had sent seven magnificently trained divisions to France. Its function was to police and garrison a global commercial empire, and, when partial rearmament began in the middle 'thirties, absolute priority had been given

---

[1] It still, however, had little more than half the strength with which a year later it was to fight the Battle of Britain.

to the needs of the Navy and Air Force and the Army had been left almost in the same state of neglect into which it had fallen in the pacifist 'twenties, when, with an armaments expenditure of less than two and a half millions compared with the Navy's thirteen millions and the R.A.F.'s seven and a half millions, its personnel had shrunk to under 150,000 men. Its artillery had little more than half the range of the latest German guns, it was without any but the lightest armour, and its men had had to do their training with flags instead of batteries and wooden dummies and hired tradesmen's vans instead of tanks and bren-guns.[1]

Not until the anxious summer of 1938—and then only on the spur of the moment and to reassure the French—had the possibility of sending two of its five divisions to the Continent in the event of a German war been considered. Even then, with the urgent needs of the other Services, little was done for the Army except to strengthen its anti-aircraft units for purposes of home defence. But in the spring of 1939, after the Chamberlain Administration had met Hitler's treacherous invasion of Czechoslovakia with a guarantee of Poland's western frontiers and the threat to Germany of a European war on two fronts, conscription had been suddenly introduced. With the knowledge that the Army's training depots could be now filled and oblivious of its almost complete lack of modern arms, the Government had promised the French to increase the initial Expeditionary Force from two to four divisions—almost the entire Regular home-strength of the country—and to reinforce it as soon as possible after the outbreak of war by a further five or six Territorial divisions. Ultimately, it intimated, thirty or more divisions would be raised. ·

Yet, though there was now no lack of potential man-power, the utmost the Ministry of Supply could hope to arm and equip for France even by 1942 were five Regular and fourteen Territorial divisions. On the outbreak of war in September, 1939, only two of these were approaching readiness. The Regular Army had only just received its peacetime complement of wheeled transport and barely half its tracked vehicles. The new National Service Army existed only on paper. Barely a month had passed since the first 30,000 " militiamen " had reported for their six months' training—raw youths from the streets who had been taught to despise soldiering and who appeared in Press photographs toasting unnaturally polite sergeants in mugs of tea or, hollow-cheeked from long un-employment, holding out their plates for their first Army dinner. Though it was expected that within a year nearly a million men would be with the Colours, one immediate effect of the National Service Act had been to hold up the training and equipment of the Regular Army, whose ranks had been thinned by the demand for instructors and specialists to teach the new units. And, by withdrawing labour from the factories, it had temporarily dislocated and retarded armament pro-duction.[1]

On the day after the declaration of war, however, the first detachment of the Expeditionary Force sailed for France. Within just over a fortnight, blanketed by security precautions so stringent and travelling by routes so devious that there was some difficulty in supplying them with rations, the 1st and 2nd Divisions—the only fully trained troops in England—had been landed in the French Atlantic ports and assembled around Le Mans, ready for the journey to their battle stations on the Belgian frontier. With them went an Air Component for co-operation with the French Army and a small Advanced Air Striking Force of light and medium bombers to attack com-munications and strategical targets in the event of a German invasion of the Low Countries.

Two further divisions, constituting a hastily-formed II Corps, though not yet trained or equipped and with nearly half its men reservists, followed at the end of September in accordance with the Government's promise to France. Together with its maintenance, supply and communications services in the rear areas, the Expeditionary Force constituted an initial reinforce-ment to the French Army of some 160,000 men and 24,000 vehicles. It was transported across the Channel, despite the threat from Lufwaffe and U-boat, without the loss of a man or weapon.

The Commander-in-Chief of this Force was Lord Gort, who

[1] The effect on Britain's first " Armoured " Division is told in three articles in *The Army Quarterly* (Vols. 45 and 46) by its then commander, Major-General R. Evans.

had handed over his post as Chief of the Imperial General Staff to the veteran General Ironside; its two corps commanders were Sir John Dill and Alan Brooke. Having to mobilise for foreign service two divisions deficient in almost every essential of modern continental war, the latter, as soon as he took up his command at Salisbury, had drawn attention to their dangerously unprepared state. Neither had had any divisional or even brigade training, and their infantry, who had learnt their battle-drill with marking-flags, had only been issued with machine-guns in the past year.[1] Their few tanks were without even such elementary equipment as wireless sets, while the artillery's new 25-pounder guns were still in process of issue and its gunners unpractised in their use. Brooke had, therefore, asked for—and received—an assurance that, though it might be necessary for political reasons to send his men overseas with their better trained and equipped comrades of the 1st and 2nd Divisions, they should remain in western France for completion and training before proceeding to the frontier. Yet as he stepped off the gangway at Cherbourg on September 29th he was met by the news that they were to move at once to the frontier. And, having been given one assurance before he left England, he was now given another by a War Office representative: that, though his Corps must go to its battle stations untrained and half-equipped, there was no possibility of a German attack before the winter. " I wonder if he is right," was his comment.

By this time Poland, with her two million fighting men, had been driven out of the war. Her air force—as large as France's —had been wiped out in a few hours, her cities and communications paralysed by continuous day bombing, and her troops, fighting with obsolete weapons and technique, overwhelmed by the speed and striking power of a modern mechanised army trained and equipped for a war of movement. The French, trained and equipped for one of inert defence, had remained behind the Maginot Line, helpless spectators of her fate, while, in deference to Paris' cautious

---

[1] In the Southern Command manœuvres of 1939 most of the Bren-gun carriers bore an inscription on their sides, "Not to be used in action. Mild steel only. Not armour plate." Lt.-Col. M. Henniker, "*Prelude to Battle*," *Blackwood's*, September, 1947. 210.

policy of non-provocation, the R.A.F. had countered the hail of bombs on Polish towns by dropping leaflets by night on the Reich. Left to defend herself without help, Poland's effective resistance had lasted little more than a fortnight. Before it ended the Russians, seeking their agreed share of the spoils, had crossed the frontier and advanced on Brest Litovsk. On September 27th—the day before Brooke sailed for France— Warsaw had surrendered. The last Polish garrison laid down its arms next day.

The commander of the II Corps, therefore, had some ground for his anxiety, for the German east-to-west communications, with their strategic railways and *autobahns*, were the best in the world. Nor was he reassured when, on October 2nd, he made the two-hundred miles journey to Lord Gort's head-quarters at Arras and saw the frontier defences which the I Corps was taking over near Lille. They consisted of nothing but a shallow tank-ditch and, at intervals of every thousand yards, alarmingly visible concrete pill-boxes, most of them unfinished owing to shortage of cement. Little wiring had been done and no rear demolitions made, and, as the Expeditionary Force was desperately short of sand-bags, it could not make even improvised defences, though vast quantities of these were being used in England to protect buildings against non-existent air raids.[1] The front allocated to its four divisions stretched for twenty-five miles, while there was a large gap between them and the nearest French force on their left. So wide a front offered no scope for defence in depth if the Germans attacked across the Belgian plain. " It surely would not take them long," Brooke wrote, " to cross the intervening ground should they decide to . . . and thus take advantage of the unpreparedness of the French and ourselves."

To make matters worse, the whole district, a densely-populated one, was swarming with Belgians, Poles, displaced Saar miners and even Italians, who had taken the place of the French reservists in the mines and cloth factories. Opportunities for spying were unlimited. And the local Communists, who for years had been clamouring for war, were now doing everything

[1] " When one remembers the lavish use made of sandbags at home in localities that will never see a bomb, it makes one's blood boil to be so short of them out here." *Diary*, 22nd October, 1939.

they could to obstruct the war-effort and undermine the morale of both civilian population and the armies.[1] " We are facing this war in a half-hearted way," Brooke wrote in his diary on October 9th. " The forward area is still crammed with civilians that ought to be evacuated, and no real serious efforts seem to be made to organise civilian labour to prepare defences that are essential. . . . I feel that the Germans would have been tackling the situation very differently." " Both the War Office and G.H.Q.," he added two days later, " appear to be thinking of the war in six months' time. Our immediate danger in the event of an attack does not appear to be fully realised."

Yet when he and Dill—the soldier whose professional judgment Brooke respected above all others—confided their fears to their Commander-in-Chief and listed the items needed to give their troops some chance of withstanding the Germans, they found him cheerfully unconcerned. Like the authorities in England he seemed unable to realise how serious the deficiencies were. No braver man than Gort ever lived. During the first War his gallantry had become a legend, and men who had fought at Cambrai remembered all their lives the imperturbable calm with which, as a young battalion commander of thirty, he had organised the Guards' counter-attack at Bourlon Wood. As a fighting soldier in the heart of an action he was incomparable; the most inspiring person, Brooke thought, he had ever known in handling a battalion in war. Yet before his appointment as Chief of the Imperial General Staff in 1937, he had never commanded any unit larger than a brigade, and he was almost wholly without Dill's and Brooke's knowledge of the science of higher command and of the latest developments in Continental warfare and armaments. The very lion-heartedness that made him great in battle was a defect in his present situation, for it rendered him blind to dangers visible to those more gifted with imagination than himself. Dill might have made his political superiors realise its dangers and urgent necessities; Gort could not.

For the position in which he found himself called, not merely for character, with which he was superlatively endowed, but

---

[1] As early as October 19th Brooke had to complain to the Prefect of Lille that his men were being tampered with by Communists.

for exceptional clarity of vision. He was in charge of Britain's
only army, yet had been placed by his Government under the
command of the French who not unjustly regarded it as a very
insignificant fraction of their force and, though they politely
concealed their professional contempt, thought of him and his
officers as inexperienced amateurs. He was not even a member
of the Supreme Allied Council, and was under the orders, not
only of the French Supreme Commander, General Gamelin,
but of both the Commander in Chief of the North-East and the
General commanding the Group of Armies on the Belgian
frontier. Though he possessed a right of appeal to London, he
was far too loyal to exercise it except when disaster was staring
him in the face. His very straightforwardness and Guardsman's
feeling for obedience tended to neutralise his natural shrewdness and to silence any doubts he may have had. Instead of
challenging the fallacious assumptions of his superiors, he
loyally and cheerfully accepted them. The French High
Command, General Spears has since written, regarded him as
a kind of friendly and jovial battalion commander, always
willing and anxious to please and ready to do everything he
was told.[1]

.   .   .   .

   The fog of unrealism in which Gort and his army found
themselves that winter would have taxed the capacity of a far
more astute mind. Those at home were thinking in terms, not
of the swift mechanised and air warfare of the mid-twentieth
century, but of the huge troglodyte armies and continuous
trench-lines of twenty years before. Having at last made up
their minds to a conflict for which, on land, they were almost
totally unprepared, the goal they had unconsciously set themselves was to recreate as quickly as possible the conditions of
Sir Douglas Haig's triumph in 1918. And if Britain's military
thought was obsessed with the past, that of France was still
more so. Twenty years' intensive study of the mistakes of
1914-18 had convinced her generals that, in the face of modern
automatic weapons, heavy casualties could only be avoided by
a scrupulous refusal to take any risks at all. Most of them had

[1] *Prelude to Dunkirk,* 47.

served on the Staff in the first War when France had lost more than a million and a half lives, and when a fanatical belief in the virtues of the offensive had caused enormous casualties. As a result the French military mind, pursuing logic further than is wise in an illogical world, had gone to the other extreme and enthroned the defensive as the secret of war. The only kind of attack acceptable to orthodox thought was one in which no movement was made without the most exact knowledge of the enemy's strength and dispositions, in which the attacker's preliminary bombardment was so annihilating and his objectives so limited that they could be attained without sacrifice, and in which every yard gained was carefully consolidated. An army had to go forward slowly and circumspectly or not at all. Above all, the will-of-the-wisp of a breakthrough must be shunned as deadly heresy. Those who, like the young General de Gaulle, argued that tanks and highly mechanised mobile groups of all arms could restore the power of the offensive, were regarded as dangerous cranks. The tank —a weapon which the French possessed in greater numbers than any other nation—was employed by them exclusively as an instrument of positional warfare to support and protect infantry in defence and in small, limited advances. Being highly vulnerable to artillery and anti-tank weapons, it was only to be used in the closest co-operation with other arms. A swift attack by armour, it was held, might overwhelm a small nation without elaborate prepared defences; it could effect nothing against a well-equipped one. Static fire-power was the lord of the battlefield, and the object of strategist and tactician alike should be to wear down the enemy's patience and induce him to lower his guard and himself attack.

While the Germans were knocking out the Poles and holding the Siegfried Line with a skeleton force of 42 weak divisions, the French with their 72 available divisions[1] had staged such a limited offensive on the Saarbrücken frontier. With infinite caution and every possible precaution against casualties, they occupied, without opposition, a chain of frontier villages in front of the enemy's main defences. The process was much

---

[1] This figure does not include the twelve divisions holding the Italian frontier or the four British divisions then assembling in western France.

praised by British Press commentators, who described it as setting " a perplexing strategic problem for Hitler," and " a game played with great skill " by General Gamelin. They were particularly impressed by the almost complete absence of casualties. " On the assurance of the High Military Command," English newspaper readers were told, " there is to be no wastage of life." Even when, as happened after the first victorious German divisions began to return from Poland, the French immediately withdrew from the ground they had gained to the shelter of their Maginot defences, the British continued to be impressed by the apparent skill of their ally and " the almost uncanny difference between the present war and the previous one."[1]

This obsession with the supremacy of static fire-power was common to all the European Staffs of the 'twenties and 'thirties. The German generals were almost as conscious as the French of the casualties of the 1914-18 offensives. But having been forbidden heavy artillery and fortified defences by the Peace Treaties, they had been driven to seeking substitutes for them. Encouraged by the reorganiser of the post-war *Reichswehr*, General von Seeckt, some of their younger officers had experimented during the 'twenties with ways of using tank groups and motorised support troops in conjunction, first for mobile defence and later for attack. When major rearmament began under Hitler these experiments resulted in the creation of three armoured or panzer divisions in which fast tanks with mobile supporting arms were grouped together, not for co-operation with infantry against fixed fronts, but for swift, independent action in a war of movement. These divisions had played the leading part in the unopposed occupations of Austria and Czechoslovakia, and, recently, in the campaign against Poland.

Yet with the re-creation of a fully equipped *Reichswehr*, the more senior German generals had reverted to the older and more conventional view of war in which they had been brought up. Now that they once more enjoyed heavy guns and masses of conscript infantry, they tended to frown on the theories of younger enthusiasts and, like the French, to favour the employ-

[1] *Illustrated London News*, 21st October, 1939.

ment of tanks in small tactical groups for the support of infantry. The *blitzkrieg* had triumphed over an unmechanised enemy without strongly prepared defences, but the German High Command no more contemplated using it against the Maginot Line than the French against the Siegfried Line. Nor, impressed by the strength of French defensive armaments, were they anxious to expose their Army on the Belgian plain; they wished, not to attack, but to be attacked. The stalemate mentality was almost as strong in von Brauchitsch and Halder, the Commander-in-Chief and Chief-of-Staff of the German Army, as in the prudent Gamelin. They had been trained in the same school.

Hitler's mind had also been conditioned by his experiences in the First World War. But it was obsessed by the fear, not of casualties, but of a repetition of the positional or trench war of attrition that had proved so fatal to Imperial Germany. For the Western democracies, with their potential resources and hope of ultimate help from the New World, a static war spelt steadily growing strength. It was because Hitler saw that for Germany it spelt defeat that he turned to the military theories, not of the older, more conventional soldiers at the head of the *Reichswehr*, but of their more radical subordinates. Before any other European leader he had grasped the immensely increased importance of the air-weapon—a realization on which all his triumphs of the past eighteen months had been based. During the Polish campaign he became fully aware of the power of another and purely military weapon. Four days after the start of the offensive he had stood amazed by the side of Guderian, the pioneer of Germany's independent armoured divisions, surveying the smashed Polish batteries that had contested the crossing of the Vistula. " Our dive-bombers did that? " he asked. " No," replied Guderian, " our panzers." And when that original-minded soldier informed him that the casualties of his four divisions were only 150 killed, he could scarcely believe him.[1]

For the *blitzkrieg* had succeeded. The completion of the Polish campaign in just under four weeks and the liquidation

[1] " I was able to show him that the smallness of our casualties in this battle against a tough and courageous enemy was primarily due to the effectiveness of our tanks. Tanks are a life-saving weapon." *Guderian* 73.

of an army of two millions had banished all Hitler's remaining hesitations as to the readiness of the Reich for major war. He became convinced, not only that German morale had completely recovered from the humiliations of 1918, but that his own intuition was as infallible in battle as in peace. He had never had many doubts about the range of his genius; now he had none. It had been he who had brushed aside his generals' fears of attacking in the East while the French Army threatened their rear, just as he had ignored their earlier fears about the occupation of the Rhineland, the *Anschluss*, and the rape of Czechoslovakia. And though, before becoming Commander-in-Chief of the German Armed Forces, he had never held any higher rank than a corporal's, he had been proved right in his contemptuous disbelief in the power of an isolated State like Poland to withstand the assault of a rearmed and resurrected *Reich*. He was convinced that he was equally correct in his estimate of the inertia and cowardice of the French. Their failure to attack while the overwhelming bulk of his army was engaged in the east showed not only that they might be induced to accept a humiliating *fait accompli* but that they could be dealt with in the same manner as the Poles.

Hitler was an opportunist, but his ultimate objectives never changed. They were unlimited power for himself and, as the means to achieve it, unlimited living space for the German race. He sought them in the historic conception of the *Drang nach Östen*—the eastward expansion of the *Reich* at the expense, first of the Versailles Treaty States, and then of Soviet Russia. Because he was a central European with little feeling for the sea, and because he had a certain admiration for England— born of her valour in the first War and her supposed Teutonic origin—he had wished to make an ally of her and leave her her naval power and empire. Her people's growing dislike of his tyranny and their reaction to his bad faith after Munich had aligned her against him. Yet, though he had made a pact with Russia and freed his hands to attack the Western Powers, his goal remained the same—not the overseas empire and sea-borne trade of Britain and France, but the continental spaces, the wheat and oil of Russia, the Ukraine and the Caucasus.

At the outset of the Polish campaign he had, therefore, ordered his troops in the West to stand strictly on the defensive and do nothing that might turn Britain's and France's nominal declaration of war into an active one. " In two months," he had declared, " Poland will be finished and then we shall have a great peace conference with the Western Powers." But though the overthrow of Russia remained his ultimate aim, after his triumph in Poland his appetite for military adventure was whetted. On October 6th, the day after he reviewed his troops in the ruins of Warsaw, he made his peace offer to the Western Powers in the Reichstag. Yet even before his speech had been drafted he was preparing for immediate military action if his overtures should be rejected. On the day that Warsaw surrendered he had asked von Brauchitsch and Halder what plans they had made for prosecuting the war in the West. When they replied that these were based purely on the defensive and that no preparations had been made for an attack, he had abruptly dismissed them from his presence.

During the next ten days, while his armies were returning from Poland, the German Leader reached his decision. If his generals used technical arguments to impede his projects, he would use his political power and titular rank as Commander-in-Chief of the Armed Forces to compel them. No professional *expertise* should weigh against his will, not even that of the General Staff and Officer Corps—from time immemorial the most sacred thing in Germany. On October 9th, while General Brooke was noting in his diary his fears of what might happen to his half-prepared, ill-equipped troops if the Germans should strike at them across the Belgian plain, Hitler was at work on a Memorandum to demolish the objections of his cautious Commander-in-Chief and Chief of Staff to an immediate offensive in the West.

It was an uncompromising document. The Poles having been eliminated, the next aim must be " the destruction of the ability of the Western Powers ever again to oppose the development of the German people in Europe." Hitler's pact with Russia and his victory in Poland had made war on a single front—the dream of every German for a century—a realizable achievement. Yet this unique opportunity could not in the nature of things, he contended, endure. For perhaps a year Russia's neutrality could be depended upon, but no treaty would ensure it indefinitely. The only safeguard against Soviet attack was irresistible German strength. The same argument applied to Germany's allies, Italy and Japan, who could only be brought into the war by the clearest proof that she was bound to win.

" Time," Hitler continued, " cannot be considered an ally; only success will be. . . . The military application of our people's strength has been carried through to such an extent that, within a *short* time at any rate, it cannot be markedly improved. . . . Any increase of our military power which can be expected in the next five years will be offset, not indeed by France, but by England, which is constantly growing stronger." And what was true in the military sphere was equally true in the economic. Germany lacked resources for a long war; she could only obtain them by a swift, decisive victory. She was particularly vulnerable in the West, where her Ruhr industries lay within easy striking distance of a strong enemy air force. Though the British were at present inferior to Germany in the air, that inferiority would not last. " The longer the war continues, the harder will be the preservation of German air superiority."

If the Western Powers would not make peace, everything pointed to an immediate offensive, not against the Maginot Line, but through Belgium and Holland. This would not only enable Germany to strike at France's flank before the British were strong enough to guard it, but would safeguard the Ruhr and place the Luftwaffe and German Navy in a position to deal the islanders " a mortal blow." With ocean bases won for the U-boats outside Germany's own narrow littoral, and England's factories and ports within easy reach of the captured Dutch and Belgian airfields, her downfall would be inevitable.

It was only the democracies who stood to gain by a stalemate in the West. The less hope they had of being able to destroy the German armed forces in battle, the more they would try to create the conditions for " a long-drawn-out war of attrition and annihilation." It was therefore useless to await their attack behind the Siegfried Line. Everything should be thrown into an all-out assault " as the one certain way of preventing a long and disastrous war." And it should be launched with lightning speed and in such strength that the French and British forces mobilising along the Belgian frontier would never be able to build up a solid front. " An offensive which does not aim at the destruction of the enemy forces from the start is senseless. To attack with weak and insufficient forces is equally useless." Boldness could alone win safety for the German people and the chance to fulfil their destiny.[1]

When the heads of the German Army heard Hitler read his manifesto, they were appalled. All their trained instincts revolted at the idea of an offensive at the outset of winter against the Force which for twenty years they had thought of as the strongest and best-equipped in Europe. Their deeply-rooted fear of modern fire-power blinded them to the lesson of the Polish campaign—obvious to Hitler and to younger officers like Guderian—that, by combining striking-power with rapid movement, a purely static fire-power could be neutralised and shattered, and that aircraft and fast-moving armour in conjunction offered the means of doing so. Even the Maginot Line, though impregnable against frontal attack, could be outflanked by a mobile fire-power sufficiently swift and strong to overwhelm in the open any opposing fire-power that lacked its mobility. For, whatever their numerical superiority in artillery and tanks, so long as the French failed to make their fire-power mobile, the Belgian plain, Hitler saw, offered as ideal a field for the *blitzkrieg* as the Polish.

In his insistence on an immediate offensive and his faith in the effects of mobile striking-power the German dictator was far nearer the classical military tradition of Prussia than his own senior commanders. The prophetic von Seeckt had preached it in the days of the *Reichswehr's* eclipse after its casualties in the great offensives of the first War. " The mistake," he wrote, " lies in opposing an immobile and almost defenceless human mass to the brutal action of material. . . . Material is superior to the living, mortal human mass, but it is not superior to the living and immortal human mind. . . . The whole future of warfare appears to me to be in the employ-

---

[1] *Nuremberg Documents*, 52-L *cit*; Hinsley, 38-42; A. Bullock, *Hitler*, 512-13; J. Wheeler-Bennett, *Nemesis of Power*, 464-5.

ment of mobile armies, relatively small but of high quality and rendered . . . more effective by the addition of aircraft." Von Seeckt's younger disciples, who had seen the Polish Army crumble under the lightning blows of the dive-bombers and panzers, knew that his teaching was true. The fifty-year-old Guderian, who had watched his tanks fulfil the dreams of years, never doubted they could achieve the same results elsewhere. " We hoped," he wrote, " that the speed of our Polish victory would bear political fruit and that the Western Powers might now feel inclined to make a sensible peace. We imagined that if this were not the case, Hitler would quickly decide on a campaign in the West. . . . The Corridor was pierced. We were available for fresh employment."[1]

. . . .

It was because he appreciated, better than any other British soldier of his time, the combined striking-power of swift-moving armour, motorised artillery and low-flying aircraft and the inability of the ill-equipped, static French and British forces on the Belgian frontier to withstand them, that Alan Brooke expected the Germans to attack in the West before the latter's deficiencies could be made good. Like Guderian and de Gaulle, he had been a protagonist of the new technique of warfare, but, whereas his German and French counterparts had been advocating their views—the one successfully and the other unsuccessfully—in armies with large numbers of tanks, Brooke had been doing so in a country which, though it had been the first to invent and use them, possessed virtually none. The experimental mobile and " armoured " division which he had commanded and started to train two years before was still in England, waiting, not only for three-quarters of its vehicles, but for guns, gun-mountings and wireless sets. The sole armour the Expeditionary Force possessed were a few slow infantry tanks and the almost absurdly light ones with which the Divisional cavalry regiments were equipped. It was short of anti-tank guns, of ammunition for them and of anti-aircraft protection,

[1] *Guderian*, 84, 73. Mr. John Wheeler-Bennett, in his brilliant *Nemesis of Power*, states that Guderian feared that " a mechanical attack in the West that autumn would bog down on account of ground conditions." This, however true later in the winter, does not seem to have been his view in October.

and lacked all means, not merely for launching a *blitzkrieg*, but
for resisting one. Nor, with so many demands on the R.A.F.'s
limited resources, could it look for any effective co-operation
and protection from the air. And, though its four divisions,
under their two very wide awake corps commanders, were now
hard at work putting up wire entanglements, constructing pill-
boxes and earthworks and strengthening the shallow tank
ditch in front of them, the territorial French troops on either
flank were making practically no preparations at all. They
seemed listless, bored and ill-cared for.

But, except for Brooke and Dill, no Allied leader, military or
civil, expected Hitler to attack at this time. When on October
12th, Chamberlain publicly rejected his peace offer, it did
not seem to have occurred to him that Hitler might meet his
refusal by an immediate offensive. Having at last accustomed
their minds to the hateful necessity of war, Britain's rulers were
now growing steadily more confident. None of the unpleasant
things they had been led to expect—massive air-raids, gas
attacks, heavy casualties—had happened, and time to complete
the country's rearmament was being afforded as though peace
was still continuing. Indeed, they were so impressed by the
miracle they had accomplished—with Hitler's help—of turning
a civilian-minded nation into an armed, or fast-arming camp,
that they tended to forget that the act of putting men into
khaki did not make them trained soldiers, or that sending even
regular troops into battle did not equip them for it. A never-
ending stream of optimistic propaganda, retailed to a censored
Press by a Government Department, concealed from the public
every item of news that could alarm or discourage and presented
a uniform picture of growing Allied strength and success. The
newspapers were full of accounts of a superlatively equipped
Expeditionary Force, with tanks advancing across the plains of
northern France, " thundering in open order, . . . ironsides, in
fact, . . . with exhausts roaring and wireless masts swaying," and
of French armies, fighting for the first time since the Napoleonic
era on German soil, carrying out, under a great military genius,
Gamelin, a process of costless and scientific attrition that was
slowly but remorselessly eating into the Siegfried Line. In
contrast, the reckless and amateur Germans were said to have

suffered immense losses in Poland through their offensive, while their internal economic situation was growing desperate for lack of petrol and sea-borne trade. Nor was it only the ignorant who were taken in by such propaganda; Britain's rulers themselves were. Even the veteran Winston Churchill, who, after vainly sounding the alarm for six years, had returned to the Admiralty from which he had mobilised the Fleet in 1914, expressed the view, in a memorandum to the War Cabinet, that the situation was far more favourable than at the start of the Kaiser's war and that Britain's policy should be to leave Hitler " to stew in his own juice during the winter while speeding forward our armaments and weaving-up our alliances."[1]

It came, therefore, as a shock when, towards the middle of October—three weeks after the Deputy Chief of the Imperial General Staff had assured General Brooke that such a thing was impossible—warnings began to reach the West of an impending attack on the Low Countries. On October 15th Brooke drew a picture in his diary of " the whole country dressed in their Sunday best and apparently oblivious that they may be sitting on a volcano." " It is hard at present to realize," he wrote, " we are at war." But that night, just as he was going to bed, he learnt by telephone that the French High Command was expecting an immediate attack through Belgium. And though the Belgians were resolved to take no step that might compromise their neutrality, the Allied Supreme Commander decided that, if they resisted, the ill-prepared Franco-British forces on the frontier should advance into their country to meet the invaders.

To Brooke and Dill this seemed madness. Their unarmoured troops could not yet hope to meet a German attack except behind the defences they were so busy strengthening. To encounter the panzers and Luftwaffe in the open plain before they completed their training and equipment would be to court the same disaster that had befallen the Poles. On the 19th Brooke's diary read:

> " Spent the morning planning for our advance into Belgium in the event of the Germans violating her

neutrality. In the afternoon attended two and a half hours G.H.Q. conference at I Corps H.Q. Before the conference Dill and I got hold of Gort and tried to make him realize the serious aspect of the contemplated move, the danger of leaving our present prepared position for one totally unprepared, and the exposure of our left flank if Fagalde's 16th Corps does not come up on the left. He will take a very lighthearted view of the situation and is too inclined to underestimate the strength and efficiency of the Germans."

Three days later, while rumours of a German attack were alternatively reported and denied, the French XVI Corps was still thirty miles to the rear. On the 27th Brooke again referred to his and Dill's difficulty in getting the Commander-in-Chief " to realize the seriousness of the situation. He refuses to face the difficulties we may be up against and makes light of them all."

On the very day that his two Corps Commanders were trying to awaken Gort to his danger, Hitler, impatient at the interminable excuses and delays of his Army leaders, summoned the Commander-in-Chief and Chief of the General Staff to the Chancellery and informed them that Operation Yellow—the code-name for the attack on the Low Countries—was to start on November 12th. So dismayed were they by the prospect that during the next week there was some talk among them and their Staff of seizing or assassinating the German Leader in order to negotiate terms with the West. A little group of retired officers of strong anti-Nazi views, led by Colonel-General Beck —a former Chief of the General Staff—tried to persuade them to throw in their lot with him. But when on Sunday November 5th, after promising the conspirators that he would join them unless the offensive was cancelled, the Commander-in-Chief had his next interview with Hitler, he was met by such a storm of reproach and abuse for his timidity that he crumpled up and returned to his headquarters in a state of collapse. After that there was no more talk of rebellion, and the preparations for an attack on Belgium and Holland went forward without further challenge by the German High Command.

As for the conspirators, their only action was to send a secret warning to the Belgian and Dutch Legations in Berlin that an attack could be expected on the 12th. There followed a week of wild alarms. By the evening of the 8th the news of the impending offensive had reached the Allies, and Brooke was notified that, as soon as it began, he was to advance into Belgium with his two divisions as far as the Scheldt and take up sixteen miles of the river near Oudenarde. This was a wider frontage than seven British divisions had held at Ypres in November, 1914, when the Germans had so nearly broken through to the Channel. " If I felt certain that the French XVI Corps would be up on my left," Brooke wrote, " it would not be so bad, but I have the gravest doubts on this account. . . . I only hope to God we do not have to hold the line of the Scheldt with such strung-out forces." ' The whole plan of the advance,' he commented afterwards, ' was fantastic and could only have resulted in disaster.'

The weather saved the British Army, which at that time had only half the strength it was to attain by the spring. The metereological report on November 7th was so alarming that the offensive was postponed, and, though orders for it continued on a day-by-day basis until the middle of January, the weather never recovered for long enough to make it possible to use the Luftwaffe. The rest of November was exceptionally wet, and early in December the coldest winter for years set in, with heavy snowfalls, fogs and almost constant frost. Yet Hitler continued to wait for a chance to attack. On November 23rd he made an impassioned speech to the principal officers of the Army, Navy and Air Force, proclaiming his intention of striking at Britain and France through Belgium and Holland at the earliest possible moment; the conditions, he declared, were more favourable now than they would ever be; in another six months it might be too late. It would cost him a million men, but it would cost the enemy as many, and the enemy could not stand it. On January 10th, following a spell of settled though still very cold weather, he ordered the invasion of the Low Countries to begin on the 17th. On that day, however, by a strange mischance, an aircraft, carrying a German staff officer with a complete operational plan of the offensive, lost its bearings and made a forced landing in Belgium. Before he could burn his papers they were seized by Belgian guards and their contents communicated to Brussels. The subsequent scare, during which the British Army stood to arms for several days, led to a strange incident recorded in Brooke's diary when, after a conference at G.H.Q., Lord Gort mysteriously introduced him " to a Mr. X who does a great deal of travelling and was very interesting." This, he revealed in his Notes after the war, was no less a person than Admiral of the Fleet Lord Keyes, the British First Lord of the Admiralty's liaison officer with the Belgian King—" dressed in most disreputable clothes "— on a secret mission to discuss the possibility of the Allies entering Belgium and taking up a new defensive line along the Dyle. However, while the Germans were still considering the situation caused by the disclosure of their plans, heavy snow began to fall and the offensive was finally cancelled. So was the proposed Belgian invitation to the Allies.

.   .   .   .

Thus the extremity of that bitter winter alone prevented Hitler from launching against an ill-equipped and ill-prepared Anglo-French Army on the borders of France and Belgium the mid-winter offensive which five years later he launched without command of the air against an exceedingly well-equipped and well-trained Anglo-American one. But for this Guderian's armour and Goering's bombers might have reached the Channel and the Belgian and Dutch airfields nine months before the Battle of Britain and when Fighter Command was still nearly twenty squadrons short of the force that was to save England in 1940.[1] " What might have happened," Brooke wrote afterwards, " if the Germans had attacked before the winter makes me shudder to think." " I only hope," he noted after the cancellation of the November offensive, " that we may now be left in peace for the next two or three months to complete the required readiness for war of the II Corps."

[1] In the last winter of the War, just after Hitler's December offensive in the Ardennes, the writer asked Lord Gort whether, had the Germans attacked in November, 1939, his troops and the French would have been better able to withstand them than in May, 1940. His reply was that they would have been far less so.

It was sorely needed. Some of the units arriving from England were almost completely untrained; one machine-gun battalion which he inspected towards the end of November Brooke described as totally unfit for war in every respect. " It would be sheer massacre," he commented, " to commit it to action in its present state." When the Secretary of State for War asked him whether he did not agree that formations should be sent to France to complete their training in order to impress the French, he replied that he regarded such a procedure as unfair to the units, to the B.E.F. and to Britain's allies. " To send untrained troops into modern war," he said, " is courting disaster such as befell the Poles."[1]

All through that bitter December, January and February, with the fields deep in powdery snow and the roads sheets of ice, while the British Expeditionary Force laboured ceaselessly at its defences, excavating, draining and revetting, making pill-boxes and tank-traps, and laying railway lines and cables along the frontier, Alan Brooke, tireless in supervising their making, had the sense that they would never be used. " I feel," he wrote, " that we are unlikely ever to defend the front we have spent so much thought and work in preparing. How can we avoid being drawn forward into Belgium? " For, since the Germans could only strike at them by invading that country, it seemed certain that, when they did so, his men would have to leave their defences and hasten, at whatever risk, to the aid of the Belgians. And this despite the fact that the latter, though now in secret communication with French and British Headquarters, continued to refuse, out of fear of provoking the Germans, to offer their would-be saviours any facilities for preparing an advance that would have to be made at the eleventh hour and under circumstances dictated by the enemy.

This was the dilemma which faced the Allies: that, while military considerations made it wise to await the German attack on their prepared frontier line, political considerations made it impossible not to try to save at least a part of Belgium. The only real issue was how much could be saved. The easiest and safest course would be to advance to the Scheldt—involving only a day's march—and hold the extreme western corner of

[1] *Diary*, 28th November, 1939.

the country, so protecting the Lille industrial area which the
Germans had occupied in the first War and which the
French were most anxious to prevent them occupying again.
The more tempting alternative was to move forward sixty
miles—probably under air attack and over roads packed with
refugees—to the line of the Dyle. This would save the Belgian
capital and the port of Antwerp and keep open communications
with western Holland if that State were attacked too. From a
military point of view it would also mean, if the river could be
reached in safety, a shortening of a dangerously extended line
and the incorporation in it of such of the twenty or so Belgian
and twelve Dutch divisions as could be saved—a nominal
accession of strength that would help to offset the steadily
rising number of German divisions in the West.

To those to whom military units were arithmetical figures of
equal value, like money or votes, and their movement a matter
of measuring miles on a map, all this seemed simple. The
Supreme War Council in Paris on November 17th resolved that,
" given the importance of holding the German forces as far
east as possible, it is essential to make every endeavour to hold
the line Meuse-Antwerp in the event of a German invasion of
Belgium." The French High Command, in whose hands the fate
of the Expeditionary Force lay, after some hesitation concurred
in this decision. The Supreme Commander took the view that
his troops could reach the line Mézières-Namur-Antwerp and
possibly even the Albert Canal and the Dutch islands beyond
the Scheldt, and told a visiting English M.P. that they would
move to the Dyle so quickly that the Belgians would not have
time to give way. General Georges, Commander-in-Chief of
the French Armies of the North-east, was more doubtful.

Brooke was not at all sanguine. " If we can get there in time
to organize ourselves properly to meet the German onrush,"
he wrote on November 19th, " it is without doubt the right
strategy. It is the shortest line possible through Belgium, saves
half that country, should give time for co-ordinated action
between the three countries provided the Belgian advance-
guards on the Albert Canal, at Liége and in the Ardennes can
hold out sufficiently long. We must, however, resolutely resist
being drawn on to try and save all Belgium by defending the

line of the Albert Canal and Liége. By trying to save the whole of Belgium instead of half, not only would we lose the whole of Belgium but probably the war as well."[1] The crux of the problem as he saw it—and of the Allies' danger—lay in the necessity, first of going forward, with inadequate air support and anti-aircraft protection, through a panic-stricken and bombed countryside whose roads they could not control, and then of defending a line which they would be given no time to prepare. For the Belgian authorities refused to offer any facilities until they were actually attacked. They wanted all the information they could get about the Allies' plan and dispositions but declined to give any about their own. They would not even allow their prospective defenders to reconnoitre their line of advance. The most they would do was to let some British officers in plain clothes visit the Dyle.

·   ·   ·   ·   ·   ·   ·   ·

It was not only Belgian lack of realism that made Brooke anxious. He was even more concerned at the unrealism of the French. Unlike the British Government and War Office and his own gallant, unquestioning Commander-in-Chief, he had no faith in the French Higher Command. He could see that the Supreme Commander was old and tired, that his lieutenants who entertained their British colleagues so hospitably were more interested in gastronomy than fighting, and that the dapper, ageing generals in their gilded képis and immaculate breeches who had been staff officers under Foch were living on the glories of the past and ignoring the present. General Spears, who had been liaison officer at French Headquarters in the first War, looking at General Georges with the eyes of memory and affection, could still believe him the embodiment of energy he had been twenty years before; could see in the smooth, complacent high priest of the defensive, Gamelin, remote from all in his ivory tower at Vincennes, the brilliant young staff officer who had followed Père Joffre like a shadow and helped to plan the miracle of the Marne. Brooke saw the hollowness of the French generals' mask of professional omniscience. Giraud—the commander of the new army formed

[1] *Diary*, 19th November, 1939.

on the British left to advance into Holland—might seem to others " a veritable tiger "; Brooke, while admitting he was a most charming personality, sized him up, with prophetic insight, as a Don Quixote who " would have ridden gallantly at any windmill regardless of consequences " and who "inspired one with little confidence when operating on one's left flank." Most of the other senior officers he met struck him as excellent company, amusing conversationalists, familiar with all the latest gossip from Paris, and thoroughly unreliable. Their type was the local District Commander—an old staff officer of Foch's, very amusing, talkative and rather like a bantam-cock, who explained that he was teaching himself English with a gramophone while shaving, and, when asked what sort of sentences it taught him, replied, " Why will you not dance with Helen? Because Helen will smoke cigarettes and I am wearing a cellulose collar."[1] The chief concern of such generals seemed to be the culinary standard of their Headquarters' Messes. " A wasted day as far as work was concerned," Brooke wrote on October 31st, " but I hope that as a result of it our good relations with our allies were more closely knitted. . . . Champagne-lunch consisting of oysters, lobsters, chicken, pâté-de-foie-gras, pheasant, cheese and fruit, coffee, liqueurs, etc. We sat down at 1 p.m. and got up about 3 p.m." "Again a heavy lunch," he recorded two days later, " with hors d'œuvres, trout, duck and mushrooms, cheese, ices, fruits, coffee and liqueurs! I hope this is the last of these lunches; they interfere with my work and my liver."

Nor was it only the French generals, with their fine brandies and magnificent Cadillac cars, who during those waiting months were weighed in the balance and found wanting. For a generation British statesmen, soldiers and diplomats had regarded the French Army as the greatest force on earth and the repository of all military wisdom. Their own troops were so few and ill-equipped that it was natural that they should do so. They had been shown, like other foreign observers, its crack regular divisions, huge guns and tanks and underground fortresses, and had been deeply impressed. They could not perceive the senile

---

[1] " I asked him if he had found this class of conversation useful in contacts with the British troops."

reality beneath the glittering exterior or realise the indiscipline and defeatism of the territorial divisions of which the bulk of the French Army in war was composed.

Alan Brooke could. He had been born and educated in France and spoke French like a native. He loved the country and sympathised with her difficulties, but he was as instinctively critical of her shortcomings as any Frenchman. On the day he landed at Cherbourg, though he wrote of the personal kindness and hospitality of the military authorities, he observed in his diary that French slovenliness, dirtiness and inefficiency were worse than ever. Before he had been in France a few days he had begun to wonder whether the French still possessed the spirit and fighting qualities that in the first War had enabled them to transcend these defects. All the outward signs of patriotism were there: total mobilisation, ceaseless official propaganda, speeches and affirmations of solidarity and the will to victory. Yet, noting the universal slackness and listlessness of the troops on the Belgian frontier, Brooke began to " entertain most unpleasant apprehensions as to the fighting qualities of the French in this new war." These misgivings were crystallized at a parade presided over by General Corap of the French Ninth Army to mark the anniversary of the arrival of the German armistice envoys in the Allied lines in 1918. ' The ceremony,' he wrote, ' took place round a monument on which was inscribed: " *Ici triompha par sa ténacité le Poilu!* " . . . Corap requested me to stand alongside of him whilst the guard of honour, consisting of cavalry, artillery and infantry marched past. I can still see those troops now. Seldom have I seen anything more slovenly and badly turned out. Men unshaven, horses ungroomed, clothes and saddlery that did not fit, vehicles dirty, and complete lack of pride in themselves or their units. What shook me most, however, was the look in the men's faces, disgruntled and insubordinate looks, and, although ordered to give " Eyes left," hardly a man bothered to do so. After the ceremony was over Corap invited me to visit some of his defences in the Fôret de St. Michel. There we found a half-constructed and very poor anti-tank ditch with no defences to cover it. By way of conversation I said that I supposed he would cover this ditch with the fire from anti-tank pill-boxes.

This question received the reply: " *Ah bah! on va les faire plus tard—allons, on va déjeuner!* " And away we went to *déjeuner,* which was evidently intended to be the most important operation of the day.' " I could not help wondering," Brooke wrote that night, " whether the French are still a firm enough nation to again take their part in seeing this war through."

All through the winter, while the Expeditionary Force laboured to complete its defences and training, the sense of French inefficiency and half-heartedness gained on Brooke. At the end of January he attended an official showing of a French Army film. " A very amateur appearance," he commented, " which compares unfavourably with the ultra-efficiency of the Germans, even as exemplified by types of German prisoners in French hands. I only hope that they still possess the same fighting qualities which they showed in the last war."[1] Like other senior British officers he visited the Maginot Line and, though much impressed, the more he saw of it the less he liked it. " The fort," he wrote of one he inspected at Welshtenberg, " reminded me of a battleship built on land, a masterpiece in its way, and there is no doubt that the whole conception of the Maginot Line is a stroke of genius. And yet! It gives me but little feeling of security, and I consider that the French would have done better to invest the money in the shape of mobile defences such as more and better aircraft and more heavy armoured divisions than to sink all this money into the ground."[2] " Most interesting," he wrote a few weeks later of Fort Hackenberg, " garrison of over 1000 men, over seven kilometres of passages, four vast great diesel engines, electric railways, electric kitchens, electric baths, automatic gun-controls, and all round an astonishing engineering feat. But I am not convinced that it is a marvellous military accomplishment. Millions of money sunk into the ground for a purely static defence, and the total fire-power developed by these works bears no relation to the time, work and money spent in their construction. Their most dangerous aspect is the psychological one; a sense of false security is engendered, a feeling of sitting behind an impregnable iron fence; and

[1] *Diary,* 29th January, 1940.
[2] *Diary,* 20th December, 1939.

should the fence perchance be broken, the French fighting spirit might well be brought crumbling with it."[1]

Behind the *malaise* of the French Army—its slovenliness, inactivity and sense of fatalism—lay the *malaise* of France herself. Deep as was their dislike of Germany, the French did not only dislike the war; they resented it. They felt that they had been pushed into it by England, several years too late and for an inadequate reason. They had not wanted to die for Danzig and the Polish Corridor and, now that these were lost, saw little purpose in continuing to fight for them. For most thinking Frenchmen hope of victory had vanished before the war began, on the day that the Russians, rejecting the West's alliance, signed their non-aggression pact with Nazi Germany. For it meant that the Poles, caught between their hereditary enemies, were doomed, and that Germany, instead of having to fight on two fronts as in 1914, would be able to concentrate their superior man-power against France and bleed her white.

The British, who were responsible for this, were themselves, it seemed to the French, the party who had prevented France from acting when she was strong enough to do so. They had sabotaged all her plans for keeping down a militant and resurgent Germany. They had induced her to evacuate the Ruhr, to withdraw her army of occupation from the Rhineland, to allow the Saar to vote itself into the Reich, to refrain from enforcing her treaty rights when Hitler remilitarised his western frontier. Yet, though it was the British who had induced her to let Germany rearm and then, when that nation had regained its wonted strength and swagger, to pick up its iron gauntlet in the name of honour, their contribution to the defence of France in the peril they had brought upon her was negligible. All they had sent her were four divisions and a promise of six more by the spring. Only a few months before the outbreak of war had they at last imposed upon themselves the yoke of conscription—a yoke which every Frenchman had borne from boyhood. And after half a year of war, while one in every eight Frenchmen was serving with the colours, only one in every forty-eight Englishmen had been called up.[2] Having failed to

---

[1] *Diary*, 6th February, 1940.
[2] E. Spears, *Prelude to Dunkirk*, I 69.

provide themselves with the means of making their challenge to Germany effective, they were now ready in its pursuit to fight to the last Frenchman and to subject an exhausted France to the same blood-letting she had suffered in the first War. " *Toujours les poitrines françaises,*" the cry went up, " always the French breasts! "

.   .   .   .

In this the French were being less than fair to the British. The latter meant, as in 1914, to wage war with all the force they possessed and to win, but they were not yet preparing for the right war. Their recipe for victory was to rely on the French and the Maginot Line to hold the Germans while they created the army they had failed to create in peace, manufactured vast stores of arms and aircraft, and made themselves as strong as they had done in the first War. Then in the fullness of time the Americans would throw in their lot with them, while Germany, starved of petrol and raw materials by their blockade, would be driven to bankruptcy, rebellion and surrender. In the meantime they had countered the German U-boat attack by a vigorous anti-submarine offensive and had not only closed the waters between Britain and France to the enemy, but had inflicted far greater losses on the German merchant-marine than the U-boats had been able to inflict on their own. There was nothing defeatist, or even defensive, about the attitude of the First Lord of the Admiralty—the sixty-five-year-old Winston Churchill. Indeed, had he been allowed his way, he would, emulating Canning and Nelson and regardless of the air-weapon, have started a naval offensive in the waters of the Sound in order to break into the Baltic—a thing the Admiralty had considered impossible even in the first War before the advent of air-power.[1]

By this time the British, growing conscious of the freedom of choice given by command of the sea, were beginning, as so often in the past, to contemplate offensive adventures for which they did not possess the military power. In November they had been gravely shocked by Russia's demand for bases in the

[1] *Churchill*, I, 323, 363-4, 458. It is significant that, despite the appalling risks to the Royal Navy of such a course, Hitler himself—no mean judge of what daring could effect—was alarmed by the danger of it to Germany.

Baltic States and by her invasion of Finland when that country refused to accede to her demands. Filled with admiration for the Finns' resistance and forgetful of the fact that, with grossly inadequate force and armaments, they were already facing the greatest military and air power in Europe, they proceeded to plan, in concert with their French allies, an expedition as fantastic as even a British Government had ever launched from its island-base. This was nothing less than the despatch of a force to seize Narvik in the Arctic Circle and thence, using the single railway across northern Norway and Sweden, to cross the top of the Baltic and reinforce the Finns. In the view of its proponents, this plan would save a democratic nation and, even more advantageous—a point which the First Lord of the Admiralty had been vehemently urging—stop at its source the all-important Swedish iron-ore traffic to Germany. The military possibilities of the expedition ever reaching its remote destination or, if it did, in the face of German sea and air command of the Baltic and of Russian land-power, ever returning, seemed to trouble the Cabinet little. The delay in despatching it arose, not from strategic considerations, but solely out of respect for the reluctance of the Swedish and Norwegian Governments to allow it to cross their territories.

The shadow of what Alan Brooke called " the Finnish wild-goose chase " began to fall on the British Expeditionary Force at the beginning of February. By that time a fifth Regular division had reached France—it had been incorporated in Brooke's II Corps—and three Territorial divisions had arrived or were on the point of arriving. " Whilst out touring round gunner units near Armentières," he wrote in his diary on the 2nd,

" I received a telephone call saying Gort wanted to see me at I Corps H.Q. at 4 p.m. I wondered if the Germans were again threatening an invasion of Holland and Belgium, and started off at once on a long drive to Douai. It was not the Germans that had stirred this time, but he wanted to tell me the results of his meetings whilst home on leave. They were not reassuring. Apparently various expeditions to other theatres of war are being considered by the highest, most of which would, it strikes me, lead to a dispersal of effort and provide better chances than ever for our losing the war. History is repeating itself in an astonishing way. The same string-pulling as in the last war, the same differences between statesmen and soldiers, the same faults as regards changing key-posts at the opening of hostilities, and now the same tendency to start subsidiary theatres of war and to contemplate wild projects. We shall apparently never apply the lessons of one war to the next."

Six days later he wrote again:

"The proposed plans fill me with gloom. They are based on the assumption that the Germans will not attack on this front during the spring. Personally I hold diametrically opposed views. Any forward move of the Germans on this front must necessarily bring operations in subsidiary theatres to a standstill, but unfortunately by then we shall have seriously reduced our strength on this front and will be less well able to meet any attack. We seem to be falling into all the errors that we committed in the last war by starting subsidiary theatres and frittering away our strength. However, there is still hope that those we propose to help will elect to be left alone and may well decline our assistance. Meanwhile the least that we shall suffer from here will be delay and confusion."[1]

This delay continued for the rest of the month while Brooke temporarily commanded a force bigger than the original Expeditionary Force. On the 11th he wrote:

"The situation in the Corps is getting more and more confused. Just as we were in the process of giving birth to the new III Corps, their recent proposed diversion to other theatres has put everything into a state of suspense. The 5th Division is awaiting orders to be pulled out into reserve, the 51st Division is in the middle of the relief of the 53rd French Division, and the 50th Division is following on close behind. We are at present handling five divisions,

[1] *Diary*, 8th February, 1940.

all in the middle of reliefs which have been partly counter-ordered, and can get no definite orders. I now discover that the last development is that Gamelin had never been informed that the British Government proposed to withdraw the 5th Division and that he is objecting to this move. This will probably lead to 'Tiny' Ironside dashing over, more Cabinet meetings, more discussions, and meanwhile we shall be left in uncertainty as to what reliefs are to be carried out or when to put divisions which are in the process of arriving in the forward areas. It is these uncertainties and counter-orders which are so killing and exhausting for the staffs, forcing them to prepare a multitude of alternative plans that are never carried out."

The confusion was only resolved in the middle of March by the Scandinavian States' refusal to agree to the project and the Finns' surrender to the Russians' terms. In the meantime the B.E.F. had lost six precious weeks of preparation and training against a possible German offensive in the spring. " There is only one front that matters in this war during 1940," Brooke wrote to Dill on February 11th, " and that is this front. It is the only front during the present year on which the war can be won or lost, and it is quite shattering to see its security endangered."[1]

The trouble was that the authorities in England failed to realise it. Lulled into false security by that winter of waiting and shadow-boxing, they had come to believe that the campaign in the West was a " phoney war " and would remain so— a continuation of the old, comforting peace-time delusion that Hitler was bluffing. ' It may have seemed " phoney " to those comfortably established at home,' Brooke wrote; ' from my point of view it was anything but " phoney." To find oneself in command of a formation unready for war, both from the point of view of training, equipment and deficiency of modern weapons; ... to be confronted with plans which were definitely unsound in the event of attack; to become daily less and less confident of the fighting value of one's allies; on top of it all, to have the firm conviction that the Germans must attack

---

[1] Brooke to Dill, 11th February, 1940, Lord Alanbrooke, *Personal Files.*

sooner or later. . . .' Again and again during those early months of 1940 he found himself arguing with those who believed that the Allies enjoyed the initiative and that the Germans were going to remain indefinitely passive.

" *January 28th*. Dewing, Director of Military Operations at the War Office, came out to-day for a tour of the front and we were out all day. I had an opportunity of pumping him as regards the War Office view of the prosecution of the war. The feeling they gave me is that, whilst concentrating on ensuring that they are going to win the war in three years' from now, they neglect to realise the dangers they run of losing it this year. Unless we get the Air Ministry and the War Office to realise that they are fighting the same war, and that their combined effort is required at the same spot, at the same time and with the same object, we are courting disaster against an enemy who adheres to the doctrine of the concentration of effort at the vital point and at the right time. To contemplate bombing the Rhine[1] at a time when the Germans are using their combined Army and Air Force effort in one mighty attempt to crush the French and British forces to clear their way into France is, in my mind, sheer folly."

" *January 30th*. . . . Martel (commanding 50th Div.) and his staff came in. He was wondering why we were not more concerned with preparing offensive measures to attack the Siegfried Line, and seemed quite oblivious of the fact that, instead of attacking this spring, we are far more likely to be hanging on by our eyelids in trying to check the German attacks."

" *February 16th*. I had a long talk with the Secretary of State[2] in the car and explained to him how dangerous

[1] A favourite project of Churchill's for " paralysing of traffic on the Rhine by the dropping and discharge of fluvial mines." Churchill *I*, 459. " Two ' wrongs,' " wrote Brooke, " will not make a 'right' in this case, and a misuse of our own Air Force will not induce the Germans into a misuse of their own Air Force, by diverting them from their proper task to that of bombing England. When the combined task of the German land and air forces is completed, and Northern France cleared of the Allies, then, and only then, will the Germans turn their air might on to England." *Diary*, 28th January, 1940.

[2] The Rt. Hon. Oliver Stanley, who had succeeded Mr. Hore-Belisha as Secretary of State for War in January.

I thought any idea of reducing the strength of the B.E.F. at this moment for any ventures in other theatres. He seemed inclined to agree. . . . He expressed the view that he thought it very doubtful whether the Germans would attack on the western front this year. I told him that I had no doubt on this matter whatever, and looked upon it as a certainty."

" *February 23rd.* To-day Venning[1] came out for a tour. He is another example of those who consider that a state of stalemate prevails on this front and that no active operations are likely to take place. I did my best to convince him that the reverse was the case."

" *February 25th.* All indications show that the War Office now look upon this front as one of stalemate. They may well have a rude awakening! "

Part of the trouble lay in the fact that Gort, by reason of his very virtues as well as of his limitations, was incapable of dissuading his military and political superiors in England from these injudicious assumptions. His loyalty and refusal to complain, and his complete imperturbability, only increased their feeling that all was well on the Western Front. Dill's attempts, as senior Corps Commander, to get him to realise the Army's weakness and danger merely led to misunderstanding. " I am afraid," Brooke wrote, " Dill feels the situation acutely. . . . He feels it his duty to inform Gort, who has not quite the same breadth of vision, and Dill feels that Gort has the impression that he suffers from ' cold feet ' and is an alarmist. It is a very sad situation; he is torn between loyalty to his Commander and loyalty to his Corps."

For with all his grandeur of character, Gort was a man not of vision, but of detail. ' He was one of those pre-eminently straight characters,' wrote Brooke, ' who inspired confidence. He could never have done anything small or mean. . . . He had one of those cheerful dispositions full of vitality, energy and *joie de vivre*, and the most wonderful charm, and was gifted with great powers of leadership. . . . I could not help admiring him and

---

[1] Lt.-Gen. (now Gen.) Sir Walter Venning, Quarter-Master-General at the War Office.

had feelings of real and deep affection for him. But I had no
confidence in his leadership when it came to handling a large
force. He seemed incapable of seeing the wood for the trees.'
He was tirelessly occupied with tactical questions such as the
proper use of hand-grenades and the number a patrol should
carry, the importance of teaching men to read tracks in the
snow, the best ways of wiring isolated posts, of patrolling and
night rifle-fire, but shrank from discussing the wider strategic
issues. When, during a visit to the Maginot Line, where
successive British infantry brigades were taking turns of duty,
Brooke tried to discuss with him the flaws in the French outpost system of defence which had led to the surprise of two
section posts, he merely replied, " Oh! I have not had time
to think of it, but, look, what we must go into is the proper
distribution of sandbags." On another occasion, after they
had visited the front together, Brooke wrote, " I think he had
a terrible longing to stop up for the night and take a patrol
out himself. His eyes were still twinkling with the excitement
of it."

Indeed with his look of a good-natured, invincible bulldog,
Gort perfectly represented the men he commanded—their
limitations and, as the event was to prove, their incomparable
virtues. ' Nobody,' Brooke wrote, ' could have been more
charming or considerate than he was, and in many respects he
was the most delightful commander to serve under, but unfortunately his brain was geared to details the whole time. He
wandered about scratching the barks of the trees and you could
never get him to come out and look at the wood as a whole.
The important points, such as the system of defence to be
adopted, lines of advance into Belgium, relative advantages
of remaining on the frontier as opposed to advancing to meet the
Germans, all such and many others he left entirely to his staff,
whilst he dealt with details such as platoon log-books, carrying
of sandbags, booby-traps. . . . Repeatedly Dill and I called for
conferences to discuss specific important points. He at once
agreed to hold such conferences, but, when we met, all these
points were handed over to Pownall or Neame to deal with.
He took practically no part in the discussion and was eager to
get on to some minor points which he had brought with him.

As the time passed, these failings became more and more disconcerting and ate deep into Dill's heart.'[1]

In the middle of April, Dill returned to England to become Vice Chief of the Imperial General Staff. Brooke was now the senior Corps Commander in France, with two newcomers, both old friends, Michael Barker and Ronald Adam, taking over the I and the newly formed III Corps. ' Dill's departure,' he wrote, ' left me in the depths of gloom.[2] . . . I had an absolute conviction that the German offensive was coming soon. I now had no illusions as to the efficiency and fighting value of the French Army. I had little confidence in Gort's leadership in the event of attack, and now Dill was gone there was no one left in the B.E.F. with whom I could discuss my misgivings freely. . . . Meanwhile we remained short of essential arms such as planes, tanks, anti-tank guns, anti-aircraft guns, wireless, and the dark clouds were gathering fast.'

In those clouds there was one silver lining for Brooke—the transformation of II Corps from the untrained, almost defenceless force it had been in the previous autumn. Its two original Regular divisions, as a result of ceaseless training, and the 5th Division which had joined it in December, had become battleworthy units, ready, even though not yet fully equipped, to stand the shock of modern war. All three were commanded by fine soldiers, and one—the 3rd—by a trainer of genius.[3] Major-General Bernard Montgomery was then a man of fifty-two, with only a year's experience as a divisional commander. But Brooke's diary that winter contains many references to the progress of the defensive works made by his division[4] and its

---

[1] *Notes on My Life*, III 103.

[2] " He leaves a terrible blank behind him and I have a horrid lonely feeling knowing that he is gone. . . . He is quite one of the finest men I have ever known." *Diary*, 18th April, 1940. ' I know of no other soldier in the whole of my career who inspired me with greater respect and admiration. An exceptionally clear, well-balanced brain, an infinite capacity for work, unbounded charm of personality but, above all, an unflinching straightness of character; these were the chief characteristics that made up one of the most remarkable soldiers of our century. I owe him an infinite debt for all I learned from him.'—*Notes on My Life*, II. 66.

[3] The 5th Division was commanded by Major-General Harold Franklyn, who played a splendid part in the retreat to Dunkirk and later became Commander-in-Chief, Home Forces; and the 4th Division by a V.C. of the first War, Major-General D. G. Johnson—an older man whom Brooke described as ' a charming and very gallant gentleman, as reliable as one could wish.'

[4] " To 3rd Division and then went for a tour of the front with Monty who wanted to show me all the new work he was starting." *Diary*, 12th February,

impressive training Exercises. ' It was a matter,' he wrote, ' of
the greatest interest watching Monty improving every day as
he began to find his feet as a Divisional Commander. . . . These
Exercises, all of them admirably run . . . were an eye-opener
to me as to his ability as a trainer. Their value was more than
proved when we finally carried out our advance, as his 3rd
Division worked like clockwork.'

It was during that winter that Brooke formed the opinion
of Montgomery that was to have such important results later
in the war, and to lead, in 1942, to Britain's first decisive
victory. It was during that winter, too, that he saved him from
the consequences of an indiscretion that might easily have
brought his career to a premature end. It arose out of an unfortunately phrased divisional order about the health and
morals of his men to which Montgomery had appended his
signature instead of leaving it to be issued by his staff. This
had caused bitter complaints from the Senior Chaplains of both
the Church of England and the Roman Catholic Church, and
the Adjutant General had informed Brooke that the Commander-in-Chief wished Montgomery to withdraw his order.
This Brooke declined to make him do. " I was dead against
such a procedure," he wrote in his diary. " Monty had already
sufficiently undermined his position as a Commander through
the issue of the document; to make him withdraw it would
be a clear indication of superior authority's disapproval which
would remove any vestige of respect his division might have for
him. . . . I told the Adjutant-General that instead I
would have him up again, express the Commander-in-Chief's
displeasure to him and impress on him again the magnitude of his
blunder. I, therefore, pointed out to Monty that his position
as Commander of a Division had been seriously affected . . .
and could certainly not withstand any further errors of this
kind. I also informed him that I had a very high opinion of
his military capabilities and an equally low one of his literary
ones! He took it wonderfully well."[1] ' Had I agreed to what

---

1940. " Met Monty at 9.30 a.m. at Lesquin and spent the day with him going
round some of his most modern defences. They have made tremendous progress
and he has some ninety pill-boxes of various kinds all under construction."
Diary, 19th April, 1940.
[1] *Diary*, 23rd November, 1939.

the Adjutant General informed me were the wishes of the Commander-in-Chief,' Brooke recalled afterwards, ' I should have . . . been forced to withdraw Monty from his division and to send him home. I should never have had the opportunities that I had in 1940 to estimate his true value and should probably have remained ignorant of them and consequently failed to recommend him for command of the Eighth Army. . . . I never ceased to thank Heaven that I saved Monty at this danger point in his career. . . . His reactions to all I said to him on that day were admirable. He thanked me for telling him where he had failed, told me that he knew he was apt to do foolish things and hoped I would always help him in a similar way in the future. What more could I have asked for? '[1]

Brooke was by now very proud of his Corps. ' I was fortunate,' he wrote, ' and could not have been better served on all sides or wished for a better team with which to face a crisis such as we were doomed to experience . . . and one which we should never have survived had it not been for the efficiency of all concerned.' It saddened him to think of the losses his men must sustain going into battle under such heavy handicaps. "Whilst talking to them," he wrote after an inspection of two battalions in which he spoke to every officer individually, " I always have the horrible feeling that I may at one time or another be instrumental in the issue of orders that may mean death to them."[2] For, though there was now no doubt of the fighting quality and efficiency of the men who were so soon to face the *blitzkrieg*, the tools their country had given them were not enough. The gravest defects of all were the lack of armour and air co-operation for ground fighting. Despite repeated requests for it Britain's only armoured division was still at home awaiting its long-promised equipment.[3] When its commander visited

[1] *Notes on My Life*, III 108-9. ' I had several more occasions during the war when I had to guard him against his own foolishness. In doing so, I inevitably had to adopt a most unpleasant attitude towards him. He never resented such reproof and always received every admonishment in the spirit in which it was intended. I could not have had an easier or more pleasant commander to handle.'

[2] *Diary*, 16th November, 1939. " It is, I think, one of the most trying sides of commanding in war, the haunting thought that you may at any time be forced to issue orders that mean probable death to your friends."

[3] It had been broken up and employed on anti-invasion and internal security duties during the winter; a proposal to concentrate it for training on the Marlborough Downs had been turned down on the ground that the gallops of the neighbouring racing stables would be interfered with. When it finally was sent

France in January Brooke was bitterly disappointed to learn how little progress had been made. Even as late as March its cruiser-tank strength was still under fifty per cent of establishment and it was without either divisional artillery or tank-bridging equipment; there was no reserve of fighting vehicles and an acute shortage of spare-parts, tank-tracks and anti-aircraft guns.

The only way in which a force so ill-equipped for mobile war could hope to defeat the Germans was by awaiting their attack in the fortified lines it had worked so hard to construct. During the winter the B.E.F.—now nearly a quarter of a million strong, with another 150,000 base and lines-of-communications troops in the rear areas—had made forty miles of anti-tank obstacles and some four hundred concrete pillboxes as well as fifty-nine airfields and over a hundred miles of broad-gauge railway.[1] It had also concentrated behind it large stores of supplies and ammunition. Yet the Allied Supreme Council and the French High Command had now finally decided that the moment the Germans attacked, the British and the French forces on their right should leave their defences and hurry forward across sixty or seventy miles of unreconnoitred and refugee-crowded road to take up a new position on the right of the Belgian Army on the Dyle, while the French reserve under General Giraud was to advance up the seaward-flank towards Antwerp and the Dutch frontier to forestall a German enveloping movement from the north. ' This move,' Brooke wrote,

' was a complicated one to be carried out on a two-divisional front in the I Corps and on a one-divisional front in the II Corps. This was due to the fact that there were not sufficient roads to allow . . . a four-divisional front. We were expecting heavy air attacks on our forward roads, and, consequently had subdivided such roads into sections to which were allotted infantry to handle possible parachutists, engineers to repair bombing damage, workshops to repair

overseas in May part of its Staff went into action in three-ply wood " mock-up " armoured—or rather unarmoured—Command vehicles. *Army Quarterly* XLV, 56-61.

[1] *The War in France and Flanders* (H.M.S.O.) 20-1.

vehicles, signals to maintain communications along the road, breakdown gangs to clear damaged vehicles off roads, hospital detachments to handle wounded, and a special road-control staff with military police to reconnoitre deviations when necessary and to see that all roads had special sign-posts along their whole length. It was an elaborate organiza-tion, but essential to carry out the movement at high speed and to avoid obstructions and delays. It had, however, one disadvantage; when finally worked out and everybody warned of their rôle, it became an inflexible organization which did not lend itself to many changes.'

The details of this advance, constantly rehearsed by his troops, was causing Brooke the gravest anxiety owing to the vagueness of the French preparations and the contradictory orders that kept arriving. On April 29th, less than a fortnight before the German attack, he recorded in his diary a G.H.Q. conference in which half an hour was spent

> " discussing the important plans of our advance into Belgium and the proposed changes, followed up with two hours of complete detail on training matters of minor importance. It is quite maddening not to be able to deal properly with the higher direction of this war without being drawn into minor details."

.   .   .   .

The German plans for the coming offensive were not those the French High Command had anticipated. In February, following the forced landing that had disclosed to the Belgian and Allied Governments details of his proposed attack, Hitler had ordered the substitution for the earlier variations of the time-honoured Schlieffen Plan of a highly original project put forward by Lieutenant-General von Manstein, at that time Chief of Staff to von Rundstedt, Commander-in-Chief of the central German Army Group on the Western Front.[1] Instead of the classic enveloping movement from the north across the

---

[1] The British official war historian of the War in France and Flanders 1939-40 attributes it to its official sponsor, von Rundstedt, but Guderian—the tank general whose genius was so largely instrumental in its success—categorically states in his memoirs that it was prepared by von Manstein. *Guderian*, 89-91.

Belgian plain, a thrust was to be made by concentrated armour through Luxembourg and the wooded hill defiles of the Ardennes to surprise and seize the Meuse crossings between Dinant and Sedan in the centre of the Allied line. While parachute troops were to overrun Holland and other attacks were to draw the main French reserves northwards, more than forty divisions, seven of them armoured, supported by massed dive-bombers, were to force the Meuse opposite the weakest point in the French line, where a gap of secondary defences was known to exist between the Maginot fortifications and the strong new lines the British had been constructing in Flanders. Then, driving across the plains of the upper Oise and Somme —ideal country for armour—they were to strike due west towards the Channel with the object of cutting off the Franco-British forces advancing into Belgium and Holland. The objective, as defined by Rundstedt and Manstein, was " to annihilate the Allied forces on land and in the air, to eliminate the continental sword of the English and then, as a second step, to attack England herself by air and sea."[1]

On paper the rival armies—each numbering some three million men—were not unevenly matched, if the thirty or more ill-prepared and still neutral Belgian and Dutch divisions were added to the ninety-four French,[2] one Polish, and ten British divisions strung out along the frontiers. In reality the Germans, as Brooke saw, were far stronger. They were a homogeneous force under a single national command and were not divided and weakened by doubts like the Belgians and Dutch and the Territorial bulk of the French Army. Because their Leader and younger generals believed in attack and had forged, in their armoured and air forces, a new offensive weapon, they enjoyed the immense advantage of the initiative. They had nearly 4000 aircraft to co-operate with their ground forces and, though their tanks were less numerous than the French, ten armoured divisions trained and grouped for mobile war. And they possessed a general reserve of forty-five divisions, more than

[1] German Army Group A, War Diary appendices, cit. *The War in France and Flanders 1939-1940.* (H.M.S.O.) 339.
[2] This is the British War Office's figure, based on French sources, for the strength of the French Army in France on 10th May, 1940. It does not include six divisions facing the Italians in the Alps. Spears, *Prelude to Dunkirk*, I 242.

three times that of the weak and scattered French reserve.
They could strike where they pleased and bring against the
chosen point a far greater weight of men and armour than could
be opposed by the defenders, strung out along hundreds of
miles of defensive front. The part of the defending line they
had selected for attack was that held by General Corap's
Ninth Army, whose troops—most of them unmechanised
reservists—had so shaken Brooke when they had marched past
him in the previous autumn, and the still weaker Second Army
to the south of it. If, by punching a hole through these sixteen
weak divisions—together holding a front of ninety miles—
Rundstedt's forty-four divisions could open a gap for his
massed, swiftly-moving armour to break through to the
Channel, the forty-three French divisions manning and in
support of the Maginot Line and Rhine defences would be cut
off from the fifty or sixty French, British, Dutch and Belgian
divisions awaiting the expected German attack in the Low
Countries. The Allies' advance into Belgium and Holland
would play into the German hands. As they raced north-
eastwards towards the Scheldt estuary and the Dyle, von
Rundstedt's armour would break in behind them, smashing
the unprotected hinge on which their advance pivoted. The
trap would be shut and the mouse in it.

Already, before they struck, Hitler had shown what could
be done with the initiative and its opportunities for tactical
surprise. On April 9th, infuriated by the attempts of the First
Lord of the Admiralty to tighten the blockade along the
Norwegian coast and so cut off Germany's supplies of Scandinavian iron-ore, he had forestalled a threatened Allied landing
in Norway by invading Denmark and seizing the principal
Norwegian ports and airfields from the sea and air. By his
coup he outwitted the Royal Navy in its own element. In a
subsequent attempt to shut the stable door after the horse was
out—or rather in—the Allies were forced to deflect forces from
France at the very moment when every man was needed there
and were given an object lesson in the cost of conducting
amphibious operations in a country where the enemy, possessing
the airfields, enjoyed command of the air.

The failure to expel the Germans from Norway and their

occupation of almost its entire coastline threw back the Royal Navy's blockading cordon for hundreds of miles, exposing Britain and her trade to new dangers. Despite the losses inflicted on the German Fleet, it gravely impaired both the country's and the Navy's prestige. " I listened on the wireless," Brooke wrote on 2nd May, " to Chamberlain's statement on our withdrawal from South Trondheim. It is a sad blow, and one which will, I think, have repercussions in the Mediterranean.[1] It is the first real conclusive proof we have had of the undermining of sea-power by air-power."

Six days after Brooke made his diary entry, a violent attack was made on Neville Chamberlain and his conduct of the war in the House of Commons. The most damaging speech of all was made by one of his own followers, many of whom voted against him in the subsequent vote of censure. On May 10th, feeling he had lost the confidence of the House, the Prime Minister resigned, and on his advice the King entrusted Winston Churchill with the task of forming a National Government. On the same day the German attack in the West began.

[1] Brooke was glad, however, at the abandonment of the Norwegian campaign. " In the withdrawal," he wrote, " and in the strategical logic of such action I already see evidence of Dill's hand on the tiller, and thank God for it."

Chapter Two

THE SAVING OF THE ARMY

*The French Army will be destroyed and the English on the
Continent will be made prisoners of war.*

RIBBENTROP

IN HIS diary and autobiographical notes Alan Brooke gives
his account of the three weeks' campaign in Belgium and
Flanders—the advance to the Dyle, the seven days' retreat to
the old lines on the Franco-Belgian frontier that the Germans,
in their break-through the French centre, had outflanked and
all but encircled, and, during the last days of May the desperate
five days' battle to reach the sea as the victorious German
hordes closed in on the apparently doomed army from every
side and from the air above. His narrative of that fiery ordeal
begins on May 9th, the day before the German attack opened,
when the Expeditionary Force was waiting in its fortified lines
on the Franco-Belgian frontier between the French First and
Seventh Armies, and when Brooke was still in his winter
headquarters at Phalempin, half-way between Lille and Douai.

' *May 9th* was a memorable day, it represented the last
day of the " Phoney War." Coming events were heralded
by several German planes that came over at about 10 p.m.,
drawing fire from all the A.A. guns. We gathered in the
garden of our billet to watch the fireworks, little knowing that
they represented the signal for a general flare-up of activity
on the Western Front.

' The start of the offensive and the manner in which I
became aware of it is best told in my own words of 10th May.'

" The German planes returned early this morning
between 3 and 4 a.m., and an infernal bombardment of

A.A. guns started. A little later Ritchie[1] came to tell me that G.H.Q. had rung up to place us at six hours' notice to move. Shortly afterwards he returned and said that the Germans had invaded Belgium and Holland at 3 a.m., and that we were at last to put into effect our famous ' D ' plan. This entails a rapid move forward to the River Dyle, east of Bruxelles. The II Corps goes on to a one-divisional front, with the 3rd Division (Montgomery) forward and the 4th Division (Johnson) and 50th Division (Martel) back.

" It was hard to believe on a glorious spring day, with all nature looking its best, that we were taking the first step towards . . . one of the greatest battles of history. All day long, planes have been droning overhead and many have been brought down, one not very far from this Corps H.Q. I spent the day checking over the orders for the move. Everything so far has been running like clockwork, and with less interference from bombing than I had anticipated. Gort came to see me in the afternoon and discussed progress made.

" 3rd Division started off at 2.30 p.m. this afternoon and by now its advance elements should be approaching the Dyle. It will, however, take some eight days to assemble the whole Corps forward.

" I move up to-morrow. Had time to look up Tom in the morning, and found him holding his own well, I thought rather cheerful about himself.[2] Thus finishes seven months of war spent at Phalempin."

' There was a great deal that lay behind those last few words. Those seven months had been spent struggling to fit the II Corps for war, with moments of intense anxiety lest it should be put to the test before it was ready. Now that the moment to test it had come at last I felt that from the point of view of training it had reached a standard that would justify full confidence in its answering the helm and giving a good account of itself. From the point of view of

[1] Brooke's Brigadier General Staff, now General Sir Neil Ritchie.
[2] Brooke's eldest son, who since April 25th had been lying desperately ill with a burst appendix and peritonitis in hospital at Rouvroy, near Douai.

equipment the situation was still lamentable, and we were still deficient in all the vital armaments of a modern army. In the air we were provided with the Lysander, an army co-operation machine; it was entirely unsuited for its task and deficient of forward aerodromes. As regards fighter protection against bombers, I understand that the few machines we had were working in support of our bombers in forward missions. I practically never saw a fighter during the rest of my time in France.

' As regards tanks, all we possessed were a few of the very slow " I " tanks and the ridiculous light tank with which the Divisional Cavalry regiments were armed. Anti-tank guns were still on a completely inadequate scale. In spite of repeated requests for anti-tank ammunition for Bofors guns to render them available for the double role of anti-tank and anti-aircraft, we had not received a single round. Tracer ammunition, essential for hose-pipe methods of engaging low-flying aircraft, were in such short supply that the few rounds available were mainly allocated to the R.A.F. The proportion of A.A. guns was also quite inadequate for the size of the B.E.F. It was certainly not comforting to realise that with such an ill-equipped army we were moving forward to engage a force equipped with all the most modern armaments manned by a personnel already war experienced.

' There was little comfort to be derived from our Allies. I had by now few illusions as to the fighting efficiency of the French. The Belgians still remained to be seen, but what I had heard about them was not promising. . . . Therefore, on that 10th day of May, 1940, as I contemplated our move forward into Belgium, my mind was far from being at rest. And yet with it all there was a feeling of relief that the period of suspense was now over, the continuous scares were over, the sword had now fallen and I felt that action would be preferable to suspense.

' On top of all the professional worries there was now the additional anxiety concerning my boy, whom I should have to leave at a period when his life seemed to be in the balance. I have still a vivid recollection of the unreality of things on that day. Was I really awake or possibly lost in some ghastly nightmare? Could it be possible that on such a glorious spring day Hell could be let loose? Thank God I was not gifted with the powers of a crystal-gazer, and the bitterness of that Hell was concealed from me.

' It had been decided a few weeks previously that Johnson, commanding 4th Division, who was getting on in age, should be relieved by "Rusty" Eastwood. In fact, on that date, Eastwood had already arrived in the country. Johnson came round to see me and, almost with tears in his eyes, implored me to allow him to remain with his division. He said that surely I could not have the heart to take his division away from him after training it all these months, when at last it was a case of fighting? I assured him that I had not the least intention of withdrawing him at the eleventh hour. He went off overjoyed and never gave me a moment in which to repent this decision.

' On May 11th I left Phalempin for good at 12 noon after an early lunch. The whole Wavrin family turned out to see us leave, and I was kissed on both cheeks by Madame, who was weeping at our departure.[1] I called on Johnson for a final word with him as regards moves of the 4th Division and then started on my journey forward.

' It was quite an experience crossing the frontier and moving into the " no man's land " which we had been looking at for so long. I had an uneventful drive to Sotteghem where I was to establish my H.Q. that night. Here I dumped my kit and went to visit my " Road Control Centre " under Brigadier Massy, to find out how the move forward was proceeding. I was informed that Alost had come in for a lot of bombing, and that unfortunately Colonel Perkins, my Assistant Quartermaster-General, had been killed by a bomb while doing a railway reconnaissance. This was the

---

[1] " During the phoney war A.B. lived in a modest manner in a ' petit chateau ' at Phalempin, with his office half a mile away. We shared the big sitting-room with the family. . . . Madame was a very intense woman. . . . After dinner as we entered the drawing-room she would, with great tact and charm, say ' Bon Soir ' and go. She ached to talk to him of course, but never really got a ' run ' till we said good-bye on 10th May and 11th when she kissed him anywhere she could. How I laughed ! " *Notes by Lt.-Col. R. Stanyforth, Military Assistant to General Brooke.*

first casualty the Corps had sustained from enemy action and was a serious loss. He was a first-class officer. . . .

'I then went on to the 3rd Division in front of Brussels where I got in touch with Monty. He informed me that the move forward had worked like clockwork, that they had arrived in the dark to find that the front allotted to them was already occupied by the 10th Belgian Division. In fact, Monty's division had arrived so suddenly that the Belgians had taken them for German parachutists, opened fire on them and seriously wounded a man of the Middlesex Regiment.

'In the very early stages of the preparation of the " D " plan a line had been drawn out and settled with the Belgians which was to represent the boundary between the Belgian and British forces. This line was known as the Gamelin Line and ran east and west on the north side of Brussels and Louvain. I asked Monty whether he had informed the Commander of the 10th Belgian Division that he was on the wrong side of the Gamelin Line and therefore must withdraw his division. He informed me that he had made this quite plain, but the only reply he got from the Belgian Commander was that his King had entrusted him with the defence of Louvain and that he would never leave his post without orders from his King. I then told Monty that I should take steps to have him removed and meanwhile to keep his division deployed. He said he certainly would do so, as he had little opinion of the fighting value of the Belgian division from what he had seen of them.

'I then left Monty and proceeded to the Embassy in Brussels to look for Needham, . . . our Liaison Officer with the Belgians. I found that he was established with the Belgian G.Q.G. in one of the Antwerp forts. It was too late to go there at that time, as I still wanted to see about moves of 4th Division. I therefore sent Needham a message instructing him to have the 10th Belgian Division withdrawn. While I was at the Embassy, Mason MacFarlane, the Director of Military Intelligence at G.H.Q. turned up, and I requested him to inform G.H.Q. on his return of the wrong position of the 10th Belgian Division. He told me that news from the front was bad, and that the Germans had broken through at Maastricht.

'I eventually returned to my H.Q. to find an order from G.H.Q. telling me to take up a front with 3rd Division between the 10th Belgian Division and I Corps. . . . This was typical of many G.H.Q. orders which were apt to be based on lack of knowledge of the forward situation. With great difficulty I got through to G.H.Q., got them to cancel this order and to agree to 3rd Division double-banking the 10th Belgian Division until such time as I could get the latter moved. There was, however, no offer from G.H.Q. to take on this task which was certainly up to them, being an inter-Allied point.'[1]

Brooke's diary for 11th May ends:

> "Not a satisfactory solution. Belgians should be made to side step to their left. A day of ceaseless alarmist rumours of Belgians giving way."

It ' was very difficult,' he added, ' to get any clear idea of what was happening on the frontier.'

Since the German pounce at dawn on the previous day most of Holland had been overrun and heavy pressure had been maintained against the Belgian Army along the Albert Canal and the frontier fortifications covering Liége and Maastricht. Three of the bridges over the Canal had been seized and the supposedly impregnable fortress of Eben Emael captured by a parachute descent on its roof. But though Holland had been paralysed by air attack and half the Belgian air force destroyed on the ground, the Luftwaffe had made little attempt to disorganise the great forward wheel across Belgium of the French

---

[1] *The War in France and Flanders* (H.M.S.O.) (64-5) refers to this lack of liaison between G.H.Q. and the forward Commands. "The poverty of intelligence at a time when it was important for commanders to be well informed, was largely due to a faulty organisation of Lord Gort's Headquarters Staff. When he . . . formed his Command Post and moved forward into Belgium, he took with him General Mason MacFarlane and two staff officers from the Intelligence Branch at General Headquarters, which was left behind at Arras. Thereafter information received direct at General Headquarters often failed to pass from the Intelligence Staff at the Command Post to formations at the front in time to be of use to them, while much of the information which divisions at the front sent into the Command Post was never passed back to General Headquarters at Arras."

and British Armies and their race to the Meuse, Dyle, and Scheldt estuary. It suited the enemy to let them drive as far into Belgium as possible, for the farther they advanced the easier they would become to cut off. Corap's Ninth Army, wheeling right to the Meuse from the pivot point of the Allied advance near Mézières, occupied with its nine weak divisions the fifty miles of supposedly inaccessible river bank opposite the Ardennes above Namur; farther to the north the French First Army, with its ten divisions, took up a twenty-five miles frontage between that town and Wavre; while the nine divisions of the B.E.F., with three in the line and the remainder in reserve, filled a seventeen-mile gap along the Dyle between Wavre and the right flank of the Belgian Army, whose eighteen or nineteen divisions, falling back from the Albert Canal, had another twenty miles to hold as far as Antwerp, beyond which seven divisions of Giraud's Seventh Army, outrunning their ammunition in their advance, had precipitated themselves across the Scheldt estuary into the Dutch islands of Walcheren and South Beveland.

Meanwhile the seven German armoured divisions, which were to force the Upper Meuse and lead the drive to the Channel, were hurrying westwards towards the river and the French frontier along the narrow twisting hill and forest roads of Luxembourg and the Belgian Ardennes, brushing aside weak French cavalry forces patrolling this supposedly untraversible country. Behind them came the thirty-seven infantry divisions of von Rundstedt's German Army Group A., and still farther back the forty-five divisions of the German General Reserve. By nightfall on the 11th, Guderian's three panzer divisions were within ten miles of the Meuse crossings at Sedan, while, thirty miles to the north, Rommel's 7th Panzer Division, on the extreme right of the German armoured advance, was about the same distance from the river at Dinant. They and three other armoured divisions advancing between them had covered fifty miles since their start from Germany thirty-six hours earlier.

Brooke's diary for May 12th—Whit Sunday—begins:

" Left Sotteghem by 7 a.m., and motored to Bruxelles

British Embassy. Here duty officer in the Military Attaché's office informed me that Louvain had been captured by the Germans. Luckily this was incorrect. Rang up Needham at Belgian G.H.Q. to try and solve the problem of 3rd Division occupying front already held by Belgian 10th Division. Gathered from him that situation had been fairly jumpy all yesterday, and he suggested that I should come and see him. I, therefore, motored to near Antwerp and found Roger Keyes in the office who suggested I had better discuss the matter with the King."

' This,' Brooke wrote afterwards,

' was fixed up in a few moments, and the Admiral took me into the King's room and introduced me to him in English. As I came in I saw no one else in the room, and Roger Keyes withdrew and left me alone with the King. I explained to him my difficulties . . . in English. I found him charming to talk to, and felt that I was making progress . . . when I suddenly heard a voice speaking French from behind my right. On turning round I found an officer there who did not introduce himself to me but went on speaking in French to the King. His contention was that the Belgian Division could not be moved, that the whole of the B.E.F. should be stepped farther south and be entirely clear of Brussels. I then turned on him in French and told him that he was not putting the full case before the King, since he had not mentioned that the 10th Belgian Division was on the wrong side of the Gamelin Line. He then turned to me, and said: " Oh! do you speak French? " I assured him that I did, and that I happened to have been born in France. By that time he had interposed himself between me and the King. I therefore walked round him and resumed my conversation with the King in English.

' This individual then came round again and placed himself between me and the King, and the King then withdrew to the window. I could not very well force my presence a third time on the King, and I therefore discussed the matter with this individual whom I assumed must be the Chief of

Staff. I found that arguing with him was sheer waste of time; he was not familiar with the dispositions of the B.E.F. and seemed to care little about them. Most of his suggestions were fantastic. I finally withdrew, and on going out I met the French general, Champon, who was the appointed Liaison Officer between the French and Belgian forces. I told him about my interview and asked him who it was I had met with the King. He told me that his name was van Overstraeten and that he was the A.D.C. to the King with the rank of Major General. I asked him where the Chief of Staff was. . . . He then told me that it was quite useless my bothering to see him, as van Overstraeten had taken all control in his hands and that he could get the King to do just what he wanted.

' Champon told me, however, that he could get the matter put right for me, as the King had to attend a conference of General Georges's that afternoon at Mons. He told me that he would inform General Georges that the 10th Belgian Division was in its wrong place and ask him to issue orders to the King for the withdrawal of this division. He kept his word and within twenty-four hours orders were issued and the matter was put right. . . .

' I left the Belgian G.H.Q. with many misgivings in my heart. As I motored back to Brussels I wondered whether the Belgians would turn out to be no better than the French. My left flank was to rest on the Belgian Army; these thoughts were consequently most disconcerting. . . .

' I then went on to lunch with Monty. I told him the result of my interview and that he would have to wait for another twenty-four hours for the orders for the withdrawal of the 10th Belgian Division. He thereupon said that it was quite all right, and that he had settled the matter for himself. I expressed surprise and asked him how he had settled the matter. He then told me: " Well, I went to the Belgian Divisional Commander and said to him: ' *Mon général*, I place myself and my Division unreservedly under your orders, and I propose to reinforce your front." He said that the Belgian Commander was delighted with this arrangement. I then asked Monty what he proposed to do if the Germans started attacking. He replied: " Oh! I then place the Divisional Commander under strict arrest and I take command." This episode is typical of Monty's resourcefulness; something had to be done, the Germans might arrive at any moment, and he certainly found a solution to settle the matter. I think I remember saying to him, " Poor Belgian Commander, how little he knows the viper he is harbouring in his breast!" . . .

' After lunch I went up with Monty through Louvain to see our proposed front. The town of Louvain had been badly bombed and was burning near the railway station. The roads were crowded with refugees streaming westwards, and these formed a queer contrast with the local inhabitants in normal church-going parties.

' We went up to a position in advance of Louvain where the 15/19th Hussars had taken up a position covering Louvain. The air was full of rumours of the rapidity of the German advance and of German victories. I did not like the number of Belgian officers whom I saw driving westwards in motor cars, but presumed they must be all staff officers.

' I then returned to the Embassy to telephone back to Gort the results of my morning trip to Belgian G.Q.G., and to give him my reasons for leaving the 3rd Division . . . on the Louvain front, covering one of the main lines of advance in to Brussels. As he asked me to let I Corps know, I started off for a long hunt in the southern outskirts of Brussels to try and find Michael Barker and his H.Q. I finally found his H.Q., but did not see him, so left a message for him informing him of my dispositions.

' I then returned to my own H.Q. near Sotteghem and found Johnson there, and obtained from him the latest news of the 4th Division which was now closing up on to the northern outskirts of Brussels. I finished my diary that evening with the following sentence:

" Results of day are not satisfactory as regards resistance put up by Belgians, but panic is less, and our air seems to be providing greater resistance." '

Brooke's entry for May 13th was made in his new headquarters in a requisitioned villa in the northern suburbs of Brussels.

"An indifferent night's sleep owing to A.A. gunfire. Ritchie came early to tell me that G.H.Q. had wired that it was now fixed up for 3rd Division to relieve 10th Belgian Division. So all my work of yesterday did bear fruit. I was ordered to hold conference with 10th Division Commander to settle details of relief. Called at Embassy on way up and was given instructions concerning boundary which was to swing right, south of Bruxelles, and was quite hopeless.

"Called for Monty but found him out, so took his G.I. with me and went to H.Q. Belgian 10th Division. Found fat little Divisional Commander and settled all details of relief with him. Then went to look for VI Belgian Corps H.Q. which I found with some difficulty. Here . . . a whole Belgian Corps. . . . was reforming after being broken up in front right in the area that the 4th Division was moving up into and where my Corps H.Q. was to move.

"I went to see Monty to ensure that relief for to-night was all right and found him quite happy and in great form. Then to Embassy to try and telephone to Pownall. Could not get either him or Commander-in-Chief as they were moving to Renaix. I then found that the Director of Military Intelligence, Mason MacFarlane, was with the Ambassador, so went round to him and explained situation of Belgian VI Corps and necessity to move it out at once. He was going on to G.H.Q. and said he would fix it up.

"Called on French VI Corps H.Q. on way back to establish liaison, as they will be on our left rear.

"Came home and sent telegram to Pownall and after dinner had talk to Gregson-Ellis[1] telling him how essential it was to move I Belgian Corps, and also arranged for conference with Commander-in-Chief and Chief of General Staff to-morrow at the Embassy at 12 noon to settle future employment of 4th and 50th Divisions.

"Belgian G.Q.G. have ordered retirement of Belgian

---

[1] Lt.-Gen. now Sir Henry Pownall, Chief of General Staff, B.E.F. and Col., later Maj.-Gen., P. Gregson-Ellis, G.S.O.1. Operations, G.H.Q.

forces to-night on to the Antwerp-Louvain-Wavre line. So to-morrow we shall be in contact with the Germans. I do not think much of the Belgian Army and am very nervous as to my left flank."

In the garden of his new billet Brooke was grimly amused to find a life-size statue of a naked boy pointing to heaven. ' I did not like this boy,' he wrote, ' there were far too many German planes in the sky to require a statue to draw attention to them.' Had he spent that day in Holland or in the Ardennes, where, under cover of a hail of dive-bombers, the mobile infantry of the panzer divisions were contesting the passage of the Meuse, he would have had even more reason to dislike the boy's reminder. For that Whit Monday—May 13th—was one of the decisive days of the war. During it the Luftwaffe, operating far to the north and south of the British Expeditionary Force, won two great triumphs, bringing about the collapse of the Dutch Army and the evacuation of the Dutch Government and smashing the resistance of the infantry and gunners of the French Second and Ninth Armies guarding the passage of the upper Meuse. Next day Rotterdam was gutted from the air and the Dutch Commander-in-Chief asked for an armistice, while at Sedan, Montherme, Givet and Dinant, despite sacrificial attempts by the R.A.F.'s bombers to stop them, the German tanks swept in a continuous stream across the pontoon bridges over the Meuse under cover of intense anti-aircraft fire.[1]

The 14th was a day of increasing tension, with the Belgians streaming back from the Albert Canal and rumours of a German break-through somewhere in the French lines to the south. Brooke's diary entry runs:

> " Left my H.Q. about 7 a.m. after seeing Johnson who was on the move up and proceeded to our new Corps H.Q. just north of Bruxelles. Left my kit there and reconnoitred a rear line and a switch. Then went to 3rd Division H.Q. and from there on to the Embassy where I had an appointment with Gort.

[1] By nightfall only 206 of the R.A.F.'s 474 planes in France remained serviceable. *Churchill* II 38.

" I met Admiral Keyes who asked me to try and in-fluence Gort to go and see the King of the Belgians in the afternoon. He told me he was having great difficulty keeping up the King's and van Overstraeten's spirits. We then had a conference and Barker from I Corps had also been summoned to come. I found, as I expected, that Gort was not really in the picture as to the troubles and difficulties which I had been having with the Belgians. Nor did he realise their very poor fighting quality. I had to impress on him the importance of insisting on the Belgians giving us sufficient room to deploy north of Bruxelles. We drew up places for holding a rear line along the Charleroi Canal through Bruxelles and for ways and means of withdrawal.

" News of the French at Dinant and at Sedan was not good, as Germans had broken through at both these points. We are still short of fighters, but I understand that three new squadrons are coming out from home . . .[1]

" In the afternoon reconnoitred Charleroi Canal line through Bruxelles. 4th Division coming up well, Second Brigade up now and on move by 6 a.m. to-morrow, 50th Division coming up to-morrow."

That evening, about seven o'clock, the first German attack was made on Montgomery's division in front of Louvain but was driven off. Of the following day, the 15th, Brooke wrote:

' bad news came pouring in with rumours and counter-rumours . . . I began by being told that the Germans had got into Louvain. This rumour had originated through the fact that some of the 10th Belgian Division during their relief in the dark were taken for Germans and shot up by the Grenadier Guards. . . . Later I was informed that the 50th Division was being withdrawn from II Corps, as it was

[1] Two days later, on the 16th, the Cabinet gave permission for four more fighter squadrons to be sent immediately to France; later on the same day, Churchill, under pressure from the French Government and High Command, asked for a further six, reducing Metropolitan Fighter Command to the in-dispensable minimum of twenty-five squadrons without which its Commander-in-Chief, Air Chief Marshal Sir Hugh Dowding, declared himself unable to guarantee the defence of Britain. *Churchill* II 38, 44-5.

required elsewhere. This was a serious blow, as in my reconnaissance of the previous day I had based my plans on its use. I now had to alter my plans.

' As I considered it now necessary to have further co-ordination with I Corps, I asked Michael Barker to come up for a conference, and subsequently called up Gort and got him to come also, thus again organising a Corps Conference. It proved a highly useful meeting. Gort began by giving us the bad news of the debacle on Corap's Ninth Army front, where the Germans had broken through south of Dinant. We were also told that Germans had penetrated at Sedan and Mézières. The French First Army on our immediate right was being heavily pressed on the Wavre-Namur gap. British I Corps was expecting an attack. Holland had now collapsed, thus freeing German troops for an advance on Antwerp, and the Belgian forces on our left were in a very shaky and jumpy condition, not to be trusted to put up any serious resistance.

' I wrote that evening in my diary:

" The B.E.F. is therefore likely to have both flanks turned, and will have a very unpleasant time extricating itself out of its present position.

" During the day several minor attacks took place on 3rd Division front with minor penetrations; . . . . these were, however, restored in every case. But Coldstream had some casualties. I have been busy drawing up plans for our withdrawal to the Charleroi Canal and from there to the Dendre, if necessary.

" There is enough to make one feel gloomy, but I must say that I still have a firm conviction that Right must conquer Wrong. . . ."

' It was now evident that, with the situation that was developing on the French front on our right, a withdrawal of the B.E.F. would soon become necessary. The withdrawal of the 3rd Division at Louvain was not an easy one, as its route of retirement was badly exposed from the north. The northern flank was the one I was uncertain about owing to the Belgian lack of fighting spirit. I therefore moved up one

brigade of the 4th Division east of the canal to protect the
3rd Division in the first stages of the withdrawal.

' On May 16th the news worsened. The German attacks
the previous day on the French First Army front had driven
their forces back, forcing a retirement which had involved
the British I Corps. I received orders from G.H.Q. to start
a retirement that night through Brussels. The 4th Division
would hold a temporary position on the Charleroi Canal
through which the 3rd Division would retire.

' After a bad night, with continual interruptions caused
by messages, orders, bombing, etc., I attended first of all a
G.H.Q. conference and then proceeded to 3rd Division
H.Q. to discuss final arrangements for its withdrawal. There
had been a certain amount of fighting on the Louvain front,
and as I arrived one of the Engineer officers who had been
killed that night was being buried in the château garden.
Monty as usual was at his best under adversity. Completely
unaffected by the seriousness of the situation and brimfull
of efficiency and cheerfulness. It was indeed easy work
settling the details of his retirement with him. I left him full
of confidence that he would bring off this rather difficult
move with complete success.

' I then proceeded to Belgian VI Corps H.Q. to co-
ordinate our retirement with them. Here I found a very
different state of affairs, and amongst the confusion that
prevailed it was practically impossible to form any very clear
idea of what the intentions of this Corps were. The day
finished with another G.H.Q. conference in the evening,
after which I returned to my H.Q. in Brussels for our last
night there. . . .'

" Now I hope," Brooke wrote that night, " withdrawal has
started, as it was to begin at 10 p.m." Everywhere except on
the British front it had been a day of disaster. Though the
Expeditionary Force had repulsed every attack, forty miles and
more to the south a fifty-mile wide gap had been torn in the
French Ninth and Second Armies, through which von
Rundstedt's seven panzer divisions were pouring. Every
attempt to stop them had failed and, as the German tanks—

their numbers magnified by rumour—drove westwards through
the Maginot Line extension and into the plains beyond, panic
seized the French, whose organisation, staff and supply system
were designed only for static, not mobile war. " Civilians and
French troops," wrote Rommel, " their faces distorted with
terror, lay huddled in the ditches, alongside hedges and in every
hollow beside the road. . . . Always the same picture, troops
and civilians in wild flight down both sides of the road . . .
a chaos of guns, tanks and military vehicles of all kinds, inex-
tricably entangled with horse-drawn refugee carts. . . . By
keeping our guns silent and occasionally driving our cross-
country vehicles alongside the road, we managed to get past the
column without great difficulty. The French troops were completely overcome by surprise at our sudden appearance, laid
down their arms and marched off to the east. . . . Nowhere
was any resistance attempted."[1] By evening Guderian's divisions, their men cheering their commanders and drunk with
victory, were from forty to fifty miles beyond the Meuse, while
to the north, keeping almost level and lapping like an iron
sea round the southern flank of the French First Army,
Reinhardt's and Hoth's two other panzer corps were heading
towards the base towns—Landrecies, Cambrai, Valenciennes,
Arras, Douai and Lille—from which only six days earlier the
Allied advance into Belgium had been launched. At 5 a.m. on
the 17th Rommel's tanks, after driving through the night,
entered Landrecies. An hour and a half later they were
approaching the outskirts of Le Cateau.

' On the morning of May 17th,' Brooke recalled,

' I received a very alarming message by despatch-rider. It
was timed 2 a.m., but had been delayed in delivery owing
to the despatch-rider losing his way. It came from Michael
Barker of I Corps and contained words somewhat to this
effect: " Situation on my right flank extremely grave, outflanked by armoured forces." I sent off a liaison officer at
once to I Corps to discover what the situation was, and
studied maps carefully with the object, if necessary, of
diverting my route of retirement in a more northerly

[1] *The Rommel Papers* 19-22.

direction. However, after sending yet another liaison officer, I finally got another message stating that situation after all was not so serious. . . .

'The night of the 17th was spent at Terlinden, but I was apparently too tired that evening to write up my diary, for on the 18th I find the following:

" I was too tired to write last night, and now can barely remember what happened yesterday. The hours are so crowded and follow so fast on each other that life becomes a blur and fails to cut a groove in one's memory."

' The 3rd Division had carried out its retirement successfully out of Louvain, and, covered by the armoured cavalry, had retired through Brussels and across the Charleroi Canal. Here the 4th Division was already holding the line of the canal. On clearing the canal the 3rd Division embussed and moved back to the line of the Dendre which it began to reach early that afternoon. Once the cavalry had been withdrawn, the bridges over the canal through Brussels were blown, and the Germans gradually closed on to this front.

' I had time, however, to motor along the bridges and to see that all the preparations were ready before the arrival of the Germans. After attending another conference at I Corps H.Q., I finally came back to my new command-post just behind the Dendre at Terlinden.'

Next morning—Saturday the 18th—Brooke's command-post at Renaix was heavily bombed. The Luftwaffe, having forced the Meuse crossings and knocked out Holland, had turned its attention to the retreating French and British Armies and was now spreading terror and destruction along the highways of Belgium and France. With the French Air Force driven from the skies and the R.A.F. Air Component reduced to half its strength and with its airfields in the path of the panzer torrent, the Luftwaffe by now had the air almost to itself. The fog of war had descended over the vast battlefield, covering, as the German tanks sped forward in vast dust clouds, all northern France and Belgium. On both sides, frightened by the pace of events and the lack of clear news, the Higher Command was

showing signs of panicking. Twice—on the evening of the 15th
and again on the morning of the 17th—Guderian's superiors,
fearful of a counter-attack, tried to stop his advance, and he
had only been able to continue by pleading the formula that
Hitler had approved when the Manstein plan was first adopted:
" Once armoured formations are out on the loose, they must
be given the green light to the very end of the road." Had it
not been that the French, bewildered by the onrush, seemed
incapable of making any attempt against their long, exposed
flanks, those precarious columns of swiftly-moving armour—
the Reich's most precious asset—would almost certainly have
been halted or recalled.

But though Churchill, who had flown to Paris on the evening
of the 16th to hearten the French Government, pleaded first
with Gamelin and later with his successor, Weygand, not to
try to stop holes but to punch them, the French were unable
to do so. " *Où est la masse de manœuvre?* " he asked the Supreme
Commander, whereupon that officer helplessly shrugged his
shoulders and replied, " *Aucune!* " It was scarcely surprising that
when the High Command showed itself so impotent to control
events, subordinate commanders, left without intelligence of
what was happening or even of what was planned, became
themselves confused and uncertain. During the 18th, the day
on which the German armoured divisions took Cambrai and
St. Quentin, Brooke had to contend with two major changes
of plan by his fellow corps-commander, who at this time was
exposed far more closely than he to the menace of the German
armour moving so swiftly round the flank of the retreating
French First Army on his right and who, though a most gallant
officer, lacked the physical strength and resilience to cope
unperturbed with the succession of contradictory reports and
rumours, the continuous lack of sleep, and the appalling shock
and pace of the *blitzkrieg*. ' He started,' wrote Brooke,

' by comparing the situation of the I Corps with that of
Smith-Dorrien at the battle of Le Cateau. He said that he
was incapable of retiring any farther and must fight it out
where he was. After considerable argument we got him to
agree that he could resume the retirement the next day. He

said, however, that the I Corps could not move the forward
elements back before noon. This plan did not suit me at all;
I disliked withdrawing in daylight and had intended withdrawing by dawn. However, to suit I Corps, I agreed very
reluctantly to wait till 12 noon.'

Yet when, after making arrangements to postpone his withdrawal, Brooke got back to his command-post, he was greeted
with the news that, faced by a new and, as it turned out false,
report of enveloping German armour, I Corps had now issued
orders for its retirement to start at dawn. ' This,' he wrote,

' put II Corps in a serious position. We were echeloned in
front of I Corps, and its early withdrawal would expose the
right of my Corps. I, therefore, sent messages to Monty and
Alex warning them of I Corps' intention and instructing
them, if possible, to conform as nearly as possible with I
Corps' moves. As matters turned out, this change of plans
seriously exposed Alexander's right flank, and a dangerous
situation might have ensued had it not been for Alex's quick
action in ordering the I Corps cavalry regiment to cover his
exposed flank.'

For one result of that day's conference was that Brooke had
had transferred to him from the overburdened Commander
of the I Corps one of his divisions—the 1st, commanded by the
forty-eight-year-old Major-General Harold Alexander.

' In taking over the 1st Division I was for the first time
having the experience of having Alexander working under
me. It was a great opportunity . . . to see what he was made
of, and what an admirable commander he was when in a
tight place. It was intensely interesting watching him and
Monty during those trying days, both of them completely
imperturbable and efficiency itself, and yet two totally
different characters. Monty with his quick brain for
appreciating military situations was well aware of the very
critical situation that he was in, and the very dangers and
difficulties that faced us acted as a stimulus on him; they
thrilled him and put the sharpest of edges on his military
ability. Alex, on the other hand, gave me the impression of

never fully realising all the very unpleasant potentialities of our predicament. He remained entirely unaffected by it, completely composed and appeared never to have the slightest doubt that all would come right in the end. It was in those critical days that the appreciation I made of those two commanders remained rooted in my mind and resulted in the future selection of these two men to work together in the triumphal advance from Alamein to Tunis.'

Brooke sympathised deeply with his fellow Corps commander and well understood the mental hell he was suffering: 'lack of sleep, irregular meals, great physical exertions of continuous travelling in all directions, rumours, counter-rumours, doubts, ambiguous orders and messages, lack of information on danger-points, and the thousand and one factors that are perpetually hammering away at one's powers of resistance.' His diary reveals only too clearly the harrowing anxiety and uncertainty to which those responsible for making decisions were subjected. Yet what is so remarkable to anyone reading his day-by-day account of his experiences is the way in which he concealed from everyone around any trace of anxiety. To his Military Assistant—his constant attendant—and to all who encountered him during the retreat, he seemed completely imperturbable.[1] It was only then that they realised their Corps Commander's full stature. All through that nightmare time, while he was confiding his doubts and fears to his journal as though to a lightning-conductor, he remained, as one of his staff put it, "poker face." He listened to what everyone had to say, made whatever modifications to his plans seemed necessary, and gave his orders with his habitual incisiveness and speed but without the least sign of being ruffled or hurried. Nothing the enemy did or threatened apparently surprised or left him without an answer, for in almost every instance he had already foreseen it. He always found time for four or five hours' good sleep, never appeared dirty, shabby or unshaven, and was always immaculately dressed. Wherever he went he conveyed the sense

[1] He concealed even his anxiety about his son's fate. " He must," wrote his Military Assistant, " have suffered hell over his son who was terribly ill during the retreat. He never showed it, even to me. I merely got what reports I could and they ceased quite soon." *Notes by Lt.-Col. R. Stanyforth.*

that the *blitzkrieg* and all the pandemonium around him were part of the normal background of a soldier's life.

Yet his diary entries during the next two days of alarm and rumour reveal the storm he was riding.

" *May 19th. Wambrechies.* Got up at 5 a.m. after a short night and, after examining reports, started off to examine our new line of defence on the Scheldt. Found travelling difficult owing to masses of refugees, but succeeded in covering the whole length of the river and in going up on to Mont St. Auber (near Tournai) to see to what extent it overlooks our new line. It is going to be a troublesome spot. I then motored on through the new H.Q. of the 1st Division to try and find out how they were getting on. Then on to the new H.Q. which we reached in the middle of an air-raid on the aerodrome, which is unfortunately just alongside of us.

" I had only just arrived when I was called to G.H.Q. for a Corps commanders' conference. It was a momentous one. The news of the French front was worse than ever; they were attempting one further counter-attack to try and restore the situation. Should this fail, it looks as if Allied forces would be cut in the centre. The B.E.F. communication to the sea would be completely exposed and so would our right flank.

"G.H.Q. had a scheme for a move in such an eventuality towards Dunkirk, establishing a defended area round this place and embarking all we could of the personnel of the B.E.F., abandoning stores and equipment. I preferred pivoting on our left flank which is secure and in contact with the Belgians; to swing our right back on to the River Lys up the now empty canal to Ypres and thence by Ypres Canal to the sea. By this means I feel that at any rate we can keep the B.E.F. as an entity and not have it destroyed by bits. If we let go our hold on the Belgians now, I feel certain they will stop fighting and both our flanks will be exposed, in which case there would be little hope. We are to meet again this evening for another conference if G.H.Q. have any more news.

" I have spent most of the afternoon in considerable anxiety trying to obtain information from 3rd and 1st Divisions as to whether they are back safe. It was not till about 7 p.m. that I began to get first reports of arrivals of leading brigades during the afternoon, but it was not till after dinner that I got final confirmation of both 1st and 3rd Divisions being on their fronts. They are very tired and will require at least twenty-four hours to sort out vehicles and to put them in a real fit state again.

" The II Corps has now covered a good hundred and fifty miles in nine days and in the process has occupied four successive defensive positions. It has entailed excessively hard work on the part of all ranks and has been exceptionally efficiently carried out.

" *May 20th. Wambrechies.* Went round in the morning to see Adam[1] and discuss with him further moves; found him in agreement with me. Then visited Monty and discussed with him yesterday's withdrawal. He had had a difficult time and had been shelled, losing his car-driver and some men of the Anti-Tank Regiment. He seemed now firmly established on his new front.

" I then visited 1st Division and saw Alexander and discussed his withdrawal. He apparently was subjected to flanking pressure owing to I Corps withdrawing too early. His 3rd Brigade, I discovered later, has lost a good deal of material, and the rear party finally had to abandon their vehicles and swim the canal owing to bridges being blown.

" In the afternoon Gregson-Ellis came to give me the latest news from G.H.Q. which included German pressure on Arras. Every possible measure is being taken to try and stem the advance of the tanks and armoured-cars in the gap they have made, but the situation still remains very serious. C.I.G.S. has flown out from London to discuss future measures. Weygand appointed Supreme Commander. Pagézy[2] has left Lille. The refugees are a desperate encumbrance on all roads."

[1] Lt.-Gen., now Gen. Sir Ronald, Adam, commanding the 111 Corps.
[2] French Commander, Lille District.

' After Gregson-Ellis had left me I had a telephone call from Pagézy asking me where my Corps was. I told him where it was, whereupon he informed me that this was all wrong and that the Germans were in Roubaix. I told him this was not the case, and that there were no Germans any-where near Roubaix. He then said that he had been in-formed by the Mayor, that he knew where they were, and implied that I did not know what the situation was on my front. He was in a very worked-up and excitable condition . . . I told him fairly bluntly that I did not have to go to the Mayor of Roubaix to find out where the Germans were.

' During the winter months we had worked out an elaborate scheme by which 800,000 of the population of Lille, Roubaix and Tourcoing were to be evacuated to north-western France in the event of a German attack. During our retirement this scheme had been put into effect, and, as I arrived back into our old Lille area, I thanked heaven that we were now rid of refugee problems. . . . I was thanking Providence too soon. . . . As I went out again in the afternoon, to my dismay I found all the roads which had been so clear of refugees on the previous day crammed with humanity moving from west to east. In fact, they were all crowding back into the area which we had so successfully evacuated. They were all haggard-looking, and many women were in the last stages of exhaustion, many of them with their feet tied up with string and brown paper where their shoes had given out; they were covered with mud from throwing themselves into the ditches every time a plane flew over. There were old men trundling their old wives in wheel-barrows, women pushing prams piled high with all their belongings, and all their faces distorted by fear, a heart-breaking and desperate sight.

' I was informed by the Préfet that these were the 800,000 people whom we had evacuated westward. They had run into the German armoured forces, and into rumours of these forces where they did not exist. Like one big wave, the whole of this humanity, short of food and sleep and terrified to the core, was now surging back again and congesting all roads at a moment when mobility was a vital element. The Préfet was most helpful. He told me that, if I directed these crowds into Lille with my military police, he would form dormitories, bakeries and butcheries to deal with them. He was as good as his word, and handled this mass of humanity exceptionally well. He remained at his post till the last moment and fell into German hands.'

With the possible exception of two days in the winter of 1941-42, May 20th, 1940, was for the democracies the most disastrous day of the war. In it, while the bewildered French expected a swing south on Paris, Guderian's armour, in a frenzy of inspired offensive, swept westwards for forty miles from the old Somme battlefields of the first War to the Channel shore, capturing both Amiens and Abbeville and, by reaching the sea, cutting the last line of communication of the northern armies—close on a million men—with Paris and the British supply-ports in Normandy and Brittany. In their advance they overran the scattered units of two recently landed Territorial divisions which Lord Gort had hastily summoned from the base areas in the south to bar their path. One British battery was actually captured with all its guns in the market square at Albert.

There was only one way to retrieve the situation: to stage a counter-attack from north and south on that severing corridor before the German infantry could reinforce the seven panzer and six supporting motorised divisions that had made it. On the day before Guderian reached the Channel, Gamelin had given orders for such an attack, and the British Prime Minister and War Cabinet and the Chief of the Imperial General Staff, while authorising as a precautionary measure the assembly of a fleet of small craft in the south-coast ports, had rejected Lord Gort's plea for a retreat to Dunkirk and called for an immediate offensive to the south, sending the Vice C.I.G.S., Sir John Dill, to French General Headquarters to help co-ordinate it. As a first step, on the 21st a small force, already assembled at Arras to prevent British G.H.Q. from being overrun by the German armour, made a sudden assault on Rommel's flanking panzer division and a supporting S.S. division of Motorised Infantry. It consisted of two tank battalions and two territorial battalions of Durham Light Infantry from the 50th Division, which, with his own 5th Division, had been hastily placed under General Franklyn with orders to hold the town and halt the German tanks to the south of it. It was far too small to achieve more than temporary success and suffered heavy casualties. Yet in a few hours of fierce fighting it not only caused a panic among the S.S. infantry but so alarmed the German Higher Command that for a whole day Guderian's armour was halted on the coast instead of being allowed, as its commander pleaded, to advance on the unprotected Channel ports to the north. And, though at dawn next day, after Franklyn's men had withdrawn into the Arras defence lines, Guderian was allowed to resume his drive on Boulogne and was already attacking that port by nightfall, the German Higher Command, from Hitler downwards, was left with an uneasy feeling that the British had teeth and that it would be unwise to risk the armour—needed for future battles against the main French armies—in attacking too closely.

But the grand southward counter-assault that the Prime Minister was urging with such spirit and vehemence was only possible on three conditions: that the retreating British Army in Belgium, now engaged in repelling heavy frontal attacks from the east, could be sufficiently disengaged to enable it to stage an offensive against the forces established in its rear; that support to make this practicable could be provided by the French and Belgians cut off with the British; and that the main French armies on the far side of the panzer corridor could launch a simultaneous counter-attack from the south. And none of these conditions were satisfied. With only four days' supplies and ammunition available, with seven of his eleven divisions[1] on the Scheldt holding a seventy-miles front against von Bock's Army Group and with the German armour astride his communications and swinging inwards behind him towards the Canal du Nord and the Channel ports, it was impossible for Lord Gort to obey the order which the Prime Minister sent

[1] One division, the 51st, was taking its turn of duty with the French Army in the Maginot Line, while the newly-landed and still incomplete 1st Armoured Division was also cut off from the Expeditionary Force by the German drive to the Channel.

him from Paris on the 22nd for the B.E.F. and the French First Army to attack next day towards Bapaume and Cambrai with eight divisions. The very earliest by which he could hope to launch such an offensive was the 26th and then only by retiring to his fortified winter lines on the French frontier and freeing sufficient divisions from the battle on his front to assail the enemy in his rear. Even this would only be possible if the Belgians on his left could carry out a planned retreat to the Yser, take over part of his line, and protect his seaward flank and the eastern approaches to Dunkirk.

Yet when on the 21st the new French Supreme Commander, General Weygand, flew to Calais to attend a meeting at Ypres with the King of the Belgians, Lord Gort and General Billotte —the Commander-in-Chief and co-ordinator of the encircled northern Armies—King Leopold had made it clear that his shaken troops were incapable of offensive action or even of any further organised movement at all.[1] Nor did the French seem in much better case. When Gort, who had not been notified of the time and place of the meeting and could not at first be found, reached it from his new command-post at Premesques, Weygand had already left for Paris,[2] and Billotte frankly admitted that, though a counter-attack had been ordered, his troops were in a state of such confusion that they were not only incapable of an offensive but could barely defend themselves. They and their channels of communication were under continuous attack from the air, and every road behind them was packed with hordes of refugees. An hour after the meeting, while negotiating such a road himself, Billotte was fatally injured in a collision, dying in hospital two days later and leaving the Allied armies in the north without anyone to co-ordinate them.

Meanwhile Brooke and his Corps were holding the left of the British line on the Scheldt, with the Belgians, whose uncertain

[1] " The King pointed out that the Belgian Army existed solely for defence; it had neither tanks nor aircraft and was not trained or equipped for offensive warfare. . . . M. Pierlot, who met the King after seeing General Weygand, says, ' The King considered the position of the armies in Flanders almost, if not quite, hopeless.' " *The War in France and Flanders* (H.M.S.O.), 105, 110-11.

[2] By submarine from Calais, his aircraft having been attacked and driven down on its way to Ypres.

appearance worried him more and more, on his left. ' On May 21st,' he wrote,

' I got up early to go round the Corps front and started with the 3rd Division, which I found well established but infernally thin on the ground. All three brigades were in the line, two of them with all three of their battalions up. The division consequently only had one battalion in reserve. I visited one of the observation-posts of the 76th Regiment R.A. and had a fairly good view. I then dropped in to the H.Q. of the 1st Coldstream to have a word with them, as they had had a bad time in Louvain, losing five officers and a hundred and sixty men. At 7th Guards Brigade H.Q. I found Jack Whitaker and had a talk with him about the fighting his brigade had been through during the retirement. Whilst I was with him a heavy bombardment broke out just south of 3rd Division on the left of the 1st Division near Peck bridge. I, therefore, went on to 1st Division H.Q. to find out what was going on. On arriving there I was informed that the Germans were across the river at Peck bridge on the 1st Guards Brigade front. I told Alexander that they must be pushed back, and that we could not allow any lodgments on our side of the river.

' I got back to my H.Q. at Wambrechies for lunch and was told that Gort was coming to my Headquarters for a G.H.Q. conference at 4.15 p.m. He started by giving us the general situation, which was extremely gloomy. The Germans were reported near Boulogne and Calais; these ports were heavily mined, there were great communication and supply difficulties, and little progress had so far been made by any attempts to close this gap in our front.

' The situation on the south and the highly extended nature of our front necessitated our retiring from the Scheldt to the frontier defences on the following evening (May 22nd). We were therefore, after all, to occupy those defences which we had spent so many months in preparing. Unfortunately we were far too thin on the ground to hold them, and it could only be a temporary measure entailing further withdrawals.

' By the evening I had reports that the situation on 1st Division front at Peck bridge had been restored, and the II Corps was everywhere on its river line. Unfortunately, penetrations of Germans still remained on both I and III Corps fronts, namely, on both flanks of II Corps.

' I started the day—May 22nd—with a Corps conference at 7 a.m. which I held at 1st Divisional H.Q. There I settled details with Monty and Alex for our further withdrawal to the frontier which was to take place that night. I also informed them as to the general situation, and warned them of the supply difficulties which faced us owing to our lines of communication to the base having been cut. I then carried out a reconnaissance of the canal lines through Lille to estimate their defensive value in case I should have to select a defensive line in this area.[1]

' The refugee problem was getting worse and worse, and I wrote that evening in my diary:

" They are the most pathetic sight, with lame women suffering from sore feet, small children worn out with travelling but hugging their dolls, and all the old and maimed struggling along."

' This continual sight of agonising humanity drifting aimlessly like frightened cattle becomes one of the worst of daylight nightmares. One's mind, short of sleep, is continually wracked by the devastating problems of an almost hopeless situation, and on top of it one's eyes rest incessantly on terrified and miserable humanity cluttering the lines of communication on which all hope of possible security rest.

' In the evening I moved Corps H.Q. from Wambrechies to Armentières in anticipation of the night's withdrawal. Armentières was not an ideal selection as it was evidently liable to draw bombs, which it did before long. It had, however, good telephone and road communications with the rest of the Corps. A new trouble was now facing us: our rear was now threatened by German tanks. It was impossible even to obtain accurate information of the situation in our

---

[1] About this time, some six hundred miles to the south, the Municipality of the little Pyrenean town of Bagnères de Bigorre was passing a resolution that they should invite General Brooke to honour them by visiting his birthplace.

rear. I knew, however, how flimsy our improvised forces were to whom the task had been given of building up a screen of defence in our rear. It was evident that at any moment German armoured forces might break through this screen and descend on us suddenly. I, therefore, established a detachment of anti-tank and anti-air guns, plus an infantry platoon, under the control of one of our G.S.O.s, with the sole task of protecting Corps H.Q.

' I was informed that evening that General Billotte had been involved in a serious motor-car accident and had been taken off to hospital. . . . Command must now rest with General Blanchard who had up to date commanded the French First Army and who was not familiar with the layout of the forces of the northern wing.

' *May 23rd.* I started my diary that evening:

" Nothing but a miracle can save the B.E.F. now, and the end cannot be very far off. We carried out our withdrawal successfully last night back to the old frontier defences and by this morning we were established in the defences we spent the winter preparing. But where the danger lies is on our right rear. The German armoured divisions have penetrated to the coast; Abbeville, Boulogne and Calais have been rendered useless. We are, therefore, cut off from our sea communications, beginning to be short of ammunition. Supplies still all right for three days, but after that, scarcity. This evening the Germans are reported to be pushing on to Béthune and on from St. Omer, namely, right in our rear."

' I spent the morning visiting divisions and found them well established in our old defensive line. The provident Monty . . . had been driving along with him some " beef on the hoof," consisting of several herds of cattle. He was establishing butcheries and bakeries, thus supplementing our limited rations. In addition he had discovered an ammunition train originally destined for Brussels which had been stopped near Roubaix or Tourcoing. It was very near the front, but they decided to endeavour to extricate it and . . . . succeeded in doing so.

'I was called to a conference at G.H.Q. and informed that I was now to take over the 4th Division again from III Corps and to hand back the 1st Division to the I Corps. I was sorry to lose Alex and had formed a very high opinion of his ability during the short time I had him under my command. On the other hand, I was very glad to have my old 4th Division back with me.

'I went over to see the 4th Division that afternoon in anticipation of taking them over again. I found that the 11th Infantry Brigade had lost fairly heavily on the previous day. The Northamptons were reported to have lost two hundred and fifty men, whilst two of the commanding officers of the brigade had been killed.

'I finished my diary that evening with:

"It is a fortnight since the German advance started and the success they have achieved is nothing short of phenomenal. There is no doubt that they are most wonderful soldiers." '

.   .   .   .

The change in the composition of his Corps to which Brooke referred was caused by Lord Gort's attempt to carry out the instructions given him from French General Headquarters and London by releasing the two Territorial divisions of General Adam's III Corps to join with the 5th and 50th Divisions in a major offensive to the south—the "penetration scheme," as it was called. But though the need to break through the German encircling lines was desperate—that day the Expeditionary Force was put on half rations, and Guderian's panzers, already besieging Boulogne and Calais, began to advance on Grave-lines and Dunkirk—the means of doing so were hopelessly inadequate. Most of the striking reserve the Commander-in-Chief was valiantly trying to assemble was already tied down in an improvised defensive battle against the encircling German armour along the forty-mile canal line between La Bassée and the sea at Gravelines—facing south-west and with their backs to their comrades who, only twenty miles away, were defending the French frontier from the main German armies advancing

from the north-east. Meanwhile, a further fifteen miles to the
south at Arras, two brigades of the 5th Division and two of the
50th, which were to have formed the spearhead of the break-
through to the south and had been fighting under General
Franklyn for three days to hold the town, were almost completely surrounded. That night, realising that they would
otherwise be lost, Gort ordered their immediate withdrawal;
with great skill they made good their escape during the hours of
darkness and rejoined the main British forces to the north.

The position of the Expeditionary Force was now desperate.
Its 200,000 fighting men, with the remnants of the French
First Army, were holding a hundred miles of a hundred-and-
thirty mile front, bent back like a long hairpin, with its north-
western end on the Dover strait at Gravelines, its bent centre
to the south of Lille and its north-eastern end on the left of
Brooke's II Corps touching the Belgian right near Menin, some
thirty miles south of the North Sea. So far the chief danger had
been from the German armour in the rear; now, with the
impending collapse of the Belgian Army, those additional miles
on Brooke's left around Ypres and Dixmude were to become
all-important. For on the 24th von Bock's Army Group broke
clean through the Belgian lines both to the north-east of
Courtrai and between Courtrai and Menin.

' *May 24th*,' Brooke wrote,

' started with a conference at G.H.Q. at 9 a.m. when we
discussed the proposed plan for attack southwards to join up
with one to be carried out by the French from the south.
The enterprise did not seem very hopeful, and I do not believe
that any of us had any confidence in its success.

' After the conference Gort left to meet Dill who had flown
over to Poperinghe. I stopped on to discuss plans with
Pownall and Adam, when Blanchard arrived. We had just
heard that Billotte had died from the results of the motor
accident. Was his mantle now to fall on Blanchard? It
seemed likely that it would, and I therefore took great interest
in looking at Blanchard to see what he was like and what
confidence he would inspire. He was standing studying the
map as I looked at him carefully, and I gathered the im-

pression that he might as well have been staring at a blank wall
. . . . He gave me the impression of a man whose brain had
ceased to function; he was merely existing and hardly aware
of what was going on around him. The blows that had fallen
on us in quick succession had left him " punch drunk " and
unable to register events. I was badly shaken and felt that,
if he was to take over the tiller in the present storm, it would
not be long before we were on the rocks.

' Whilst at G.H.Q. reports came in of German attacks on
Hazebrouck,[1] and the wireless had the optimistic report that
the southern French attack had reached Bapaume, which
unfortunately turned out to be incorrect.

' From G.H.Q. I motored up to see the 3rd and 4th
Divisions and found them all well. The continual visits to
the divisions I found essential, both to keep in touch with
the ever-changing situation, and also to keep them informed.

' Visits of this kind during periods of disaster are not easy.
. . . The moment you step into the H.Q., all eyes are on you,
endeavouring to read your mind and to discern how grave
the situation may be from the look on one's face. It is, therefore, essential to submerge all the feelings of anxiety that are
literally tearing out one's insides, and to carry an outward
appearance that radiates confidence and assurance. It is not
an easy matter, but one on which morale depends. I was
immensely impressed during those trying days to find the
magnitude of the influence which one can exercise on subordinates by maintaining a confident and unperturbed
exterior.

' Adam dropped in during the evening, having spent the
day discussing plans for the southern attack. He informed
me that the Germans had stopped their advance on Hazebrouck. Just as I had finished tea, German bombers came
over at low altitude and proceeded to bomb the main street
in Armentières, which ran parallel to the one my billet was
in. Several bombs fell unpleasantly close and started fires
raging in Armentières. We had practically no fighter or
A.A. protection and the town was completely at the mercy

[1] Where the German armour from the West was attacking the Territorial
divisions of General Adam's III Corps.

of low bombers. The streets began to be encumbered with demolished houses, broken vehicles, dead horses and men.

' Last thing in the evening I received an alarming report that the Germans had penetrated the Belgian front between Menin and Courtrai. This was in my immediate left front, just off the 4th Division, although I still had the River Lys as an obstacle to guard my left. Any penetration towards Ypres would put the whole of the B.E.F. in the most precarious position, with both flanks turned and its rear threatened. The last lines I wrote that evening were:

" I hope this news is not correct, but I feel very nervous about this flank as I have no reserves in hand should my flank be exposed." '

For in the course of that day the situation confronting the British Army changed dramatically. " Now," wrote Rommel on the 23rd, " the hunt is up against sixty encircled British, French and Belgian divisions."[1] But during the 24th, while a brigade of Rifles—taken from the Armoured Division, and hurriedly ferried over from England to Calais—fought desperately to deny the town to the Germans and retard their eastward advance, the panzers, already across the Gravelines-St. Omer-Béthune-La Bassée water-line in several places, were halted by orders, first from von Rundstedt and then from Hitler himself.[2] Disquieted by the stubbornness of Franklyn's defence of Arras and by rumours of an impending British counter-attack against the panzer corridor, and anxious to prevent his armour—which he needed for early operations against the main French Armies—from being damaged in forcing a heavily canalised and partially flooded area unsuitable for tanks, he and the High Command had decided to use the panzers merely to hold the British right between La Bassée and the sea, while throwing von Bock's Army Group

[1] *Rommel Papers*, 34.
[2] Guderian himself was most indignant. " The order," he wrote, " contained the words: ' Dunkirk is to be left to the Luftwaffe.' . . . We were utterly speechless. But since we were not informed of the reasons for this order, it was difficult to argue against it. The panzer divisions were therefore instructed: ' Hold the line of the canal. Make use of the period of rest for general recuperation.' . . . Hitler and, above all, Goering, believed German air supremacy to be strong enough to prevent the evacuation of the British forces by sea." *Guderian*, 117, 120.

from the east into the vacuum created on the British left by the disintegration of the Belgian Army. The Expeditionary Force would still be held firmly in a long and narrowing corridor between the German armour to the west and the main German masses to the east, but instead of the capture of its last remaining door to the sea at Dunkirk being left to Guderian, the *coup de grâce* should be delivered from the east through the broken Belgian armies and the fatal gap beyond towards Ypres and the North Sea. Instead of being rolled up from the north-west behind Adam's III Corps, it would be encircled and smashed from the north-east round the back of Brooke's corps. And while von Bock cut the last roads between Lille and Dunkirk, the Luftwaffe's dive-bombers would render the port untenable and stop any remnants who managed to escape through the closing jaws of the trap from reaching England. What had nearly been accomplished at first Ypres in November, 1914, and been thwarted by the almost inconceivable courage of seven decimated British divisions, should now be accomplished with new weapons against those divisions' still more imperilled successors.

Brooke's diary for the 25th—a day of fateful decision—begins:

> " During the night I received information at 2 a.m. that the German penetration through the Belgian front was growing rapidly and that the Belgians were not offering much resistance. I came to the conclusion that this was the beginning of a German offensive intended to push right through to our left rear and to join up with the armoured divisions which must have just about shot their bolt.
>
> " Went to G.H.Q. to obtain reinforcement of a brigade to hold the line of the Ypres-Comines Canal. I had already sent a machine-gun battalion for 3rd Division there. With great difficulty I finally extracted this brigade."

' I remember well finding it difficult at that time to make Gort realise the danger to our left flank, or the fact that from now on the whole security of the B.E.F. would depend on this flank. I had few illusions by then as to the fighting value of the Belgians. Gort's first reactions were that I should put two machine-gun battalions to hold the extensive front from Comines to Ypres both inclusive.[1] I pointed out to him that their defensive power at night would be practically nil. . . . G.H.Q. on that morning were still absorbed with the prospects of the southern attack. . . .

'From G.H.Q. I went to visit Johnson at 4th Division H.Q. and whilst I was there our liaison officer with the 1st Belgian Division came in. He had a very gloomy account of the fighting put up by the Belgians; so much so that I wrote in my diary:

" Personally I am convinced that the Belgian Army is closing down and will have stopped fighting by this time to-morrow. This, of course, entirely exposes our left flank." '

' From the 4th Division I went on to see Monty at 3rd Division H.Q. and to keep him informed as to the situation. He had his H.Q. in a small villa, and, as I walked through the dining-room to the drawing-room he was in, I noticed that his staff were very busy with some papers round the dining-room table. After seeing Monty and on walking back through the dining-room, by way of making conversation I said to them: "You seem to be very busy round that table." Whereupon one of them replied: " Oh! yes, we have some most interesting documents here." On making further enquiries from them I discovered that one of our patrols working across the Lys River had run into a German Staff car. The driver had been killed, but the German Staff officer had escaped. On examining the car a leather wallet was found containing many documents and a small boot-jack. . . . I asked them if they had a German interpreter amongst them, and was informed that one of them knew a little of the language. To their disgust I told them to put all the papers back into the wallet and to give it to me so that I could take it direct to G.H.Q. to be examined.

' As I drove along towards G.H.Q. I remembered the papers which Meinertzhagen had planted on the Turks for

[1] Nearly nine miles.

Allenby by riding into no man's land and allowing himself to be shot at, pretending he was wounded; as he galloped away with his arms round his horse's neck, he dropped a pocket-book which had been artistically prepared with false information. I wondered if the Germans were up to some such trick and then remembered the boot-jack in the wallet. I thought it was highly unlikely that the Germans would have thought of placing a boot-jack in the wallet, whilst on the other hand, it was highly probable that a German staff officer might have tight boots requiring a jack to pull them off.

' On arrival at G.H.Q. I handed over the wallet to White-foord, who was Intelligence G.S.O.1., and asked him to have the papers interpreted as quickly as possible. I then pro-ceeded to attend a G.H.Q. conference. . . . As soon as the conference was over I got hold of Whitefoord to find out what he made of the German documents. He said that he had only had time to glance through them, but they contained one order connected with a holding attack on the defended front east of Lille, and an assault by a whole Corps to be directed on the front of Ypres-Comines. In addition, there was a document of general importance concerning German general dispositions. I told Whitefoord to give full details to Gort, and told him personally of the important part. From now onward I had less difficulty in obtaining reinforcements for this front.

' The German staff officer was Lt.-Col. Kinzel (later Lt.-Gen.) serving on von Brauchitsch's staff as liaison officer with Sixth Army. His instructions were to report at least twice a day on the picture on Sixth Army front. Un-doubtedly he drove into the front line, as it is so easy to do when the situation is fluid and you come up from the rear to gain information. He had in his wallet two priceless docu-ments: the first of immediate importance to the B.E.F. in the shape of Orders to Sixth Army for an attack on the following day. The second one was of the very greatest im-portance to the War Office—a document of the highest military security classification, of which only twenty copies were issued, and only four . . . . went into the field. The copy lacked six pages dealing with the Saar, Poland, Denmark and Norway, but with these exceptions it gave a complete picture of the Army Groups, Armies, Corps and Divisions of the German Army, with Commanders-in-Chief, Chiefs of Staff. Its speedy transmission to the War Office made it possible for the first time to obtain a clear grip of the Order of Battle of the German Army—a grip which was never subsequently lost.'

At the G.H.Q. conference which Brooke attended while the captured documents were being examined a full awareness was shown for the first time of the gravity of the threat to the British left. " I found," he wrote that night in his diary, " the atmosphere entirely changed and was at once presented with the 5th Division for the defence of the Ypres-Comines Canal. They have now realised the danger I warned them about this morning. The penetration scheme is temporarily abandoned." The reconnoitring staff-officer whom Brooke had interviewed that morning at 4th Division headquarters had reported that the only Belgian soldiers to be seen were sitting about in cafés and had given up any idea of fighting, while the main Belgian forces were withdrawing under enemy pressure northwards.[1] Through the gap there was now nothing to prevent von Bock's men from pouring westwards across the old Ypres battlefield to link hands with the German armoured divisions beyond Cassel and Hazebrouck. In the light of this threat of encirclement, Dill, who had arrived from England at Gort's headquarters, had telegraphed to the Prime Minister that morning that any Allied offensive to break out to the south could be no more than a very minor affair.

Impressed by Brooke's repeated warnings of what would happen unless immediate steps were taken to close the breach on his left, Lord Gort now decided that he could no longer carry out the instructions of the French High Command and his own Government. On his sole responsibility he cancelled the orders

---

[1] This was confirmed by a report at 6.30 p.m. that evening by the British Military Mission at Belgian Headquarters. "German attack . . . to-day drove back Belgians right to Gheluwe. Gap exists between Gheluwe and Lys which Belgians cannot close. Last reserves used already." *The War in France and Flanders 1939-40* (H.M.S.O.), 148.

for a break-out and at once transferred one of the two divisions scheduled to take part in it to help Brooke defend the Army's remaining lifeline to the north.[1] Having felt for some time, and rightly, that the only hope of saving his troops was to retreat at once on the one port left them, this brave, simple and honourable man had decided to stake everything, including his own honour, on keeping open the road to Dunkirk and withdrawing along it while there was still time.

Whether, however, the B.E.F. could cover those forty or fifty miles down a narrowing corridor little more than fifteen miles wide, with two numerically superior German armies on either side, and with the roads down which it was to retreat under constant air-attack and packed with refugees and traffic, depended on whether the II Corps could simultaneously hold off its assailants from the east and extend its left flank in time to prevent the enemy from flooding through the gap between it and the sea. Only lightning action could avert the greatest disaster of British military history. ' Strategically,' Brooke wrote of the situation that faced him that evening,

' I was in a most precarious situation. My Corps was strung out on an extended front from Halluin on the Lys through Tourçoing and Roubaix. Some six miles on my left rear the Germans were to deliver an attack commencing on the following day on the Ypres-Comines front of some 15,000 yards. On this front I had only one infantry brigade and one machine-gun battalion. To make matters worse, the withdrawal of 3rd and 4th Divisions to reinforce the newly threatened front could only be done by the circuitous

[1] The official history of the *War in France and Flanders 1939-40* (pp. 148-9), and Sir Winston Churchill in his *Second World War* (II 74-6), go further than this and imply that at 6 p.m. on the 25th Gort ordered the transfer of both divisions. " At six o'clock," the former states, " Lord Gort had already taken what was perhaps the most fateful action during the whole campaign. Without waiting to ask authority from the French commander, he ordered the 5th and 50th Divisions to abandon preparations for the attack southwards on the 26th and to move at once to the threatening gap between the British and Belgian armies. By doing so he saved the Expeditionary Force." " At 6 p.m.," writes Churchill, " he ordered the 5th and 50th Divisions to join the II British Corps to fill the impending Belgian gap." This seems to be an anticipation of what happened. The 5th Division was transferred to II Corps by an order issued at 8 p.m., but it was not till next morning, after Brooke had carried out a personal reconnaissance near Ypres, that he secured a brigade of the 50th Division, and not till the evening of the 26th that he obtained the rest of the division.

routes round and through Armentières. . . . All roads
were crammed with refugees and detachments of disorganised French forces retiring from the Valenciennes
area. . . . I remember during the next two days seriously
considering destroying my diary as I did not want it to
fall into German hands, and this seemed quite a possible
eventuality. . . .

' During the day I had had my Corps H.Q. removed from
Armentières to Lomme on the western outskirts of Lille. It
was fortunate that I had done so, as my diary for that day
ends with the following lines:

" Armentières has been very heavily bombed and we are
well out of it; half the town is demolished, including the
madhouse, and its inmates are now wandering about the
country."

' These lunatics let loose . . . were the last straw. With
catastrophe on all sides, bombarded by rumours of every
description, flooded by refugees and a demoralised French
army, bombed from a low altitude, and now on top of it all
lunatics in brown corduroy suits standing at the side of the
road grinning at one with an inane smile, a flow of saliva
running from the corner of their mouths, and dripping
noses! Had it not been that by then one's senses were numbed
with the magnitude of the catastrophe that surrounded one,
the situation would have been unbearable.

' Several years later, whilst dining at Chequers one week-
end, Churchill said to me the receptive capacity of a man's
brain to register disaster is like a 3-inch pipe under a culvert.
The 3-inch pipe will go on passing the water through under
pressure, but when a flood comes the water flows over the
culvert whilst the pipe goes on handling its three inches.
Similarly the human brain will register emotions up to its
" 3-inch limit " and subsequently additional emotions flow
past unregistered. This simile of his reminded me of my
feelings during those last momentous days in France before
Dunkirk. I had reached a stage when the receptive capacity
of my brain to register disasters and calamities had become
numbed by successive blows. It is a providence of nature that

it should be so, otherwise there would be more mad people in this world.

'The best cure under conditions of this kind is activity of mind and body to plan and work and strive throughout the twenty-four hours of the day; never to despair, never to allow oneself to think that there can be no solutions, never to pay attention to constant rumours that are mostly wrong, but to concentrate all one's powers and all one's ability with just one object in view—to save the situation.

'I was faced with an intensely interesting problem of saving our left flank, and I became entirely absorbed in all its ramifications. I had at last secured the 5th Division and had ordered it to move up on to the line of the Ypres-Comines Canal during the night. I had told Franklyn who commanded the division that he was to take over the 34th Infantry Brigade and the machine-gun battalion that he would find on that front. I now knew from the captured order that the attack on the Lille front on my 3rd and 4th Divisions was intended to be a holding attack, and in any case the defences we had built during the winter with trenches covered by wire entanglements gave this front greater resisting power. I argued out, therefore, on the night of the 25th that, should I become too hard pressed on my new left front, I could probably reinforce from the right.

'*May 26th.* I started early on what was destined to be one of the most arduous days of my life, a day during which every minute had to be lived intensely and every ounce of one's vitality thrown into the day's work. Accompanied by Ronnie Stanyforth we set out for 5th Divisional H.Q. in Ploegsteert Wood. We had to pass through Armentières which was being heavily bombed and sprinkled with incendiaries. On arrival at Franklyn's H.Q. we were greeted by more bombers and spent five minutes at the bottom of a ditch waiting for the departure of the bombers which were flying over at a low altitude. I was informed at Headquarters that the 5th Division were at that time arriving on their front. The right brigade was already up and busy taking up a position whilst the left brigade was in the process of moving in. I then proceeded to the line of the canal to see how the deployment was getting on. I found the left brigade in process of debussing and urged them to exercise all speed to get in on their front. As I wanted to know what the Belgian situation was on my left, I decided to motor on in the hope of finding some Belgian H.Q., or at least some Belgian troops.

‘On arrival in the vicinity of Zillebeke I came across some French soldiers and, on inquiring from them what formation they belonged to, was informed that they were part of the 1st French Motorised Division. I then asked

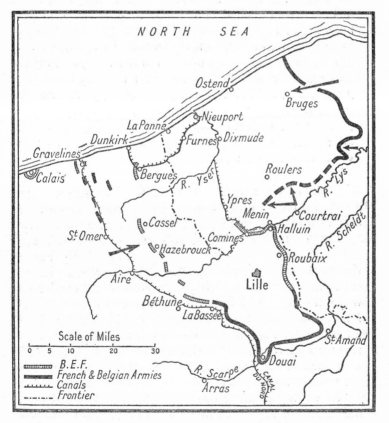

THE POSITION ON MAY 26th
The arrows indicate the main German thrusts

them where the division was and was told by them that it was in Valenciennes. I then asked them what part of the division they represented and they informed me that they were the Divisional Postal Service. This conveys some idea of the confusion that prevailed. I informed them that if they remained where they were they would soon be taken prisoners, and suggested they should waste no time in withdrawing.

' Of Belgian soldiers I could find none. The only sign of defensive preparations was a mass of railway trucks parked close together along the Ypres-Zonnebeke railway line, which I believe were intended as an anti-tank obstacle. Of troops of any kind I could find none, nothing but an eerie void.

' As a matter of fact, Herbert Lumsden[1] with the G.H.Q. armoured cars had been moved up to this front, and my car was actually observed by one of his armoured cars and reported back to him. It is a pity that G.H.Q. never notified me that he was on my left or instructed him to report to me the result of his observations. Considering that in the final stages G.H.Q. were out of touch with the situation, I think that the best plan would have been to have placed the Armoured Car Regiment directly under my orders. It was this lack of mobile troops that was inducing me to carry out a personal reconnaissance which, as we shall see, nearly had a bad ending.

' Finding no troops on my left, I determined to examine the defensive value of the Ypres-Comines Canal. I knew the canal was still empty and in an incomplete condition but considered that, taken in combination with the railway line that ran parallel with it, it should have some defensive value. I decided, therefore, to motor along it and to examine it as I went along. The road ran on the east side of the combined railway and canal line, and I had arrived at a point just north of Houthem when the road crossed by a bridge over the railway and canal.

' As we turned on to this road I noticed a couple of our men near the bridge running along in a crouching attitude. I only wondered vaguely why they were crouching as we

[1] Col., afterwards Lt.-Gen., Lumsden, commanding the 12th Lancers.

drove along over the bridge and turned south into Houthem.
We had barely cleared the bridge when there was a heavy
explosion immediately behind us which I attributed to a
bomb. I told the driver to accelerate through the village,
where we encountered four more explosions which I again
attributed to bombs. I told the driver to turn west by a road
out of the village and, when clear of the houses, to stop. I
then got out to see where the planes were that were chasing
us, only to be confronted by an empty sky. Ronnie and I
were bewildered as to where the bombs had come from and
were gazing into the sky when suddenly we heard that well-
known whistle of an approaching shell, followed by four
crumps between us and the village.

' The situation was now clear. The Germans had evidently
started their attack on Houthem and we had had a very
narrow escape from being captured or shot up. I always
attribute the first explosion we heard behind us to our
fellows blowing up the bridge we had just come over, having
already been informed of the approaching Germans. If this
is the case, which I have never been able to confirm, we had
narrowly escaped arriving just too late to cross the bridge.

' The important fact . . . . was that the Germans had
already gained contact with the centre of the 5th Division
front at Houthem, whilst the left of the 5th Division was only
just finishing its debussing, and on its left a complete void with
no Belgian forces. The situation was extremely critical. I,
therefore, dashed back to G.H.Q. to endeavour to obtain
more troops, and was allotted one brigade of the 50th
Division, which I directed to move up to cover Ypres and
join up with left of the 5th Division.'

At this time Brooke was co-ordinating the movements both
of his own Corps and of the 1st Corps on his right and in
retreat behind him, without orders from above and on his own
sole responsibility. The Army's signals communications had
almost completely broken down, and every road in the
corridor along which it was retreating was under machine-
gun attack from the air and from dive-bombers. Most of
Brooke's orders were given by word of mouth and only con-

firmed afterwards in writing, or sent by relays of Motor Contact officers of whom he usually had two or three with him. His only regular attendant was his Military Assistant, Colonel Stanyforth. " He never took a Staff Officer in his car with him," wrote the latter, " but usually only myself. He would occasionally ask me to remember things, but not very often. He had got the whole thing fixed in his mind all the time, and only wanted someone to find the way and deliver him at his destination in the shortest possible time and to keep an eye open for *boche* bombers. He was curious about this, as he would sit in front of a glass window but he would get out of his car. He lay under a cottage fence near Ypres, having abandoned the car with thirty-six *boche* bombers passing over our heads at five hundred feet at the most. . . . Otherwise, he was really rather silly in his lack of attention to bombs. He sat in a window on the second floor of a house in Armentières while the whole of the adjacent and parallel street was destroyed, though not all the time as I *made* him sit on the floor. He and Monty used to confer in glass houses with the bombs flying about like wasps! "[1]

.   .   .   .

It was during this day—the 26th—that the full extent of the Army's peril was at last realised in England. The churches were packed with worshippers and a special Service of Intercession was held in Westminster Abbey.[2] A telegram had been sent from the War Office approving Gort's decision to retreat on Dunkirk and authorising him " to operate towards the coast forthwith in conjunction with the French and Belgian armies." The Rifles defending the citadel at Calais in front of the Gravelines waterway were ordered to fight to the last man, and instructions were given to the Admiral commanding at Dover to put into immediate effect the improvised plans for an evacuation, beginning with base and non-combatant elements that night. In view of the immense strength of the Luftwaffe and the fact that once Calais fell—and its fall was now a matter

---

[1] *Notes by Lt.-Colonel R. Stanyforth.* " He did ask me to get his tin hat out of the car when we were caught on the beaches at La Panne in a big raid, but that was the only exception."

[2] " In my stall in the Choir I could feel the pent-up, passionate emotion, and also the fear of the congregation, not of death or wounds or material loss, but of defeat and the final ruin of Britain." W. Churchill, *Second World War* II 87.

of hours[1]—the short sea-route between Dunkirk and Dover would be within range of German guns, the Admiralty was anything but optimistic about " Operation Dynamo," as it was christened. But it was hoped that it might be possible, if a bridgehead round Dunkirk could be held so long, to evacuate 45,000 men in the course of the next two nights. After that, it was felt, the shore would be unapproachable even if the port had not fallen.

Whether the British Regular divisions on the Franco-Belgian frontier could reach it was, however, far more doubtful. " I must not conceal from you," Lord Gort had reported to the Secretary of State for War that morning, " that a great part of the B.E.F. and its equipment will inevitably be lost." During the day the Panzer Corps facing the Gravelines-La Bassée waterline was given permission to resume its eastward drive, and throughout the 26th, 27th and 28th the Germans were attacking on both sides of the narrowing sack out of which the British and First French Armies were struggling to escape. While the divisions at the southern or bottom end of it withdrew northwards, leap-frogging by night behind the comrades guarding its two sides, four British divisions, facing westwards, fought off von Rundstedt's Army Group, while another four under Brooke, facing eastwards, fought off von Bock's. Owing to the watery and broken nature of the terrain and the reluctance of the German commanders to sacrifice their armour against opposition so fierce and stubborn,[2] the pressure from the west was less sustained than that from the east, though it was severe enough to produce at least three actions—those of the Gloucesters and the Oxfordshire and Buckinghamshire Light Infantry at Ledringham, Hazebrouck and Cassel— worthy of a place among the great epics of British military valour in adversity.

Farther to the south, in its heroic stand, the 2nd Division was reduced to the strength of a single brigade. The main weight of the attack, however, came across the open plain from

---

[1] It fell that night after the last ammunition of its defenders had been expended.

[2] By this time von Rundstedt had lost nearly fifty per cent of his armoured strength. *The War in France and Flanders* (H.M.S.O.) 227. " The enemy," ran the war-diary of the XXXXI Panzer Corps, " are fighting tenaciously and, to the last man, remain at their posts." *Idem*, 191.

the east, and it was here, where Brooke's quickness of brain and decision were pitted against the German High Command, that the future of the British Army was decided.

His diary for the 26th continued:

> " Then attended G.H.Q. conference where we were informed of instructions received from home for the evacuation of the B.E.F. We discussed plans for this operation, and I spent the rest of the day in conference finishing off plans for this withdrawal. It is going to be a very hazardous enterprise and we shall be lucky if we save 25 per cent of the B.E.F. We are bound to suffer heavily from bombing. I have already been put into the ditch three times to-day to avoid bombing attacks. The Germans have carried out incessant air attacks on Armentières and surrounding towns."

' The situation was now becoming even more complicated and I was faced with the twofold problem of establishing and holding a defensive flank facing eastwards . . . whilst at the same time undertaking the gradual evacuation of the Corps to the Dunkirk area. The initial stages were to be the most difficult ones, as my right was thrown well forward into the Halluin-Roubaix salient. The retirement would depend entirely on the 5th Division holding the impending attacks, which by the evening were already making some headway into Comines. Matters were further complicated by the paucity of roads, since to the west we were hemmed in by the armoured forces. I should consequently have to make use of roads perilously near the fluctuating battle on the 5th Division front.

' It was either on this visit to G.H.Q. or the following day that Ambrose Pratt,[1] commanding the Heavy Artillery of I Corps, came to me and asked me whether I should like the support of a Corps Artillery. I thought at first that he was joking, and asked him whether the I Corps had no use for his services. He informed me that apparently not, since he

---

[1] Col. (later Maj.-Gen.) F. W. H. Pratt. Lord Alanbrooke seems to be wrong in his date here. According to his diary entry for the 25th, he " picked up I Corps H.A. behind Ploegsteert Wood that evening," and it was placed under his orders that night.

was receiving no orders from them, ... that his Corps Artillery were just west of Ploegsteert Wood and had plenty of ammunition. This was almost too good to be true and a truly heaven-sent reinforcement at a critical moment. I told him to report to Franklyn and to remain at 5th Divisional H.Q., to deploy his artillery to cover Ypres-Comines Canal and to give all possible support to the 5th Division. He accomplished this task admirably, and the success of the defence owes him a great debt of gratitude for the part played by his artillery.

' From G.H.Q. I proceeded to 4th Division where I instructed Johnson to hold one brigade ready to reinforce 5th Division at short notice should this become necessary. I passed on from there to visit Monty and to keep him in the picture with the most recent developments. I also discussed with him the retirement which he would shortly have to carry out. During the course of the evening the remainder of 50th Division was allotted to me and directed to Ypres to extend defence northwards.

' Late that evening Corps H.Q. was suddenly disturbed by two rounds from a 25-pr. fired in quick succession. As these shots came from the Corps H.Q. defence I felt certain that we were receiving a visit from German tanks which were by then in Arras and the vicinity. However, on making inquiries I was informed that we had fired on a French tank, one of their heavier " Char B "; the shells had burst on the exterior, nobody had been hurt and after an exchange of salutations the French tank had gone on its way.

' *May 27th*, after a few hours disturbed sleep I drove up to Bondues to hold a Corps conference with 3rd and 4th Divisions to discuss the plans for their withdrawal, to allot to them their roads and the timings of their moves. I next went to 1st Division H.Q. to see Alexander as the 1st Division had in error been moving on 3rd Division road. Alex was in my old Wambrechies billet and was as usual completely composed and unperturbed.

' From there across the Lys to Ploegsteert Wood to see 5th Division. I found Franklyn out visiting brigades, but had a long talk with Grover, his G.S.O.1. Division was now established along line of canal and in contact with Germans all along its front. Touch had not yet been established with 50th Division on its left. Its right was being heavily shelled in Comines where situation was somewhat obscure.

' My next visit was to 50th Division H.Q. on outskirts of Ypres, where I found Martel who informed me that Haydon[1] with the 150th Infantry Brigade was in position, but had not yet been able to establish touch on his right with the 5th Division. Martel had come up quickly with his division, the other brigade was not far off, and it was a tremendous relief to see this dangerous gap filling. I placed Martel in command of the remnants of the French *Division Lourde Motorisée*, which we had found north of Ypres, of the machine-gun battalion of 4th Division which I had moved to this front, and of course, his own two infantry brigades. We were only just in time. The western approaches to Ypres were already being shelled, and as we drove away we passed the body of an unfortunate small boy of about eight or ten who had just been killed by a shell.

' Motored back to G.H.Q., passing through 5th Division H.Q. again to inform them of situation on 50th Division front, and to impress importance of 5th Division gaining touch with the 50th. Was informed that the Germans had penetrated into Comines and that the situation was critical on southern portion of 5th Division front. As G.H.Q. had no further reinforcements, I proceeded to 4th Division to instruct Johnson to move brigade I had told him to have in readiness as soon as possible to reinforce 5th Division. He informed me that " Bubbles " Barker's brigade would be moved round at once and placed under orders of 5th Division.

' As I had heard that the 1st Division had already started withdrawing three battalions from the line and that these battalions were somewhere west of Ploegsteert Wood, I decided to endeavour to secure their assistance. After some hunting I found I Corps H.Q. in one of the old Lille forts, and I obtained Michael Barker's agreement. I therefore

---

[1] Lt.-Gen. Sir Giffard Martel and Brig. C. W. Haydon.

proceeded again to Wambrechies to see Alexander to request him to issue orders to these battalions to come under orders of 5th Division and to move forward at once. Alexander, as I expected, co-operated at once, and these three battalions[1] played a great part in restoring the situation on the right of the 5th Division front.

' From 1st Division I motored back again to G.H.Q. and this time secured seven infantry tanks which were despatched at once to 5th Division front.

' I had now set all that was possible in motion to reinforce 5th Division, so returned to my headquarters at Lomme to keep Ritchie, my B.G.S., informed of the various moves I had carried out, and to discuss orders for withdrawal with him.

' Having seen to these details, I again returned to 1st Division H.Q. to discuss with Alexander his future moves and to find out at what points I could gain contact with him during our retirement.'

General Franklyn has recorded his recollections of Brooke's decisive intervention to save his division that day. It was the only time that he ever saw him show any sign of the intense strain he was undergoing. The 5th Division was being attacked by three German divisions and, had any point of its long tenuous line given way, the whole Expeditionary Force would have been swept away in irretrievable disaster. " When Brooke visited me at 10 a.m. that morning," Franklyn recalled, " he studied the situation in silence—it was very bad —and then all he said was, ' What are you going to do about it? ' I replied, ' I'm not worried about my left, but I am uneasy about the 143rd Brigade on my right—they have given and are being pushed back.' "

" Without a word Brooke left. He apparently went straight to H.Q. I Division (I Corps) who were to withdraw to the Lys the night, 27th/28th May, ordered Alexander to send three battalions at once to suport 5th Division, and sent them to support 143rd Brigade at Comines and the situation was restored. Brooke's action in ordering up these reinforcements

[1] 3rd Grenadier Guards, 2nd North Staffs, 2nd Sherwood Foresters.

from I Corps on his own responsibility saved the situation which was ultimately restored by midnight."[1]

' From there,' Brooke continued,

' I proceeded to Bondues to see Monty at 3rd Division H.Q., as I wanted to find out how he was getting on with the preparation for the very difficult move that lay ahead of him. He had to evacuate his present position and lead his division under cover of darkness across the Lys just east of Armentières, past Ploegsteert Wood, and up by second-class roads northward within 4,000 yards of the fluctuating front of the 5th Division, to north of Ypres, where he was to prolong our eastern defensive flank north of the 50th Division. It was a task that might well have shaken the stoutest of hearts, but for Monty it might just have been a glorious picnic. He told me exactly how he was going to do it, and was as usual exuberant in confidence. There is no doubt that one of Monty's strong points is his boundless confidence in himself. He was priceless on this occasion, and I thanked Heaven to have a commander of his calibre to undertake this hazardous march.

' I now returned to my H.Q. at Lomme to collect a few papers, leaving Ronnie Stanyforth with the car at the gate of the house serving as our H.Q. As I came back to the car he pointed to a body lying in the gutter on the opposite side of the road and said: " They have just shot that chap." When I said: " Who shot him? " he replied: " Oh! Some

---

[1] That evening, with the situation still hanging in the balance, Brooke on his second visit to Franklyn heard that the left brigade of the 5th Division was in difficulties. He again asked, " What are you going to do about it? " Franklyn, who was beginning to feel the strain replied, " This sort of thing has been happening all day, please leave it to me." Brooke left without further comment. Franklyn mentioned this incident, not by way of criticism, but to illustrate how difficult it is not to show anxiety as to how a subordinate will handle a critical situation. Thereafter there was no further questioning as to how the battle should be fought but constant encouragement, and, when it had been won, the warmest appreciation.

In summing up Brooke's quality as a commander Franklyn said, " He gave his orders clearly and decisively and one was left in no doubt as to his intentions. He delivered to divisional fronts supports when and where most needed and without being asked for them. Brooke showed his great tactical ability under the most difficult circumstances and later proved himself to be the best strategist among the allies. He would have made a great Commander-in-Chief in the field." *Communicated by Gen. Sir Harold Franklyn.*

of these retiring French soldiers; they said he was a spy, but I think the real reason was that he refused to give them cognac! " This gives some idea of the lack of discipline in the French retirement, which at times looked more like a rout. This lack of discipline and demoralisation was by no means universal, and some of the formations were living up to the very highest traditions of the French Army. . . . However, . . . these instances of rapidly deteriorating morale were a factor of major importance when taken in combination with the demoralised refugees. The combined effect of these two undermining factors might well have played havoc with the morale of the men of the B.E.F. had it not been for that indescribable quality of detachment and staunchness of the British soldier. He can sympathise with misery, he can rub shoulders with demoralised allies and suffer on their account; he can be subjected to untold fatigues and hardships in the face of disaster, and yet none of these factors affect his balance. To my mind, it is this factor more than any other that has saved us from many disasters and has contributed most to the successes of the British Army. Never have I had greater admiration, respect and affection for the British soldiers than during those anxious days of our retirement from Louvain to Dunkirk.

' I decided to pay one more visit to G.H.Q. before closing my H.Q. at Lomme, to inform them of my moves and to ascertain their intentions. I consequently motored off once more to the small château east of Armentières, but on arrival there found they had left without leaving any indication as to where they were off to. This was the last that I saw of any member of G.H.Q. till my arrival at La Panne, although I sent my Brigadier General Staff to attend a conference on the following day.

' I now turned back towards Lomme along the main Armentières-Lille road. It was practically blocked with four lines of French Army traffic moving against me towards Armentières, two rows of horse-drawn vehicles and two rows of motorised ones. The drivers were unshaven, and with the growth of several days on their faces, their clothes were covered with mud. I saw no officers in charge or any attempt on the part of N.C.O.s to control this mob. With great difficulty, by travelling mostly on the footpath, I managed to work my way back to Lomme with the sickly smiles of dribbling lunatics in corduroy occasionally looming up in the failing light at the car window.

'The sight of that uncontrolled mass of French Army vehicles sent a cold chill through my heart as I thought of Monty and his 3rd Division carrying out their precarious night move. This mob of vehicles might well bring the 3rd Division to a standstill should they overflow on to the roads I had allotted to it.

'I reached Lomme and, after attending to final details with Neil Ritchie, I closed down my H.Q. and moved off to a command-post which I had had established at the Ferme de l'Alouette, just north-west of Ploegsteert Wood, and on the road on which the 3rd Division was to move.

'I had been unable to visit 5th Division since the morning, so proceeded to see Franklyn and discussed the day's fighting. I found him very tired but running an excellent show. He had had a very trying day with continual German attacks, resulting in the loss of ground but had retained his front intact. The only point that was causing me serious alarm was the junction between the 5th and the 50th Divisions. Franklyn informed me that satisfactory contact had not been established. The 10th Brigade under " Bubbles " Barker had up to the present failed to restore the situation. I cannot remember at present whether it was at this juncture, or possibly a little earlier, that I ordered the 4th Division to despatch the 11th Infantry Brigade under Kenneth Anderson to reinforce 5th Division and instructed it to be placed on Wytschaete Ridge to cover the rear of the junction between the two divisions.

'Having discussed questions of future withdrawal with Franklyn, I then returned to the Ferme de l'Alouette. I had ordered Johnson to move his H.Q. to the Ferme du Rossignol, only a few miles east of me, so that he would be handy to fix details on the next day for his further moves.

'I wrote that night:

" It has been an anxious day. Bad congestion on roads
due to French forces spreading over on to roads reserved
for us. Belgians have practically given up fighting so that
security of eastern flank of retirement rests with II Corps."

' I was evidently too tired and too depressed to give full
vent to my feelings.'

. . . .

That night was the climax of the retreat. Everything depended on whether Montgomery's 3rd Division could be
extricated from its perilously exposed position in front of
Roubaix—nearly fifty miles from Dunkirk and in the heart of
the German Sixth Army[1]—and transferred by daybreak to its
new position, twenty-five miles to the north beyond Ypres, to
fill the gap on the left of the 5th and 50th Divisions and prevent
the enemy from sweeping across the Yser to cut the road to
Dunkirk. It was the evening of the Belgian surrender.[2] During
that midnight vigil at his command post at the Ferme
de l'Alouette, Brooke's Military Assistant saw his chief appear
worried for almost the only time in the retreat. The latter
himself wrote of it:

' There was little possibility of sleep that night, as the
3rd Division were moving past and I repeatedly went out to
see how they were progressing. They were travelling, as we
had so frequently practised for our night moves, with lights
out and each driver watching the rear of the vehicle in front
of him, which had the differential painted white and lit up
by a tail-lamp under the vehicle. The 3rd Division through
constant practice had become most proficient at this method
of movement. However, with the congestion on the roads,
road-blocks outside villages, and many other blocks caused
by refugees and their carts, the division was frequently
brought to a standstill. The whole movement seemed un-
bearably slow; the hours of darkness were slipping by;
should daylight arrive with the road crammed with vehicles

[1] During the day Rommel had written to his wife, " We're busy encircling
the British and French in Lille at the moment." *Rommel Papers*, 39.
[2] King Leopold asked for an armistice late that afternoon and capitulated
at midnight.

the casualties from bombing might well have been disastrous.

'Our own guns were firing from the vicinity of Mount Kemmel, whilst German artillery was answering back, and the division was literally trundling slowly along in the darkness down a pergola of artillery fire, and within some 4000 yards of a battle-front which had been fluctuating all day somewhat to our disadvantage. It was an eerie sight, which I shall never forget. Before dawn came, the last vehicles had disappeared northwards into the darkness, and I lay down for a few hours disturbed sleep, but kept wondering how the 3rd Division was progressing.

'*Dawn May 28th.* My first care when daylight came was the situation on the 5th Division front. I proceeded to see Franklyn and discovered that the situation on his left, at junction with 50th Division, was still unsatisfactory. Germans were apparently infiltrating between the two divisions. I gave verbal instructions for the further withdrawal that night and then proceeded to see Johnson at 4th Division H.Q. to instruct him to co-ordinate his retirement with that of the 5th Division. The 4th Division was to send one brigade to a covering position along the railway line from Ypres to Poperinghe, whilst the remainder of the 4th Division was to head for the River Yser. The 5th Division was at that time to go north and man the canal in continuation from the flank of 3rd Division.

'From the 4th Division I proceeded to the outskirts of Ypres to see Martel and to find out from him what the situation was on his right and whether his 50th Division had yet gained touch with the 5th. Here I saw Haydon, who commanded the 150th Brigade, who informed me that he had failed to gain contact with the 5th Division and had consequently thrown back his right flank. I instructed Martel to send the 4th Northumberland Fusiliers at once to clear up the situation and to gain contact with 5th Division.

'The situation on the Ypres front seemed satisfactory, and all attacks on this front had been held. I therefore proceeded north to find out how Monty had completed his dangerous night flank march. I wrote the following that evening:

" Found he had, as usual, accomplished almost the impossible and had marched from Roubaix to north of Ypres. A flank march past the front of attack, and was firmly established on the line with the French *Division Lourde Motorisée*, to his north."

' In spite of many checks throughout the night, the division has kept moving steadily north, and, if it had not been for the very high standard of night marching which the division had reached from constant exercises under Monty, I am convinced that it would never have completed this dangerous move.

' It was with a feeling of intense relief that I found Monty in position. It meant that the first, and the most difficult stage of the move of the II Corps had been accomplished. The 5th Division, plus all the reinforcements that I had given it, had held during the dangerous period of the withdrawal of the 3rd and 4th Divisions from their advance positions. I now had a continuous defensive flank with 5th Division on right, 50th Division in centre and 3rd Division on left, stretching from Comines to well north of Ypres, and the French *Division Lourde Motorisée* extending farther north.

' After congratulating Monty on the success of the move, I headed back to my command-post at the Ferme de l'Alouette to see Ritchie who had left early for a conference at G.H.Q. where apparently very little was settled. I then closed my command-post and sent Neil Ritchie back to Vinckem, south of Furnes, to open up a new one.

' During the days of our move from Louvain to Dunkirk I commanded the Corps principally by word of mouth, by continually visiting the various Divisional H.Q.s and giving the orders direct for moves. I periodically returned to my command-post where I kept Neil Ritchie informed as to what I had done, and got him to send out confirmatory orders whenever possible. Even then the situation changed so rapidly that I had frequently to return again to a Divisional H.Q. to alter some point in the confirmatory order or of my own oral instructions. Neil Ritchie was quite invaluable during this period, was always thinking ahead, and I could not have wished for a better staff officer. Always calm, never rattled and with a sense of humour to relieve some of the more gloomy situations.

'My next move was covered in my diary:

> "Down again to 5th Division H.Q. to find out situation after day's hard fighting. Division had held on by its eyelids. 17th and 13th Infantry Brigades greatly reduced by casualties, 10th and 11th Infantry Brigades supporting them. I Corps Artillery, which had been left behind to help, had fired 5,000 rounds of medium artillery ammunition in thirty-six hours. Line had held, thank God, otherwise 5th and 4th Divisions were lost and II Corps would have been rolled up."[1]

'Franklyn had put up a very fine show and the 5th Division had fought admirably. It had been a very heavy task for Franklyn for, in addition to his own division, I placed under his orders two brigades of 4th Division, three battalions from 1st Division, one Machine-gun battalion from 3rd Division, seven Infantry tanks and the I Corps Heavy Artillery.

'Now came the task of withdrawing the 4th and 5th Divisions. They were so closely interwoven by now that I ordered Franklyn and Johnson to co-ordinate their withdrawal together. The 5th Division was to withdraw to the Dunkirk perimeter, whilst the 4th Division was to send Hawkesworth with his 12th Infantry Brigade in advance to Dixmude and the rest of the division to follow to that vicinity.

'I then returned to 50th Division and instructed Martel to throw back his right flank from the Canal to rest at Poperinghe where it should come into contact with 1st Division. He was to retain this covering position throughout the next day to allow 5th and 4th Divisions to retire through his division and to cover their retirement.

'Having completed my dispositions for the next stage of our retirement, I motored off to La Panne to see Adam who was organising the embarkation. He informed me that he

---

[1] It was on this day that the Prime Minister, announcing the Belgian surrender in Parliament, declared, "The House should prepare itself for hard and heavy tidings."

had just had a message that a column of Germans had arrived at Nieuport. He had rapidly formed an improvised force for its defence.

'This was a disconcerting bit of news. I thought that I had checked the German advance westward in the battle that had been raging in the Ypres-Comines area, but here was a new force which had evidently been advancing along the coast. I sent off instructions at once to divert Hawkesworth and his 12th Infantry Brigade from Dixmude to Nieuport, and remainder of 4th Division to follow, so as to cover perimeter defence from Furnes to Nieuport.

'On returning to my new command-post at Vinckem, I received a despatch-rider sent off by Monty with the same news about the Germans being in Nieuport. Monty had picked up this information from Herbert Lumsden's Armoured Cars; he knew enough about my plans to realise at once the importance of this new and unexpected development. He had consequently sent off a despatch-rider at once, and in order to make doubly certain that the news should reach me he also despatched his G.S.O.1., " Marino " Brown, in a car. A very wise precaution which unfortunately ended in a tragedy. The roads were very badly congested with disorganised elements of the French Army, which had lost all discipline and were completely out of control. We have only the account of Brown's chauffeur as to what happened. Apparently the road was so badly jammed with French transport vehicles that it was impossible to pass. Knowing the urgency of the message he was carrying, apparently Brown got out of his car, leaving it on the side of the road with his chauffeur, and proceeded on foot in order to regulate the traffic and to induce some discipline into the French transport. Shortly after he had been left, the chauffeur heard a revolver shot somewhere up the road, and a little later on he was informed by one of our men that there was a dead Colonel lying on the side of the road. He went to see and found that Brown had been shot dead. Further details remain shrouded in mystery and will never be cleared. Probably Brown had difficulty in clearing the road, he was known to have a hottish temper, and he may

well have used the rough of his tongue on some of this
rabble. This may have resulted in one of these demoralised
Frenchmen drawing a revolver and shooting him. It was a
real tragedy, as he had a brilliant future. . . .

' It was after 11 p.m. when I returned to my command-
post and, after having some food, waited till 1 a.m. for the
arrival of the general commanding the 2nd *Division
Lourde Motorisée*, and who had been placed under my
orders. . . . Apparently his division had lost all its tanks and
now consisted only of a column of buses and workshops, with
a certain number of men with rifles. The whole outfit was
more of an encumbrance than anything else, its fighting value
was practically nil, whilst its power of blocking roads with
its huge vehicles was unlimited.

' *May 29th*. My diary for this day begins:

" Received Order from Gort that I was to proceed
home and hand over my Corps so as to be available for the
task of reforming new armies. Went to see Gort to find out
whether this was an order, as I wanted to remain with
Corps. Told it was an order which I must obey. Got him
to agree that I could stop till I had finished retiring Corps
into perimeter defence covering embarkation."

' The order, I believe, came from the War Office and may
well have been a right one under the circumstances, but it
did not make it any the easier to obey. After having struggled
with the Corps through all its vicissitudes, and having
guided it to the sea, I felt like a deserter not remaining with
it till the last.

' My first task on this day was to head south again to see
Martel and Monty and to find out the situation on their
divisional fronts. I found the 50th Division established on
its new front with its right flank resting on Poperinghe.
Apparently the retirement had been successfully carried out
and resulted in the Germans attacking a village, after a
heavy bombardment, which the division had previously
evacuated.

' I motored on into Poperinghe to ensure that contact had
been established with 1st Division. Poperinghe was in a

most unpleasant condition. It had been badly bombed and almost every street we tried to go down seemed to be blocked by a house that had been blown into it. There was the unpleasant feeling that the bombers might well return any moment and that in that case there was every chance of being trapped like a mouse between two demolished houses. Finally, we got out to the west side of the town but found no signs of troops of any kind. I therefore returned to Martel and told him to move the Northumberland Fusiliers to cover that flank, and to send out the 13th/18th Hussars . . . . on an observation role.

' Called in on Monty and found that the 3rd Division were in no difficulties. I discussed with him the further retirement that night on to the perimeter defence. I wrote in the diary:

" Congestion on roads indescribable, French Army become a rabble and complete loss of discipline. Troops dejected and surly, refusing to clear road and panicking every time a *boche* plane comes over."

' I still marvel that amongst those surroundings our men remained completely unaffected. I never saw a single case of loss of discipline or of panicking. . . . On arrival near the perimeter we were destroying guns and vehicles, ... and there was even that additional cause that might have undermined their morale.

' After leaving Montgomery I returned to Eisenberg to see the 5th Division and to find out whether they had succeeded in extricating themselves successfully. I found them on the Yser all well but with the 13th and 17th Infantry brigades greatly depleted by the heavy fighting they have been through.

' On returning to my château to pick up some papers I was met by Ciriez, our French Liaison Officer. He was in an infuriated condition and livid with rage. He informed me that a squadron of French cavalry had entered the château grounds, had commenced to shoot their horses and to throw their arms into the moat of the château. He had dashed out to ask them why they were doing this, and they informed him that the Germans were on the outskirts of the village, and they did not wish to be captured with their arms. He informed them that there were no Germans within twenty miles, that they were a disgrace to the French Army, and a few more very appropriate home truths. He told me that it had the right effect, they mounted again and rode off.

" Went back to La Panne to see how embarkation was proceeding, found arrangements quite inadequate and of a most Heath Robinson nature. Saw Gort and asked him to get Admiralty to produce a few Marines and more landing craft."

' This impression, as written down that evening, was, I think, inevitable. The Navy were working wonders to produce the craft they had, but, when measured in relation to the numbers that had to be evacuated and the limited time available for this process, it all seemed painfully inadequate.

' While Ronnie Stanyforth and I were watching the slow process of embarkation, a heavy bombing raid came over. We retired into the sand-dunes at the edge of the beach and lay there watching the effects of the bombing. It was a most awe-inspiring sight.

' The beaches, which were crowded with men, were being plastered with bombs. A black cloud of smoke soon shrouded the whole beach and was punctuated by vivid flashes as new bombs burst and threw up jets of sand and what appeared like human bodies, but luckily turned out to be greatcoats and clothing abandoned by men who had embarked. When the bombers had safely departed I went down on to the beach, expecting to find a regular shambles. To my surprise, I found only a few men who had been seriously wounded. The bulk of them were smothered with sand which they were busy extracting from their ears, eyes, noses, necks and sleeves. The men had all flattened themselves out on the beach, and I presume that the effect of the bombs had been greatly damped down by sinking into the loose sands before bursting. It was indeed fortunate, or the casualties would have been much more serious. We also watched another raid directed against the shipping lying off the beaches, and this time the results were far more serious. One destroyer was hit amidships by a dive-bomber; the bomb must have penetrated into the ammunition magazines, as there was a terrific explosion followed by a column of smoke which mushroomed over the ship. As the smoke cleared, the destroyer had entirely disappeared. Such a sight was not a cheering one for those on the beach awaiting embarkation.

' I worked my way eastwards along the perimeter to visit Johnson and to find out from him how the 4th Division were getting on in Nieuport and along the rest of the front. I gathered from him that there had been some heavy fighting in Nieuport, but that the situation was then well in hand. The arrangements for the final withdrawal into the perimeter that night had still to be settled, and I therefore proceeded to visit Monty and Martel to give them their orders for this final move. The 5th Division was also to withdraw that night and come into reserve within the perimeter.

' Whilst these moves were taking place the 2nd French *Division Lourde Motorisée* was to remain in its present position and cover the eastern flank of the move. Just as I had finished issuing all the orders and interviewing all concerned, the trouble started.

' I received a message from the general commanding 2nd *Division Lourde Motorisée*, informing me that he had received orders from General Blanchard that he was to proceed to La Panne to embark his division. He proceeded to state that he was conforming with this order and moving his division at once. I got Neil Ritchie to draft out an order to him telling him that I gave him a direct order that he was NOT to commence moving before midnight, explaining that if he moved sooner he would completely throw out all arrangements for the retirement of the II Corps. I then got hold of his liaison officer, who was to carry back this message and told him " that if his General disobeyed my order and I caught him, I should have him shot." He did disobey this order, but took good care that I did not catch him.

' I cannot do better than quote the last few lines of my diary for that day:

" An officer of the 3rd Division came in to say that

Germans had got in behind the 5th Division on the Yser. To complete troubles, the 32nd French Division cut in from the west right across the lines of retreat of 50th, 5th and 3rd Divisions. Utter confusion on all roads and complete jam. However, matters finally sorted themselves out, and during the night 3rd Division took over the centre portion of the sector covering Furnes, 50th Division took over the western sector, and 5th Division went into reserve. The retreat from the river Dyle, east of Brussels, to the perimeter round La Panne was completed."

' That last night was one of many anxieties, and to this day I do not know how the final chaos of that night sorted itself out. The confusion at one time was quite indescribable and it was not till well after daylight that the final moves were completed.

' It was only nineteen days since we had left our Lille area to march to Brussels. Those nineteen days had been filled with continuous moves and much fighting in the later days. The Corps had been surrounded by every possible de-moralising influence, panicking allies, terrified refugees, liberated lunatics, retirements in front of a victorious enemy, endless long marches, and little or no sleep. And yet in spite of these factors, the five divisions that I was fortunate enough to have under my command (the 1st, 3rd, 4th, 5th and 50th Divisions) behaved magnificently throughout the retreat. Had it not been for those priceless qualities of the British soldier to which I have previously referred, I am convinced that such a flank march in the face of the enemy could never have been accomplished.

' I should be the very last ever to belittle the wonderful performance of the Navy in extricating the B.E.F. from Dunkirk. But whereas the Navy has received all the credit that was due to it, the B.E.F.'s part in the retreat from Brussels to Dunkirk has been somewhat put in the shade. . . . I sincerely hope that at some future date historians will give the B.E.F., and the British soldiers before all others, the credit that is due to them for having brought off a masterly retreat under most adverse conditions.

' This was destined to be my last night in France . . . and it was spent at Adinkerke, but certainly not in peaceful repose.

' We now come to May 30th, my final day with the II Corps. My diary that evening was written on board the destroyer that took me home and begins with:

" Went round all four divisions to ensure that defence of sectors was complete, and to find out what strength of Corps remained.

3rd Division	—	13,000 strong.
4th Division	—	12,000 strong.

Very satisfactory considering what we had been through.

" 5th Division only two brigades, 17th and 13th both very weak, about 600 per brigade.

" 50th Division a little stronger and two brigades of about 1,200 each.

" There is no doubt that the 5th Division in its fight on the Ypres-Comines Canal saved the II Corps and the B.E.F.

" I can hardly believe that I have succeeded in pulling the four divisions out of the mess we were in, with allies giving way on all flanks. Now remains the task of embarking, which will be a difficult one."

' After ascertaining condition of the Corps I proceeded to see how embarkation was getting on and " found the whole thing at a standstill through lack of boats." Sykes, who was handling the beaches and embarkation, was doing his best, but was having a very difficult task.

' I now had to make the necessary dispositions for the command of II Corps after my departure. I had no hesitation in selecting Monty to succeed me. . . . I then selected Kenneth Anderson from 11th Infantry Brigade to succeed Monty in command of 3rd Division, and Horrocks, at that time commanding machine-gun battalion, to succeed Anderson.

' Dear old Barney Charlesworth[1] surpassed himself for our

---

[1] Brooke's A.D.C., Captain A. K. Charlesworth, who had joined him in February. ' I had never met him before, and he was recommended to me by Ronnie Stanyforth. If he had been sent to me direct from Heaven he could not have been better chosen. He became one of my most intimate friends and

final lunch, and with great joy he informed us that we had
" petit poussin " and asparagus for our last lunch. The
poussin had been slaughtered to save them from *boche* hands,
and the asparagus was growing in the garden of our abandoned
billet. Unfortunately this lovely meal was somewhat spoilt
by the most awful stench that periodically blew in through
the window from the inflated bodies of three cows that had
been killed by a bomb a few days previously.

' After lunch came the difficult moment to decide what to
abandon. I had a brand-new pair of Huntsman breeches and
an equally new pair of Maxwell's Norwegian boots. However, I thought this would be an awkward attire to swim in,
and it seemed more than probable that we might have to take
to the water before we had done with the coming night's
trip. I therefore very reluctantly stripped these off and
replaced them by a pair of slacks and easy shoes, and then
felt I was ready for any swimming contest.

' My despatch-rider, who had been accompanying my car
ever since we started moving, ready to carry messages at
any moment, was less fainthearted. As soon as I was gone,
he changed into my breeches and boots and risked drowning
sooner than miss such a chance. I am glad to say that his
valour was rewarded and he was reported as having landed
safely with them on. I hope he survived the war to enjoy
them; he had certainly thoroughly deserved them.

' During the retreat from Brussels to Dunkirk perimeter
I had seen little of Mansergh, my Chief Administrative
Officer. He had gone ahead and had been working marvels
in handling the administrative services and evacuating all
that was not required at as early a date as circumstances
admitted. He had killed himself with work and could
hardly keep awake whilst talking to me. Suffering from
internal ulcers, he had shown the most wonderful
tenacity in carrying on with his work when many another
would have reported sick. To my great distress he was killed

remained with me till he was killed in an aeroplane crash on our way to Yalta
Conference. I owe him an untold debt for all his true help and assistance during
those years. A trusty confidant as safe as a clam, to whom I could confide my
innermost views on most matters without any fears of leakage.' *Notes on My
Life*, III 119.

by a bomb after having embarked and whilst waiting to start the journey home. A great loss to the Army and quite especially so to all his friends.

' *Afternoon May 30th.* The time came for a final tour of the four divisions and to say good-bye to their commanders. It was a very trying trip, I hated leaving them at this juncture after we had shared so many trials and perils together. I also could not help wondering how many I should see again. As matters turned out, they all survived to render further great services to their country.

' Before embarking I attended a final G.H.Q. conference[1] with Gort, and to hear latest news from the War Office. I found Gort undecided as to how to continue evacuation. To my mind there was only one solution, namely, gradually to shorten the perimeter from the east westward. Namely, to withdraw II Corps westward within I Corps perimeter, to evacuate II Corps first, and then to repeat the process within the I Corps itself by divisions.

' I did not, however, like to press my point too strongly lest it be considered that I was trying to have II Corps evacuated at the expense of the I Corps. The governing factor was that the port of Dunkirk was at the western end and must be held till the end. This geographical fact dictated the procedure to be followed, and pointed to the eastern end as the first to close inwards. I think that Gort was convinced by my arguments, and that the procedure followed was very similar to what I had recommended.

' Having said good-bye to Gort and promised him to give full particulars at home concerning the remaining evacuation of the B.E.F., I walked down the beach towards the sea. On the way I met Herbert Lumsden, who with his excellent 12th Lancers was controlling the beach and organising embarkation parties.

' The final departure is perhaps best taken from the words I wrote on the destroyer that evening:

" Went down to beach at 7.15 p.m. and was carried out to open boat, and with Ronnie Stanyforth and Barney

[1] 1800 hours, 30th May, 1940

Charlesworth we paddled out to the destroyer and climbed aboard. There I found Adam, to my great joy. We have been waiting till 10 p.m. before starting, rather nerve-racking as Germans are continually flying round and being shot at. After seeing yesterday the ease with which a dive-bomber can sink a destroyer, it is an unpleasant feeling.

" Later.—We never started till 12.15 a.m. At 3 a.m. we were brought up short with a crash. I felt certain that we had hit a mine or been torpedoed. But she remained on an even keel, and after some shuffling about proceeded slowly on. I heard later from the Commander that he had three routes to select from: one was under gunfire from the coast, one had had a submarine and mines reported on it, and the other was very shallow at low water. He chose the latter and hit the bottom, damaging a propeller slightly. Finally arrived Dover at 7.15 a.m. Wonderful feeling of peace after the last three weeks."

' Had I not been completely exhausted I could have written a great deal more about that last journey home. Those five long hours at anchor with repeated visits from German bombers, the crash of bombs on the sea, the continuous firing of A.A. guns, and the horrible sight of the destroyer being blown up by a bomb which we had witnessed the previous afternoon continuously before our eyes. I am not very partial to being bombed whilst on land, but have no wish ever to be bombed again whilst at sea. I have the greatest admiration for all sailors who so frequently were subjected to this form of torture during the war.

' *May 31st*. After a good wash-up, shave and breakfast, Adam and I went up to Dover Castle to see Bertie Ramsay, who was busy handling the vast fleet of small ships that were carrying out the evacuation of the beaches. I had not seen him since we worked together at the Imperial Defence College, and it was a godsend that we had worked so closely together during those two years. Had we not known each other as we did, it would, I feel certain, have been much more difficult to arrive at the changes in his dispositions that were necessary.

' He was planning for one more superhuman effort during the coming twenty-four hours and then to close down. I told him that this would not cater for all that still had to be moved, that he would have to endeavour to carry on with the effort for several more days. He was most wonderfully understanding and only too ready to do all that he could, and yet I could see that he had serious doubts as to the possibility. Adam and I gave him the fullest picture we could of what remained at Dunkirk, of what the conditions were, and what would probably be required. I still have the most vivid recollection of the wonderful relief of finding a man of Ramsay's calibre handling this difficult situation. I know no other sailor whom I would sooner have seen responsible for extricating my old Corps and the B.E.F. Providence was indeed kind that we should have known each other so well before this critical interview on which so much depended.

' The interview with Ramsay over, Adam and I drove off by car on our way back to London. That drive has always remained so deeply engraved in my memory that time has had but little effect on it. It was a most lovely English spring morning, with all the country looking as it only can in spring. Everywhere around us were those spring sights and smells of nature awaking after her winter slumbers. The contrast of this lovely sunlit country and its perfect peacefulness when compared with those Belgian roads crammed with distressed and demoralised humanity, horizons shrouded in smoke-clouds from burning villages, continuous rumbling of guns, bombs and aircraft, smashed houses, dead cattle, broken trees and all those war scars that distort the face of nature. To have moved straight from that inferno into such a paradise within the spell of a few anguished hours made the contrast all the more wonderful. That drive will always remain one of my most cherished memories.

' On arrival in London we drove straight to the War Office, where I saw Dill who had now become C.I.G.S., " Tiny " Ironside having been passed on to the command of Home Forces. I explained to Dill the situation in Dunkirk as I had left it, told him all that remained to be moved, and informed him of my interview with Bertie Ramsay in Dover and the steps he was taking to meet the situation.

' When I had finished my talk with Dill the reaction of the last three weeks began to set in, and I felt desperately tired and sleepy. During those last weeks it had been a case of snatching sleep at odd moments. Thank Heaven I was able to take full advantage of any opportunity that I could snatch. For all that, I began to suffer from uncontrolled sleepiness. I caught the train down to Hartley Wintney and had to walk up and down the compartment to keep awake and in my fear of overshooting the station.

' On the platform I found my wife and two children to welcome me. It all felt like the most wonderful dream. I drove home with them when I had a nursery tea with them, after which I retired to bed and to one of the very deepest sleeps I have ever had.'

Chapter Three

THE FALL OF FRANCE

*" Never give in, never give in, never, never, never, never. . . .
Never yield to force; never yield to the apparently overwhelming might of the enemy."*

WINSTON CHURCHILL

"I WOKE at home," Brooke wrote of the day after his return
from Dunkirk, " from a long sleep of well over thirty-six
hours and felt wonderfully refreshed, and on 1st June set
out for the War Office to find out what I was wanted for."
There he learnt to his relief and joy that his old friend Admiral
Ramsay had fulfilled all his promises, that another 68,000
troops had been ferried across the North Sea during the past
twenty-four hours, and that the evacuation was still proceeding
rapidly. In all, before the operation closed on June 4th,
366,000 men, 224,000 of them British, were rescued by the
Royal Navy from what had seemed certain destruction or
capture. While they waited for ships they stood in long, patient
queues by the waterside or sheltered in impromptu holes in the
sand, while overhead dive-bombers roared and screamed and
fantastic air-battles were fought out in the midst of gigantic
pillars of drifting smoke and fountains of water. By some
miracle of courage, improvisation and seamanship all these
thousands of men were embarked and taken from the delirium
of modern war to the quiet and ordinariness of England, to
neat railway carriages and smiling policemen and girls holding
up cups of tea, so that they might live to fight another day—
on the sands of Alamein and the beaches of Tunisia. ' As I
look back on those last days before Dunkirk,' Brooke wrote, ' I
still marvel at the fortune we had, and I shall always remain
convinced that, had it not been for the guiding hand of an

Almighty Providence, the B.E.F. would never have left the shores of France. Repeatedly throughout the war I realised the influence of this same guiding hand, this same superhuman Power, watching and guiding the destiny of humanity. Had the B.E.F. not returned to this country, it is hard to see how the Army could have recovered from this blow. The reconstitution of our land forces would have been so delayed as to endanger the whole course of the war.'

' It must be remembered that the majority of our future leaders were at that time all with the B.E.F. . . . and many others who played a very great part in the re-raising of our forces, their training and their leading to ultimate victory. I can speak with personal experience, as in the months and years to follow, both in my capacity as Commander-in-Chief, Home Forces, and as Chief of the Imperial General Staff, one of my major difficulties arose from the paucity of real high-class leaders. The First World War had unfortunately taken the cream of our manhood. Those that had fallen were the born leaders of men, in command of companies or battalions. It was always the best that fell by taking the lead. Those that we had lost as subalterns, captains and majors in the First World War were the very ones we were short of as colonels, brigadiers and generals in the Second World War. Had we, therefore, been deprived of the existing leaders of the Army before Dunkirk, it may be imagined how irreparable this loss would have been. There were also the warrant officers and non-commissioned officers—men who were also quite irreplaceable when it came to training and shaping new units. Time and again throughout the years of the war I thanked God for the safe return of the bulk of the personnel of the B.E.F.'[1]

It was in this mood of thankfulness that Brooke entered the War Office on June 2nd in answer to the summons of his friend, the new Chief of Imperial General Staff. ' I was still overcome,' he wrote,

' by the wonderful transformation from war to peace. The

[1] *Notes on My Life*, III, 193-4.

awful load of responsibility had been laid aside, the night-mares of anxiety were gone, roads were free from refugees, demoralisation no longer surrounded me on all sides, it was another glorious English summer day. From every point of view life had suddenly assumed a wonderfully rosy outlook, and I walked into Dill's room . . . with a light heart.

' I sat in that chair next to the C.I.G.S.'s table which I was to know so well later on, and asked him what he now wished me to do. His reply was: " Return to France to form a new B.E.F." As I look back at the war, this was certainly one of my blackest moments. I knew only too well the state of affairs that would prevail in France from now onwards. I had seen my hopes in the French Army gradually shattered throughout those long winter months; I had witnessed the realization of my worst fears concerning its fighting value and morale and now I had no false conceptions as to what its destiny must inevitably be. To be sent back again into that cauldron with a new force to participate in the final stages of French disintegration was indeed a dark prospect.

' I asked Dill whether I could refit the 3rd and 4th Divisions so as to bring out some seasoned troops. He said that there was no time for this, that I should be given the 51st Division, the 52nd Division, the remnants of the Armoured Division, Beauman's[1] force, and the 1st Canadian Division. After some discussion he agreed to push on with the re-equipping of the 3rd Division and to send them on as soon as possible. . . .

' My Corps Headquarters was dispersed all over England after its arrival back from Dunkirk. Chaos prevailed, and it was not an easy task assembling personnel. Dill asked me who I should like as my Chief of Staff, and I suggested Pownall, as he had had experience. I found, however, that he could not be spared, as Gort required him for the writing of despatches. I finally selected Eastwood who was available and also stipulated for Neil Ritchie to be with me again.

' After a long discussion with Dill about all preliminary details I was told that Anthony Eden, who was then Secretary

[1] Brigadier, subsequently Maj.-Gen., A. B. Beauman, commanding the troops protecting the British base depots in Normandy and now in command of an improvised division helping to defend Normandy.

of State, wished to see me. He was very charming and sympathetic as to all the difficulties that lay ahead of me, and finished by asking me whether I was satisfied with what was being done for me. I think I astonished him by replying that I was far from satisfied. That the mission I was being sent on from a military point of view had no value and no possibility of accomplishing anything. Furthermore, that we had only just escaped a major disaster at Dunkirk and were now risking a second.

' I continued by stating that possibly this move had some political value. . . . There might be some reason connected with the morale of the French Government and efforts to maintain them in the war. All that was not for me to judge, but I wanted him to be quite clear that the expedition I was starting on promised no chances of military success and every probability of disaster. It was for him to judge whether these risks were justified. . . . I left his room with the clear conviction that what I was starting on was based purely on political requirements, and from what I had seen of the French up to date I had very great doubts as to any political advantages to be gained.'

For Brooke knew what awaited those of the 140,000 troops still in France who were now not to be evacuated, and those others whom the Prime Minister, in his resolve to sustain the French Government, was proposing to send back there. Convinced that the collapse of the French Army was imminent, he could see no prospect before them but death or captivity. There were plenty of Frenchmen ready to die for their country, but as their leaders had completely failed to prepare and organise them to resist the *blitzkrieg*, what had formerly been the finest army in Europe was now, for all practical purposes, a herd of sheep in process of being rounded up by wolves. No intervention by Britain's scanty land or air forces could save it. Whatever the political arguments, what Brooke was being ordered to do seemed to his soldier's mind folly, for, having committed the nation's entire available military armament to France and lost it, its rulers in seeking now to dispatch its last remaining armed troops to help the

French achieve the impossible were staking, to no purpose, its very existence. With the Channel ports in their hands the Germans were now between England and the French Army and could throw their entire weight against either. Britain could only send aircraft and troops to defend Paris and France at the expense of leaving herself defenceless against air-attack and invasion. At that moment she needed every weapon and man she possessed if she was to survive during the desperate weeks while she was re-equipping her Dunkirk army and making good the heavy losses her air force had suffered during the retreat and the evacuation.

Brooke was a soldier, bound to carry out whatever orders he was given. But he left Eden in no doubt as to what he thought. Bernard Paget, Ironside's Chief of Staff, who encountered him outside the Secretary of State's room, noticed how strained and worn he looked. Yet, though he knew his mission was hopeless, the new Commander-in-Chief threw himself into his task with his customary concentration. ' The next few days,' he wrote,

' were busy ones for me. . . . I established a temporary head-quarters in the old Cavalry Barracks in Aldershot and there we gradually assembled. Both Ronnie Stanyforth and Barney Charlesworth rejoined me there as A.D.C.s, Neil Ritchie turned up, and we soon had very much the same set-up as we had had before, except for the loss of Mansergh and Perkins on the administrative side, both of whom had unfortunately been killed in France.

' I was informed that on arrival in France I should take command of all British Forces and that I should come under the orders of General Weygand. My rôle was to support the French. The situation in France as far as British Command was concerned was slightly involved. In the first place, there was General de Fonblanque who was in command of the Lines of Communication troops of the original Expeditionary Force. In addition, there were Generals Karslake and Marshall-Cornwall[1] who had been sent out to assist in taking control. I was told that on my arrival I could either

---

[1] Maj.-Gen. P. de Fonblanque, Lt.-Gen. Sir Henry Karslake, and Lt.-Gen. (now Gen. Sir James) Marshall-Cornwall.

retain them out there or return them home, whichever suited me best.

'On June 11th I was summoned to Buckingham Palace by the King and awarded the K.C.B. . . . for my services in France. On June 12th all was at last ready for my departure. I motored over to Beaumont Barracks in Aldershot with my wife and there was the heart-breaking wrench of parting again. I left at 11.30 a.m. and motored to Southampton with "Rusty" Eastwood, where we arrived at 1 p.m. We had a considerable hunt to find the "Duty Boat" by which we were to travel. It turned out to be a dirty little Dutch steamer only capable of 12 knots with no arrangements for food on board. Considering the fuss that the War Office had been making to get my Headquarters out quickly, I felt they might have produced something faster in the way of transport!

'We arrived in Cherbourg at 9.30 p.m., to be told that it was too late, that we should have to anchor in the stream and might disembark at 6 a.m. the next day. When the pilot-boat came alongside, I said I would go ashore in it. I was informed by the French officials that this was quite impossible; that passengers were strictly forbidden from travelling on the pilot's boat. It was evident that the war had not yet reached Cherbourg.

'I had sent repeated messages to Gervase Thorpe, who was in command at Cherbourg, instructing him to come and fetch me off. Apparently he had never been even warned by the War Office of my arrival. At last he turned up about midnight, pouring rain, pitch dark and an air-raid on, with every A.A. gun in Cherbourg blazing away for all they were worth. After being first of all rushed to a dugout, in spite of my remonstrating that I did not believe there was a single German plane about, I was finally taken to the château in which Thorpe was established at 2 a.m. It was an unpleasant return to France from every point of view.'

Brooke's instructions were the same as those that had been given to Lord Gort when he sailed for France in September, 1939.

" The rôle of the force under your command is to co-operate in the defeat of the common enemy under the Supreme Command of the French *Commandant-en-Chef de l'Ensemble des Théâtres d'Opérations*. His Majesty's Government have agreed that the latter may delegate the immediate command of your force to a subordinate French commander, of rank not below the Commander of a Group of Armies, as he considers necessary. You will, however, at all times have the right of direct access to the French *Commandant-en-Chef*.

" In the pursuit of the common object, the defeat of the enemy, you will carry out loyally any instructions issued by the French commander under whose command you may be serving. At the same time if any order given by him appears to imperil the British Expeditionary Force, it is agreed between the British and French Governments that you are to be at liberty to appeal to the British Government before executing that order.

" It is the desire of His Majesty's Government to keep the British Forces under your command as far as possible together. If at any time the French High Command finds it essential to transfer any British troops outside the area of operation of your main force, it should be distinctly understood that this is only a temporary arrangement."[1]

The military situation at that moment could scarcely have been worse. The Germans had wasted no time in following up their victory. A week before Brooke's return to France—and on the day the Dunkirk evacuation ended—they had opened a new offensive against the French armies south of the Somme. Attacking with greatly superior forces and an overwhelming ascendency in armoured striking-power and in the air, their tanks by June 9th had reached Rouen and the Seine. The only response by the French High Command was an inert defence. Instead of forming a mobile reserve by withdrawing from the Maginot Line, where a third of its remaining divisions were still shut up in their now useless forts, General Weygand staked everything on trying to hold a thin, over-extended line with

[1] *The War in France and Flanders.* (H.M.S.O.) 297.

nothing behind it. Like Hitler in a similar position four years later, the seventy-four-year-old Generalissimo met the onslaught of superior and better-equipped force by the fatalistic expedient of ordering outnumbered units to fight to the death where they stood. The inevitable result was that those who obeyed their orders were either surrounded or killed while the weaker fled, carrying panic and disorder along every highway.

Of the three British divisions still fighting in France, one—the 51st or Highland Division—was thrown away altogether by this strategy of despair. Separated from the Expeditionary Force while serving in the Maginot Line, it had been transferred to the seaward flank of the French armies in Normandy where, when the Germans attacked on June 5th, it put up a fight worthy of the highest traditions of Scotland. One of its units—a Territorial battalion of the Argyll and Sutherland Highlanders—lost 23 officers and 500 men in a single day without yielding ground.[1] But by June 11th, as a result of Weygand's refusal to allow it to withdraw across the Seine while there was still time, almost the whole division had been first penned in the Havre peninsula and then surrounded at St. Valéry-en-Caux, where on the day that Brooke returned to France it had been forced to surrender after an unsuccessful attempt by the Navy to rescue it. The so-called " Beauman " Division and what was left of the 1st Armoured Division, part of whose tanks and supporting infantry had been lost at Calais, withdrew, after heavy casualties, across the river westwards.

On the day before the panzers entered Rouen, the German armies struck at the main French forces on the Aisne. Next day Italy entered the war. By the morning Brooke disembarked at Cherbourg, Guderian's tanks were across the Marne, and Weygand's armies were everywhere disintegrating. During the 13th, fearful of the dissolution of the one force capable of preserving order—and property—the Generalissimo advised his Government, which had fled to Tours, to seek an armistice.[2]

Meanwhile Churchill, whose purpose it was to inspire the despairing French Ministers with his own resolution, had landed on the airfield at Tours. It was his fifth visit to France

---

[1] *The War in France and Flanders.* (H.M.S.O.) 273.
[2] *Weygand*, 128-9.

since the German offensive began and his second in three days. By now even he saw little prospect of saving the French Army but he still hoped to persuade the Reynaud Government to continue the fight from North Africa and, above all—for Britain's security depended on it—to prevent France's Navy from falling into German or Italian hands. Neither his courage nor his generous refusal to answer unjust reproaches and recriminations were able to effect anything, and he returned to England with the knowledge that powerful elements in the French Government and Army were working for a separate peace. Among the subjects he had discussed both on this and his previous visit had been the possibility of making an Anglo-French redoubt in the Breton peninsula, where under cover of sea-power an Allied force might continue to hold a small corner of France until Britain had created new armies. But, though tentatively favoured by Reynaud and his bolder Ministers, it had been dismissed as militarily impracticable by General Weygand,[1] and before Churchill left for England on the 13th the French Prime Minister, who was about to move with his Government to Bordeaux, told him that it was too late to organise it.

While the British Prime Minister was at Tours making his last attempt to revivify the spirit of France's rulers, the new Commander-in-Chief of the British Forces in France was battling his way through streams of refugees from Cherbourg, first to Le Mans—his Headquarters—and then to Briare, beyond Orléans, the temporary Headquarters of the French Supreme Command. On the previous night, parted once more from his wife, he had resumed his diary, and his entry for the 13th began with a laconic account—written that night at Briare—of his 340 miles journey from Cherbourg.

"Left at 8 a.m. for Le Mans which we did not reach till 2 p.m. but were glad to arrive alive in spite of dangerous driver. Refugees again swarming everywhere, and heart-

---

[1] "Mr. Churchill then brought up once more the question of a bridgehead on the Atlantic, a variation of the theme of a Breton redoubt. I explained why I did not think it reasonable to base any hopes on devices of that sort." *Weygand*, 121. Churchill referred to it as "a kind of Torres Vedras line across the foot of the Brittany peninsula." *Churchill*, II, 169.

breaking to find oneself back amongst them. At Le Mans found de Fonblanque, Karslake, and Swayne.[1] . . . Asked de Fonblanque for particulars of base organisation."

'To my consternation,' he wrote,

'I found that there were still some 100,000 men from the original B.E.F. Lines of Communication Troops. In addition, masses of dumps of clothes, equipment, vehicles, stores, petrol, etc. I instructed him to keep on evacuating home as many of this unarmed personnel as he could, only retaining personnel essential for maintenance of the four divisions. I also gathered final news about the fate of 51st Division at St. Valery, and I ordered home at once the remnants of this division. The 52nd Division I was told had one brigade fighting with the French Tenth Army and the rest of the division awaiting orders. Beauman was also commanding a mixed force with the French Tenth Army. Marshall-Cornwall was with its Headquarters.

'Having ascertained the dispositions of the various forces I was then in a position to accompany Swayne—Liaison Officer with General Georges—who was waiting to take me on to Weygand's Headquarters. We had already covered some 170 miles in coming from Cherbourg and another 170 miles lay in front of us. To cover 340 miles of refugee-infested roads is an unbelievable ordeal. When we arrived in the vicinity of Orléans we met the main stream of refugees fleeing from Paris. We had to do a long detour to avoid the town which was a solid block of cars. Every petrol pump was empty and surrounded by cars with empty tanks unable to move. Roads were continually double banked, with cars interlocked, necessitating continual descents from the car to carry out traffic-control duties in order to clear a passage. A never-ending and exhausting business.

'At last, shortly after 8 p.m. I reached Howard-Vyse's[2] Headquarters; he was our Liaison Officer with Weygand. I was informed that it was too late to see him that evening

---

[1] Col., now Lt.-Gen., Sir John Swayne, Head of British Military Mission to French G.Q.G.

[2] Maj.-Gen. Sir Richard Howard-Vyse, Head of British Military Mission with French High Command.

and that I should have to wait till next morning. Meanwhile, I collected all the news I could from Howard-Vyse, and as a result of all I had gathered during the day I finished my diary that night. . . .'

" From all I can gather, I can see no hope of the French holding out longer than the next few days."

' I started June 14th by going to see Weygand. . . . In his Memoirs[1] he has dealt with this meeting, and I do not think that his memory has served him as well as my diary. I wrote that evening:

" Went to see Weygand at 8.30 a.m. Found him looking very wizened and tired with a stiff neck from a car smash on previous evening. He said he would speak very frankly. That the French Army had ceased to be able to offer organised resistance and was disintegrating into disconnected groups. That Paris had been given up and that he had no reserves whatever left. He then stated that at the Inter-Allied Council it had been decided to hold a position covering Brittany in front of Rennes. That consequently I could concentrate the Canadian Division in the vicinity of that place and that instructions would be issued to Tenth Army Commander to manœuvre British troops under his command during the retirement, so that I could collect them in the vicinity of Le Mans. He then suggested that I should go with him to Georges' Headquarters to draw up an agreement for this manœuvre."

' I therefore started off in the car with him for Georges' Headquarters, and, as we were trundling along, he turned to me, and said: " This is a terrible predicament that I am in." I was just preparing to answer that I could well understand how heavy the responsibility must be to be entrusted with the task of saving France in her distress. To my astonishment he continued with: " Yes, I had finished my military career which had been a most successful one." I remained dumb and unable to make any adequate remark; it seemed impossible that the man destined to minister to

[1] *Weygand,* 135-142.

France in her death agonies should be thinking of his
military career.

' When we arrived at Georges' Headquarters and I met
him again, I could not help thinking how much water had
flowed under the mill since I met him last, touring the
II Corps front. Our next meeting place was to be in Algiers,
some two years later. He was looking very tired and haggard,
but as charming as ever. He asked me if I would like to see
the situation on the front, and took me to a large wall-map
with a line running across France, showing latest fighting
reports. On this line was drawn in red chalk several sausage-
shaped indentations along the line. I asked what these represented and was informed by him that they were penetrations
by German armoured forces. I looked at the scale and saw
that they were penetrations of some fifty to a hundred
kilometres on a frontage of twenty to thirty. I asked him
what reserves he had and, holding his hands up in a gesture
of desperation, he replied: " Absolutely none, not a man,
vehicle or gun left! " What I was seeing on that map and
what Georges was saying confirmed what Weygand had said,
that the French forces were disintegrating into groups, groups
that might well offer some resistance. But any form of co-
ordinated attack from those forces as a whole was no longer
to be hoped for.'

' We then turned to the question of the defence of Brittany,
and Weygand explained that a line was to be held stretching
through Rennes with its flanks resting on the sea. While he
was talking I had pulled out my pocket-dividers, and, setting
them to 50 kilometres, I measured this line and made it out
to be some 150 kilometres. I drew Weygand's attention to
this and he said that it could not be as much. I therefore
measured the distance again under his eyes and said that to
defend a front of 150 kilometres we should require at least
fifteen divisions. Where were they to come from? I had at
the most four divisions, and that was assuming that those
forces with French Tenth Army would still be available.
He said that a few divisions might possibly be found from
the Tenth Army. I pointed out that the plan as far as I
could see had no hope of success. Weygand agreed that the

idea was " fantastic," and Georges, I think, qualified it as
" romantic! " I therefore said that if we, as military men,
considered this scheme as doomed to failure with the resources available, it was up to us to represent this fact clearly
to the Inter-Allied Council. Whereupon he gave me to
understand that this had already been done; that it was
now to be considered as an order. As I had been placed
under Weygand's command, there was now no alternative
left but to comply with this order, and at the same time to
notify my Government.'

' An order was then drawn up providing for the defence
of Brittany as described, and this document was signed by
Weygand, Georges and myself. While this document was
being prepared, Georges and Weygand proceeded for a short
walk in the grounds of the château, no doubt to discuss the
state of the French Army and the approaching end. I had
had a long conversation with Swayne in the car on the
previous day and he had informed me that there was great
anxiety in the minds of Georges, Weygand and Pétain lest
some form of mutiny should develop. . . .'

' I felt rather like Alice in Wonderland, so much had
happened in the last twenty-four hours! All my worst fears
were being confirmed as regards the rapidly waning fighting
value of the French Army; it could be seen clearly that the
end was imminent. . . . At that time we were within three
days of the moment when Pétain ordered the French Army
to stop fighting. With this situation facing me, I had been
told of an Inter-Allied plan to hold Brittany, a plan which
had never been mentioned to me before my departure. What
is more, the defence of Brittany entailed holding a line some
150 kilometres long with only four divisions as a maximum,
with possibly three or four badly-mauled French divisions
from the French Tenth Army. There were no existing
defences on this line, no anti-tank ditch, no wire, practically
no anti-tank guns to defend it with, and quite inadequate
A.A. defences for the ports destined to act as bases. On top
of it all, it was more than probable that the Germans would
reach this line long before we could deploy our forces
along it.

' Immediate action was essential if we were to save the British forces in France. Whilst the document was being prepared for our combined signatures, I prepared a message for Howard-Vyse to take home, and instructed him to fly back to England as quickly as he could. He was to inform Dill of the situation and to tell him that the only course left open was to stop sending any further troops and to instruct me to evacuate the rest.'[1]

That morning the Germans had entered an undefended Paris. While Brooke was drafting his telegram to the War Office, Air Marshal Barratt, the Commander-in-Chief of the British Air Forces in France, was making a similar report to the Air Ministry recommending the immediate evacuation of his squadrons. Brooke's account of the day continues:

' Having completed my interviews with Weygand and Georges, I started back on my 170-mile journey through those refugee-congested roads. The situation on the road was no better than the previous day, and we had to deal with continual traffic-jams. My moves are covered by my diary notes. . . .'

" Arrived back at Le Mans at 4 p.m. and called up Dill to explain the situation and request that the flow of troops out to this country should be stopped at once. He informed me that this had already been done. I then told him I considered the Brittany scheme a wild project which was quite impossible, and that there was only one course open to us, namely, to re-embark the Expeditionary Force as quickly as possible. He said he would see the P.M. as he had not heard of the Brittany scheme, and would call up later. Later he informed me that the Brittany scheme was

[1] The message read: " Weygand stated organised resistance has come to an end. French Army disintegrating disconnected groups. He told me of decision taken by Governments yesterday to attempt to hold Brittany. He, Georges and I are in complete agreement as to military impossibility of this with troops which can be made available. Strongly recommend decision should be reconsidered as it can only lead to further losses of British troops without hope of result. Present plan is to hold back drafts and corps troops at Rennes and that the others should reassemble in that area after falling back fighting with 10th Army on Le Mans. Recommend Nos. 1 and 2 Mission should be withdrawn as Weygand and Georges will have no effective control." *The War in France and Flanders*, 1939-1940. (H.M.S.O.) 299.

off[1] and that I was to proceed with the embarkation of troops not under orders of French Tenth Army. I requested him to let Weygand know, as I was still under his orders, which he said he would do."

' The above brief notes written later in the evening do not contain the full gist of my conversation with Dill. I had in the first place given him a full account of my visit to Weygand and of my impressions of conditions prevailing in the French Army. I had repeated to him what Weygand had told me in the morning and which I have already quoted from my diary, namely, " That he said he would speak frankly. That the French Army had ceased to be able to offer organised resistance and was disintegrating into groups. That Paris had been evacuated and that he had no reserves whatever left.' "

' Weygand in his Memoirs accuses me of having misrepresented him by stating that the French Army was disintegrating, and that he had never made any such statement. It is unlikely that I should have invented the statement I made in my diary. . . . The very fact that the French Army was stopped fighting by Pétain within three days of our conversation points to the fact that the Army as a whole was not far from disintegrating at the time we were discussing the situation. Furthermore, one look at Georges' map was sufficient to confirm my mind to that effect. From the moment that I received orders that the Brittany scheme was off and that I was to embark the Expeditionary Force, it was evident that I could no longer remain under Weygand's orders. I stressed this point with Dill, and made it clear to him that as long as I was under Weygand's orders I must comply with the Brittany plan.

' On receiving Dill's instructions I sent orders for those Canadian formations that had already landed to return to Brest and to re-embark. The 52nd Division, less the brigade group with the French Tenth Army, was to proceed as soon as possible to Cherbourg, leaving a force in the neck of the

[1] " Dill had referred this matter to Winston Churchill, who said there was no such agreement between the Governments." *Diary*, 16th June, 1940.

Cotentin peninsula to cover the embarkation and the final withdrawal of the remainder of the division and those forces fighting with French Tenth Army when the situation justified their withdrawal. The unserviceable and non-fighting elements of the Armoured Division were to be moved to Nantes, and the Lines of Communication Troops, some 7,000 at Le Mans, 65,000 at Nantes, 20,000 at Rennes, etc., were to be dispersed to various ports as soon as possible. I also sent a message to Jimmy Cornwall to come and see me. . . .

'Just before dinner, as I was about to have a final interview with James Drew[1] and John Kennedy, his C.R.A., the telephone bell rang and I found myself talking to Dill on that very indifferent line which had been kept going between Le Mans and London. I naturally thought he was calling up from the War Office, but as a matter of fact he was with Churchill at 10 Downing Street. He asked me what I was doing with the 52nd Division, and I gave him an account of the dispositions which I have just described and which I had agreed with him on my previous talk. He replied: " The Prime Minister does not want you to do that." And I think I answered: " What the hell does he want? " At any rate, Dill's next reply was: " He wants to speak to you," and he handed the receiver over to him. To my surprise, I found myself talking to Churchill on this very bad line of communication.[2] I had never met him, I had never talked to him, but I had heard a good deal about him!

'He asked me what I was doing with the 52nd Division, and, after I had informed him, he told me that that was not what he wanted. I had been sent to France to make the French feel that we were supporting them. I replied that it was impossible to make a corpse feel, and that the French Army was, to all intents and purposes, dead, and certainly incapable of registering what was being done for it. However,

[1] Maj.-Gen., later Sir James, Drew, commanding 52nd Division.
[2] The diary-entry made that night reads: " Just before dinner (about 8 p.m.) called up by Dill who was at 10 Downing Street and put P.M. on to me. I had a difficult discussion with him as regards the evacuation of the 2nd Brigade of 52nd Division. He considered they might be used to assist the French or fill the gap between Tenth Army and Army on its right (some 30 miles!) At last I got him to agree to what I was doing." *Diary*, 14th June, 1940.

he insisted that we should make them feel that we were supporting them, and I insisted that this was quite impossible and would only result in throwing away good troops to no avail. He then asked me whether I had not got a gap in front of me. When I replied that this was correct, he asked whether the division could not be put into the gap. I told him that, as the gap was some thirty to forty miles broad at that time, and would probably be some forty to sixty miles to-morrow the remainder of the 52nd Division would be of little avail in trying to block this widening chasm. I said that it would again inevitably result in the throwing away of good troops with no hope of achieving any results.

' Our talk lasted for close on half an hour, and on many occasions his arguments were so formed as to give me the impression that he considered that I was suffering from " cold feet " because I did not wish to comply with his wishes. This was so infuriating that I was repeatedly on the verge of losing my temper. Fortunately, while I was talking to him I was looking through the window at Drew and Kennedy sitting on a garden seat under a tree. Their presence there acted as a continual reminder of the human element of the 52nd Division and of the unwarrantable decision to sacrifice them with no attainable object in view.'

' At last, when I was in an exhausted condition, he said: " All right, I agree with you." '

' In Volume II of Churchill's *Second World War*, on page 171, he deals with this incident:

" On the night of June 14th, as I was thought to be obdurate, he " (General Brooke) " rang me up on a telephone line which by luck and effort was open, and pressed this view upon me. I could hear quite well, and after ten minutes I was convinced that he was right and we must go. Orders were given accordingly."

' This interpretation of what happened is interesting. In the first place he states that I rang him up. This was hardly likely, as I did not know him and had never spoken to him. All my communications were direct with the C.I.G.S. His statement did not, however, disclose . . . . that, without

sufficient knowledge of conditions prevailing on that front
at that time, he was endeavouring to force a commander to
carry out his wishes against that commander's better judgment. With all his wonderful qualities, interference of this
nature was one of his weaknesses. . . . The strength of
his powers of persuasion had to be experienced to realise
the strength that was required to counter it.

'Having completed this difficult conversation with
Churchill, I now turned to Drew, and, with a sense of great
relief over the result of my struggle, gave him his final orders
for his retirement to Cherbourg. I then had interview with
the commander of the Air Forces working with me, fixing up
with him for fighter protection over Cherbourg from
squadrons based on the Channel Islands.

'After dinner I had another talk with Dill confirming all
that I was doing. He informed me that an order had been
sent by him placing me on my own and no longer under
Weygand. . . . Worn out, at midnight, I retired to bed for
a few hours' sleep.

'I was not destined to sleep long, as at 3 a.m. on June 15th
I was called and told that General Marshall-Cornwall had
arrived. I told him to take command of the British Forces
operating with the French Tenth Army. He was to continue
operating with the French Army as long as it had some
cohesive fighting value. Whilst rendering all possible help
to the French, he was to direct the axis of his retirement on
Cherbourg. I allotted one Motor Transport column to
render the 157th Brigade of the 52nd Division mobile.
Beauman's force and the Armoured Division were already
provided for.

'I got up at 6.30 a.m. after a poor night's sleep, and, after
an early breakfast, ordered my headquarters and that of the
Lines of Communication back to Vitre. We were too exposed
where we were. There was a very wide gap in the French
Army immediately in front of us. The *Armée de Paris* was
supposed to link up between the French Tenth Army, which
was retiring along the coast, and the French Seventh Army
which had its left flank east of Paris. I wrote that evening
in my diary:

" We are still very exposed here to raids from armoured cars or tanks, and have practically no protection. We may consequently have to move farther back before long. It is a desperate job being faced with over 150,000 men and masses of material, ammunition, petrol, supplies, etc., to try to evacuate and dispose of, with nothing to cover the operation except a crumbling French Army."

' It was an uncanny feeling with no system of observation of my own and no one to send out, never knowing accurately what the situation was in front. In addition, continuous rumours and counter-rumours, to which it was wisest to close one's ears. On my way back from Le Mans to Vitre I went round to the villages which had been occupied by the advanced elements of the Canadian Division to make quite certain that they had received their orders to return to Brest to re-embark. I found their rear-parties just departing and satisfied myself that all was well.

' Now began a very difficult and trying period due to continual interference with my plans from home. As I reached Vitre and had re-established telephone communication from London, I was instructed that the two brigades of the 52nd Division now at Cherbourg were not to be embarked without orders from the United Kingdom. I wrote:

" This can achieve nothing but lead to chaos. It means that Jimmy Cornwall will probably arrive on the rest of the crowd before they have had time to be evacuated. After lunch I had another talk with Dill and was again told that for political reasons it is desirable that the two brigades of 52nd Division should not re-embark for the present. In the evening I was told that shipping was available at Cherbourg to remove Drew's brigades, but that owing to the War Office restriction it could not be made use of. We are wasting shipping and valuable hours. At present bombing is not serious; at any moment it may become so.

" After dinner I had another talk with Dill and Anthony Eden and pointed out to them that from a military point of view we were committing a grave error. We are wasting shipping, valuable time and opportunities when air interference is not serious. Subsequently was again called up by Dill and informed that I could embark some of the gunners of 52nd Division and Royal Engineers at Cherbourg, provided I retained the infantry of the two brigades.''

' I do not blame Dill in the least for this interference, as he fully realised the dangers of interference at a distance. The interference was political, I am convinced. . . . What difference could it make embarking artillery and engineers instead of infantry at this stage? We were luckier than we deserved. Fortunately Cherbourg was not bombed during those dangerous days of embarkation, or we might well have suffered a few more tragedies such as the sinking of the *Lancastria* at St. Nazaire. . . .'

' On Sunday June 16th I got up at 6 a.m. after six good hours' sleep which had been badly wanted. I received orders that I could now start embarking the two infantry brigades of the 52nd Division—a very welcome bit of news, as I might at any time now have Jimmy Cornwall and his troops arriving on top of 52nd Division in Cherbourg. The War Office still refused to let Jimmy Cornwall withdraw his force from the Tenth Army, and he was to remain with them till they began to disintegrate.

' I communicated with Barratt, who was in Nantes, to find out whether I could do anything more for him as regards shipping his ground-personnel. He stated all was well, and we agreed together that, if we had to go, we might well be forced to do so suddenly. I then instructed de Fonblanque to get in touch with the Navy to ensure that the sweeping of Brest area for mines which Germans had been laying was not left entirely in French naval hands; the Admiralty to be warned to be prepared to do some sweeping in the event of an armistice putting a stop to all action on the French part.

' The rest of the morning was taken up with arrangements for evacuation, orders placing each Port Commander responsible for continuing embarkation of stores, equipment and personnel up to the last moment; De Fonblanque as General Officer Commanding Lines of Communication to remain responsible as long as communications held. I also received a message from Cornwall telling me that the Tenth Army was still working on the Brittany scheme and expecting our co-operation. I therefore let Dill know, asking him to ensure that Weygand realised we were no longer working on this scheme.

' In the afternoon I moved my Headquarters to Redon (north of St. Nazaire) and had some difficulty in opening up communication again with the War Office. That evening Drew called up from Cherbourg to let me know that half his troops were embarked, and that the remaining half would embark next day.

' Dill informed me in a telephone conversation that Weygand was not satisfied that I should have departed from our signed agreement, namely, the one to hold Brittany. I reminded Dill that I had told him of this agreement, but that it was based on the supposition that the Inter-Allied Governments had agreed that Brittany should be held. As I had been told that there was no such agreement and had been told to commence evacuating Expeditionary Force, I considered I was no longer tied . . . and had asked Dill especially that I should be removed from Weygand's orders and the matter made clear to him. I wrote that evening:

> " I had specially asked Dill to let Weygand know, as I was under an obligation of the document I had signed. I understood that this had been done and that the order taking me from under Weygand's orders included such information. However, I do not mind what accusations may be made against me. If I were faced with the same situation again I should act exactly the same way, and am convinced that any other course of action could only result in throwing good money after bad."

' When I look back now on those anxious days my opinion is exactly the same. Had I accepted Weygand's orders concerning Brittany and worked on them, deploying the Canadian and 52nd Divisions through Rennes and retained

Lines of Communication organisation to support them and all other details concerned with such a defensive line, we should indeed have been lucky if we had evacuated a quarter of what we did.

' That evening I sent Neil Ritchie home as I had no further use for him, and it was no use risking good officers at such a time when the unforeseen might occur at any moment.

' Late in the evening Briggs, who was functioning as Jimmy Cornwall's G.S.O.1., arrived at my H.Q., with the most recent information of conditions on French Tenth Army front. These were not reassuring.[1] He was looking very tired and had been having a hard time.'

The diary entry for June 16th ends:

" Barratt called me up this evening stating that he did not consider that we were getting R.A.F. personnel off quick enough. I assured him that they were getting their fair share of available shipping space and was just as anxious as he was not to remain in this country an hour longer than necessary.

" Midnight reports of embarkation are good. Some 45,000 have been embarked in last twenty-four hours, 12,000 previous twenty-four hours, giving total of just under 60,000 for forty-eight hours. Transportation hopeful of reaching 60,000 figure in next twenty-four hours, which should complete evacuation."

That night Marshal Pétain succeeded Reynaud as Prime Minister and authorised immediate negotiations for a ' Cease-fire.' Before dawn Guderian's tanks had reached the Swiss frontier east of Besançon, cutting off the Maginot Line and its half-million garrison and support-troops from the rest of France. Meanwhile, nearly a thousand miles away, the Red Army, seizing its opportunity, had started to overrun the Baltic republics and was preparing to invade Rumanian Bessarabia. On Monday June 17th, Brooke wrote:

' I started what was destined to be my last day in France

[1] At 17.35 hours that evening, 16th June, General Georges sent a telegram to Weygand at Bordeaux: " *Situation encore agravée . . . Nécessité absolue prendre décision.*" *Lyet*, 140.

for many long years of struggle to return. In the early morning I received information from Cornwall that the French Tenth Army was in full retreat and that he was retiring the British forces under his command to Cherbourg. Apparently Tenth Army were heading towards Laval and Rennes. Barratt's air reconnaissance had reported Germans in Orléans and tanks advancing from there on north bank of the Loire. Fighter squadrons were ordered to move that day from Dinant to the Channel Islands to be in a position to protect the Cherbourg embarkations.

'I instructed Naval Officer to have a destroyer in St. Nazaire ready to take me and remnants of my Corps H.Q., should necessity arise. I also instructed de Fonblanque and the Naval Commodore to push on with all speed with the loadings that day as we were unlikely to have more than some twenty-four hours to clear ports. The air was full of every conceivable report, including a persistent one that a party of Germans was advancing on Redon, where we were at that time. Such disintegration was beginning to prevail on all sides that I should not have been surprised to see a party of Germans in armoured cars driving up to our front door at any time. The absence of any form of screen of observation covering us gave one an unpleasant feeling of insecurity.

'The early part of the morning was taken up with orders and instructions for speeding up the embarkation.'

"At 10 a.m. put call through to Dill to tell him of situation of French Tenth Army front and of Jimmy Cornwall's move on Cherbourg. First reaction of Dill was that Jimmy should have remained with French Tenth Army. However, as this Army is in full retreat and as the forces of Jimmy Cornwall are based on Cherbourg, and further since Jimmy said that any pressure from the Germans would result in disintegration of the French Tenth Army, I cannot see that any other course was open to him. Dill then said that he hoped that, if French wished, they should be given opportunity of retiring in this direction. I assured him that Jimmy had already been instructed to that effect. I then gave him figures of re-embarkation and asked him what he wished me to do, as I could not see that I was performing any useful purpose stopping on out here. He seemed to consider that my presence out here was important from a political point of view, which I fail to see as I am not in contact with any French forces nor under the command of any French formation. He then suggested that I should proceed by sea to Cherbourg to find out how evacuation was proceeding there. Finally, informed me that he would call me up about 3 p.m., to let me know what I was to do. Telephone line to War Office very bad and interrupted by bombing attack on Rennes.

" At 10.30 a.m. called up Barratt to fix up details with him as regards his final moves and embarkation of party of R.A.F. defending Nantes. Issued instructions to de Fonblanque as G.O.C. Lines of Communication to remain here as long as his signal communication and enemy situation admitted of his serving a useful purpose and then to proceed home. Individual Port Commanders at Cherbourg, St. Malo, Brest, St. Nazaire, Nantes and La Rochelle have already received orders to continue embarking men and material to the last moment."

So far, all Brooke's preparations for the inevitable had been made and on his own initiative. Only on the afternoon of the 17th did he learn—and then, not from French Headquarters, but from London—that France had already offered to surrender and that he and his troops might be interned at any moment under the terms of a German-Franco armistice. ' At 1.15 p.m.' he wrote:

' I received a call from Dill asking me whether I had heard that Pétain had sent out a broadcast message ordering all French forces to stop fighting pending the establishment of an Armistice. I told him that I had not heard a word about it. I suggested that we should now concentrate on getting personnel out of France. I had instructed de Fonblanque to do his best to load as many vehicles as he could, and some of the M.T. ships were in process of being loaded. We decided that it was more important to save the men than the vehicles, and that we should now take steps to do so. I had previously asked Dill whether the moment had not come to withdraw my H.Q., but he had considered that for political reasons it had better remain a little longer. He now considered that those reasons were no longer valid and that we might embark that evening.

' Shortly afterwards, Méric, one of my French liaison officers, burst into my room and collapsed in a chair shaken from head to foot with sobs of tears. When he had sufficiently composed himself he repeated to me the news of Pétain's broadcast which I had just heard from Dill. It was a strange situation to find oneself in. Here I was operating with Allies, and in command of a force sent to their assistance in their final struggles. And when the end came, they never even had the decency to inform me officially that the French forces had ceased fighting. They just abandoned the British forces in France to their fate and left them to extricate themselves as best they could in the face of an unopposed victorious German Army.

' I do not suggest that at such a critical moment they should have assisted us in extricating our forces, but I do consider that under the circumstances they could easily have given me forty-eight or even twenty-four hours' notice of such a possible contingency and advised me to speed up the embarkation. Throughout that last trip to France I had the unpleasant feeling that the French High Command knew only too well that the French forces in France were doomed, and that it was a matter of very little concern to them how many of the British troops were sucked down with them in the whirlpool of this catastrophe. Looking back on those days I thank Heaven that from my first contacts with Weygand I appreciated the imminence of the disaster, and in spite of opposition from home, took the dispositions I did. Had I not, I feel certain that we should have saved very little of the British forces at that time in northern France.

' From now onwards the situation was clear and with all speed everything was got out that could be in the last few remaining hours. I called up Barratt to let him know that I should be shortly closing down my headquarters.

' About that time, one of my liaison officers whom I had sent to Cherbourg to gather news of embarkation, returned with the news that he had been unable to reach Cherbourg. He had found himself in the rear of a German column closing on that place and had only narrowly escaped being captured. It was therefore evident that I was now cut off from the Cherbourg detachment and that the embarkation of this place would now rest in Cornwall's hands.

' At 2.45 p.m., I got through once more to the War Office but unfortunately I found Dill was out. At 3.30 p.m., I tried again and this time was informed that our communications with London had been cut with no possibility of getting through. Whether this was due to the German advance or bombing I could not ascertain. Being now no longer in touch with London it was unnecessary to remain in Redon, and I therefore moved down to the outskirts of St. Nazaire to get ready for our embarkation that evening.

' I sent Allen, our Naval Officer, on ahead to find out when and where the destroyer would be available. He returned about an hour later with the news that the *Lancastria* had just been sunk with some 6,000 men on board. The destroyer that had been detailed for me had gone to the rescue of these men and was no longer available. I could choose between the *Ulster Sovereign* sailing next morning, and an armed trawler, capable of taking just my H.Q., and some of de Fonblanque's officers, which could sail at once but would be required for escort duty of a convoy. I selected the latter.

' I then moved into St. Nazaire where I found " Turtle " Hamilton in charge of the naval side of the embarkation. He was most obliging and helpful in our search for the armed trawler, H.M.T. *Cambridgeshire*. She had also gone to assist in in the *Lancastria* rescues, and it was sometime before she could be found. When she did arrive, it was after saving nine hundred men from swimming in fuel oil, and conveying them to another transport. During their time on the trawler they had most of them stripped off their oil-soaked clothing. The whole trawler was covered in that foul-smelling black treacly substance, heaps of clothes on the decks oozed out oil, whilst in the tiny cabin below the carpet was soaked with it, the walls covered with impressions of every part of the human anatomy printed in brown on the white walls; bandages, cotton-wool, iodoform, blood and the all-permeating smell of fuel oil. Ronnie Stanyforth came to me and said: " The one reason why I like to serve you as A.D.C. is owing to the comfort and luxury that we travel in! " '

' I brought with me a party of thirteen, including de Fonblanque, Eastwood, the French liaison officers, etc. We brought with us no food, and the crew of this trawler could not have been kinder and better hosts. They shared all they had with us, and it just lasted us out for the journey.

' After embarking we lay at anchor in the harbour until 4 a.m., during which time there were several more air-raids. We were sleeping on deck and " Rusty " Eastwood had his roll of bedding alongside of mine. The A.A. Lewis guns on the bridge were firing furiously. Suddenly I heard a thump, followed by a grunt of discomfort from Eastwood. I asked him if he had been hit, he replied: " Yes, by a Lewis gun drum thrown from the bridge, which landed on my stomach! " '

All through the 18th the *Cambridgeshire* steamed slowly with its convoy round the Brittany peninsula. ' We spent the whole of this day,' Brooke wrote,

' on the trawler, mostly lying on the deck in the sunshine and thanking God that we were safely out of France for the second time. Luckily it was a lovely calm day, and, in spite of the stink of fuel-oil, conditions were quite pleasant. Suddenly in the middle of this peaceful scene we were disturbed by piercing yells emanating from the lower parts of the trawler. The screams drew nearer and finally the individual responsible for them emerged on the deck. It was one of the stokers, a young boy who had been so seriously affected by the men of the *Lancastria* drowning in fuel-oil that he had temporarily become unhinged. He started tearing round the deck shouting, " Can't you see they are all drowning? Why are you not doing anything? Oh, God, we must do something for them." We caught him and held him down, and then hunted for some bromide to give him, but there was none. We therefore got several aspirins and ground them down in some milk and poured it down his throat. He gradually quietened down and slept for a couple of hours, when the whole procedure had to be repeated.

'I gathered from the captain that he had done excellent work on the previous day and had saved a lot of men himself personally. He had then done a turn of stoking and had gone to bed. He must have been of a highly-strung disposition and the sight must have been too much for him and temporarily unhinged him. I do not wonder at it, for from all accounts the sinking of the *Lancastria* was a tragedy beyond description in which some three thousand men perished. The trawler had certainly done wonderful work in saving 900, just as many as she could carry. In doing so she had used up all lifebelts, life-rope, rafts and life-saving gear of every description. We travelled slowly some six knots per hour and escorted a convoy of some half-dozen transports . . . I wrote that day in my diary:

> " It is an extraordinary contrast to find oneself sailing along on a lovely day surrounded by a calm sea, with no refugees, no columns of troops, no problems and no decisions to make. A wonderful enforced rest."

Brooke finished his last day's account of his voyage—begun in the trawler on the 19th—in the midnight train from Plymouth to London on June 19th/20th:

> " Yesterday evening the sea became very choppy just about our high-tea time. However, I put away the buttered toast and sardines and succeeded in keeping them down, which is more than some of the others did.
>
> " From Ushant we took a very wide sweep out westwards to avoid minefields. We are in a bad way if we should strike a mine, bomb or torpedo, as the whole of the salvage gear is gone in the rescue of survivors of the

Lancastria. We have no small boats, rafts, life-belts, life-buoys, or anything.

"It has been quite amusing travelling on this trawler, and getting a first-hand idea of what life on an armed trawler is like. The crew are a very good lot, very cheerful, and have been very good in making us as comfortable as is possible. They come from Lewes, Lincoln and London, but seem to mix together very well. The one that went queer yesterday is still in a bad way and suffering from a complete nervous breakdown, continually shouting about saving people.

"At 6 p.m. we at last drew near to Plymouth and the Admiral's (Dunbar Nasmith) barge . . . came out to meet me.[1] I transferred into it with Eastwood and Ronnie. We sailed through Plymouth Bay, full of memories of my time there with 8th Infantry Brigade. . . . At last we set foot on British soil again and thanked God for again allowing us to come home. . . . We went up to Admiralty House where the Admiral gave us tea, and then provided us with baths and dinner. . . . I called up Dill and told him I was home and fixed up to see him at 9 a.m. next morning. Finally we caught the midnight train for London."

As soon as he reached London on the 20th Brooke went straight to the War Office. He was greeted with an enquiry as to why he had not saved more vehicles and equipment. It was only a week since he had set out on his journey from Cherbourg to Weygand's headquarters. In those seven nightmare days he had rescued three fighting divisions, which, had he carried out the Government's original instructions, would all have suffered the fate of the Highland Division. His prescience, decision and moral courage had made possible the evacuation of nearly 150,000 British troops, more than three hundred guns and another 47,000 Allied servicemen. Those embarked at Cherbourg and St. Malo—the most threatened ports of all—had been brought home without the loss of a life or ship. For the efficiency of this second evacuation, which brought the total

[1] The last British troops had embarked from France twenty-four hours before. The official history of the *War in France and Flanders* (p. 301) is mistaken in saying Brooke landed at Southampton.

of men carried out of France by the Navy to more than half a million, the highest credit was due to the Lines of Communication chief, General de Fonblanque, who died, worn out by his exertions, a few days after reaching England. ' To my mind,' Brooke wrote, ' the country owes him and his staff a great debt of gratitude.' But from start to finish, the will and vision that had saved the rest of the British Expeditionary Force had been Brooke's.

Chapter Four

THE STRONGHOLD

" So to-day—and O if ever
Duty's voice is ringing clear,
Bidding men to brave endeavour,
We will answer, ' We are here! ' "

HARROW SCHOOL SONG
sung by Winston Churchill while a boy
at Harrow School

BROOKE SPENT the six days after his return from France at his Hampshire home, during one of which he was summoned to Downing Street to lunch with the Prime Minister. ' It was the first of many meals we had together,' he recalled, ' and left a vivid impression on my mind. We lunched together at a small table for two, and he cross-questioned me about my last trip to France, my impressions of the French and details of my final evacuation.'[1] Then on June 26th Brooke returned to harness, taking up the appointment of General Officer Commanding-in-Chief, Southern Command, which he had relinquished to go overseas in the autumn of 1939. At that time, for a man with his love of sport and nature, it had seemed the most attractive command in the British Army. But at midsummer 1940 its prospects were of a very different kind. From the North Cape to the Pyrenees, half-encircling the British Isles, stretched a vast arc of hostile coastline, from which two thousand long-range bombers, more than a thousand medium and dive-bombers, and fifteen-hundred fighters threatened their skies. Two-thirds of them were being fast concentrated on the shores of the Channel within a few minutes flying-time of southern England. They were known

[1] ' As we finished lunch he said he must go now and consult his two experts on France, and on my way down I ran into Duff Cooper and Spears.' *Notes on My Life*, III, 221.

to out-number the R.A.F. by at least three to one. Behind them were a hundred and thirty victorious divisions, ten of them armoured.

To repel this force the only troops available, apart from twelve almost totally un-equipped and raw training divisions, were the thirteen or fourteen badly mauled divisions which had been evacuated from northern and western France. Their men possessed nothing but their personal arms, for almost everything else had been left behind. The Army had lost nearly 1200 field and heavy guns, 1350 anti-aircraft and anti-tank guns, 6400 anti-tank rifles, 11,000 machine-guns, 75,000 motor vehicles and almost every tank it possessed, as well as vast quantities of ammunition. Scarcely enough remained to equip two divisions. At St. Margaret's Bay near Dover—the most threatened beach in England—Churchill, a week after the fall of France, found only three anti-tank guns covering five miles of coast.

Nor was Britain threatened only with invasion. Her sea communications were at the enemy's mercy. An over-populated, heavily industrialised island, dependent on ocean transport for two-thirds of her food and most of her raw materials, she could now only import by running the gauntlet of enemy U-boats, surface warships and aircraft established, as a result of Hitler's victories, in every harbour and on every airfield of Europe's western seaboard. Her life-lines were threatened at their home-water terminals, not only, as in 1914-18, from the east, but from north, south and even west. The blockader of the Continent had become the blockaded. And the vital sea-route that bound her to her eastern dependencies and dominions—to Egypt, the Persian and Iraq oil-wells, India, Malaya and Australasia—was outflanked for nearly four thousand miles of its course by a hostile shore: in the Biscay bay, in the Mediterranean, in the Red Sea. With the French Fleet and French North Africa at best neutral and at worst aligned against her, with Italy possessing on both shores of the central Mediterranean a geographical position that virtually cut that sea in half, and with that ambitious Power's large Air Force and Navy of six battleships, twenty-three cruisers and more than two hundred destroyers and submarines, Britain's historic naval dominance seemed as threatened in Europe's southern waters as in its northern.

Meanwhile, in the Nile Valley 55,000 British and Imperial troops with some two hundred obsolescent aircraft were left, through the defection of the French armies of Syria, Tunisia and Morocco, to face the attack of 415,000 Italian troops, based on Libya to the west and Abyssinia and Eritrea to the south of them, supported by an Italian air force of seventeen hundred first-line aircraft—nearly five hundred of them already in Africa. With the Mediterranean Fleet withdrawn to Alexandria, Malta was left an isolated outpost, only sixty miles from the Sicilian coast and eight hundred from the nearest British base. Even Gibraltar was dominated by the guns of Franco's Spain. It was scarcely surprising that most of the American Service chiefs regarded Britain at this time as a bad risk. The French High Command, conscious of how quickly its own Army had collapsed, predicted that within three weeks her neck would be " wrung like a chicken's."

Brooke's forces in Southern Command consisted of a single Corps headquarters, one regular division—the 4th—and two territorial divisions. The coastline he had to defend stretched from West Sussex to Wales. " The main impression I had," he wrote after his first day at Wilton, " was that the Command had a long way to go to be put on a war-footing. . . . The more I see of conditions at home, the more bewildered I am as to what has been going on in this country since the war started. It is now ten months, and yet the shortage of trained men and equipment is appalling. . . . There are masses of men in uniform, but they are mostly untrained: why, I cannot think after ten months of war. The ghastly part of it is that I feel certain that we can only have a few more weeks before the *boche* attacks."

For the next three weeks, Brooke worked unceasingly to strengthen the coastal defences and—what he regarded as more important—to form a reserve for mobile operations. ' My days,' he wrote, ' were spent touring the coastline, visiting defences and formations, changing unsuitable officers, and trying to instil a greater war atmosphere.'[1] He established a

[1] *Notes on My Life*, IV, 223.

central striking force on Salisbury Plain, organised Exercises,
attended conferences for Divisional and Area commanders,
and inspected the beach-defences of the entire south coast
from Plymouth to West Wittering. " Called up late last night,"
he wrote on June 30th, " and invited to lunch at Chequers with
P.M. to see Paget "—Ironside's Chief-of-Staff. " Suggested
Paget should come here instead, which he did. Had long talk
with him, telling him what I wanted for the defence of Southern
Command, namely, another Corps H.Q., another division,
some armoured units and a call on bomber squadrons. Some
of these things I may get. At any rate, I rubbed into him
the nakedness of this Command taken in relation to the new
situation in western France."[1]

For it was from across the Channel against southern England,
not across the North Sea against East Anglia—the area where
at the moment the defending forces were most strongly concentrated—that Brooke expected attack to come. Everywhere
he was struck by the lack of drive and preparedness, and by the
slowness and unfitness for the pace of modern war—of whose
shock and speed they had little conception—of many of the
older commanders. " Why do we in this country," he asked after
a two-hour conference with Local Defence Volunteer leaders,
" turn to all the old men when we require a new Volunteer
force? Old men spell delay and chaos. I wonder," he added,
" whether I have reached the age to stand clear and let
younger men replace me? "[2]

.   .   .   .

But there was one Englishman for whom advancing years
spelt neither delay nor indecision. Winston Churchill was
now in his sixty-sixth year. Though he had repeatedly warned
his countrymen that the peril facing them from across the
North Sea could only be met in closest co-operation with the
French Army, now that it was broken and peril threatened
them from across the Channel itself, he bade them be of good
heart. The voice that spoke for England in that hour was

[1] As a result, he received a further Corps headquarters, commanded by his
lieutenant of the Dunkirk retreat, General Franklyn, and an Australian brigade.
[2] *Diary*, 29th June, 1940.

neither repentant nor submissive. It was angry, defiant and utterly resolved. It was not concerned with the possibility of defeat but only with certainty of victory.

For though for those who were not Germans there seemed that summer only one way of safety—instant and unconditional surrender—and for those who delayed only one fate—certain and imminent destruction—Britain possessed assets which, by making her people conscious of, Churchill was able to mobilise in her defence. She was still an island surrounded by a tank-ditch of stormy, tidal water. The fleets and naval bases of France and the French Empire had been lost to her, her sea-terminals were outflanked by the conquest of Norway and the shores of the Biscay bay, her blockade of Europe had been thrown back for thousands of miles. Yet the spirit and efficiency of the Service that had won her naval ascendency remained and, though the physical tasks her seamen were called upon to face were greater than any in her history, they were not—as the event was to prove—beyond their powers. And though the Navy could no longer hold the narrow seas unless the air over them was also held, the Royal Air Force in the course of its brief existence had built up a tradition and skill that matched those of the senior Service. All but three of its fighter squadrons had been thrown into the battle over northern France and Dunkirk, and during May and June several hundred highly trained pilots had been lost. But though at the beginning of July Metropolitan Fighter Command could only put into the air forty-two of the sixty first-line squadrons which the Air Ministry had stated to be essential for the country's safety, its members did not regard the odds against them as too high. During the Dunkirk evacuation they had inflicted two-to-one losses on the enemy, and they believed that fighting over their native land they could do still better.

As for Britain's third line of defence, the Army, it at present, it is true, lacked arms. But if these could be found while the Navy and Air Force held the enemy at bay, it, too, could play its part in saving the country if the Luftwaffe should make a bridge across the Channel for the panzers. After the fall of France and the loss of nearly all Britain's military equipment there was only one country which could help to fill the gap between what she needed in her immediate plight and what her own factories were making.   Not the least of Churchill's services in 1940 was to awaken in the American President the conviction that weapons sent to England would not be wasted. Despite the belief of many of his Service chiefs[1] that, as she was doomed, to sell her weapons from America's scanty armoury would be to compromise the safety of the Western Hemisphere, Franklin Roosevelt responded to a faith and courage that matched his own.   Under pressure from the White House the American Army released from its First World War reserves half a million rifles, 80,000 machine and tommy-guns, 900 75-mm. field-guns, and enough ammunition for them to meet a few weeks' fighting.   They were hurried to the eastern seaboard, loaded on to waiting British ships and reached England during July.

Churchill did not seek only arms.   He raised a new civil defence force and armed it, with shotguns, pikes and maces. Impressed by the part played in the fall of France by the passivity of the civil population and the ease with which small numbers of armoured troops and parachutists had secured control of vast areas in advance of their armies, he appealed to the nation for volunteers to defend its streets and villages.   To the half million men who instantly responded he gave the name of Home Guard and the slogan, " You can take one with you! "   In the same spirit he insisted that " the people should be accustomed to treat air-raids as a matter of ordinary routine."   And, offering them " blood, toil, tears and sweat," he called on his countrymen in factory and field to work as never before to make good the deficiency in their armaments.   His appeal met with the response it deserved.   " They would rather perish in the common ruin," he bade the Foreign Secretary tell a neutral who offered to act as peace-intermediary, " than fail or falter in their duty."

For their duty, he taught them, was to save not only them-

---

[1] Major Walter Bedell Smith, Assistant Secretary of the General Staff, described the transfer to Britain of America's reserves of 75-mm. guns as " dangerous to the national defence " and a transaction which might well one day involve " everyone who was a party to the deal . . . hanging from a lamp-post."   *U.S. Army in World War II; Strategic Planning for Coalition Warfare*, 17.

selves but mankind. Like Pitt, when Napoleon's Grand Army was waiting to cross the Channel, he pointed to the historic path of their salvation. " We have become the sole champions now in arms," he declared, " to defend the world's cause." He bade them take the offensive and strike with a pebble at Goliath. He did not hesitate to take risks. When the new French Government, seeing in it a valuable bargaining counter, refused to remove its Fleet out of reach of possible German control, sooner than allow any chance of its becoming aligned with the Axis navies, he ordered it to be attacked and disarmed in its own harbours. On July 3rd a British squadron sank or drove aground three French battleships under the guns of Mers-el-Kebir in Algiers. Five days later another battleship was attacked and damaged at Dakar. " The fighting spirit of His British Majesty's Fleet," wrote the Italian Foreign Minister, " is alive and still has the aggressive ruthlessness of the captains and pirates of the seventeenth century. Ambassador Bastianini, who is back from London, says that the morale of the British is very high and that they have no doubts about victory, even though it may come only after a long time."[1]

Faced by such a response, the German conqueror hesitated. He had expected the British to accept their allies' defeat, overthrow their Government and join with him as a junior Aryan partner in policing the world. He did not want their enmity until he had dealt with the Slavs and, if necessary, the Americans. He needed them to keep down the East until he was ready to conquer it from them. " He would like an understanding with Great Britain," reported Ciano; " he knows that the war with the English will be hard and bloody." Yet, though he had ordered the Luftwaffe to give them a taste of the medicine that was coming to them if they proved obdurate, and, on the night after France fell, sent nearly a hundred German aircraft over England, he still waited for a change of heart.

At the beginning of July the pressure was intensified. British shipping in the Channel and port-installations in southern England were repeatedly bombed; Brooke in his diary recorded a dive-bombing attack on Portland and Weymouth and air-raids on Bristol, Plymouth, Falmouth and Purbeck. The news-

[1] *Ciano Diaries*, 4 July, 1940.

papers were full of pictures of tanks, motorised guns and trucks, packed with proud, fanatic-looking, young Germans, passing in endless processions through the streets of cowed French and Belgian towns; of great black bombers and troop-carriers with hooked crosses swarming overhead; of pitiful staring refugees wandering about the rubble of their former homes. But it seemed to have no effect on the islanders and on the man who had become their spokesman. And, as their defiance persisted, the world realised with a thrill that England was going to fight. " And now," Churchill declared on July 14th, " it has come to us to stand alone in the breach and face the worst that the tyrant's might and enmity can do. . . . We are fighting *by* ourselves alone; but we are not fighting *for* ourselves alone." Not since Elizabeth had anyone spoken to the English like this. Even an enemy felt " behind that façade of beautiful words and strong affirmations . . . a will and a faith."[1]

. . . .

Three days after his broadcast the Prime Minister visited Southern Command. On July 17th Brooke collected him from Gosport, where he had been lunching with the naval Commander-in-Chief, and drove with him on a tour of inspection along the Hampshire and Dorset coasts, finishing up at eight in the evening near Wool. " He was in wonderful spirits," Brooke wrote, " and full of offensive plans for next summer. We had a long talk together, mostly about old days and his contacts with my two brothers, Ronnie and Victor, of whom he was very fond."[2] Churchill refers to this afternoon in his war memoirs. " All the afternoon I drove with General Brooke

---

[1] *Ciano Diaries*, 286, 20th August, 1940.

[2] Major Victor Brooke (1873-1914), ten years older than Alan Brooke and the youngest of his five elder brothers, was a subaltern in the 9th Lancers when Churchill joined the 4th Hussars. He was Alan's chief hero and did much to shape his character. " I formed a warm friendship with him," Churchill wrote, " in 1895 and 1896. His horse reared up and fell over backwards, breaking his pelvis, and he was sorely stricken for the rest of his life. He . . . perished gloriously from sheer exhaustion whilst acting as liaison officer with the French Cavalry corps in the retreat from Mons in 1914." *Churchill*, II, 233-4. Brooke's second oldest brother, Ronnie (1866-1925), was, in Churchill's words, " a rising star in the Army " before the Boer War, when he became Adjutant of the South African Light Horse with Churchill as his Assistant Adjutant. " Together we went through the fighting at Spion Kop, Vaal Krantz and the Tugela. I learned much about tactics from him. Together we galloped into Ladysmith on the night of its liberation. . . ." *Idem*, 234.

who commanded this front. His record stood high. Not only had he fought the decisive flank-battle near Ypres during the retirement to Dunkirk, but he had acquitted himself with singular firmness and dexterity in circumstances of unimaginable difficulty and confusion when in command of the new forces we had sent to France during the first three weeks of June. . . . We were four hours together in the motor-car on this July afternoon, 1940, and we seemed to be in agreement on the methods of home defence."[1]

Two days later, while inspecting defences in the Isle of Wight with Auchinleck, Brooke received a message to proceed at once to London to see the Secretary of State. At the time he was eating sandwiches on the southernmost beach of the island, but hastily swallowed his last mouthfuls and set off at once. He reached the War Office at 7 p.m. and, after waiting twenty minutes, was summoned to Anthony Eden's room.

'I was shown in . . . and informed that I was to take over command of the Home Forces destined to meet the impending invasion at once. "Tiny" Ironside was to be created a Field Marshal, given a peerage and retired, and Gort was to be made . . . Inspector of Training.

'I knew well enough the dangers we were exposed to, the probability of an attempt to invade these islands, the unpreparedness of our defences, the appalling lack of equipment, and the deficiency of training and battle-worthiness in the majority of our formations. The idea of failure was . . . enough to render the load of responsibility almost unbearable. Perhaps the hardest part of it all was the absolute necessity to submerge all one's innermost feelings and apprehensions and maintain a confident exterior. To find oneself daily surrounded by one's countrymen, who may at any moment be entirely dependent for their security on one's ability to defend them, to come into continuous contact with all the weaknesses of the defensive machinery at one's disposal, to be periodically racked with doubts as to the soundness of one's dispositions, and with it all to maintain a calm and confident exterior is a test of character the bitterness of which must be experienced to be believed.'

[1] *Churchill*, II, 233-4.

That night Brooke wrote in the journal he kept for his wife:

> " I find it very hard to realize fully the responsibility
> that I am assuming. I only pray to God that I may be
> capable of carrying out the job. The idea of failure at this
> stage of the war is too ghastly to contemplate. I know that
> you will be with me in praying to God that he may give
> me the necessary strength and guidance."

The day of the new Commander-in-Chief's appointment was
the day of Hitler's final peace offer to England. Two weeks
before, the Fuehrer had told the Italian Foreign Minister that
if the English refused his offer he would unleash upon them " a
storm of wrath and steel." " I can see no reason," he announced on July 19th, " why this war need go on. . . . Possibly
Mr. Churchill will brush aside this statement of mine by saying
it is merely born of fear and doubt of final victory. In that case
I shall have relieved my conscience in regard to things to
come." " Late in the evening," reported Ciano, " when the
first cold English reactions to the speech arrived, a sense of ill-
concealed disappointment spread among the Germans." On
the 21st, while Brooke was spending his first day as Commander-
in-Chief, Hitler informed the heads of his Fighting Forces that
the decisive stage of the war had been reached.

The plan for the invasion—Operation " Sea Lion "—had
been prepared by the German Naval Staff during the winter.
It had been propounded to Hitler by Admiral Raeder on the
day after the panzers reached the Channel. But it was not till
July 16th—a month after the fall of France and only three days
before he made his final peace offer—that the Fuehrer issued
his first directive. " As England, in spite of the hopelessness of
her military position, has so far shown herself unwilling to come
to any compromise, I have therefore decided to begin to prepare
for, and if necessary carry out an invasion."[1] Its object he
defined as being " to prevent England being used as a base
from which to continue the war against Germany." Now, on
July 21st, he ordered the operation to be completed by September
15th, before the equinoctial gales. It would be one, he
pointed out, of exceptional difficulty and daring. " A de-

---

[1] *Nuremberg Documents*, 442-ps. cit. *Hinsley*, 67-8.

fensively and utterly determined enemy faces us and dominates the sea-area which we must use. Forty divisions will be required; the most difficult part will be the continued reinforcement of material and stores." The prerequisites he defined as complete mastery of the air and the creation of a sealed corridor across the Straits of Dover by means of minefields and long-range batteries on the French coast. For the present the Luftwaffe was to continue softening Britain's south-coast harbours and probing her air defences. Then, in the first week of August, it was to hurl its whole weight against the R.A.F. " It will take between a fortnight and a month," a Luftwaffe general reported to the Chief of the Army Staff, " to smash the enemy air force."

Brooke reached his Headquarters at St. Paul's School on the afternoon of July 20th. His first day there was spent in making the acquaintance of his staff, picking up the threads of his task and suffering, at the instance of the Ministry of Information, what he called " photographs and cine-men." Ironside had already left, but his Chief-of-Staff, Bernard Paget, Brooke wrote,

> ' was thoroughly familiar with all dispositions and able to put me in the picture. I could not have wished for a more helpful and loyal Chief of Staff, and am deeply grateful to him for the efficient way in which he ran the Headquarters.'

As his predecessor had taken his furniture with him from the Headmaster's empty house and no official accommodation was available, Brooke put up temporarily at the Naval and Military Club in Piccadilly, moving a few days later to the Army and Navy Club in Pall Mall."[1]

Brooke did not believe a minute was to be lost if the defending troops were to cope with the speed and violence of even a small armoured invading force. The existing anti-invasion plan was the conventional one of linear defences in depth, with a strong G.H.Q. anti-tank line covering London and the Midlands behind which the enemy was to be held until the central reserves could be moved up for a counter-attack.

[1] ' It is fortunate that I did so, as the rooms of the Naval and Military were hit by a bomb shortly afterwards and I should probably have been bumped off.' *Notes on My Life*, IV, 225.

Brooke's view was that swift offence was the only answer to the German threat, and that the right policy was to create mobile reserves near the coast to strike back at the enemy immediately wherever he landed and drive him into the sea before he could consolidate. On the 22nd he spent the day at the headquarters of the General Officer Commanding-in-Chief Eastern Command,[1] whose defences ran from Sussex to the Wash. ' This front,' Brooke wrote,

' was cut in two by the River Thames, comprised the main danger-area from the point of view of invasion, and was much too extensive for one man to control. I did not like it from the start and had it split into two Commands before long. I also discovered that much work and energy was being expended on an extensive system of rear defence, comprising an anti-tank ditch and pill-boxes, running roughly parallel to the coast and situated well inland. This static rear-line did not fall in with my conception. . . . To start with, we had not got sufficient forces to man this line, even if we had wanted to do so. To my mind our defence should be of a far more mobile and offensive nature. I visualised a light line of defence along the beaches, to hamper and delay landings to the maximum, and in rear highly mobile forces trained to immediate aggressive action intended to concentrate and attack any landings before they had time to become too well established. I was also relying on heavy air-attacks on the points of landing. . . .

' Another form of defence which I found throughout the country and with which I was in total disagreement consisted of massive concrete road-blocks at the entry and exit of most towns and of many villages. I had suffered too much from these blocks in France not to realise their crippling effect on mobility. Our security must depend on the mobility of our reserves, and we were taking the very best steps to reduce this mobility. . . . I stopped any further constructions and instructed existing ones to be removed where possible.'

The rest of Brooke's day is described in his diary.

" Lunched at St. Paul's and went on to Horse Guards

[1] Lt.-Gen., now Gen., Sir Guy Williams.

to see Bertie[1] and to discuss with him his problem of the defence of London area. From there on to the Cabinet War Room where I may have to be near the P.M. if an invasion starts. . . . Back to St. Paul's where I remained till 7.30 p.m. finishing off work.

" I then drove to the club and walked to 10 Downing Street to dine there with the P.M. Just by ourselves at the end of a long day's work was rather trying. But he was very nice and I got a good insight into the way his brain is working. He is most interesting to listen to and full of the most marvellous courage considering the burden he is bearing. He is full of offensive thoughts, but I think he fully realises the difficulties he is up against. He said that he wondered if England had ever been in such straits since the Armada days. He refers to Hitler always as ' that man'! I must say that it is very hard to see where we are heading for, but I have implicit faith in God that whatever happens it is for the good of mankind in the long (and perhaps distant) run."

" *July 23rd.* Left Hendon by plane for York 9.30 a.m., arrived 10.30. Adam had both Corps commanders, Holmes and Alexander,[2] to meet me and we had a discussion lasting about an hour on organisation of defences. Then motored to Scarborough and inspected defences from there to Bridlington. . . . Motored back to York, and, after tea with Adam, flew back landing Hendon at 6.45 p.m. . . ."

" *July 24th.* Flew to Chester, leaving 9.30 arriving 10.40 a.m. ' Copper '[3] met me at Sealand airport, discussed defences of Liverpool, Birkenhead, etc. We then got into another plane and flew over sea up to near Blackpool and Preston, inspecting possible landing-grounds on sands. After lunch motored out to see Jimmy Cornwall at his Corps H.Q. Finally flew back reaching Hendon at 7.45 p.m.'

" *July 25th.* Spent a day in the office. Had intended to

---

[1] Lt.-Gen. Sir Bertram Sergison-Brooke, commanding the London District.
[2] Lt.-Gen., now Gen., Sir Ronald Adam; Lt.-Gen., now Gen. Sir William George Holmes; Lt.-Gen., now Field-Marshal Earl, Alexander.
[3] Gen. Sir Robert Gordon-Finlayson, G.O.C.-in-C., Western Command.

start for Edinburgh to-night but had to put it off owing
to Chiefs of Staff meeting to-morrow afternoon at 4 p.m.
which I must attend. . . ."

" *July 26th*. Worked in office during the morning. In
afternoon went to see Dill at the War Office at 3 p.m., and
from there on to the Chiefs of Staff meeting. Main subject
of discussion was the priority of use of fighters in the event
of invasion. I came away feeling less confident. . . .
The attitude of representatives of the Naval Commander
brought out very clearly the fact that the Navy now realises
fully that its position on the sea has been seriously undermined by the advent of aircraft. Sea supremacy is no
longer what it was, and in the face of strong bomber
forces can no longer ensure the safety of this island
against invasion. This throws a much heavier task on
the Army."

" *July 27th*. Caught night-mail to Edinburgh. Had
breakfast with Carrington[1] and then went on to visit the
46th Division. Found it in a lamentably backward state
of training, barely fit to do platoon training and deficient
of officers. . . . Saw Wimberley's[2] brigade of the 5th
Division and was much impressed by it. Returned to
London by night-mail. . . ."

'Fortunately,' wrote Brooke of his constant journeys
round Great Britain at this time,

'air travel made it possible to tour defences rapidly. . . . I
set my programme of tours so as to cover the whole of the
coast-line first, getting a picture in my mind of the main
danger points, examining the defences, visiting units, and
above all, meeting commanders of corps, divisions and
brigades. I was soon able to decide what changes were
necessary in the command of formations. Having completed
my tour of the coast line, I then concentrated on the organisa-
tions in reserve, such as Nosworthy's Corps, the Canadian
Corps, the New Zealanders. . . . I discussed the rôle they

[1] Lt.-Gen., now Sir Robert, Carrington, General Officer Commanding-in-
Chief, Scottish Command.
[2] Brigadier, later Maj.-Gen., Douglas Wimberley, who afterwards commanded
the Highland (51st) Division at Alamein.

were to play in the event of invasion and inspected units and formations to assess their value in the event of an attack. I was seriously disturbed by the prospect of German airborne landings on the South Downs, to be carried out in combination with landings and destined to prevent the timely arrival of my counter-attacking forces. To guard against such an eventuality, mobile forces such as Brocas Burrows' brigade were retained on the South Downs, ready to deal at once with any airborne landings.

' There was, however, one point above all others that constituted a grave danger in the defensive organisation. . . . There was no form of Combined Command over the three Services. . . . There were far too many commanders. The Navy had the C.-in-C., Home Fleet, C.-in-C., Nore, C.-in-C., Portsmouth, C.-in-C., Plymouth, C.in-C., Western Approaches. The Army had the C.-in-C., Home Forces; and the Air Force had the A.O.C. in C., Fighter Command; the A.O.C. in C., Bomber Command, and the A.O.C. in C., Coastal Command. There was no co-ordinating head to this mass of commanders beyond the Chiefs of Staff Committee and the Admiralty, Air Ministry and War Office.'

' It was a highly dangerous organisation. Had an invasion developed, I fear that Churchill would have attempted as Defence Minister to co-ordinate the action of these various Commands. This would have been wrong and highly perilous, with his impulsive nature and tendency to arrive at decisions through a process of intuition as opposed to " logical " approach. . . . He held periodic conferences of Commanders-in-Chief, which were attended by all the coastal naval Commanders-in-Chief, . . . thus giving the naval side too great a preponderance in these discussions when the Army was represented only by one member, and the R.A.F. by three.

' I soon discovered that the Home Fleet, in the event of an invasion, had little intention of coming farther south than the Wash. As destroyers were also being drawn off to protect Western Approaches, the naval defence in the Channel and southern waters did not appear to be . . . . able to offer the required interference with German landing opera-

tions. On the other hand, the Admiralty and naval commanders were inclined to criticise freely Army dispositions. . . .
Had I listened to these criticisms I should have had to employ practically the whole of my forces solely for the defence
of naval bases by concentrating men on the beaches in
their vicinity.'[1]

For close though its watch was of the enemy's ports and of
his three thousand miles of conquered coastline, the Royal
Navy, which in 1914 had been able to guarantee the country
against any invasion except an isolated raid, was now facing
a fearful dilemma. So long as Britain and her allies controlled
both sides of the Straits of Dover, the North Sea, across which
invasion could alone have come, had been open only to
the north where, secure from air attack in their Orkneys base,
the battleships of the Home Fleet were able simultaneously to
afford protection to the covering destroyer and light-cruiser
screen to the south and counter any attempt of the German
surface warships to break out northwards into the Atlantic.
But now, not only had this second task been complicated by
the German seizure of Norway and its long coastal corridor, but
the sea-area across which invasion could come had been
doubled by the enemy's occupation of the French coast.
Under protection of shore-based aircraft the German battle-
cruisers and pocket battleships could pass from the North
Sea into the Channel to cover an invasion while the British
battle-fleet could not follow them through the bottleneck
between the Thames estuary and Dutch and Belgian coasts and
the still narrower Straits of Dover without running risks from
air-attack that might destroy its command of the sea altogether.
It could continue from its northern base to support the light
craft guarding eastern England, but it could only give support
to the destroyer screen in the Channel by detaching part of its
strength—already reduced by the despatch of additional battleships to the Mediterranean—and basing it on Liverpool or
Plymouth. The Straits of Dover had ceased to be a British
naval barrier, as in the First World War, and had become a
German trap-door. The enemy could invade from either side

[1] *Notes on My Life*, IV, 229-230.

of it at choice, and the Commander-in-Chief of the Home Fleet, six hundred miles away in the Orkneys, could not guard both North Sea and Channel without dividing his forces.

And, though the German surface-fleet has suffered heavily in the fighting off Norway, the Admiralty did not know how heavily. It was known to have on the stocks, nearing completion or possibly already commissioned, two battleships— the *Bismarck* and *Tirpitz*—more powerful than any British warship. Every link in the Navy's chain of defence was dangerously stretched. Not only was the battle-fleet prevented by the new factor of shore-based air-power from giving adequate protection to the destroyers whose business it was to sink and engage invaders and their escorts, but the destroyers were too few for the task imposed on them by the enemy's control of the French coast. During the fighting in the spring and early summer sixteen of them had been sunk and forty-two damaged, or roughly half the destroyer strength in home waters. Though these losses were being made good in the dockyards, it was natural that the Commanders-in-Chief of south-coast naval bases should feel anxious lest sudden descents should result in their being attacked from the land and that they should bombard the Commander-in-Chief of the Army for troops and guns needed for the defence of the country as a whole.

.　.　.　.　.　.　.　.

For the moment everything depended on whether the Royal Air Force could defeat the Luftwaffe's attack or, if that proved impossible in the light of the odds against it, hold it at bay long enough to enable the Army, now re-arming, to repel an invasion which the Navy could no longer by itself prevent. Two years before when, in the summer of Munich, its new steel-frame, eight-gun fighters had just started to come from the assembly-lines, the R.A.F. had had to confront, with only five Hurricane and no Spitfire squadrons and without the aid of a Radar warning system, a first-line force of nearly fifteen hundred modern bombers too fast for interception by its few hundred slow and obsolescent wooden biplanes. Had the Germans at that time seized the airfields of the Low Countries and thrown the Luftwaffe against England, there would have

been nothing to prevent London and the industrial towns of
the Midlands being subjected to the same uninterrupted day
bombing that later destroyed Warsaw and Rotterdam. Now,
with only a hundred more first-line bombers than it had
possessed in 1938, the Luftwaffe had to defeat a force of forty-
nine modern Spitfire and Hurricane squadrons whose mobility
had been increased out of all measure by the creation of a
Radar network round the coasts.

Yet even with these advantages the odds against the British
fighters were at least two to one. On August 2nd, in obedience
to Hitler's instructions and to clear a way across the Channel,
Goering ordered the Luftwaffe to bring the R.A.F. to action
and destroy it. Nearly fourteen hundred first-line bombers and
thirteen hundred fighters were by now concentrated on the
airfields of northern France and the Low Countries. On
August 8th the attack began. On the first day twenty-eight
German aircraft were shot down for a loss of twenty British;
on the third day the comparative losses rose to thirty-five and
thirty-two. At first the enemy effort was still directed against
Dover, Portland and the Channel convoys. But on the 12th,
in order to force Fighter Command to deploy its full strength
in defence of its bases, it was switched from the ports to the
Radar stations, airfields and aircraft factories of south-eastern
England. During that day six heavily escorted bomber formations damaged five Radar stations and three airfields, one of
which—Manston in Kent—was temporarily put out of action
altogether. In the fight to defend them thirty-six raiders were
destroyed for the loss of twenty-two R.A.F. fighters. Next day
another seventy-one were shot down for a loss of twenty-seven.

Six weeks before, after its heavy casualties in France, the
R.A.F. could not have inflicted—or sustained—such losses.
By this time, however, Fighter Command had recovered its
strength. Thanks to far-sighted planning by the Air Staff
before the war and the drive of the new Minister of Aircraft
Production, Lord Beaverbrook, the number of fighters reaching
the squadrons from the factories had risen from two hundred
and fifty in April to nearly five hundred by July. Air-Chief-
Marshal Dowding's operational strength in Spitfires and
Hurricanes, down to 331 after Dunkirk, was now 620, giving

him a total of 704 serviceable first-line fighters, with a further
289 in reserve compared with only 36 on June 4th. Though this
was barely half the force the Air Staff had asked for to ensure
the safety of the country in the altered strategic conditions
created by the fall of France,[1] it was felt in the Service that if
the Radar stations could continue to give warning, it might
prove enough to keep the Luftwaffe at bay and enable the
Navy to hold the Channel. It would be a near-run thing,
depending mainly on the quality of the defending pilots and
aircraft. But thanks to the standards by which Lord Trenchard's
lieutenants had built and trained the R.A.F. in the pinchbeck
years between the Wars, the R.A.F. believed it could do it.
If it failed, invasion was certain.

When the Battle of Britain began Brooke had been in the
saddle for little more than a fortnight. He was still far from
confident of his ill-equipped troops' ability to repel invasion,
and was having the utmost difficulty in building up mobile
reserves. In particular, he was desperately short of armour; of
the seven hundred tanks sent to France only twenty-five had
returned. Subject to the overriding priority for fighters everything was being done to get new tanks from the factories
quickly, and during June and July more than three hundred
had been delivered. But on August 10th, just as the Battle of
Britain was beginning, Brooke was summoned by the Secretary
of State for a conference with General Wavell, who had flown
from the Middle East to seek armour to halt the now imminent
Italian march on Alexandria. As a result of an intensely brave
decision made that day by the Prime Minister and C.I.G.S.,
one regiment of heavy, one of light and one of cruiser tanks
were taken from the Forces awaiting invasion and allocated
to the defence of the Nile Valley.

'This,' Brooke wrote afterwards,

'does not seem much when considered from the point of
view of the later years of the war, but in those early days
even this small contribution constituted a large proportion
of the total of my armoured forces. To make matters worse
Beaverbrook, who was Minister of Aircraft Production, began

[1] *The Royal Air Force*, 1939-1945. (H.M.S.O.) I, 156.

to form an army of his own to protect aircraft factories in the event of invasion. He acquired a large proportion of armour plating for the production of small armoured cars called " Beaverettes," with which he equipped Home Guard personnel of factories for their protection. This was at a time when I was shouting for every armoured vehicle I could lay my hands on with which to equip Regular forces. The whole conception was fantastic. How could individual factories have held out, and what part could they have played once the main battle for this country was lost? "

This realisation that to try to be strong at every point was to be weak at all was the essence of Brooke's strategy. He had to defend more than two thousand miles of coastline in Great Britain and Northern Ireland, of which at least eight hundred miles were assailable—a frontage twice as long as that which the joint French, British and Belgian armies had failed to hold in May. For this he had, in theory twenty-six, and in practice only about fourteen weak divisions. And though the Germans could not simultaneously attack all that vast coastal circumference, provided they could cross the sea at all they had a wide choice of landfall, for, owing to their geographical position, they could dominate the air over the landing beaches everywhere between the Wash and Bristol Channel.

From Narvik to Biarritz the foe was now ready. The swastika rose over the Channel Islands; Mussolini's legions, outnumbering Wavell's few by nearly ten to one, prepared to march into Somaliland and Egypt; the Japanese sharpened their swords at the gates of Hong Kong. While the procession of barges floated down the rivers and canals of Europe towards the Channel ports, the columns of grey and steel moved to their appointed places, and the great, black, laden aeroplanes gathered on the airfields of northern France, Belgium, Holland and Norway. It was part of the strategy of invasion to keep the defenders guessing, and a continuous stream of rumours and reports, any one of which might be true, flowed into G.H.Q., London, from the Continent. Three days after the Commander-in-Chief had been compelled to surrender part of his scanty armour to defend the Nile Valley, and just as he was about to fly from London to the south-west, he received news of an impending attack on Scotland. " Swayne," he wrote on the 13th,

> " called up early to inform me that Admiralty had received accurate information that Germans in Norway had embarked on night of the 11th and that they expected invasion in the north."[1]

Later that day, after inspecting coastal defences from Exmouth to Weymouth with the Prime Minister, Auchinleck and Montgomery, Brooke witnessed an air battle over Portland that might have been the prelude to a descent on the Dorset coast.

> " We found a German plane which had just come down. Pilot was all burned up, but, as 500-lb. bomb was in the débris which was burning, we did not stop long. Finally flew back from Weymouth, arriving Hendon at 6 p.m. Went to St. Paul's School to find out situation before going home."

Meanwhile another report arrived that Austrian mountain divisions had been seen in the Pas de Calais equipped with mules for climbing the Kentish and Sussex cliffs.

On August 15th, the Luftwaffe struck the all-out blow—the *Adlerangriff* or eagle-attack—which was expected to destroy the R.A.F. as the Polish, Belgian and French air forces had been destroyed. Eighteen hundred aircraft, nearly thirteen hundred of them fighters, attacked England in successive waves. The feature of the day was a raid on the Tyne by a hundred bombers and seventy escorting fighters from Norway and another on the Yorkshire coast. Imagining that every available fighter would be thrown into the battle over south-eastern England, the Germans expected to find the north bare to their assault and to be able to subject its factories and harbours to an inferno of uninterrupted low-level bombing. But true to the classic principles of war, Dowding had kept in reserve seven squadrons, temporarily withdrawn for rest from the south, and stationed them in the north-east to guard against the blow.

[1] *Diary*, 13th August, 1940.

As the bombers with their escort of slow long-range fighters neared the Northumbrian and Yorkshire coasts, they were assailed by Spitfires and Hurricanes warned of their approach by Radar. Though most of them managed to cross the coast, they were forced to jettison their bombs at random, doing little damage except to houses and losing nearly a quarter of their number. Altogether in the day's fighting the Luftwaffe lost seventy-six aircraft or more than twice the defenders' thirty-four. And though, in the confusion of continuous lightning dives and pursuits, both sides seriously overestimated the other's losses,[1] the Germans suffered their first decisive defeat of the war. So shaken were they by their casualties, especially among the bombing crews, that Goering issued an order that no aircraft should fly with more than one officer and that, to economise effort, attacks on Radar sites should be discontinued in favour of airfields and factories. In this, however, he profoundly miscalculated. For the Radar stations were Britain's eyes and enabled the R.A.F. to parry his blows despite the odds.

As it happened, Brooke had arranged to fly north on August 15th in his slow, unescorted Flamingo to spend two days inspecting the defences of Lincolnshire, Yorkshire and Tyneside.

> "*August 15th.* Left Hendon at 8.30 a.m. and arrived at Sutton Bridge on the Wash at 9 a.m. where I was met by Adam and Kelso.[2] Proceeded to inspect western defences of the Wash up to Skegness. . . . On up to the Humber, doing Grimsby and Immingham docks. Picked up plane again at Grimsby aerodrome and flew over Humber, examining forts and Spurn Head defences. Then flew up coast to Hornsea before starting inland for York where we arrived at 8 p.m. Stopped the night with Adam."

[1] Owing to the fact that on hotly contested days several pilots inevitably claimed the same machine, during the Battle of Britain the British claimed the destruction of 2,698 enemy aircraft and actually destroyed 1,733, while the Germans claimed 3,058 and destroyed 915. *The Royal Air Force*, 1939-1945. (H.M.S.O.) I, 190.

[2] Brig., now Maj.-Gen., J. E. Utterson-Kelso—a brilliant trainer of troops who, while serving under General Alexander, was one of the pioneers of the battle-school.

" *August 16th.* Left York 8.30 a.m. by air for Middles-borough where we picked up car. . . . We then went to Redcar, which we did in detail, crossing Tees by suspension bridge and working up the coast through Seaton and Sunderland which had been heavily bombed on previous day. Lunched South Shields, crossed Tyne by ferry to North Shields and worked up coast through Blyth to Amble. Finally picked up plane at Ackburgh aerodrome at 5.15 p.m. Dropped Adam in York and was back at Hendon at 7 p.m. Went to office before coming home."

Though no more raids were made on the North, that day southern England was assailed by 1720 aircraft, more than three-quarters of them fighters. By the 18th the Germans in ten days of battle had lost 367 aircraft, Fighter Command 183 and another 30 on the ground. During the last week of August, following five days of cloud, the Luftwaffe closed in on the inner ring of section stations round London, sending over from a thousand to sixteen hundred aircraft a day in its resolve to break the R.A.F. Meanwhile a dispute had arisen between the German Navy and Army Commands about the execution of " Sea Lion." On the ground that its strength was inadequate to win control of any larger sea-area, the Navy wished to confine the landings to the Straits of Dover, where great guns erected on the French cliffs, aided by minefields and U-boats, would create, it was hoped, a corridor through which successive waves of invaders could be ferried into Kent. The Army, whose Intelligence had grossly overestimated British military strength,[1] contended that an attack on so narrow a front would be suicidal and asked for landings along the whole southern coast from Ramsgate to Lyme Regis, with 100,000 men in the first wave and 160,000 in the second. This, the Navy pointed out, would require two million tons of shipping and was logistically impossible even with command of the Channel. On August 27th, therefore, a compromise was imposed by Hitler, under which an initial landing of eleven divisions was to be made between the North Foreland and the Isle of Wight. But in the last resort

---

[1] The Operation Order issued by von Rundstedt's Army Group " A " at the beginning of September estimated Brooke's forces at thirty-nine divisions. M. Shulman, *Defeat in the West*, 49.

—for neither Hitler nor his Navy or Army was prepared to run the risks involved until this condition had been fulfilled—everything depended on the elimination of Fighter Command from the skies over southern England and its sea approaches.

During the closing days of August and the first of September, it looked as though the R.A.F., its strength sapped by attrition, was nearing its end. In order to compel the British fighters to attack at a disadvantage, the Germans were now sending their bombers against the controlling sector stations with escorts six or seven times their strength. Though repeatedly victorious, the defenders were suffering far heavier casualties than they could replace, and by September 3rd the available pilot strength of Fighter Command had sunk from 1438 to 840. If the rate of attrition continued for a further two or three weeks, German air control over the Channel and Britain's southern cities would be assured.

Brooke's diary reflects the impact of that struggle as the German attacks drew closer to the capital. He spent the week-end of August 17th with the Prime Minister and Lord Beaverbrook at Chequers, and two days later carried out an Exercise to test the control of his defences. On the 24th, just as he was leaving London to visit his reserves on Salisbury Plain, the first bombs fell on the capital.

> " *August 24th.* As I left home at 8.30 an air-raid warning started. Motored through a deserted London with only air-raid wardens about. Arrived at Hendon aerodrome to find it deserted except for the defending troops. After some eleven minutes Fighter Command reported road safe, so I started off in my Flamingo, flying very low for Andover which we reached at 9.45 a.m. Definite signs of bombing here. Motored to Tidworth, where I inspected battalions of 60th and Rifle Brigade. Then motored to West Lavington to inspect 1st Army Tank Brigade. From there to Warminster where I saw 3rd Armoured Brigade, including Bays, 9th Lancers and 10th Hussars. Finally to Chisledon to see Queen Victoria's Rifles which are just reforming after their Boulogne fight. Flew home from near there."

" *August 25th. Sunday.* After a night of air-raid warnings went to the office in the morning and spent afternoon at home. As I write this we are again in the middle of an air-raid warning."

" *August 26th.* More air-raids during the night. Worked in the office all day and left by the 7.30 p.m. from Euston for Inverness. No dining-car and an air-raid of two hours which entailed going to bed in the dark. . . ."

" *August 27th.* Arrived in Inverness two hours late. Met by Alan Cunningham (commanding 51st Division) and Chalmers commanding Area. Flew to Wick where I inspected defence of aerodrome. Then examined neighbouring beaches. Next by car to Skitten aerodrome, Thurso and beaches close by and on to Castletown aerodrome. After discussing defences flew back to Evanton near Invergordon, there met battalion commander and discussed defence of aerodrome. Finally flew back to Inverness. . . ."

" *August 28th.* Motored to Kenton aerodrome; after discussing defence on to Lossiemouth aerodrome. Also looked at beaches nearby. . . . Looked at beaches and on to Dyce aerodrome. Finishing off with Black Watch battalion in Aberdeen. . . . and beaches north of it. Caught 6.40 p.m. train back to London. . . ."

" *August 30th.* Left Hendon at 9 a.m. and flew to Worcester where we arrived at 9.50 a.m. Motored on to 2nd London Division H.Q. to see Signal Exercise. . . . Exercise took us right along valley of the River Usk towards Pembroke. Finally picked up plane again at aerodrome west of Pwll. Had lovely fly back along the Bristol Channel, passing over Cardiff, Bristol, Reading, Henley, Maidenhead. Took one hour and five minutes to return. On landing at Hendon was informed that they had just been watching an air-battle over the aerodrome. We did not miss it by much."

． ． ． ． ． ． ． ．

'The pilots of Fighter Command' Brooke wrote, 'were putting up a performance for which they will remain famous throughout history. There were, however, grave doubts as to whether they could last the course.' On September 1st reports began to come in from R.A.F. photographic reconnaissance of hundreds of barges moving towards the Scheldt and Straits of Dover. Every day during the week the number of vessels photographed in the harbours between Flushing and Havre mounted steadily; on August 31st there were eighteen barges in Ostend, on September 2nd seventy, on the 4th a hundred and fifteen, on the 6th two hundred and five. By that night the concentration of shipping along the French and Flemish coasts was so great that Home Forces issued the preliminary Invasion Alert—" Attack probable within the next three days."

That evening, after a visit to the 1st Armoured Division, Brooke was summoned to Chequers. When he arrived at eight o'clock, his diary records, he

> " found Mrs. Churchill and Dill in hall. Told by him that P.M. had gone to rest, dinner to be at 8.45 p.m. Finally sat down to dinner at 9 p.m. . . . Party consisted of Dill, Ismay, P.M. and self. P.M. warmed up and was most entertaining for rest of evening. First of all he placed himself in the position of Hitler and attacked these shores while I defended them. He then revised the whole of the air-raid warning system and gave us his proposals to criticise. Finally at 1.45 a.m. we got off to bed."
>
> " *September 7th.* All reports look like invasion getting nearer. Ships collecting, dive-bombers being concentrated, parachutists captured, also four Dutchmen on the coast.[1] Drove in from Chequers with Dill. On arriving in office was sent for to attend Chiefs of Staff meeting to discuss latest intercepted message concerning German plans for putting down fog. Back to St. Paul's to discuss expansion of Armoured Forces. Finally dined with Bertie after sending out order for ' Cromwell ' State of Readiness in Eastern and Southern Commands."

But though Alert No. 1—" Invasion imminent and probable within twelve hours "—was sent out, and in some places the Home Guard rang the church bells to announce that the enemy

---

[1] They had landed in a rowing-boat to try to ascertain the movements of Brooke's central reserve in the Ipswich-London-Reading-Oxford area. *Churchill* II, 275-6.

had landed, the condition insisted on by Hitler and the German Admiralty before the Invasion Army embarked had not been fulfilled. Fighter Command was still in being. And, though its numbers were dwindling fast, in the course of the day a remarkable change came over the air war. It was due primarily to Churchill. A fortnight earlier, on August 24th, the first bombs had fallen in the central London area. Though the maximum force available for bombing Germany was scarcely a tenth of what the Luftwaffe could send over England and the distance from its airfields to the German capital six times greater than that between the French coast and London, the Prime Minister had without hesitation proposed the bombing of Berlin. On the night of the 25th eighty-one British aircraft set out, twenty-nine of which reached their objective. Other night raids followed and, though the damage was small, their effect on Hitler's temper was extensive. On September 4th he announced his intention of wiping out London.

Thus, at the moment when growing damage to its control system and airfields and, above all, the cumulative exhaustion of its pilots were causing Fighter Command the gravest anxiety, the enemy made a fatal mistake. By calling off his bombers from the hard-pressed sector stations and loosing them on the capital, Goering gave the country's air defenders the breathing-space they needed. On September 8th—the day on which Brooke's Headquarters sent out the " Cromwell " alert—successive German formations, sailing up the Thames and ignoring the Kentish and Essex airfields, dropped their bombs on the factories, warehouses and working-class dwellings of Woolwich and Dockland. Forty of the raiders and their escorts were shot down, but immense damage was done in the crowded industrial areas and streets of East London, and huge fires were started. That night, by their light, two hundred and fifty bombers flew in again over the capital, dropping 350 tons of bombs and 13,000 incendiaries. For the next week the Germans attacked it day and night. But, though able to drop their bombs without interference in the dark—for there were as yet virtually no night-fighters and London had been stripped of anti-aircraft defences to guard the airfields and aircraft factories—their attempts at systematic target-bombing by day were invariably frustrated by the Spitfires and Hurricanes. Freed from the harassing task of defending their own airfields and control stations, the latter were able to attack with new vigour, while their numbers, reinforced from the training squadrons and factories, steadily recovered. Acting on fresh orders they now concentrated exclusively on Goering's bombers. The ratio of aircraft destroyed rose rapidly once more in Britain's favour.

"*Sunday, September 8th.* Heavy bombing of London throughout the night, the whole sky being lit up by the glow of fires in London docks. Went to the office in the morning where I found further indications of impending invasion. Everything pointing to Kent and East Anglia as the two main threatened points. Went over to Ferney Close for lunch and spent the afternoon and evening in complete paradise with you. . . . Motored back at 8.30 p.m. with air-raid on. Searchlights working in all directions, and a glowing red sky over London. It seemed so strange leaving you and all the wonderful peace and happiness connected with our contented lives to return here for what may well be one of the most eventful weeks in the history of the British Empire."

" I called in at St. Paul's School on the way back, and found that all reports still point to the probability of an invasion starting between the 8th and 10th of this month. The responsibility of feeling what any mistakes or even misappreciations may mean to the future of these isles and of the Empire is a colossal one and . . . staggers me at times. I wish I had more completely trained formations under my orders. But for the present there is nothing to be done but to trust God and pray for His help and guidance."

" *September 9th.* Spent part of the morning in the office, then attended Chiefs of Staff meeting at 10.15 a.m. Returned to St. Paul's School where I worked till lunch. I then lunched with Sir Findlater Stewart to meet Sir John Anderson at the Athenæum. After lunch went to War Office for Selection Board meeting. Returned to St. Paul's

School to see Pownall and continued with office work. Finally left office at 7.45 p.m. and returned to club. Hope for quieter night than last one which was a continuous bombing of London. I counted over sixty bombs fall in vicinity in one hour. Two in St. James's Park, one in Buckingham Palace, Madame Tussaud's destroyed, South Kensington Natural History Museum, many power stations, stations, hospitals, etc."

" *September 10th.* Left Hendon at 10 a.m. for Doncaster. Rather a bumpy journey. Met Adam, Alexander and Percival at the aerodrome. Proceeded to watch an exercise between two Infantry brigades of 42nd Division. Finally left for Hendon again at 6.15 p.m. and landed just after an air-raid warning at 7 p.m. . . . Last night again indiscriminate bombing of London. Still no invasion to-day. I wonder whether he will do anything during the next few days?"

" *September 11th.* Called up early; whilst shaving told that Dill and Anthony Eden wanted to see me at 10 a.m. So went round to War Office to be told that P.M. had been somewhat disturbed by Admiralty paper concerning security of guns mounted in vicinity of Dover. He proposed to visit that sector of the coast to-morrow. Returned to office and worked there rest of day. Evidence of impending invasion has been accumulating all day, more ships moving west down the Channel, intercepted cypher messages, etc. It is still possible that it may be a bluff to hide some other stroke. The next day or two are bound to be very critical."

" *September 12th.* Left the Rag shortly after 8 a.m. and proceeded to pick up Dill and then on to Holborn Viaduct Station which we reached with some difficulty owing to results of night's bombing. Here we joined the P.M.'s train for Shorncliffe. On the way had long talk with P.M. on the organisation of defences on the Narrows. . . . Proceeded to examine 9.2-in. railway guns, coast guns, defence to Dungeness. Then back to Dover for lunch in the castle with Bertie Ramsay. After lunch P.M. wanted to watch air-fight but there was none to see. . . . Party consisted of P.M., First Sea Lord, First Lord of Admiralty, Dill, " Pug " Ismay and self. P.M. was very pleasant and as usual most refreshing and entertaining. His popularity is astounding, everywhere crowds rush up to see him and cheer him wildly, encouraging him with shouts of ' Stick it! ' "

" *September 13th.* Another night of bombing and A.A. fire, but a rainy morning and signs of break in the weather. Spent morning in the office studying increasing evidence of impending invasion. Lunched with Imperial Chemical Industries at Nobel House, where I found them all in the basement sheltering, as Buckingham Palace had just been attacked by a dive bomber. After lunch returned to office, where King-Hall came to see me about defence of aircraft industry. Finally returned to club at 8 p.m. During dinner air-raids started again and A.A. barrage is now going full blast. To-day bombs have been dropped in Horse Guards, House of Lords, War Office, etc. Everything looks like an invasion starting to-morrow from the Thames to Plymouth. I wonder whether we shall be hard at it by this time to-morrow evening?"

" *September 14th.* A quieter night on the whole, but plenty of A.A. fire. Went to see 31st Independent Brigade commanded by Smythe. Got back to the office about 5 p.m. Ominous quiet! German shipping moves greatly reduced and air action too. Have Germans completed their preparations for invasion? Are they giving their air force a last brush and wash up? Will he start to-morrow, or is it all a bluff to pin troops down in this country while he prepares to help Italy to invade Egypt, etc.? "

" *September 15th.* Still no move on the part of the Germans. Everything remains keyed up for an early invasion, and the air war goes on unabated. This coming week must remain a critical one, and it is hard to see how Hitler can now retrace his steps and stop this invasion. The suspense of waiting is very trying, especially when one is familiar with the weakness of one's defences. Our exposed coast line is just twice the length of the front that we and the French were holding in France with about eighty divisions and the Maginot Line. Here we have twenty-two divisions of which only about half can be looked upon as in any way fit for any form of mobile operations. Thank God the spirit is now good and the defeatist opinions expressed after Dunkirk are no longer prevalent. But I wish I could have six months more to finish equipping and training the forces under my command. A responsibility such as that of the defence of this country under existing conditions is one that weighs on one like a ton of bricks, and it is hard at times to retain the hopeful and confident exterior which is so essential to retain the confidence of those under one and to guard against their having any doubts as regards final success. . . . Heavy air-raid on at present and A.A. guns going full blast. Unfortunately the full moon remains uncovered by any clouds. Buckingham Palace was again hit to-day."

' It should not be thought that I considered our position a hopeless one. . . . Far from it. We should certainly have had a desperate struggle and the future might well have hung in the balance, but I felt that, given a fair share of the fortunes of war, we should certainly succeed in finally defending these shores. It must be remembered that, if my diary occasionally gave vent to some of the doubts which the heavy responsibility generated, it was the one and only outlet for such doubts.'

.   .   .   .

From September 8th to the 10th conditions for moon and tide on the south-eastern coast were almost ideal. " No one," Churchill broadcast on September 11th, " should blind himself to the fact that a heavy full-scale invasion of this island is being prepared with all the usual German thoroughness and method, and that it may be launched now—upon England, upon Scotland or upon Ireland, or upon all three. . . . We must regard the next week or so as a very important period in our history. It ranks with the days when the Spanish Armada was approaching the Channel and Drake was finishing his game of bowls; or when Nelson stood between us and Napoleon's Grand Army at Boulogne." Yet the enemy still failed to strike. The German Foreign Minister assured satellite diplomats in Berlin that the blow would fall any day, Mussolini told Ciano that it was a certainty and ordered his generals in Libya to march on Cairo the moment the first patrol landed in England, while Hitler told the world, " If people in England are asking ' Why doesn't he come,' I can put their minds at rest. He's coming! "

But though the invasion Commander-in-Chief, von Rundstedt, expected to reach the Gravesend-Reigate-Petersfield-Portsmouth line within a week of landing, his naval counterpart, Admiral Raeder, was insistent that the preliminary condition for invasion had not been fulfilled. " There is no sign," he reported on the 10th, " of the defeat of the enemy's Air Force over southern England and in the Channel area." Next day Hitler, who had already postponed the date from the 15th to the 21st, postponed it again till the 24th. Although six batteries of long-range guns on the Calais cliffs were now firing at shipping in the Straits and even bombarding Dover, the chance of establishing a quick shuttle service for ferrying troops and tanks across the Narrows had passed. Not only had the British Army become a fighting force which only a major battle could dislodge, but the Navy, having made good the damage suffered during the evacuation, was far stronger in the Channel than in July. The battleship *Revenge*, based on Plymouth, was cruising in the Western Approaches, and growing numbers of destroyers, frigates and patrol boats were operating off the invasion ports. Heartened by the purchase from America of fifty First World War destroyers in return for naval and air bases in the Atlantic colonies, the Admiralty had stripped the ocean convoys of escorts in order to strengthen the flotillas on the enemy coasts. And, having a month earlier delayed the assembly of the invasion fleet by bombing the Dortmund-Ems canal, Bomber Command had switched its attention to the waiting barges in the harbours of Flushing, Ostend, Dunkirk, Calais and Boulogne. Every available aircraft was thrown in against the crowded target—the "Blackpool Front," as it became called—only a few minutes from the English coast. On the night of the 13th alone eighty barges were sunk at Ostend.

On September 14th Hitler again conferred with his naval Commander-in-Chief. Though urged to do so, he refused to call off the invasion until the Luftwaffe had made one more attempt to break the R.A.F. Next day, confident that Fighter Command was down to its last few hundred aircraft, Goering launched on London the most concentrated attack of the whole battle. More than a thousand sorties were made against the capital and the proportion of fighters to bombers sent over was five to one. But the defenders seemed more, not fewer, and their attack on the bombers more devastating than ever. Though Churchill, watching the fight from the Control Room of No. 11 Fighter Group at Uxbridge, saw the R.A.F.'s last reserves thrown in, no formation was able to destroy its target, and fifty-six raiders, including thirty-four of the heavily-guarded bombers, were shot down for a loss of twenty-four.

" Still no invasion," Brooke wrote on the 16th. " Rumour has it that to-night is to be the night. He is certainly being infernally busy in the air and six bombs have come whistling down fairly close to the Rag.[1] . . . Dined with Bertie at the Orleans and walked home in middle of heavy air-raid with sky lit up by burning houses in direction of Charing Cross."

' I have the most vivid recollections of that dinner in the Orleans Club before it was bombed to bits. I had a strong conviction that we were on the eve of the invasion. . . . After dinner I walked back from the Orleans round through St. James's Square to the Army and Navy Club. Only a few yards to go, but that distance has never seemed longer. I had not even got a hat on, and there was a real inferno of a bomb raid, a continual roar of falling bombs and A.A. fire, and through the middle of it that unpleasant vicious hum of A.A. splinters as they came raining down.'

" *September 17th.* Still no invasion, and to-day a mild hurricane which should be stirring up the Channel well. Continual raids last night with heavy anti-aircraft fire. Bombs dropped in Burlington Arcade, Bond Street, Berkeley Square and Park Lane, etc.

" Inspected 42nd Division with brigades in Maidenhead,

[1] The Army and Navy Club where he was sleeping.

Newbury, and Oxford. A good division which will require a good deal more training. Returned at 6.15 p.m. and put in an hour and a half in the office. Now back at the club after dinner and back again into our usual air-raid with the droning of German planes, the crash of bombs and heavy roll of A.A. barrage. It is hard to believe that it is London."

But on that very day, unknown to Brooke, Hitler threw up the sponge. The equinoctial gales were at hand, and, despite replacements, the strength of the air-formations operating against England were by now five hundred below establishment. The casualties among the crews were even more serious. Continuance of such losses could only blunt the weapon with which Germany dominated the Continent.[1] As the High Command needed ten clear days' notice to launch the invasion, it was decided to postpone it *sine die* while continuing to maintain the threat of it and the nightly raids on London. Having failed to capture Britain's Army in France, to penetrate her Navy's guard and to destroy her Air Force, the only way to end the war seemed to be to break the spirit of her people.

" *September 18th.* Another day without invasion. Wind has dropped and weather unfortunately finer. Spent the day in the office with a series of interviews. First Pope to settle future of Armoured Corps. Then Pownall to discuss Home Guard. Then Nosworthy to talk about methods of counter-attack with IV Corps. . . . Last night heavy bombing again, considerable damage in Oxford Street. Every indication continues to look like an invasion being staged, ready to be launched at any time. I wish the weather would really break up."

" *September 19th.* An unpleasant night with heavy bombing in the West End. . . . This morning when going to Hendon we found most roads closed—Piccadilly, Regent Street, Bond Street, North Audley Street, Park Lane. Big cranes round the Marble Arch, etc. Finally left Hendon at 10 a.m. and in twenty minutes had covered seventy miles to Mildenhall. Spent the day . . going round

[1] Already Britain's production rate of aircraft had overhauled Germany's.

the 52nd Division which I found in good form but still
very short of transport. Got back to Hendon just before
7 p.m. and went to St. Paul's for an hour in the office. At
8 p.m. air-raid warning started again and has been on
ever since. Heavy bomb has just fallen in the vicinity
which shook the whole club building."

" *September 20th.* Another night of raids. Went to see
Oliver Leese [and his 29th Independent Brigade. . . .
After lunch returned to the office. . . . Finished by 8 p.m.
and returned to club. . . ."

" *September 21st.* Spent the day in the office. In the
morning had an interview with Director of Military
Training to settle details of the Command Company
Commanders' Course. Then Freyberg came to say good-
bye before starting again for the Middle East. In the
evening came up to see Dill for a long talk. Air-raids
going full blast again to-night. This evening P.M. sent me
paper which had come from Sam Hoare from Spain giving
details of a talk with a reliable American who had
just come from Germany. Speaking on the 7th of this
month he said he was certain that Hitler would attack
within a fortnight. To-day the 21st must be the last day
of that fortnight. Weather prophets predict a quieter
sea."

" *Sunday September 22nd.* After a night of almost continuous air-raids, which did *not* prevent me having a very
good night's sleep, I went to the office and finished work
quickly. Then went home, where I found you all singing
hymns in the drawing-room. It was a wet day but it
might have been brilliant sunshine for the joy of being
back with you. . . . Returning in the evening . . . the
approach to London looked like approaching Dante's
Inferno, continuous flashes of guns and sparks of bursting
shells in the sky with haloes of searchlights."

" *September 23rd.* Still no invasion! A day in the office
with continuous work from 9 a.m. to 8 p.m. without much
let-up. At present again our usual continuous night
raid. . . ."

" *September 25th.* . . . Rather a worse night of ' bumps

and crumps' than usual, with several unpleasantly close. The Savile Row, Burlington Gardens area was again receiving much attention. Spent a day in the office and amongst other things reinforced the North Foreland-Dungeness front by an additional Brigade group and Machine-Gun battalion. It is that narrow neck of sea that constitutes a danger point now that he has all his shipping assembled on the French coast opposite to it. It is very hard to fathom what he really intends to do and whether he still contemplates invasion. The conditions are still very good for it and the sea remains abominably calm."

" *September 26th.* Left the club at 8 a.m. for Hendon. Delayed on the way there owing to results of last night's air-raids. . . . Flew to Old Sarum where we picked up Auchinleck and Ritchie. From there we flew to St. Eval which we reached shortly after 10 a.m. Here Franklyn and Charles Allfrey met us and we proceeded towards Land's End examining the defences of St. Ives and Penzance beaches, also Falmouth defences. Then back by car to St. Eval where we took off for Old Sarum at 5.30 p.m. and dropped Ritchie, going on to Hendon where we arrived just after 7 p.m. and only just in time, as it was getting dark and a ground mist was rising. Reached club about 7.30 p.m., having covered about six hundred miles in the twelve hours."

" *September 27th.* Left club at 8.30 a.m. and, after many obstructions from last night's bombs, reached Hendon just as the air-raid warning started. However, we called up Fighter Command who reported Germans are attacking Biggin Hill and that we could fly north safely. Flew to Liverpool taking one hour and ten minutes owing to head wind. Met by ' Copper ' and Mansergh commanding Tank Brigade. Then went to see Exercise. . . . From there on to see Lumsden and his Armoured Brigade. Then flew back to Hendon, and on to office to work till 8 p.m. To-day is anniversary of my departure for France from Salisbury and our parting outside the County Hotel. I can see your car driving off now when I shut my eyes and can again feel that ghastly desolation that froze into my heart at our having to part."

"*September 28th.* A day spent in the office which included several visits—Pownall coming to say good-bye on going to Ireland, 'Rusty' Eastwood coming to take over from him. Budget Lloyd came to discuss training. Holden to tell me about Beaverbrook's latest attempts at raising a special army of his own. Still always indications of impending invasion. And up to the present no signs that the Germans are proposing to give up the attempt. . . ."

"*September 29th.* . . . This next week should, I feel, bring the matter of invasion to a head. If he intends to try it on I don't feel that he can leave it much later. . . . But I wish the weather would deteriorate. . . ."

By this time, however, not only had the invasion barges—twelve per cent of whose strength had been destroyed—been moved to a position of safety and harmlessness, but the Battle of Britain, which was to have been the prelude to invasion was over. In a day of major operations against the capital on September 27th, the Luftwaffe had lost more than forty-five aircraft to the R.A.F.'s twenty-eight; on the last day of the month it lost another forty-seven to twenty. Thereafter it confined itself to dropping bombs on London in the dark—an activity for which its crews had never been trained nor its aircraft equipped. On October 12th, in great secrecy, Operation "Sea Lion" was postponed till the summer of 1941.

.   .   .   .

II

For a few weeks, until winter set in, the Commander-in-Chief continued to note reports of intended landings and his suspicions of the enemy's intentions. " Still no invasion," he wrote on October 13th. " I am beginning to think that the Germans may, after all, not attempt it. And yet! I have the horrid thought that he still may bring off some surprise on us." Reassured, however, by the spectacle in every street and field of men in khaki—of whose preparedness for modern war they knew only what official propaganda told them—his phlegmatic countrymen had by now dismissed the invasion as a Nazi bogey; early in October Brooke recorded, a little wryly, a visit by an official of the Jockey Club " who wished to carry on the Newmarket race-meetings as if no war existed." Even the King, who entertained him to lunch at Windsor to discuss plans for defending the Castle against paratroops, spoke of his hopes of returning to Sandringham in one of the most exposed coastal areas in the country.

" *October 16th.* . . . Spent the day with the 1st London Division going round Ramsgate salient, the bay immediately south of it, Deal, etc. The more I look at that salient the more I dislike it. We are definitely too weak there, but I have nothing else to add to that part without depleting other fronts dangerously."

" I have now all moves prepared to get divisions back to train but do not yet dare to do so. The most recent reports point to preparations for an invasion-try on foot, a force being assembled in the Scheldt on a programme lasting some seven days. The information is fairly reliable, but it is difficult to believe that the Germans would attempt a serious invasion at this time of the year. Luckily at present it is raining and an overcast sky, so we may have a less disturbed night than the last two."

" *October 17th.* Evidence is amassing . . . of an impending invasion of some kind or other. Rotterdam is filling up with shipping. I have asked for it to be heavily bombed and for continuous reconnaissance of the Scheldt. . . ."

" *October 24th.* Another quiet night with little bomber activity, and not much doing during the day. Is this the lull before the storm? To-morrow is supposed to be a dangerous date from the point of view of moon and tide. . . . The weather is certainly very unfavourable for the launching of any large-scale attack. And yet it would be unwise to surmise that all was safe. It is just possible that under the cloak of Hitler's visit to Franco on the French-Spanish frontier, when all eyes are turned in that direction, a sudden blow might be directed at England."

None, however, fell, and the general belief grew that, though Hitler might resume his attempt to invade in the spring, his next move would be in the Mediterranean. General Graziani's " Army of Egypt," outnumbering the British in the Western Desert by five to one, had by now advanced to Mersa Matruh, a hundred and fifty miles from Alexandria, making Mussolini, who hoped to enter Cairo like a Roman Emperor, " radiant with joy."[1] It was decided therefore to transfer still more of Brooke's scanty armour to the Nile Valley and he was informed that by the end of November he would have to part with the whole of the 1st Armoured Division. With so little with which to defend herself and her vast, exposed empire, Britain could not afford to let tanks or aircraft stand idle in one part of the world while they were urgently needed in another. Yet the dilemma for those entrusted with the responsibility of holding both the United Kingdom and the Middle East was that the armies of the Axis lay between and could strike at either, and that armour and aircraft, once shipped from England to Egypt, could not be brought back in time should the enemy make another invasion attempt.

Meanwhile the Luftwaffe persisted in its attempt to break the nation's morale by destroying London. Though it could no longer do so by day, for sixty-seven nights it bombed the capital without a break. Except once or twice, when his

[1] *Ciano,* 17th September, 1940.

journeys of inspection took him so far afield that he was forced to spend a night in Scotland or the North, Brooke invariably returned to sleep in London while there remained any possibility of a German landing. His nights, therefore—spent in the Army and Navy Club in the heart of Whitehall—were anything but quiet.

"*October 14th.* Left office at 8 p.m. in middle of heavy air-raid with sky lit up by flares. Arrived outside club to find the whole street littered with glass, and car unable to drive down Pall Mall. The Carlton Club had been hit by a bomb and set on fire. It is burning hard now and my room here is thick with smoke from it. There are several fire-engines working and they seem to be getting it under control. . . . The moon is unfortunately far too bright."

"*October 15th.* The Germans were very active last night in these parts. Besides burning out the Carlton Club, they hit the Monico, Burton's and the church in Piccadilly, landed one in St. James's Square and one on the steps at the bottom end of Regent Street. There they unfortunately killed Admiral Tower, my chief naval liaison officer. . . . To-night they are hard at it again. . . ."

"*October 16th.* The most noisy night we have had yet and I was kept awake till 3.30 a.m. by continual bombing. Several pretty close, including a parachute mine in St. James's Park, which blew in all the windows of Buckingham Palace and most houses surrounding the Park. . . ."

" It is a queer life," Brooke noted after a month of it, " knowing that bombs are being carted about the sky over one's head and may be released at any moment. . . . One can only thank God for the Providence that guards over one, and leave the whole matter in His hands."[1] Not till November 11th was he able to start his diary with the words: " Pouring rain and up to now a lovely quiet night with no bombers." Only then, when the Germans began to switch their attack to the ports and the industrial Midlands, did he move to less exposed sleeping-quarters at St. Paul's School, Hammersmith—a far quieter part of the town. ' I remained,' he wrote, ' till the 17th of November

[1] *Diary*, 8th November, 1940.

in rooms of the Army and Navy Club facing out on to Pall Mall and always slept in my bed no matter what the bombing was like.'

How great the strain was for a man bearing his burden of work and responsibility can be seen from an entry for a Saturday in that November.

> "*November 16th.* A real unpleasant night, and from midnight to close on 5 a.m. there was almost incessant bombing of the vicinity of the Rag. The Orleans Club only about 150 yards away was hit; another dropped in bottom of St. James's Street, two in St. James's Square, one in Duke Street, two in Lloyds Bank, one in the Carlton and one in Hamptons, besides several in St. James's Park. Hamptons caught fire and burned nearly most of the night with noisy arrival of fire-engines. I got up to look out of the window; it was a weird sight looking east to see the end of the street one blaze of flame. . . . Got up feeling very sleepy, spent day in the office and at 5 p.m. started for Ditchley Park, Enstone, . . . where the P.M. was spending the week-end instead of Chequers owing to the full moon and the fear of night attacks by bombers. I dreaded the thought of being kept up till 2 a.m. by the P.M. in my sleepy mood. However, I slept in the car on the way out, and the evening went off better than I had hoped for and I was in bed by 2 a.m."

.   .   .   .

For Brooke the main activity of that winter was training, ceaseless, tough and regardless of weather, to turn a half-amateur Army into a professional one and ensure that, when the spring came, Britain would no longer be as defenceless on land as it had been in the previous summer. At first the Exercises he organised were aimed at repelling invasion; later, as the danger receded, the stress shifted to fitting selected contingents of Home Forces for active service overseas. Some of these Exercises were large-scale theoretical ones to test the higher Command; others were conducted in the field on a divisional, brigade or even battalion level. An example of the former was recorded in the diary for the first week of January 1941.

"*Sunday January 5th, 1941.* . . . In evening went over to Staff College for the big Exercise on Armoured Forces that I am running there. . . . Gave opening address after dinner. Very large gathering, all five Army commanders, six Corps commanders and all Armoured Divisional commanders and Armoured Brigade commanders. After opening address we had a lecture by Military Intelligence, War Office, on German Armoured Divisions."

"*January 6th.* Lecture in the morning on Armoured Divisional organisation, Signal lay-out and Administrative organisation. After lunch demonstration of parachutist gliders, bridging, and various types of armoured vehicles. After dinner Dill came from War Office and gave an excellent lecture. He was in better form than I had seen him for a long time."

"*January 7th.* A hard day. Started with Ritchie on Air Co-operation and spent rest of day on running our Armoured Divisional Exercise. I found it a heavy strain listening to successive answers and making up criticisms and serving up remarks as we went along. Snow and very cold."

"*January 8th.* Finished up final situations of Armoured Exercise and then made my final remarks. The latter gave me an opportunity of instilling a little more offensive spirit into the Army and also of expressing my views as regards the present stagnation of higher training. . . . Put in afternoon in office. Quiet night with no bombing. . . ."

"*January 9th.* Spent day in the office catching up on back work. Nasty clear moonlight night and Germans active again."

A week later a similar Exercise was held at Minley—an annexe of the Staff College—for the commanders of all armoured units down to brigade level.

More often these Exercises were conducted, not in the class rooms of Camberley, but in the wintry landscape of the shires and wolds where Britain's Army lay awaiting an invader. There

were few weeks that winter and in the following summer when
Brooke did not attend one or more of these[1] or spend at least
a day watching or visiting some battle or training school.
Four days after the Armoured Corps exercise was over, in
bitterly cold weather he directed an invasion test under as
realistic conditions as possible.

> " *January 22nd.* Did a tour of inspection of the 55th
> Division till about 3 p.m. and then motored back to
> London to take part in our large-scale Home-Defence
> Exercise which began to-day. We have moved the whole
> Administrative G.H.Q. to our Battle H.Q. and I am
> sleeping in my battle dug-out next to my office for the
> next three nights. So far in the Exercise the Germans have,
> invaded the Canary Islands, Iceland, and Ireland."
>
> " *January 23rd.* Home Defence Exercise in full swing
> all day with invasion developing all over the coast from
> Scotland to Devon. Headquarters moving smoothly."
>
> " *January 24th.* Another day of hard fighting in the
> Exercise. The Secretary of State and the C.I.G.S. came
> round in the afternoon to see how the Exercise was going."
>
> " *January 25th.* Closed down the Exercise at 1 p.m. and
> went home for the week-end. Glad to get out of the
> stuffiness of my underground office and bedroom."

After which, the Commander-in-Chief recorded, he spent
Sunday at home " carpentering and blowing my nose owing
to a cold."

Recalling this period of intensive training in a letter to
Wavell later in the war, Brooke wrote,

> " I agree with you that we are not anything like as
> tough as we were in the last war. There has been far too
> much luxury, safety-first, Red-Triangle, etc., in this
> country. Our one idea is to look after our comforts and
> avoid being hurt in any way. That is why during the
> whole of my time in command of Home Forces I insisted
> on protracted Exercises lasting several days, in all weathers,

---

[1] " Got up at 5.15 a.m. to watch 1st Armoured Division exercise. Exercise
based on one I had carried out theoretically during the winter." *Diary,* 1st May,
1941.

winter and summer, and with long marches of thirty miles and over."[1]

It involved for the Commander-in-Chief dividing his time between long office hours in a blitzed and blacked-out city and days in wet or snow-covered fields, preceded and followed by long journeys by rail, road and air.

" *January 2nd.* Left Hendon by air for Liverpool at 11 a.m. Weather bitterly cold and the country below covered in snow. Met by " Copper," and visited one of the new Beach Infantry brigades with him. Then inspected his new battle-headquarters and remained in his office with him till 8.30 p.m. . . . Streaming cold and feeling rotten."

" *January 3rd.* Left at 9 a.m. to visit Junior Leaders' School, Company Commanders' School and one battalion (K.O.S.B.) of the 5th Division. Weather still bitterly cold and my cold in the head streaming. Caught 3 p.m. train from Crewe, arrived Euston three hours late with nasty head produced by cold. . . ."

" *January 21st.* Started at 10 a.m. to visit 55th Division. Found them busy doing a Divisional Training Exercise with tanks which finished after lunch. . . . Very cold and slushy snow all over the Cotswold hills still. . . ."

" *January 28th.* Up at 6.30 a.m. to watch march of 15th Division in the dark. Very unpleasant day and cold in my head bad."

" *February 25th.* Left Kings X at 10 a.m. for York where I arrived at 1.40 p.m. and was met by Adam. We then proceeded in direction of Bridlington to watch Exercise carried out by 2nd Division. Very cold and whole country covered with snow. . . ."

" *February 27th.* Left again at 8.45 a.m. for Lincolnshire to see Exercise of 1st Division near Louth. A poisonous day. Bitter cold, rain and sleet driven by a north wind that was sweeping over a snow-covered country. . . ."

' I had often admired the railway-posters of summer-resorts recommending *Bright Breezy Bridlington* and it certainly lived

[1] Brooke to Wavell, 5th July, 1942.

up to that reputation on that February day. . . . Under such conditions it is hard to maintain the enthusiasm of troops in training. And yet those winter Exercises were essential, and and I have the most vivid recollection of that heartening enthusiasm displayed by all ranks under the most trying conditions.'

Whenever possible, in order to crowd the maximum of work into his day, Brooke flew. During his first year as Commander-in-Chief he covered 14,000 miles by air and motored 35,000 miles in his own car and about the same distance in other people's. While in the air he always studied the map, so as to make himself master of the country he might one day have to fight over. Much of this flying was carried out under adverse weather-conditions. " Blizzard of rain was blowing and impossible to see across aerodrome," he wrote of one journey in October 1940,

> " waited for rain to blow over and then got on board, but starboard engine refused to start. ' Booster coil ' was fused; this entailed more delay to replace it, and it was 4.10 p.m. by the time we got off. Very strong head-wind and damnably rough. . . ."[1]
>
> " *May 13th*, 1941. Finished meeting at 1.30 p.m. I rushed for Hendon where I took off for the Orkneys at 2 p.m. . . . Only reached Glasgow at 6.30 p.m. . . . Told weather conditions were very bad so had to strike across to east coast, hitting Dundee and working up the coast past Aberdeen and round via Lossiemouth and Nairn. Finally arrived at Inverness at 7.45 p.m. Took off again in five minutes and, after a very good fly, landed at Kirkwall at 8.50 p.m."

In the middle of the winter, when flying became too uncertain to be relied on, Brooke made his longer journeys by train, with all the delays caused by enemy bombing.

> " *November 28th*, 1940. . . . From Bridlington returned to York where I visited Mechanised Transport School. . . . I then caught 5.50 p.m. train back to London and only

[1] *Diary*, 9th October, 1940.

arrived at King's X at 3.15 a.m., five hours late on a four-hours' run. This was due to an air-raid on Liverpool which caused train to run dead slow."

At the start of Brooke's second winter as Commander-in-Chief, realising the heavy burden imposed by such journeys, the Prime Minister provided him with a special train—" Rapier " —so that he could combine office work with his journeys. 'He had realised,' Brooke wrote, 'how much continuous travelling I had to do and very kindly on his own arranged for this. It would have been a God-send had I had it earlier, but as it was, it turned out most useful during the rest of the war and was used regularly by Paget when he succeeded me. ... It had a dining-car divided into two compartments, making a very comfortable sitting-room and dining-room, the sitting-room being well fitted up with writing-table, sofa and chairs. There was also a full sleeping compartment, and a truck to take a car.' On November 19th, 1941, Brooke recorded his first—and only—day's journey in it.

.   .   .   .

Much of Brooke's time as Commander-in-Chief was spent trying to improve the Army's still hopelessly inadequate equipment. His political chiefs, whose military experience dated from days when mechanization had been in its infancy, were apt at this stage of the war to assume that all the Army needed was plenty of tanks, rifles and field guns, and to forget that land fighting now called for almost as many precision-instruments as sea and air fighting. At the beginning of 1941 his forces were still without the most elementary requirements. Scarcely anything had been done before 1939 to equip the Army for Continental warfare, the little that had been extemporised for it had been lost in Dunkirk, and the other two Services, as the country's first line of defence, were inevitably being given first claim on production. After a Commanders-in-Chief's conference in January 1941, Brooke wrote,

' I raised the lamentable lack of arms that still prevailed after one and a half years of war. Shortage of rifles, .303 ammunition, tracer ammunition, Bofors rifles and their

ammunition, anti-tank guns, tanks, armoured cars, etc.
This did not please Winston at all, and after the meeting
he complained to Dill that he considered it most ungrateful
of me to complain of lack of equipment after all that had
been done for me. . . . I considered that I had every right,
and indeed it was my duty to draw attention to the shortages that prevailed.'[1]

During 1940 vast numbers of men had been called up, put
into khaki and drafted into the Infantry—the only branch of
the Army able to absorb and train them. But, as the defeat of
France had proved, hordes of immobile infantry armed with
the weapons of the past were useless against highly trained,
highly mechanised, mobile forces armed with the latest
weapons of speed and destruction. And to maintain an Army
in the field against the *blitzkrieg* a vast organization had to be
created in its rear of workshops and mobile repair-units, stores
and ordnance depots, roads, railways and docks to make good
the appalling wastage of modern war and ensure that the
fighting man had the weapons, ammunition and spare parts he
needed on the day of battle.

So long as the Army was based on the United Kingdom
with its civilian factories, communications, supply and medical
facilities, the half-equipped infantry masses whom Brooke
commanded possessed a striking-power far greater than they
could enjoy overseas. Even a single infantry division, formerly
of 15,000 men, serving abroad, now absorbed 42,000 men,
a large proportion of them skilled craftsmen, in addition to
Corps, Lines of Communication and Base troops required to
support it. The demand on man-power and material of an
Armoured Division—and Britain's long-term military policy
was to create as many of these as possible—was even greater.[2]
To fight the Germans on equal terms the Army needed

[1] *Notes on My Life*, IV, 250.
[2] At a royal inspection at Newmarket in the autumn of 1941, when new
technical equipment for the Army was beginning at last to flow from the factories,
Brooke remarked to General Martel, the Commander of the Royal Armoured
Corps, "Heavens, we should all get the sack if Winston could see all that
transport ! What on earth is that ? " " Divisional Signal Waggon, sir." " Looks
to me more like a Rajah's Purdah Waggon ! " *Communicated by Lt.-Col. R. Stanyforth,
Lord Alanbrooke's Military Assistant.*

electricians, instrument-makers, fitters, blacksmiths, armourers, wheelers, turners, coppersmiths and a whole host of trades- men.   When, after sixteen months as Commander-in-Chief, Brooke became professional Head of the Army, one of his early steps was to establish a new corps—the Royal and Electric and Mechanical Engineers or R.E.M.E.—to service repair the new instruments of reconnaissance, movement and fire-power without which, the best troops in the world were helpless against those possessing them.

Commanding Britain's principal army—the force which would both have to defend her in the event of invasion and out of which her overseas armies would have to be formed— Brooke's responsibility for setting the pattern of future equip- ment and armament was very great. His task would have been far easier had the country been at peace, as it had been in the years when the R.A.F. was rearming itself with new fighters. But as the Army was already engaged in a campaign which necessitated constant replacements to meet the wastage of desert warfare, the factories were forced to go on manufacturing obsolescent weapons and equipment instead of switching over at once to the production of the new prototypes for which Brooke and his fellow-generals were asking.   And it was difficult for any parliamentary politician, particularly one as impatient for results as the Prime Minister, to acquiesce in the accumulation of reserve tanks, equipment and spares—essential for any sustained battle—when existing first-line formations were waiting for them. Of the meetings summoned by the Prime Minister in the summer of 1941 between the makers of tanks and those responsible for their use in action, Brooke wrote on June 19th:

> "Attended 'Tank Paliament' run by P.M. at which I pressed for a better spare-part organization and for the necessity of maintaining some twenty per cent spare armoured fighting vehicles per formation. This was not appreciated by the P.M. who likes to put the whole of his goods in the front window."

'This failure to provide adequate spare-parts for tanks, accounted for many of our failures and early difficulties in armoured fighting in North Africa. . . . Had Winston listened to me at this period we should have avoided a great deal of the spare-part chaos which prevailed in Egypt at a later date and which literally brought operations to a stand-still. Unfortunately Beaverbrook aided and abetted in this false spare-part outlook.'[1]

Brooke's diary for 1941 contains repeated references to his attempts to improve the quality of British tanks and of the weapons for destroying enemy ones.

" *April 29th.* . . . Went to Bisley to see demonstration of new anti-tank weapon. Mainly based on the new " cutting explosive " and was very much impressed by the results. Am going to press hard for their rapid development. . . ."

" *Saturday May 10th.* . . . Went on with Martel to Luton to see the new heavy tank (some 35 tons), the A.22., which is now nearing completion. Had a drive round and took over the steering from the dual-control seat of the howitzer gunner. Then visited factory to see tanks constructed on motor-car principle. The tank promises extraordinary well. I wish we had a hundred of them. . . ."

" *June 3rd.* Left Hendon at 10.15 a.m. for Birmingham where I was met by Lord Nuffield and went round the factory making the Mark VI cruiser tank and also inspected the mock-up of the Mark VIII cruiser. . . ."

" *June 18th.* . . . Left Hendon at 10 a.m. and flew to Netheravon. From there motored to Larkhill to see demonstration of anti-tank weapons. I was disappointed with the standard reached and shall start a campaign to improve matters."

" *June 19th.* Interviewed a Mr. Glancy, an American business man, on tank production in the U.S.A. and the desirability of instilling it with more drive. . . ."

" *July 10th.* After an early breakfast I left for Hendon at 8 a.m. From there I flew to Netheravon to go to Larkhill to watch some anti-tank trials. Some improvement since I last saw them but much more improvement required. Took off from Netheravon again

[1] *Notes on My Life*, IV, 271, 281.

at 12.30 p.m. for London where I arrived in time for late lunch."

" *July 19th.* In the morning Mr. Thomas from Nuffield Works came with models of Bofors mounted on tank which I had asked him for. I had a meeting of experts to examine it, but, as it cuts across the cruiser-tank production, I decided to mount it in a wheeled vehicle for the present."

" *September 9th.* Left 8 a.m. for Hendon. Weather very thick and only just able to take off for Netheravon. Motored on to Larkhill for anti-tank trials and conference on improvements. Anti-tank shooting beginning to make some progress. Had 2 pr., 6 pr., 75 mm., Bofors and 3.7 A.A. guns all firing. Very glad to find that Bofors with Kenison Predictor came up to my expectation. . . . Left for Netheravon at 12.45, landing Hendon 2 p.m. . . ."

" *November 7th.* Spent the morning in the office with various interviews. After lunch went to see Kenison's most recent inventions and the possibility of applying modern anti-aircraft methods for anti-tank purposes. I feel that there is a great deal to be done to improve anti-tank shooting of all kinds."

" *November 10th.* Motored to Salisbury Plain in the morning to see further anti-tank demonstration. I think we have made some progress in the last six months."

A subject to which Brooke devoted almost as much time was air co-operation with ground troops. His experiences in France had made him a fanatic about this. He maintained the closest relations with Fighter Command, at whose Headquarters at Stanmore he had worked before the war when commanding Anti-Aircraft Command and whose Commander-in-Chief, Air Chief Marshal Sir Sholto Douglas was an old friend, having been his fellow Instructor at the Imperial Defence College. " After lunch," he wrote on June 4th, " went out to Stanmore to discuss with Sholto Douglas the question of protection of fighter aerodromes and also the question of fighter support for military forces in the event of invasion. I found him all out to help and full of assistance. It is a great help having worked with him for two years at the Imperial

Defence College." Later that year Brooke was greatly struck by a demonstration Sholto Douglas arranged for him by cannon-firing fighter aircraft attacking lorried infantry and guns.

> ". . . Most impressive. There is no doubt that the single-seater multiple machine-gun fighter is destined to play a serious part in ground attacks. Left to their own devices they could destroy long columns even spaced out at 150 yards between vehicles. I must take steps to provide for their protection in future. The cannon-aircraft may, when equipped with a heavier gun . . . become a formidable weapon against tanks."

Brooke was always pressing for specially trained and equipped squadrons to serve with the Army, and here he found himself at cross-purposes with the R.A.F. planners, whose aim was to achieve the end he sought, not by the use of aircraft operating under direct military command as under the German system, but by winning unchallenged strategic and tactical control of the air.

> " *December 9th, 1940.* In the afternoon conference by Anthony Eden on the new Army Co-operation Command of the Air Force. . . . Deplorable situation as regards Army Co-operation generally. No machines and not likely to materialise for some time. . . ."
>
> " *May 13th, 1941.* . . . Attended second 'Tank Parliament' 10 Downing Street. Beaverbrook took the chair to start with when we discussed maintenance and spare parts. Next item was Air Co-operation, and assembly was enlarged for this. . . . Before we had finished I became a bit heated and attacked Air Ministry strongly as regards recent attitude towards Army Co-operation. P.M. backed me strongly and meeting was great success."

Of this meeting Brooke wrote afterwards:

> ' This was at a time when the . . . . attitude was growing fast that the war could best be won by a vast bombing effort. . . . The Air Ministry looked upon the re-entry of the

Army on to the Continent as most improbable and probably quite unnecessary. As a result, the main effort was directed towards production of large four-engine bombers quite unsuitable to Army Co-operation. The old Army Co-operation planes were dead, no new ones were being produced and, what is more, method and doctrines of co-operation between land and air were going to the wall. It was from the Army's point of view a continuous battle, and one that was not easy to fight, as the Air Ministry took the attitude that they, at any rate, were actively engaged in killing Germans, and that it was improbable that the Army would be able to do so in Europe.'[1]

Yet, despite his differences with the Air Ministry, Brooke was the most air-minded of soldiers. He was always trying to train troops to use the air, and he became the chief British exponent of the use of airborne forces.

> " *December 3rd, 1940.* Paget picked me up at 7.30 a.m. and we motored to Tilshead where we met Montgomery. We first of all saw the use of parachutists. Thirty-two were dropped by four planes from a height of about 500 feet. Only one man was slightly hurt by twisting his knee. I was very much impressed and feel certain that we must develop an Airborne Brigade with the least possible delay, probably in Canada."

Just before he ceased to be Commander-in-Chief, Brooke took that fine officer, Major-General Browning, from the Guards Armoured Training Group and appointed him to command the first British Airborne Division. Another remarkable soldier whom he employed on the same pioneer work was Brigadier, now General, Sir Richard Gale, commander of the earliest Parachute Brigade.

.   .   .   .

While Brooke was trying to secure for the Army the weapons it would need if it ever returned to the Continent, he was selecting and training the commanders who would one day

[1] *Notes on My Life*, IV, 272.

lead it in the field. One of the objects of the Exercises he was always holding was to enable him to test the quality of his subordinates and replace those who, in his opinion, would be unable to stand the shock of modern war. At first he was often far from satisfied; " a very useful exercise," he wrote of one operation at Ipswich in November, 1940, " judging by the number of mistakes I saw." " Rather a sleepy and podgy division," he reported on another seen soon afterwards, in a bitter north wind, in the West Country. Later he became better pleased. " Spent the day inspecting the 9th Armoured Division," he wrote on March 19th, 1941. " It is making great strides and should make a grand division eventually."

Most of those who held high command in the latter years of the war served under Brooke in Home Forces. Among those he picked for promotion were Brian Horrocks, the future commander of the 10th Corps at Alamein, and Richard McCreery who was to become Chief of Staff in the Middle East and Tunisia. Many senior officers failed to come up to his exacting standards; " it is lamentable," he wrote, " how poor we are in Army and Corps commanders; we ought to remove several, but Heaven knows where we shall find anything very much better. . . . The flower of our manhood was wiped out some twenty years ago and it is just some of those that we lost then that we require now." But three of his principal commanders enjoyed his full confidence: Bernard Paget—the hero of the Norwegian campaign—who was his Chief of Staff during the invasion autumn and whom he later recommended to succeed him at Home Forces, and the two imperturbable soldiers who had served under him in France, Harold Alexander and Bernard Montgomery. The first of these at first commanded a Corps in the north of England and later became G.O.C.-in-C., Southern Command; the other, in the spring of 1941, was given the crucial anti-invasion front in south-east England. ' Monty,' Brooke wrote, ' came to lunch with me as I wanted to put him into the picture with regard to the Corps he was taking over from " Bulgy " Thorne on the dangerous salient of the coast. It was always a pleasure to hand over any job to him; he was so quick at grasping all the essentials and so very pleasant to deal with.'[1]

.   .   .   .

Until the Germans struck at Russia in the summer of 1941 Brooke's first concern was the defence of Britain against invasion. Even after Hitler's attack on Russia, the thought of it was never far from his mind, for, if the U.S.S.R. went the way of France—and from July till November there seemed every possibility she might—a far more formidable attempt on the British Isles was certain. The steady withdrawal of forces from Britain, especially of trained forces, to fight in other parts of the world was a source of continuing anxiety to the Commander-in-Chief.

" *March 13th, 1941.* . . . The rumour season is beginning to accentuate itself. Where are the Germans going to push next? I would not be surprised to see a thrust into Russia. In many ways this is far the most promising line of action. However, wherever the next thrust may be on the Continent it is certain that the process of attempted strangulation will continue with attacks on trade routes, Western Approaches, western ports and Industry. And if these attempts are sufficiently successful, eventually invasion will be attempted. Meanwhile the preparation of our Forces makes good progress."

" *April 4th.* . . . Just heard that I am to lose another Tank brigade. . . .'"

" *April 21st.* Left Ferney Close 8 a.m. Arrived office at 9.15. Spent an hour doing office work. Then attended meeting of Minister for Home Security (Herbert Morrison), attended by Ministers for Health, Education, Food, Transport, Scotland, etc. . . . We were discussing desirability of allowing holiday-makers to visit East Coast. From the arguments put forward one might well have imagined that no war was on."

" . . . . After lunch attended Secretary-of-State's conference till 5 p.m. Followed by visit from . . . Martel to

[1] *Notes on My Life,* IV, 268.

discuss impending withdrawal of some sixty cruiser tanks
. . . . for the Middle East. It is an appalling blow as far
as the defence of this country is concerned. . . ."

" *October 27th.* . . . Another extraction of armoured
forces from this country this evening in the shape of a
brigade from the 6th Armoured Division. When will
War Office learn not to break up armoured formations
which it has taken months to build up? "

In the light of later events and of the immense maritime
preparations that had to be made before Britain and America
were able to stage a cross-Channel invasion in 1944, Brooke's
fears in 1940 and 1941 may seem to have been needless. But
in view of the deficiencies in military armaments and the
bleakness of the global situation, it was only natural that he
should warn his political superiors of the danger of relaxing
anti-invasion precautions or of withdrawing too large a
percentage of the country's inadequate mobile and armoured
forces. He had several clashes over this with the Prime
Minister, whose mind was now wholly set on the offensive.

" *Sunday February 2nd, 1941.* . . . Had to leave at 6 p.m.
to go over to Chequers where I was due for the night.
. . . . Party consisted of P.M. Mrs. Churchill and
daughter, Anthony Eden and wife, Attlee, Professor
Lindemann, and secretary. After dinner epidiascope was
produced and I had to give a lecture on our recent Home
Defence Exercise. They were all three very interested
in it and the P.M. very flattering about the defensive
measures that had been taken. But he would not acknowledge that an invasion of this country on that scale
was possible in the face of partial sea-control and local
air-control."

' I had to . . . explain exactly what the German dispositions
had been for invasion and what measures I had taken to
counter their moves. Winston's reactions were very typical.
He was quite flattering about the dispositions I had taken,
but he criticised the scale of the German attack. He considered that the umpires had exaggerated the German threat

of invasion. He even implied that this had been done in order to influence him into considering the threat greater than it really was. I assured him that this was not the case; that no one connected with the Exercise even knew that he would wish to be made familiar with it. I pressed on him the fact that from the umpires' point of view it was essential to test out the defence with the fullest possible threat. Nothing that I said had much effect; his suspicious nature had been roused.'[1]

A few months later, when Britain's military forces were becoming increasingly involved in the Middle East, a proposal of Brooke's to stage a large-scale Exercise in London against possible parachute landings was turned down by the Cabinet on the ground that it was unnecessary and would alarm the public. ' I had been worried,' he wrote,

> ' by the possibility of the Germans combining an air-borne attack on London with their invasion. There was ample room for a series of parachute landings in the large London Parks. The more I examined those possibilities the more I realised the chaos which such landings would create. If they occurred at night it would be necessary to rush troops into London, and their arrival would clash with the morning flow of men, women, milk, vegetables, fruit, fish, etc. I therefore prepared an exercise to test out the very complicated arrangements required to minimise the chances of chaos. . . . '[2]

Even though by then the tide of war had receded and was flowing eastwards, it might return at any time, and Brooke, who had seen the fall of France, knew, better than any man, the full force of the shock Britain would have to face.

" Left Ferney Close this morning," he wrote in his diary after a brief spell of leave,

> " and motored back to London with a distinct ' going back to school ' feeling. Rather a sinking at heart at the thought of shouldering again the burden of responsibility

[1] *Notes on My Life*, IV, 253.
[2] *Notes on My Life*, IV, 277.

and all the worries and doubts which . . . are not always easy to keep down. . . . Have I really taken the proper dispositions for the defence of this country? Am I sufficiently insured in the South-East? Can I reinforce this corner without taking undue risks in the North? Am I under-appreciating the air threat? Ought I to further denude the beaches to cover the aerodromes? If I do, am I opening the door to sea-invasion? Will the air-support be as efficient as the Air Ministry would like us to believe? How long will the Navy take to concentrate its forces in Home waters? Shall we be able to hold the thrust of Armoured divisions in Kent during this period? These are all questions where a wrong answer may mean the end of life as we have known it in this country and the end of the British Empire."

. . . .

After his failure in the autumn of 1940 Hitler was faced by a dilemma. If he attempted to invade England and failed, he would lose not only much prestige and the whole of Germany's available shipping, but, by depriving himself of the means of making another attempt, release the growing British Army and Air Force for operations elsewhere. As he put it, he was " in the position of a man with only one round left in his rifle; if he missed, the situation would be worse than before." If, on the other hand, he left the islanders alone, with the support of their backers in the United States they would grow steadily stronger, particularly in the air, and ultimately confront him with that major war on two fronts it had been his object to avoid.

For to the east of the Reich, incorporating the plains of eastern Poland and the Ukraine and the Caucasian oilfields he had resolved to conquer, lay the Communist Empire of Russia, with its vast resources and population and its Ten Years' Plan of industrialisation, threatening Hitler with a mechanised military power that would presently surpass his own. Sooner or later, if he delayed his eastward march, he knew he would have to face a Russian attack—a possibility of which he had been unpleasantly reminded during his summer campaign in the West when the U.S.S.R. had annexed the Baltic States and Rumanian Bessarabia. For all their fear of his victorious Army and professions of friendship, the Soviet leaders were only playing for time. It seemed, therefore, essential for the German leader, if he could not induce Britain to make peace, either to rid himself of her by sudden invasion, or, alternatively, to keep her growing air and land forces tied down by the threat of it until the Soviet colossus had been dealt with.

In the winter of 1940-41 and spring of 1941, however, there was an alternative. It was one which both the Head of the Luftwaffe, Goering, and the German naval Commander-in-Chief, Raeder, were pressing on Hitler. This was to join Italy in attacking Britain's weakly-held bases in the Mediterranean and Middle East, capture the Suez Canal and the Persian and Iraq oilfields, and, cutting the last link of the Balkan States and Turkey with the West, either force them to throw in their lot with the Axis or use them as an involuntary corridor through which to encircle the Black Sea, establish air-bases within striking distance of the Caucasian oil-wells and outflank Russia from the south. One German Army Group under von Rundstedt, it was suggested, should advance through Spain to occupy Gibraltar, Algeria and Tunisia, another under von Bock cross through Italy into Tripolitania to conquer Egypt, and a third under von List drive through Jugoslavia and Greece to the Bosphorus and Anatolia.[1]

It was this that those responsible for Britain's strategy most feared. And, despite their inadequate armaments, under Churchill's bold leadership they had taken immense risks to prevent it. At a time when their Fleet was desperately strained both to defend Britain and keep open her global trade-routes, they had doubled their naval forces in the Mediterranean and sent part of their scanty armour to hold the Nile Delta and Suez Canal—the link between Asia and Africa, the Mediterranean and Indian Ocean on which, more than any other spot on earth except Britain itself, the defence of the free world depended. Even before the Battle of Britain had been won and the threat of invasion lifted, they had realized that their strategic problem had ceased to be parochial and become

[1] M. Shulman, *Defeat in the West*, 56-7.

global. Their business was not merely to defend their own shores but to maintain a ring of salt water and desert round the forces that had conquered Europe. While with her left arm Britain guarded her home seas and skies, with her right, half-encircling the Continent, she had to hold the Atlantic waters, the Straits of Gibraltar, the Egyptian desert, the Eastern Mediterranean and Middle East. So long as she did so, despite their domination of Europe, Hitler and Mussolini could not conquer the world. Short of knocking her out by invasion or attacking Russia, they had to break that outstretched arm before they could overrun Asia and Africa.

Yet in the winter of 1940-41 this did not seem difficult. Britain's arm was dangerously weak and extended, the striking power of Germany and Italy tremendously strong. Four battle-ships in the eastern Mediterranean and two in the western, based on Alexandria and Gibraltar, and some 55,000 British, Indian and Commonwealth troops and two hundred aircraft in the Nile valley were all that stood between the Axis and its goal. And not only was Italy, with her dominating strategic position and African bastions, in an ideal position to isolate and destroy these inadequate forces, but the German Army which had overwhelmed France was free to drive through Spain to Gibraltar, seal the Mediterranean off from the west and pour into French North Africa. The Spanish dictator was a declared friend to Germany and Italy and under great obligations to them. Yet when that October Hitler met Franco at Hendaye and asked him to join the Axis, that shrewd despot, aware that Britain had defeated the Luftwaffe and still held the seas around Spain, had been curiously evasive. He had been full of assurances but had promised nothing. And, though Hitler was very angry,[1] he did not consider it worth while to shatter his ideological façade of a New Order in Europe or start another Peninsular War by forcing his way through the territory of a Fascist and ostensibly friendly State.

Instead, he left the Mediterranean to his ally, Italy. In this he was unfortunate. Some years before he had observed to the Italian Foreign Minister that, while the English complained

---

[1] After his nine hours' interview with him, the Fuehrer had said that, sooner than go through such an ordeal again, he would rather have three or four teeth out. Ciano, *Diplomatic Papers*, 402.

that Germany and Italy were led by adventurers, England herself, which had been led by adventurers in the days when she had made her empire, was now ruled by incompetents. But, when it came to war, this was just what she was not. At that moment, in charge of her forces in the Mediterranean and Middle East were three commanders of the highest daring— Andrew Cunningham, Commander-in-Chief of the Eastern Mediterranean Fleet, Archibald Wavell commanding the Middle East Ground Forces, and Richard O'Connor who, under the latter, directed the small Western Desert Force facing General Graziani's vast Italian host in Libya and Western Egypt. The first of these, with the assistance of a squadron operating under Admiral Somerville in the Western Mediterranean, established from the start such a moral ascendency over the Italian Fleet that, despite its central position and the Regia Aeronautica, it was unable to prevent the British from holding on to Malta and even passing occasional convoys through the Sicilian Narrows to reinforce Egypt and reassure Greece and Turkey. And when in November the Italians, with a surprising lack of military success, struck at Greece across the Adriatic, Cunningham not only protected the Greek archipelago and islands from invasion but, with an attack by torpedo-carrying aircraft on the Italian Fleet in Taranto harbour, sank or immobilised three of its six battleships and transformed the balance of sea-power in the Mediterranean in the course of a night. When a month later Graziani, furiously prodded by an impatient Mussolini,[1] started to move forward with his long strung-out army of nearly a quarter of a million men to occupy Alexandria and deprive the Navy of its base, O'Connor, backed by the skill and daring of a few hundred R.A.F. pilots, fell on his advance-guard at Sidi-Barrani with a single Indian Infantry division and one weak Armoured division from England and completely destroyed it. Though his Indian division was at once withdrawn by Wavell to attack the Italians in Eritrea and Abyssinia, with a raw Australian division in its place and in a campaign conducted five or six hundred miles from his base and sustained

[1] " Never," wrote Italy's Foreign Minister of the reluctance of his country's generals to advance, " has a military operation been undertaken so much against the will of the commanders." *Ciano Diaries.* 291.

by captured enemy transport, O'Connor proceeded to encircle and storm one after another of the Italian coastal strongholds in Libya and Cyrenaica, finally, after a hundred and fifty mile dash across unreconnoitred desert with his dwindling armour, rounding up the remnants of Graziani's host. Altogether, with never more than two divisions at his disposal, this astonishing soldier advanced five hundred miles and, at a cost of less than 2000 casualties, destroyed ten Italian divisions and captured 130,000 prisoners, 400 tanks and 850 guns.[1] And though the opportunity offered by his victories of driving on to Tripoli and, by securing air-bases, restoring Britain's control of the central Mediterranean, was subsequently thrown away in order to send an expeditionary force to Greece, their impact and that of Cunningham's and Somerville's naval victories had a profound effect not only on Italian morale, but on neutral, and particularly Spanish and Turkish, opinion. Meanwhile, during the early months of 1941, two other small Commonwealth armies under Wavell's orders, one attacking from the north under General Platt and the other from the south under Andrew Cunningham's brother, Alan, closed in on Italian forces four or five times their size in Eritrea and Abyssinia and by the early summer had liquidated them, taking another 185,000 prisoners and restoring the Ethiopian Emperor to his throne.

The intervention of the British in Greece was less successful. Here, instead of Italians, they encountered the Germans, with their superbly trained troops and military air-power. Here, too, instead of standing guard outside the sea-cage in which the Axis conquerors of Europe were held, out of motives of chivalry they thrust their fingers inside it. " Are we again going to have ' Salonika supporters ' as in the last war? " Brooke asked in his diary ; " why will politicians never learn the simple

---

[1] " One can search the annals of war from the earliest times and not find a greater victory than this." C. N. Barclay, *Against Great Odds*, 70. Field Marshal Sir John Harding, who was O'Connor's Chief of Staff, has written of this campaign, " Although he had the invaluable support and wise advice of Field Marshals Wavell and Wilson to aid him, the plan of battle was hatched in General O'Connor's brain, the tactical decisions on which success or failure depended were his, the grim determination that inspired all our troops stemmed up from his heart; it was his skill in calculating the risks, and his daring in accepting them, that turned what might have been merely a limited success into a victorious campaign with far-reaching effects on the future course of the war." *Idem*, v-vi.

principle of concentration of force at the vital point and the avoidance of dispersal of effort? "[1] Not only were the British driven out of Greece, again losing almost all their military equipment as in Norway and France, but, as a result of this dispersal of their slender Middle East forces, they failed to hold the island of Crete and the airfields which O'Connor had captured in western Cyrenaica, both of vital importance to command of the Eastern Mediterranean. The evacuation of Crete in May in the face of the Luftwaffe involved losses that neutralised the advantages won by a brilliant earlier naval victory over the Italians off Cape Matapan and that, suffered by any commander less rock-like than Cunningham, would almost certainly have involved the withdrawal of the British Fleet from the Mediterranean. And the disregard of O'Connor's warning against attempting to hold the Tripolitanian-Libyan frontier with a skeleton force nearly resulted in the loss of Egypt. Weakened by the withdrawal of almost all their tanks and guns to aid Greece and attacked by German armour which had reached Tripoli in the latter part of February under Rommel, the British in Africa had been thrown back in rout for three hundred miles and besieged in the little Italian port of Tobruk, won earlier by O'Connor. O'Connor himself, sent back to help his successor retrieve the disaster he had predicted, was taken prisoner two nights after his return to the desert. Only Wavell's firmness saved the Delta itself from being overrun.

Yet Britain's chivalry in the eastern Mediterranean that spring had consequences that, even if unintended, damaged Germany more than herself. For Hitler had by now resolved to attack Russia, and the diversion of armoured and airborne troops to smash the Jugoslav and Greek resistance and drive the British out of Greece and Crete, delayed the start of his

[1] *Diary*, 11th November, 1940. 'I lamented Dill's departure with Anthony Eden to the Middle East,' Brooke wrote of the departure of the Foreign Secretary and C.I.G.S. in February; 'a journey that was destined to take them to Greece and Dill to Jugoslavia, and one that influenced our operations in Greece and Crete. This is one of the very few occasions on which I doubted Dill's advice and judgment, and I am not in a position to form any definite opinion as I was not familiar with all the facts. I have, however, always considered from the very start that our participation in the operations in Greece was a definite strategic blunder. Our hands were more than full at that time in the Middle East, and Greece could only result in the most dangerous dispersal of force.' *Notes on My Life*, IV, 256.

Russian offensive, though the forces involved were only a minute fraction of the immense German and satellite armies assembling on the fifteen hundred mile western frontier of the U.S.S.R. And the very daring of Britain's offensive operations in the Middle East caused the German leaders to think her stronger in that theatre than she was and deterred them from attacking Turkey and so securing the Middle East oil-wells and a dominating position on Russia's southern flank. On June 22nd the impatient German dictator launched his armies in a frontal assault on the U.S.S.R. Barred by the tenuous ring of British sea-power from breaking out of Europe into southern Asia and Africa, he struck eastwards, like Napoleon, across the boundless plains of Russia.

. . . .

In all this, as in the events of the previous summer, Churchill's influence had been decisive. He had not overruled the Chiefs of Staff Committee—his constitutional and expert advisers in strategic and Service matters—but, in his capacity as Minister of Defence, had dominated it by his courage, resolution and energy. To save England and the free world he had been prepared to take immense risks, and had taken them. At times, in the orders sent to Wavell and Andrew Cunningham and the extent of the commitments he had urged them to assume with inadequate forces, he had appeared to disregard the bounds of what was militarily practicable and to court disaster. Yet the proof of the pudding was in the eating, and the end of Britain's perilous year alone found her still holding the seas and the Middle East, and with her enraged assailant, like a bull maddened by a skilful toreador, charging blindly at the giant mass of Russia.

Nor had Churchill only secured his country an involuntary ally in the east. He had gone far to win her another in the west. His spectacular yet uncomplaining stand and generous understanding of the American peoples' difficulties had broken through the rigid isolationalism in which they had stood a year before and done much to cause them to offer to their struggling fellow democracy almost every help short of war itself. They had begun in the summer of 1940 by allowing the

Roosevelt Administration to sell Britain reserves of guns and destroyers; then, stirred by Churchill's appeal for arms, they had started to re-gear their heavy industry to make armaments and aircraft. Later, in March, 1941, when Britain's last dollar reserves were nearing exhaustion, they had passed in their Congress the President's far-sighted Lease-Lend act to supply her with the tools she needed for victory without money payment. They were still outside the ring, but they were by now leaning on the ropes and shouting encouragement. And though, in conformity with time-honoured American military tradition, their Army chiefs regarded the British Army as a rather antiquated force officered by stiff-necked amateurs who could never be a match for German professionals,[1] reassured by the Battle of Britain and the Londoners' fortitude in the blitz they had joined with the retiring Naval Commander-in-Chief, Admiral Stark—a staunch supporter of Britain—in formulating a global policy under which the defeat of Germany was to be regarded as the United States' first strategic priority and the policing of the Pacific against Japan, her particular bugbear, as a secondary task until the Nazi power in Europe had been destroyed. Though the United States was still neutral, her Government and people had by the summer of 1941 accepted the thesis of which the British Prime Minister had made himself the world's spokesman: that Nazi Germany was mankind's enemy and must be destroyed. In January secret Anglo-American staff conversations, though still only of an exploratory character, were held in Washington; in March American officers visited England to select bases for their forces in the event of a future war. By the summer British warships were being repaired in American dockyards and the U.S. Navy had started to patrol the western Atlantic. And in August the Prime Minister, accompanied by the Chiefs of Staff, conferred with the President of the United States and his naval and military advisers in an American cruiser off the Newfoundland coast. The political

[1] At the end of September 1940 General Marshall, Chief of the American Army Staff, reminded his colleagues of the Air Corps, who had been much impressed by the R.A.F.'s victory, that in the first War the Germans " had always been six months ahead of the Allies." *U.S. Army in Second World War, European Theatre of Operations*, II, 24.

result of their collaboration was published as the Atlantic Charter.

.   .   .   .

During that year Brooke saw a good deal of the Prime Minister. Sometimes, though not as often as in the invasion summer, he was joined by him on his inspections. " Spent leave at Ferney Close," he wrote of a seven days' holiday in July,

> " except for Friday 25th when I motored to Tidworth with Martel to meet the P.M. He was coming down to see the 1st Armoured Division to say a few words to them to let them know that he realized the losses they had sustained in having to send some hundred and fifty tanks to the Middle East. Everywhere he had an astounding reception. He drove in my car between troops lining both sides of the road, all of them cheering him as he went and shouting, 'Good old Winnie!' His popularity is quite astonishing."

Early in 1941 Brooke moved from his General Headquarters at St. Paul's School into special underground Battle Headquarters near the War Cabinet Room at Storey's Gate. ' The headquarters,' he wrote,

> ' was deep down in the basement and covered over with a thick apron of reinforced concrete. . . . All offices were well fitted out with special ventilators, telephones, message conveyors, map rooms, etc. It was in every way an excellent battle headquarters. . . . As the Chiefs of Staff Committee also met in the same building, and Winston had a flat in it as well, interviews were facilitated and work speeded up.'[1]

A few weeks later, when the Prime Minister moved into his flat, he insisted on showing it to the Commander-in-Chief.

> " *February 10th.* Went straight to Windsor Castle . . . for interview with the King, and to give him details of our ' Victor' exercise. He displayed great interest in all

[1] *Notes on My Life,* IV, 249.

details, and was as usual quite charming. Then up to London where I did office work till lunch when the Prime Minister and "Pug" Ismay came to lunch with us. He was in great form and did a complete tour of my Headquarters after lunch, visiting every single department. He finished up by inviting me to see his new flat in the building, and we visited his study, sitting-room, dining-room, Mrs. Churchill's bedroom, bathroom, his own, kitchen, scullery, etc."

'He was just like a small boy,' Brooke added, 'showing his new toy and all it could do.'

The qualities that most impressed Brooke about Churchill in these early days of their association were his courage, wonderfully stored memory and inexhaustible energy. Several times in these early months he remarked with amazement on this last quality. "P.M. in great form," he wrote on May 27th, 1941, after one of his Tank parliaments,

> "and on the whole a very successful meeting. It is surprising how he maintains a light-hearted exterior in spite of the vast burden he is bearing. He is quite the most wonderful man I have ever met, and it is a source of never-ending interest, studying him and getting to realise that occasionally such human beings make their appearance on this earth—human beings who stand out head and shoulders above all others."

Every now and then Brooke was summoned to spend a week-end with his chief at Chequers. Having so much to do and because his Sundays at home with his wife meant so much to him, he did not always welcome these summonses, and his early references to them are often perfunctory.

> " *October 11th, 1940.* After a night's heavy bombing, with one or two fairly close to the Rag, started for Hendon. Much delayed by roads blocked by unexploded bombs. Flew to Old Sarum where Auchinleck met me and took me on to Monty's H.Q., where I attended part of his ' Officers' Week ' and said a few words. Received message whilst there asking me to dine and sleep Chequers. Flew

back to London, changed and packed bag. Put in another hour in the office and then left for Chequers. There I found P.M., Mrs. Churchill, Randolph C., Mrs. Sandys, Miss Churchill, " Pug " Ismay, Tim Pile and secretary. Sat up till 2 a.m. P.M. . . . . discussing probable course of war, likelihood of German move in Mediterranean, also reason for failure of Dakar expedition. He has a wonderful vitality and bears his heavy burden remarkably well. It would be impossible to find a man to fill his place at present."

Later, as the strain of preparing for an invasion lessened, Brooke gave more space to these visits.

" *Sunday March 9th, 1941.* Spent day at home. In the evening departed for Chequers at 6.15 p.m. arrived there at 7.45 p.m. House party consisting of P.M., Mr. Menzies (P.M. of Australia), Sandys and his wife, P.M.'s youngest daughter, Professor Lindemann, etc."

" P.M. suffering from bronchitis, came down to dinner in his ' siren suit,' a one-piece garment like a child's romper-suit of light blue. He was in great form and after dinner sent for his rifle to give me a demonstration of the ' long port ' which he wanted to substitute for the ' slope.' He followed this up with some bayonet exercise! "

' It was one of the first occasions on which I had seen Winston in one of his real light-hearted moods. I was convulsed watching him give this exhibition of bayonet exercises with his rifle, dressed in his siren-suit and standing in the ancestral hall of Chequers. I remember wondering what Hitler would have thought of this demonstration of skill at arms.'[1]

" *April 27th, 1941.* Got up early to attend 5th Armoured Division conference. . . . Had to leave early as I was due at Chequers for the night, . . . where I arrived 7 p.m. P.M. was broadcasting at 9 p.m., so we had to wait for dinner till 9.50 p.m. He was in great form after his broadcast and kept us up till 3.30 a.m. Party consisted of Margesson

(Secretary of State for War), Kennedy (Director of Military Operations), "Pug" Ismay, Professor Lindemann, Mrs. Randolph Churchill and secretary. Kennedy tried to give P.M. a discourse on strategy in which he contemplated a fairly free evacuation of Egypt! This infuriated the P.M., and we had some trouble calming him down. However, I had good opportunities of discussing my troubles, such as shortage of man-power, loss of tanks transferred to Egypt, danger of concentrating authority for destruction of petrol, danger of forming multitude of detachments from main effort for such efforts as fire-fighting, clearing of houses, agriculture, etc., which can equally well be done by civilians. Also stressed present very unsatisfactory air situation."

'The Kennedy incident was a very typical one. Poor old John had only intended to express that there might be worse things to lose than Egypt. It was, however, at once taken up by Winston as being a defeatist attitude, and Kennedy was relegated amongst those "many generals who are only too ready to surrender, and who should be made examples of like Admiral Byng!" The more Kennedy tried to explain what he meant, the more heated Winston got, and I was very thankful when we rose from the dinner table and went into the hall to discuss other matters.'

. . . .

Brooke at this time had no part in the direction of global strategy, which was the responsibility of his military superior, the Chief of Imperial General Staff, and the Chiefs of Staff Committee on which the latter sat with his colleagues, the First Sea Lord and Chief of Air Staff. But in the early summer of 1941, just after the disastrous evacuations of Greece and Crete and when Wavell, with utterly inadequate forces, had been having to conduct simultaneous campaigns in the Western Desert, Syria, Iraq, and Abyssinia, he wrote of the Prime Minister's attempts to prod that long-suffering commander into a major offensive in Libya.

"*June 17th.* . . . At 12 noon one of the P.M.'s meetings

of his Commanders-in-Chief. . . . The P.M. began with
a survey of the world situation which was interesting. To
my horror he informed us that the present Libyan operation
is intended to be a large-scale operation! How can we
undertake offensive operations on two fronts in the Middle
East when we have not got sufficient for one? From the
moment we decided to go into Syria we should have put
all our strength in the front to complete the operation with
the least possible delay. If the operation is not pressed
through quickly, it may well lead to further complications."

For Dill in his difficult task as C.I.G.s, Brooke had the most
profound sympathy, realising the almost impossible burden he
was bearing, made all the heavier by the fact that his wife had
had a paralytic stroke and during the blitz winter was slowly
dying.[1] For all his brilliant intelligence his great friend
and hero, Brooke saw, was temperamentally unfitted to work
with anyone as overwhelming and impulsive as Churchill: in
some ways he was almost too straightforward, in others too
sensitive and finely strung. He became involved in incessant
argument, and the clash of it both angered the Prime Minister
and wore Dill down.

Before Russia was attacked the Prime Minister's opportunities
for indulging his passion for the offensive were confined by
the nature of the war to the Eastern Mediterranean and to
occasional small-scale Commando raids on the French, Dutch
and Scandinavian coasts and islands.[2] But with the series of

[1] ' Possibly if Dill had had a happier home life at that time he could have
weathered the friction with the politicians better. As it was, every visit home to his
wife in Windsor was a desperate ordeal. She could not make herself understood,
he kept guessing what she could mean, usually unsuccessfully, and finally with a
disappointed look in her eyes, she used to throw her head back on her pillow.'
Notes on My Life, IV, 245-6. "It is pathetic," Brooke wrote in his diary on
November 22nd, 1940. "He is urgently in need of a rest, cannot, I think, face
going home for a week's leave, and, if he goes elsewhere, he feels he must go
visiting troops, as he can't bear doing nothing and being left with his thoughts."

[2] Brooke, like most professional soldiers, was dubious about the wisdom of
separating the Commandos' training from the general body of Infantry. In
September he spent three days at the Combined Operations Training Centre
at Inverary in the western Highlands with the then Director of Combined
Operations, Admiral of the Fleet Lord Keyes. ' My impression,' he wrote, ' was
that a good start was being made, but that,' as he noted in his diary at the time,
" the training was far too stereotyped to fit in with varying conditions of our

disasters that befell the Russian armies in the late summer and autumn of 1941, a demand arose that the Army in Britain, which to the uninitiated appeared to be doing nothing but train and await invasion, should intervene on the Continent to save Russia from the fate of France. The Prime Minister, always anxious to attack the enemy and sensitive, like all politicians, to public opinion, sympathised with this demand and, though he knew how backward the country was in military armaments, sought eagerly for some way to meet it. As early as July 2nd—a fortnight after the German offensive began—Brooke was summoned to the Chiefs of Staff Committee to discuss possible raids on the Continent, and on September 8th he was asked to consider what he described as ' a mad scheme put up by the Joint Planning Staff '—a body which the Prime Minister, in his capacity as Defence Minister, had taken under his particular charge—' for a feint attack on the Cherbourg peninsula to relieve the pressure on the Russians.'[1]

By October the Russian position seemed almost desperate. And, as every serious soldier in Britain was convinced of the impossibility of a landing on the French coast, where the Germans had at least four times as many divisions as the British could hope to land, the Prime Minister turned his mind to Norway. Here, he argued, if a lodgment could be made so far outside the range of British fighters and in the face of German air-power—a thing which only he believed possible—it would have the double effect of distracting German attention from Russia and easing the difficulties of escorting the convoys which Britain and America were sending to Murmansk round the North Cape of Norway. At this time, conscious that if the Russians collapsed, the Army he commanded would have to face an early invasion-attempt, Brooke was engaged in the most ambitious anti-invasion Exercise he had yet conducted.

' It was known under the code-name of " Bumper " and

---

possible operations: still thinking much too small in all our plans." ' The whole of my visit to Roger Keyes was on his part to try and convince me that our Commando policy was right. He failed to do so, and I remained convinced till the end of the war that the Commandos should never have been divorced from the Army in the way they were. Each division should have been responsible for maintaining a divisional battle patrol capable of any Commando work that might be asked of it.' *Notes on My Life*, IV, 294-5.

[1] *Notes on My Life*, IV, 292; *Diary*, 8th September, 1941.

comprised the Armoured divisions, nine Infantry divisions and two Army brigades. On September 27th I had an interview with the Press to explain the scope of the Exercise. The following day I established my Control Centre at Oxford. Laurence Carr[1] was commanding the Eastern Force (representing Germans) that had landed in East Anglia, whilst Alexander commanded the Forces opposed to him. I had appointed Monty as Chief Umpire and he was quite excellent. The exercise lasted till October 3rd, and was of great value.'[2]

Its course is described in the diary.

" *September 28th, 1941.* Left at 3.30 p.m. for Oxford to establish my Control Centre for the manœuvres. Am living in the hotel with office, etc., just outside."

" *September 29th.* Left early to fly from Cowley (Oxford) to Norwich. But weather bad and did not get off till 9 a.m. Very dirty weather and forced to fly very low most of way. Went to see German H.Q. and had talk with Carr. From there motored on to II Corps H.Q. and XI Corps H.Q. to find out situation. Then flew . . . to Reading where second car met me and took me round to South Command H.Q. where I discussed Alexander's plans with him. Returned to Oxford where I ran conference at 8 p.m. on day's fighting. Then Admiral Ramsay came to dinner and I described situation to him afterwards."

" *September 30th.* Spent day touring front and visiting various headquarters by car and by air. Bertie Ramsay came with me. Dill turned up for final conference after dinner. Manœuvres going very well and day most interesting."

" *October 1st.* Again rushing round by air from 8 a.m. to 7 p.m. and conference till midnight after dinner. . . . Sad mishandling of armoured force by Higher Command."

" *October 2nd.* Another day of manœuvres. Spent all day motoring and flying about. Have now ordered manœuvres to close down at 6 a.m. to-morrow. They have

[1] Lt.-Gen. Laurence Carr, G.O.C.-in-Chief, Eastern Command.
[2] *Notes on My Life*, IV, 295.

been a great success. I am delighted with the way
Armoured divisions have come on, but very disappointed
at the way Higher Commanders are handling them; they
have all got a great deal to learn, and the sooner they learn
the better."

But on the day after he returned from this Exercise and before
the subsequent conference of commanders could be assembled
to discuss it, Brooke was called upon to consider a far more
urgent matter.

> " *October 3rd.* At midnight received special messenger
> from the War Office with orders to carry out examination
> for attack on Trondheim and preparation of plan of
> attack. The whole to be in by next Friday! Also that
> I was to dine to-night at Chequers and spend night there
> to discuss plans. I motored back to London in the morning
> and spent most of the afternoon studying details of the
> plan."

> " At 6 p.m. picked up Dill at the War Office and drove
> to Chequers discussing details with him on the way.
> Dudley Pound, Portal and Attlee formed the party. We
> sat up till 2.15 a.m. discussing the problem, and I did my
> best to put the P.M. off attempting the plan. Air support
> cannot be adequately supplied and we shall fall into the
> same pitfall as we did before."

> " *October 4th.* Resumed discussion at 11 a.m. and went
> on till 1 p.m. I think P.M. was beginning to weaken on the
> plan. Returned to London and made arrangements for
> conference on Monday to start discussing plan. Finally
> motored home in time for dinner. Very weary after hard
> week short of sleep."

' The plan for the capture of Norway had already been
examined by the Chiefs of Staff Committee, and had been
turned down as impracticable owing to insufficient air
support for the operation. Now, at Chequers, I, in my
capacity of Commander-in-Chief Home Forces, had received
orders from him to prepare a detailed plan for the capture
of Trondheim, ready to the last button. A commander for

the expedition was to be appointed by me and the plan was to be sufficiently ready only to require the order to start. I was given one week to prepare it. I said that, if I was to do so, I must have the Commander-in-Chief, Home Fleet, Air-Officer-Commanding Fighter Command, Air-Officer-Commanding Bomber Command, Minister of Transport and several others at my disposal for repeated conferences during the week. I was told that they were all to be made available.'

' It was an unpleasant assignment. I had been told by Dill of the results of the Chiefs of Staff inspection of the problem, and I felt convinced that I should arrive at similar conclusions. It was going to entail a great deal of wasted work on the part of many busy people. Personally I was in the middle of the final work connected with " Bumper " Exercise, and my time already fully booked up.'[1]

The diary describes what followed.

" *October 6th.* Left home 8 a.m., foggy. Conference at 11 a.m. in Cabinet War Room at which I presided. Following were present: Commanders-in-Chief, Home Fleet, Fighter Command, Bomber Command, Coastal Command, Army Co-operation Command, Quartermaster-General, Minister of Transport, my own Staff, etc. The more we examine the problem of Trondheim, the more certain I am that it would be folly to attempt it. . . ."

" *October 7th.* Had intended to fly to visit the Dutch forces, but the whole country was wrapped in fog the whole morning and I had to postpone the visit. I therefore spent the day preparing notes for my final Conference on my long Exercise of last week which takes place at the Staff College next Friday morning."

" *October 9th.* . . . The whole morning had been taken up with another of my meetings preparing the Trondheim operation. . . . Our final survey of the operation convinced us more than ever of its impracticability. I now have been warned to attend Chequers next Sunday again at 6 p.m. I have to start for Newcastle the same night."

[1] *Notes on My Life*, IV, 296-7.

" *October 10th.* Left at 8 a.m. for the final conference of our large " Bumper " Exercise. We held it at the Staff College. There were some two hundred and seventy Service officers attending it. I began by turning to Montgomery to act as historian, and then I followed on with criticisms. A great relief to have it over. The last fortnight has been a hard one with the large Exercise and the P.M.'s task on top of it to examine Trondheim operation."

' Monty had been the Chief Umpire throughout the Exercise, so I . . . . made him narrate the whole course of events. He did this admirably and produced a masterly picture of the various phases. . . . I then followed him with my criticisms of the operations, bringing out the failures of various commanders. The Exercise was of the greatest value and a landmark in the higher training of that year.'[1]

" *October 11th.* Had a troublesome morning going through the final appreciation of Trondheim for the P.M. After lunch Tovey (C.-in-C. Home Fleet) and Brind, his Chief of Staff, came round and we again went through the whole appreciation. I don't like its final shape and would have liked to recast the whole thing. But my conclusions would still remain the same that the operation is impracticable."

" *Sunday October 12th.* After having made all arrangements to go to Chequers and for special train to collect me at Wendover station at 1.45 a.m., I suddenly received message during afternoon that P.M. wanted us at 10 Downing Street instead. Went there at 6.30 p.m. All Chiefs of Staff, Tovey, Sholto, Paget and I attended. P.M. very dissatisfied with our Appreciation. Told me that he was expecting a detailed plan for the operation, and instead of that I had submitted a masterly treatise on all the difficulties. He then proceeded to cross-question me for nearly two hours on various items of the Appreciation, trying to make out that I had unnecessarily increased the difficulties. However, I was quite satisfied that there

[1] *Notes on My Life*, IV, 300.

was only one conclusion to arrive at. Finally left at 8.30 p.m., dined at club and embarked on train at 11 p.m.

Of this meeting—in the course of which, according to General Paget, the Prime Minister, looking angrily at him and Brooke, remarked, " I sometimes think some of my generals don't want to fight the Germans! "—Brooke wrote subsequently:

' At 6.30 p.m. we assembled at 10 Downing Street. The P.M. was already in the Cabinet Room, and I saw at once from his face that we were in for the hell of a storm! He had with him what he used to classify as some of his " colleagues," usually Anthony Eden, Attlee, Leathers on this occasion, and possibly a few others. On my side of the table I had the various Naval and Air Commanders-in-Chief who had collaborated with me, Paget, who was nominated as commander of this Expedition, and some of my staff.'

' When we were all assembled he shoved his chin out in his aggressive way and, staring hard at me, said: " I had instructed you to prepare a detailed plan for the capture of Trondheim, with a commander appointed and ready in every detail. What have you done? You have instead submitted a masterly treatise on all the difficulties and on all the reasons why this operation should not be carried out." He then proceeded to cross-question me for nearly two hours on most of the minor points of the appreciation. I repeatedly tried to bring him back to the main reason—the lack of air-support. He avoided this issue and selected arguments such as: " You state that you will be confronted by frosts and thaws which will render mobility difficult. How can you account for such a statement? " I replied that this was a trivial matter and that the statement came from the "Climate Book." He at once sent for this book, from which it at once became evident that this extract had been copied straight out of the book. His next attack was: " You state that it will take you some twenty-four hours to cover the ground between A and B. How can you account for so long being taken? Explain to me exactly how every hour of those twenty-four will be occupied? " As this time had been

[1] *Notes on My Life*, IV, 300-1.

allowed for overcoming enemy resistance on the road, removal of road-blocks and probable reparation to demolition of bridges and culverts, it was not an easy matter to paint this detailed picture of every hour of those twenty-four. This led to a series of more questions, interspersed with sarcasm and criticism. A very unpleasant gruelling to stand up to in a full room, but excellent training for what I had to stand up to on many occasions in later years.'

'The meeting finished shortly after 8.30 p.m. and for the second time Winston had been ridden off Trondheim. . . .'[1]

What finally deterred the Prime Minister from his project— one that he wished to launch because the Russians were *in extremis*—was, General Paget recalls, Brooke's sudden abandonment of his opposition on military grounds and his skilful passing of the ball to the First Sea Lord. He was prepared, he said, to waive all his objections about lack of air-cover, the time of year, climatic conditions, etc., provided that Admiral Pound would agree to send the Fleet into Trondheim fiord in support of the landing. At this everyone looked at the First Sea Lord, who, as was often the case in long committee meetings, had begun to doze. But, at the mention of the Fleet, the old man, to whom the security, traditions and transmitted wisdom of his Service were life itself, awoke to full activity and shook his head vigorously. On this the Prime Minister, who had a deep respect for Pound and his judgment and for all naval wisdom, desisted from his plan.[2]

Churchill was nothing if not magnanimous. A fortnight after this stormy scene he asked Brooke to stay the night at Chequers.

" *Sunday October 26th.* At 6 p.m. left for Chequers where I arrived about 7.45 p.m. I found that the only other guest was Lindemann. Dinner lasted on till about 11 p.m. by the time we had finished having snuff, etc. After dinner the P.M. sent for his dressing-gown to put over his ' siren-suit.' The dressing-gown is a marvellous garment, rather like Joseph's many-coloured robe. We then proceeded upstairs where he had a small cinema. There we watched

<hr/>

[1] *Notes on My Life*, IV., 300-1.
[2] Communicated to the author by General Sir Bernard Paget.

Russian and German films till about midnight. We then
came down and spent from midnight to 1 a.m. with an
explanation of ' Bumper ' Exercise which I had to give."

" The P.M. then dismissed Lindemann and told him he
wanted to speak to me. He proceeded to discuss impending
operations in North Africa and Mediterranean and all the
hopes he attached to them. From that he went on to
discuss defence of this country against invasion and the
strength of the forces left for this purpose. I told him of
the forces I had, of being very short of tanks if we went on
sending them to Russia as proposed. He assured me that
I should have some 4,000 tanks in this country by the
spring. Finally at 2.15 a.m. he suggested we should proceed
to the hall to have some sandwiches, and I hoped this
might at last mean bed. But, no! We went on till ten to
three before he made a move for bed. He had the
gramophone turned on, and in the many-coloured dressing-
gown, with a sandwich in one hand and watercress in
the other, he trotted round and round the hall, giving
occasional little skips to the tune of the gramophone. On
each lap near the fireplace he stopped to release some
priceless quotation or thought. For instance he quoted a
saying that a man's life is similar to a walk down a long
passage with closed windows on either side. As you reach
each window, an unknown hand opens it and the light
it lets in only increases by contrast the darkness of the
end of the passage."

' Considering the burden of responsibility he was bearing,'
Brooke added, ' his lightheartedness was unbelievable.' Next
morning he accompanied the Prime Minister to a demonstration of the " Bombard," a mortar in which the latter was
much interested. ' It was a good example of the interest he
took in all sorts of details. I think it was on this occasion that
the Bren-gun he carried in his car was pulled out so that
he could practise with it. He would certainly have sold his
life dearly if it had ever come to that.'[1]

· · · · · · · ·

[1] *Notes on My Life*, IV, 307.

A few days after this visit Brooke heard rumours that great changes were impending and that Dill, whose relations with the Prime Minister had been growing steadily more strained, was to be superseded. On November 13th he had a long, melancholy talk with the man whom he had long regarded as Britain's foremost soldier. Dill told him that he was sure that his days as C.I.G.S. were numbered and that, though Brooke was the man to whom he would like to hand over, he understood the choice of a successor lay between three of his subordinates: Lt.-Gen. Sir Frederick Pile, the G.O.C.-in-Chief Anti-Aircraft Command, Lt.-Gen. Sir Bernard Paget, the G.O.C.-in-Chief South-Eastern Command who had just been nominated to command in the Far East, and Major-General Archibald Nye, Director of Staff Duties at the War Office— a younger man still in his forties and a staff officer of great ability to whom, despite lack of seniority and of experience of command in the field, the Prime Minister had taken a strong fancy and was believed to favour.[1]

On the same evening Brooke received an invitation to stay at Chequers on the following Sunday. He was a little surprised, having stayed there so recently, but assumed it was to be told of Dill's departure and the appointment of his successor. He spent the Sunday morning as usual at home, painting and reassembling his daughter's goat-cart—a vehicle whose repair seems to have taken much of his leisure that winter—and left for Chequers at 5.30 p.m. On arrival he found that the party consisted of Captain Lord Louis Mountbatten, who had now succeeded Roger Keyes as head of Combined Operations; the Prime Minister's scientific adviser and familiar, Professor Lindemann or Lord Cherwell, as he had recently become; and the Military Secretary of the War Cabinet, Lt.-Gen. Ismay. After dinner, at which Mrs. Churchill was present, the Prime Minister took Brooke to his study and told him that, as Dill had had a hard time and was a tired man, he had made up his

---

[1] 'From many points of view he would have made an excellent C.I.G.S. A first-class brain, great character, courage in his own convictions, quick worker with very clear vision. As C.I.G.S. he would, however, have had the very serious handicap of being on the junior side and would consequently have had some difficulty in handling men such as Wavell, Auchinleck, Alexander, Monty and Paget who were considerably senior to him.' *Notes on My Life*, IV, 311.

mind to relieve him by making him a Field Marshal and Governor of Bombay.

" He then went on to say," Brooke wrote,

" that he wanted me to take over . . . and asked me whether I was prepared to do so. It took me some time to reply, as I was torn by many feelings. I hated the thought of old Dill going and our very close association coming to an end. I hated the thought of what this would mean to him. The magnitude of the job and the work entailed took the wind out of my sails. The fact that the extra work and ties would necessarily mean seeing far less of you tore at my heart strings. And finally a feeling of sadness at having to give up Home Forces after having worked them up to their present pitch."

" The P.M. misunderstood my silence and said: ' Do you not think you will be able to work with me? We have so far got on well together.' I had to assure him that these were not my thoughts, though I am fully aware that my path will not be strewn with rose petals. But I have the greatest respect and real affection for him, so that I hope I may be able to stand the storms of abuse which I may well have to bear frequently."

" He then went on to explain the importance he attached to the appointment, and the fact that the Chiefs of Staff Committee must be the body to direct military events over the whole world. He also stated that his relations with me must from now on approximate to those of a Prime Minister to one of his Ministers. Nobody could be nicer than he was, and finally, when we went to bed at 2 a.m., he came with me to my bedroom to get away from the others, took my hand and looking into my eyes with an exceptionally kind look, said: ' I wish you the very best of luck.' "

" I got into bed with my brain in a whirl trying to fathom the magnitude of the task I am about to take on. . . . . If it was peace time I should love to try it, but in war the responsibility is almost overwhelming. The consequences of failures or mistakes are a nightmare to

think of.   I pray God from the very bottom of my heart
that He may give me guidance and be at my side in the
times I may have to go through. . . . Many, many thoughts
kept galloping through my head and by 4 a.m. I was still
tossing about without sleep."[1]

' Reading over those lines brings back vividly that night
at Chequers.   There is no doubt that I was temporarily
staggered by the magnitude of the task I was undertaking.
Let it be remembered the situation we were in at that
time. . . . We were faced with a possible invasion across
the Channel, with increasing difficulties in the Middle
East, a closed Mediterranean, dark clouds growing in the
Far East and a failing Russia driven back to the very gates
of Moscow.   The horizon was black from end to end with
only one shaft of light in the possible entry of America into
the war.   To pick up the strategic reins at the War Office at
such a moment was sufficient to cause the deepest anxiety.
Added to that was the certain trial of working hand in hand
with Winston in handling the direction of war.   I had seen
enough of him to realise his impetuous nature, his gambler's
spirit, and his determination to follow his own selected path
at all costs, to realise fully what I was faced with.'

' I can remember clearly that after he had taken me away
to his study and had offered me this appointment, he left
me alone temporarily to rejoin the others.   I am not an
exceptionally religious person, but I am not ashamed to
confess that as soon as he was out of the room my first
impulse was to kneel down and pray to God for guidance
and support in the task I had undertaken.   As I look back at
the years that followed I can now see clearly how well this
prayer was answered.'

" To-day," Brooke wrote three days later, " the papers
published Dill's departure and my appointment to C.I.G.S. . . .
I suppose I ought to be very grateful and happy at reaching
the top step of the ladder.   I can't say that I am.   I feel a heavy
depression at Dill going. . . . I had never hoped or aspired to
reach these dizzy heights, and now that I am stepping up on

[1] *Diary*, 16th November, 1941.

to the plateau land of my military career the landscape looks cold, bleak and lonely, with a ghastly responsibility hanging as a black thundercloud over me. Perhaps I am feeling liverish for want of exercise to-day! "[1]

[1] *Diary*, 19th November, 1941.

Chapter Five

WINTER
OF OUR DISCONTENT

I tell you naught for your comfort,
Yea, naught for your desire,
Save that the sky grows darker yet
And the sea rises higher.

G. K. CHESTERTON

THE NATION to the direction of whose military affairs
Alan Brooke had been called had been at war now for
more than two years. After suffering the most disastrous
reverse she had ever experienced, she had made a wonderful
recovery. Britain's economy was now fully mobilised for war.
Though the process of re-tooling her peace-time industries for
mass arms-production was only at the stage which Germany had
reached in 1938, the deficiencies from which her fighting men
had so long suffered could be expected to be made good in
another year, as the tanks, guns, bomber-aircraft and technical
apparatus began to pour at last from the factories. And
behind her own were those of the United States, where a
people still living on a peace-time economy had started to
turn their boundless productive capacity to the manufacture
of the weapons Britain needed for victory. Even in the past
year they had sent her 2,800 aircraft, 1,000 tanks and nearly
13,000 lorries.

Yet, in spite of her people's endurance and achievement,
Britain's strategic situation at the end of November, 1941,
was almost as precarious as it had been a year earlier. After
destroying all military resistance in Western Europe, Hitler
had transferred the older age-groups to the factories to make

submarines and weapons for the destruction of England. Between the summer of 1940 and the end of 1941, his U-boat fleet had increased fivefold and its toll on shipping had risen from around a hundred thousand tons a month to more than three hundred thousand. Since the outbreak of war the British Merchant Marine had lost nearly eight million tons or more than a third of its pre-war tonnage. Meanwhile the German surface-fleet which, apart from two old battleships fit only for use in the Baltic, had entered the war with two battle-cruisers and three commerce-raiding or " pocket " battle-ships, had been reinforced by the most powerful warship in the world. The 42,000-ton *Tirpitz*, her trials completed, was now in commission, tying down in the Orkneys two of the Royal Navy's strongest and fastest battleships[1] to pursue her if she broke northwards into the Atlantic. The situation at sea would have been still graver but for the sinking six months earlier of her sister-ship, the *Bismarck*—cornered by the Home Fleet during a premature foray against the Atlantic convoys in the course of which she had sent to the bottom Britain's giant battle-cruiser, the *Hood*, and damaged her latest battle-ship. As it was, while one part of the German surface fleet threatened the Atlantic convoys from one end of Europe's conquered coastline, the other, consisting of the battle-cruisers, *Scharnhorst* and *Gneisenau*, threatened them from the other at Brest, where, after sinking twenty-two British merchant-ships in the spring, they were now—watched night and day by submarines and reconnaissance aircraft—awaiting another foray.

Thus, with the entire European coastline in German hands from the North Cape to the Spanish frontier, and the Mediterranean cut by Italy's geographical position and her possession of nearly a thousand miles of North African shore, the Admiralty was facing graver difficulties than at any time in its history. Not only, with its overworked destroyers and escort-vessels and the aircraft of R.A.F. Coastal Command and the Fleet Air Arm, had it to wage a never-ceasing battle against Ger-

---

[1] " The whole strategy of the war turns at this period on this ship, which is holding four times the number of British capital ships paralysed, to say nothing of the two new American battleships retained in the Atlantic." Prime Minister to Gen. Ismay, 25th January, 1942. *Churchill*, IV, 98.

many's ocean-going submarines, but it had to guard the Atlantic convoys against sallies from surface-warships, while simultaneously containing an Italian fleet operating under shore-based air-cover from an impregnable central position in the Mediterranean. Because Germany's battleships and heavy cruisers were free to slip either along the Norwegian coastal corridor or out of the western French ports into the Atlantic, every important convoy approaching or sailing from Britain had to be guarded, not only by cruisers, destroyers and frigates—all of them in short supply—but by at least one capital ship. Reduced between the wars by economies and the unrealist formulas of international Disarmament Conferences and Treaties, the Royal Navy had not only to contain the Axis, but to face the latent threat of two powerful neutral Navies—those of Britain's former allies, France and Japan. To this had been added the necessity of escorting the convoys carrying arms and supplies to Russia along a nightmare sea-route threatened, not only by submarine and shore-based aircraft, but by warships lurking in the Norwegian and Arctic fiords.

Nor did the Navy any longer enjoy its traditional advantage of swift interior lines. Because the Mediterranean sea-route to the East was cut by the Sicilian Narrows, except for an occasional convoy escorted by a major fleet—and since the Luftwaffe's intervention in the Mediterranean even this had become virtually impossible—Britain had to supply her forces in the Middle East and India and maintain her trade with the Orient by the sea-route round the Cape of Good Hope. This multiplied four-fold the length of the voyage to Egypt and doubled that to India, imposing an immense strain on her shipping and drastically reducing its troop and supply carrying capacity. Meanwhile, while holding the western Mediterranean with a small roving battle-squadron based on Gibraltar, the Admiralty had to supply its main Mediterranean fleet at Alexandria through the Suez Canal across 13,000 miles of ocean. Here since 1940 Andrew Cunningham had guarded Egypt, the Levant and Cyprus and protected the flank and communications of the Desert Army with a dwindling force of which, after the Greek and Cretan evacuations, only three battleships and three cruisers remained. A fortnight before Alan Brooke entered on his new duties, one of the battleships, the *Barham*, was sunk by U-boats, a pack of which had entered the Mediterranean, while at the other end of that sea Admiral Somerville's Force " H " simultaneously lost its solitary aircraft-carrier, the *Ark Royal*, through the same cause.

Altogether since the beginning of the war the enemy had sunk three British capital ships, three aircraft-carriers, thirteen cruisers and sixty-two destroyers. At the end of November, 1941, the Royal Navy had only nine serviceable battleships and battle-cruisers—all but four of them a quarter of a century old—and four fleet-carriers. Two other battleships were refitting in home ports, and three more, out of reach of air-raids, in America. Two new ones, laid down after the expiry of the Washington Treaties in 1937, were on the stocks and were expected to be ready within a year, while another, the *Duke of York*, was on the point of commission. Of the nine in service, two were at Alexandria, two at Gibraltar, two on convoy duty in the Atlantic, and one—the powerful new *King George V*—at Scapa Flow keeping watch on the *Tirpitz*. Her consort, the *Prince of Wales*, and the battle-cruiser, *Repulse*, had just been despatched to Singapore, at grave risk to home waters, in an eleventh-hour attempt to prevent the Japanese from striking at Britain's rear.

For a storm was gathering there that threatened disaster as dire almost as that which had faced her in the summer of 1940. Britain was confronted at last with that major naval war in the Far East to which for a generation her Government and people had shut their eyes and against which her Admiralty had repeatedly warned them. By their surrender in 1921 to the American proposals for naval disarmament, her statesmen had accepted a 5/3 ratio of battleship-strength with Japan, leaving her Eastern empire and sea-communications at the mercy of that highly industrialised Power should the Royal Navy ever become involved alone in a major European war. When in the 'thirties such a war became a probability and Japan began to intrigue with the Fascist States, the politicians and the Treasury, interpreting only too well the nation's ostrich-like optimism, refused to meet the threat of a two-ocean war with a two-ocean fleet and trusted instead to the military barrier of French Indo-China and the benevolent neutrality of the American Pacific Fleet to prevent any attack on the costly new naval base at Singapore. As a result, after the collapse of France, Britain had had to fight the war at sea against Germany and Italy with no margin of safety at all, leaving her Eastern possessions and Indian Ocean communications—doubly vital because of the closing of the Mediterranean—unguarded against a potentially hostile fleet of ten battleships and as many fleet-carriers—a force almost as large as the entire available British battle-fleet.

In this predicament the Government had relied wholly on the friendship of the United States and the deterrent of its advanced naval and air base in the Philippines—fifteen hundred miles north-east of Singapore and on the flank of the Japanese sea-communications to the south. Though the Philippines were only held by very light forces and the American battle-fleet was nearly five thousand miles away at Pearl Harbour in the Central Pacific, its presence there had so far proved sufficient to keep the Japanese from attacking the British and Dutch East Indies. For the past five years Japan had been struggling to conquer the primary lands of the immense subcontinent of China—a conquest for which her armies needed American oil and British and Dutch rubber, tin and oil. To avoid a challenge which she could not at that time meet, Britain in the summer of 1940 had taken the step of closing the Burma road—the only channel by which China could be supplied from the outer world. And, though strongly disapproving of Japan's Chinese ambitions, the Americans had continued to sell her petrol and oil. For at that time both the English-speaking democracies had been anxious to do everything possible to prevent an extension of the war to the Pacific. Fortunately the Japanese had had their hands full. Despite the conclusion of a military pact with Germany and Ribbentrop's repeated attempts to persuade them to strike, they had remained warily neutral.

But after the Germans' attack on Russia and their rapid advance on Moscow and Leningrad, the attitude of Tokyo changed. Neither the German nor Japanese war-lords trusted one another, but the simultaneous absence of the British Navy and Russian Army from Eastern Asia offered Japan an opportunity not likely to recur. And, alarmed by the ominous Japanese occupation in July, with Vichy connivance, of French Indo-China—an ideal base for attacking the Philippines, Indonesia and Singapore—and angered by the growing interference with their Chinese trade, the Americans had that autumn instituted a trade embargo against Japan so stringent that the latter's statesmen were faced with the alternatives of either abandoning their attempt to conquer China or of seizing by force the oil and raw materials they needed from the British and Dutch East Indies. Increasingly dependent on America for finance and munitions, the British and the exiled Dutch Government felt bound to join in that embargo. From that moment a Japanese attack on Malaya and Indonesia became a probability and almost a certainty. As Japan was not only a great naval Power but a great military and air one as well, with seventy field-divisions and more than 2,600 first-line aircraft, the defenders of the British Eastern empire were faced with a grim prospect. Though that empire had been created and maintained by sea-power, they had no fleet with which to defend it, while the only substitute for one, and for which they had long been asking—a strong force of modern aircraft —had been denied them. Against the 700 first-line aircraft which Japan was known to have assembled in Indo-China for an attack on Malaya, the Singapore authorities could only oppose 150 slow, ill-armed and obsolescent planes. The aircraft that might have been sent to the Far East that autumn and winter and the ships that might have carried them there were bespoken for the convoys to Murmansk with which Britain was trying to sustain the Russian front and appease the anger of the Kremlin at her inability to launch an invasion of the Continent.

Instead, the defence of Malaya had been left to the Army, which over the past year had managed to collect there thirty-two miscellaneous infantry battalions, or the equivalent of three weak and ill-armed divisions. They were drawn mainly from Australia and India and were neither equipped nor trained for jungle warfare. Even had they been, they could scarcely have defended indefinitely a long narrow jungle peninsula, dependent on sea-communications, against an invading army from French Indo-China and Thailand with almost unchallenged command of the sea and air. In the absence of sufficient shore-based aircraft there was only one way in which Malaya and Singapore could be protected—the despatch from England of a strong fleet including aircraft-carriers. Prior to the fall of France it had always been contemplated that, should the Japanese attack the Allied rear, until America entered the war the task of containing Italy in the Mediterranean should be left to the French while the British Mediterranean Fleet moved to Singapore to defend the East Indies. But with France lost and her naval base at Kamranh Bay, dominating the South China Sea and the approaches to Singapore, in Japanese hands, and with America still uncommitted, there was no means by which a solitary Britain, her hands already full in Europe, could afford naval protection to the British and Dutch East Indies. The First Sea Lord, Sir Dudley Pound, therefore, proposed to withdraw a battleship from the Eastern Mediterranean and send it immediately with an aircraft-carrier, not to Singapore—which it was obvious so small a force could not defend if the Japanese Navy moved against it in strength—but to Ceylon, where, acting on the defensive, it could give temporary protection to Britain's sea-communications through the Indian Ocean to Egypt, India and the Persian Gulf oil-refinery. Here, as soon as these could be spared, it could be reinforced by the four slow, unmodernised " R " class battleships and, later, as replacements became available, by one or two of the newer ships. But until then, with Japan's fleet of fast modern battleships and carriers lying between the scattered British, Australian and Dutch light naval units in the East Indies and the still uncommitted American Fleet six thousand miles away in Pearl Harbour, it seemed to an experienced sailor like Pound impossible to contemplate anything more than a purely defensive strategy in the Indian Ocean.

Such a policy, however, was anathema to the Prime Minister,

who, like David with his sling, believed that offence was the way to deal with an overpowering enemy. Relying on what he described as " that kind of vague menace which capital ships of the highest quality whose whereabouts is unknown can impose on all hostile naval calculations,"[1] he proposed instead to send one of Britain's two strongest and fastest battleships—the newly-commissioned *Prince of Wales*—accompanied by a battle-cruiser, the *Repulse*, and a single aircraft-carrier, to lie in wait near Singapore and pounce on any Japanese warships approaching that port. This proposal was supported on political grounds by the Foreign Office, which felt that the arrival of the *Prince of Wales* in Far Eastern waters, if attended by enough publicity, might deter Japan from war.[2] The First Sea Lord, who was growing old and tired, and the Chiefs of Staff Committee of which he was Chairman, felt unable to withstand these powerfully argued considerations, and the *Prince of Wales* sailed for the Cape in the last week in October. She was joined at Colombo on November 28th by the *Repulse*. The aircraft-carrier was damaged by an accident and unable to sail, and there was no other available to take its place. At the end of the month the two unescorted battle-ships, neither properly prepared for war in the tropics, were hastily approaching Singapore.

.   .   .   .

Such was the global position on Monday December 1st when Alan Brooke left his Hampshire home at eight in the morning to drive to the War Office to begin his new task. After reading telegrams from the war-fronts from nine till half-past ten, he attended the Chiefs of Staff meeting, after

[1] " We should inculcate the true principles of naval strategy, one of which is certainly to cope with a superior force by using a small number of the best fast ships." Prime Minister to First Sea Lord, 29th August, 1941. *Churchill*, III, 773.

[2] " With the object of keeping Japan quiet we are sending our latest battleship, *Prince of Wales*, which can catch and kill any Japanese ship, into the Indian Ocean, and are building up a powerful battle squadron there." Prime Minister to Stalin, 4th November, 1941. *Churchill*, III, 469. General Smuts was more prescient. On November 18th, when the *Prince of Wales* was at Cape Town, he telegraphed to the Prime Minister expressing his concern at the division of Allied naval strength between Pearl Harbour and Singapore into " two fleets each separately inferior to the Japanese Navy. . . . If the Japanese are really nippy, there is here an opening for a first-class disaster." *The War at Sea*, 1939-45. (H.M.S.O.) 558.

which he and his colleagues—Admiral Pound and Air Chief Marshal Portal—were summoned by the Prime Minister to 10 Downing Street to discuss the possibilities of forestalling a Japanese invasion of Thailand and a threatened withdrawal of Australian troops from the Middle East to defend their own country. At six o'clock, after spending the afternoon preparing his brief, he attended the usual Monday evening meeting of the War Cabinet, to which he gave a résumé of the week's fighting in the Middle East and Russia. This went on till dinner, after which, at 9.30 p.m., there was another meeting of the Chiefs of Staff Committee which continued till after midnight.

Next day the situation in the Far East grew worse and Japanese submarines were reported moving south from Saigon. During the day Brooke attended two more Chiefs of Staff or C.O.S. committees, and, on December 3rd and 4th, in addition, two tense meetings of the War Cabinet and Defence Committee, presided over by the Prime Minister, to discuss the Foreign Secretary's impending visit to Moscow and what further aid he could offer the Kremlin from Britain's strained resources. Some members were in favour of offering tanks, others aircraft, others two divisions from the Middle East to hold the Caucasus in the event of a German break-through. But the difficulty with all these suggestions was that anything Britain gave the Russians was bound to be at the expense either of her Libyan campaign, now in a highly critical stage, or of her threatened and still almost undefended outposts in the Far East. The new C.I.G.S. told the War Cabinet that even the despatch of three hundred Churchill tanks by the end of June—the Prime Minister wanted to send five hundred—would dangerously denude the country of armour. For should the Red Army collapse, he pointed out, invasion might follow quickly and tank battles be fought on British soil similar to those now taking place in the Western Desert. Though this contingency made little impression on the Prime Minister, it left some of his colleagues very thoughtful.

For the chances of Russia holding out seemed at that moment highly problematical. By the beginning of November, having advanced five hundred miles in four months and destroyed or captured over two million men,[1] the Germans appeared to be on the point of repeating in the east their triumphs of the previous year in the west. Despite, however, Hitler's repeated claims that Russia's resistance was at an end, and though her capital was almost within gun-fire, her second city, Leningrad, encircled, and her third and fourth cities, Kharkov and Kiev, in enemy hands, she was still holding out. Since the fall of the first winter snows in October the German advance had been dramatically slowed down, and there were rumours of an impending Red Army counter-attack. But of the latter's ability to survive till the spring and, still more, of its capacity to resist a renewed offensive in the summer of 1942 there was no certainty and little hope. If the Germans could reach the Caucasus and its oil-wells, now only five or six hundred miles from their advanced airfields, the power of Russia to offer resistance would be at an end. In that case, not only would Britain face a renewed and far more formidable threat of *blitz* and invasion, but her whole position in the Middle East, including the Persian and Iraq oil-wells, would be threatened by major attack from the north.

In his autobiographical notes Brooke summed up the problems that confronted him in those first days of office.

' I was taking over at a difficult moment as far as the Far East was concerned. Dark clouds had been gathering fast on this horizon and everything pointed towards an early entry of Japan into the war. On the other hand, it was essential that we should take no step that might precipitate hostile action with Japan without the entry of the U.S.A. into the war. . . . I had discussed the possibility of Japan entering the war with Dill. He had told me frankly that he had done practically nothing to meet this threat. He said that we were already so weak on all fronts that it was impossible to denude them any further. . . . I think he was quite right in his dispositions and that he could not have done more, . . . but it left us in a lamentably dangerous position on the entry of Japan into the war.

[1] The Germans claimed to have destroyed the fantastic figure of ten million Russians. A. Bullock, *Hitler*, 606.

'It is interesting to . . . think that the despatch of land
and air forces to operate with the Russians on their southern
front was being seriously considered at this time. The conception was a wild one, as, in the first place, there were no
troops that could be spared . . . , and secondly, their employment on that front would have entailed countless administrative problems which had not even been looked
into.'

Even at that anxious time, though the country's overseas
forces were short of shipping, aircraft, tanks and battle-spares
of all kinds, the Minister of Defence and Chiefs of Staff
Committee were considering projects, at the former's instance,
for landings on the Norwegian, Sicilian, Italian and French
North African coasts, which, even if successful, would have
only further aggravated such shortages. 'I remember well,'
Brooke wrote, 'being appalled in those early days . . . to find the
lack of a definite policy for the prosecution of the war. We
worked from day to day a hand-to-mouth existence . . . that
swung us like a weathercock.'

To the new C.I.G.S. the nation's proper strategy seemed
obvious. It was to concentrate offensive effort in the place
where it could inflict the maximum injury on the enemy,
and continue to employ it there. Of the Government's wish
to offer two divisions to Stalin he wrote in his diary on
December 3rd: "This would probably mean having to close
down the Libyan offensive, whereas I am positive that our
policy for the conduct of the war should be to direct both
military and political efforts towards the early conquest of
North Africa. From there we shall be able to reopen the
Mediterranean and to stage offensive operations against
Italy." 'Already on my third day as C.I.G.S.,' he recalled
afterwards, 'I had a clear-cut idea as to what our policy
should be . . . It was plain to me that we must clear North
Africa to open the Mediterranean, and until we had done so
we should never have enough shipping to stage major
operations.'

For sea-transport was the governing factor in British
strategy, and everything hinged on it. Owing to the immense

loss of time involved in the double voyage round the Cape, there were only enough ships to transport between 40,000 and 50,000 troops and airmen out of Britain a month—barely enough to make good the normal wastage of battle and sickness of her overseas war-fronts and garrisons. And once they were embarked on their journey these became lost to the war for two or three months, and the ships that carried them for twice as long. The country's first objective, therefore, Brooke felt, should be to exert pressure on the one front where numbers and logistics favoured the British and not the German Army, and, by regaining the Cyrenaican airfields won by O'Connor's victories of a year earlier, secure air-cover for the Malta convoys and press on to Tripoli to expel the Italians and Germans from Africa. In this lay the importance of Malta and the justification of the losses sustained in supplying it by convoys from Gibraltar and Alexandria in the teeth of the Luftwaffe, Regia Aeronautica and Italian Fleet. Its stubborn defence, after Rommel had recovered the Cyrenaican airfields and driven the British back to Egypt, and the forays made by the Navy and R.A.F. from its battered harbour and airfields had alone prevented the central Mediterranean from becoming an uninterrupted Axis corridor across which unlimited reinforcements and supplies could be ferried for the conquest of Egypt. For from this minute island, only sixty miles from the Sicilian coast, British submarines and aircraft had been taking nightly toll of the Italian supply-ships that maintained the German Army in Africa. Recently, at the Prime Minister's instance and in the hope that with its help the Desert Army would reconquer Cyrenaica and drive on to Tripoli, the Admiralty had taken the risk of sending back to Malta a small force of light cruisers and destroyers to strike at Rommel's supply line. By sinking thirteen ships, including two urgently needed tankers, it had swung the desert battle in Britain's favour and enabled Auchinleck to relieve the besieged garrison of Tobruk at the end of November.

For Brooke was not alone in realizing the importance of the North African theatre. It had been the scene of the country's principal military effort ever since the defeat of the enemy's

invasion attempt in 1940.[1] The Prime Minister had built the
highest hopes on it. For months he had been urging General
Auchinleck and his Desert Commander, General Cunningham,
to launch an early attack, and, on the day it opened—November 18th—he had proclaimed to the world that the Desert
Army was about to add a page to history that would rank
with Blenheim and Waterloo. And beyond that victory his
far-ranging mind had envisaged a dazzling series of triumphs
—the expulsion of the Germans and Italians from Tripoli, an
invitation from the French authorities to enter Tunisia and
North-West Africa, and a descent on Sicily and Sardinia
from Malta. Indeed so sanguine was he that, despite the
gloomy view taken of this last operation by the naval and
military Commanders-in-Chief at Cairo, he had hoped to
embark on it by the end of the year.[2]

Yet though he felt the importance of pressing on with the
African offensive, he felt as strongly the call of other campaigns. At the beginning of the year, when O'Connor's
victories had opened the road to Tripoli, he had opted for a
campaign to aid Greece. Since the attack on Russia, he had
been insisting on the overriding importance of sending her
tanks and aircraft needed for the desert war and of using
Britain's over-strained shipping resources to carry them round
the North Cape to Murmansk. With equal conviction he
had been pleading for a second front in Norway and landings
in Italy—Operations " Anklet " and " Truncheon." He
wanted to fight the enemy at once with everything he had.
Brooke saw that to attempt so much was impossible. " I
tried," he wrote two days after Churchill had called him to
his side, " to begin to make him realise that we must have
one definite policy for the conduct of the war. I must get
the P.M. to see the advantages of a real North African
offensive policy."[3]

[1] As far back as August, 1940, the Chiefs of Staff—then under the chairmanship of Air Chief Marshal Sir Cyril (now Marshal of the Royal Air Force Lord)
Newall—informed American official military observers: " We regard the elimination of Italy as a strategic aim of the first importance. The collapse of Italy
would largely relieve the threat to the Middle East and free our hands at sea to
meet the Japanese threat." *Strategic Planning for Coalition Warfare*, 23.
    [2] *Churchill*, III, 479, 487, 488-9.
    [3] *Diary*, 3rd December, 1941.

Yet though he realized that the only way to wrest the initiative from foes who enjoyed the advantages of superior numbers and weapons was to concentrate at the one point where geographical circumstance and logistics did not favour them, it was impossible for Britain at that moment to do so. Hitherto her problem had been to contain the Axis Powers within a ring out of which they were trying to break. But now, at the moment Brooke was called to the nation's strategic counsels, those thinly-held besieging-lines were threatened with an attack, not merely from within, but from without, and by an assailant of immense strength.

On Sunday December 7th, the blow fell. Two days before, when the foreign military attachés were presented to him, Brooke noticed that the Japanese seemed gloomy. " I wonder," he noted in his diary, " whether we shall have them with us much longer." On the Saturday there was no Chiefs of Staff meeting, and, after working in the office all the afternoon, he was preparing to leave for home when, about five o'clock, a cablegram arrived from Singapore reporting that two convoys of transports, escorted by cruisers and destroyers, had been sighted sailing westward from Saigon.

> " As a result First Sea Lord at once called a meeting of Chiefs of Staff. Cadogan[1] from Foreign Office came also. We examined situation carefully, but from the position of the transports it was not possible to tell whether they were going to Bangkok, to the Kra Peninsula, or whether they were just cruising round as a bluff. P.M. called up from Chequers to have results of our meeting phoned through to him. Second message came in while we were there, but it did not clear up situation in the least and it only said that convoy had been lost and could not be picked up again. Put off going home, dined at club, returned to War Office after dinner. Back to my flat expecting to be called out again . . ."

Next day, while the Chiefs of Staff sat in continuous session discussing with representatives of the Foreign Office the

---

[1] The Rt. Hon. Sir Alexander Cadogan, Permanent Under-Secretary of State for Foreign Affairs.

various ways in which war might come and trying to ensure that under any given circumstances the United States would also be brought in, the Japanese resolved all doubts. Almost simultaneously their far-flung forces, moving outwards in a vast arc, had attacked, not only British Malaya and Hong Kong, but the American Philippines and Pearl Harbour. " All our work of the last forty-eight hours wasted," Brooke noted; " the Japs themselves have now ensured that the U.S.A. are in the war! "

To the Prime Minister even the disaster that had befallen the American Navy seemed of far less consequence than the fact that the United States was now ranged on Britain's side. On the same day he learnt that the last despairing attempt of Hitler's advance-guard to capture Moscow—launched in falling snow and Stygian darkness five days before—had failed, that the temperature on the Russian front had fallen to 40 degrees below zero, and that Stalin and Zhukov had launched their long-prepared counter-attack. That night, he wrote, he went to bed saturated and satiated with emotion and sensation and slept the sleep of the saved and thankful. When at a Chiefs of Staff meeting next day someone continued to advocate the same cautious approach to America that had seemed politic when her intervention was in doubt, he answered with a wicked leer in his eye, " Oh! that is the way we talked to her while we were wooing her; now that she is in the harem, we talk to her quite differently! " ' It was gems such as the above,' Brooke added, ' that often turned some of the blackest and long-drawn night meetings into far more bearable gatherings.'[1]

Yet, though America's entry into the War had immeasurably increased the possibilities of an ultimate Allied victory, the manner in which it had been brought about had greatly increased the chances of immediate and perhaps irretrievable disaster. Churchill's vision was on the horizon rather than on the shambles at his feet. On that December morning Japan had struck simultaneously at the United States' advance-base in the Philippines and at its Pacific Fleet five thousand miles away. While General MacArthur's bombers were being

[1] *Notes on My Life*, V, 325.

mown down on Clark Field, seven out of America's nine battleships in Pearl Harbour—or nearly half her capital ships —were sunk or put out of action. All hope of the American Fleet advancing to the relief of Malaya and the East Indies had gone. On the same day part of the small R.A.F. and R.A.A.F. contingent in Malaya was destroyed on its airfields, and Japanese troops landed in southern Thailand near the Malayan frontier. Next day an enemy detachment, crossing the narrow Kra isthmus, reached the shores of the Indian Ocean, seized the British landing-ground at Point Victoria and cut the air-route by which reinforcements from India and Europe were flown to Singapore.

"This has entirely upset balance in the Pacific and leaves the Japs master of the ocean until we can assemble some forces there," Brooke wrote after a late sitting of the Chiefs of Staff two days after Pearl Harbour. "We, there- fore, examined possibilities of sending British battleships to restore the situation." But next morning, December 10th, brought the worst news of the War since the fall of France. The *Prince of Wales*, which the Prime Minister had told Stalin could "catch and kill any Japanese ship," had been sunk together with the *Repulse* by torpedo-carrying aircraft while trying, without air-cover, to intercept a fleet of transports off the Malayan coast. Churchill's bold gamble to save Singapore had gone the way of Narvik, Greece and Crete. "It means," Brooke wrote that night, "that from Africa eastwards to America through the Indian Ocean and Pacific we have lost command of the sea."

The Prime Minister never flinched. Disaster brought out all that was greatest in him. His one idea now was to hasten to America to take counsel with his friend and ally, President Roosevelt. On the day after Japan struck he had obtained the Cabinet's permission to cross the Atlantic and had been somewhat chagrined by a telegram from Washington sug- gesting that for security reasons it might be better to postpone his visit till the New Year. But he was not to be deterred, and by the 12th he had got his way and was off, with hatches battened down against the winter gales, in the *Prince of Wales's* newly-commissioned sister-ship, the *Duke of York*. He took

with him the Minister of Supply, Lord Beaverbrook, the First
Sea Lord and the Chief of Air Staff, leaving the new C.I.G.S.
to act as chairman of a caretaker Chiefs of Staff Committee
in England with the Vice Chiefs of Naval and Air Staff as
his colleagues. Brooke was naturally disappointed but, being
hardly in the saddle, it was only, he wrote, to be expected.

Before Churchill sailed, however, he persuaded him—
at a meeting in Downing Street on the afternoon of the 11th
—to take with him as his permanent representative at Washington the man whom above all others he trusted and admired,
his predecessor, Sir John Dill.[1] ' This agreement,' he wrote,
' was not arrived at without a good deal of discussion. . . .
I had to press for this appointment and point out to him that,
with Dill's intimate knowledge of the working of the Chiefs
of Staff Committee and of our strategy, there could be no
better man to serve our purposes in Washington at the head
of our Mission. Thank heaven I succeeded in convincing
Winston, as few men did more in furthering our cause to final
victory than Dill. From the very start he built up a deep
friendship with Marshall and proved to be an invaluable
link between the British and American Chiefs of Staff. . . .
I look upon that half hour's discussion with Winston at 10
Downing Street on December 11th as one of my most important
accomplishments during the war or at any rate amongst
those that bore most fruit.'[2]

.   .   .   .

Thus within a fortnight of his entering on his duties Brooke
found himself left, under the Deputy Prime Minister, in charge
of the British war-machine in London " to grip," as Churchill
put it, " the tremendous problems that awaited him,"
while his political chief and colleagues crossed the Atlantic
to settle in conference with the Americans how those

[1] " In the afternoon went to Downing Street to see P.M. about sending Dill
to U.S.A. as Head of our Mission there, that is to say for him to go with P.M.
and then remain there. P.M. agreed." *Diary*, 11th December, 1941.

[2] *Notes on My Life*, V, 345. Under the original arrangement he was to have
had the title of Deputy Defence Minister. But later the Prime Minister changed
his mind and appointed him Head of the British Military Mission. ' With a man
like Dill,' Brooke commented, ' it did not matter what you called him: he did
what he considered was required of him.'

problems should be solved. " Had a real good afternoon at the office," he wrote on the day they sailed from the Clyde, " and at last began to get level with some of my work." It was all the heavier because the Vice Chief of Imperial General Staff was with the Foreign Secretary in Moscow, the Deputy Chief with the Prime Minister and Dill on the high seas, and the Director of Staff Duties on a mission to the Middle East. Almost every night that month Brooke was forced to return to the office after dinner to wrestle till midnight or after with seas of paper. The amount he had to read was so great that it affected his eyes.

One relief, however, in his chairman's absence, was the rapidity with which he was able to get through committee work. In the Deputy Prime Minister, too, who now presided over the War Cabinet, he found a political chief as expeditious in conducting business as himself. " Afternoon Cabinet meeting at 5 p.m.," he wrote on the 15th, " and Defence Committee meeting at 6 p.m. which lasted till 8 p.m. . . . run by Attlee very efficiently and quickly."

The next few weeks were a strategist's nightmare. Three days after the Prime Minister sailed, Brooke wrote in his diary, " Far East situation far from rosy! I doubt whether Hong Kong will hold out a fortnight and Malaya a month." The garrison of the former—six British and Canadian battalions without air-cover, facing the assault of three divisions—had been driven from the mainland on to the congested and heavily bombed island before his colleagues sailed for America. The Philippines were invaded on the day after the sinking of the *Prince of Wales*, and Borneo, with its Dutch and British oilfields, a week later. On December 18th the city of Penang, on the west coast of Malaya, after being wrecked by dive-bombers, was occupied by the Japanese, now advancing swiftly down both sides of the peninsula towards Singapore.

On the same day a dreadful naval disaster occurred in the Eastern Mediterranean. Following the loss of the *Ark Royal*, *Barham*, *Prince of Wales* and *Repulse*, Admiral Cunningham's two remaining battleships, the *Queen Elizabeth* and *Valiant*, were holed in Alexandria harbour by time-bombs affixed by Italian " frogmen." This brought the loss or disablement of

British and American capital ships in a month to fifteen or nearly half their combined battle strength in all oceans. Next day, while trying to intercept a convoy of German and Italian supplies bound for Tripoli, three British cruisers and four destroyers from Malta—the " K " force which the Prime Minister had induced the Admiralty to base on the island—were caught in a minefield. A further cruiser was sunk in the same week by U-boats. Simultaneously a German Air Corps, withdrawn from Russia—where flying had temporarily become impossible—opened an all-out assault on Malta. Except for the island's defiant guns and empty harbour nothing remained in the two thousand miles between Gibraltar and Alexandria of Britain's mastery of the Mediterranean but three cruisers and a handful of destroyers and submarines.

The effect on the African campaign was disastrous. With Malta immobilised and his Mediterranean supply-line re-opened, Rommel was in a position to strike back at Auchinleck's over-extended army, already more than six hundred miles from its base at Alexandria. And at the very moment when, with Tobruk relieved, the British began to advance at long last across Cyrenaica, an urgent demand had arisen for the deflection of reinforcements from the desert war to the Far East. " Informed by ' Pug ' Ismay," the C.I.G.S. wrote on December 11th, " that the P.M. now wanted to send the 18th Division to Rangoon to attack Japs in Kra Isthmus, being now convinced that we have enough troops for the North African business." Two days later Churchill from the Atlantic cabled the acting Chiefs of Staff Committee in London to start moving men and material into India and to reinforce with air from the Middle East as soon as the battle in Libya had been won. A pull-devil, pull-baker contest now developed between the two theatres of war, both dependent on a fantastically long supply-line. " The more I look at the situation," Brooke wrote on the 20th, " the more I dislike it. My hopes of carrying on with the conquest and reclamation of North Africa are beginning to look more and more impossible every day. From now on the Far East will make ever-increasing inroads into our resources."

By Christmas Eve things were worse.

" Another hard day. Chiefs of Staff meeting in the morning. The situation beginning to become difficult. Winston, arrived in Washington far from the war, pushing for operation by U.S.A. and ourselves against North Africa and banking on further success of Middle East offensive towards Tripoli. On the other side Duff Cooper in Singapore by his demands inspiring the Australians to ask for more and more for the Far East. In the middle Auchinleck struggling along with the forces at his disposal and sending optimistic personal and private messages to P.M., little knowing that his activities must shortly be curtailed owing to transfer of air and sea reinforcements from Middle East to Far East."

" At 3 p.m. Defence Committee meeting to settle aerodrome defence and ' scorched earth ' policy in Malay peninsula. . . . Had hoped to get home for Xmas, but impossible now owing to urgent necessity for Chiefs of Staff meeting to-morrow morning. So dined quietly with Barney and now off to an early bed."

" *December 25th.* Xmas Day and my first official day as C.I.G.S. Went to War Office at 9.30 where I spent two hours studying paper prepared by Joint Planning Committee on relative importance of our new Far East commitments taken in relation with the Middle East. At 11.30 went to Chiefs of Staff meeting to discuss same paper. I had to prepare wire to P.M. with reference to his desire to carry out " Gymnast " operation (i.e. reinforcements to French North Africa in event of being called in). Problem complicated by the fact that it does not look as if we are likely to be called in, and secondly that P.M. now is toying with the idea of carrying out such a plan against resistance, and finally owing to the fact that shipping available does not admit of both occupying North Africa at request of French and reinforcing Far East sufficiently to secure Singapore, Burma, and Indian Ocean communications. We have laid down that first of all in importance comes security of this country and its communications and after that Singapore and communications through Indian Ocean. This is correct, as, if the latter go, the Middle East or possibly India may follow suit. Committee lasted till 6 p.m. News received this evening that Hong Kong had fallen on Xmas Eve.

"*December 26th.* Usual C.O.S. meeting when we discussed various points connected with reinforcing of Far East and Fiji Islands, etc. In afternoon rung up by Attlee to find out whether we were ready for a Defence Committee to keep Australians quiet as they were fretting about reinforcements for Singapore. Told him we had better wait till we had reply from P.M. Later Mr. Bruce[1] asked to see me and I had to explain to him what we were doing for the Far East. He went away satisfied. Just before dinner wire from P.M. for Auchinleck came in which necessitated holding impromptu Chiefs of Staff meeting after dinner. Finally interview with Secretary of State and bed at midnight. Very weary."

"*December 27th.* A long and wearying Chiefs of Staff meeting with a series of difficult problems mainly connected with the P.M. and his Chiefs of Staff Committee in U.S.A. brewing up a series of discrepancies with what we are preparing here. In afternoon a Cabinet Defence Committee meeting. Lasted till 7.30 p.m. I then escaped home in the hope of being allowed to spend a quiet Sunday and recuperate from the effort of the last three weeks. Got home by 8.45 p.m. A very peaceful evening."

For as, with the turn of the year, the Japanese fanned rapidly outwards in the islands of the South-West Pacific and the Eighth Army followed up Rommel's retreating forces to Agheila—the farthest point reached in O'Connor's advance of the previous year—an alarmed Australian Government began to clamour for the withdrawal of its divisions from the Middle East to defend Singapore, New Guinea and its own threatened shores. Just as the deflection of forces to Greece at the moment of O'Connor's victory had dashed the hopes of the first Cyrenaican offensive, so the weakening of effort

---

[1] The Rt. Hon. S. M. (now Viscount) Bruce, Australian High Commissioner.

brought about on sea and land by the pressure of events in the Far East helped to destroy the more ambitious expectations built on the second. Brooke already realised how delusive these were.

"*January 9th, 1942.* Chiefs of Staff meeting this morning where we had representatives from Middle East to discuss with them the possibility of carrying out ' Acrobat ' (i.e. attack on Tripoli) in spite of delays that had occurred in capture of Cyrenaica and new situation in the Far East. In view of the fact that this operation cannot be carried out for six weeks and that during this period reinforcements may well flow into Africa from Italy, I am beginning to wonder whether the operation is on. At any rate I feel that it ought, if possible, to be connected with the operation for occupying North Africa on the invitation of the French. But, first secure your invitation! "

Five days after making this entry Brooke heard that the plans of the Prime Minister and President for a landing in French North Africa had been put off for lack of shipping. The moment for the offensive had passed; the time had come to draw in and hold fast to what was essential until the storm had been weathered and a real counter-offensive was possible. Even as he was writing, Rommel's Afrika Korps, re-equipped from the now unmolested Tripoli convoys, was preparing to strike back. In the next three weeks it advanced three hundred miles, racing the Eighth Army back to Gazala and recovering nearly all the ground and more than all the prestige won by the British in the Christmas campaign. The hopes of " Acrobat "—the operation that was to have swept to the Tunisian frontier and cleared the Axis out of Africa— were fading like a desert mirage.

In the same month the Japanese, enjoying complete command of sea and air, overran the whole of Malaya as far as the narrow strait dividing it from Singapore, bottled up General MacArthur's Philippine army in the starve-acre Bataan peninsula, invaded the Celebes and Burma, and, by effecting landings in New Britain, the Solomons and New

Ireland, started to cut the communications between Australia and the United States. It was not surprising that the C.I.G.S., seeing the pattern of events ahead, began his diary for 1942 with a prayer. " Started New Year," he wrote, " wondering what it may have in store for us. One thing I fully realise is that it has got about as much work in store for me as I can possibly cope with. I pray God that He may give me sufficient strength to devote the energy that it will require." Would it prove possible, he asked, to " ward-off the onrush of Germany on the one side and Japan on the other whilst the giant of America slowly girded his armour on? "

.   .   .   .

Meanwhile three thousand miles away in Washington the Prime Minister and Brooke's colleagues had been formulating with the American leaders the Western Allies' strategy. With the unco-operative and suspicious totalitarians in the Kremlin there seemed little possibility of concerting plans for common action; they regarded their allies with unconcealed distrust, denied them even the most elementary information and were only prepared to take what they could get without offering anything in return except their own stout fight for survival. But the Americans and British spoke the same language, held the same ideals and were separated from one another only by the ocean whose rule they shared. A common strategy for victory was both practicable and essential, and it was to concert it with Roosevelt and his Service advisers that Churchill and the other two Chiefs of Staff had crossed the Atlantic.

Earlier in the year it had been agreed in tentative Anglo-American staff conversations that, if the United States went to war, the two democracies should join in defeating Germany before turning against Japan. This decision had been confirmed at the Atlantic meeting in August. But the indignity of Pearl Harbour had made Japan the arch-enemy to every American, and it was a matter of grave doubt whether such a policy, however strategically sound, could now be honoured. Yet as soon as the Prime Minister reached the White House, with splendid courage and loyalty the President and General Marshall, Chief of the American Army Staff, affirmed their belief that the prior defeat of Germany was the key to victory. "Once Germany is defeated," Roosevelt wrote on Christmas Eve, "the collapse of Italy and the defeat of Japan must follow."

What was as admirable was the American leaders' resolve to pool with Britain all their resources, military and economic, and employ them under a single unified command. To Churchill's delight they at once proposed two far-reaching measures to give unity to the Allied councils: a Declaration of War Aims to be signed by all the associated Powers—henceforward, at his suggestion, to be called the United Nations; and a single Command for all the forces resisting Japan in the South-west Pacific and South-east Asia. To supervise the latter it was also agreed that a Combined Chiefs of Staff organisation, fashioned on the British model, and comprising the British Chiefs of Staff and their American counterparts, should be set up in Washington. Under the President and Prime Minister, this body was to plan the strategy, allocate the man-power, supplies and munitions, and co-ordinate the communications of the two English-speaking nations and their dependencies as though they were one. It was to meet whenever major decision was necessary, and the British Chiefs of Staff, in their absence in London, were to be represented by a team of deputies under Sir John Dill.

What was more, the American leaders made it clear that they intended to wage war with all the resources they possessed. In the opening days of the New Year the President announced a "Victory" production programme of 45,000 aircraft, 45,000 tanks, 20,000 anti-aircraft guns, 15,000 anti-tank guns and 500,000 machine-guns for 1942, and nearly twice as many for 1943. And to transport its armies and their supplies across the seas, the United States was to build eight million dead-weight tons of merchant shipping in the first year and ten million in the second.

Yet though the potential resources of America were boundless and the self-confidence of her leaders as great, her military forces were still negligible. Like Britain, she had been strong only at sea, and now the greater part of her battle-fleet had been put out of action for many months. Her arsenals were empty, and even her vaunted heavy bombers were equipped with only 100-lb. bombs. The President's list of the weapons America was planning to make—though no less than her tremendous capacity—was also an admission of what she lacked. Her leaders and people had no idea of what modern war involved and of how unprepared they were for it. The British visitors to Washington that Christmas, fresh from their own austere war-economy, were staggered by the luxury of the American capital: the swarming cars like beetles in every avenue, the huge newspapers, the piled-up food in the restaurants. " This country is the most highly organised for peace you can imagine," Dill wrote to Brooke. " Everything is done on a grand scale. I have never seen so many motor cars, but I have not seen a military vehicle. . . . And yet amid all this unpreparedness the ordinary American firmly believes that they can finish off the war quite quickly—and without too much disturbance. . . . Never have I seen a country so utterly unprepared for war and so soft."[1]

By English standards American inter-Service administration seemed completely unorganised. Even the President—the Commander-in-Chief of the Armed Forces—had no secretariat and no regular private secretary. The lack of system extended right through the Government machine. The Navy and Army acted as independent Powers, often pursuing diametrically opposite courses. When the United States Joint Chiefs of Staff—hastily-formed on the British model—met their British counterparts at their first combined meeting, there was not even an agenda or anyone responsible for taking the minutes. " There are no regular meetings of their Chiefs of Staff," Dill told Brooke, " and if they do meet there is no secretariat to record their proceedings. They have no joint planners and executive planning staff. . . . Then there is the great difficulty of getting the stuff over to the President. He just sees the Chiefs of Staff at odd times, and again no record. There is no such thing as a Cabinet meeting, and yet the Secretaries for War, Navy, etc., are supposed to function. At present this country has not—repeat not—the slightest conception

---

[1] Dill to Brooke, 28th December, 1941; 3rd, 9th January, 1942. Lord Alan-brooke, *Personal Files*.

of what the war means, and their armed forces are more unready for war than it is possible to imagine. Eventually they will do great things, but the difficulty is going to be to hold cards of re-entry to enable them to play their strong suits when they have collected them. . . . The whole organization belongs to the days of George Washington who was made Commander-in-Chief of all the Forces and just did it. To-day the President is Commander-in-Chief of all the Forces, but it is not so easy to just do it."[1]

Nor had the grand plan of operations which the American Chiefs of Staff presented to their British colleagues for dealing with the tornado of destruction sweeping across the British, Dutch and American possessions in Asia any relation to the immediate realities of the situation. It was far too optimistic. While in the Atlantic American troops were to garrison Iceland and Northern Ireland and with their British allies effect a landing in French North Africa, the combined American, British, Dutch and Australian sea, land and air forces in the South-west Pacific were to be placed at once under a single Supreme Commander with an inter-Allied staff politically responsible to some still undefined international authority to be set up in Washington. This Command, called A.B.D.A., which had emanated from the mind of General Marshall—a great believer in unity of command—was to comprise, not only the East Indies, Malaya and the Philippines but New Guinea and Burma, which were to be separated from their natural supply-base in Australia and India.[2] It was to hold an island barrier stretching for nearly four thousand miles from the Sumatra Straits and the entrance to the Indian Ocean to the island groups north-east of the Coral Sea and Australia—New Britain, New Ireland, Bougainville, the Solomons, Guadalcanal—and beyond them, tapering away into the illimitable South Pacific, the Fijis and Samoa. Denying the Japanese the rubber, oil and raw materials of Borneo, Java and Sumatra, three of the world's largest islands,

---

[1] Dill to Brooke, 3rd January, 1942. Lord Alanbrooke, *Personal Files.*
[2] " The area allotted to Wavell . . . . is continually giving trouble," Brooke wrote, " owing to original mistake of including Burma and not including Australia and New Zealand. I expect that we shall gradually be forced to change these back again." *Diary,* 12th January, 1942.

it was to secure the threatened naval base of Singapore, defend the Burma road to China, halt the Japanese advance towards Australia, and, after fulfilling these tasks, relieve MacArthur's forces in the Philippines and assist the Chinese.

But, in the face of unchallenged Japanese sea and air power, the territories comprised in this vast area could no longer be controlled, let alone defended, as a single unit, since their sea communications lay at the enemy's mercy. Japan, which had already broken the barrier in several places, could concentrate wherever she chose and destroy the defenders— immobile for lack of shipping—one by one. Receiving hourly reports that revealed only too clearly what Churchill called " the hideous efficiency of the Japanese war-machine " and the impotence of their own and the United Nations' forces in South-east Asia, the British leaders in Washington saw this clearly, but were so impressed by the importance of creating Anglo-American unity and of saving Singapore by hook or crook that they felt compelled to accept the American proposals. And the Prime Minister, though he pointed out the difficulties, was moved by the President's wish to confer the Supreme Command in South-east Asia on an Englishman— General Wavell. His Service advisers took a less sanguine view of the offer. " It would, I think, be fatal," Dill wrote to Brooke, " to have a British commander responsible for the disasters that are coming to the Americans as well as ourselves. . . . Never was a soldier given a more difficult task. . . . It is of the first importance that we should not be blamed for the bloody noses that are coming to them."[1]

To Brooke, transmitting across half the globe the executive orders for plans in whose shaping he had had no part, all this caused feelings akin to despair. The proposals for holding the Japanese seemed to him not only unrealistic but highly dangerous. Without command of either sea or air there could be no possibility of saving Indonesia, and little of saving even Singapore which, however strong when buttressed by the sea-power it was made to sustain, was indefensible without it. By deflecting to the retention of the untenable such meagre rein-

[1] Dill to Brooke, 28 Dec. 1941, 3 Jan. 1942. Lord Alanbrooke, *Personal Files.*

forcements and shipping as were available, the Washington planners were imperilling Burma and its oilfields and, still more important, what lay beyond. The essential thing was to preserve Britain's sea communications in the Indian Ocean by directing to wherever they could best help to do so every vessel, man and weapon within reach. For once those communications went, everything would go, including India, the Middle East and its oil, and the all-important siege-lines round the Axis in Europe. The Allies were faced with that " option of difficulties " which lies at the root of every strategic problem; they had to sacrifice the lesser for the greater, to know—what Wellington defined as the hallmark of a great commander—" when to retreat and to dare to do it." " Personally I do not feel that there is much hope of saving Singapore," wrote Brooke on December 17th, " but feel that we ought to try to make certain of Burma." On the day after the *Prince of Wales* and *Repulse* were sunk he had, therefore, persuaded his colleagues and the Prime Minister to transfer that country from the Malayan to the Indian Command and, by routing the 18th Division, then at the Cape, to Bombay, to place it at the disposal of the Commander-in-Chief, India, for use either for reinforcing Burma or, alternatively the Persian Gulf, should the Germans break through the Russian Caucasian front and threaten the Abadan oil. This arrangement was now to be reversed by the Washington Conference's transference of Burma to A.B.D.A. and its decision to attempt to hold Singapore and the Dutch and British East Indies without either a battle-fleet or control of the air. To Brooke the separation of Burma's defence from its natural supply-base in India and its transfer to Java, two thousand miles away in the middle of a threatened archipelago, seemed unreal. " The whole scheme wild and half-baked," he wrote two days before the end of the year, " and only catering for one area of action, namely the Western Pacific, one enemy Japan, and no central control. . . . Cabinet was forced to accept P.M.'s new scheme owing to the fact that it was almost a *fait accompli*."

Equally unrealistic, Brooke had felt, in the light of the Japanese Fleet's threat to the Allies' position, had been the

Prime Minister's and President's premature project for an Anglo-American landing in French North Africa, with or without Vichy's connivance. The only strategic purpose of " Gymnast," as it was called, could be to reopen the Mediterranean, and this could only be achieved in conjunction with a British victory in the Western Desert and not at a time when the Middle East base was itself in danger. The Prime Minister's " elated and optimistic mood," as Brooke called it, had not appeared to him justified, being based on hopes of an advance from Cyrenaica into Tripolitania which could no longer be sustained now that the warships, troops and supplies required for its success were being deflected from the Middle to the Far East. The shipping available to the Allies was obviously inadequate to supply Singapore, Burma and the Middle East during the next six months and simultaneously transport a major amphibious force across the Atlantic, even if sufficient American troops had been trained and equipped to assist the two British divisions waiting in England for this hazardous operation. So much that was proposed in Washington that Christmas seemed to bear the impress of minds which had still to grasp the complex logistics on which the planning of modern war depended. With the U.S.A. unable for many months to play any but an insignificant part in the fighting, it seemed unwise, by centering strategic control in Washington, to subordinate to those who were still only beginners the hard-won knowledge, organization and battle experience of the British High Command. Compelled to accept, and struggling to adjust to the realities of the situation the plans continually arriving from Washington, the new C.I.G.S. felt that the Prime Minister and his colleagues were selling their " birthright for a plate of porridge! "[1]

Yet in this he was being unjust to them. The Prime Minister had accepted his Allies' proposals, not on military grounds but, as he explained in a letter to Attlee, because " We are no longer single, but married." What mattered was that the United States, with its isolationist tradition, natural interest in the Pacific and blazing anger against Japan, should from the start adopt the habit of working with Britain to a common

[1] *Diary*, 9th February, 1942.

end, and that that end, if not the immediate means, should be clearly envisaged. The rest would follow, as the greatest industrial Power in the world, with its vast productive capacity and reserves of skilled manpower, transformed its economy from peace to war. The real achievement of " Arcadia," as the Washington Conference was called, was not the impracticable A.B.D.A. Command in the Pacific nor even the creation of a Combined Chiefs of Staff for the two nations. It was the decision that the Pacific war should be a holding war and that the first objective of America should be the defeat of the Axis in Europe. To secure this Churchill was rightly prepared to sacrifice almost anything.

For when it came to the political direction of war—to seeing and expressing its broad, fundamental truths in terms that men and nations could understand and translate into action —the Prime Minister had no equal. That Christmas he spoke to Congress of the troubles and tribulations that lay before the English-speaking peoples, proclaiming his conviction that they could together create a force there could be no resisting. " What kind of a people do they think we are? " he asked of the Japanese. " Is it possible they do not realize that we shall never cease to persevere against them until they have been taught a lesson which they and the world will never forget. . . . He must indeed have a blind soul who cannot see that some great purpose and design is being worked out here below, of which we have the honour to be the faithful servants. . . . The best tidings of all is that the United States, united as never before, have drawn the sword for freedom and cast away the scabbard."[1] " Here's to 1942," he told the American pressmen on New Year's Eve. " Here's to a year of toil— a year of struggle and peril, and a long step forward towards victory! "

.   .   .   .

On January 17th, after five weeks' absence, this great leader returned to a Britain faced with accumulating disaster. He had insisted, at the last moment and at some personal risk, on flying home from Bermuda and so arrived unannounced

[1] W. Churchill, *The Unrelenting Struggle*, 337-9.

one morning at Plymouth a week earlier than was expected.[1] Brooke in his diary described the crowd of Ministers in black slouch hats and astrakhan collars assembled at Paddington to greet him, and the evening Cabinet meeting at which he gave them an account of his American impressions. Next day he was summoned from his Sabbath rest to motor over snow-covered roads to dine alone with Mr. and Mrs. Churchill and their daughter Mary at the Annexe at Storey's Gate. " A very pleasant quiet homely dinner," he noted, " he could not have been nicer. After dinner went to his study where I remained with him till after midnight discussing the possibilities of Singapore island holding out. Also drew his attention to the dangers of Rangoon."

That evening marked the beginning of the long partnership between these two men. Brooke already realised how formidable its difficulties must prove. As Commander-in-Chief, he had learnt something of his leader's lightning changes of mood, untiring, stubborn will, and passionate intensity. " Difficult times with the P.M. I see clearly ahead of me," he wrote in his diary on New Year's Day, " I pray God to help me by giving me guidance as to how to handle the situations which are certain to confront me." Even in his first week of office, before Japan entered the war and Churchill sailed for America, he had had a foretaste of his impetuous, stormy temper. It had happened at a midnight Chiefs of Staff meeting, with the Lord Privy Seal, Mr. Attlee, and the Foreign Secretary, Anthony Eden, in attendance, when the Chief of Air Staff had tried to stop the Prime Minister from committing himself irrevocably to a promise to transfer ten squadrons from North Africa to Russia at the end of the Libyan offensive. " This produced," Brooke wrote,

" the most awful outburst of temper. We were told that we did nothing but obstruct his intentions, we had no

[1] " Usual Chiefs of Staff meeting when we discovered that the P.M. was flying through from Bermuda and had landed at 9 a.m." *Diary*, 17th January, 1942. The flying-boat, owing to a slight variation in its course, was at one time heading for Brest and was only saved from the German batteries by a timely alteration of course. *Churchill*, III, 628-9.

ideas of our own and, whenever he produced ideas, we produced nothing but objections, etc., etc. Attlee pacified him once, but he broke out again; then Anthony Eden smoothed him temporarily, but all to no avail. Finally he looked at his papers for some five minutes, then slammed them together, closed the meeting and walked out of the room. It was pathetic and entirely unnecessary. We were only trying to save him from making definite promises which he might find hard to keep later on. It is all the result of over-working himself and keeping too late hours. Such a pity ! God knows where we should be without him, but God knows where we shall go with him ! "[1]

Yet when the Chiefs of Staff met next morning they were greeted with a memorandum from their unpredictable chief couched in almost identical terms to those they had begged him to accept the night before. He would browbeat his advisers, but, provided they stood up to him, he was not prepared to overrule them. It was his instinct to pursue the daring course, and, in his dealings with his Allies, the magnanimous one. And he was deeply suspicious of what he called " resistances," particularly from his Service chiefs. " Those damned planners of yours," he once said to Brooke of the Joint Planning Staff, " plan nothing but difficulties." He was always afraid that opportunities to attack would be lost, by excessive prudence, inertia, " the usual helpless negation." It was a legacy partly from his experiences as a young soldier and Cabinet Minister after the long Victorian peace, when many senior military commanders had been hidebound and obstructionist and when his imagination and adventurous spirit had been thwarted by conservatism and playing for safety. It was the legacy, too, of the bitter years when he had been a voice crying in the wilderness, vainly warning his countrymen against " the dangers of yielding to soft, easy and popular expedients and the dark places into

---

[1] *Diary*, 4th December, 1941. ' This was the first serious storm that I came into contact with, and when I saw him slam his papers together and walk out of the room, without even saying " Good night," it made a deep impression. I was destined to weather many more such storms.' *Notes on My Life*, V, 323.

which we have been led thereby."[1]   And it was an inherent part—however troublesome to his advisers—of his service to England.   It had been Churchill's passionate and reiterated refusal to take " No " for an answer when " No " would have involved certain defeat that had placed his country for ever in his debt.

It was his duty as Defence Minister to probe and sift the official advice tendered to him by his Service chiefs—most of whom had been young lieutenants when he had first become a Service Minister[2] thirty years before—and he would have been a different, and lesser, man had he spared them.   In doing so he was instinctively testing their plans by making them oppose him and argue them out in the teeth of his powers of debate and invective.   If he found himself convinced they were right, he would himself become the spokesman of the very arguments he had so fiercely criticised.   Both consciously and unconsciously, he was always testing his subordinates by the sternest of tests.   ' How often,' wrote Brooke, ' have I seen Winston eyeing me carefully, trying to read my innermost thoughts, searching for any doubts that might rest under the surface.'   In the last resort, his decision and his alone stood between the nation and disaster.   Even when he seemed most unreasonable and exacting, it was impossible, Brooke wrote, ' not to be filled with sympathy for him when one realised the colossal burden he was bearing and the weight of responsibility he shouldered.'[3]

For the traits that made Churchill so hard to work for arose, not from lack of heart or consideration, but from absorption in his task of saving the nation and the single-mindedness with which he pursued his object.   He had so much on his shoulders —so much more than any other man—that he had little time to consider the convenience of others.   His mind, interested in everything pertaining to the human lot, cast a searchlight into every cranny of the nation's life.   Nothing came amiss to it, and no-one could predict—least of all the Ministers,

[1] *Churchill*, III, 447.

[2] Like Sir Bertram Ramsay—the admiral who directed the Dunkirk evacuation and D-Day landings—who was the son of his old commanding officer in the 4th Hussars and had been first seen by him as a child on the barrack square at Aldershot.   *Idem*, II, 240.

[3] *Notes on My Life*, IV, 289, VII, 536.

bureaucrats and Service chiefs upon whose activities it was turned—when and where it would light. Two days after Pearl Harbour and on the day that the *Prince of Wales* and *Repulse* were lost, and when the entire British and American position in the Pacific was crumbling, this amazing Prime Minister dictated, *inter alia*, three searching minutes to ensure that sweet-rationing should not be introduced unnecessarily, that timber-felling companies should not be allowed to denude woodlands without consideration for the appearance of the countryside, and that young women in the A.T.S., serving with A.A. batteries, should not be roughly treated and should receive every kind of minor compliment and ornament for good service.[1]

When it came to the planning of military operations this tireless energy presented those responsible with a most difficult problem. It was a part of Churchill's greatness—and of the human attributes that are the accompaniment and, at times, reverse of greatness—that he was constitutionally incapable of not intervening with his entire heart, soul and mind in any operation, great or small, of which he had cognizance, whether strategical, administrative or technical. And since, as Minister of Defence he was responsible to Parliament for the entire conduct of the War, and since there was almost no martial activity in which—himself once a soldier, a military historian, and at one time political head of each of the three Services— he was not intensely interested, it followed that his and the nation's official advisers were subject to his questioning, entreaty, interference and, when necessary, reproach at every hour of the day and night. Enjoying, despite his sixty-seven years, a wonderful and unflagging vitality and health, and possessed of boundless curiosity and of a boyish and, at times, almost impish pugnacity and zest, he subjected them, often without realising it, to a continuous, harrowing and exhausting, if stimulating, martyrdom. The extraordinary hours he per- sisted in keeping, in glorious defiance of conventional Whitehall routine, made their ordeal all the more severe, since, while they were forced on the one hand to carry out their admini- strative work as heads of their Departments during the ordinary

[1] *Churchill*, III, 754-5.

hours of Service and bureaucratic practice, they were expected to share in the long and exuberant night-life of their chief who, spending most of the daylight hours of morning in bed, reading and dictating despatches and memoranda and giving audiences, and refreshing himself after his Cabinet and parliamentary duties with an evening siesta, awoke to full and volcano-like activity—ten times greater than that of any ordinary being—at the hour when most men, exhausted by the day's labour, were seeking recreation or sleep. In those hours of the night, often continued till three or four in the morning, there poured from him a never-ending stream of ideas, projects, questionings, information, anecdotes and commentary on life and human nature. More often he spoke of the war and of the many and resourceful ways by which he hoped to win it.

Yet on a man bearing an immense executive load, who had been working since nine in the morning at high pressure at office-desk and in committee, these midnight sessions imposed an immense strain. " As I look back on them," wrote Brooke of his visits to Chequers, " I remember best long drawn-out evenings and a desperate longing for bed as these evenings extended well into the morning hours. There were times . . . of intense interest, and one could be certain of boundless hospitality, but at the end of a very hard week's work to be kept up till the small hours of the morning was, to put it mildly, a very trying procedure." When the American Chief of Staff, General Marshall, stayed with the Prime Minister for the first time, and dinner was followed by a review of the war which went on till 2 a.m. and then by a film which lasted till 2.45 a.m., " his face," Brooke wrote, " was a study. . . . He was evidently not used to being kept out of his bed till the small hours of the morning and not enjoying it much. . . . I wonder how he would have liked to work permanently with Winston, and be kept out of bed three or four nights a week."[1]

" My day starts at 9 a.m. and seldom finishes before midnight," Brooke told a friend, " whilst it frequently goes on

[1] *Diary*, 10th April, 1942. ' He certainly had a much easier life of it with Roosevelt; he informed me that he frequently did not see him for a month or six weeks. I was fortunate if I did not see Winston for six hours.' *Notes on My Life*, V, 381.

till one or two in the morning. . . . Have now finished two months as C.I.G.S. and it feels as if it had been ten years! " During the early weeks of 1942 the association between him and his chief was tried as few successful partnerships can ever have been tried. For that winter disaster rained on them as fast as bombs a year before. From the beginning of January until the end of March Brooke's diary is the chronicle of the worst succession of defeats in British history. January 30th, he wrote, was one of the dark days of the war. " News bad on all sides. Benghazi has been lost again, and Singapore is in a bad way. The defence is retiring into the island to-night. I doubt whether the island can hold out very long." Three days later he had to record " most unpleasant remarks by various Ministers in connection with defeats by our forces. As we had retired into Singapore Island and lost aerodromes, besides being pushed back in Libya, I had a good deal to account for, and found it hard to keep my temper with some of the criticisms that were raised." " Politicians," he wrote to Wavell, " prefer to be fed on victories than gorged on reverses." On February 9th there was a further " unpleasant Cabinet meeting. The news had just arrived that the Japs had got into Singapore Island. As a result, nothing but abuse for the Army. The Auk's retreat in Cyrenaica is also making matters more sour. . . . At 10.45 p.m. I was sent for by P.M. to assist him in drafting a telegram to Wavell about the defence of Singapore and the necessity for staffs and commanders to perish at their posts." ' The drafting of this telegram,' Brooke commented, ' was not an easy one, as I always consider it dangerous to interfere with a commander at a distance when you cannot be fully familiar with all the aspects of the situation confronting him.'

" *February 11th.* The news of Singapore goes from bad to worse, and now poor Archie Wavell has injured his back.[1] P.M. sent for me this evening to discuss with him last wire from Wavell about Singapore from whence he had just returned. It was a very gloomy . . . and depressing wire as regards the fighting efficiency of the troops in

[1] He had fallen off a jetty in the dark and broken two bones.

Singapore Island. It is hard from here to see why a better defence is not being put up, but I presume there must be some very good reason. I can't see the place holding out more than a day or two now. The losses . . . will be vast, not only in men but in material. I have during the last ten years had an unpleasant feeling that the British Empire was decaying and that we were on a slippery decline. I wonder if I was right? I certainly never expected that we should fall to pieces as fast as we are, and to see Hong Kong and Singapore go in less than three months plus a failure in the Western Desert is far from reassuring. We have had a wonderful power of recuperation in the past; I wonder whether we shall again bring off a comeback?"

'It is only,' Brooke wrote afterwards, 'by living through such periods of ghastly doubts when loaded with responsibility that one can realise how they eat into one's soul.'

During February 11th the Japanese Commander-in-Chief summoned Singapore to surrender. Though the demand was ignored, it was clear to everyone in the city that resistance could not be continued for more than a few days. "We are paying very heavily now," Brooke wrote, "for failing to face the insurance-premium essential for the security of an Empire. This has usually been the main cause for the loss of empires in the past." That night the German battle-cruisers *Gneisenau* and *Scharnhorst*, accompanied by the light cruiser *Prinz Eugen*, left the shelter of Brest, where they had been lurking since the previous spring, and started to run up the Channel. All next day, hugging the French, Belgian and Dutch coasts under continuous shore-based air protection, they steamed towards the North Sea, passing through the straits of Dover while the Royal Navy and Royal Air Force tried in vain to intercept and sink them. By the 13th they had reached port in Germany. Not since Von Tromp sailed up the Channel with a broom at his mast-head had the English felt so humiliated.[1] About the same time disaster met the convoy

[1] The fact that both battle-cruisers were damaged by air-laid mines in the North Sea was unknown at the time.

which Andrew Cunningham was attempting to run from Alexandria into Malta—down now to its last reserves of oil. Every ship in it was sunk. " These," wrote Brooke that night, " are black days! "

On the same day the evacuation began of all technical and specialist troops from Singapore, now under continuous bombing and shell-fire. Few reached safety, most of them being drowned or captured by the Japanese. Next morning the Governor reported that the streets were full of dead and dying and that within twenty-four hours its million inhabitants and 70,000 defenders would be without water. That afternoon, Saturday, February 14th, the Prime Minister telephoned from Chequers to Brooke at the War Office asking him to prepare a telegram for Wavell authorising him to allow surrender as soon as he judged further resistance to be useless.[1] On the 15th, the city capitulated. Loss of command of sea and air had left the garrison helpless. " The greatest disaster to British arms which our history affords," Churchill called it. " For the first time in this war," wrote Goebbels, " the English are obliged to hoist the white flag in grand style."

The Prime Minister met the disaster magnificently. In a real crisis, Brooke wrote, he was always at his best and stood all the heavy shocks without flinching. On January 29th he had faced his critics in the House of Commons with a superb fighting speech, demanding a vote of confidence, and had won it by 464 votes to one. " Provided we all stand together," he said, " and provided we throw in the last spasm of our strength, it looks, more than it ever did before, as if we were going to win." Brooke, who was summoned to his bedside when he was preparing his speech, found him propped on the pillows in his red and gold oriental dressing-gown, his few hairs ruffled on his vast domed head, a cigar sticking out of his mouth, his finished breakfast-tray beside him and the bed littered with papers and despatches. ' The red and gold dragon dressing-gown in itself,' he wrote, ' was worth going miles to see, and only Winston could have thought of wearing it. He looked rather like some Chinese Mandarin. . . . The

---

[1] " I discussed matter with other Chiefs of Staff and then sent off wire." *Diary*, 14th February, 1942.

bell was continually being rung for secretaries, typists, steno-graphers or his faithful valet, Sawyers.'[1]

After the fall of Singapore and the passage of the German battle-cruisers through the Channel, it seemed to Roosevelt and Harry Hopkins, watching from across the Atlantic, that the Prime Minister was facing the decisive crisis of his career. He was being pressed by domestic critics to hand over the Defence Ministry to an independent Minister, and by left-wing elements and his American allies to allow Congress to take over the government of India—a step which he believed would leave that country at Japan's mercy. There was talk of an adverse vote in the House and even of his succession by Eden or Cripps. But though at a dinner given by Eden, at which Brooke was present, he expressed his readiness to resign in favour of the former, he continued to weather the storm, for there was no-one who could take his place or match his courage and resilience. A few days later, after reading Churchill's speech in Parliament, Goebbels commented, "The same old stuff. A certain hopelessness finds expression . . . But his slogan of ' Blood, Sweat and Tears ' has entrenched him in a position that makes him totally immune from attack. He is like a doctor who prophesies that his patient will die and who, every time the patient's condition worsens, smugly ex-plains that, after all, he prophesied it."[2]

Brooke's diary tells the story of the days immediately follow-ing the fall of Singapore.

" *Monday February 16th*. . . . Arrived War Office 9.15. Read all wires and briefed for C.O.S. till 10.30. Then C.O.S. till 1.30 p.m. . . . . Busy afternoon studying re-percussions of fall of Singapore on flow of reinforcements. By 5 p.m. Cabinet meeting from which I escaped at 7 p.m. Considering that we have lost Singapore, en-dangered Rangoon, allowed *Gneisenau* and *Scharnhorst* to sail up the Channel and lost three transports trying to reinforce Malta, I was expecting that the Services would meet with some sarcastic remarks! However we got off far lighter than I expected."

[1] *Notes on My Life*, V, 348.
[2] Goebbels. *Diary*, 52.

" 7 p.m. to 8 p.m. working up for Defence Committee. 9 p.m. C.O.S. meeting till 10 p.m. when Defence Committee under P.M. started and lasted till after midnight; mainly concerned with decision as to whether attempts should be made to reinforce Java. Strategically this would be definitely unsound under present conditions. Politically it may be difficult not to do so. Provisionally decided to send Australian Division back to Australia and 70th Division to Burma and Ceylon. P.M. on the whole is in a very good mood."

"*February 17th.* Another hectic day. Started with C.O.S. at which we had visit from Dutch Admiral and had to discuss with him the fact that we were recommending that Java should not be reinforced by Australians. Then had to proceed to 10 Downing Street to see P.M. concerning Wavell's last wire. Found him in a dejected mood and he said that he was just back from dealing with a troublesome House. I am afraid that he is in for a lot more trouble."

" After lunch one and a half hours with Sinclair and Weeks to discuss results of their Committee. Then half an hour with Secretary of State, mainly to discuss political situation and demand for a Defence Minister independent from the P.M. An absolute impossibility with a personality such as his.[1] Then at 6 p.m. another half an hour with the Dutch Admiral, followed at 6.30 p.m. by a second Pacific Council meeting which lasted till 8 p.m. As I had expected, it was a more difficult meeting than the previous one. But on the whole the Dutch took it wonderfully well that they could expect no Australian reinforcements."

---

[1] " Frequently when the situation was bad there were suggestions that a separate Chairman for the Chiefs of Staff should be found or a Deputy Defence Minister interposed between the P.M. and the Chiefs of Staff. None of these alternatives was either possible or necessary. To my mind the P.M. in war must always deal direct with the Chiefs of Staff and the members of the C.O.S. must defend their actions personally in the Cabinet, using their Chairman as spokesman. The introduction of an outside Chairman will never smooth over differences between members of the C.O.S. if these exist. Should there be such differences there is only one course, to change some or all of the members of the C.O.S. It is essential that these three men should work as a perfect trinity." *Notes on My Life,* V, 358.

" After dinner back to War Office for another three hours' work. Am getting more and more worried by old Dudley Pound as First Sea Lord. With . . . him it is impossible for the C.O.S. to perform the functions it should in the biggest Imperial War we are ever likely to be engaged in. He is asleep during 75 per cent of the time he should be working."

For, in the crisis facing the Empire, the growing slowness and somnolence of the chairman of the Chiefs of Staff Committee constituted a serious impediment. " A futile meandering C.O.S. meeting," Brooke's diary for next day began, " with practically no major points and with Dudley Pound half asleep." The old seaman, now on the threshold of his 66th year, had been bearing the burden of office and nocturnal hours since the outbreak of war and, for all his immense professional knowledge, ability and shrewdness, the strain was too much. Unknown to his colleagues, or even himself, he was suffering from the disease—a tumour on the brain—that was to kill him and against which, out of a sense of duty, he continued to struggle till he died. Alone of the Chiefs of Staff he was responsible, not only for the operational control of his own Service but for its direction in battle, and, while his days were occupied in committee and conference, his nights were spent on a camp-bed at the Admiralty supervising the fight against the U-boats. It was not surprising that he sometimes dosed off in committee, looking, Brooke observed, " like an old parrot asleep on his perch."[1]

The position at sea was now almost desperate, with the Japanese threatening to break into the Indian Ocean and attack the convoys to India and the Middle East, and the U-boat fleet in the Atlantic sinking shipping at a rate that was dislocating the entire ocean communications of the United Nations. Presented with the opportunity of a lifetime, the German submarine commanders had fallen like wolves on

[1] *Diary*, 3rd February, 1942. ' Had I known that he was probably already suffering from the disease he died from, I should certainly not have made these remarks. . . . They are not intended as any personal criticism of this very fine sailor who at the time was a very sick man and who continued working till he died of overwork. He was the most charming of colleagues to work with, had it not been for this failing of slowness and sleepiness.' *Notes on My Life*, V, 358.

the unprepared and unescorted American coastwise traffic in the Caribbean and along the eastern seaboard of the United States. That February the Allies' losses in all oceans rose to 679,000 tons—the highest monthly figure so far of the War. The German admirals were jubilant, and their chief, Raeder, though still unaware that not a single British battleship remained afloat in the Mediterranean, urged the Fuehrer to launch an all-out spring offensive on Malta and the Nile valley in order to effect a junction between the Germans and Japanese.[1]

Acutely sensitive to this threat, Brooke referred repeatedly to the chairman's inability to cope with the business that poured in on the C.O.S. from every part of the globe. What it involved in additional work and strain is shown by his diary entries for the last week-end in February—a week after the fall of Singapore.

> " *Saturday February 21st.* A bad day. C.O.S. meeting from 10.30 a.m. to 1.30 p.m. and again from 4 p.m. to 7 p.m., and finally Pacific Council from 9.30 to 11.30 p.m. And all to do the work which could have been done by one man in one hour. And what's more, when finished the work was not worth the paper it was written on. All connected with the use of Dutch shipping in Java in the final stages of the evacuation, the use it was to be made of and the desirability or otherwise of risking it under Japanese bombing without adequate protection. I know well from personal experience that, whatever we may say, the man on the spot is in the end the only one who can judge . . . ."

> " *February 22nd.* The night continued to be as damnable as the day! Barely was I asleep when the First Sea Lord called me up at 1.45 a.m. about destination of convoy with 7th Australian Division aboard. It is at present between Colombo and Rangoon, marking time pending approval from Australia to use it in Burma. An approval which we are unlikely to obtain in spite of appeals from P.M. and President of U.S.A. As a result we shall probably lose Burma."

[1] *Hinsley,* 199; *Churchill,* IV, 122, 265-6.

"Barely was I asleep when the telephone rang again at 3.30 a.m. to tell me a car was coming down with message from Wavell. Nothing very special in it beyond statement of conditions in Java which are rapidly getting worse. Finally as I was trying to take an extra half hour in bed on Sunday morning, third telephone call to inform me that we were to have a C.O.S. meeting at 10.30 to consider Wavell's telegram."

.   .   .   .

Having failed to save Singapore, the British now proceeded to lose Burma. As Brooke had foreseen at the time of the Washington Conference, by deflecting forces from one inadequately held position to another they had merely created new holes which needed plugging in their turn. Presented with the choice of where to use the only division available for immediate reinforcement of the Far East—one which happened to be on its way to the Middle East round the Cape—they had staked everything, and under the circumstances almost inevitably, in a desperate bid to save Singapore and, braving the Japanese control of sea and air, flung it into the island just in time to be captured. It had been an intensely difficult decision, for both on the score of imperial prestige and communications, the great naval base seemed of supreme importance, and the Australian Prime Minister had cabled that its evacuation would be regarded by the Commonwealth as "an inexcusable betrayal." Yet with the American Pacific Fleet immobilised and the only available British battleships at the bottom of the sea, Singapore was not only untenable but useless. It would have been militarily wiser, Brooke thought, to have sent such slender reinforcements as there were to Burma in order to secure its oilfields and the approaches to India and to keep open the road to China.[1] Yet politically, as he saw, it was almost impossible for the Government to do so.

The loss of Burma and Java—the headquarters of the ill-fated A.B.D.A. Command—and of all the remaining British

[1] " I still feel now that if we had concentrated on reinforcing Rangoon that Burma might have been held." *Notes on My Life,* V, 332.

and Dutch East Indian islands followed in swift succession. "Burma news bad," Brooke wrote on February 18th, three days after the fall of Singapore. "If the Army cannot fight better than it is doing at present we shall deserve to lose our Empire." A week later, while three retreating British brigades were trapped and destroyed through the premature destruction of the only bridge over the Sittang, the dreadful battle of the Java Sea began in which almost the entire naval forces of A.B.D.A. were wiped out, leaving Australia wide open to invasion. From Burma General Chiang Kai-shek added a friend's insult to an enemy's injury by cabling President Roosevelt that never in his life had he seen such confusion, unpreparedness and degradation.[1]

The Prime Minister and Chiefs of Staff did their best to stem the tide, first by vainly trying to persuade the Australian Government to allow one of its divisions returning from the Middle East[2] to be deflected to Rangoon, and then by sending out to the Far East at twenty-four hours' notice the finest general the C.I.G.S. could recommend.

"*February 19th.* Received reply back from Wavell saying that he was prepared to accept Alexander . . . as Commander-in-Chief Burma. . . . After lunch was sent for by P.M. who said he agreed to Alexander being sent out. So made all arrangements and interviewed Alexander this evening and fixed up plans to fly him out direct to Cairo to-morrow. Shall try leaving Hutton as Chief General Staff; if this does not work shall have to carry out a change. Only hope Alexander arrives out in time, as situation in Burma is becoming very critical. Troops don't seem to be fighting well there either which is most depressing. . . ."

"*February 20th* . . . Burma news getting worse. Very doubtful if we succeed in holding Rangoon. Tanks due to arrive to-morrow may help to restore situation."

[1] *White House Papers*, II, 518.

[2] 'It must be remembered that this was the first time that Australia had been directly threatened and allowance must be made for the degree of nervousness created by this threat. Looking back on the event, I still feel that the arrival of this division in Rangoon at that time might well have restored the situation and saved Burma.' *Notes on My Life*, V, 361.

" I cannot see," he added on the 27th, " how we are going to go on holding Rangoon much longer."

Alexander arrived on March 5th but too late to save Rangoon, from which he withdrew his troops only just in time to avert encirclement. On the day he evacuated the Burmese capital the Japanese landed in New Guinea and began their advance on Port Moresby. A day later the Allied army in Java laid down its arms, among them 13,000 British, Australian and American troops and airmen. To the Australians and Indians the invasion of their countries now seemed only a matter of weeks, and Japanese broadcasts, dwelling on the fate awaiting them, counselled a speedy and separate peace and prophesied Axis victory parades in the streets of London and New York. While Australian statesmen spoke of scorched earth and of defending their under-populated continent to the last man, the Congress Party in India clamoured for an immediate declaration of independence, and its prophet, Gandhi, advocated non-resistance. " England," declared Goebbels, " is on the toboggan! "

PART TWO

The Winning of the Initiative

" The high tide," King Alfred cried
" The high tide and the turn ! "
G. K. CHESTERTON

Chapter Six

THE C.I.G.S.

His work was beyond praise and reward.
SIR JAMES GRIGG

O N THE evening of March 5th, 1942, just over a fortnight
after the fall of Singapore, Alan Brooke learnt from
the Prime Minister that he was to take Dudley Pound's
place as chairman of the Chiefs of Staff Committee. In the
ordinary course the First Sea Lord would have retained the
chair until his retirement, when it would have passed to the
Chief of Air Staff under the customary rotation practice.
Brooke's appointment only three months after he joined the
Committee was a measure of the impression his despatch of
business had made on the Prime Minister and his colleagues.
It meant that henceforward he would not only preside at the
Chiefs of Staff· meetings but, as their spokesman, play a
much larger part in shaping their joint strategy and in help-
ing to guide the Prime Minister and Government.

It also meant that he would have far more influence on
Anglo-American strategy and in restraining transatlantic
over-eagerness. At the end of February, to his relief, the
area which A.B.D.A. had been formed to defend having
passed into the hands of the enemy, the Command itself was
dissolved. Its official existence ended on the 23rd, on the eve
of the forlorn and disastrous battle of the Java Sea, when
Wavell, after volunteering to stay and fight it out with the
" stout-hearted Dutchmen," was ordered by the Chiefs of
Staff to return to India. " It is now quite clear," wrote
Brooke, " that we can at last dissolve the A.B.D.A. organisation and run the war on a rational basis. So far there is very
little that was settled in Washington that is surviving the test

of time. Burma has gone back to India Command, A.B.D.A. and ANZAC become one, Pacific Council goes west and, for the matter of that, so does the Combined Chiefs of Staff. And thank God for it! We shall now run the war with two main spheres of interest, the Americans running the Pacific up to Asia including Australia and New Zealand, and the British running the opposite way round the globe including the Middle East, India, Burma and Indian Ocean."[1]

Yet, though right about the demise of A.B.D.A. and the Pacific Council, Brooke was mistaken in supposing that the Combined Chiefs of Staff had ceased to exist. For the moment what he called " the false arrangements made in Washington " had become a dead letter, and control of Britain's war-effort in Europe, the Middle East and Burma reverted, under the nominal supervision of the Combined Chiefs of Staff, to the well-tried organisation in Whitehall that had grown up since the first World War around the Chiefs of Staff Committee and the War Cabinet Secretariat. Yet one child conceived in the romantic Anglo-American honeymoon of Christmas 1941, survived. The Combined Chiefs of Staff might for the moment be only a name, but it was ready to grow when circumstances allowed. ' I had little faith in this organization at the time,' Brooke wrote afterwards, ' I think mainly due to the fact that it had been set up in Washington with the U.S.A. as the predominant partner whilst they had . . . not much knowledge in the running of a war and certainly little experience. My views altered completely as time went on and I grew to have the greatest faith in the Combined Chiefs of Staff organization as the most efficient that had ever been evolved for co-ordinating and correlating the war strategy and effort of two allies.' The creation of a directing organ consisting of the supreme military, naval and air leaders of the two nations, not only made a concerted inter-Allied effort in world-wide operations possible on a scale never before attempted, but ensured that the President and Prime Minister would receive the continuous and responsible advice of a professional body whose corporate authority it was almost impossible to disregard.

[1] *Diary*, 22nd February, 1942.

Brooke's appointment to the chairmanship of the C.O.S. was part of a wider re-organization of the nation's central war control. A fortnight earlier, and four days after the fall of Singapore, drastic changes had been made in the War Cabinet.

> "*February 19th.* After lunch was sent for by P.M. who
> . . . showed me his new Cabinet . . . . A smaller one and
> much more efficient. Beaverbrook is out of it . . . He is
> off to America. Cranborne and Moyne both out of War
> Cabinet, Stafford Cripps and Oliver Lyttelton have been
> introduced, Kingsley Wood and Greenwood pass out.
> Apparently Secretaries of State of Services are also out,
> but am not yet certain. With a small War Cabinet like
> that we might be able to get on much faster. . . ."

Changes were also made at the Ministries for War, Colonies, Aircraft Production and Economic Warfare, while a new Ministry—that of Production—was formed to eliminate bottle-necks in supply, co-ordinate the needs of the three Services and represent Britain on the Control Boards recently set up in Washington to allocate munitions and materials to the Allies and theatres of war in accordance with strategic needs.

Of these changes the one that affected Brooke most was the resignation of David Margesson, who had been Secretary of State for War since the end of 1940, and his replacement by James Grigg, the Permanent Under-Secretary for War. It was an unusual appointment, for Grigg was a regular Civil Servant, but for Brooke and the Army it proved a very happy one. Having been Churchill's private secretary for five years at the Treasury, Grigg understood his mind and methods of work and was able to give the C.I.G.S. much valuable advice. His knowledge of Army administration freed Brooke, too, from a host of unnecessary distractions and enabled him to con-centrate on his main task of formulating and guiding strategy. The two men, who were both given to the same devastating frankness, completely understood and trusted one another. 'Thus started,' Brooke wrote, 'a long association with P. J. Grigg for which I thank heaven. I received nothing but assistance and support during the whole of our time together and could not have asked for anyone better to work with.

One of the quickest and ablest brains I have ever met. A slightly suspicious nature at times until one had gained his confidence. A heart of gold!' "I hardly remember," Grigg wrote of their association, "a single harsh word between us."

On Monday March 9th, after dealing with the usual morning rush of telegrams from the war-fronts—most of them gloomy—Brooke presided over his first Chiefs of Staff Committee. "First C.O.S. in which I took the chair," he noted that night. "Went off all right, and both Portal and Pound played up very well." 'This,' he wrote afterwards, 'is putting it mildly. Dudley Pound was usually late for our C.O.S. meetings and I rather dreaded taking his chair in his absence, but to my surprise dear old Dudley on this morning made a point of arriving before the appointed time, and I found him already sitting in my chair with his chairman's seat empty. This was typical of the man. I feel certain this gesture on his part was done on purpose to make matters easier for me and to impress on me how ready he was to serve under my chairmanship. I was deeply grateful to him. Portal also never showed the slightest sign of disappointment which he was well entitled to feel at my assuming the chair. Thus started a long tour of the chairmanship of the C.O.S. which lasted till the end of the war and my retirement.'[1]

Brooke was an admirable chairman for a body that had to deal with a flood of questions requiring clear, immediate answers. Two years before in France, when Commander of the II Corps, he had been noted for his brief business-like conferences, and he got through the Committee's agenda in half the time taken by his predecessor. He checked, his colleague Portal recalled, all irrelevance in discussion and conversation. He was prompt, incisive, yet patient, courteous and conciliatory. He was also very firm. His mind worked at tremendous speed and so enabled him to extract at once the essential points from any problem, however complex and technical. He had a way in committee, while others were talking, of sitting back listening with half closed eyes, usually taking off his spectacles to rest his sight. When everything

---

[1] *Notes on My Life*, V, 368. 'Peter Portal remained on the Committee the whole of the time, and Dudley Pound, on his death, was succeeded by Andrew Cunningham. I could not have wished for more delightful colleagues.'

relevant had been said, he would give his own views in a few sharp staccato sentences, to put the matter in perspective. Nor did he ever leave anyone in the slightest doubt about his opinion. If he disagreed with a colleague he said so, sometimes with no more than a curt, " I flatly disagree! " And though he indicated his reasons lucidly and concisely, he refused to be drawn into argument over secondary or minor matters. He always kept strictly to the point. Having made up his mind, he rarely changed it, but, if shown to be wrong, admitted it without hesitation.

The Chiefs of Staff Committee—the supreme battle headquarters of the Armed Forces of Great Britain, the Commonwealth and Empire, and of the Allied Forces in exile—met every morning in the Cabinet War Room in Great George Street, close to Storey's Gate and St. James's Park. It debated, until unanimous agreement was reached, an endless succession of problems affecting every theatre, aspect and department of the war, and then issued through its members the necessary executive orders to the Service and Theatre Commanders to give its decisions effect. Each of its three members had a dual function, individually as professional head of his own Service and official adviser to its Minister, and collectively and individually as one of a trinity responsible for advising the War Cabinet and Minister of Defence on defence policy as a whole. Acting together they constituted, in the words of the Warrant which each received on appointment, " a Super-Chief of a War Staff in Commission." They had not only to plan and direct the strategy of the war but to advise the Defence Minister on every question that had any bearing on it—foreign policy, scientific developments, industry, labour, shipping, raw materials, Commonwealth, Indian and Colonial relations—and to examine and prepare reports on all matters referred to them by the Cabinet or Prime Minister. They were assisted by a Vice Chiefs of Staff Committee, to which, in order to free their minds for the supreme direction of the war, they delegated the handling of matters of secondary importance, and by two inter-Service staffs—the Joint Planning Staff to whom they referred the study of all proposed operational plans, and the Joint Intelligence Staff from whom they received day-by-day reports on the military situation and the enemy's dispositions. Their meetings were attended, though not as a voting member, by the Military Secretary to the War Cabinet and Chief Staff Officer to the Defence Minister, Lieutenant-General Sir Hastings Ismay—affectionately known to his colleagues as " Pug." They were served by the permanent Secretariat of the War Cabinet, who also officiated for the Defence Committee and all the other committees set up by that body to supervise and co-ordinate the manifold war activities of a parliamentary nation. It was the function of these highly-trained officials, both military and civil, to summarise the conclusions reached in committee in a form which could become the basis of immediate executive action. As a versifying official had put it,

> " And so while the great ones depart to their dinner,
> The secretary stays, growing thinner and thinner,
> Racking his brain to record and report
> What he thinks that they think that they ought to
> have thought."

Though the Prime Minister constantly strove to persuade them to adopt his strategic views and brought to bear on them all his remarkable powers of oratory, invective and persuasion, he would never overrule the Chiefs of Staff's unanimous opinion on any purely military matter. The controversies over Antwerp and Gallipoli, which had so nearly shipwrecked his career in the first War, had made a deep impression on him, and he attached the greatest weight to the official support of his Service advisers. He entrusted to them immense powers and would not allow even the Cabinet to criticise them. "Anything which might affect the running of the war, even in the slightest degree," wrote one of them, " was referred to them for an opinion; . . . anyone criticising the Chiefs of Staff, no matter how high his position, was likely to find the Prime Minister's heavy guns turned against him."[1] And though, as Defence Minister, he occasionally presided over their meetings, he never acted as the Chiefs of Staff's mouthpiece in the War Cabinet. He requested their attendance at its meetings and left them to present it with regular weekly surveys of the

---

[1] Lord Cunningham of Hyndhope, *Sailor's Odyssey*, 584-5.

activities of their Services and, in their corporate capacity, through their chairman and spokesman, with professional advice on all strategic and operational matters.

Brooke's appointment to the chairmanship of the Chiefs of Staff Committee was accompanied by the addition to it, at the Prime Minister's instance, of the new Chief of Combined Operations, the 41-year-old naval captain and acting Vice-Admiral, Lord Louis Mountbatten. His function—one on which Churchill set great store—was to develop the technique of inter-Service raids and landings on the enemy's coasts in preparation for those larger operations which it was hoped one day Britain, with the backing of her transatlantic ally, would be able to undertake. He attended all meetings of the C.O.S. and had the special responsibility of advising on matters connected with the organisation and technique of Combined Operations whenever such matters were discussed. Brooke, who admired him and enjoyed his stimulating company, at first regarded his presence on the Committee as rather a waste of time. ' We could easily,' he wrote, ' have called him in to attend any meetings where matters connected with organization were being discussed. . . . His appointment as Chief of Combined Operations, however, was excellent, and he played a remarkable part as the driving force and main-spring of this organization. Without his energy and drive it would never have reached the high standards it achieved.' Lord Mountbatten recalls the kindness with which Brooke, nearly twenty years his senior, went out of his way to make him feel at home. The C.I.G.S. often disagreed with him and his ideas and, as Mountbatten put it, " bit him hard." But he had the gift of expressing disagreement without arousing rancour, and he received from the younger man a steady affection and loyalty.

．　．　．　．　．　．　．　．

It was characteristic both of the Prime Minister and the new chairman of the Chiefs of Staff Committee that, at a time when Britain seemed to be sinking into an ever deeper slough of disaster, both should be thinking of how they could take the offensive. The one pinned his hopes on harassing the enemy at every possible point—by Commando raids, by growing air-bombardment, by striking at once and everywhere; the other on patiently husbanding and building up resources at a single decisive point so as to be able at the right moment to launch, not an abortive attack that could not be sustained, but one that could be carried through to a finish. Only the clearing of the North African coast and re-opening of the Mediterranean could in his view do this by restoring to the maritime Powers the mobility and freedom of action they had lost through the closing of that sea. The prize was the initiative the enemy had enjoyed since 1939—the golden fleece of war. No lesser objective, Brooke believed, was worth the sacrifice of men and materials.

Hitherto, apart from the Prime Minister's heroic directives, first issued in the forlorn summer of 1940, for the training of commandos and the building of landing-craft for amphibious operations, Britain's only hope of winning the war had been by attack from the air. Until the summer of 1941 she had been fighting single-handed against a far better armed enemy in control of almost the entire western coastline of Europe and with a population at least three times her own. Even after Russia's entry into the war, until the Red Army's counter-attack at the end of the year it had seemed unlikely that Britain could look to any permanent military aid in Europe. She had, therefore, based her plans on the air and, having won the Battle of Britain and gained fighter ascendancy over the Channel, had started to build a force of four-engined bombers which it was believed would one day mete out to the Germans, with interest, the hell they had inflicted on others. The objective was still remote, for this force at present consisted only of some fifty heavy and two hundred medium bombers, and, owing to the difficulties of target-finding at night and the strength of the German air-defences, it had been able so far to accomplish little. Despite the Government's determination to mount a major air offensive at the earliest possible moment, the British aircraft industry, concentrated almost exclusively between 1938 and 1940 on fighter pro-duction, was still not geared to turn out heavy bombers in large numbers. Yet under the direction of the Chief of Air Staff, Sir Charles Portal—a former Commander-in-Chief of

Bomber Command—massive preparations were being made for an assault on the German homeland. Offering as they did the only prospect of winning the war for a Britain fighting alone, they were enthusiastically supported by the Prime Minister.

But at the end of 1941, with the Russian stand before Moscow and the entry of the U.S.A. into the war, the position had changed. For the first time it had become possible to look forward to the day when a British Army would once more take the field on the Continent beside the armies of allies with the necessary man-power to match a foe with the advantage of interior lines and the control of the entire industrial production and transport system of the Continent. If the Russians could hold out until an unarmed United States could mobilise, train and transport across the Atlantic a mechanised army, instead of having to deal with only fifty million Britons, a hundred and fifty million Germans and Italians would have to face a combined attack by more than three hundred million Russians, Americans and Britons. An invasion of Hitler's " Fortress Europe " from west, east and south would then become a practical possibility. And for this a British Army, trained and equipped to fight on the Continent, would be needed.

Until now the Army had played a comparatively small part in the Government's calculations for winning the war. Though much the largest of the three Services, it had counted for less in the struggle for survival than the Navy or Air Force. The first call on the nation's resources and skilled man-power had been naval and aerial. With the gradual extension of the call-up the Army by now numbered two and a quarter million men, with 900,000 more in the Commonwealth, Indian and Empire Forces, and a million and a half part-time soldiers in the Home Guard. Yet only a small proportion of these were front-line troops organised in mobile field-units. After more than two years of war there were still only half a dozen divisions in the country fully armed and equipped to fight the Germans on the Continent, and only two—kept in permanent readiness to occupy the Atlantic Islands or French North Africa in the event of an Axis move through

Spain or against Vichy—able to proceed overseas at immediate notice. Of the thirty-two divisions or their equivalent which comprised Home Forces, nearly a third were beach-defence units without motorised transport, while at least half a million men were engaged in anti-aircraft duties and on the defence of factories, ports and shipping. The only immediate expansion that could be expected of the country's striking force was an increase in the proportion of armour, and this had been drastically slowed down by the despatch of hundreds of tanks to Russia.[1] Compared with the two hundred or more German and satellite divisions with which Hitler was attacking Russia, the British field-army in the United Kingdom was still almost ludicrously small and, though better trained and armed, no larger than the Expeditionary Force which had been so unceremoniously bundled out of the Continent eighteen months before with the loss of its entire equipment. Even the forty-nine reserve or resting divisions which Hitler kept to garrison Western Europe against a possible British landing were five or six times more numerous.

The main function of Home Forces, apart from guarding the country from invasion and training for an unknown future, was to provide reinforcements and replacements for the British armies overseas. Every month between 40,000 and 50,000 soldiers and airmen—the maximum number for which shipping was available—were sent out of Britain to maintain her global field forces and garrisons. There were an astonishing number of these—in Northern Ireland, Iceland, Bermuda, the West Indies, Gibraltar and Malta, West and East Africa, Abyssinia, Eritrea, the Sudan, Egypt, Palestine, Syria and Cyprus, Iraq, Persia, Arabia, Mauritius, India, Ceylon and, before their capture by the Japanese, Burma, Malaya, Borneo and Hong Kong. To a greater or lesser, and constantly varying, degree, all served the strategic end of containing the Axis and of guarding the Naval and Air Force bases which secured the world's seaways. Though, except in the Far East, few of them had yet been attacked, all were liable to possible naval, air or military raids; one fear against which Brooke had to

---

[1] Under the agreement made with the Kremlin in the autumn of 1941, Britain was to supply by June, 1942, 2,250 tanks, 1,800 aeroplanes and 1,800 Bren-gun carriers. *British War Production* (*H.M.S.O.*), 119.

guard that winter was a Japanese descent on the Falkland Islands, where an enemy base would have had disastrous effects on the South Atlantic convoys and the supply of the Middle East and India. All these places had to be maintained, not only with troops but with modern armaments, munitions and technical equipment. This called for vast quantities of shipping and, in view of the rate of U-boat sinkings, which rose in March to over three-quarters of a million tons, made it impossible to undertake any new military operation without creating shortages somewhere. It was this that rendered the Prime Minister's projects for new expeditions so dangerous.

By far the most important British military force overseas was in the Middle East. Operating at the point where Africa joined Asia and the Suez Canal linked the Mediterranean with the Red Sea and Indian Ocean, the Command controlled from its headquarters in Cairo an area seven or eight times the size of the United Kingdom. Ever since 1940 a continuous stream of troops and supplies had been flowing into it, not only from Britain, but from India, Australia, New Zealand, South Africa, Rhodesia and the African colonies. By the time Brooke succeeded Dill it comprised nearly three-quarters of a million troops. Only a fraction of these—about 100,000 men —were in contact with the enemy in the Libyan desert. The rest were scattered over the vast area between the Turkish and Russian frontiers and the oceans that Britain patrolled. A large proportion of them, though that veteran of a less mechanised age, the Prime Minister, could only with the greatest difficulty be brought to recognise the fact, were not first-line combatants but artificers, engineers, labourers, dockers, administrative and lines-of-communication workers required for sustaining modern war in a primitive and remote land.

Of the sixteen field divisions of Middle East Command, six[1] were now locked, four hundred miles to the west of Alexandria, in a swaying battle in the Libyan desert with Rommel's German-Italian army. Two more divisions, fifteen hundred

---

[1] Or rather their equivalent, for much of the Eighth or Desert Army had been broken up at this time into small, semi-independent units.

miles to the south, were mopping up the last pockets of resistance in the liberated territories of what till that summer had been the Italian East African Empire. Two divisions were in Palestine and Syria to lend moral support to Turkey and prevent an Axis descent on the Levantine coast from the Italian Dodecanese, while four more, three of them Indian, were in Iraq and Persia to counter a possible German advance through southern Russia and the Caucasus against the oil-wells of the Anglo-Iranian Oil Company on whose refineries, tankers and desert pipe-lines all the British forces operating in this region depended.

Three German armoured or mobile divisions under Rommel now formed the hard core of the so-called Italian Army of Egypt which was preparing for a new advance to the Suez Canal to break the ring which still kept the Western Axis confined in Europe and the North African desert. Here, too, the British Desert Army, after the collapse of its winter offensive, was gathering strength for another bid to regain the Cyrenaican airfields without which convoys to a starving Malta could not be passed through the Axis-dominated waters between Sicily and Africa. But, owing to the demands of mechanised warfare and the immense length of Britain's ocean and desert supply-line, the maintenance of this front involved an appalling drain on resources. From the start the desert war had developed into a tank battle in which, on that illimitable ocean of rock and sand, victory went to the side which could mount and maintain the largest and heaviest-gunned force of armour. For this, enormous quantities of transport, supplies and fuel were required, and the wastage in that bumpy, sandswept wilderness had become a Quartermaster-General's nightmare. At the time Alan Brooke became C.I.G.S. there were nearly a hundred thousand wheeled vehicles on the Middle East establishment.[1]

Nor were the British yet the equals of the Germans in tank and mechanized warfare. Their tanks were weaker in fire-power and armour, they lacked mobile front-line workshops for servicing damaged vehicles and were short of up-to-date anti-tank and anti-aircraft weapons and spares of every

[1] *British War Production* (H.M.S.O.), 118.

kind—points which Brooke had been trying to impress on his political chiefs for the past eighteen months. Their opponents had been mass-producing these for years and had by now a large veteran army trained in their use.

.   .   .   .

Such was the instrument which, in his joint capacity as C.I.G.S. and chairman of the Chiefs of Staff Committee, Brooke had to use and re-fashion to help hold the great Axis offensives of 1942 and, when the time came, seize the initiative. His assumption of the chairmanship of the C.O.S. coincided, not only with the nadir of the Allies' fortunes, but with the beginning of the change—at first unperceived—from a defensive to an offensive strategy. This was neither a coincidence nor merely the result of America's entry into the war and the increased resistance of Russia—though without these it would have been impossible. It sprang largely from a proper use of the Western Allies' land forces. Sea and air operations, essential both for halting the aggressor and for providing a springboard for offensive action, could not, in the existing state of technical weapons, by themselves destroy him. For this armies were necessary to storm the walls of his fortress and grapple with him inside it.

Though acutely aware both of the importance of sea-power and of the air, Brooke saw that the Army must now increasingly take the lead. Before the war could be won it had to do in the west what the Russians were doing in the east. His Washington counterpart, Marshall, and the American Service chiefs saw this also, but, over-estimating through inexperience their powers, failed to appreciate how this could alone be effected with the comparatively small military and shipping resources at present available. Over the whole field of global strategy the three Arms of land, sea and air had to be brought to bear on the enemy as one force in pursuit of a carefully planned, limited but realisable objective, and, as defence changed to attack, with the Army playing an ever more important part. For this there must be unified command, not only at Storey's Gate and Washington, but in every individual theatre of war. In the defence of Ceylon, for instance—that

key-point in the Indian Ocean whose retention was so essential
if Britain's hopes for a Middle East offensive were not to be
destroyed by a Japanese advance to the Persian Gulf and Red
Sea—Brooke saw that, though the part of the Navy and Air
Force was more important than the Army's, the three must
act as one and take their orders, not from their respective
Service Departments in London, but from a single Supreme
Commander on the spot, himself responsible to the Combined
Chiefs of Staff. Five days before he took over the chairmanship
of the latter he had sought to impress this necessity on his
colleagues.

> " *March 4th.* A long and protracted C.O.S. taken up
> mainly with a heated argument as regards relative
> advantages between a single commander or generalissimo
> as opposed to the usual trinity of the three Services. I was
> supporting the former and was being strongly opposed
> by Chief of Naval Staff and Chief of Air Staff—the case
> in point being Ceylon and our attempt at producing a
> Military Commander instead of the usual Civil Governor.
> The argument itself and impossibility of arriving at any
> agreement convinced me more than anything else that I
> was right. But argument went on for close on two hours."

' The point,' Brooke wrote afterwards, ' was a minor one, but
one where a single commander seemed essential. In time of
war a civil Governor was out of place for Ceylon, which had
become a point of great strategic importance. A military
Governor was essential to control all the Services connected
with the immediate defence of this base.' Though a sailor
was eventually appointed, Brooke got his way on the main
issue—a circumstance which was to have dramatic consequences.

While Brooke was responsible as chairman of the Chiefs of
Staff Committee to the Prime Minister for the strategic
direction of the war, as Chief of the Imperial General Staff
he was responsible to the Secretary of State for War for the
fighting efficiency, and organization of the Army. Much of the
routine administration—swollen to many times its peace-time
size—was taken off his hands by his very able Vice Chief,

Lieutenant-General Sir Archibald Nye—a man he trusted implicitly. ' I could not have wished,' he wrote, ' for anybody better. He was brilliantly able and full of character, and yet I could leave the country with absolute confidence he would do his level best to maintain the identical policies which he knew I wanted.' Some months after Brooke took up his duties he and Grigg called in to assist with questions of equipment and organization a distinguished industrialist and Territorial officer who had served as his Director of Equipment at Home Forces, Ronald Weeks, and who was now given the title of Deputy Chief of the Imperial General Staff and the task of bridging the gap between the producer and user of military equipment. Together—Nye on the planning, training and operational side and Weeks on that of organization, scientific development and the assignment of armaments and munitions—they freed the C.I.G.S. from a mass of detail which would otherwise have clogged his capacity for clear thought and decision.

Yet the ultimate responsibility for everything affecting the operational control and efficiency of the Army remained Brooke's. All his strategic plans turned on its being trained and equipped for its functions. For until the Americans had made a force capable of taking the field against the *Wermacht*, the brunt of winning the initiative in the West was bound to fall on Britain. From the Arctic to the Black Sea the Red Army was pinning down and bleeding some five million German and satellite troops; over the whole of the rest of the globe, on sea, land and air, the responsibility, first for holding and then for attacking Japan, Italy and Germany rested on the two Western democracies, only one of which was yet mobilised for war. While the Russians engaged Hitler's central masses, the sea-powers had to contain Japan in the Pacific, Indian Ocean and along the thousand-mile Burmese frontier and simultaneously to take the offensive in Africa and Europe so as to win bridgeheads for future attack on Hitler and Mussolini And unless the opportunity offered by Russia's resistance was seized, it might be lost for ever. If the Kremlin yielded or made terms, the enemy's entire military man-power would be freed to defend Europe's southern and western approaches.

The British Army had, therefore, to be used, and at the earliest possible moment, as the spearhead of an attack or series of attacks. For this it needed equipment and arms, as well as training and generalship, equal to the best the *Wermacht* could employ against it. How far it still was from possessing these the North African campaign showed. To secure them, and at a time when shortages both of manpower and raw materials were becoming serious for all three Services, Brooke had to overcome much opposition and even prejudice. At this stage of the war the Army, compared with the other Services, lacked glamour; it had had few victories and, owing to the handicaps under which it had had to fight, had suffered a humiliating succession of defeats. And because in his youth the Prime Minister had been a soldier and because many of his then seniors had been stupid and obstructionist, he not only tended to be more critical of the Army than of the other Services but was sometimes unconsciously unjust to it. When the Expeditionary Force had been all but surrounded in 1940 he had written of it and its commander, " Here is a general with nine divisions about to be starved out, and yet he cannot send a force to clear his communications . . . Our tanks recoil before their field-guns, but our field-guns do not like to take on their tanks."[1] During his first few months as C.I.G.S., when the country was smarting under reverses in Malaya, Burma and North Africa, Brooke was often subjected to this kind of criticism from his political master and found it hard to keep his temper. ' He came out continually,' he wrote, ' with remarks such as: " Have you not got a single general in the Army who can win battles, have none of them any ideas, must we continually lose battles in this way? " . . . In the middle of a Cabinet meeting he would turn to me and say, " Pray explain, C.I.G.S., how is it that in the Middle East 750,000 men always turn up for their pay and rations, but when it comes to fighting only 100,000 turn up. Explain to us exactly how the remaining 650,000 are occupied? " '[2]

[1] Prime Minister to Gen. Ismay, 24th May, 1940. *Churchill*, II, 71-2. " I must know at earliest," he wrote to the C.I.G.S. next day, " why Gort gave up Arras and what actually he is doing with the rest of his army. . . . He must not allow himself to be encircled without fighting a battle."

[2] *Notes on My Life*, V, 352; VI, 439. ' Not exactly an easy answer to give in the middle of a Cabinet meeting.'

While C.I.G.S., Brooke continued to take the keenest interest in the development of weapons and equipment and their supply. After spending the morning in the Chiefs of Staff Committee grappling with disasters in the Far East, Africa or the Atlantic, he would see an industrialist about a new gun, drive out to Shoeburyness to watch an anti-tank rocket being tested, or preside over the special General Staff Committee which under his chairmanship was studying the development of armour. All the time that with his colleagues he was taking steps to hold the Japanese, Rommel and the U-boats, he was making provision for battles that would have to be fought in a year or two years' time in Africa, Italy and France. Already his mind was on the D-Day beaches. "Dined with Dr. Dalton,"[1] he wrote after interviewing the captain of the sunk *Repulse* on a dark January day, " and discussed with him his sabotage activities in Europe . . . and also the question of raising local forces in Europe to be armed and equipped at the last moment. There is a great deal to be done in this direction at present and I don't feel we are doing anything like enough." " After dinner," he ended his diary two days later, " back to War Office and long talk with Nye on the organisation of Airborne Division and instructed it to be pushed on to the utmost and be given preferential treatment."

Brooke continued at the War Office to follow his practice as Commander-in-Chief of going on tour as often as possible. Even during the Singapore crisis he found time, in the intervals of hectic C.O.S. meetings, to visit Paget's and Montgomery's headquarters to watch the " Victor " Exercises which Home Forces were then staging. " Dashed off to Hendon after Cabinet meeting and flew to near Catterick to inspect the 42nd Division," runs one entry in his diary. " After a heavy day in London, I caught the 5 p.m. train for Penrith and went to Lowther Castle to watch demonstrations of tanks employing searchlights to blind the enemy in attack and defence. Spent from midnight till 4 a.m. and then returned to London by 10.45 a.m. Arrived just in time for Chiefs of Staff meeting."[2]

[1] The Rt. Hon. Hugh Dalton, Minister of Economic Warfare, *Diary*, 6th January, 1942.
[2] *Diary*, 18th February; 5th May; 11th June, 1942.

Except when he was on tours of inspection Brooke reached the War Office punctually at nine every morning. Before the C.O.S. Committee met at ten-thirty, he would study the latest information from Washington and the situation and intelligence reports from the war-theatres. Then with his Vice Chief, the Director of Military Operations and the Director of Military Intelligence, he would go through the War Office briefs for the C.O.S. meeting. Every operational plan affecting the Army passed through his hands before being submitted to that body and, after it had been agreed, was issued by him in the form of executive orders to his subordinates. " The responsibility for taking the initiative and making the plans," General Nye wrote, " rested with the C.I.G.S., the approval was given by the Minister of Defence, the responsibility for action rested with the C.I.G.S., and the action was taken by the various Departments of the War Office under his direction and the various Commanders-in-Chief at home and abroad."[1]   Sometimes there would be two, or even three, meetings of the C.O.S. Committee in the day, another perhaps of the Defence Committee, and, on at least one evening a week, of the War Cabinet, presided over by the Prime Minister or in his absence by the Deputy Prime Minister, Mr. Attlee. In between these and interviews with the many military and civil personages who had a claim on his time, it was the C.I.G.S.'s duty to deal with an infinite variety of questions affecting the Army's war-effort in every corner of the world: demands for troops, allocations of shipping, equipment, weapons and organization, appreciations of future plans, and reports from the Joint Planning and Joint Intelligence Committees. Occasionally, too, he had to attend formal meetings of the Army Council presided over by the Secretary of State to consider questions of routine and administration. Once a week when in London he lunched with his old friend and fellow-gunner, the Adjutant General, usually walking back to the office with him through St. James's Park, to keep in touch with the work of his department. He also regularly discussed questions of supply with the Quartermaster-General and the Deputy and Vice Chiefs of the Imperial General Staff.

[1] Communicated by Lt. Gen. Sir Archibald Nye.

" The amount of work he got through during the day," wrote his Vice Chief of Staff, " was simply prodigious, and ... he had somehow to find the leisure to *think*. The greatest danger confronting all people in high positions during the war was that the pace was so great, one had to deal with the immediate problem under one's very nose. It was incredibly difficult to find the time to sit back and reflect, to pick up all the odd strands and to weave them together to determine where we were going and what our policy should be." It was in this that Brooke was so successful. He refused to let himself be overwhelmed. A lesser administrator would have had to burn the midnight oil, but, save when the pressure of external events made it impossible, he kept regular hours. " He was abstemious, quick, tidy and exact," wrote Ian Jacob of the War Cabinet Secretariat, " and liked dealing with things quickly and getting them over and done with." Once he had surmounted the chaos of the first few months and reduced things to a system, he seldom stayed at the War Office after seven o'clock or took official papers home to his flat. He made his staff prepare summaries of all documents that had to be mastered and then cross-examined them at high speed about the details. His subordinates never thought of him as a rushed or harassed man; even in the greatest press he remained calm and unruffled. There were times, as his diary reveals, when he was near breaking-point. Yet no-one who witnessed his methodical, unhurried application to the task of the hour could ever have supposed so.

" The last few months since I took over this job here," Brooke told a friend, " have been about the grimmest of my life. We seem to lose a new bit of the Empire almost every day, and are faced with one nightmare situation after another." " This process," he told another, " does not make Cabinet Ministers any more attractive. But Winston is a marvel; I can't imagine how he sticks it." Yet though he begged such intimates to write to him occasionally about birds and fish and not about human beings who could think of nothing better than continually waging war, Brooke admitted that he found his new work thrilling. Though it constituted an enormous burden on a man approaching his sixtieth year, it was a challenge to every professional skill and qualification he possessed. His whole career had been a preparation for it. " It is no small thing and it is certainly unusual," wrote Sir James Grigg, " that the professional head of the Army should be a man who is admitted, nay proclaimed, by every other soldier of magnitude, to be beyond doubt the most accomplished soldier in the Army."[1] " Brookie," as they called him, was held in immense respect and, indeed, awe by all his subordinate commanders. Not only resolute but stern and unrelenting, he was their master and he never left them in any doubt about it. General Dempsey recalls that the only time he ever saw his formidable chief, Montgomery, put out during the fighting in western Europe in 1944 was when he received a warning from the C.I.G.S. " We can't do that," he would say, " we've had the red light from Brookie! "

* * * * * * * *

At the moment that the expansion of the war made the Army's role of paramount importance, it became Brooke's business to select the commanders of Britain's field forces. It was already fighting in Cyrenaica and Burma; at any time it might have to do so in Ceylon and Madagascar, in Persia, Anatolia and French North Africa, in Norway and on the Channel coast, in Britain itself. To pick good men to command it was an essential part of the C.I.G.S.'s duty, and in this he was seldom mistaken. His experience of command and sound judgment of men stood him in good stead. He did not find the task easy, for, as he often complained in his diary, the real leaders of his generation, the platoon, company and battalion commanders of the first War, had had their ranks so thinned that there were not enough survivors of quality to go round. Yet once he had picked a man and he had proved himself, he trusted him and left him completely free. When the subordinate was facing the enemy, he did so even when he was not sure of him. ' I consider,' he wrote, ' that a commander should be carefully chosen and then left to run his own show without interference except to encourage, or relieve him if he fails.'

[1] Sir James Grigg, *Sunday Times*, 27th January, 1946.

Nor was his part in this passive. He protected his subordinates from the interference of others and gave them steady support and encouragement. " I should like first and foremost," he wrote to Wavell that March, " to let you know how thrilled we have all been watching the way you handled the A.B.D.A. Command. Of all the sickly triplets to be given to hold, I can imagine no worse."[1] Reading Brooke's correspondence with the Commanders-in-Chief of Britain's field armies, one can see the confidence they had in him. Sometimes he had to reprimand, and sometimes to dismiss men who had failed or were incapable of holding their own in modern war. It was an ordeal he disliked intensely. ' It was very strange how differently individuals varied under this ordeal,' he wrote. ' Some took the blow wonderfully well and realised that if they were being relieved it was due to some shortcoming or other. Others . . . were inclined to think that they could be nothing but perfect in their handling of their job and that consequently the error rested with those who failed to appreciate their high qualities and were dismissing them.'[2] Brooke never let anyone leave without appreciating clearly the reasons why a rebuke or change had become necessary. " A false idea of his own value," he wrote of an interview with one officer, " and consequently some difficulty in making him realise that he had reached his ceiling." Yet though ruthless towards anyone who behaved unworthily, he could be wonderfully tender when, as sometimes happened, a good man had to be relieved of his command through no fault of his own. " Finally dined with ——," he wrote in his diary that February, " whom I had to write to yesterday, informing him that owing to his age he would have to retire soon. Seldom have I hated writing a letter more and seldom have I received a nicer answer."

Britain's principal commanders at the time that Brooke took charge of her military affairs were Sir Claude Auchinleck in the Middle East, the latter's predecessor, General Wavell, in India, and Bernard Paget, who had succeeded Brooke in command of Home Forces. Alexander and Montgomery were

---

[1] Brooke to Wavell, 21st March, 1942. Lord Alanbrooke, *Personal Files*.
[2] *Notes on My Life*, VI, 474.

then both corps commanders under the latter. The most important at that moment was Auchinleck, who was in charge of the operations for expelling the Axis from North Africa. Brooke had a high regard for his character and ability, but was very doubtful about his choice of subordinates. Just before Rommel counter-attacked in January he wrote to warn him of his intelligence staff's " highly coloured optimistic reports " and its exaggerated estimates of enemy casualties. " These," he wrote, " are apt to create a spirit of unwarranted optimism amongst politicians, which is followed by one of doubt as to the veracity of our statements." After the loss of Benghazi he wrote again:

> " First and foremost I should like to offer my deep sympathy at the setback that your forces have suffered. I can so well imagine what a deep disappointment this must be to you. Looking at Rommel's counter-stroke from the detached point of view, I cannot help feeling that . . . over-optimistic intelligence played a large part in accounting for your troubles . . . It is not my own impression, but one that I have gathered from all quarters."

Further than this he was not prepared to go, feeling that a commander in the field should be free to pick his subordinates and enjoy, so long as he retained command, the confidence of those who had appointed him.

But though he refused to interfere with those in command, he insisted as operational head of the Army on being kept fully informed of what was happening in the field. On taking office he found that telegrams were passing between the Prime Minister and the Commander-in-Chief Middle East of whose contents he was not being notified. It was an irregularity that he took immediate steps to correct. " It is, of course, very desirable," he wrote to Auchinleck, " that you should send private telegrams direct to the P.M. in reply to his and keep him informed as to the general course of events, yet I do not think that this should in any way affect the normal channels which should exist between you and the War Office. The extensive use of private telegrams has caused confusion here at times owing to important messages never reaching either Director of Military Operations, Director of Military Intelligence or myself. In addition to the flow of military information and instructions connected with the use of reserves, etc., direct communication between you and the P.M. is apt to make my position difficult at times. I therefore hope that, whilst maintaining the necessary flow of information by direct messages to the P.M., you will ensure that such a procedure does not affect the normal channel of communication to me which should exist between us."[1] For he was resolved that no military information should be communicated to Ministers that was not communicated to those officially charged with the direction of operations, and that instructions should only be given by those directly responsible for giving them. The basis of an Army and of the successful conduct of war was discipline, and it was the essence of discipline that the chain of command should not be interfered with. On this point the new C.I.G.S. was adamant.

\   •   •   •   ā   ā   ā   ā   ā

As soon as he assumed responsibility as the Prime Minister's principal strategic adviser, Brooke was confronted with his two besetting failings—his incurable wish, as he put it, " to stick his fingers into every pie before it was cooked," and his eagerness to do everything simultaneously instead of concentrating on one thing at a time. His habit of urging commanders in the field, without first-hand knowledge of the realities facing them, to attack before they were ready or to hold what could not be held, called for all Brooke's powers of tact and firmness. There were times when Churchill seemed aware of this tendency himself; " it is no good," he said of Wavell that January, " appointing a Supreme Commander if you have to spend your time teaching him to supreme command; I want to keep the flies away from the meat! "[2] Yet he continued to bombard that long-suffering officer with telegrams, regardless of the fact that, as Supreme Commander of A.B.D.A., he was not responsible merely to the British

[1] C.I.G.S. to Auchinleck, 10th December, 1941. Lord Alanbrooke, *Personal Files*; *Notes on My Life*, V, 328.
[2] *Diary*, 22nd January, 1942.

Government but to an international body in Washington. In the same way, at a time when reinforcements intended for Egypt had been deflected to the Far East and when he himself was urging the withdrawal of aircraft from the Middle East to reinforce India and the Russian front,[1] he persisted in trying to prod the cautious Auchinleck into a premature offensive, though he knew that the Chiefs of Staff were opposed to it. "Another bad Monday . . . , " Brooke wrote on March 2nd; " found P.M. had drafted a bad wire for Auchinleck in which he poured abuse on him for not attacking sooner." ' Without it being possible for him to be familiar with all aspects of the situation . . . . he is trying to force him to attack at an earlier date than is thought advisable and, what is more, tried to obtain his ends by an offensive wire. Thank heaven we were able to stop the wire and re-word it.'

Nor was the Prime Minister discouraged by rebuffs; foiled in one attempt, he tried another. On March 8th—the day before Brooke first took the chair at the Chiefs of Staff Committee—he wired Auchinleck suggesting that he should return to England for immediate consultation—an invitation which the Commander-in-Chief declined on the grounds that his presence was indispensable in Cairo. "Considered Auchinleck's refusal to come home at this morning's C.O.S.," Brooke wrote on the 13th:

> " Drafted letter to P.M. about it; however, he called up from Chequers and I had to tell him about it. He was infuriated and once again suggested relieving him of his command. Would not agree to Auchinleck's suggestion that I should go out with Chief of Air Staff. . . . In the afternoon another call from Chequers, P.M. saying he would now send telegram to Auchinleck.

1 " At 6.30 p.m. C.O.S. meeting under the P.M. at which I argued strongly against sending aircraft to Russia from Middle East . . . at a time when we are at our wits' end how to build up adequate air forces for the Middle East and Far East." *Diary*, 25th March, 1942. " Returned . . . . to find P.M. was seeing First Sea Lord and Chief of Air Staff at 4 p.m. Decided to go round to 10 Downing Street to attend this meeting. Glad I did, as I was able to influence withdrawal of aircraft from Middle East to India which P.M. was intending to carry out. As he had decided on a Libyan attack in May, it was madness to withdraw fighters from Middle East for India now in spite of all risks Calcutta might run." *Idem*, 27th March, 1942.

I shudder at what he may put in it, and we shall have to vet it to-morrow morning! "

In a subsequent letter to Auchinleck, Brooke referred to the trouble that his refusal to return home for consultation was causing and to the Chiefs of Staff's decision to send out the Vice-C.I.G.S., to report. Though it was impossible to tell him everything that had happened without being disloyal, he was most anxious that Auchinleck should feel that he was being supported from home. " I hope," he wrote of Nye's impending visit, " you will give him a full picture of your existing situation with its difficulties and prospects. Without such a full picture it will be very hard to make the P.M. understand reasons for delays. Matters have not been any too easy in that connection lately, as you may have noticed from recent telegrams. But I can assure you that this has not been due to the fact that we have not given full consideration to all the points you have raised. . . ."

" It is very exhausting," Brooke wrote again on March 24th, " this continual protecting of Auchinleck." Though his faith in the Middle East Command and Staff was growing more and more shaken, he did not yet feel justified in changing its commander. Instead, he sent out Major-General McCreery, one of the finest Armoured Divisional commanders in Home Forces, to advise on tank warfare and the maintenance and handling of armoured forces.[1] For he felt that it would merely be gambling to adopt the Prime Minister's impulsive proposal to replace Auchinleck by Gort, whom after the fall of France he had relegated to the shelf, or by Nye, who, though a brilliant staff officer, had had no experience of command in the field.

The Prime Minister's inclination to attack at every point

---

[1] As early as January 21st he had written to the Commander-in-Chief, Middle East: " I am worried . . . that you have not got a first-class Armoured Force officer on your staff. . . . There is a colossal amount of work for him in the re-equipping and reforming of your armoured divisions and army tank brigades, and in the provision of general advice on armoured matters." And again on Friday 4th : " The distribution and general state of readiness of your armoured forces at the time of Rommel's counter-attack is, I feel, an example of lack of advice on important matters connected with the handling of armoured forces. I do hope you will reconsider the advisability of appointing an Armoured Forces Major-General on similar lines to your Chief Gunner and Sapper." Lord Alanbrooke, *Personal Files.*

within reach was equally embarrassing. With the Axis Powers seeking a decision against a desperately strained Britain and Russia before America could be mobilized and armed for major war, everything turned, while holding their drives, on building up sufficient reserves to be able to counter-attack at the moment when the foe was over-extended and off his balance. The Churchillian instinct for what the eighteenth century called " diversions,"[1] though in the classic tradition of British " salt-water " strategy, constituted a constant threat to Brooke's policy of husbanding the country's forces for a decisive effort. The danger, as he saw, was that the Prime Minister would involve the country in too many minor enterprises, all swallowing up ocean transport. " The situation as regards shipping," he wrote on February 4th, " is most disturbing and one which the P.M. will not face. And yet it is the one situation which will affect our whole strategy during the coming year." Even while the triumphant Japanese were driving forward from Hong Kong to New Guinea and Australia and from Indo-China to Singapore, Burma and India, and at a time when the sea-transport available was manifestly insufficient to maintain simultaneously the Middle East and Far East fronts and the flow of supplies to Russia, the Prime Minister, with irrepressible optimism, continued to canvass schemes for an invasion of French North Africa, a landing at Cherbourg and a descent on Norway, in addition to an expedition to Madagascar to forestall its seizure by the Japanese. " I had to go round to see P.M. at 10.30 p.m.," Brooke wrote after a hard day towards the end of March, " and was kept up till 1 a.m. discussing possibilities of some form of offensive in North France to assist Russia. . . . The universal cry to start a Western Front is going to be hard to compete with, and yet what can we do with some ten divisions against the German masses? Unfortunately the country fails to realise the situation we are in."[2] As for the Prime Minister's Norwegian project it remained for Brooke a recurrent night-

[1] His projects for these were so numerous that when, in a cable to the Minister of State in Cairo, he mentioned the name of the C. S. Forester novel he had just been reading, Middle East Headquarters assumed that " Hornblower " must be the name of some new operation.

[2] *Diary*, 30th March, 1942.

mare. ' Why he wanted to go back and what he was going to do there . . . we never found out. The only reason he ever gave was that Hitler had unrolled the map of Europe starting with Norway and he would start rolling it up again with Norway . . . It had no strategic prospects of any kind and yet he insisted on returning to it. Heaven knows what we should have done in Norway had we landed there! '[1]

Yet even this fantastic project, as it seemed to Brooke and his colleagues, served Britain's ends so long as it was not translated into reality. By his perpetual readiness to attack, even at the most depressing times, Churchill not only kept up the courage and faith of the British people but distracted and confused the enemy. He never allowed discomfiture or disappointment to dim his conviction that his adversary was also suffering embarrassment and that it was only necessary to persevere in striking at him to force him into folly and on to the defensive. And frequently his courageous sense of what the foe was fearing proved right. Even in those dark winter days of 1942, when the British Empire and its command of the sea seemed crumbling away, by a strange paradox the German leaders were in the depths of gloom. Their eastern army had suffered a million casualties and had only narrowly escaped a disaster as great as that of 1812; shortages of petrol, manpower and raw materials were impeding production; the long, cold, dark winter on the Russian front was profoundly depressing the nation's morale, including Hitler's.[2] Even the passage up the Channel of the *Scharnhorst* and *Gneisenau*, which so shocked and angered the British, caused the German leader intense anxiety. "We are all trembling," wrote Goebbels, "lest anything happen to them. It would be terrible if even one of these three ships were to share the fate of the *Bismarck*." And the object of their break-out through the Straits of Dover was not, as was supposed in England, to attack British commerce but to defend the German conquests in Norway from

[1] *Notes on My Life*, V, 403.
[2] See Goebbels' *Diary*, 22nd, 24th January; 6th, 7th, 10th February; 3rd, 6th, 8th, 16th, 20th March, 1942. " This long, hard, cruel winter . . . put not only the German Wehrmacht but especially its Supreme Commander under a cruel strain. It is nothing short of a miracle that we stood it. . . . Sometimes, the Fuehrer said, he feared it simply would not be possible to survive." *Idem*, p. 88-9.

the purely hypothetical attack which Churchill was seeking to launch. " If the British go about things properly," Hitler wrote to his naval Commander-in-Chief, " they will attack northern Norway at several points, . . . take Narvik if possible, and thus exert pressure on Sweden and Finland. This might be decisive for the war. The German Fleet must therefore use all its forces for the defence of Norway."[1] Thus it came about that at the very moment when, in pursuit of a joint Japanese-German-Italian global strategy, Hitler's surface ships should have been used in offensive operations against the British supply lines in the Atlantic, they remained in the Norwegian fiords to serve a purely German and defensive end.

.　　.　　.　　.　　.　　.　　.　　.

Throughout March the succession of disasters in the Far East continued. On the 7th the invasion of New Guinea began and Rangoon was evacuated; the last resistance in Java ceased next day. Within three weeks all Lower Burma was lost. At sea, with Singapore and the Sumatra Straits in their possession, the Japanese were ranging far into the Indian Ocean, sinking and bombing as far as the Cingalese and Indian coasts, and on land, in full cry after Alexander's army, were bearing down on the gates of the Raj. " It is not easy," Churchill wrote to Roosevelt, " to assign limits to the Japanese aggression."[2] With the failure that month of Cripps' mission to India and ever mounting tidings of British disaster, the vast, restless subcontinent seemed on the verge of revolution, with many of its nationalist leaders preaching co-operation with the enemy, and Britain's allies, America, Russia and China, adding fuel to the fire by ill-timed ideological propaganda about the doom of an outworn imperialism and the inevitability of immediate " liberation." Only the firmness of the Viceroy and the loyalty of the Indian Army stood between the land and anarchy.

On the closing day of the month the tired, exasperated C.I.G.S. wrote in his diary:

" The last day of the first quarter of 1942—fateful year

[1] *Hinsley*, 195-8. Ciano's diary for 7th February, 1942, makes the same point.
[2] *Churchill*, IV, 169.

in which we have already lost a large proportion of the British Empire and are on the high road to lose a great deal more of it. During the last fortnight I have had for the first time since the war started a growing conviction that we are going to lose this war unless we control it very differently and fight it with more determination. . . ."

" I wonder if we shall muddle through this time like we have in the past? There are times when I wish to God I had not been placed at the helm of a ship that seems to be heading inevitably for the rocks. It is a great honour to find myself entrusted with such a task, and the hope of saving the ship a most inspiring thought and one that does override all others. But may God help me and guide me in my task! "

'After writing these words,' Brooke recalled, 'I must have slept soundly and woke up refreshed, for the following evening on April 1st I continued in the following strain ':

" Looking back at what I wrote last night I wonder whether I was liverish. Life looks yellow at times, but as long as one can prevent one's thoughts and actions from being tinged with yellow, all is well. We have got to choose between pulling through or sinking, and it does not take long to make that choice! "

Chapter Seven

SEARCH FOR A PLAN

Ships! ships! All we need is ships.
GENERAL EISENHOWER

O N APRIL 1st, 1942, the American Secretary for War,
Henry Stimson, and the Chief of Army Staff, General
George Marshall, presented President Roosevelt with
a plan for an early Anglo-American invasion of northern
France. It had been drafted by the newly promoted head of
the Army Plans and Operations Staff, Major-General Dwight
Eisenhower. Based on the doctrine laid down by the President
and Prime Minister at Christmas that " the U.S. should adopt
the strategic defensive in the Pacific and devote its major
offensive effort across the Atlantic," its objects were to keep
Russia in the war by drawing German ground and air forces
from the eastern to a western front, and to provide a theatre
where American forces could be employed at once to destroy
the Axis in Europe before turning against the Japanese aggressor
in the Pacific. Ignoring the earlier Anglo-American proposals
put forward at the Arcadia Conference for clearing the North
African coast in the coming year, it envisaged the despatch to
the United Kingdom during the summer of either two armoured
or three infantry divisions—the largest force for which shipping
was available—and by the spring of 1943 of at least 400,000
troops and airmen, roughly as many, that is, as the British had
built up in France by 1940 under cover of the French Army.
If ships could be found to transport the additional troops whom
the U.S. would by then have trained, this force could be
increased to a million men or as many as thirty divisions. With
eighteen British divisions and supported by powerful British and
American air forces operating from south-eastern England, it

344

was to cross the Channel at its narrowest point, storm the German coastal defences and establish a Second Front in Europe. If, as seemed likely, the plight of Russia necessitated earlier action, a preliminary landing—Operation " Sledge-hammer "—was to be made in the present summer. It was recognised that this would have to be carried out mainly by British troops and that its cost would probably be sacrificial. But it was hoped that it might establish a bridgehead which could be held during the winter until the larger-scale invasion—Operation " Round-up "—could be launched in 1943.

In a memorandum to the President written a week earlier, General Marshall, who was strongly backed by Secretary Stimson, had explained the reasons why such an operation seemed preferable to any other the Western Allies could undertake. Both men—the one aged 61 and the other 72—had served as colonels in France in the First War and had been impressed, like most senior officers at the time, with the importance of concentrating on the one front where a decisive victory could be won, and the danger of dispersing it on " diversions " like Salonica and Palestine. Both felt that what had been true of the first war must be true of the second, and that it was necessary to resist the weakness of their political chief and his fellow amateur strategist in Downing Street for fancy projects such as " Gymnast "—the proposed landing in French North Africa, which to Stimson seemed " the wildest kind of dispersion debauch."[1] In his memorandum to the President, Marshall described northern France as the one place in the world " in which a powerful offensive can be prepared and executed by the United Powers in the near future . . . where the vital air superiority over the hostile land-areas preliminary to a major attack can be staged, . . . and in which . . . the bulk of the British ground forces can be committed to a general offensive in co-operation with the United States forces." " Successful attack in this area," he concluded, " will afford the maximum of support to the Russian front . . . The bulk of the combat forces of the United States, United Kingdom and Russia can be applied simultaneously only against Ger-

[1] *Stimson*, 214.

many, and then only if we attack in time. We cannot concentrate against Japan."[1]

Though based on the broad principle laid down at the Arcadia Conference, the Marshall Memorandum involved a reversal of the deployment policy which, under pressure of disasters in the Pacific, the United States had till now pursued. Of the 132,000 American troops embarked since the beginning of the year, only 20,000 had gone to the Atlantic bases in Northern Ireland and Iceland. Nearly all the rest had been sent to the Pacific to stem the Japanese tide. With their battle-fleet temporarily immobilized and an ocean arc to defend of more than seven thousand miles, stretching from the Aleutians through Midway and the Hawaiians to the Fijis, New Caledonia, Australia and New Guinea, the American admirals were seeking to use air-striking power in place of battleship-power by converting every island in the Japanese path into a stationary aircraft-carrier. For this, in addition to their own carrier-borne aircraft, they needed heavy Army bombers, garrisons of troops or marines to hold the islands, and vast quantities of shipping to carry men and equipment to them and maintain them. Their champion on the American Joint Chiefs of Staff Committee was the new Commander-in-Chief and Chief of Naval Operations, Admiral Ernest King, a tough 63-year-old salt of strong views and uncompromising temper who had grown up with the American Navy and was intensely jealous of its independence. Though fully aware of the immense difficulties to be overcome, he was already planning for the distant counter-offensive which, based on Australia and the central Pacific islands, was to avenge Pearl Harbour, regain the Philippines and destroy Japan. " It is time," he said on taking office, " to toss defensive talking and thinking overboard; our days of victory are in the making—we will win this war." Despite a nominal acceptance of the Chiefs of Staffs' thesis of " Germany first," his recipe for doing so was to concentrate amphibious striking-power in the Pacific as quickly as possible, first to halt and then to hit Japan.

The decisive factor governing all troop and supply move-

[1] *Strategical Planning for Coalition Warfare*, 1941-1942, 185; *White House Papers*, II, 524-5.

ments, both for America and Britain, was shipping. The U-boat sinkings in the western Atlantic and Caribbean were having a disastrous effect on the rate at which the United States could deploy both the forces it was training and the armaments it was making for itself and its allies. Owing to the distances across which everything had to be carried, the Navy's demands for its Pacific campaigns threatened to make nonsense of the Administration's policy of " Germany First." These demands were backed, though with varying emphasis, by an American public opinion eager for revenge, by an anxious Australian Government, and by the great popular hero, General MacArthur, who since his evacuation from Corregidor and appointment as Supreme Commander of the South-west Pacific, had been advocating an early counter-offensive in that area both to check the Japanese advance on Australia and to secure island bases for future offensive action. The President's acceptance of Marshall's and Eisenhower's cross-Channel plan constituted, therefore, a recognition at the highest level that, the Navy's difficulties notwithstanding, the United States was going to stand by the principle laid down at the start of the war. Its endorsement on April 1st by the American Joint Chiefs of Staff was only rendered palatable to King on the ground that, by putting pressure on the British to join in an early all-out assault on Western Europe, the full resources of the United Nations would be released for action against Japan sooner than would otherwise be possible.

For the President's decision also marked the rejection by America of the British contention that no frontal attack on Germany was possible for a long time and then only if the Reich's military strength had been drastically weakened by Russian resistance. It marked, too, the by-passing of a more detailed and far less sanguine appreciation of the possibilities of a cross-Channel attack drawn up by the Combined Planning Committee of the Combined Chiefs of Staff, which, in deference to the facts pointed out by its British members, had stressed the limitations imposed on any invasion by shortage of cargo shipping and landing-craft. There was little prospect, it had been shown, of enough of the latter, for any successful

landing either in 1942 or 1943.[1] For this reason, sooner than
refer the War Department's plan back to the Combined
Chiefs of Staff, the President had decided that his confidential
emissary, Harry Hopkins, should proceed with Marshall at
once to London to press it on the British Prime Minister and
Chiefs of Staff. On April 4th the two left Baltimore by clipper
for Bermuda and England.

.   .   .   .

During the week in which Marshall's planners were preparing figures to show that a successful Anglo-American
invasion of France was practicable, the British Chiefs of Staff
were struggling with the threat to their Indian Ocean and
Middle East communications which had resulted from the
American disaster at Pearl Harbour and the immobilisation
of the American battle-fleet. With Yamashita's army closing
in on the last American survivors in the Philippines and the
whole of the Dutch and British East Indies, Singapore, Malaya
and the Sumatra Straits in her hands, Japan was showing
signs of preparing a westward advance across the Indian
Ocean to seize Ceylon, cut the Persian Gulf oil supplies, and
link hands with her European partners in the Middle East.
Desperately short though the Navy was of capital ships to
meet the emergency, the Chiefs of Staff and Admiralty had
withdrawn five of the older battleships from the Mediterranean
and Atlantic, together with two large aircraft-carriers and one
small one, and sent them to the Indian Ocean. At the beginning of the last week in March the former Commander of
Force H in the Western Mediterranean, Admiral Sir James
Somerville, had arrived in Colombo to take over this hetero-
geneous fleet and consult with the flag-officer commanding
the Ceylon station, Sir Geoffrey Layton. As a consequence of
Brooke's plea for a single Supreme Commander in the island,
the latter had recently been appointed Commander-in-Chief
of all the British forces there. The C.I.G.S.'s contention had
been justified by the vigour with which, invested with the
powers of unified command, Admiral Layton had improvised
the island's defences, not only requisitioning private property

[1] *Strategic Planning for Coalition Warfare, 1942-1943.* 180.

to make airfields, but, in the nick of time, ordering the diversion to Ceylon of two squadrons of Hurricanes on their way to Java, where they would inevitably have fallen into the enemy's hands.

Confronted by the fact that the Japanese, fresh from their victory in the Java Sea, had just occupied the Andaman Islands—only six or seven hundred miles from the Indian and Cingalese coasts—and by a report that they were planning a carrier-borne attack on Colombo, Admiral Somerville had decided to leave that port at once and to concentrate his highly vulnerable fleet, part of which was still on its way from the Cape, in the open sea near Addu Atoll, a coral-island lagoon six hundred miles south-south-west of Ceylon. After his exploits with Force " H " no-one could accuse him of lack of daring, but as four of his five battleships were slow and unconverted veterans of the First World War, and as there was no hope of reinforcements from Europe for many months, he was in no position to take risks. The security of the supply-lines to the Middle East and India depended on his keeping the Eastern Fleet in being and not allowing it to be caught like the *Prince of Wales* and *Repulse* or the American battleships at Pearl Harbour. For, with the *Tirpitz* threatening the North Atlantic, and the Eastern Mediterranean unguarded by a single capital ship, the Navy was without reserves.

Of all this the chairman of the Chiefs of Staff Committee was painfully aware. On April 2nd—the day after the President's decision to strike at Germany across the Channel—he had a heated argument in the C.O.S. Committee with the First Sea Lord. " I could not get him to realise," he wrote, " how essential it is for us to have a concerted plan with the Americans as regards the actions of our naval forces. Without such a plan we run grave risks of being defeated in detail." That night, without informing his colleagues, the old sailor allowed the Prime Minister to send out instructions that the French battleship, *Richelieu*, was to be attacked and sunk if it attempted to sail from Morocco to Toulon. All next day, Good Friday, the Chiefs of Staff struggled to get the order withdrawn, knowing that the naval position was almost desperate and that the intervention of Vichy France and the

Toulon Fleet might prove fatal. Luckily the *Richelieu* never came out and the matter was not put to the test. But when, after spending Easter Day at home, Brooke returned to the office on Monday morning, he found the situation ominous in the extreme.

"*April 6th, 1942*.... On reaching C.O.S. I discovered that most of the Japanese Fleet appeared to be in the Indian Ocean and our Eastern Fleet retiring westward. Up to present no sign of transports. I don't like the situation much, as we are very weak in the Indian Ocean.[1] I have been trying to get First Sea Lord to fix up with Americans some counter-move towards Japan to cover the very predicament that we are in, but he has failed to do so up to present. At any rate the air action over Ceylon was successful yesterday and we downed 27 Japs."

"*April 7th*. C.O.S. at which we looked into the unpleasant situation created by entrance of Japanese Fleet into Indian Ocean. Just what I had been afraid of and had been trying to get First Sea Lord busy about doing the whole of last week. Also frantic calls for air support from Wavell[2] which according to Portal there is little chance of meeting. I suppose this Empire has never been in such a precarious position throughout history. I do not like the look of things. And yet a miracle saved us at Dunkirk and we may pull through this time. But I wish I could see more daylight as to how we are to keep going through 1942."

"A very gloomy Cabinet meeting. Both Bevin and Alexander reporting Labour discontentment at course of war and difficulty at not being able to give them a full account."

' All my plans for clearing North Africa, opening Mediter-

---

[1] " Once Japanese battleships, aircraft-carriers, submarines and the Japanese naval air force are based on Ceylon, the British will be forced to resort to heavily escorted convoys if they desire to maintain communication with India and the Near East. . . . The Suez and Basra positions are the western pillars of the British position in the Indian Ocean. Should these positions collapse under the weight of concerted Axis pressure, the consequences for the British Empire would be disastrous." Raeder to Hitler, 13th February, 1942. cit. *Hinsley*, 199.

[2] Now back at his old post as Commander-in-Chief, India.

ranean and threatening Southern Europe now seemed very far. We were fighting for our lives to stop gaps. Cairo was none too safe, Persia was threatened with its precious oil by German advance in South Russia, India's eastern flank was threatened, vital communications through Indian Ocean might be cut at any moment, and Australia and New Zealand even open to attack.'[1]

. . . .

Yet, thanks to the timely action of the island's Commander-in-Chief, what had happened in the Ceylon skies over Easter proved one of the turning points in the war. On the evening of Easter Saturday a warning had been given by a Catalina flying-boat, just before it was shot down, that a fleet of four fast Japanese battleships and five aircraft-carriers, with a large force of cruisers and destroyers, was approaching Colombo. Layton had acted with speed and decision. During the night the merchant shipping in the harbour was hurried to sea, and the thirty-six Hurricanes requisitioned to defend the island were made ready for battle. Shortly before eight o'clock on Easter morning fifty Japanese bombers, escorted by an equal number of Zero fighters, roared in from the south, expecting a second Pearl Harbour. In the fighting that followed half the bombers were shot down for the loss of the same proportion of the defending force. But though damage was done to the harbour and dock installations, and two British cruisers and a destroyer were sunk by low-bombing aircraft, the attackers returned to their carriers with their mission unaccomplished. Through the foresight shown by the Chiefs of Staff and the presence of mind of the two admirals to whom the island and the Eastern Fleet had been entrusted, the air defences of Ceylon—the key to the Indian Ocean—remained unbroken and the fleet safe at sea. For the first time since the start of the Japanese war a major assault by the Rising Sun had been repulsed.

Yet the danger to the Indian Ocean and Britain's communications with India and the Middle East had not passed. All next day, unaware that his fleet was outnumbered by two

[1] *Notes on My Life*, V, 379.

to one in carrier strength and gun-power, Admiral Somerville, who had been watering at Addu Atoll when the news of the attack reached him, sought the enemy while the enemy sought him. Disaster was only averted because the British admiral continued on his eastward course to rescue the survivors of the sunk cruisers. But for this, Nagumo, seeking him far to the west, might have gained a victory that would have given Japan control of the Indian Ocean, isolated the Middle East, and brought down the Churchill Government. Next day an anxious Admiralty hastily ordered Somerville to withdraw his slow and out-gunned battleships to the African coast.

.　.　.　.　.　.　.　.　.

It was against this background of anxiety that on Wednesday April 8th, following a tense C.O.S. Committee, Brooke went to Hendon to meet General Marshall and Harry Hopkins, who, after being held up over Easter in Bermuda, had landed at Prestwick on the previous evening. That night he dined with the Prime Minister in their company at 10 Downing Street.

> " Attlee also present there and Anthony Eden came after dinner. Neither Hopkins nor Marshall disclosed their proposed plans for which they have come over. However, it was an interesting evening and a good chance to get to know Marshall. Did not get back till 1.30 a.m."

According to Hopkins, their host spent the evening ranging over the American Civil War and First World War and never came to grips with the business for which they had come, though the Chief of the Imperial General Staff, he noted, got into it enough to indicate that he had a great many misgivings.

Yet earlier that afternoon, according to the same authority, as the Americans had privately unfolded their plan, the Prime Minister had given it a most favourable reception. Hopkins, an experienced politician, doubted if he was serious, but the simple, straightforward soldier Marshall was deeply impressed. Though Churchill mentioned the objections of his Chiefs of Staff to a premature attack, he indicated that he was prepared, in spite of everything, to go along with them.[1]

In this the Prime Minister showed his understanding of the transatlantic mentality, as well as his sense of the overriding importance of Anglo-American unity, but may have opened a door to future misunderstanding. The Americans were in deadly earnest about their wish to attack. They were a people accustomed to hustling and getting things done, and, after four months of defeat and humiliation, they were resolved to strike back. At that moment their forces in the Philippines were at their last gasp and their ships were being sent to the bottom in scores by U-boats. They wanted revenge, they wanted results and they wanted to fight. They had not left their homes and embarked on an unwonted trade merely to hang about in training camps; they wished to engage the enemy at the earliest possible moment and end the war. As the President put it, the nearest point at which they could do so—the shortest distance from the United States for supply-lines for any front anywhere—was the French coast opposite England. " What Harry and Geo. Marshall will tell you all about," he had written on April 3rd, " has my heart and mind in it." Using England as a springboard, the armies of the Western democracies were to storm Hitler's fortress from the Channel and bring the War in Europe to a close. Six divisions were to go ashore on the first day and, reinforced at the rate of 100,000 men a week, break swiftly out of the beach-head to seize first the line of the Oise-St. Quentin and then the port of Antwerp. Only by such means could the pressure on the Red Army be relieved and Russia kept in the War. For to the President the elementary strategic fact of 1942 was that the Russians were killing more Axis personnel and destroying more Axis material than all the other twenty-five United Nations put together and must be helped at all costs. A few days later—on the 11th—he cabled Stalin that he was putting forward a " very important military proposal involving the utilisation of our armed forces in a manner to relieve your critical western front."

[1] *White House Papers*, II, 528. Hopkins is the sole authority for this conversation. There is no reference to it in Sir Winston Churchill's own history of the War.

On April 9th, the Marshall Memorandum was presented to the Chiefs of Staff Committee.

> " Started C.O.S. at 9 a.m. as Marshall was due at 10.30 a.m. He remained with us till 12.30 p.m. and gave us a long talk on his views concerning desirability of starting a western front next September and that the U.S.A. forces would take part. However, the total force which they could transport by then only consisted of two and a half divisions, no very great contribution! Furthermore, they had not begun to realise what all the implications of their proposed plan were . . . I liked what I saw of Marshall, a pleasant and easy man to get on with, rather over-filled with his own importance. But I should not put him down as a great man."

' These first impressions of mine about Marshall,' Brooke wrote afterwards, ' are interesting and of course incomplete. They were based on the day's discussions, which had made it quite clear to me that he had up to date only touched the fringe of all the implications of a re-entry into France. In the light of the existing situation his plans for September of 1942 were just fantastic.'[1] Marshall seems to have formed much the same impression of Brooke, for he told Hopkins that, though he might be a good fighting man, he lacked Dill's brains.[2]

> "*April 10th.* A very busy day which started with usual C.O.S. meeting, mainly concerned in trying to save India from the Japs; a gloomy prospect with loss of command of sea and air. Lunched with Adam and in evening had another C.O.S. meeting to discuss Joint Planning Staff report on Marshall's scheme for invasion of Europe. Then out to Chequers for dinner and the night. Harry Hopkins and Marshall there, also three Chiefs of Staff. We were kept up till 2 a.m. doing a world survey but little useful work."

[1] *Notes on My Life*, V, 381. The head of the American Navy, Admiral King, had come earlier to the same conclusion about his colleague's views on amphibious operations. " Marshall appeared to think that landings were easily managed." Whitehill, *Admiral King*, 114.
[2] *White House Papers*, II, 528.

"*April 13th*. A bad C.O.S. with much loss of time and interruption. Trying to frame a reply for Marshall . . . Cabinet 5.30 p.m. attended by Harry Hopkins, Marshall, and Casey. Afterwards meeting to settle final details of reply to Marshall. Only got away after 8 p.m. and had Marshall to dinner with me. The more I see of him the more I like him."

"*April 14th*. Another very busy day. Marshall attended Chiefs of Staff meeting at which I stated our reply to his Memorandum and handed over document to him. We then had a Cabinet meeting to settle new programme of arms for Russia. . . . At 5 p.m. a meeting under Oliver Lyttelton to try and settle conduct of strategy and production. Then back to War Office for interview with Archie Nye and a rush home to change for dinner at Savoy with Anthony Eden, de Gaulle, Peake and self. A difficult dinner in many ways as there was no knowing where de Gaulle might want to lead us to. From there back to Downing Street for a Defence Committee attended by Hopkins and Marshall. A momentous meeting at which we accepted their proposals for offensive action in Europe in 1942 perhaps, and in 1943 for certain. They have not begun to realise all the implications of this plan and all the difficulties that lie ahead of us. The fear I have is that they should concentrate on this offensive at the expense of all else. We have therefore been pressing on them the importance of providing American assistance in the Indian Ocean and Middle East."

At this midnight meeting of the Defence Committee, attended by Hopkins and Marshall, it was agreed that the President's proposals should be accepted by Britain in principle. Churchill formally welcomed the American resolve to treat Germany as the main enemy, but dwelt on the importance of safeguarding India and the Middle East. After Marshall had outlined his plan and stated his belief that the difficulties of providing the necessary shipping and landing-craft could be overcome, Brooke reminded the Committee of the immediate problem in the Indian Ocean. For if Japan's advance along the southern shores of Asia was not halted, it would cut off three-quarters of a million fighting men in the Middle East, leave India with its vast reserves of man-power at her mercy, and bring about the dreaded junction of the Axis partners and the exchange of raw materials they both needed. Turkey would be surrounded, the Russian oil supplies in the Caucasus would be threatened from both south and north and those of Persia and Iraq be lost to Britain and the West. Completely isolated, Russia would then be forced to surrender, and any cross-Channel assault on Germany—freed from the British blockade and a war on two fronts—would become impossible.

The meeting ended with agreement that planning should start at once to build up American military and air forces in Britain for a major cross-Channel offensive in 1943 and for a possible emergency landing in 1942. In order to meet the British point about the danger of any further Japanese advance towards the Middle East and its communications, a limited measure of American air-support was also to be given in India and the Indian Ocean. Churchill spoke of the two nations, bound by this " momentous proposal," marching forward together " in a noble brotherhood of arms," while Hopkins cabled Roosevelt that the British Government had accepted the main American position. To the statesmen it seemed that what Hopkins called a " meeting of minds " between the Chiefs of Staff had been achieved.

But neither Marshall nor Brooke shared this illusion. As the former pointed out in a letter home, agreement had only been reached in principle and most of the participants held " reservations regarding this or that." " Great firmness," he added, would be required to avoid " further dispersions."[1] And though, for the sake of concentrating the largest possible force in the British Isles, the American Army chief was prepared to take a calculated risk in the Pacific, his British *vis-à-vis* had made it clear that he regarded the defence of the Indian Ocean as a first and overriding priority.[2] Nor had the latter and

[1] *Strategic Planning for Coalition Warfare*, 1941-1942. 189.

[2] The Chief American Planner, Eisenhower, had seen the need for this more clearly than his chief, Marshall. " Over simplification of the Japanese problem because our primary objective lies elsewhere," he had written on February 28th, " is likely to discount the enormous advantages that will accrue to our enemies through conquest of India, the domination of the Indian Ocean, the severing of

his colleagues committed themselves to a cross-Channel operation in 1942 or even in 1943 but merely to the desirability of launching one if, and only if, conditions at the time made its success seem probable. What, in effect, the British Chiefs of Staff had agreed to do was to start preparing plans, in conjunction with the U.S., for an invasion of Europe whenever it became a practical operation, and to welcome in the meantime the maximum concentration of American military and air strength in England—the place where it would be most valuable, whether Russia held out and made an invasion of the Continent possible or whether she collapsed and left Hitler once more free to attempt an invasion of England.

As for the so-called plans for storming the coast of northwestern Europe in the face of thirty or forty German divisions and destroying the enemy in what the American planners airily described as the " general area of Calais-Arras-St. Quentin-Soissons-Paris-Deauville," Brooke, with his knowledge of modern war, knew how insubstantial such dreams at present were. The Americans had not begun to grasp the complexity of the logistical problems involved or the existing German superiority in armaments, particularly tanks. ' With the situation prevailing at the time,' he commented, ' it was not possible to take Marshall's " castles in the air " too seriously. . . . We were hanging on by our eye-lids. Australia and India were threatened by the Japanese, we had temporarily lost lost control of the Indian Ocean, the Germans were threatening Persia and our oil, Auchinleck was in precarious straits in the desert, and the submarine sinkings were heavy. . . . We were desperately short of shipping and could stage no large-scale operations without additional shipping. This shipping could only be obtained by opening the Mediterranean and saving a million tons through the elimination of the Cape route.'[1]   Even if the Americans proved able to ship the necessary troops, aircraft and material across the Atlantic by the dates they proposed, there were not enough landing-craft to carry them and their British comrades across the tidal

all lines of British communications to the Near and Middle East and the physical junction of our two principal enemies." *Strategic Planning for Coalition Warfare,* 157-8.

[1] *Notes on My Life,* V, 383-4.

waters of the Channel and maintain them through open beaches. Yet without a port there was no other way of establishing a bridgehead in France. Even by 1943 the most that could be looked for in landing-craft would only suffice to create a two-division front.

On the following day, April 15th, Brooke continued his conversation with Marshall.

"After lunch I had Marshall for nearly two hours in my office explaining to him our dispositions. He is, I should think, a good general at raising armies and at providing the necessary link between the military and political worlds, but his strategical ability does not impress me at all. In fact, in many respects he is a very dangerous man whilst being a very charming one. He has found that King, the American Naval Chief of Staff, is proving more and more of a drain on his military resources, continually calling for land-forces to capture and hold land-bases in the Pacific. . . . MacArthur in Australia constitutes another threat by asking for forces to develop an offensive from Australia. To counter these moves Marshall has started the European offensive plan and is going one hundred per cent all out on it. It is a clever move which fits in with present political opinion and the desire to help Russia. It is popular with all military men who are fretting for an offensive policy. But, and this is a very large ' but,' his plan does not go beyond just landing on the far coast. Whether we are to play *baccarat* or *chemin de fer* at Le Touquet . . . . is not stipulated. I asked him this afternoon—Do we go west, south or east after landing? He had not begun to think of it."

' My conversation with Marshall that afternoon,' he commented afterwards,

' was an eye-opener. I discovered that he had not studied any of the strategic implications of a cross-Channel operation. He argued that the main difficulty would be to achieve a landing. I granted that this would certainly present grave difficulties, but that our real troubles would start after the landing. We should be operating with forces initially weaker than the enemy and, in addition, his rate of reinforcement would be at least twice as fast as ours . . . His formations were fully trained and inured to war whilst ours were raw and inexperienced. I asked him to imagine that his landing had been safely carried out, and asked him what his plans would then be . . . I found that he had not begun to consider any form of plan of action or . . . to visualise the problems that would face an army after landing . . . Nor could he understand that until the Mediterranean was opened again we should always suffer from the crippling shortage of sea-transport. It was evident that if Russia cracked up, the Germans would concentrate the bulk of their forces in France and would make an invasion quite impossible. Under these circumstances our only hope would be to operate in Africa.'

Brooke's diary continued:

" Later in afternoon attended an American sherry party at Claridges to meet Marshall. Finally dined 10 Downing Street. The King had been invited to meet Marshall and Harry Hopkins, also Pound, Portal, Mountbatten, Ismay and Hardinge[1] and self. After dinner heated discussion as to possible future of German plans. I propounded possible German move through Eastern Mediterranean with sea and airborne attack against Cyprus and Syria. I suggested this might be alternative if Germany did not feel strong enough to attack in Russia. The King very interested, and resulted in good argument with Winston."

" *April 16th.* Important Chiefs of Staff meeting at which we discussed plans for this year's invasion of Continent in collaboration with the Americans and also plans for 1943. The plans are fraught with the gravest dangers. Public opinion is shouting for the formation of a new Western Front to assist the Russians. But they have

[1] The Hon. Sir Alexander (now Lord) Hardinge, Private Secretary to the King.

no conception of the difficulties and dangers entailed. The prospects of success are small and dependent on a mass of unknowns, whilst the chances of disaster are great and dependent on a mass of well-established facts. Should Germany be getting the best of an attack on Russia, the pressure for invasion of France will be at its strongest, and yet this is just the most dangerous set of circumstances for us."

On April 17th, well pleased with what they had achieved, the Americans flew home.

"Short C.O.S. from which I went round to No. 10 Downing Street to say good-bye to General Marshall before his departure for U.S.A. He was very charming as usual and hoped I would be able to return his visit."

During the nine days he had been in England, Brooke had been trying to size Marshall up. Dill in his letters from Washington had described him as a man who improved immensely on acquaintance—straight, clear-headed, and loved by all: not a strategist, perhaps, but a military organiser of the highest ability, full of character and humour. 'There was a great charm and dignity about Marshall,' Brooke wrote, 'which could not fail to appeal to one; a big man and a very great gentleman who inspired trust but did not impress me by the ability of his brain.' Though, during the four years they worked together as heads of the British and American armies and chief military advisers to their respective Governments, he continued to be critical of Marshall's strategic outlook and Marshall of his, he came more and more to see him as " a great man, a great gentleman and a great organiser." The two soldiers met as the protagonists of contending points of view, each rooted in his country's military past. But their differences were those of men of honour seeking the same end.

In a letter of characteristic generosity written after the war, Marshall described Brooke as " determined in his position, yet amenable to negotiation, generous in his judgments and delightful in his friendship. He worked from a wide experience, particularly in France and in the opening phases of the Second World War. He had had a hard schooling in the battles of the Somme in earlier years and had suffered the shock of the highly modernised Nazi Army. This, for a year or more in our earlier negotiations, made it difficult for him to meet our theory and battle inexperience with his practical and rather desperate experience. All of this washed away as the war developed and we came more and more into mutual understanding." Brooke reciprocated these feelings. Without the great Virginian's strength of purpose and administrative ability the American armies could never have been made so swiftly the instrument of victory they became. Between Pearl Harbour and D-Day Marshall did for America, and on a far vaster scale, what Carnot did for Revolutionary France and Kitchener for Britain. At the moment all this was in the future, and Brooke could only see a very likeable but over-confident advocate of courses that would almost certainly end in disaster, not only for America but Britain. Having already to restrain Churchill's passion for premature offensives, he had now, it seemed, to restrain that of his American colleague as well.

Yet though Brooke acted as a brake on both, it was not, as Marshall supposed, because he was averse to returning to France. He merely saw, with his habit of exactly calculating means to ends, that no plan for invading Western Europe could succeed if it interfered with the preliminary operations essential to its execution. He shared the American belief that the ultimate key to victory was a successful landing in France, yet knew how delicately the scales would have to be adjusted to make it possible. The steps of his graduated strategic policy were first to hold the enemy's drives—in the Indian Ocean, the Atlantic, the Mediterranean and African desert, and, if necessary, in the Caucasus—and then, when the requisite force had been assembled at the decisive point, to defeat Rommel and clear the North African coast preparatory to using the shipping so released to threaten Europe's southern shore. Every successive stage demanded the most far-sighted planning, not only of military effort but of industrial production and sea transport. For, in the light of Axis strength, the margin between success and failure was so narrow that no resource could be misdirected or applied at the wrong place or moment. Otherwise there would not be enough shipping, men, aircraft, guns, tanks and supplies at the point of opportunity when the opportunity came.

. . . .

In April, 1942, the immediate threat to Brooke's plan lay in the Indian Ocean. During the first two days of his conferences with Marshall the thought of it haunted his diary.

> " *April 9th* . . . Large Japanese naval forces are in the Indian Ocean operating with carriers and have sunk two cruisers and one aircraft-carrier in the last two days . . ."
>
> " *April 10th.* A very busy day which started with usual C.O.S. meeting, mainly concerned in trying to save India from the Japs; a gloomy prospect with loss of command of sea and air."

It was this that had created the paradox of the British Prime Minister and C.I.G.S. having to remind their American colleagues that, before they could attack in Europe, the Japanese must first be held. It arose out of initial American unpreparedness and carelessness in the one sphere where they might have been expected to restrain Japanese power. Because of the surprise, in the face of every warning, of the Pacific Fleet at Pearl Harbour, the British, with their hands already full in Europe and Africa, had lost the East Indies, Malaya and Burma and now seemed on the point of losing India and Ceylon. Even a month after Marshall's visit to London, Brooke was writing to Wavell: " The Americans seem to be taking a long time to get into their swing, and their share of the war at sea is not very conspicuous yet. This is what worries me most, as I feel that if we could once produce a reasonably satisfactory situation at sea in the Indian Ocean, we should reduce your dangers and troubles by 75 per cent."[1]

By this time Somerville's battleships had been withdrawn to the African coast, Mandalay had gone up in flames, the Burma road had been cut, and the survivors of Alexander's

---

[1] Brooke to Wavell, 5th May, 1942. Lord Alanbrooke, *Personal Files.*

army, with half a million refugees, had started on their retreat
across six hundred miles of roadless jungle and mountain to
the Indian frontier—the only escape route left now Britain
had lost her sea highway.   In India, where the Viceroy,
Linlithgow, stood like a lonely rock against the waves of non-
resistance, panic swept the country.   Multitudes, fearful of
air-raids, fled from the eastern cities; invasion and revolution
seemed imminent.   From Wavell, most taciturn and least
alarmist of commanders, came urgent reminders that without
aircraft the defence of the sub-continent was impossible.   " It
certainly gives us furiously to think," he wrote, " that when
after trying with less than twenty light bombers to meet an
attack which has cost us three important warships and nearly
100,000 tons of merchant shipping, we see that over two
hundred heavy bombers attacked one town in Germany."
Meanwhile the Australian Government, confronted by
imminent invasion, demanded the return of its remaining
forces in the Middle East or, alternatively, an increase in the
numbers of American troops and aircraft in the Antipodes.
Struggling with grossly inadequate shipping resources to
balance the needs of India and Australia with those of the
Middle East, Brooke and his colleagues were at their wits' end
to keep the balance.

Yet, unknown to them, the menace to India and the Middle
East, though not yet to Australia, had already begun to
recede.   On April 9th, even before the American emissaries
left London, in a second air battle over Ceylon Layton's
remaining Hurricanes and six Fulmer fighters from the Fleet
Air Arm, defending the naval base of Trincomalee against
more than a hundred Japanese planes, inflicted such further
losses on them that three of Nagumo's five carriers were forced
to return to Japan to refit.   Though in its four days in Cingalese
and Indian waters the Japanese fleet sank thirty merchant
ships and caused a panic in Calcutta, where half a million
tons of British shipping were lying, for the moment it had
shot its bolt.   While Churchill was addressing urgent appeals
to Roosevelt for diversionary action in the Pacific and for
the despatch of American reinforcements to Scapa Flow to
release more British battleships for the Indian Ocean, the

Japanese admiral turned home. The centre of gravity between Japan and the Anglo-Saxon Powers shifted back to the Pacific and away from the danger-point to Britain's future offensive.

As it did so, the reviving power of the United States first made itself felt in the Pacific. On April 18th, American Army bombers, launched from a carrier's deck, appeared out of the blue over Tokyo and bombed the Japanese capital. At the same time, though the damaged battleships of the Pacific Fleet still lay eight thousand miles away in the Californian dockyards, American carriers and cruisers began to move southwards towards the Coral Sea to meet a threatened attack on Port Moresby and the island approaches to Australia. Here at the beginning of May there occurred in the waters south of the Solomons a naval battle of a new kind. In it the contending fleets never caught sight of one another yet inflicted heavy losses, not by the guns of warships, but by the torpedoes and bombs of aircraft operating from fleet-carriers. Though the honours were even, the action in effect was a Japanese defeat. For the transports that were to have captured Port Moresby were forced to turn back and the advance on Australia was halted.

Even before the battle was decided and while the Japanese and American naval pilots and gun-crews were still seeking one another amid vast spaces of sea and air—it was the day that Corregidor, the last American outpost in the Philippines, surrendered—Brooke sensed that, though Burma had been overrun, the danger to India had temporarily passed. " I feel," he wrote to Wavell on May 5th, " that Japan, after clearing up Burma, should turn against China to liquidate that long-standing commitment of hers . . . now that she is well placed to do so. In doing so, she will ensure the raw products she still requires and will at the same time free more of her forces for the next blow. Meanwhile I see her operating in the Pacific in the hope of extending her hold over New Guinea and groups of islands to the east. From such a stronghold she would be in a position to carry out seaborne raids on India and Australia and to worry our sea communications whilst awaiting our final defeat by Germany. I do not see her entangling herself in an all-out offensive against either India or Australia."[1]

. . . .

While Brooke was writing, British troops and Commandos, under the guns of the battleship *Ramillies*, were starting to land in Diego Suarez Bay in French Madagascar. The fleet that carried them had left Britain in the utmost secrecy towards the end of March in order to forestall a Japanese attempt to establish a submarine base on the Middle East supply-line. For two months Brooke's diary had contained references to this operation—the first offensive undertaken by the Western Allies since the start of the Japanese war.

"*April 23rd, 1942*. A very difficult C.O.S. connected with the proposed operation against Madagascar . . . The change of Government in France and arrival of Laval puts a new complexion on the enterprise. The repercussions are more likely and may be more serious. We have to take into account the possibility of Bizerta being handed to Axis Powers, or possibly the French Fleet, or Gibraltar heavily bombed and the flow of aircraft interfered with, or Dakar falling into Axis hands. All . . . would have a serious adverse effect on our power to proceed with the war . . ."

"*April 24th*. A short C.O.S. which started at 10 a.m. to consider advisability to put Madagascar operation on. We then had to go on to discuss the operation with P.M. and Foreign Secretary at 11 a.m. and finally with Defence Committee at 12 noon. . . . Personally I feel we have little to gain by carrying out the operation. The main object is to deny the base of Diego Suarez to the Japs, and I don't feel they are likely to go there. . . . However, Winston decided for it for the present . . ."

[1] "Do you agree with any of the above?" Brooke to Wavell, 5th May, 1942. Lord Alanbrooke, *Personal Files*. In a letter to Marshall written three days later, MacArthur expressed the same view. The soundest course now for Japan, he wrote, was to attack southward, securing her position in the Pacific, before attempting any large operation against India. MacArthur to Marshall, 8th May, 1942. *Strategic Planning for Coalition Warfare*, 215-16.

For, the issue being a political rather than a purely military one, the last word lay with the Defence Minister.

" *May 1st.* A short C.O.S. fixing final details as regards announcing carrying out of Madagascar attack on Tuesday morning . . . Sent for by P.M. in the evening to discuss with him Wavell's latest wire. He is protesting strongly at the fact that land, sea and air forces for the defence of India are not being built up quicker. This is partly due to the Madagascar operation. Personally I wish we were not carrying it out . . . With the new Laval Government we may suffer a good deal from the reactions. However, I put the matter clearly to P.M. and Anthony Eden, and they said they did not apprehend any special reaction from Laval."[1]

" *May 4th.* . . . C.O.S. concerned with final arrangements for attack on Madagascar which takes place to-morrow morning early . . . P.M. then invited all the Chiefs of Staff to lunch at 10 Downing Street where he arrived a little late from Chequers. He was in good form and said he felt elated, I think probably mainly with excitement at thought of attack on Madagascar."

Though resisted by the French, the landing was successful and the anchorage captured with less than four hundred casualties. Yet, as Brooke had foreseen, even for this minor diversion a price had to be paid. For, with the competing needs of the Desert campaign, the defence of the Indo-Burmese frontier and the protection of the Persian-Iraq oil-wells against a German drive through the Caucasus, Britain could ill afford to employ forces in southern and eastern waters on any operation not absolutely essential. Because of Madagascar, reinforcements and shipping-space needed to maintain the flow of reinforcements to India and the Middle East were held up, while the troops who landed there contracted malaria. What was worse, the *Ramillies*—one of the battleships assembled with

[1] Eden's view and that of the Foreign Office was that, if the Vichy Government wanted the Germans in North Africa—which he did not believe—Laval would provide the excuse regardless of Britain's actions. ' As matters turned out,' Brooke wrote after the war, ' they were quite right and the reactions were negligible. On the other hand, I still feel the operation was unnecessary and that the Japs never contemplated going there.' *Notes on My Life,* V, 393.

such difficulty to hold the Indian Ocean—was torpedoed by a Japanese submarine while lying in the captured harbour and put out of action for several months.

The trouble was that Britain and America had still more on their hands than they had ocean transport to sustain. Shortage of shipping was the Achilles heel of all their projects. That May and June more than a million and a half tons were sunk by U-boats, bringing the total for the half year to over four million tons. The maritime Powers' dilemma lay in the distances across which they had to carry troops and materials and the U.S. Navy's lack of escort vessels and disastrous delay in organizing convoys along the crowded sea-lanes of the eastern American coast. The loss in tankers was particularly grave, since oil was the main sinew of armoured and mechanised war. In the first quarter of 1942 more than 600,000 tanker tons were sunk in the western Atlantic—a rate of wastage which threatened to bring the Allied war effort to a complete standstill. On June 19th General Marshall pointed out to Admiral King that nearly a quarter of the ships allocated to the Army for July had already been sunk, that 22 per cent of the bauxite fleet and 20 per cent of the Puerto Rican fleet had been destroyed, and that tanker sinkings were averaging 3.5 per cent per month or more than 40 per cent a year. " The losses by submarines off our Atlantic seaboard and in the Caribbean," he wrote, " now threaten our entire war effort."[1]

.   .   .   .

It was this that made the problem of helping Russia so hard and bedevilled the relationship, never easy, between an intensely suspicious Moscow and the Western democracies. Both armies on the Eastern Front, after narrowly escaping destruction—the Russians in the autumn and the Germans at Christmas—had only with difficulty survived what had been one of the worst winters of the century. The horrors of the campaign passed description; in Leningrad the people, dying in thousands, were declared by the exultant Nazis to be living on jelly made from human flesh.[2] In April, prematurely aged

[1]*Whitehill*, 246-7.   [2]Goebbels, *Diary*, 21st April, 1942.

and grey, Hitler had ordered a renewal of the offensive as soon as the ground dried. In the second week of May, in the hope of forestalling him and of relieving pressure in the Crimea, the Russians themselves struck near Kharkov.

For a few days it looked as if the dreaded German summer offensive might be stayed. " I cannot see," Brooke had written to Wavell on May 5th, " where the Germans are to raise a large enough mass of manœuvre of reasonably fresh troops to launch the full-scale offensive to finish off Russia and penetrate to the Caucasus. The forces may be there, but they are hard to find and there are very few signs of them at present. Certainly, as regards adequate German air forces for such an operation whilst at the same time maintaining the required air forces facing this country and in the Mediterranean, I fail to see where the Germans are to find them."[1]   Yet, though nearly half Hitler's air force and about a quarter of his ground forces were guarding and garrisoning western Europe or fighting Britain in the Mediterranean, by concentrating the bulk of his armour on the southern sector of the Eastern Front he hoped by the winter to overrun the Donetz industrial basin and the Kuban cornfields and, driving to the Caucasus and Caspian, possess himself of the oilfields without which Russia could not fight. Six German and two satellite armies, three of them armoured, were assembling under von Bock between Kursk and Kharkov, while to the south three more armies under von Manstein, after capturing the naval base of Sebastopol and the Kerch peninsula, were to sweep round the north-eastern shores of the Black Sea.

The Red Army's attempt to smother the offensive failed. On May 19th, when its drive had reached the outskirts of Kharkov, von Bock counter-attacked and in the last ten days of May encircled and destroyed most of the attackers. At the beginning of June the Germans opened their assault on Sebastopol. The Russian leaders were under no illusion as to the gravity of the threat or of the blow they had to meet. They pressed fiercely for the fulfilment of Western promises of arms and for an immediate invasion of Europe to draw off divisions from the Eastern Front. Being half-Orientals,

[1] Brooke to Wavell, 5th May, 1942. Lord Alanbrooke, *Personal Files*.

they also seized the opportunity to try to blackmail Britain and the United States into recognising the annexations they had carried out at the beginning of the war at the expense of Poland and the Baltic republics. On May 21st, after a perilous flight over the enemy lines, the Russian Foreign Minister, Molotov, reached London on his way to New York, to conclude a treaty of alliance with Britain and press for a Second Front.

Brooke was in Northern Ireland when he arrived, inspecting an American training exercise. Narrowly escaping being recalled that night to attend a Defence Committee meeting that went on till two in the morning, he met Molotov next day at a luncheon party at 10 Downing Street. 'Not very impressive to look at,' he noted, 'and with a slight impediment in his speech, yet gave one a feeling of distinct ability and shrewdness.' Four days later, on May 26th, he was present when the treaty with Russia was signed.

> ". . . Went out to lunch at Russian Embassy to meet Molotov again. A memorable lunch party held prior to signing of new Anglo-Russian Treaty. Lunch attended by P.M., Eden, Attlee, Stafford Cripps, Oliver Lyttelton, Evatt,[1] Bevin, John Anderson, Chiefs of Staff, etc. Many toasts and many speeches. Somehow the whole affair gave me the creeps and made me feel that humanity has still many centuries to live through before universal peace can be found."

' I had evidently,' he commented, ' not yet become hardened to the insincerity of statements contained in the speeches of statesmen and politicians on such occasions.'

Yet, though Russia secured a tacit acceptance of her Baltic annexations and the British saved their faces by omitting all reference to post-war frontiers in the treaty, thanks to the firm front of the British Chiefs of Staff Molotov failed to obtain any promise of a landing in 1942. He was told about the preliminary plans for " Sledgehammer " and " Round-up " and given a long, eloquent lecture by the Prime Minister on the difference between a land and sea Power and the way in

[1] Rt. Hon. H. V. Evatt, Australian Minister for External Affairs.

which the new weapon of the air had increased the difficulties of amphibious operations. A few weeks earlier, when the Anglo-American decision was taken to prepare for an invasion of Europe, Churchill had spoken of the whole coast from the North Cape to the Spanish frontier as lying open to Britain's and America's attack.[1] Yet, as he admitted to the Russian Foreign Minister, in reality the air weapon had made this untrue. Whereas in the past sea-power had given its possessor freedom to land anywhere, a landing in force was now impracticable in the teeth of air-opposition unless that opposition could be neutralised from the air. And, whereas the Germans could move the whole of their air strength in France and the Low Countries to any threatened point within a few hours, the British and Americans could only launch an attack where the Continent lay within reach of their fighters in southern England. This reduced their choice to the Pas de Calais and part of the Normandy coast—both strongly held by the enemy.

During the past three months, even before the Americans' visit, the British Chiefs of Staff had repeatedly examined the problem of how to take the weight off Russia's shoulders.

" *March 10th, 1942.* Long C.O.S. with Mountbatten attending for first time. We discussed the problem of assistance to Russia by operations in France, either large raid or lodgment. Decided only hope was to try and draw off air force from Russia and that for this purpose raid must be carried out on Calais front. Now directed investigation to proceed further . . ."

" *March 28th.* A difficult C.O.S. to handle. Paget and Sholto Douglas were both there and Mountbatten. We were discussing ways and means of establishing new Western Front. I had propounded theory that a Western Front to be of use must force withdrawal of force from Russia. That it was impossible with the land force at our disposal to force the Germans to withdraw land forces from Russia, but that we might induce them to withdraw air forces. But to do this a landing must take place within

[1] *Churchill*, IV, 287.

our air umbrella, namely in vicinity of Calais or Boulogne. Mountbatten was still hankering after a landing near Cherbourg, where proper air support is not possible. Finally I think we convinced him sufficiently to make his visit to Chequers that evening safe . . ."

'. . . . Dickie's visits to Chequers were always dangerous moments and there was no knowing what discussions he might be led into and . . . let us in for. He was most loyal and on those occasions frequently asked me what he was to say that night to the P.M. As it was not easy to predict what he might be asked, it was not possible to guard against all eventualities. On Monday morning he always gave us a full account of what had happened to him.'[1]

" *March 30th.* . . . Chiefs of Staff in morning to discuss proposed raid to Bayonne . . . After dinner had to go round to see P.M. at 10.30 p.m. Was kept up till 1 a.m. discussing possibilities of some form of offensive in northern France to assist Russia in the event of German attack being successful, as it will probably be. A difficult problem. This universal cry to start a Western Front is going to be hard to contend with, and yet what can we do with some ten divisions against the German masses? Unfortunately the country fails to realise the situation we are in."

Politically the position was growing more and more difficult, ' part of Press,' Brooke wrote, ' influencing public outlook in the direction of a Western Front, Albert Hall meetings, Trafalgar Square meetings, vast crowds shouting for immediate help for Russians. Many seemed to imagine that Russia had only come into the war for our benefit. Certainly very few of them realised that a premature Western Front could only result in the most appalling shambles which must . . . reduce the chances of ultimate victory to a minimum.' The country could not understand why its soldiers could not relieve the burden on Russia. Churchill himself, the shocks and disasters of the winter forgotten, was in his most belligerent mood. " Here in the thirty-third month of the war," he told

[1] *Notes on My Life,* V, 375.

a crowd of 25,000 outside the Leeds Town Hall, " none of us is weary of the struggle, none of us is calling for any favours. . . . Whatever we have got to take, we will take; and we will give it back in even greater abundance."

For that spring the Prime Minister's appetite for adventurous courses had been whetted by three brilliant Commando raids organised by Mountbatten's Combined Operations Command, one of which had blown up the main dock-gate of the naval and submarine base at St. Nazaire. " The process of trying to control the Prime Minister's actions," Brooke wrote to Wavell on May 5th, " is fraught with difficulties and uncertainties." Next day, after travelling all night from Cumberland, where he had been attending a demonstration of searchlight tanks, the C.I.G.S. reached the morning Chiefs of Staff meeting only just in time to turn down a project for a landing in Alderney by the Brigade of Guards.[1] He was still resisting the proposal five days later.

> " *May 11th.* . . . Chiefs of Staff mainly concerned with various combined operations which Chief of Combined Operations is planning . . . At 12 noon we had meeting under P.M. to discuss the giving up of the attack on Alderney and raids planned as alternatives."

The alternative, submitted to the Chiefs of Staff by Combined Operations two days later, was an ambitious scheme for a raid on Dieppe in July, partly to gain experience of landing on open beaches with modern technical equipment and partly to force the Germans to commit their air force to battle.

> " *May 13th.* Main interest of morning's C.O.S. was examination of projected large-scale raid for vicinity of Dieppe. Little did I ever think in the old days of my regular journeys from Newhaven to Dieppe that I should have been planning as I was this morning."

Yet even this did not satisfy the Prime Minister. Ten days later, on Saturday May 23rd—the second day of Molotov's visit—Brooke and Mountbatten spent three hours with him " discussing invasion possibilities." " He was carried away,"

[1] *Diary*, 6th May, 1942.

Brooke wrote, " with optimism at times and established lodg-ments all round the coast from Calais to Bordeaux with little regard to strength and landing facilities. We both lunched with him and did not get away till 3.30 p.m." ' This meeting with Winston was typical of many others when all difficulties were brushed aside, and many unpleasant realities, such as resources available, were scrupulously avoided.'[1]

For of a successful invasion in the conditions of 1942 Brooke could see no hope whatever. As early as May 8th—three weeks after the American visit—he noted that, after a detailed examination of the problem, the Commander-in-Chief, Home Forces, and the Chief of Combined Operations reported that the landing-craft available were totally insufficient. There were scarcely enough to land four thousand men at a time. Until more assault-vessels could be built—and they still only stood tenth on the American shipbuilding list[2]—a cross-Channel bridgehead was a mere pipe-dream that could only end in the death, capture or ignominious re-embarkation of the entire force engaged. Nor could it give relief to Russia by forcing the withdrawal of troops from the eastern front. Twenty-five German divisions were already stationed in France and the Low Countries. Even if landing-craft had been available to carry them and their equipment there, Britain at the outside had only ten divisions trained and equipped for cross-Channel operations, and the utmost America could provide by the autumn were two.

Even Churchill's optimism and desire to help his allies could not surmount facts so stubborn. Though he was resolved with the Americans to attack in 1943, and was as conscious as Roosevelt of the need to keep Russia in the war, he had never been a " westerner " and knew what the price of a premature frontal assault against prepared positions must be. For all his hatred of " resistances " by his military advisers, he was not prepared, for purely political reasons, to batter his head and England's against a stone wall. He, therefore, let Molotov depart for Washington without the assurances for which he had come. " The Prime Minister in very good form," Brooke wrote that night, " and quite ready to appreciate that

[1] *Notes on My Life.* V, 401.   [2] *White House Papers*, II, 558.

it is impossible to establish a front with landing-craft only capable of lifting 4,000 men in first flight. He was very amenable to reason, but inclined to transfer the scene of action to northern Norway, which we are now to examine."[1]

For Churchill's offensive spirit was not to be stifled because an attack in one particular place was for the moment impossible. He had every intention of invading France when the time was ripe, and, on May 30th, two days after sending Roosevelt a report on his conversation with Molotov, wrote—though in another connection—his famous directive on the construction of floating piers.[2] In the meantime his mind was busy with other projects. On the night of June 4th, while the British Eighth Army and Rommel's Afrika Korps were grappling with one another in the Western Desert, he and Brooke sat together from half past ten till one in the morning discussing operations for capturing, not only northern Norway, but Petsamo, Spitzbergen and Rangoon. He also referred to the plan for winning control of French North Africa and re-opening the Mediterranean that he had discussed with the American President at Christmas. " We must never let ' Gymnast ' "—the Arcadia Conference's name for an Anglo-American landing in Morocco—" pass from our minds," he wrote to Roosevelt on May 28th.

But at the moment his chief hope was northern Norway—that romantic land of fiord, mountain and snow so conveniently adjacent to the Russian front and on which during the past three years his thoughts had so often dwelt. To this project, a kind of Arctic Salonika—one which in Brooke's view offered no strategic prospects of any kind—he now reverted with a wonderful and compelling enthusiasm. He named it " Operation Jupiter " and throughout the summer months continued to press its claims on the Chiefs of Staff. His " constructive plan," he called it. It would give the Russians a " second front," protect the northern convoys, impress Sweden and Finland, and, as the victorious British advanced gradually southward over one mountain range after

---

[1] *Diary*, 27th May, 1942.

[2] " They must float up and down with the tide. . . . Let me have the best solution worked out. Don't argue the matter. The difficulties will argue for themselves. W. S. C. 30-5-42." *White House Papers*, II, 552.

another, " unroll the Nazi map of Europe from the top." All that had to be done was " to oust the enemy from the airfields and destroy their garrisons," land the troops with enough supplies to last them for three or four months, and then survive through the Arctic winter. The Chiefs of Staff's axiom that it was impossible to land anywhere without superior air strength he brushed aside with characteristic spirit. "Without in any way disputing the desirability of having superior air-power and fighter cover, it may be questioned whether it is indispensable if the objective is of sufficient value and there is no other way. . . . It seems unlikely that more than one-fifth or one-sixth of the transports and covering craft would be sunk. A military attack is not ruled out simply because a fifth of the soldiers may be shot on the way."[1]

As, however, the Battle of the Atlantic was in a highly critical stage, most of the German surface fleet and a quarter of the U-boat fleet were concentrated in Norwegian waters under cover of shore-based aircraft, and every inch of available shipping space was urgently needed to carry supplies and reinforcements to the one British army as yet actively engaged with the Germans, the opposition of the Chiefs of Staff and their chairman to this scheme of the Prime Minister's remained adamant. So did that of the Americans, struggling with the insurmountable logistical problems of simultaneously supplying their Pacific forces and building up a great army in England for the invasion to which they had so light-heartedly committed themselves. For, as Brooke had foreseen, with each week that passed the shipping problem appeared more intractable. Despite the immense shipbuilding programme which had been launched in the United States at the beginning of the year and which had already equated new American construction to British, the loss and damage to Allied vessels exceeded replacements for the first half of 1942 by nearly three million tons. After allowing for imports of raw materials and foodstuffs—kept by rationing to an indispensable minimum— Britain's Merchant Marine barely sufficed to carry round the Cape the 40,000 or 50,000 men, who, with their accompanying

[1] To General Ismay for C.O.S., 13th June, 1942. *Churchill*, IV, 312-16.

weapons, vehicles and equipment, had to be sent every month to maintain her armies and air forces in the Middle East and India. America's much smaller Merchant Marine had all it could do to supply the Pacific war, even with the help of the *Queen Mary* and *Queen Elizabeth*, whose building the British Government had fortunately subsidized against just such a contingency before the war and whose size and speed enabled them to carry up to 15,000 men each, if necessary unescorted. It was impossible even to assemble enough tonnage to get the weapons and munitions promised to the desperately pressed Russians. The shipments through the Arctic Circle to Murmansk had only reached about half the total agreed in the autumn, and one out of every four cargoes despatched was being sunk. So anxious were Western statesmen to sustain their ally that, though their original undertaking had not included sea transport, they persisted in accepting losses of the most frightful kind. During the winter the nightmare voyage round the North Cape to Murmansk—the only route open to Russia except the single-track line through the Persian highlands—had proved more dark and uncomfortable than dangerous, but, with the longer days, the convoys were attacked continuously, not only by packs of U-boats, but by aircraft and surface warships operating from the Norwegian fiords. Protection against these, including the giant battleship, *Tirpitz*, depended on the Royal Navy, whose entire battle and cruiser strength in home waters had to be deployed, at grave risk, to support the passage of each convoy. These perils and losses were increased by the Russian refusal even to allow American fighter aircraft to be flown across Siberia.

Brooke had always doubted the wisdom of sending Russia weapons of which British troops engaged against the enemy stood in need. " Personally," he wrote, " I consider it absolute madness. We have never even asked Russia to inform us of the real urgency of these reinforcements."[1] Ninety per cent of the equipment sent her consisted of tanks, aircraft and vehicles urgently required in the Middle and Far East. ' When we consider,' he commented after the war, ' that a fair proportion of tanks for Russia were destined to be sunk in transit by

[1] *Diary*, 25th February, 1942.

submarine action and that the Russian maintenance of mechanical vehicles was poor, it is doubtful whether the tanks sent there achieved much. . . . We kept on supplying tanks and aeroplanes that could ill be spared and in doing so suffered the heaviest of losses in shipping conveying this equipment to Arctic Russia. We received nothing in return except abuse for handling the convoys inefficiently. We had absolutely no information as to what the Russian situation was as regards equipment. Russia even refused to keep us informed as to the distribution of her forces. . . . I do not pretend for one moment that Russia was not playing a vital part in the war and bearing the maximum brunt of the land warfare. I agree that it was essential to retain her in the war and to assist her to do so, but this would in no way have precluded our getting fuller value for what we were doing.'

The pressure on Britain, however, to maintain this costly traffic was terrific. With Russia enduring so much and the Western Allies sheltered from the full impact of war, it seemed politically impossible for them to refuse her any aid within their power. While supplies piled up in American and British ports for lack of ships to carry them, and laden ships waited for convoys, the Government was bombarded with demands, not only from Stalin, but from Roosevelt. Even Churchill's magnanimous patience towards his allies was momentarily strained. " With very great respect," he replied to one urgent appeal from the White House, " what you suggest is beyond our power to fulfill . . . I can assure you, Mr. President, we are absolutely extended." Yet seven days later he cabled Stalin: " We are resolved to fight our way through to you with the maximum amount of war materials." He did so despite the advice of the War Cabinet and Chiefs of Staff; it was a political decision, he told the latter and, for political reasons, had to be accepted: " I share your misgivings, but I feel it is a matter of duty."[1] Of 84 ships despatched on the Murmansk run that April and May only 58 got through. In a single convoy in June, 23 out of 34 ships were sunk, 130,000 out of 200,000 tons of cargo went to the bottom and thousands of

[1] To Gen. Ismay, for C.O.S., 17th May, 1942. *Churchill*, IV, 233-4.

seamen perished miserably in icy seas or of frost-bite in open boats.

.   .   .   .

While ships needed to reinforce and supply Britain's own battle-fronts in the Middle and Far East were breasting their way through Arctic waters to aid the surly Russians, a still more intractable convoy problem faced the Royal Navy in the Mediterranean. Here Malta and its defenders were nearing the end of their resources. The retreat of the Desert Army from Cyrenaica in February had again left the final and most dangerous lap of the island's eastern supply-line without air protection, and the Mediterranean Fleet, after its winter losses, was without either battleships or carriers. The western supply-line through the narrow bomb-alley between Tunisia and Sicily and Sardinia had never been usable except under convoy of at least one fleet-carrier and attendant battleship, and with the loss of the *Ark Royal* and the departure of Admiral Somerville's Force " H " to fight the Japanese, these were no longer available. At the end of March, despite a brilliant action in which four British light cruisers from Alexandria turned back an Italian battle-fleet, only 5,000 out of 25,000 tons of fuel and ammunition sent out reached the island. For the next three months no supplies got through at all, either from east or west.

Early that spring, seeing in it the obstacle which alone prevented Rommel from building up strength to tumble the British out of Egypt and secure the Suez Canal, the German admirals had prevailed on Hitler to transfer 400 first-line bombers from Russia to Sicily in order to shatter Malta's naval installations and airfields preparatory to a sea and airborne invasion. Under Field-Marshal Kesselring, the ablest of Germany's air commanders, an all-out assault on the island began. By the end of April its dwindling force of fighters, engaged almost incessantly against odds, had almost ceased to exist. The only way of replenishing it was by borrowing an American aircraft-carrier—for Britain's were all engaged either in the Arctic or Indian Ocean—and sending her through the Straits of Gibraltar with decks packed with Spitfires to be flown off the last two hundred miles. When this first happened, the German and Italian raiders had an unpleasant surprise. But the respite was only temporary. Within a few weeks the dockyard and naval base had been rendered unusable and the attacks on Rommel's supply-line had ceased altogether. Whereas during December only 20,000 tons of the 40,000 seaborne tons sent to supply the latter had reached him, during April and May more than a quarter of a million tons of Axis munitions, armaments and oil were carried across the Mediterranean.

Towards the end of April, when it had become clear that Malta might be subjected at any moment to a full-scale airborne attack and invasion, Brooke decided, in view of its vital importance to his strategic plan, that it was necessary to relieve the 63-year-old Governor, Lieutenant-General Dobbie, by a younger man. Dobbie's fortitude during the island's two years' siege had won the admiration of the entire Empire, but the strain on him was intense and he could not be expected to carry it indefinitely. As his successor Brooke proposed the Field-Marshal and V.C. who had commanded the British Army in France—his former chief, Lord Gort. The very limitations which had handicapped Gort as Commander-in-Chief, made him the ideal man for inspiring and directing the defence of a besieged fortress.

" *April 21st, 1942.* . . . After dinner sent for to 10 Downing Street to discuss successor for Dobbie in Malta as apparently strain is beginning to tell on him. Also possibility of getting convoys into Malta."

" *April 22nd.* We went on this morning with the problem of convoys to Malta and at 12 noon attended Defence Committee when we went on with the problem without much success. Recommendation had also come in that Dobbie should be changed. P.M. was not for it, but, in view of the recommendation from all the Services, I pressed for it and recommended that Gort should be sent to Malta as Commander-in-Chief. P.M. would not agree at first but called me up after lunch to say that he had come round and agreed."

It was characteristic of Gort that without a thought of self he at once accepted.

.　ⁱ　.　ⁱ　ⁱ　ⁱ　ⁱ　ⁱ

In the last resort everything turned on the offensive which Auchinleck was due to launch in the Libyan desert. For without the recovery of Benghazi and the airfields of the Cyrenaican bulge, Malta could not be revictualled, and, unless Malta could be relieved and the naval and air attack resumed on Rommel's supply-line, Egypt itself would soon be in danger. Ever since the winter's setback Churchill had been urging the Commander-in-Chief, Middle East, to renew his attack. It came, therefore, as a shock when at the end of the first week in May this universally respected soldier, on whose appointment a year earlier the Government had built such high hopes, proposed that, instead of attacking, he should send reinforcements to India and remain on the defensive. The Prime Minister was furious. It was only with the utmost difficulty that Brooke was able to persuade him not to demand Auchinleck's immediate recall and his supersession by Alexander, then in the last stages of his race against the Japanese and the rains through the jungle defiles to the Indian frontier.

> " *May 7th.* I was sent for on the way to C.O.S. meeting to see P.M. in bed about wire which has come in from Auchinleck about the date of his attack which he is again putting right on ahead to July or August. P.M. as usual very upset about the whole business, wishing to bring Alexander back to take over half of Middle East."

' That morning's meeting with Winston was typical of many others. He was a wonderful sight in bed, with large cigar in his mouth, hair somewhat ruffled, bed littered with papers and messages and alongside of the bed one of those large cuspidors to drop his cigar ends in. On this morning he was in one of his dangerous moods; the Auk had roused him properly with his proposed postponement of his attack. The situation required handling delicately;

in his upset state he might well take some wild decision which it would then be very hard to wean him from.'[1]

" *May 8th*.   An unpleasant day!   Difficult C.O.S. meeting, first of all considering Auchinleck's wire in which he proposes to put off his attack from May 15th to June 15th.   I do not like his message; it is . . . purely based on number of tanks and not on the strategical situation.   He never takes into account danger that Malta is exposed to through his proposed delays . . ."

" Cabinet meeting at 3 p.m. to examine Auchinleck's wire.   I had to open the ball and stated that I did not consider that we could order the Auk to attack about May 15th against his advice.   That we should give him till June 15th, tell him to co-ordinate his attack with running of convoy to Malta, whilst being prepared to take advantage of any limited attack enemy might make as expected towards end of May.   P.M. asked opinion of all attending meeting and finally drafted reply himself, in which he said that Chiefs of Staff, Defence Committee and Cabinet were unanimously of opinion that attack should, if possible, be delivered before end of May . . ."

" *May 10th*.   Called up after breakfast by Director of Military Operations to be told that I was wanted for Cabinet meeting at 6 p.m. and Chiefs of Staff meeting before that to discuss latest wire from Auchinleck.   He had again stuck his toes in and was refusing to attack till a later date and had sent in a . . . telegram in which he entirely failed to realise the importance of Malta and over-estimated the danger to Egypt in the event of his being defeated.   We framed a proposed policy at C.O.S. in which we laid down that we considered that the value of Malta was under-estimated, whilst his argument against attack was not very convincing.   Finally we suggested that he should be allowed to wait to take advantage of possible limited German offensive for Tobruk to put in a counter-stroke, but that the June convoy to Malta should be the latest date, as this afforded the last opportunity of assisting in the supply of Malta.

[1] *Notes on My Life*, V, 395.

" At Cabinet meeting I made statement of our decision. P.M. then asked individual opinion of each Minister, who practically all agreed to our proposals. P.M. then withdrew to draft a proposed wire which he read out on his return. We did not quite like it, so Chiefs of Staff were asked to withdraw to consider it and redraft it, which we did. Our proposal was accepted."

To the instructions contained in this telegram[1] Auchinleck agreed, though he still held that delay would strengthen his chances. Subsequently the Prime Minister likened him to the man who mixed a powder to blow into a sick bear's throat and let the bear blow first. He made one last attempt to spur him into anticipating Rommel's attack by an analogy taken from the life of his favourite commander, Napoleon. There is a reference to it in Brooke's diary for May 25th:

" Fairly quiet day, only disturbed by one telephone call from the Prime Minister after dinner to discuss telegram based on battle of Austerlitz, which he wanted to send Auchinleck and wanted my advice. I advised him not to send, but doubt whether he will take this advice as he wants to discuss it further with me."

This he did next day as they drove back together from a luncheon at the Russian Embassy. It was too late. That night the German tanks flung themselves out of the moonlit dust at the British outposts near Bir Hacheim.

The battle that followed seemed to justify Auchinleck's belief that, despite improvements in its armour and supply position, the Desert Army was not yet strong enough to impose its will on the enemy. Until Malta could be relieved and the

---

[1] It is printed in *Churchill*, IV, 275-6. " The Chiefs of Staff, the Defence Committee and the War Cabinet have again considered the whole position. We are determined that Malta shall not be allowed to fall without a battle being fought by your whole army for its retention. The starving out of this fortress would involve the surrender of over 30,000 men, Army and Air Force, together with several hundred guns. Its possession would give the enemy a clear and sure bridge to Africa, with all the consequences flowing from that. Its loss would sever the air route upon which both you and India must depend for a substantial part of your aircraft reinforcements. Besides this, it would compromise any offensive against Italy, and future plans such as ' Acrobat ' and ' Gymnast.' Compared with the certainty of these disasters, we consider the risks you have set out to the safety of Egypt are definitely less, and we accept them."

naval and air attack on the Axis Mediterranean supply-line renewed, the Germans could replace their losses, particularly in tanks, more quickly than the British with their extended communications and shortage of shipping. The expectations which had been formed of massive deliveries of American aircraft and armour to the Middle East had not been realised, partly owing to the prior call of Russia and partly owing to the fact that they were now required by the Americans themselves. Immeasurable as had been the enlargement of British hopes through Russia's and America's entry into the war, the immediate effect had been to retard the rate at which Britain's armies could be re-equipped.

For since the day when Churchill had asked the United States for the tools with which to finish the job, Britain's strategic plans had depended almost as much on American war production as on her own. To meet the new situation created by United States belligerency a Combined Munitions Assignment Board had been set up under the Combined Chiefs of Staff to allocate all assignment of raw materials and munitions " in quantity and priority whether to Great Britain and the United States or other of the United Nations, in accordance with strategic needs." But under pressure of the rapid expansion of America's armed forces such priorities were being increasingly ignored, and in April Oliver Lyttelton, who had been appointed British Minister of Production, had gone to Washington to stress the urgent needs of his countrymen who were still having to bear the brunt of the Western Powers' effort in the field. The point in which the British were most seriously affected was in the air, where the demands of Russia and the need to provide operational types for training America's growing air forces had involved a drastic cutting down of aircraft deliveries to British combat formations, particularly in the Middle East.[1] This in turn was having repercussions on the desert war. In the latter part of May the American Chief of Army Air Force, General Arnold,

[1] On March 30th General Arnold recommended that any increase in allocations to the Soviet Union " should be met by an even further reduction in commitments to the British," to which Secretary Stimson agreed that the immediate step was to cut air allocations to the British. *Strategic Planning for Coalition Warfare*, 207.

arrived in England to try to resolve the deadlock. Despite, however, the excellent liaison and friendship established between him and his British counterpart, Air Chief Marshal Portal, there remained a fundamental clash of outlook and policy, the British believing that their hard-won experience would enable them to make better use of the aircraft, the Americans that their own airmen ought to get into action at the earliest possible moment.   " Transactions," wrote the C.I.G.S. on the 26th, " are not going over well."

.   .   .   .

The dilemma of American and British leaders alike was that their commitments were still far heavier than the means for carrying them out. The Anglo-American agreement to prepare for an early invasion of Europe had increased these without doing anything to enlarge the means of meeting them. Because the Americans had undertaken to assemble a force of 3500 operational aircraft in Britain by the spring of 1943, they could no longer afford to allocate to the R.A.F. the planes—a third of the latter's estimated supply for 1942— which they had agreed to make for it and on which it had been counting. The same decision to subordinate everything to a cross-Channel invasion aggravated the competition for the R.A.F.'s resources between Bomber Command, the Royal Navy and the Army. That spring the British Air Staff's area-bombing policy had been inaugurated with the disappearance in flame and rubble of the first two German towns selected for the fate of Rotterdam and Warsaw. Though Bomber Command's new chief, Sir Arthur Harris—a man of bulldog resolution after Churchill's own heart—had as yet only a fraction of the armada of 4,000 heavy bombers which had been planned, his and Portal's eyes were steadily fixed on the distant vision that had sustained them as they watched the London blitz from the Air Ministry roof two years before[1] and which, in the teeth of many set-backs and difficulties, its officers and men had been gallantly pursuing for two barren, unrewarding years.

---

[1] " I said out loud as we turned away from the scene: ' Well, they are sowing the wind.' "   Sir Arthur Harris, *Bomber Offensive*, 52.

Yet at the very moment that the new four-engined bombers were starting to flow from the production lines, both the Admiralty and War Office began to clamour for the deflection of air effort to naval and military ends. In order to defeat the mounting U-boat offensive, the First Sea Lord asked both for increased allocations of long-range aircraft to Coastal Command and for the bombing of German submarine bases. In order to build up a force able to storm and maintain itself in north-western Europe in the face of the *blitzkrieg,* the C.I.G.S. demanded a tactical air force without which he was convinced from bitter experience any bridgehead in France would become a death-trap.

" With the P.M. in his present mood and with his desire to maintain air-bombardment of Germany," Brooke had written before the American visit, " it will not be possible to get adequate support for either the Army or the Navy."[1] The decision to start immediate preparations for a cross-Channel operation aggravated the dispute about air-support for the Army because it made it so much more urgent.

> " *April 13th.* A bad C.O.S. with much loss of time and interruption trying to frame up reply for Marshall. Then lunch with Portal and Freeman to settle ' off the record ' the differences between Army and Air Force. Evidently little hope of arriving at any sort of settlement."
>
> " *April 29th.* . . . At 6.15 I went to Cabinet meeting where we were intended to discuss the future operations on the Continent. But instead we got involved in a heavy discussion on Army Support from the Air. I became involved in heated discussion with Secretary of State for Air. . . . However P.M. backed me up, and rubbed into Sinclair the necessity for devoting more love and affection to those Air Forces destined for Army requirements."
>
> " *May 18th.* . . . Lunched with Sinclair, Grigg and Portal to discuss Army Air requirements. We made no headway at all, and are exactly where we were before. The situation is hopeless and I see no solution besides the provision of an Army Air Arm. . . ."

[1] *Diary,* 19th March, 1942.

' I always felt that this lunch party had been organised between Sinclair and Grigg because it was considered that I was being obdurate on the question of lack of co-operation on the part of the Air Ministry. I think, however, that as a result of this lunch Grigg realised, better than he had before, the lamentable situation that prevailed as regards air co-operation with the Army. I know that I had up to then always been strongly opposed to a separate Army Air Arm, and it was only out of despair at seeing nothing done for the Army that I had reluctantly altered my views.'[1]

" *May 19th.* Difficult Chiefs of Staff meeting at which we discussed Army and Navy air requirements. It lead in the first place to heated arguments between me and Portal, and subsequently between Pound and Portal. I had obtained agreement on a certain number of points but had to carry forward several for the Defence Committee to settle. It is a depressing situation, and the Air Ministry outlook is now so far divorced from the requirements of the Army that I see no solution to the problem except an Army Air Arm. . . ."

" We are now reaping the full disadvantage," Brooke wrote to Wavell, who was bombarding him with requests for military aircraft, " of an all-out independent air policy directed towards the bombing of Germany. As a result we are short of all the suitable types of aircraft for support of the other two Services. It is an uphill battle to fight, as the Air Ministry at once takes cover behind the War Cabinet's continual desire for an all-out policy of bombing directed against Germany."[2] Yet both Brooke and Portal were seeking the same end by different means: the command of the air over the battlefield on which the British Army would have to fight in Western Europe. The decision to attempt an invasion within the next year made it seem indispensable to each of them to carry his point, though the means for doing both at once were not as yet available. The C.I.G.S. felt that air-ground co-operation was as necessary for victory as tanks and artillery. The Chief of Air Staff knew

---

[1] *Notes on My Life*, V, 399.
[2] Brooke to Wavell, 5th May, 1942.   Lord Alanbrooke, *Personal Files.*

that, once command of the air had been won, everything else would be added and was opposed to tying up machines and men in non-operational training at the moment when he needed to employ every available aircraft, airman and factory in the air offensive against the Luftwaffe.

.   .   .   .

Though chairman of the British Chiefs of Staff Committee, Brooke was only *primus inter pares*. He could not command either his British colleagues or their American partners; he had in every case to convince them and his political chief as well. It was only natural for Americans to regard Britain as a rather unimportant partner in industrial production—the sphere in which they had long led the world in peace—and to expect to dictate its operation in war. It was natural for them, with their transatlantic belief that all things were possible, to suppose that they could deal with the Germans without learning from the slow, war-weary " Limeys." It was hard enough to persuade them to contemplate a strategic plan that was sufficiently graduated to surmount each obstacle in turn. It was far harder, with so many competing priorities and a still half chaotic administrative organization on the other side of the Atlantic, to get those who directed American production to ensure that the necessary weapons and equipment—tanks, aircraft, guns, ammunition, lorries, repairing-units, and, above all, landing-craft and shipping—were produced far enough in advance and in sufficient numbers to be ready for each required operation at the right time and place. Yet because of the logistics of modern war no operation could succeed without the closest long-term planning, not only of shipping and troop-movements but of production priorities.

In the early summer months of 1942 his Mediterranean policy must at times have seemed to Brooke unattainable. He was being subjected to pressures almost impossible to resist and which he had no means of resisting except by persuasion. On the one hand was his political master, set on pursuing every course, likely or unlikely, that offered any chance of inflicting injury on the enemy, and his two Service colleagues, each, for the best of reasons, intent on what seemed at that

moment an overriding priority—the defeat of the U-boat and
the pursuit of the long-prepared offensive that was to win
command of the air.   On the other hand were the American
Army planners, obsessed by their resolve to concentrate everything on an operation that Brooke saw as the last, not the first,
step for destroying Germany and at the expense of all the preliminary operations needed to make it possible.   Backing them
were the Russians, who were both unable and unwilling to
grasp the difficulty of amphibious operations and the present
inadequacy of Britain's and America's shipping and military
resources, and who, in their single-handed struggle with the
German Army, were in such extremities that they were clamouring, regardless of consequences, for a sacrificial landing on the
Channel coast in the hope, however illusory, that it might
draw off some part of the immense forces opposed to them.   And,
to complicate matters still further, there were the American
admirals, intent on their campaign against Japan and urging
their military colleagues and the President to force a showdown on the temporising and ultra-cautious British and, in
default of their agreeing to stake everything on an immediate
cross-Channel invasion, to transfer the entire offensive strength
of America to the Pacific.   The United States tended at this
moment to speak with three voices: that of the War Department which, represented by Marshall and Stimson, was bent
on getting the maximum troops, aircraft and equipment to
England in the minimum time at the expense of all other
commitments;   that of King and the admirals, interested
primarily in the Pacific;   and that of the President, who set
out his viewpoint in a letter that May to General MacArthur,
after the latter had been pleading the cause of the Australian
Government and of his own South-west Pacific strategy.

" I fully appreciate the difficulties of your position.   They
are the same kind of difficulties which I am having with
the Russians, British, Canadians, Mexicans, Indians, Persians
and others at different points of the compass.   Not one of
them is wholly satisfied but I am at least succeeding in
keeping all of them reasonably satisfied and have so far
avoided any real rows."[1]

[1] *Strategic Planning for Coalition Warfare*, 214.

As soon as General Marshall had returned to America in the middle of April, he had set himself, with characteristic thoroughness, to implement the agreement made in London. When, under pressure from MacArthur and the Australians, the President showed signs of yielding to entreaties for the allocation of aircraft to the Pacific that would have seriously reduced the American air-contribution to " Round-up," he had staked his career to preserve the absolute priority of " Bolero," as the American build-up in Britain was called. " If new commitments and continuous reinforcement of secondary theatres," he wrote, " are to interfere with the execution of these plans, the faith of the British in our firm promises will be destroyed, co-ordination will be lost and the success of the plan will be doomed. . . . We must remember that this operation for 1942 depends primarily upon British forces and not our own. They have far more at stake than we and are accepting very grave hazards to which our own risks are not comparable. They have accepted the ' Bolero ' project with a firm understanding that it would be the primary objective of the United States. If such is not to be the case, the British should be formally notified that the recent London agreement must be cancelled. I present this question to you as Commander-in-Chief and request that you discuss the matter with Admiral King, General Arnold and me, and give us a formal directive for our future guidance."[1] Faced with such uncompromising honesty, the President agreed that " Bolero " should have absolute priority over all other commitments, even that of security in the Pacific.

Such was the position at the end of May when, disappointed in his hopes of securing the promise of an immediate Second Front from the British, Molotov arrived in Washington determined to secure one from the Americans. His representation of Russia's plight and of the magnitude of her impending ordeal made a deep impression on the President. After stressing the immense superiority of the Germans in aircraft and armour, he asked bluntly whether the Western Allies could undertake to land enough troops in France to draw off

---

[1] Memo. Chief of Staff for President, 6th May, 1942. *Strategic Planning for Coalition Warfare*, 218-19.

forty German divisions, adding that, if they could, the war would be decided in 1942. " If you postpone your decision," he said, " you will have eventually to bear the brunt of the war."

To this the President returned a categorical answer. He authorised Molotov to tell Stalin that he expected the formation of a Second Front in the present year and added that every effort was being made to create conditions for an early invasion and that the United States already had the troops trained, the munitions, the aircraft, and the armoured divisions. All that was needed was shipping and landing-craft. Next day, May 31st, the President, in conference with Marshall and King, read a cable that he proposed to send Churchill, naming August as the latest date for a landing. Marshall, though he believed that a 1942 invasion of Europe would be forced on the Western Allies by Russia's condition, felt that this was too specific and might arouse legitimate British resistance. None the less, the telegram was sent.

. . . .

During the week-end in which the President all but committed himself to a cross-Channel invasion in August, the British Chief of Imperial General Staff was spending a quiet Sunday at his home at Hartley Wintney. It was his wife's birthday, and she asked him to help her take a swarm of bees. ' My wife had never taken a swarm before,' he wrote,

' but after reading about it in the book felt full of confidence. Certainly more than I did! No excuses availed and I was roped in as assistant, provided with a veil and a pair of gardening-gloves full of holes. My wife climbed up the step ladder and detailed me to hold the skep upside down under the swarm ready to receive the bees when she shook the pear-tree bough that they were on. Things, however, did not go according to the book. Half the bees fell into the skep and the remainder lit all over us. They soon penetrated our defences and busily attacked my wife's neck and my wrists. Suddenly she shouted, " I can't stand it any longer," and fled into the house. I felt that honour was now satisfied and followed in her wake, shedding bees in all directions.[1]'

It was in a somewhat similar spirit that the British received their allies' proposal that they should storm Hitler's western wall in two months' time and confront an army of twenty-five divisions with a first-wave landing of only 5,000 men. On June 5th, in the light of Roosevelt's telegram, the Chiefs of Staff once more discussed the various possibilities of relieving Russia, either by a lodgment or a " tip and run " raid, and found none of them offered any hope of achieving their purpose. When Molotov arrived in London on his way home, he found his hosts as non-committal as on his earlier visit. They agreed, with alacrity, to the issue of a joint communiqué proclaiming that " full understanding " had been " reached with regard to the urgent tasks of creating a Second Front in Europe in 1942." But at the meeting at which the draft was agreed, the Prime Minister handed the Russian Foreign Minister an *aide-mémoire* stating that, though preparations were being made, it was impossible to say whether the situation would be such as to make the operation feasible and that no promise could be given. And on the day that the communiqué was released in London and Moscow, the Prime Minister, in terms he had submitted to the Chiefs of Staff three days before, proposed in the War Cabinet that there should be no substantial landing in France until the Germans had been demoralised by a further set-back in Russia and unless it was intended to remain there. " P.M. in good form," Brooke wrote that night, " and carried Cabinet with him in the proposed policy that we do not move to France in strength except to stop there, and we do not go there unless German morale is deteriorating."

For though the British leaders were still uncertain whether their allies could withstand the impending German offensive, they were beginning to feel more confidence in what the year might bring forth after the winter's disasters. The Russians had proved their fortitude; and, while the ordeal

[1] *Notes on My Life*, V, 405-6. ' When we finally reached the safety of her bedroom I had to pull twenty-two stings out of her neck and a dozen had to be removed from my wrists.'

before them was likely to be severe, it could hardly prove worse than that which they had surmounted in the past year. Nor, though the fear of it haunted the minds of his political masters and of the Americans, did Brooke believe that the Russians were likely to make a separate peace. They had tried the experiment of a deal with their fellow-totalitarians once, and, however much they might try to blackmail their allies by the threat of another, survival and self-interest alike depended on the defeat of the invaders. The British were containing—in the Mediterranean, France, Scandinavia and the Low Countries—nearly half Hitler's air force and at least fifty Axis divisions. And though, save in Libya, not actively engaged on land, in the air—alone among the United Nations —they were carrying the war into the Reich itself, subjecting its industries to a new and growing drain and compelling the Germans to maintain a million men in their defence. That spring the R.A.F.'s pulverisation of the Baltic ports of Lübeck and Rostock had given to friend and foe alike an indication of the difficulties Germany might find in supplying her armies in the field.[1] In April the first of Britain's Lancaster four-engined bombers had appeared over Germany—a portent for the future. And on May 30th Air-Marshal Harris struck his first real blow at a major German town, sending nearly a thousand bombers, including training aircraft, to saturate the defences of Cologne. Six hundred acres of the city were left in ruins, nearly as many as had been destroyed in all the previous raids on Germany put together. And fifteen hundred miles away in the Libyan desert the Eighth Army was holding, and, despite its not very satisfactory system of command and supply, had defeated the German attempt to forestall it and drive it from its prepared positions in Cyrenaica. Rommel's drive had failed and Tobruk had been held. Only with heavy losses had his armour battered its way back to safety through the minefields. On the last day of the month, Auchinleck

---

[1] " This Sunday has been thoroughly spoiled by an exceptionally heavy raid by the R.A.F. on Lübeck. . . . Eighty per cent of the old part of the city must be considered lost. . . . I have been shown a newsreel of the destruction. It is horrible. . . . We can't get away from the fact that the English raids have increased in scope and importance; if they can be continued for weeks on these lines, they might quite conceivably have a demoralising effect on the population." Goebbels, *Diary*, 30th, 31st March, 4th April, 1942.

from Cairo signalled, " Well done, Eighth Army! " It remained now to be seen whether Ritchie's tired men, having held the enemy's drive, could themselves seize the initiative and, by advancing to Benghazi and the airfields of western Cyrenaica, win the necessary air-cover for the convoys that were about to cross the Mediterranean to revictual Malta.

Meanwhile the Japanese threat to the Allies' besieging lines, so desperate to all appearances at Easter, had receded. Not only was Ceylon held and India reinforced by aircraft and troops, but the enemy fleet had vanished from the Indian Ocean. And during the first week of June dramatic news came from the central Pacific. The American carrier-fleet, though outnumbered and still without battleship support, had defeated a Japanese attempt to seize Midway and, in doing so, inflicted losses on the enemy as decisive as they were unexpected. Four Japanese fleet-carriers, while attempting to repeat their surprise at Pearl Harbour, had been sunk in mid-ocean with the loss of only one American carrier. As a result, the supporting battleships and transports, no longer protected by aircraft, had been forced to turn back. Japan had lost her decisive advantage in carrier strength, and, with thirteen fleet-carriers and fifteen escort-carriers building in American dock-yards, the U.S.A. could look forward in a not too distant future to air supremacy in the Pacific. Despite their eleven battleships, victorious Army and far-flung island bases, the Japanese no longer possessed a secure flank for an advance on Australia or the Middle East. For all their enormous strength, they could not expand further without command of the air.

Midway was one of the decisive battles of history. By removing the Japanese threat to the besieging ring round Europe, it made it possible for the Allies to embark on that succession of cumulative actions in the Mediterranean through which Brooke saw that Hitler's continental fortress could be sapped and stormed. On one factor, however, everything depended: the integration of the Anglo-American war effort to make possible the preliminary stages of this process. And this had still to be achieved. On June 3rd Lieut.-General Eisenhower, who had been sent to London with the American air-chief, Arnold, to study the progress of the Anglo-American planning for " Sledgehammer " and " Round-up," reported, " It is necessary to get a punch behind the job or we'll never be ready by spring 1943 to attack. We must get going."[1] On the same day the British Chief of Combined Operations, Lord Louis Mountbatten, arrived in Washington to explain why a cross-Channel operation in 1942 was impossible.

The division between the two nations did not arise so much from the refusal of the British to commit themselves to Operation " Sledgehammer," almost the entire burden of which was bound to fall on them and which, it was growing increasingly clear, was certain to end in disaster unless the Germans were first decisively defeated in the east. Marshall was a just man and, though still dangerously optimistic about the capacity of raw American troops to land from the sea and encounter a superior and veteran German army, he was a highly competent professional soldier with a mastery of logistics and military administration. But what stuck in his throat and that of his political chief, Stimson, was that, after the agreement made in London in April and the prodigious efforts he had been making to increase shipping allocations and re-arrange schedules for the " Bolero " build-up, the British should be showing increasing signs of declining to carry out, not only " Sledgehammer in 1942," but " Round-up in 1943 " too. The first indication of such a repudiation, as it seemed to the American War Department chiefs, had appeared in the telegram which Churchill had sent Roosevelt at the end of May, announcing that he was sending Mountbatten to Washington to explain the difficulties encountered in planning " Sledgehammer." " I have also told the Staffs," he said, " to study a landing in the north of Norway, the occupation of which seems necessary to ensure the flow of our supplies next year to Russia." " This cable," commented Harry Hopkins's biographer, " provided the first danger signal to Roosevelt and Hopkins, Marshall and King, that British thinking was beginning to veer towards diversionary operations far removed from the main point of frontal attack across the Channel."[2] The suspicion was reinforced by the very strength of the case which Mountbatten presented against " Sledge-

[1] *Strategic Planning for Coalition Warfare*, 196.   [2] *White House Papers*, II, 559

hammer" and his contention that, without a far larger number of landing-craft than there was any chance of providing in 1942—and, as the Americans were well aware, in 1943—there was no hope either of creating a bridgehead that could be held against the German divisions already in France or of forcing a withdrawal of any additional divisions from the Russian front—the primary object of the operation.

* * * * * * * *

After the Cabinet's decision on June 11th not to attempt a landing unless it could be launched with sufficient strength to be sure of remaining, further and early consultation with the Americans had become essential. It became even more so when during the same week events in the Mediterranean and Western Desert took a turn which neither ally had anticipated. On June 9th, after receiving the good news of Midway, the Prime Minister and Chiefs of Staff decided to send General Auchinleck two additional divisions, one of them armoured, which were on their way round the Cape to reinforce India or Australia against a Japanese invasion. On the very next day, however, Rommel resumed the offensive, and, keeping his tanks closely concentrated, fell on the dispersed British armour and in two days inflicted on it such a series of blows that by June 12th the British infantry in the desert were left without tank protection. On the 13th, following a final disastrous battle round the "Knightsbridge" box and faced by a situation of the gravest peril, Auchinleck and Ritchie ordered an immediate retreat on the Egyptian frontier. All Churchill's and Brooke's hopes for the offensive were dashed.

Simultaneously the two convoys intended to revictual Malta met with disaster. On June 14th, the western convoy, escorted by a battleship, two carriers, three cruisers and seventeen destroyers, was attacked from the air off Sardinia, where the heavier units of the escort, after suffering severe loss, were forced to turn back. Next day Italian cruisers and destroyers joined in the attack on the merchant ships, only two of which got through to the island. The rest were sunk. The eastern convoy never arrived at all. Attacked by Italian battleships as well as by swarms of German aircraft and U-boats, it was driven back to Alexandria, after losing a cruiser and three destroyers and two of its eleven merchant ships. Thus only two out of the seventeen supply-ships sent reached Malta. The island's survival, the implementation of Brooke's plans for re-opening the Mediterranean, and the maintenance of the British base in Egypt were all in jeopardy.

Chapter Eight

HANDS ACROSS THE SEA

*The American mind runs naturally to broad, sweeping,
logical conclusions on the largest scale. . . . The British
mind does not work quite in this way.*

WINSTON CHURCHILL

'O N JUNE 13TH, 1942,' Brooke wrote in his autobiographical notes, ' my first trip to America began to take shape.' " The P.M.," he recorded that night,

" called me up on the telephone and told me he was thinking of starting for Washington on Thursday next and would like me to come with him. He considered Roosevelt was getting a little off the rails, and some good talks as regards Western Front were required."

' I had slipped home on June 14th in the hope of a quiet Sunday, but this was not to be. My diary records ':

" A Sunday disturbed by many calls from the P.M. who was much disturbed at bad turn taken by operations in the Middle East. Rommel certainly seems to be getting the better of Ritchie and is out-generalling him."

" *June 15th.* A real unpleasant Monday. Left Ferney Close at 8 a.m. and drove straight to Huntsman where I ordered thin uniform for Washington. Then to War Office when P.M. called me up during my briefing for C.O.S. and delayed me badly. C.O.S. till 1 p.m. Then lunch and ordered thin shirts and tried on suits. . . . 3.30 to 4.30 p.m. conference with Weeks, Watson and Nye on organisation of forces for next year's offensive. 5.30 p.m. Cabinet meeting, and very gloomy owing to bad news from Libya and from Malta convoys. Lasted till 7.30 p.m. After dinner an hour's hard work before 10.30 p.m. meeting with P.M. at 10 Downing Street. Just back at 1.30 a.m. And we did *nothing* except meander round from Burma to France and back. Also discussed impending visit to Washington and nearly decided to start to-morrow morning at 11 a.m. Now postponed till Wednesday at any rate."

' The following day, June 16th, is worth quoting as exemplifying the continual changes in plans that were so characteristic of Winston's moves.'

". . . C.O.S. this morning. First of all an interview with Joint Intelligence Committee, then a visit from Donovan from U.S.A. to explain the organization of their Secret Service. . . . Then discussions on the command of 'Round-up' operation, and also of the part to be played by Mountbatten and his party. . . . Then went out to dine with Bertie Brooke and was called up whilst I was there and told that the P.M. contemplated starting to-morrow. None of my thin clothes will be ready in time and all money and coupons wasted. But worst of all I shall miss my dinner with you to-morrow evening."

' The uniform was a serious matter as the temperature in Washington in June is like a Turkish bath and I had no thin uniform except what I had just ordered.'

On the morning of Wednesday June 17th the final decision was taken and the time of departure fixed for that night. The Eighth Army was in full retreat, its vehicles streaming in interminable column along the highway to the Egyptian frontier while the Germans closed round Tobruk, and the R.A.F., withdrawing from each improvised airfield at the last possible moment like a bird before a cat, kept up an attack on the enemy so fierce and continuous that there was scarcely any molestation of the defeated army from the air. The next few days were bound to be critical. But by flying the Atlantic instead of going by boat, the Prime Minister and C.I.G.S. would only lose control of the war for twenty-four hours, and, with the need for consultation with Washington so urgent, the hazard seemed worth it. " In case of my death in this journey I am about to undertake," Churchill wrote to the King, " I avail myself of your Majesty's gracious permission to advise that you should entrust the formation of a new Government to Mr. Anthony Eden."[1]

Brooke's diary tells the story of the flight:

" Decided early that by 10.30 a.m. a final decision was to be given as to whether we started for America at 12.15 p.m. . . . Attended C.O.S. when we received the verdict that we were off. Went back to War Office and flat to pick up kit and Barney met me at Euston Station with two half-finished suits."

" Travelled up to Stranraer in P.M.'s special train; very comfortable. Had meals alone at table with him and thus able to settle many points in anticipation of talk with Roosevelt. Arrived Stranraer about 10.30 p.m. when latest news was telephoned through to P.M. Then went by motor-boat to the Boeing Clipper. Huge flying-boat, beautifully fitted up with bunks to sleep in, dining-saloon, steward's office, lavatories, etc."

' I find that I did not mention two little episodes in my diary which nevertheless have remained very clear in my memory as being typical of Winston. We were walking down the quay to embark in the motor-boat to take us to the Clipper. He was dressed in his zip-suit and zip-shoes, with a black Homburg hat on the side of his head and his small gold-topped malacca cane in his hand. Suddenly, almost like Pooh-Bear, he started humming, " We are here because we're here—We're here because we're here! " This little song could not have been more appropriate. It was at a time when the Atlantic had not been so very frequently flown,[2] we were both somewhat doubtful why we were going, whether we should get there, what we should achieve while we were there, and whether we should ever get back. We were facing a journey of twenty-seven hours in the air, and

[1] *Churchill*, IV, 337.

[2] The first ferry-service across the North Atlantic had been initiated by the R.A.F. in the winter of 1940. *Royal Air Force 1939-1945* (H.M.S.O.) II, 146-7.

might reasonably have some doubts as to whether we should reach our destination.'

' The next incident was on our arrival in the flying-boat. He sent for the steward and said to him: " The clock is going to do some funny things while we are in the air; it is either going to go backwards or forwards, but that is of little consequence, my stomach is my clock and I eat every four hours! " As I had to share every one of these meals with him, and, as they were all washed down with champagne and brandy, it became a little trying on the constitution.'

' To return to the diary ':

" Party consists of P.M., his doctor, his A.D.C., secretary, clerk, butler, detective, " Pug " Ismay, myself and my staff officer, Stewart.[1] At 11.30 p.m. we took off. Just saw a bit of the Irish coast and then at 5000 ft. found ourselves above the clouds. At 12.30 wonderful red sky from sun just below the horizon. Slept very comfortably after paying a visit to the pilot in his driving-compartment on top bridge."

' Our departure had been especially delayed till after dark owing to the danger of meeting a German Focke-Wulf plane, apt to cruise over the Western Approaches. I have a most vivid memory of the thrill of the start of that flight. Looking out over a sea of cotton-wool clouds with a pink tinge from the red sky and the silver wings of the Clipper reflecting this glorious colour, and with it all the wonderful feeling of sailing out into the boundless spaces of the Atlantic.'

" *June 18th.* Had long morning in bed as the clock was going back, and breakfast was not available till 11 a.m. (about 8 a.m. real time). Still flying over blankets of clouds till about 12.30 when we found the sea again and shortly afterwards flew over a large convoy of some thirty-five ships. P.M. in tremendous form and enjoying himself like a schoolboy! . . . As I write we are over the Atlantic, and within about an hour's flying time of Newfoundland."

---

[1] Brigadier G. M. Stewart, Director of Plans, War Office, afterwards killed flying home from the Casablanca Conference.

" *Later.* Now over Newfoundland which we reached after 14½ hours flying. Beautiful clear sky and able to get a wonderful view of the country. We flew direct to Gander, the new airport, and, after circling over it to have a good look, we flew on in a more southerly course."

" *Later.* Hit land off Cape Breton Island, and on to Nova Scotia. Unfortunately cloudy again and unable to see the ground. Flying at 5000 ft. now, but came over Newfoundland at 1500 ft. so as to see the country well."

' And what a bleak country, nothing but rock and water with a few woods. The coast line was interesting with small fishing villages at long distances apart.'

" *Later.* After leaving Cape Breton Island ran into heavy fog and bumpy conditions till we reached Cape Cod. By then we found that adverse winds had delayed us and that we should now have no time to divert our course to have a look at New York. We therefore flew straight on to Washington and landed on the Potomac after being 26½ hours continuously in the air."

" Met by Halifax, Lee, Dill, etc. Dill is very kindly putting me up. Halifax asked me to dine, so had to rush to Dill's house to bath and change before going on to Embassy, where P.M. is stopping. Have only just returned at 1.45 a.m. which is equivalent to 7.45 a.m. by English time, by which I have been working the rest of the day."

Our arrival in Washington is one more of those episodes which remains almost as clear in my mind as if it had been only yesterday. The sight of this beautifully laid-out town in the hazy light of the evening; the Potomac looked like a small silver ribbon running through the middle of it, so small at that height that it seemed quite impossible for the large Clipper to find sufficient space to accommodate it. And yet when the time came it slid down on to the water like a great swan, and there we were in contact again with the more solid elements of this earth. I found it hard to realise that in one hop I had moved through space from Stranraer Loch to the Potomac.'

Early next morning Churchill flew to Roosevelt's family home at Hyde Park. Here, free from prying eyes, as the President " poised and backed his car on the grass verge of the precipices above the Hudson," the two statesmen, before turning to the strategic situation, addressed their minds to the momentous question—then known by the secret code-name of ' Tube Alloys ' and made urgent by reports of German experiments with heavy water[1]—as to whether the attempts of British and American scientists to release atomic energy should be carried a stage further by the erection of plant in the United States for making an atom bomb. Meanwhile in the Washington heat Brooke and Dill discussed with their American colleagues of the Combined Chiefs of Staff the equally momentous and still more urgent question of whether there should be a landing in Europe in 1942.

" *June 19th*. Left here at 10 a.m. and drove to the C.O.S. offices when I found Dill and had a long talk with him. At 12.30 p.m. attended a Combined Chiefs of Staff meeting at which I gave a statement of reasons for our visit which was connected with some of the doubts expressed by the President to Mountbatten. We then had a lunch given by the Combined Chiefs of Staff. After lunch had another interview with Marshall and his staff at which we made further progress towards defining our policy for 1942 and 1943. Found we were pretty well of the same accord as to the general outlook. Came back to Dill's room, and then did some shopping. Dined with Dill in his house. On the whole made fair progress to-day, but am a little doubtful as to what P.M. and President may be brewing up together."

" *June 20th*. Stinking hot day! Went up to the office in the morning where I looked through minutes of yesterday's meetings. Then attended another Chiefs of Staff meeting at 11 a.m. Here I met Admiral King[2] for the first time.

---

[1] " I received a report about the latest developments in German science. Research in the realm of atomic destruction has now proceeded to a point where its results may possibly be used in the present war. . . . It is essential that we should keep ahead of everybody." Goebbels, *Diary*, 21st March, 1942.

[2] Admiral (later Fleet Admiral) E. J. King, U.S. Chief of Naval Staff and Commander-in-Chief.

Meeting was, I think, a success; at least as military men we were in agreement as to the policy we should adopt. But we fully appreciated that we might be up against many difficulties when confronted with the plans that the P.M. and President had been brewing up together at Hyde Park. We fear the worst and are certain that North Africa and North Norway plans for 1942 will loom large in their proposals, whilst we are convinced that they are not possible. . . . "

" From there we went on to lunch with General Marshall. A very pleasant quiet lunch in a delightful house amongst the trees. After lunch we went to see the Lee Memorial—his old house kept exactly as it was when he inhabited it. I was thrilled with it and could easily transfer myself back to the days when he was there. I could almost see him going through the crisis of his life deciding on which side he would fight. The slave quarters were also very interesting. Then back to the office, and on to a sherry party given by Dill for me to meet all the Dominion and British officers employed in Washington. Finally dined with the Under-Secretary for War, where the Secretary[1] was dining."

' This dinner was my first opportunity of meeting Stimson, Secretary for War. I found him an exceptionally charming man to meet, and certainly a fine administrative brain, but with a limited strategic outlook. He was one of the strong adherents of breaking our heads in too early operations across the Channel. Consequently a strong supporter of Marshall.'

With the Eighth Army in retreat and Malta and Egypt in deadly peril, with the battle of the Atlantic undecided, and the Germans, triumphant in the Crimea, massed for their drive to the Caucasian oil-wells, Brooke was between the devil and the deep-sea. On the one hand was his political chief pouring into the ears of the American President projects for diversions which, however admirable in themselves, could only end in disaster if they were not sustained by sufficient shipping or if, by prematurely deflecting resources from what at the moment

[1] H. L. Stimson, U.S. Secretary for War.

were vital points, they made it impossible to hold the Middle East bastion. On the other were his American colleagues, in their wish to save Russia at all costs, impatiently seeking the impossible and preparing to present Hitler with a victory that would retrieve all his past mistakes and restore the Reich to the power and prestige it had enjoyed in 1940. It was useless to expend shipping and resources on capturing one end of the African Mediterranean littoral if the other, with the Suez Canal, was allowed to pass into enemy hands. For the next few months every available vessel was going to be needed to rush men and supplies round the Cape to enable Britain to hold the Nile valley and Persian oil-refineries and keep intact the further half of the broken sea-route to the East until, by a resumption of the Desert offensive and a landing in French North Africa, it was possible to open the rest of it. The plan which the Prime Minister and President had discussed so hopefully at Christmas before the Japanese victories was only the second, not the first, of the ascending steps of that Mediterranean offensive which Brooke saw as the pre-requisite for a successful invasion of Europe. To take it if the imperial base in the Middle East had passed into Axis hands would in his view be a step in the air. The overriding immediate need was to hold Egypt.

For this reason, while discouraging his American colleagues from committing themselves to premature action in Europe in 1942, Brooke felt it wiser to do nothing for the moment that could weaken their resolve to build up their forces in Britain quickly—Operation " Bolero "—for cross-Channel operations in 1943. He pointed out, however, that, if by then the Russians had been forced to make peace, an invasion of France would be out of the question and the Allies would have to launch their blow elsewhere. In the meantime, the forces they were assembling in England would secure their European base from invasion. With the issues of the battles raging in Russia and Libya undecided and the submarine campaign at its height, the professional Service leaders of both nations at that moment felt that it would be wise to wait and see for a little and, in the meantime, build up a strategic reserve in England to meet any contingency, rather than commit themselves to an immediate operation—whether in France, Africa or Norway—that would make continuing and possibly disastrous demands on their inadequate shipping and available military resources.[1] At their meetings on June 19th and 20th, therefore, the Combined Chiefs of Staff agreed that the proposal to build up strength in Britain should be adhered to, that " the locality, strength and availability of means " for a landing in 1942 should be further studied, but that, since it would delay preparations for the real attack later, it should be undertaken " only in case of necessity or of an exceptionally favourable opportunity." This, thanks to Brooke and Dill, was at least an approximation to the British decision of June 8th.

Yet at this point the Prime Minister's invincible optimism and power of recoil in disaster again exercised a decisive influence on the course of the war. On the day that Churchill had flown to Hyde Park, the seventy-four-year-old American Secretary of War had sent the President a solemn, urgent letter. Deeply disturbed by Mountbatten's visit of a fortnight before and convinced that Churchill and " his team " had come over to wheedle his political chief—already an instinctive " diversionist "—from the straight and narrow path of frontal attack into " the wildest kind of diversionist debauch," Stimson urged upon him " a steady, rapid and unrelenting prosecution of the ' Bolero ' plan, . . . the surest road, first to the shaking of Hitler's anti-Russian campaign of '42 and, second, to the ultimate defeat of his armies and the victorious termination of the war." "Geographically and historically," he argued, ' Bolero,' was the easiest road to the centre of our chief enemy's heart. The base was sure. The water barrier of the Channel under the support of Britain-based air-power is far easier than either the Mediterranean or the Atlantic. The subsequent overland route into Germany is easier than any alternate. Over the Low Countries has run the historic path of armies between Germany and France."[2]

[1] *Strategic Planning for Coalition Warfare*, 237-44. "As professional officers the Chiefs of Staff were uncomfortably aware how quickly military situations could change and how important it was to have uncommitted reserves in the field and at home. In this respect they were more cautious than the President and the Prime Minister."

[2] *Stimson*, 217-19. By " Bolero " he meant either " Sledgehammer " or " Round-up "—the names agreed for the 1942 and 1943 landings respectively

But Roosevelt was assailed that week-end by a more powerful memorialist than Stimson. On Saturday Churchill handed him a Note which he supported with all his armoury of eloquence.

" We hold strongly to the view that there should be no substantial landing in France this year unless we are going to stay. No responsible British military authority has so far been able to make a plan for September 1942 which had any chance of success unless the Germans became utterly demoralised, of which there is no likelihood. Have the American Staffs a plan? At what points would they strike? What landing-craft and shipping are available? Who is the officer prepared to command the enterprise? . . . In case no plan can be made in which any responsible authority has good confidence, and consequently no engagement on a substantial scale in France is possible in September, 1942, what else are we going to do? Can we afford to stand idle in the Atlantic theatre during the whole of 1942? Ought we not to be preparing within the general structure of " Bolero " some other operation by which we may gain positions of advantage, and also directly or indirectly to take some of the weight off Russia? It is in this setting and on this background that the French North-West Africa operation should be studied."[1]

That night, instead of remaining, as had been arranged, at Hyde Park till Sunday, the two great " diversionists " set off together for Washington in the President's special train. Brooke's diary tells the story of what happened next day.

" *June 21st (Sunday).* Had planned a nice quiet morning with Dill, but it was not to be. ' We had put on old clothes and intended visiting Mount Vernon.' As we dropped into the office we were warned that I had to lunch at White House with the President. (' We had not expected P.M. and President back in Washington till that evening.') Shortly afterwards ' Pug ' Ismay called up to say that P.M. wanted to see me at once, and that he was very upset

and which the American political leaders confused with the code name given to the prior build-up of American forces in Britain.
[1] *Churchill*, IV, 342-3.

at the decisions we had come to with the Combined Chiefs of Staff meetings. Found him a bit peevish, but not too bad and, after an hour's talk with him, had him quiet again. Then went with him to see the President. I was very much impressed by him. A *most* attractive personality. Harry Hopkins and Marshall also turned up, and we had a general discussion of all the possible offensives in France, Africa and Middle East."

' This meeting with Roosevelt made a very vivid impression on my mind. I was dressed in a very old suit for my day out with Dill and, when I found I was to meet the President, I implored Winston to let me slip home and change into uniform, but he would not let me go and said he wanted me.'

' When I walked into the President's room I felt very ill at ease, being in such slovenly clothes. He was sitting at his desk and, after Winston had introduced me, I apologised for being so badly dressed and gave him the reasons. He replied, " What's wrong with you? Why not take your coat off like I have, you will feel far more comfortable? " It was so nicely said that it at once made me feel at ease and broke down all my discomfort. On all the occasions that I met him he was perfectly charming to me.'

" At 1 p.m. we adjourned for lunch when I met Mrs. Roosevelt. During lunch he said to me, ' When I was a boy a certain Sir Victor Brooke came to stop with us at our home, Hyde Park; is he any relation of yours? ' I then discovered that my father and Douglas had stopped with his father and he remembered them well. I could not help wondering what Father would have thought if he had known then the circumstances under which Roosevelt and his youngest son would meet in the future."

" After lunch we had another long conference lasting till 4.30 p.m. In the middle the tragic news of the loss of Tobruk came in."

' I can remember this incident as if it had occurred yesterday. Churchill and I were standing beside the

President's desk talking to him, when Marshall walked in with a pink piece of paper containing a message of the fall Tobruk. Neither Winston nor I had contemplated such an eventuality and it was a staggering blow. I cannot remember what the actual words were that the President used to convey his sympathy, but I remember vividly being impressed by the tact and real heartfelt sympathy which lay behind these words. There was not one word too much nor one word too little.'

' Marshall at once got to work to see what he could do to furnish some tangible signs of their sympathy in the shape of active assistance. As we shall see, he proposed in the first place sending the First American Armoured Division to the Middle East. This division was only partially trained, and it would have entailed forming an American front in the Middle East. Consequently it was decided to send three hundred Sherman tanks and a hundred self-propelled guns at once to the Middle East. These tanks had already been issued to the Armoured division and had to be withdrawn from them for this purpose. Anybody knowing what it entails withdrawing long-expected weapons from fighting troops just after they have received them, will understand the depth of the kindness that lay behind this gesture.'

' I always feel that the Tobruk episode in the President's study did a great deal towards laying the foundations of friendship and understanding built up during the war between the President and Marshall on the one hand and Churchill and myself on the other.'

' The diary continues ':

" After the meeting I had three-quarters of an hour with Harry Hopkins and then came back to Dill's house via the office."

' This sentence is, I think, worth expanding. As I was walking out of the President's room, Hopkins said, " Would you care to come round to my room for a few moments' talk? I could give you some of the background which influenced the President in the statements he has just made and the opinions he has expressed." I went with him, expecting to be taken to his office. Instead, we went to his bedroom where we sat on the edge of his bed looking at his shaving-brush and toothbrush, whilst he let me into some of the President's inner thoughts.

' I mention this meeting as it was so typical of this strange man with no official position, not even an office in the White House, and yet one of the most influential of men. A man who played a great and nebulous part in the war as the President's right-hand man. A great part that did him all the more credit when his miserable health is taken into account.'

" We had an early dinner and went back to the White House by 9 p.m., when we had a meeting with President, P.M., Dill, Marshall, King, Harry Hopkins, Little, Ismay and self. Discussed results of submarine warfare and necessity for greater action on . . . . preventative measures. Then the proposed operations in the Pacific. Finally the Middle East position and accepted offer of American Armoured division for Middle East. This may lead to a U.S.A. front in Middle East at expense of the European front. Did not finish till 1 a.m. A little cooler this evening, thank heaven, as heat has been oppressive all day."

"*June 22nd.* Held a conference in the morning to discuss the use of the U.S.A. aircraft-carrier *Ranger* in connection with convoys to Russia, to Malta, and aircraft to Takoradi for the Middle East. Also discussed the implications of sending U.S.A. Armoured division to Middle East and effect on " Bolero." Then did some shopping and lunched with Dill, after which we went to Mount Vernon to see Washington's home, most interesting. It is kept very much as it was in his day, and makes it possible to bring him to life before one's eyes. I now want to read all about him."

' During this afternoon I saw my first Kentucky Cardinal, a most lovely bird that I had always longed to see after reading Lane Allan's book of this title and his " Aftermath." '

" After tea back to the office and finally dined at the Embassy to meet Winston and various Naval, Army and

Air officers on the Mission here. Winston made me drive back with him to the White House in the President's car to discuss the need to relieve Neil Ritchie. I felt this was bound to come and was prepared for it. I am devoted to Neil and hate to think of the disappointment this will mean to him."[1]

" *June 23rd.* Went to office in the morning and at 2.30 p.m. on to the White House to attend a meeting of President, P.M., Harry Hopkins, Marshall, Arnold,[2] ' Pug ' Ismay and self. We discussed what could be done to reinforce the Middle East rapidly by diverting U.S. Air Forces from India to Middle East, and also details concerning sailing of an Armoured division from this country."

" Afterwards I visited the Museum with Dill. We finally went round to the White House at 7.40 p.m. in anticipation of entraining for to-morrow's Army demonstrations. However, after waiting some time we were informed that the special train had met with a misadventure and would not be able to start for another two hours or so. We were therefore invited to dine with the President who was in very good form. After dinner we went to the train which was air-conditioned and beautifully cool."

This visit to the training camp at Fort Jackson in South Carolina of the Prime Minister and C.I.G.S.—now urgently needed in England to cope with the crisis caused by the fall of Tobruk—was an addition to their programme made at the special request of Marshall and Stimson, who were anxious to convince them that the American levies, trained by trans-

---

[1] ' Neil Ritchie had been my Chief of Staff in France in 1940 through all the Dunkirk days, and on my return to France through Cherbourg. I had the very highest opinion of him, but to my mind he should never have been given command of the Eighth Army at the time he was appointed to it. He had never yet commanded even a division in action, let alone a Corps. To be given an Army Command in an emergency at that stage of his career was testing him too highly. When he returned to England I posted him back to a division to regain confidence in himself and he very shortly afterwards qualified for a Corps which he commanded admirably. It was a great pity that he was ever placed in such a position. . . A very fine man who did a wonderful " come-back " after suffering a serious blow.' *Notes on My Life,* VI, 420, 442.

[2] General H. H. Arnold, Chief of U.S. Army Air Force.

atlantic mass-production methods, were fit to take their place in the battle-line against Hitler's veterans. The day was very hot, and the training-ground reminded Churchill of his subaltern days in the plains of India in the 'nineties. Brooke, to whom they may have recalled similar experiences of a decade later, wrote:

"*June 24th.* Slept well and had good breakfast on the train. Then a short conference with Marshall and the P.M. At 11 a.m. we arrived at Camp Jackson in South Carolina. Met at the station by Guard of Honour, bands and masses of cameras and correspondents."

' As we got out of the train there was a fleet of cars to take us round for the day, and, as there was a vacant seat in one of the rear cars, Marshall very kindly suggested that Sawyers (the P.M.'s butler) should accompany us. From then onwards Sawyers became one of the party.'

". . . Drove out to Receiving Field when we were shown three combat-teams from 8th, 30th and 77th Divisions respectively. Fine hard-looking men. We were next shown a parachuting display by over 600 parachutists. Only three casualties, one leg broken, one sprain, and one suspected skull fracture. We were then shown individual training by 77th Division, after which we had lunch on the train. We then went to field-firing range and watched a disappointing exercise. Finally flew back some 350 miles from Owen Fields, Columbia, reaching Washington a little after 7 p.m."

'. . . Winston had changed into his zip-suit on the plane and put on a Panama hat for his arrival. The brim of the Panama was turned up all round and he looked just like a small boy in a suit of rompers going down the beach to dig in the sand. Sawyers took up a position in the middle of the plane and refused to let him pass. Winston asked him: " What's wrong, Sawyers, why are you getting in my way? " . . . Sawyers replied: "The brim of your hat is turned up, does not look well, turn it down, turn it down! " . . . Winston, rather red and looking angry, turned the brim down. Thereupon Sawyers stood to one side muttering to himself, " That's much, much better, much better! ". . . ' [1]

' The diary entry ended ':

" A very interesting day. I drove round with Stimson, the Secretary of State for War. . . . The American system of individual and elementary training seems excellent, but I am not so certain that their higher training is good enough, or that they have yet realized the standard of training required."

' They certainly had not,' Brooke commented, ' and had a lot to learn. I next met them in Northern Ireland and they still had a lot to learn, but seemed to prefer to learn in the hard school of war itself. As a result they learned a great deal more in North Africa. But in the art of war, as in polo, lawn tennis, golf, etc., when they once got down to it they were determined to make a success of it.' Churchill's reaction, as recorded by Hopkins, was that, though amazed by Marshall's assembly-line methods of mass-production and enthusiastic at the exercises he saw, he remained profoundly unconvinced of these young divisions' present ability to compete with the Germans. It took, he told his hosts, two years to make a soldier. Yet when his personal Chief of Staff, General Ismay, expressed the view that to put these troops against the Germans would be murder, he replied: " You're wrong. They are wonderful material and will learn very quickly."

" *June 25th.* Went round to the office by 8.45 a.m. when we had a Joint Staff meeting to discuss American reinforcements to the Middle East. Cunningham had

[1] *Notes on My Life*, VI. There is a delightful reference to the Prime Minister's relations with this faithful man-servant in Sir Ian Jacob's diary of the journey to Casablanca and Adana in January, 1943. Sawyers looked after all the Prime Minister's personal wants, including the twenty or thirty packages with which he invariably travelled. On emplaning at Castel Benito on the way home, Sawyers produced drinks for the party from the bomb-bay and afterwards assisted the Prime Minister to undress in that cramped space. ' It was quite a business hoisting him into his perch and undressing him. At one stage I heard Sawyers say: " You are sitting on your hot-water bottle. That isn't at all a good idea." To which the P.M. replied: " Idea? It isn't an idea, it's a coincidence." ' Sir Jan Jacob, *Diary*, 5th February, 1943.

just arrived to replace Admiral Little.[1] At 9.30 we went round to a Combined Staff meeting when we examined alternatives for providing an American armoured division for Middle East, a project both P.M. and President were very keen on. Marshall put forward a new proposal to provide three hundred Sherman tanks and a hundred 105-mm. self-propelled guns together with two train-ferry ships to take the lot out to Middle East. Marshall then lunched with Dill and I had a very satisfactory talk with him, explaining to him that, after examining his proposal, I was all for accepting it, but that I might have great difficulty to get the P.M. to accept it as he would wish to conform to the President's desire to produce fighting troops instead of equipment. He agreed situation might be delicate and hoped I would do my best."

" At 2.45 p.m. I went round to the White House to put new proposal before the P.M.—Dill, Little, Evatt,[2] Cunningham and Ismay were also present. Things went better than I had expected and I was able to convince the P.M. that the military aspect of the problem and its advantages (of receiving at once all this new equipment) outweighs the political considerations (of an American front in the Middle East). I then telephoned to Marshall who was delighted with the result. Then dashed off to see a demonstration of the new American rocket-gun ('the first model of the Bazooka'). I was very much impressed by it, and consider that it should be rapidly developed in large numbers. Then returned to Dill's house to pack and dine."

" At 8.15 p.m. assembled at the Embassy under Secret Service arrangements and motored to Baltimore where we found our Clipper drawn up along the quay like a ship. By 11 p.m. we were off, having taken off in the dark, and were flying over the lights of Baltimore heading for Newfoundland."

" *June 26th.* Had an excellent night's sleep and got up at 6.30 a.m., as we were due to arrive at Botley at about

[1] Admiral Sir Andrew Cunningham, now Admiral of the Fleet Viscount Cunningham of Hyndhope, and Admiral Sir Charles Little, Head of the British Admiralty Delegation in Washington.
[2] Rt. Hon. H. V. Evatt, Australian Minister for External Affairs.

8 a.m. and were expected to breakfast first. Flew over a very swampy and water-logged part of Newfoundland, finally arriving at Botley, a small village of wooden houses and wooden church. Very good landing and went ashore for a couple of hours whilst the Clipper took on petrol."

" Our party is much the same—P.M., his doctor Sir Charles Wilson, Martin his secretary, Thompson his Flag Lieutenant, his butler, a clerk, detective and ' Pug ' Ismay. In addition my staff officer Stewart, Jacob[1] whom we are fetching back, and Harriman who has joined the party."

" We are at present well above the clouds sailing out into the Atlantic."

" It has been a very interesting trip and real good value. I feel now in much closer touch with Marshall and his staff, and know what he is working for and what his difficulties are. Also meeting King makes it easier to realise the difficulties of obtaining close co-operation between the land and sea forces of America. Especially so when King looks out over the Pacific principally, whilst Marshall has his eyes turned towards Europe."

" Then meeting the President was a matter of the greatest interest. There is a wonderful charm about him. But I do not think that his military is on a par with his political sense. His military conceptions and plans are not based on a full grasp of all the implications. As a result he favours plans which are not possible owing to their administrative aspects. On that account Marshall has difficulties and is forced to disagree with the President."

" I found it difficult at the first few meetings to be able to appreciate the degree of importance to attach to the President's military suggestions and I did not know how Marshall would react. With the President and P.M. planning on their own in the White House, it made it difficult at first to carry on business with Marshall. However, I finally got on sufficiently intimate terms with him to be able to discuss freely with him the probable reactions

---

[1] Colonel Ian Jacob, Military Assistant Secretary of the War Cabinet, now Lt.-Gen. Sir Ian Jacob, Director-General of the B.B.C.

of both President and P.M. to the plans we were discussing. There is no doubt that Dill is doing wonderful work and that we owe him a deep debt of gratitude."

' These remarks of mine about my early relations with Marshall are interesting. His relations with the President were quite different from my relations with Winston. The President had no great military knowledge and was aware of this fact and consequently relied on Marshall and listened to Marshall's advice. Marshall never seemed to have any difficulties in countering any wildish plans which the President might put forward. My position was very different. Winston never had the slightest doubt that he had inherited all the military genius of his great ancestor, Marlborough. His military plans and ideas varied from the most brilliant conceptions at the one end to the wildest and most dangerous ideas at the other. To wean him away from these wilder plans required superhuman efforts and was never entirely successful in so far as he tended to return to these again and again. I am convinced that on many occasions Marshall imagined that I was in agreement with some of Winston's wilder ideas; it was not easy for me to explain how matters stood without disloyalty. On several occasions I believe that Marshall thought I was double-crossing him. It is in this respect amongst others that Dill was such an invaluable help. Marshall had the highest respect for him and I was devoted to him; consequently he was in a unique position to reduce difficulties between us. . . .'

" *Later.* Still above the clouds and approaching Ireland. It has now become dark and although only 10 p.m. by my watch it is 4 a.m. by English time."

" *Later.* Shortly after writing above I went up to sit in the Second Pilot's seat where I found the P.M. Beautiful moon shining over a sea of clouds; as the moon was nearly full, the scene was beyond words. Shortly afterwards the clouds began to break and the sea again became visible, with only patches of clouds lying about. Then out of the darkness dark patches loomed up on the horizon which turned out to be the north-west corner of Mayo.

We soon struck the coast, only just visible in the moonlight. P.M. was as thrilled as I was. We skirted the north coast of Mayo and sailed in just south of the mouth of the River Erne, and on right over the middle of Lough Erne, hitting the north coast about Killadeas. On over Armagh, north corner of Lough Neagh, and just north of Belfast. Then across the channel and back to Stranraer Loch where we made a perfect landing at 11.10 p.m. by American time, but 5.10 a.m. by British time. The journey home had taken just twenty-four hours from Baltimore."

' Now that the air has become one of the regular mediums for transatlantic journeys, a crossing by air makes little impression on one. But at the time of the flight described in my diary regular services had not yet been established and we had not left very far behind those memorable pioneer flights. Both the journey over and back left unforgettable memories in my mind. I remember as if it was yesterday the pilot coming to me and saying: " We have just passed the point of no-return ". . . .'

' I also remember clearly when, up with the pilot and Winston staring into the darkness trying to make out if we could see land, the pilot saying that if our land-fall was correct we should soon see a lighthouse. And then suddenly flickering out of the darkness was a small spark of light. We had crossed that vast expanse of water and struck the exact spot we hoped for.'

' My feeling during that moonlight flight across Northern Ireland can well be imagined. I was spellbound looking down on Lough Erne and remembering the days I had fished there for pike. Then passing over Colebrooke[1] and all the memories it conjured up, whilst Belfast wrapped in the morning mist, pierced by columns of smoke, raised a lump in my throat and a desperate longing for days of peace.'

' We then landed and got into the P.M.'s train, where I slept till 12 noon (British time). Then got up, had lunch, and went through a mass of papers that had been sent up to

[1] His father's ancestral home, the residence of Alan Brooke's nephew and close friend, Sir Basil Brooke, Prime Minister of Northern Ireland—now Lord Brookeborough.

meet us. At 4.45 p.m. we arrived at Euston to be met by Mrs. Churchill and daughter, also large assembly of Cabinet. I then drove back to flat where I left kit. From then on to Cabinet meeting at 5.30 p.m. when P.M. gave an account of our trip, and I was made to give a statement also. After that went to War Office, picked up more papers and drove home and was given a wonderful welcome by you and the two young. Such a joy to be back with you."

. . . .

The facts that faced the C.I.G.S. on his return to England were grim. "The Middle East situation," he wrote on June 28th, "is about as unhealthy as it can be, and I do not very well see how it can end." All but a fraction of the British armour in the desert had been destroyed, Tobruk had surrendered with 33,000 men—the second major military capitulation of the year—and the Eighth Army, now far inside the Egyptian frontier, was still retreating. Two days before an attempt by Auchinleck, who had taken personal command, to stand at Mersa Matruh had failed despite a brilliant action by Freyberg's New Zealanders, hastily brought up from Palestine. By the 28th, having lost another 6000 prisoners and immense quantities of war material, the defeated army was at Alamein, nearly four hundred miles from its starting point at Gazala and only sixty from Alexandria. Meanwhile, under Admiral Harcourt's orders, the Mediterranean Fleet had evacuated the port[1] and withdrawn for safety to the Red Sea. Reinforcements of men and armour were on their way round the Cape, but it would be weeks before they could all arrive. And meanwhile a new and still graver threat to the Middle East was developing from the north.

For on June 23rd, having concentrated nearly three hundred divisions in the east, the Germans had broken the Russian lines on a wide front and begun their drive to the Volga and Caucasus. And as the grey storm of men and armour swept eastwards, Churchill's prophecy of eighteen months before—

---

[1] Because the harbour could now be bombed under enemy fighter-cover and because the Suez Canal might be blocked behind it.

that Hitler might tear vast provinces out of Russia and march to the gates of India—seemed on the point of fulfilment. In the next two months the Russians were to fall back more than four hundred miles, to abandon the Maikop oilfield and see the invaders reach the banks of the Don and Volga. Their allies, defeated in the desert and struggling on every sea to maintain their ocean communications, could only watch in growing anxiety. In a single week at the beginning of July Britain and America lost 400,000 tons of shipping in the Atlantic, while Churchill, faced by the destruction of two-thirds of the last Russian convoy to Murmansk and by a complete *non possumus* from the Admiralty, was compelled to inform Stalin that further sailings would have to be suspended till September.

The political situation appeared almost as unhealthy as the military. The Government had just suffered a resounding defeat in a by-election, and a much-respected Conservative back-bencher had placed a motion on the Order Book that the House had lost confidence in the direction of the war and that its control should be taken from the Minister of Defence and given to a professional soldier or sailor directly responsible to Parliament. As always, Churchill fought back fiercely and insisted on a vote of confidence. On July 2nd, after a magnificent fighting speech, he defeated the motion of censure by 475 votes to 25. But tempers remained strained, and for some time both Government and High Command were under continuous criticism. Brooke had his share of it in the War Cabinet; at a meeting on the 29th he found the Minister of Labour " full of uneducated peevish questions about the Middle East operations, continually asking questions on points that I had just explained." Though later, when he got to know his formidable critic better, he formed the highest opinion of him,[1] at this time he found it " infuriating to listen to men who had no idea how to handle the situation laying down fantastic theories as if they were past-masters in the art of strategy." " A dreadful exhibition of amateur strategy by Cabinet Ministers," he wrote again at the end of the first week in July, " the P.M. unfortunately

[1] ' I was evidently in a peevish mood at this Cabinet meeting. My remarks about Bevin are most unfair, and on the whole he was always of the greatest assistance and one of the Cabinet Ministers for whom I had the greatest respect and admiration.' *Notes on My Life*, VI, 429.

not in his usual form and unable to keep them in order. A most depressing and lamentable evening."

So grave was the situation in the Middle East that Churchill was all for flying out there at once with the C.I.G.S. and proposed to do so as soon as the debate in the House was over. On July 3rd Brendan Bracken, the Minister of Information, stopped Brooke in the lobby outside the Cabinet room and begged him to use his influence with the Prime Minister to prevent him going. Brooke needed no persuading, for he dreaded the impact of the Prime Minister's presence in the middle of a battle. "Had about three-quarters of an hour with Winston . . . ," he recorded that night, "trying to convince him that he should not try to fly out to Gib. and through the Mediterranean in a Liberator, and secondly, that he should wait till situation consolidates a little more in Egypt before flying out." His impatient chief accepted the advice with reluctance, and avenged himself by tilting at the Middle East Army and its commander in the War Cabinet. "I had an uphill task," Brooke wrote,

"defending him and pointing out the difficulties of his present position. Also the fact that any rash move on his part at the present time would very quickly lose us Egypt. However, P.M. was in one of his unpleasant moods, going back over old ground and asking where the 750,000 men in the Middle East were, what they were doing, and why they were not fighting. Afterwards. . . , with that astounding charm of his, he came up and said to me, ' I am sorry, Brookie, if I had to be unpleasant about Auchinleck and the Middle East.' "

For, the clouds having lifted a little, the Prime Minister was already clamouring for a renewal of the attack. On July 1st Cairo had been in a panic, with the railway stations thronged with refugees and smoke rising from the gardens of G.H.Q. and the British Embassy as their staffs burnt their files. But though few in Egypt now expected it, Auchinleck and his men —fighting in the British Army's spiritual home, the last ditch—held the Nile Delta. Holding the one position on the coast where the Qattara quicksands, forty miles to the south, formed a flank to the desert, and only sixty miles from their base at Alexandria, they clung grimly to the defences which their Fabian commander, like Wellington at Torres Vedras, had prepared against the day of disaster. With the sudden extension of their communications, the Germans found they had outrun both their supplies and, for the moment, their physical powers. Rommel had shot his bolt.

Thus, though the situation remained critical, by the second week in July the chief anxiety of the Chiefs of Staff had become once more to restrain the Prime Minister's impulse to attack too soon. Like a terrier momentarily released from the grip of a more powerful dog, his one idea was to fly back at the enemy's throat. On the 11th Brooke had difficulties over " an unpleasant wire " which he had drafted to Auchinleck and which the ever-tactful General Ismay vainly spent the morning trying to dissuade him from sending. Next day Brooke mentioned another long " conversation with P.M. on telephone after breakfast in which . . . he at last agreed to alter his wire and split it, sending half to the ' Auk ' and half to Corbett "— Auchinleck's Chief of Staff.[1] Simultaneously the C.O.S. Committee was called upon to consider yet another plan for invading Norway. This time the Prime Minister proposed that the operation should be entrusted to the Canadians.[2]

Nor was Churchill alone in contemplating an offensive while the shipping situation remained desperate and the gates of the Middle East unsecured. The most insistent of those demanding immediate action, and the hardest to resist, were the Americans. Profoundly dissatisfied with what they regarded as the procrastinating and opportunist English attitude of the Prime Minister and C.I.G.S. towards their brain-child, " Sledgehammer," they were now insisting that a definite decision should be taken at once. Accustomed, with their vast pioneer and expanding economy, to setting themselves impossible targets and then going all out to achieve them, they

[1] *Diary*, 11th July, 1942.
[2] " It having been suggested . . . that, with his more flexible and fertile brain, McNaughton would find a way out when the Chiefs of Staff had failed. After lunch I sent for him to my office and informed him privately how matters stood, as I did not want him afterwards to imagine that we were suggesting that the Canadians should undertake an operation which we considered impracticable." *Diary*, 9th July, 1942.

could not understand the hesitations of their allies. To them ifs
and delays were merely signs of half-heartedness. It had been
agreed in Washington in June that, while preparations on the
largest possible scale for an invasion of France in 1943 should
be pressed forward with speed and energy, efforts should also
be made to overcome the difficulties in the way of a preliminary
cross-Channel operation in 1942. It is true that, at Churchill's
instance, the possibilities of alternative action in North Africa,
Norway or the Iberian peninsula were also to be considered
by the Combined Chiefs of Staff. But by the middle of July
Marshall and his chief, Stimson, had become so exasperated
by the continued indefiniteness of their British colleagues and
their reminders of the difficulties that would confront a
cross-Channel operation even in 1943, that they were in the
mood, to use an Americanism, to " fish or cut bait."[1] Strongly
supported by Admiral King, who since his victory at Midway
had been clamouring for a major offensive against the Japanese,
they urged the President to offer the British the alternatives of
a landing in France that autumn or a transfer of the main
American effort from the Atlantic to the Pacific. In Roosevelt's
homely idiom, they proposed to force the issue by threatening
to " take up their dishes and go home."

Roosevelt's own attitude was more balanced. He continued
to insist that Germany was the major enemy and would have
to be destroyed before the United States could concentrate
against Japan. He refused to believe that the British were
lukewarm about an invasion of the Continent, though he was
disturbed by their reluctance to act in the present year. But,
as action of some sort in 1942 was essential to help the Russians,
he maintained that, if " Sledgehammer " could not be mounted
before the winter, the possibilities of immediate American inter-

[1] " A telegram has come from Great Britain indicating that the British War
Cabinet are weakening and going back on " Bolero " and are seeking to revive
" Gymnast "—in other words, they are seeking now to reverse the decision which
was so laboriously accomplished when Mr. Churchill was here a short time ago.
This would be simply another way of diverting our strength into a channel in
which we cannot effectively use it, namely, the Middle East. I found Marshall
very stirred up and emphatic over it. He is very naturally tired of these constant
decisions which do not stay made. This is the third time the question will have
been brought up by the persistent British, and he proposed a showdown which I
cordially endorsed. As the British won't go through with what they agreed to,
we will turn our backs on them and take up war with Japan." *Stimson*, (Diary, 10th
July, 1942.) 220.

vention either in French North Africa or Egypt should be explored. " I do not believe," he told Hopkins, " that we can wait until 1943 to strike at Germany. If we cannot strike at ' Sledgehammer,' then we must take the second best—and that is not the Pacific . . . ' Gymnast ' . . . . would secure Western Africa and deny the ports to the enemy; it would offer the beginning of what would be the ultimate control of the Mediterranean; it is the shortest route to supply."[1] The seed sown by Churchill in Washington had fallen on fruitful ground.

Next day Hopkins, Marshall and King received orders to proceed at once to London. They were to discuss with the American Service chiefs already there—Eisenhower, Mark Clark, Spaatz and Stark—and with the British Chiefs of Staff the possibilities of " Sledgehammer" and do everything possible, for the sake of relieving Russia, to carry it through. But if, as a result of unshakable opposition to it of those on the spot, they became convinced that it was not practicable then—and then only—they were to determine upon some other place where American troops could fight in 1942. " I hope for total agreement," the President ended, " within one week of your arrival."

With these instructions his emissaries set out next day to fly the Atlantic, landing at Prestwick in the early hours of July 18th and proceeding at once by special train to London. " It will be a queer party," Brooke wrote, " as Harry Hopkins is for operating in Africa, Marshall wants to operate in Europe, and King is determined to stick to the Pacific."[2] On the 17th his diary reads:

" Spent most of the Chiefs of Staff meeting preparing for visit of Harry Hopkins, Marshall and King who are on their way over now, arriving early to-morrow morning. They have come over as they are not satisfied that we are adhering sufficiently definitely to plans for the invasion of France in 1943 and if possible in 1942. In my mind 1942 is dead off and without the slightest hope. 1943 must depend on what happens to Russia. If she breaks and is overrun, there can be no invasion and we should then be

[1] White House Papers, II, 603-4.
[2] Diary, 15th July, 1942.

prepared to go into North Africa instead. But Marshall seems to want some rigid form of plan which we are bound to adhere to in any case."

. . . .

At 7.50 a.m. on Saturday the 18th Brooke went to Euston to meet the visitors who, determined to avoid temptation from the great " diversionist " and to spend the week-end in consultation with the American planners in London, had refused Churchill's invitation to stop at Chequers.[1] Later he attended a long Chiefs of Staff sitting to settle points for discussion with them on Monday. " At 4 p.m.," he wrote, " when I was getting near end of my work and thinking of soon going home, I was informed that all the Chiefs of Staff were wanted at Chequers for the night. Arrived there just in time for dinner. Pound, Portal, Mountbatten, Ismay, Cherwell and self. After dinner a long sitting reviewing the whole war and relative advantages of various fronts. This lasted till 2 a.m. when we were taken to see a film. Finally in bed by 2.45 a.m." It was decided that the Americans should be informed that the only feasible operation for 1942 was " Gymnast " but that, by making it a British as well as an American undertaking, it should be possible to land as far east as Algiers, two hundred miles inside the Mediterranean, and so establish the flank of a future Second Front in Europe. With this firm agreement between Prime Minister and Chiefs of Staff it was proposed to confront the visitors on Monday.

Brooke's diary tells the story of what happened:

" *July 20th.* . . . At 12.30 we went round to 10 Downing Street to meet the American Chiefs of Staff with the P.M. We had originally intended to meet them at 10 a.m. ' off the record ' for a private talk, but the P.M. very suspicious and had informed me at Chequers that Marshall was trying to assume powers of Commander-in-Chief of

---

[1] Hopkins was subsequently persuaded by the Prime Minister to reconsider his refusal and, leaving Marshall and King in London, to spend Sunday at Chequers. " The Prime Minister," he reported to Roosevelt, " threw the British Constitution at me with some vehemence. As you know, it is an unwritten document, so no serious damage was done." *White House Papers*, II, 608.

American troops, which was the President's prerogative."

" After lunch at 3 p.m. we met Marshall and King and had long arguments with them. Found both of them still hankering after an attack across the Channel this year to take the pressure off the Russians. They failed to realize that such action could only lead to the loss of some six divisions without achieving any results. The next argument was that we should take advantage of German pre-occupation in Russia to establish a bridgehead for 1943 operations. Had to convince them that there was no hope of such a bridgehead surviving the winter. Next discussed alternative operation in North Africa, which they are not much in favour of, preferring the Pacific."

" Rushed back to War Office to see Secretary of State, Vice Chief of Imperial General Staff, Deputy Chief of Imperial General Staff, Director of Military Operations, Director of Military Intelligence, and Military Secretary. After dinner put in two hours' hard work and was then sent for to 10 Downing Street. There I found Hopkins, Harriman and Beaverbrook with the P.M. He kept me up, alone with him, after the others had left, giving him till 1 a.m. results of my talks with Marshall and King."

" *July 21st.* A short C.O.S. which started at 10 a.m. leading up to a meeting at 11 a.m. with American C.O.S. Disappointing start. Found ourselves much where we had started yesterday morning, except that Marshall admitted that he saw no opportunity of staging an offensive in Europe to assist Russians by September. He missed the point that after September the Russians might be past requiring assistance and that the weather, at any rate at that season, was such as to make cross-Channel operations practically impossible. We went on arguing for two hours, during which King remained with a face like a Sphinx, and with only one idea, to transfer operations to the Pacific. Finally we parted at 1 p.m. and I felt we had made little headway. We are to meet again at 11 a.m. to-morrow. . . ."

" . . . At 11 p.m. I had to go back to 10 Downing Street. Both Eden and Hopkins were there, and I was not allowed to join them for fear that Marshall and King should hear of it and feel that I had been briefed by Hopkins against them according to President's wishes. P.M. therefore came up to Cabinet Room to see me and to find out results of our morning meeting. Got home by 12.30 a.m."

"*July 22nd.* Started with C.O.S. at 10 a.m. and was sent for by P.M. at 10.45 to discuss proposed draft of telegram to hurry the ' Auk ' on to attack. I had telegram read to me by shorthand writer and asked to see it in type to save time and to try and stop its despatch. At 11 a.m. met American Chiefs of Staff again. They handed in a written memorandum adhering to an attack on Cherbourg salient as the preliminary move to a general attack in 1943. The memorandum drew attention to the advantages, but failed to recognise the main disadvantage that there was no hope of our still being in Cherbourg by next spring. I put all the disadvantages to them. They did not return to the attack, but stated that they would now have to put the matter up to the President and wished to see the P.M. first. I therefore fixed up for a 3 p.m. meeting with the P.M. and went round to explain to him how matters stood, and to discuss with him the most profitable line of action. . . ."

" At 3 p.m. we all went to Downing Street and remained there till 4 p.m. P.M. informed American Chiefs that he was in agreement with the opinion of his Chiefs of Staff, and would put the whole matter before the War Cabinet at 5.30 p.m."

" At the Cabinet meeting I had to open the ball by putting results of all our meetings before the Cabinet, and then marshalling the case against the Cherbourg attack in 1942. I had no trouble in convincing the Cabinet who were unanimously against it. American Chiefs are therefore now wiring to America and we are waiting for next phase of our meeting. I hope they will not be as exhausting as the last seven hours of discussion."

" This evening Chiefs of Staff gave dinner to Americans at Claridges. On the whole, went well."

" *July 23rd.* My birthday—59! I don't feel like it. A

difficult C.O.S. at which we discussed the necessary measures to guard against German attacks through Persia on Abadan oilfields should Russian resistance break. Then lunched at Ritz with Turkish Ambassador. He spent most of the meal explaining to me the various reasons why Turkey could not under any circumstances throw her lot in with the Germans. He did not entirely convince me."[1]

" Whilst lunching received message that P.M. wanted Chiefs of Staff to meet him at 10 Downing Street at 3 p.m. Arrived there to be told latest developments in our negotiations with Americans. Roosevelt had wired back accepting fact that Western Front in 1942 was off. Also that he was in favour of attack in North Africa and was influencing his Chiefs in that direction. They were supposed to be working out various aspects with their staff and will probably meet us to-morrow. Winston anxious that I should not put Marshall off Africa by referring to Middle East dangers in 1943. Told him I must put whole strategical picture in front of Americans. Foresee difficulties ahead of me."

" Auchinleck started new attack day before yesterday, and not very happy with progress he is making. This evening had Marshall to dine with me, and got P. J. Grigg, Venning and Weeks to dine with me. Marshall in very pleasant and friendly mood."

The drama of what happened that day has been told in Sir Winston Churchill's history and in more detail in the White House Papers of Harry Hopkins and the life of Admiral King. Marshall and King had found that their Army and Air chiefs in London were ready, with reservations,[2] to attempt " Sledge-

---

[1] " I was unnecessarily suspicious and unbelieving." *Notes on My Life*, VI, 448a.

[2] " I personally favoured, at that time, the third course of action; that is, the attempt to seize a small bridgehead on the north-west coast of France. However, I told General Marshall that the project was a hazardous one and that my only real reason for favouring it was the fear of becoming so deeply involved elsewhere that the major cross-Channel attack would be indefinitely postponed, possibly even cancelled. Almost certainly any 1942 operation in the Mediterranean would eliminate the possibility of a major cross-Channel venture in 1943. Later developments have convinced me that those who held the " Sledgehammer " operation to be unwise at the moment were correct in their evaluation of the problem. Our limited-range fighter craft of 1942 could not have provided sufficiently effective

hammer." Their idea was that it should be directed against the Cotentin peninsula, where they believed it might be possible to capture Cherbourg and hold it as a port of entry throughout the winter. But Admiral Stark, the American naval Commander-in-Chief in European waters, did not believe the operation was practicable on what by the autumn—the earliest date when it could be staged—would have become a dangerous lee shore, while the British Prime Minister and Chiefs of Staff were adamant in their refusal to attempt it. Hopkins, therefore, on the 22nd, cabled Roosevelt that no agreement on " Sledge-hammer " could be reached. That evening they received the President's instructions to seek an alternative agreement on some other operation against the European enemy that would involve American troops in 1942. " We are naturally disappointed," Hopkins replied, " but goodwill prevails nevertheless. Now that the decision has been made we are hard at work on the next steps. I believe that our people will finally turn to an expanded ' Gymnast.' "[1]

On July 24th agreement between the Allies was reached. " Gymnast," rechristened by Churchill " Torch " and enlarged to include landings inside the Mediterranean and as near the Tunisian frontier as possible, was to become the first Anglo-American offensive operation approved and directed by the Combined Chiefs of Staff. It was to have an American Supreme Commander—Eisenhower—who was unofficially told of his new mission by General Marshall at Claridge's Hotel on the 26th, a combined Anglo-American staff, and a British task commander to lead the drive of its eastern advance-guard to Tunis and Bizerta. In the words of the American Lease-Lend administrator then in England, there was to be " complete co-operation and sharing of leadership, fighting men, ships and battle equipment."[2]

Brooke's diary continues:

> " *July 24th.* During our C.O.S. meeting we received a note from Marshall saying that American Chiefs of Staff

---

air cover over the Cotentin or Brittany peninsulas against the German air strength as it then existed." D. Eisenhower, *Crusade in Europe,* 79.

[1] *White House Papers,* II, 611.

[2] Stettinius, *Lease-Lend,* 204.

would be ready to see us at 12 noon. I was a bit nervous as to what they might have been brewing up since our last meeting. . . . However, they produced a paper containing almost everything that we had asked them to agree to at the start. We sat with them till 1.30 p.m. and only made minor alterations to their draft. We then parted till 3 p.m. When we met again to examine the redraft, we settled that the British C.O.S. should present the paper to the P.M. and to the Cabinet for their approval before final signature by them and Americans as a ' Combined Chiefs of Staff Document.' They all agreed to giving up immediate attack on Continent, and to prepare plans for attack on North Africa to be carried out if re-entry into Europe was impossible next year. In order to obtain this we were prepared to accept an American armoured division in Persia and to stand certain cuts in proposed air allotments. At 4.30 p.m. we met P.M. and I put Memorandum to him. He was delighted with it and passed it at once. At 5 p.m. Cabinet meeting . . . to discuss Stalin's reply to stopping Northern Convoy and intimation that Western Front was not possible. It was an unpleasant reply."[1]

" Then P.M. got me to put our Memorandum to the Cabinet. From the start things went wrong. . . . I perspired heavily in my attempts to pull things straight and was engaged in heated arguments. . . . In the end I triumphed and had the Memorandum passed without a word altered. Any change would have been fatal. The Americans had gone a long way to meet us, and I should have hated to have to ask them for more."

" A very trying week, but it is satisfactory to feel that we have got just what we wanted out of U.S. Chiefs. Just been told that I am for Chequers to-morrow night."

" *July 25th.* At the C.O.S. we examined advisability of completing the Madagascar expedition, now that negotiations have failed, with the minimum disturbance to future operations in Burma and in North Africa. After lunch interview with Paget to inform him of results of week's

---

[1] " I got a rough and surly answer." *Churchill,* IV, 241.

work. Then saw Andy McNaughton to find out how his
planning of the North Norway (Canadian) expedition was
getting on. Found out he was asking for five divisions,
twenty squadrons and a large fleet. Was then sent for by
P.M. who wanted to hear results of our morning meeting
with Marshall and King. I told him we had fixed up
question of command of North Africa. U.S. to find
Supreme Commander, with British Deputy. Under him
two Task Force Commanders, one U.S. for Casablanca
front and one British for Oran front. I wanted Alexander
for Task Force Commander. He wanted him to be both
Deputy Supreme Commander and Task Force Commander. Had an hour's argument with him from 6 p.m.
to 7 p.m.; finally had to stop as it was time to start for
Chequers. Arrived there at 8 p.m. Party consisted of
P.M., Mrs. Churchill, Marshall, King, Harry Hopkins,
Harriman, three Chiefs of Staff, ' Pug ,' Martin and
Tommy. After dinner the Americans were shown Cromwell's death mask and Queen Elizabeth's ring.[1] They
then left by special train for Scotland to fly to America.
After they left we were shown a good film, *The Younger
Pitt*, and then two hours' talk and bed at 2.45 a.m. Dog
tired and grateful this week is over."

The Second Front, 1942—Alan Brooke's bugbear since the
spring—was out of the way. So was the strategical deadlock
between the British and Americans. The latter believed that
the substitution of " Torch " for " Sledgehammer " in 1942
meant the postponement of " Round-up " from 1943 to 1944
or perhaps for ever. The British C.I.G.S., who had always
regarded an invasion of France across the Channel as the
crowning act in the plan he had envisaged but doubted
whether it would be possible in 1943, made no attempt to
challenge this view. Both allies agreed that the build-up of
American ground and air forces in Britain—" Bolero "—was to

---

[1] " Before dinner, in the light of the long summer evening, they admired the
exterior of the house built like some Elizabethan houses with the ground plan of
an E. Mrs. Churchill showed King a ring worn by Queen Elizabeth which
contained a secret recess that led to speculation about poison. After this excursion
into the past the showing of a British war film brought the company back to
1942." *Whitehill*, 198.

continue as fast as possible but that for the moment everything, except the defence of the indispensable Middle East bastion, was to yield to " Torch." It was hoped, Roosevelt cabled on the 24th, to put 80,000 American infantry and air force personnel into the initial operation before the end of October. " I cannot help feeling," he wrote to the Prime Minister, " that the past week represented a turning point in the whole war and that now we are on our way shoulder to shoulder."

Chapter Nine

A MOMENTOUS JOURNEY

May what you are at have the success which courage and imagination deserve.

FIELD MARSHAL DILL TO
WINSTON CHURCHILL
1st August, 1942

EVER SINCE his return from America Brooke had been longing to go to the Middle East to see for himself what was wrong. He was the head of the Army, responsible to the Government for its conduct and efficiency in the field, and now, for the third time since he had assumed charge of its affairs, it had suffered a major defeat. In the one theatre of war where it had been actively engaged since the debacle of Singapore and Burma, it had lost the bulk of its armour and been driven back for four hundred miles, with the result that the Nile Delta and the Canal were in imminent danger at the moment that a new threat was developing from the north against the oilfields on which the whole Middle East, as well as India, depended. Whether the cause of the Desert Army's failure lay in its leaders, its equipment or its morale, it was hard to decide at a distance of thirteen thousand miles by sea and four thousand by air. And though a continuous stream of men and armour—despatched earlier at Brooke's instance—was on its way round the Cape to reinforce it, he was gravely disquieted. ' It was quite clear,' he wrote, ' that something was radically wrong but not easy at a distance to judge what this something was, nor how far wrong it was. . . . The crisis had now come and it was essential that I should go out to see what was wrong. But for this I wanted to be alone.'[1]

[1] *Notes on My Life*, VI, 430.

431

The thought of his mission had been constantly in Brooke's mind while he waited for the Americans and during their visit to London. Three days before they arrived, on July 15th, he obtained the Prime Minister's leave to go, finding him " in a very pleasant mood " as they sat together discussing the war in the garden of 10 Downing Street. ' I had by then learnt,' he wrote, ' that if you wanted to get Winston's agreement to something, you might have to wait several days for a propitious moment. To ask at the wrong moment was to court disaster. Once you had received a negative reply it was almost impossible to get him to alter his verdict. I had been waiting for days, very precious days, to ask him if I might go to the Middle East on my own. I knew that the odds would be heavily against getting his sanction. That he would say he could not spare me, whilst in the back of his mind the real reason would be that he would hate me to go off on my own without him. . . . Meanwhile the situation in the Middle East was not improving; and the Auk was suggesting giving the Eighth Army to Corbett. It was essential that I should go out to see for myself what was really wrong. . . . Fortunately, that lovely evening sitting in the garden of 10 Downing Street I found him in one of his amenable moods. I jumped in at once and, to my joy, got his approval.'

The moment, therefore, the Americans left, Brooke made his preparations for an immediate start. In addition to probing the Middle East and Desert Commands he wished to assure himself about three other matters: the readiness of Gibraltar to serve as a base for operations against French North Africa; the defence of Malta; and the ability of the small and scattered British forces in Persia and Iraq to protect the oilfields if the Russian front in the Caucasus collapsed. He wanted, too, if there was time, to go on to India to discuss this last problem— the most pressing of all at that moment—and the defence of the Burmese frontier with its Commander-in-Chief, General Wavell. For all these reasons he decided to fly by the shortest and most dangerous route, crossing the whole length of the Mediterranean and calling at Malta where the garrison and its gallant Governor, Lord Gort, were fast nearing the end of their resources. It meant taking risks, for engine failure anywhere over the hundreds of miles of sea controlled by the enemy would entail certain capture or death.

But on July 30th, the day before he was due to leave, Brooke learnt, at the Chiefs of Staff morning committee that the Prime Minister had decided to go to Cairo too. Immediately after the meeting he was summoned to his presence and told the reasons for this sudden change of plan. A few days earlier he had found him deeply depressed at the Eighth Army's failure to drive the enemy back from Alamein, " pouring out questions as to why the Auk could not have done this or that." Now, faced by a further failure of the tired, punch-drunk Army to dislodge Rommel from his position at the gates of Egypt and by the realisation that months might elapse before another offensive was staged, the Prime Minister's impatience with what he regarded as the inexplicable inertia of Middle East Command had become uncontrollable. Only his presence, he felt, could galvanise it into reversing the decision of Knightsbridge and recovering the initiative. Instead, therefore, of waiting for the C.I.G.S.'s report and then following him out by the safe but longer air-route across West and Equatorial Africa, he proposed to set off within the next few days and, flying straight from Gibraltar across the North African desert, reach Cairo at the same time.

There was another reason for the Prime Minister's decision. With the swift German sweep across the southern Steppes towards the Volga and the Caspian, the Russian demand for a Second Front was growing every day more insistent, and the British Ambassador was urging the need for immediate personal contact with the Kremlin at the highest level. With his habitual courage Churchill felt that he ought to break the unwelcome news to Stalin in person and explain the reasons for the substitution of " Torch " for " Sledgehammer." He had therefore cabled the Russian dictator that morning, proposing that he and the C.I.G.S. should meet him as soon as they had finished their business in Cairo. It meant an end to Brooke's hopes of going to India and of forming calm, unhurried judgments about the Middle East Command before making his recommendations. He would now have to take decisions affecting the whole future of the war with his impetuous master at his elbow. ' *L'homme propose*,' he wrote, ' *et Dieu dispose*.'[1]

Late that night, after the Prime Minister had kept him up till 1 a.m. discussing the details of his journey and his plan for disguising himself at Gibraltar with a grey beard, Brooke made the last entry in the sixth of the little lock-up pocket-books in which he kept his diary. " Shall start new book to-morrow," he wrote, " as I dare not risk being caught with this one should we be caught or crash." A few hours later he presided at the usual morning Chiefs of Staff meeting and gave his final instructions at the War Office. The story of the journey on which he set out that evening is told in his diary and auto-biographical notes.

" *July 31st* 1942, *Portreath. 300 miles—1¾ hours*. . . . At 5.30 p.m. left for Hendon with Adam and Peter ' (Dunphie) '. There we found Cranborne[2] and Achieson. The latter two were to come with us to Malta. We were given a Flamingo and had a very good flight down to Portreath in Cornwall where we arrived about 7.45 p.m. We were given a good dinner, and I am now off to bed for a few hours' sleep before taking off for Gib. at 2 a.m. to-morrow morning. It is a most lovely night and I don't feel inclined to go to sleep."

' Adam, the Adjutant-General, was coming along with me to Cairo, and from there we were to have gone on to India together, but now the new Moscow plans had upset these plans and we were destined to part in Cairo.'

" *August 1st.   Gibraltar.   1500 miles—7 hours*. After a doubtful two hours' sleep, called and given breakfast at 1.30 a.m. We then embarked and by 2 a.m. were off into the darkness. I did not sleep over well as plane was very noisy. At a few minutes before 9 a.m. we saw tops of mountains sticking up out of a sea of clouds. Shortly afterwards clouds cleared and the ' Rock ' was visible before us. We flew round it once, ... which was interesting. Mason-

---

[1] *Notes on My Life*, VI, 452.

[2] Viscount Cranborne, Secretary of State for the Colonies, now Marquess of Salisbury.

MacFarlane[1] and his staff met us on landing. Bath and breakfast after which I toured defences and tunnels with Mason-Mac. Large lunch with Admiral, Air Marshal, etc., after which another tour of defences till tea. We then went out in the motor launch and did a tour of the ' Rock ' by sea. All most interesting. Tremendous tunnelling work has been accomplished since beginning of war. Practically all stores, hospitals, distilleries, ammunition and accommodation for garrison has been tunnelled out of the main rock. In addition a full-size lorry road connecting the east and west sides of the ' Rock.' "

" After dinner we were given a demonstration of barrage A.A. fire and searchlights. Finally emplaned at 11 p.m. and slid off into the dark."

' For the next hop it was essential to reach Malta before dawn, otherwise there were chances of being shot down by Italian fighters. Dill and Eden on their way to Greece had missed the island, overshot it and had to turn back to find it, only reaching it just in time. I was specially anxious to visit Gort in Malta as I knew he was in a depressed state, feeling that he had been shoved away in a corner out of the real war and in danger of his whole garrison being scuppered without much chance of giving an account of themselves. His depression had been increased by the fact that he insisted on living on the reduced standard of rations prevailing in the island in spite of the fact that he was doing twice as much physical and mental work as any other member of the garrison. Owing to the shortage of petrol he was using a bicycle in that sweltering heat, and frequently had to carry his bicycle over demolished houses.'

' I wanted to tell him about the plans for new Command in the Middle East with an advance westward, combined with American-British landing in North-west Africa moving eastward, destined to meet eventually. I wanted to make him feel that if all this came off he would find himself in an outpost of an advance instead of the backwater he considered himself in. I felt certain that to be able to look forward to something definite would do much to dispel his gloom.'

[1] Lt.-Gen. Sir Frank Noel Mason-MacFarlane, Governor of Gibraltar.

Had Brooke known the secrets of the German General Staff, he would have had even more to tell his old chief about the island's part in the overall strategy of the war. For that spring it had been agreed by Hitler and Mussolini that Malta was to be invaded from Sicily by four airborne divisions, two of them German, with a seaborne expedition guarded by the Italian Fleet as soon as the bridgehead had been secured. This operation had been planned for July, but, after the capture of Tobruk, Hitler had postponed it till September on the ground that it would involve needless loss if, as then seemed probable, Rommel could capture Egypt and the Canal without it.[1] The fight put up by the British in Crete a year earlier was still vivid in his memory and he shrank from the risks and sacrifices of another operation over the sea. Like most Germans, his strategic outlook was continental and, despite the entreaties of his admirals, he failed to grasp the close connection between Malta and the battle Rommel was preparing to wage for the Nile Delta. It was because Churchill and the British Chiefs of Staff were so well aware of it that at that moment the Admiralty was preparing to send a major fleet into the western Mediterranean to fight a convoy through to Valetta at all costs.

" *August 2nd. Malta. 1250 miles—6½ hours.* A very comfortable smooth flight. I had borrowed ear-plugs from Mason-Mac. to drown noise of engines which I found affected my ears during previous night's flight. I slept on and off and was snoozing properly when I woke to find the plane bumping badly and thought something had gone wrong till I realized that we were landing in Malta in the dark. It was just before dawn. Gort had sent Munster (his A.D.C.) to meet us, and Park, the Air Officer Commanding, was there also. We drove up to Gort's house where we had some tea and then went off to bed for a four hours' sleep till 10 a.m. Then discussed business with Gort till lunch. Told him of future plans in Africa which interested him very much."

" For lunch Park and Leatham, the Admiral, came, also

[1] Shulman, *Defeat in the West*, 59-60.

Beckett, the Commander Royal Artillery.[1] After lunch went down to the docks and to Valetta. The destruction is inconceivable and reminds me of Ypres, Arras, Lens, at their worst during the last war. We travelled about in Admiral's barge and examined wrecks of last convoy. Finally examined new dock workshops which have been mined into the rock. Had tea with the Admiral in charge of docks. Five air-raid alarms during the day, but no serious bombing. Finally at 10.45 p.m., just as we were about to start, a German plane came over but did not remain."

'It had been a very hot and tiring day, all the more so after a hard day in Gib. and two nights' flying without much sleep, sitting up with a wooden box between my legs. The visit had been well worth while and, I think, brought a new hope to Gort. The conditions prevailing in Malta at that time were distinctly depressing, to put it mildly. Shortage of rations, shortage of petrol, a hungry population that rubbed their tummies looking at Gort as he went by, destruction and ruin of docks, loss of convoys just as they approached the island, and the continual possibility of an attack . . . without much hope of help or reinforcements.'

That evening, while Brooke was waiting to fly the twelve hundred miles from Malta to Egypt, the Prime Minister, who had left England with the Permanent Secretary to the Foreign Office[2] eighteen hours earlier, was heading south-east from Gibraltar towards French North Africa escorted by four long-range fighters. Operation " Bracelet," as his mission was called, had gravely alarmed the sixty-seven-year-old statesman's colleagues and medical advisers, but no one had been able to withstand his determination to go. Beneath the two American Liberators that bore him and his entourage towards Cairo and distant Moscow lay the barren, mountainous land that he and his allies had committed themselves to surprise and conquer. Presently, in Churchill's words, " darkness cast her shroud over the harsh landscape," and the Liberators, parting from their

[1] Air Chief Marshal Sir Keith Park, Admiral Sir Ralph Leatham and Major-General C. T. Beckett.
[2] The Rt. Hon. Sir Alexander Cadogan.

escorts, turned eastwards on their flight across the African desert. About the same hour Brooke resumed his journey:

> "*August 3rd. Cairo. 1250 miles—7½ hours.* We took off into the dark at 11 p.m. and had a very peaceful journey in spite of the fact that we ran right down "Bombers' Alley" between Crete and Cyrenaica. We flew at between eight to ten thousand feet as on the previous days. Just as the day was breaking we struck the mouth of the Delta just east of Alexandria and flew inland to look for an aerodrome on Alexandria-Cairo road. Unfortunately we struck a low blanket of clouds and could not get down for an hour, during which time we flew round in the morning sunshine over a sea of clouds. I had not slept much as my legs were rather cramped. . . ."

> " Finally we descended at about 6.30 a.m. and found a large gathering on the aerodrome awaiting P.M. who was due shortly.[1] Miles Lampson, Casey, Tedder, naval captain, Chief of General Staff, and Lindsell. We did not wait for P.M. but drove in the 25 kilometres to Cairo and the Embassy where I had a shave, bath and breakfast. P.M. then turned up delighted with his trip and looking remarkably fresh. He has got his doctor with him[2] who tells me he was a little worried about his pulse."

> " Went over to G.H.Q. after breakfast and had a long talk with Corbett, the Chief of General Staff. . . . Also had a long talk with Messervy, who was interesting on recent fighting. At lunch Smuts turned up having flown up from Pretoria. He was astounding good value and full of wit in answering P.M.'s remarks."

> " After lunch snatched three-quarters of an hour's sleep before going to meet Auchinleck, who was coming back from the front. Had a short talk with him before attending one of his C.-in-C. meetings. At 5.30 p.m. he

[1] Having struck the Nile near El Fayum, sixty miles to the south of Cairo, the Prime Minister's plane was approaching from the opposite direction. "There in the pale glimmering dawn," he wrote of that morning, " the endless winding silver ribbon of the Nile stretched joyously before us. Often had I seen the day break on the Nile. . . . Never had the glint of daylight on its waters been so welcome to me." *Churchill*, IV, 412. Sir Winston is mistaken in supposing it was on the 4th of August that he reached Egypt; it was Monday the 3rd.

[2] Sir Charles Wilson, now Lord Moran.

came over to the Embassy and we had a long interview with the P.M., after which he (the P.M.) called me in for further talks. He is fretting that there is to be no offensive action till September 15th, and I see already troublesome times ahead."

" After dinner, when I was dropping with sleepiness (I had had three sleepless nights sitting in the plane and two hard days in Gib. and Malta) P.M. again called me in and kept me up till 1.30 a.m. Back to the same arguments that Auk must come back to the Command of Middle East and leave the Eighth Army. Exactly what I have always told him from the start. Then he argued strongly for Gott to take over, whilst I know that Gott is very tired. Finally suggested that I should take it over. . . ."

' It is interesting to note that Winston was already selecting Gott without having seen him. Personally, I knew Gott very well indeed and had the highest opinion of him. He had been Second-in-Command to " Bubbles " Barker in the battalion of the 60th K.R.R. attached to Aldershot Armoured Brigade when I commanded the 1st Mobile Division. He was a brilliant commander, but had been in the Desert since before the beginning of the war and was beginning to feel the effects of it. He was no longer as fresh as he might be. . . . I did not feel, therefore, that Gott, in his present state was the man to instil a new spirit of self-confidence in the Eighth Army. It would require someone like Montgomery, bounding with self-confidence and capable of instilling this confidence to all those under his command. At any rate, I wanted to see Gott for myself to find out how tired he was before putting him down definitely as unfit for the Eighth Army.'

' Winston's suggestion that I should take over the Eighth Army personally gave rise to the most desperate longings . . . . I had tasted the thrill of commanding a formation in war whilst commanding II Corps in France. For sheer thrill and freedom of action it stood in a category by itself and not to be compared with a staff appointment. . . .'

" *August 4th.* Met Auchinleck at 9 a.m. and had a short

talk with him before proceeding to attend a joint Commanders-in-Chiefs' conference with him, Tedder and the Admiral. We discussed the relative importance of Egypt as opposed to Abadan, and all agreed that the latter's importance was paramount. Then returned to the Embassy at 12 noon to have an hour with Smuts at which we discussed the relief of South African Brigade from Madagascar at the earliest possible date, the transformation of South African Division to armour, and the situation here. He has a good opinion of the Auk, but considers that he selects his subordinates badly and that several changes are desirable. Most of the changes he suggested coincided with my own views. He is the most delightful old man with a wonderfully clear brain."

" I then lunched at the Mohammed Ali Club with the Auk, Tedder and the Admiral. . . . After lunch returned to G.H.Q. for long discussion with the Auk. A most useful one. I fortunately found that he was in agreement as to the necessary changes:

(*a*) New Commander for Eighth Army—Montgomery.
(*b*) New Chief General Staff to be selected *vice* Corbett.
(*c*) "Jumbo" Wilson[1] too old and to be replaced by Gott.
(*d*) Quinan . . . . to be replaced by Anderson.

These changes should lead to improvements, but I must still pass them through the P.M. and there will be the difficulty."

' The relative importance of Egypt as opposed to Abadan was a subject to which I had given a great deal of thought. All the motive-power at sea, on land and in the air throughout the Middle East, Indian Ocean and India was entirely dependent on the oil from Abadan. If we lost this supply, it could not be made good from American resources owing to shortage of tankers and continuous losses of these ships through submarine action. If we lost the Persian oil, we inevitably lost Egypt, command of the Indian Ocean and endangered the whole Indian-Burma situation.'

[1] General Sir Henry Maitland (now Field Marshal Lord) Wilson, G.O.C. Ninth Army.

The diary for August 4th continued:

"Came back to Embassy at 5.45 p.m. for large conference under P.M. attended by Smuts, Auchinleck, Wavell, the Admiral, Tedder, Casey, Jacob and self. P.M. reviewed the whole situation and explained plans for offensive in North Africa with Americans and its relation to Western attack in Middle East. On the whole he was fairly sound in most of his arguments. Finally he cross-questioned Auchinleck as to probable date of his offensive. I could see that he did not approve of his replies. He is again pressing for an attack before Auchinleck can possibly get ready. I find him almost impossible to argue with on this point. Conference lasted two and three-quarter hours. Just had time to rush off for a bath before 9 p.m. dinner."

"After dinner I was dragged off into the garden by P.M. to report results of my day's work. As I expected, my work was not approved of. Montgomery could not possibly arrive in time to hurry on the date of the attack. I told him no one else could. He then pressed for Gott. I told him that I had discussed him with Auchinleck who did not consider him up to it, and also that he was too tired. I then told him about the project for moving Wilson as too old. He then said I was failing to make use of two of the best men; Gott and Wilson. He then said that he knew neither of them but that Eden had told him so. I got level with him this time by suggesting that it was not astonishing that Eden should select old 'Green Jacket' officers! This went home all right and he saw the logic of it and was very nice."

"However, he kept me arguing till 1 a.m. and we have got to get up at 4.45 a.m. to-morrow. Moscow party is growing, Wavell is coming and probably Harriman."

' The day had been a fruitful one, and the various talks I had had assisted in clearing my mind. . . . The talk with Smuts had been most instructive. . . . I had been surprised that the Auk was prepared to accept Monty in command of Eighth Army. I had expected some opposition, but I felt some very serious doubts as to whether an Auk-Monty combination would work. I felt that the Auk would interfere too much with Monty; would ride him on too tight a rein, and would consequently be liable to put him out of his stride. As I was very anxious to place Monty in command of the Eighth Army, I felt this might necessitate moving the Auk to some other command. . . .'

' Jumbo Wilson I knew intimately. We had sat at neighbouring desks at the Staff College in 1919. I was well aware of his exceptional ability, but had heard from all sides that he was showing signs of ageing and had lost his drive. I had been misinformed and should not have attached such importance to rumours. Luckily I discovered my mistake in time and made full use of him during remainder of the war.'

" *August 5th. 250 miles. 1½ hours flying.* Was called at 4.45 a.m. and had early breakfast to admit of a start at 5.45 a.m. with P.M. and his doctor from Heliopolis aerodrome. There we emplaned for Burg el Arab aerodrome (about twenty miles west of Alexandria). P.M. in great form in spite of early start. We were met at aerodrome by Auchinleck, Tedder and Coningham, Air Officer Commanding.[1] The Auk took the P.M. in his car, and I travelled with Tedder and Coningham. We drove right up to El Alamein where we met the Australian and South African Divisional Commanders. We then motored back along the road when Australians came to meet the P.M. They all seemed delighted to meet him."

" We then motored on to Eighth Army H.Q. where the Auk gave us a light breakfast, and we also met Gott, Briggs commanding 5th Indian Division, and Inglis commanding the New Zealand Division as Freyberg is still wounded. After breakfast P.M. started for home, and I stopped on to continue my trip. . . . I then went on . . . . for a further tour. We started down the famous central ridge on which such heavy fighting has taken place recently. Lunched with Briggs at 5th Indian Division H.Q. It was he who commanded the brigade that fought its way out of Benghazi."

[1] Air Vice-Marshal—later Air-Marshal Sir—Arthur Coningham.

" From there I motored south to Gott's H.Q. and had a useful talk with him. There is no doubt that a rest home would do him a lot of good, and I do not feel that he would yet be ready to take over the Eighth Army. He requires more experience. However, I do not know what opinion the P.M. formed of him and how much he will press for him instead of Monty."

" I then motored back to Eighth Army H.Q. where I had tea with the Auk. It has been an interesting day. I was impressed by the dispersal which the air forces on the Army, with all its evil consequences as regards maintenance and control. The lack of any real bold features also surprised me; I had expected that the various ridges would be more marked. It is a strange life that this Army leads in the desert, but the men look fit and hard. I was much impressed by the beauty of the turquoise blue of the Mediterranean. The colour is caused by the specially white sand along this coast line."

" Left the Auk about 5 p.m. and motored back to Burg el Arab, where I emplaned again for Heliopolis. On the aerodrome I found Adam, who had come down to settle plans for to-morrow. Again a late night with bed only after 1 a.m."

' My interview with Gott had confirmed my suspicions, but not until I had nearly finished my tour with him and we had discussed every kind of topic. It was not till we were sitting at tea together that he began to open out his heart to me. He said, " I think what is required out here is some new blood. I have tried most of my ideas on the *boche*. We want someone with new ideas and plenty of confidence in them." I knew Gott well enough to know that he would never talk about having " tried most of his ideas " unless he was tired and had temporarily lost some of his drive. This confirmed my opinion that he was probably not the man to lead the Eighth Army in an offensive to turn the tide of the war. It was going to be very difficult to convince Winston and Smuts that Gott was tired. From all the enquiries both had made they had been informed on all sides that Gott was the man for the Eighth Army.[1] Personally I had a strong feeling that Montgomery was far better qualified for the job. This conviction was, however, not strong enough to insist that at all costs Monty should be appointed instead of Gott. I was prepared to press as strongly as I could and to leave it at that. It is not easy to be absolutely certain between the relative qualifications of two very able commanders.'

"*August 6th. Cairo.* One of the most difficult days of my life, with momentous decisions to take as far as my own future and the War was concerned. Whilst I was dressing and practically naked, the P.M. suddenly burst into my room. Very elated, and informed me that his thoughts were taking shape and that he would soon commit himself to paper. I rather shuddered and wondered what he was up to!"

"Ten minutes later he burst into my room again and invited me to breakfast with him. However, as I was in the middle of my breakfast by then, he asked me to come along to his bedroom as soon as I had finished. . . . When I went round he made me sit on the sofa whilst he walked up and down. First of all, he said, he had decided to split the Middle East Command in two. A Near East taking up to the Canal, and a Middle East taking Syria, Palestine, Persia and Iraq. I argued with him again that the Canal was an impossible boundary as both Palestine and Syria are based administratively on Egypt. He partially agreed, and then went on to say that he intended to remove the Auk to the Persian-Iraq Command as he had lost confidence in him. And he wanted me to take over the Near East Command with Montgomery as my Eighth Army Commander. This made my heart race very fast! He said he did not require an answer at once, and that I could think it over if I wanted. However, I told him without waiting that I was quite certain it would be a wrong

[1] "Only Gott remained of the original men, and he stood out like a giant in this bitter, thankless fighting, the one great name left on the British side, the one man who had survived death, capture or major error. . . . He was the last of the old desert rats to go. He was a great man for England." Alan Moorhead, *A Year of Battle*, 247, 252.

move. . . . Another point which I did not mention was that, after working with the P.M. for close on nine months, I do feel at last that I can exercise a limited amount of control on some of his activities and that at last he is beginning to take my advice. I feel, therefore, that, tempting as the offer is, by accepting it I should definitely be taking a course which would on the whole help the war the least. Finally, I could not bear the thought that Auchinleck might think that I had come out here on purpose to work myself into his shoes."

' I could not put the real reasons to Winston. . . . Whether I exercised any control or not, I knew by now the dangers to guard against. I had discovered the perils of his impetuous nature. I was now familiar with his method of suddenly arriving at some decision as it were by intuition without any kind of logical examination of the problem. I had, after many failures, discovered the best methods of approaching him. I knew that it would take at least six months for any successor, taking over from me, to become as familiar with him and his ways. During those six months anything might happen.'

' I would not suggest that I could exercise any real control over him. I never met anybody that could, but he had grown to have confidence in me, and I had found that he was listening more and more to any advice I gave him. These considerations stood out clearly in my mind and played the major part in forming my decision. They were reasons which I could not put before Winston. I had therefore to rely on other arguments such as my lack of knowledge of desert warfare. I should, however, have been ready to chance this shortcoming and do not believe that it would have rendered me unfit for the appointment.'

The diary entry continued:

" P.M. was not pleased with this reply, but accepted it well."

" At 10.30 a.m. we had a meeting with P.M., Lindsell, Adam and Corbett to examine details concerning the

" tail " of the Army. It was not a happy meeting, and he rather lost his temper with Corbett before it was over. Smuts attended. After the meeting I took Adam, Lindsell and Corbett on to the lawn to decide action to take to meet P.M.'s requirements."

" After lunch Smuts asked if he could see me for a bit, and we retired to a quiet room. He then started on the same story as the P.M. in the morning, telling me what importance he attached to my taking it (the Command of Near Middle East), and what a wonderful future it would have for me if I succeeded in defeating Rommel. I repeated exactly what I had said to P.M. Thanked him for his kindness and told him that he really did not know me well enough to be so assured I could make a success of it. However, he answered that he knew I had taken a leading part in saving the B.E.F. in France. At last I got him to agree that Alexander was a better selection than me."

" I have been giving it a great deal of thought all day and am *quite* convinced that my decision was a right one, and that I can do more by remaining C.I.G.S."

" Then went round to G.H.Q. where I had interviews with Lumsden, Freyberg and " Jumbo" Wilson. Then on to an Adjutant General's meeting to lay down policy for amalgamation of units owing to the shortage of reinforcements. Whilst there was sent for by the P.M. to meet him and Smuts and to read their final decision. The telegram was to the War Cabinet, recommending a splitting of the Middle East into Near East and Middle East. Auk to vacate the former and take over the latter. Alexander to take over Near East, Gott to take over the Eighth Army. Ramsden to leave, Quinan to leave, Corbett and Dorman-Smith also to go. Considering everything, this is perhaps the best solution. I accepted it. Alexander is to fly out at once to take over . . . . and for us to see him before we leave for Moscow."

" Went back to G.H.Q. and gave talk on world situation. After that had half-hour with Casey.[1] Then back here for

---

[1] The Rt. Hon. Richard Casey, Minister of State, Middle East.

bath and another interview with P.M. to see his last telegram."

' As I had written that evening in my diary, it had been
one of the most difficult days in my life, and one with
devastating heart-burnings. I had been offered the finest
Command I could ever hope for and I had turned it down.
During the last nine months with Winston I had repeatedly
longed to be my own master, to escape from the terrific
burden of C.I.G.S. work in war, and to return to the open
air again to exercise command in the field. And now I had
had my chance to fulfil these wishes and I had turned down
this chance. I knew my decision was a right one, and that
was some consolation, but it fell far short of soothing the
bitter despair that I felt that night.'

' It had been difficult turning it down when Winston
offered it, but I felt I must do so at once. If I took time for
my decision I might not retain the strength of character to
resist. . . . It had been hard to resist Winston's pressure, but
it was doubly difficult to resist that of Smuts. I was a
tremendous admirer of his, and any word he spoke carried
immense weight with me. He could not have been more
charming and painted a wonderful picture of the great field
that lay open to me if I accepted: I had an opportunity of
turning the tide of the war and of my name going down to
posterity as the man who had played the major part in
leading our Forces towards final victory. He said he was
confident from what he had seen and heard about me that
I was capable of leading the Middle East Forces to victory.
I must confess that whilst listening to him . . . my resolutions
of the morning were shaken. For a few moments I hesitated
and then, thank heaven, I remained firm. Looking back I
am certain that my decision, hard as it was, was the right
one and that, by remaining on as C.I.G.S., I was able to
render greater services to my country than if I had accepted
the more attractive alternative. I had many heart-gnawing
regrets, but at any rate the satisfaction of feeling that I had
chosen the right course. There is no doubt in my mind that
Winston never realized what this decision cost me. . . . '

' The split of the Middle East Command was one I had been pressing for for some time, but not for a boundary on the Suez Canal. Such a split was quite unsuitable. In addition to the administrative consideration, strategically Syria, the Lebanon and Palestine formed part of Egypt's eastern flank of defence against any advance through the Caucasus or Turkey. The case of Iraq and Persia was quite different. There lay the oil, and consequently all the motive-power for Middle East, Indian Ocean and India. Up to the present, as no threat had existed on this flank, both Iraq and Persia were the poor brethren in the Middle East family. The situation was now changing and the Germans were in the Caucasus, but a readjustment of outlook is a slow process. Cairo was seriously threatened by Rommel on the west, and any dangers on the east seemed more nebulous and distant. And yet of the two the oil was by far the more important strategic objective. . . . We may thank Heaven that Hitler failed to appreciate its importance and threw away forces at Stalingrad which might have played a far more decisive rôle had they been directed on Persia and Iraq. These considerations had convinced me that Iraq and Persia must be detached from the Middle East and given a separate Commander whose sole preoccupation would be the security of the oil.'

'. . . This memorable day finished with my agreement with Winston's wire to the Cabinet. Most of it was entirely in accordance with the advice I had given him. The only major point in which it varied was in the appointment of Gott instead of Montgomery to the Eighth Army. I had very serious misgivings concerning Gott's appointment in his tired state, but was not at that time sufficiently convinced of the degree of this disadvantage to oppose the appointment. I may have been weak; in any case Fate took the matter in its hands within twenty-four hours of our decision.'

" *August 7th. Cairo.* Spent most of the morning with Wavell discussing various problems connected with India, and getting his advice on the situations which we are faced with here. At 12 noon P.M. sent for me to see reply from

Cabinet to his wire concerning changes. They are quibbling at the split in the Command. Their arguments were not very conclusive, and we were able to deal with them fairly easily. Spent afternoon with Adam and Wavell and in interviews with Corbett and Dorman-Smith."

" Just as I was starting for home for dinner I received the news that Gott had been killed this afternoon, being shot down whilst flying back from Burg el Arab. A very hard blow coming on top of all the planning we had been doing. He was one of our linch pins. I do feel frightfully sad for Mrs. Gott."

. . . He was flying back on the Burg el Arab-Heliopolis route, considered so safe that no escort had been found necessary for Winston when we flew out. It happened to be an individual German plane driven out of the high altitudes in combat and dashing home in the lower altitudes. It came across the slow transport plane on its way and shot it down in flames. . . .'

' Looking back on those days with the knowledge of what occurred at Alamein and after it, I cannot but feel that the whole course of the war might have been altered if Gott had been in command of the Eighth Army. In his tired condition I do not think that he would have had the energy and vitality to stage and fight this battle as Monty did. It might well have resulted in stalemate on this front, a failure to achieve a turn in the tide, possibly resulting in a further failure to unite British and American Forces in North Africa.'

" After dinner, P.M., Smuts and I had a conference as to how the matter should be settled. I pressed for Montgomery to replace Gott. Had some difficulty; P.M. rather in favour of Wilson. However, Smuts assisted me, and telegram has now been sent off to Cabinet ordering Montgomery out to take command of Eighth Army. I hope I may get Alexander and Montgomery out soon, so that I may settle details of Corps Commanders and Chiefs of Staff with them."

"Harriman[1] arrived to-day together with some Russians. They are to accompany us to Moscow. Also Maxwell, the American General, is to join us. . . . I am longing to finish tying up this front and to get on to Russia, and am having rather a job to keep the P.M. on the move."

' Matters were now settled as I wanted, with Alex in command of Middle East and Monty with Eighth Army. I knew both of them well and felt certain that this combination should work well. It now remained to find a successor . . . as Chief of Staff. I at once thought of Dick McCreery, whom I had sent out to the Auk as his Adviser on Armoured Forces. . . . I knew his ability well and I also knew that he had acted as G.S.O.1. of the 1st Division. . . . I therefore decided to suggest him to Alex as soon as he arrived. . . .'

The news had still to be broken to Auchinleck that he was to be relieved of his command—at that moment, after the post of C.I.G.S., the most important in the Army. For all concerned it was an intensely distasteful decision. Everyone admired him as a man of the highest character and splendid talents. But though, when he had taken command himself, he had twice saved the Eighth Army from disaster, his subordinates' ill co-ordinated attempts to solve the problems of a mechanized Desert campaign had resulted in neglect of the cardinal principal of war—concentration. Divided into small detachments and without an adequate striking reserve or " mass of manœuvre," the Desert Army had been defeated in detail by a more decisive and ruthless commander who never dispersed his forces and made a point of keeping them, and above all, his armour, under his immediate control. It was this even more than deficiencies in tank construction and superior German guns and front-line workshops that had caused the repeated failure of Britain's hopes in the Desert. It was this that made Churchill stride up and down his room in the Embassy at Cairo crying, " Rommel, Rommel, Rommel! What else matters but beating him! " For all its courage, the Eighth Army had lost confidence in its leaders and, as a result, in its capacity for victory,

---

[1] Averell Harriman, President Roosevelt's Special Representative in Great Britain and Chairman of President's Special Mission to U.S.S.R.

and had come to see its adversary as an invincible figure who was bound, almost as though by magic, to get the better of it.

It was time to break that spell. It was to do so that the Prime Minister and Alan Brooke had come to Egypt.

"*August 8th.* I was called early to go round to P.M.'s bedroom as he had received reply from Cabinet. They had now agreed, rather reluctantly, to splitting of Command, but disliked nomenclature. Middle East Command should remain Middle East Command, and new one to be called Persia-Iraq Command. Perhaps they are right. However, Montgomery was fixed and his replacement by K. Anderson was settled.[1] Jacob was then sent off with P.M.'s letter to Auchinleck and instructed to bring back a reply.[2] P.M. and I, with Harriman, then accompanied Dick McCreery in a visit to 8th, 9th and 24th Armoured Brigades. All of them awaiting issue of tanks. Fine lot of men looking very fit. . . ."

" Returned here at 2.30 p.m. late for a large lunch attended by three of our Russian friends who are to accompany us on our journey to Moscow. I had a long talk to the Russian general after lunch. Then back to office to tell Wavell most recent developments, and on to the U.S.A. G.H.Q., where I met General Maxwell and was given a full account with films of their recent survey of the trans-African route."

" Back to Embassy to see Jacob and P.M. Result Auchinleck refuses new appointment and prefers retirement. . . ."

". . . Back to Embassy again to receive a long lecture from the P.M., with all his pet theories as to how essential it is for Alex to command both Middle East and Eighth Army. I again had to give him a long discourse

---

[1] As Commander of 1st Army for " Torch."

[2] " I felt," wrote Jacob, " as if I were just going to murder an unsuspecting friend. After offering the condolences of the Prime Minister and C.I.G.S. on the death of General Gott, I handed the C.-in-C. the letter I had brought. He opened it and read it through two or three times in silence. He did not move a muscle and remained outwardly calm and in complete control of himself. . . . I could not have admired more the way General Auchinleck received me and his attitude throughout. A great man and fighter." Sir Ian Jacob, *Diary*, 8th August, 1942.

on the system of the chain of command in the Army. I fear that it did not sink much deeper than it has before. . . ."

' I had for some time tried to make Winston understand the military chain of command in the Middle East, and the fact that the Commander-in-Chief Middle East was responsible for all Middle East fronts, bases, administration, inter-Service contacts and local political considerations and came directly under the orders of the Chiefs of Staff, whilst the Commander of Eighth Army was responsible for the handling of forces allotted to him by Commander-in-Chief Middle East for use in the Desert against German and Italian forces and remained responsible to the C.-in-C., M.E. I certainly did not want Winston to suggest to Alex that he was to command the Eighth Army direct as well as Middle East. This would upset the chain of command and confuse the control . . . and I did not want Alex to be encouraged to interfere with Monty.'

" *August 9th. Cairo.* Had settled to breakfast with P.M. on his terrace at 8.30 a.m. At 7.15 a.m. his valet (Sawyers) called me to inform me that the P.M. was awake and wanted to know when I should breakfast. I replied 8.30 a.m. as settled. The valet was horrified and replied, ' But, Sir Alan, the Prime Minister likes to breakfast when he wakes up! ' I replied that, if that was so, I regretted that he would have to breakfast alone, as I intended to breakfast at 8.30 and turned round for another snooze."

" At 8.30 I went round. He had finished but bore me no ill-will. We were expecting Alexander, and I badly wanted to see him before the P.M. got hold of him, and had instructed for him to be brought round to my room. Unfortunately he arrived while I was having breakfast on verandah. The P.M.'s flag-lieutenant whispered in my ear that he had arrived, but P.M. overheard and had then to be told that Alex had gone off to the lavatory! Finally I got an opportunity and dashed out to see him. I wanted to warn him as regards the P.M.'s conception of the Command of the Middle East as opposed to that of the

Eighth Army which he mixes together. I then brought Alex in to P.M. and we had a long talk, after which I had a long go with Alex by himself. . . ."

" *August 10th.* Breakfast with Alex on the terrace, P.M. keeping us company. Then call from the Auk to G.H.Q. . . . Came back here to collect P.M. at 11 a.m. to visit map room at G.H.Q. Interview with Wavell and back to lunch. Visit from Gatehouse[1] at 3.30 p.m.; then sent for Dick McCreery to congratulate him on being Chief of General Staff (to Alex) and to give him a few words of advice. . . . Back to Embassy to discuss transport with P.M. and Lindsell from 5 to 6 p.m. Then Wavell to discuss with P.M. and me the new Iraq-Persia Command and its possible inclusion in India Command."

" Now I have finished packing, as we start off on our new venture to Moscow to-night shortly after midnight."

.   .   .   .   .   .

" *August 11th, 1942. Teheran. 6½ hours—1300 miles.* We left the Residency (Cairo) about midnight and drove out to the aerodrome where we emplaned in three Liberators. P.M. with his doctor and retinue in one. I had with me in my plane Cadogan (of Foreign Office), Wavell, Tedder, Jacob, and one other. We were kept waiting till after 2 a.m. before taking off; why I do not know."

" I had a fair sort of bed rigged up in the bomb-racks and slept pretty well. Unfortunately I had no sort of window and was unable to look out when daylight came. I should have liked to see the Persian mountains."

' The Liberators we were flying in were far from comfortable. We were crammed into the bomb-rack where there was very little head-room and barely room to stretch out. I discovered later in other flights that there was a more comfortable little compartment near the tail where there was more head-room and also windows to look out from. Our party was unnecessarily large, and Winston on these

[1] Major-General A. H. Gatehouse, commanding 10th Armoured Division.

occasions loved to accumulate a large number of Generals, Admirals and Air Marshals. . . .'

" About 8.30 a.m. we landed and drove to the Legation where we washed and had breakfast. We were to have gone on after an hour, but, owing to our late start last night, it became evident that we could only reach Kuibyshev[1] to-night and could not reach Moscow. It was therefore decided that we should spend the day here and leave early to-morrow morning for Moscow. P.M. consequently went off to lunch with the Shah whilst we lunched in the Legation."

" After lunch we came up to a delightful spot in the hills where the Legation staff live. Beautifully cool, trees and a lovely clear stream running through the garden. In the centre of the garden a most beautiful old Persian tent, and almost in the tent a small blue tiled pond of clear water with gold-fish in it. When compared with the surrounding arid country, a real paradise. . . ."

". . . Went down again to Teheran this afternoon for a meeting at 6 p.m. with the P.M., attended by Harriman and several Americans, to discuss advisability of handing over the development of rail and road communications in Persia to the Americans. On the whole, this seems advisable, but we are to make a final decision on returning to Cairo."

' The communications through Persia which we discussed with the Americans were those leading from the Persian Gulf to the Caspian, which constituted the southern supply route to Russia. Both the rail and road communications were very poor and unable to handle all the war-equipment it was desirable to deliver. It seemed a very reasonable share in this general effort that the Americans should take over this task.'

" We were given a most excellent dinner by the Holmans in that most lovely Eastern setting. Sitting under a very

[1] " The German armies were now so near the Caspian that our course was set for Kuibyshev, keeping well away from Stalingrad and the battle area. *Churchill*, IV, 427.

old Persian tent with a lovely blue tiled pool . . . . with roses round it and gold fish swimming about. We started with caviar, and went on with excellent fresh brown trout."

" Early to bed, ready for an early start."

"*August 12th. Teheran. 2½ hours. 400 miles.* Called at 4.45 a.m., breakfast at 5.15 and left the house at 5.30 to emplane by 6 a.m. As a matter of fact, owing to usual delays on the aerodrome, we did not take off till 6.45. After we had taken off I crawled to a rear part of the Liberator from which it is possible to see out, and had a good view of the country. After we had been up for an hour we were told that one of the four engines had gone wrong, and that the adjustable propeller blades were stuck. We had to turn back, and spent a long time cruising round to reduce the overload of petrol before landing. The plane was examined and we were informed we could not go on before to-morrow morning. So back we went to the Legation. We were, on the whole, fortunate as the trouble was a serious one and might have set fire to the plane."

" After lunch I had a first-class sleep and bath, and then tea followed by a walk through bits of Teheran with Cadogan and Archie Wavell. We have now dined and are making for an early bed as we are by way of taking off in a Russian plane at 5 a.m. Our pilot is the Russian who flew over the North Pole, going from Russia to America."

' It had been a disappointing day. I had seen Winston's plane disappearing in the distance as it headed for Moscow while we turned back to Teheran. I did not like seeing him go off out of my sight without knowing how we were going to follow him.'

' Our burning of petrol flying round over Teheran was not all bliss. We had such a heavy load of petrol in order to make Moscow in one hop that we should have crashed our under-carriage had we tried to land. At first it was quite interesting studying the Shah's lovely gardens from the air, and looking down on to the various Embassy grounds. This pleasure began to pall as it became more and more bumpy with the increasing hot-air currents. It was a relief when we finally landed.'

' The night in Teheran, short as it was, was not pleasant, very hot and many sand-flies that penetrated the mosquito net.'

" *August 13th. Moscow. 13 hours. 1800 miles.* Called at 3.30 a.m., breakfast 4 a.m. and off to aerodrome by 4.30 a.m. There we found a very fine Douglas aeroplane beautifully fitted up inside with eight arm-chairs and two couches, also large table. A very nice Russian pilot, interpreter and crew."

' Our Russian pilot was a grand specimen of manhood, about 6 ft. 6 in. tall and proportionately built of fine physique. A perpetual light-hearted smile on his face. We were also to discover that as a pilot he was equally light-hearted. His method of take-off was to fly low to the end of the runway, then to turn with a terrific bank, the inside wing almost cutting the daisies. He then headed back to where we had taken off and made the plane do a flip-flop as a good-bye to his friends.'

" At 5.30 we started off flying for Kazvin, very desolate sandy desert plain with high mountains to the north. At Kazvin we turned north to pass through the mountains and struck the Caspian Sea near Pahlevi—a wonderful change of scenery as we approached the Caspian. Instead of a bare treeless desert and hills one suddenly comes into wooded hills and green fields. A very attractive scenery which looked lovely from the plane. We then followed the west coast of the Caspian Sea till we reached Baku at 8 a.m. Then we landed to have a fill of petrol and took off again at 8.45. It is a bigger place than I had expected, and very interesting seeing all the oil-wells. I am writing in the plane which is bumping about a bit and hence bad writing."

" We flew right up the west coast till we came to the

swamps at the mouth of the Volga. Miles and miles of small lakes and marshes. We finally reached Astrakhan and crossed the Volga north of it. We then again came into miles of marshes followed by a sort of desert. It became unpleasantly bumpy about that time. At 3.15 p.m. we landed at Kuibyshev, the rear capital. We had been expected here for some time and were given a reception on the aerodrome with masses of hors d'œuvres, including caviar and vodka! "

' We had been very fortunate in finding that there was a Russian plane flying back to Moscow ready to take us with them. Having a lower radius of action than the Liberator we had to come down twice for petrol at Baku and Kuibyshev. We flew up the west coast of the Caspian, whilst the route we were to have taken had we flown with Winston was on the right bank. I was very much impressed by the comfort of this Russian plane after the discomfort we had been subjected to in the Liberator.'

' Whilst in Baku our pilot was instructed to fly low under 200 ft. and to hug the line of the coast to avoid any German fighters that might be about, as their troops were now in the centre of the Caucasus. This suited me admirably as we had a wonderful view of that strip of flat ground some ten to twenty miles wide between the Caucasus and the Caspian which provides one of the main lines of advance from Russia into Persia. I was very anxious to see what kind of defences were being erected by the Russians. I did not expect very much. If the burglars are in your house, you are not very likely to take special precautions to prevent them from going into your back yard, even if the road through this yard leads to the grocer, butcher and ironmonger. I had, however, expected to find more than what I saw, which consisted of only one half completed anti-tank ditch, badly revetted and without any covering defences. The work was unfinished. A working party of about a hundred men and two general-service horsed wagons were at work. Beyond that nothing to be seen, not a man, gun, lorry, tank or defence of any kind. In fact the back door seemed wide open for the

Germans to walk through for an attack on the Russian southern supply-route and, more important still, on the vital Middle East oil-supplies of Persia and Iraq.'

' The marshes in the deltas of the Volga made me long to visit them for purposes of photography. I could see white egrets, herons and duck flying about as we skimmed past, flying low. On arriving at Kuibyshev I was very much impressed as we circled round to see all the work that was going on in the way of factory construction. Everywhere new works were springing up out of the ground. When we landed we found a strange reception awaiting us. In one of the aerodrome buildings was a lunch evidently prepared for Winston who had been expected the previous day. The meal had been left in the hope that at any rate we might turn up on the next day to eat it up! The corners of the sandwiches had begun to curl up, the open sardine tins had lost their lustre, and the whole meal had a faded appearance. However, the caviar was good and some of the vodka had to be consumed, a serious risk in view of the bumpiness of the trip.'

The diary for August 13th continues:

" We took off again at 4.15 p.m., flew over the town, crossed the Volga again, and flew over the most lovely forest where I spotted an eagle hovering below. We are now over more open country, but the plane is bumping about a lot. Must stop."

" We finally arrived in Moscow at 8.30 p.m., having been some thirteen hours in the air and fifteen hours travelling."

' As we arrived in Moscow our light-hearted pilot gave vent to his feelings. He flew all-out straight at the main hangar and, just as I thought he intended to wipe us all out, he pulled his joy-stick right back and we shot almost vertically up into the sky. Poor Cadogan at that moment was stooping over his suit-case to close it up, and the sudden change in direction flattened him out like a dead frog on the floor. I shall never forget the injured look on his face as he rose up from the floor! '

" We were met at the airport by a large gathering including our Ambassador, Shaposhnikov, the Chief of Staff, also the General Commanding Moscow, and a mass of Press correspondents. Anders, the Polish general, was also there. We had to have groups taken, etc."

" Then drove to the hotel for a quick change and to dine with the P.M. in his house just outside Moscow. Found him very well and on the whole pleased with his interview with Stalin yesterday."[1]

" At 11 p.m. we were due to go and meet Stalin in the Kremlin. It was very interesting meeting him, and I was much impressed by his astuteness and his crafty cleverness. He is a realist, with little flattery about him, and not looking for much flattery either. Our meeting consisted of Stalin and Molotov and P.M., Cadogan, Wavell, Tedder, Jacob, self and two interpreters. We remained there till about 1.45 a.m. when I was dropping with sleepiness, having been up since 3.30 a.m. The discussion ranged mainly round our inability to establish a Second Front, and the fact that they cannot understand why we cannot do so. To-morrow at 3 p.m. I am to hold a military meeting with their Chiefs of Staff to go further into the matter with them. At 6 p.m. they are to give us a demonstration of their new mortar."

" I do not feel that this evening's meeting was on the

---

[1] This interview is described in Churchill's history and in the report which Harriman cabled next day to President Roosevelt. The Prime Minister had come to bring to " this sullen, sinister Bolshevik State " in its hour of agony the news that there could be no Second Front. He insisted on proceeding to the Kremlin the moment he landed, " scorning all suggestions that he might like to have a few hours' rest." The start of the conference had been " bleak and sombre," with the Prime Minister explaining the Western Allies' limitations in landing-craft and shipping, and Stalin replying with taunts, asking why the British and Americans were so afraid of the Germans and saying that a man who was not prepared to take risks could never hope to win a war. But, when Churchill turned to the British bombing offensive against German cities, the tension began to ease, and when he went on to unfold the secret plans for " Torch," the Russian dictator had become intensely interested and had even exclaimed, after his guest had drawn a picture of a crocodile with a soft underbelly, " May God prosper this undertaking! " To Churchill's surprise he then went on to enumerate several reasons in its favour: that it would hit Rommel in the back, overawe Spain, cause fighting between Germans and Frenchmen, and expose Italy to the brunt of the war. The meeting had left the visitors much impressed by " the Russian dictator's swift and complete mastery of a problem hitherto novel to him." *Churchill*, IV, 429-45; *White House Papers*, II, 616-618.

whole much of a success, or that it will do much towards drawing us much closer together. The two leaders, Churchill and Stalin, are poles apart as human beings, and I cannot see a friendship between them such as exists between Roosevelt and Winston. Stalin is a realist if ever there was one; facts only count with him. Plans, hypotheses, future possibilities mean nothing to him, but he is ready to face facts, even when unpleasant. Winston, on the other hand, never seems anxious to face an unpleasantness until forced to do so. He appealed to sentiments in Stalin which do not, I think, exist. Altogether, I felt we were not gaining much ground. . . ."

" Personally I feel our policy with the Russians has been wrong from the very start . . . . We have bowed and scraped to them, done all we could for them, and never asked them for a single fact or figure concerning their production, strength, dispositions, etc. As a result, they despise us and have no use for us except for what they can get out of us."

Of this midnight interview between the Prime Minister and the Russian dictator, Brooke wrote afterwards:

' It had been a long and tiring flight lasting some fifteen hours. I was longing for a bath, light dinner and bed. It was not to be—as I stepped out of the plane I was handed a message from Winston to come at once to dine with him, to go on to the Kremlin at 11 p.m.'

' Tired as I was I would not have missed that meeting between Stalin and Winston for anything in the world. Everything of that meeting is still vivid in my memory. We were shown into a sparsely furnished room of the Kremlin, which reminded me of a station waiting-room. I think the only picture on the wall was that of Lenin. Stalin, Molotov and the interpreter entered and we sat at a long table.'

' We were soon involved in heated discussions concerning Western Second Front, and Winston had made it clear that such an offensive was not possible for the present but would be replaced by operations in North Africa. Stalin then began to turn on the heat and through the interpreter he passed a lot of abusive questions such as: " When are you going to start fighting? Are you going to let us do all the work whilst you look on? Are you never going to start fighting? You will find it is not too bad if you once start! " etc., etc.'[1]

' The effect on Winston was magnetic. He crashed his fist down on the table and poured forth one of his wonderful spontaneous orations. It began with: " If it was not for the fighting qualities of the Red Army . . ." And then went on to tell Stalin exactly what his feelings were about fighting and a lot more.'

' Stalin stood up sucking at his large bent pipe, and with a broad grin on his face stopped Winston's interpreter and sent back through his own: " I do not understand what you are saying, but by God, I like your sentiment! " '

' Looking back on that episode I am convinced that Stalin insulted Winston with the purpose of finding out what his reactions would be, and of sizing up what kind of a man he was. He very soon discovered what Winston was made of, and I am certain that this outburst of Winston's had impressed Stalin and started feelings of admiration for what he discovered was a true fighting man. At any rate, from that moment onwards the relations between the two improved and there grew up between them certain bonds of mutual admiration and appreciation based on the highly-developed fighting qualities which both of them possessed.'

' My views of Stalin as formed at that first meeting were fairly correct and were confirmed and expanded by future meetings. I was still too close, when I wrote my diary, to the events of that evening to be able to assess their full value. Looking back on that night in the Kremlin, I am certain that it played an important part in laying the foundations for a certain mutual understanding which grew up between these men and which greatly facilitated the co-ordination of our plans. I still feel, however, that we started off on the wrong leg in our first negotiations with Moscow. We gave everything unconditionally and never asked for anything. We were dealing with a semi-Asiatic race with innate bargaining

[1] According to Sir Ian Jacob who was present, Stalin made his remarks " in a very low gentle voice, with an occasional gesture of the right hand, and never looked the Prime Minister in the face." *MS. Diary*, 13th August, 1942.

instincts. The supplies of equipment, etc., should have been counter-balanced by greater co-operation. During the whole of the war I never received a Russian order of battle showing their dispositions. . . .'

" *August 14th. Moscow.* Had a bit of a rest and breakfast at 9 a.m. with caviar and every other description of food.[1] After breakfast did a short tour of the town to see the Kremlin, Lenin's Tomb, the Red Square, etc. Also did a little shopping. At 11 a.m. Anders, the Polish general, came to see me and we discussed the evacuation of the Polish Forces from Russia to Persia. It is now in full swing."

" At 12 noon I went round to see the P.M. and found him with a headache. Not very pleased at results of last night and rather depressed at results of last convoy to Malta which sustained heavy losses. Lunched with P.M. and sat next to American Ambassador. At 2.30 p.m. started off to see demonstration of new rocket-mortars. Shaposhnikov and Voroshilov were both there. Quite a useful type of weapons which we might well make use of. Returned about 7 p.m. and was informed that Stalin's dinner at the Kremlin would not take place till 9 p.m."

' Our life in Moscow was from one aspect somewhat that of prisoners. We each had a guard armed with revolvers perpetually in attendance. They stood outside one's room in the hotel and accompanied one everywhere, always shadowing one's footsteps.'

' Anders' visit was of some interest. I had last seen him at that sherry party of Sikorski's at Claridge's. He had been sent back to Russia to extract the Polish prisoners captured by the Russians in their invasion of Poland when co-operating with the Germans. When he came into my hotel

[1] " I . . . found a meal ready which consisted of caviar, cake, chocolates, preserved fruit, grapes and apparently none of the normal breakfast dishes. I was just wondering whether I could possibly face caviar at that time of the morning when . . . coffee and an omelet appeared and all was well. Leslie Rowan told me that when he asked for an egg and bacon, they produced four eggs and nine rashers of bacon—all very nice, except that one remembers that the vast majority of the population are practically starving." Sir Ian Jacob, *MS. Diary,* 14th August, 1942.

sitting-room he beckoned to me to come and sit at a small table with him. He then pulled out his cigarette case and started tapping the table and speaking in a low voice. He said: " As long as I keep tapping this table and talk like this we cannot be overheard by all the microphones in this room! " I must confess that till then I had not realised that my sitting-room was full of microphones. I learned to realise that all rooms in Moscow had ears. Anders then proceeded to tell me that, hunt as he might, he could not discover a large consignment of Polish prisoners which comprised most of the men of distinction in most walks of life. He had followed one clue half-way across Siberia and then it fizzled out. He said he was certain that they were either being liquidated in one of the Siberian Convict Camps or that they had been murdered. It turned out that he was correct. This was the batch of prisoners that the Russians murdered and that the Germans found later on, Goebbels exploiting this find to the utmost.'

' Anders wanted me to fix up a meeting for him with Winston so that he might assist him in getting authority from Stalin to establish assembly-areas for other collections of Polish prisoners and for their despatch to Persia. He told me that their condition was deplorable, most of them being in a half-starved condition. I had an opportunity of cor-roborating this fact later on in Teheran.'

' The mortar-rocket demonstration was quite interesting and the weapons very effective for area bombardments, such as the plastering of Company localities. They consisted of slides mounted at an angle on lorries from which groups of rockets could be fired. The heavier rockets were actually fired out of the wooden crates in which they were packed. The crate was put in a rack at an angle of some 45 degrees and then the lid of the crate removed, the rocket being fired electrically. On returning from Moscow I got the War Office to apply for details and diagrams of these rockets through the Soviet Embassy, but we never received any reply to our enquiries.'

The evening's banquet was held in Catherine the Great's

magnificent State rooms in the Kremlin. It was the night before the Germans crossed the Don at Kalach, fifty miles from Stalingrad; the Maikop oilfields in the Caucasian foothills had been abandoned a week earlier. There were about a hundred present, including most of the members of the *Politburo* and many of the leading Russian generals not engaged at the front.

The British and American guests were received by Stalin, dressed, as usual, in a short lilac-coloured cotton tunic and with his trousers stuffed into his boots. Brooke, having heard something of Kremlin banquets from earlier visitors to Moscow, was a little apprehensive.

"From the beginning vodka flowed freely and one's glass kept being filled up. The tables groaned under every description of hors d'œuvres, fish, etc. Stalin sat at the centre of the table with P.M. on his right and Harriman on his left, then came an interpreter, then myself and Voroshilov on my left with a foreign office official beyond. Molotov was opposite Stalin, and started proposing toasts within five minutes of our having sat down. Then toasts went on continuously. My turn came about third or fourth and I replied by proposing health of Red Army, after which I was left in peace. Archie Wavell replied in Russian which met with great success."

"The evening dragged slowly on, many members getting somewhat the worse for wear! I got so bored and so disgusted looking at food that I almost felt sick. There were nineteen courses and we only got up at 12.15 a.m. having been three and a quarter hours at the table. Luckily the evening rapidly drew to a close, as P.M. said he was feeling too weary to attend a film which had been provided for him."

"By the end of dinner Stalin was quite lively, walking round the table to click glasses with various people he was proposing the health of. He is an outstanding man, that there is no doubt about, but not an attractive one. He has got an unpleasantly cold, crafty, cruel face, and whenever I look at him I can imagine his sending off people to their doom without ever turning a hair. On the other hand, there is no doubt that he has a quick brain and a real grasp of the essentials of war. He strikes me as ageing and beginning to show distinct signs of wear."

" By 2.15 a.m. I was in bed and very grateful to have got off as lightly, having expected to be kept up till 4 a.m."

' I was in dread,' Brooke recalled afterwards,

' of this banquet all day and shuddered at the idea of having to spend the evening dodging the effects of vodka. It turned out to be a complete orgy as I described in my diary. Continual toasts throughout the dinner, and a table groaning with food, mostly of a fishy and oily nature. During the first hour we must have got through at least a dozen toasts. Luckily I had a jug of water in front of me, and when I was not being watched I filled up my glass with water instead of vodka. By that means I had at least halved the vodka consumption. At this time Voroshilov said through his interpreter, " This white vodka is no good. I am sending for yellow vodka! " I thought that he must have spotted me juggling with the water jug, but he had not, he genuinely preferred yellow vodka. The new drink arrived with a large red chili, about the size of a large carrot, floating in the jug. Voroshilov filled my glass and his and said, " No heel taps," to which I replied, " Oh, no, you know your yellow vodka, I have never tasted it and shall therefore sip this first glass." This I proceeded to try to do, but after a couple of sips I found it impossible to swallow any more; it was just like drinking liquid cayenne pepper and completely choked up one's throat. I told Voroshilov that I should stick to the white, but he said that he would now take to the yellow and proceeded to throw down two glasses in quick succession.'

' The result did not take long to show itself. His forehead broke out in beads of perspiration which soon started to flow down his face. He became sullen and quiet, sitting with a fixed stare straight to his front, and I wondered whether the moment had arrived for him to slip under the table. No, he retained his seat, but took little further interest in the proceedings.'

'The evening wore away slowly and I felt more and more despondent. In front of me amongst the many fish dishes was a small sucking pig covered with a blanket of white sauce. He had a black truffle eye and an orange peel mouth. He was never eaten, and as the evening slipped by his black eye remained fixed on me, and the orange peel mouth developed a sardonical smile. I can still see that pig now if I shut my eyes.

'Towards the end of the banquet Stalin took up the running from Molotov and started a round of toasts. He filled his glass with vodka and must have had his eye on Voroshilov . . . . for he descended straight on him. He came and stood alongside of him holding his glass on high and started his toast with a broad grin on his face. Voroshilov had to stand whilst his toast was being proposed. . . . He held on tight to the table with both hands, swaying gently backwards and forwards with a distant and vacant look in his eyes. The critical moment arrived—Stalin held up his glass for Voroshilov to click with his. Voroshilov must have seen at least half a dozen glasses, a worried look came on his face, he tried to concentrate his thoughts, finding that impossible he trusted to luck and lunged forward at one of the many glasses he was seeing. Fortune was with him and he clicked the right one. Stalin walked off to fill his glass another dozen times for further toasts, whilst Voroshilov with a deep sigh sank back on to his chair.

'The end came at last and I rose from the table thanking Heaven that I still had full control of my legs and my thoughts!'

"*August 15th. Moscow.* Took an easy morning in bed after our late last night. Then went for a short walk round to the Red Square with Archie Wavell. At 11 a.m. we went to the P.M.'s house for a final talk before our military interview which was timed for 12 noon."

"Then we met Voroshilov and Shaposhnikov with one other general and interpreters. We consisted of Archie

Wavell, Tedder, Maxwell (U.S.A.), one U.S. airman, Jacob and self. Our meeting lasted till 2.30 p.m. For two and a half hours I argued against the possibility of establishing a Western Front in 1942. It was very uphill work, as they had no intention of being convinced and hoped to convince us that we were wrong. As they have not got the vaguest conception of the conditions prevailing in France or England, nor any real idea of the implications of amphibious operations, it was a hopeless task from the start.[1] We remained quite friendly but entirely unconvinced."

" They then gave us lunch, during which time I had a talk with Shaposhnikov, who looks terribly ill and worn out. He has been Chief of the Staff since the start and is a sick man suffering from his heart or something. He is very charming to talk to and I should think quite a sound staff officer. Voroshilov is an attractive personality, but the typical political general who owes his life at present to his wits in the past."

" After our meeting I went to report to P.M. and then back to the hotel, hoping to be called for another meeting to discuss the Caucasus situation, and when I raised this point this afternoon I was told by Voroshilov that he had no authority to discuss it. He said he would endeavour to obtain authority from the Government to meet us at 5 p.m. to discuss this side of the problem."

" There is no doubt that they are anxious to get all they can out of us, but at the same time have no intention of giving us the smallest help of any kind. They are an astonishingly suspicious type of people and make it very difficult to arrive at that close co-operation in war which is

[1] " The meeting began by a very clear account by the C.I.G.S. of the various projects which had been considered by ourselves and the Americans for operations in Europe and of the conclusions to which we had come after long and anxious discussion. Marshal Voroshilov and Marshal Shaposhnikov then gave their views on the formation of a Second Front. . . . Their remarks showed only too clearly how totally unable the Russians are to appreciate the nature of large-scale operations across the sea. They began straight away by saying they were not in a position to go into the details of shipping and thus begged the question from the start. They then suggested that we should immediately move all the divisions now in England and land them in France, preferably at Cherbourg." Sir Ian Jacob, *MS. Diary*, 15th August, 1942.

so essential. This visit may have done some good in forging some bonds of greater confidence between us, but on the whole it is highly unsatisfactory. We have never really got down to discussing the main problems of this war or how we can best circumvent our common difficulties. We agree easily enough that those difficulties exist and must be overcome, but since we approach them from diametrically opposed points of view, solutions are hard to find."

" At 6 p.m. I went over to visit the British Mission under Admiral Miles, and from there went on for a second meeting with Voroshilov to discuss the question of the defence of the Caucasus. He had now received permission from Stalin to discuss this point, but was still as sticky as could be. I then said that I had been frank with him as regards the strength of British forces, and expected equal confidence on his part."

" He then agreed and said that there were twenty-five Russian divisions in the Caucasus with corresponding tank and air forces. This is the same figure as quoted by Stalin, but I am certain it is not the truth. We then discussed possibility of sending air reinforcements to the Caucasus. This he took greater interest in, but was definitely looking the ' gift horse in the mouth ' till I again got annoyed with him and got him into a better mood. In the end we got agreement concerning machinery to carry out the required preparations to receive the air forces if they can be spared for this front."

" Rushed back after a touching parting with Voroshilov and Shaposhnikov, and dined with Admiral Miles at his flat. Have now returned and am getting ready for an early bed in anticipation of an early start to-morrow morning. I am leaving Moscow with no regrets. If Moscow represents Bolshevism, we must certainly look for something better. Even making full allowance for war and its effect, the dejection, drabness and lack of any sort of *joie de vivre* is most marked."[1]

[1] " I never saw a single shop window . . . and nearly all the buildings are drab and shabby. There are not as many people walking in the streets as one would expect . . . they all look extremely poor and seedy. . . . We drove through the streets entirely regardless of red and green lights or of policemen and pedestrian-

'I found that the discussion with Voroshilov and Shaposhnikov was very heavy work. Voroshilov evidently understood nothing about it and his military knowledge was painfully limited, as exemplified by his questions which were entirely childish. There was no difficulty in dealing with the questions, but the reply was never absorbed and the same question was reiterated unendingly.

'I gathered that Voroshilov's position with Stalin was based more on personal friendship and early contacts. I believe that in the early days when Voroshilov commanded a battalion, Stalin was attached to his unit as the Political Commissar. . . . The foundation of an understanding between them was set up in these days and cemented during the purge of generals. . . . Whatever the relations were, they were certainly not based on his value as an adviser on military matters. I do not remember a single instance in which Stalin sought his advice in all our meetings. Shaposhnikov was a very different type. I believe he had been an officer in the Czarist Armies, and had graduated at their Staff College. If so, he had evidently turned Communist and thrown in his lot with them. A pathetic figure, evidently dying fast of some complaint since he only lasted a few months after our interview. He had a well-trained military brain and his questions were far more to the point than those of Voroshilov.

'Throughout our discussion Wavell was most useful to me, as he could understand Russian. He wrote down a few notes as they spoke and pushed them over to me even before the interpreter had time to get to work. I thus had a few additional seconds to frame my replies in.

'After two and a half hours of it I saw clearly that we could go on arguing till the cows came home without making any headway. I therefore said that it was useless continuing our talk on the Second Front, that I had given them all the strong reasons that made such an operation impossible in 1942, that the operation could not take place, and that I had nothing more to add to what I had already said. . . .

---

crossings. If there are pedestrians in the way, so much the worse for them. . . . The drivers treat the citizens like so many cattle." Sir Ian Jacob, *MS. Diary*, 14th August, 1942.

'After having given me his reply of twenty-five divisions in the Caucasus, a number which I suspected as a gross exaggeration, I decided to test Voroshilov's veracity over the defences of the Caucasus. I knew that he would not realise that I had flown up the west coast of the Caspian instead of following the east coast as Winston had done. I therefore began by asking him questions concerning the central passes, but I could not check his answers. I then turned to the main approach route between the Caucasus and Caspian. Here I drew him on and extracted out of him details of their strong lines of defence with anti-tank ditches and concrete pill-boxes for anti-tank-guns and machine-guns—a complete pack of lies from what I had been able to see for myself. . . . I was thus able to estimate the amount of faith one could attach to any of his statements.'

While Brooke was bidding farewell to the Russian Marshals and preparing for an early bed, the Prime Minister was at the Kremlin. He had gone there at seven o'clock to take leave of Stalin. He, too, had asked about the Caucasus passes, and, in reply, the Russian dictator, spreading out a map, had answered with quiet confidence, " We shall stop them; they will not cross the mountains." Afterwards to his surprise Stalin had invited him to join him in his private apartments for drinks. Here the two men remained closeted for more than six hours. There was only one break in the night's good fellowship when the host, after " a rough and rude remark " about the destruction of the last Arctic convoy, asked if the British Navy had no sense of glory. At that moment, two thousand miles away, the last of five crippled survivors of a fleet of fourteen merchantmen was entering the battered harbour of Malta after Admiral Syfret's escorting squadron had lost a third of its carrier and cruiser strength in forcing a passage through three days and nights of continuous bombing and U-boat attack in the presence of the Italian battle-fleet. But, true to his policy of making every allowance for the stresses through which the Russians were passing, Churchill contented himself with pointing out that he had had some experience of naval affairs and that, while Russia was a land animal, Britain was a sea one. After that the two statesmen spent the rest of the night in friendly and jovial conversation, chaffing one another and Molotov, who had joined them, ranging over the field of war, and even discussing Churchill's favourite project of a landing in northern Norway, which they agreed, without reference to their military advisers, " should be done if possible."[1] Before they parted Stalin confided to his guest as a great secret that he was planning a counter-offensive before the winter. The Prime Minister was left with the impression, not only that the Russians would hold out, but that he and Stalin had established a relationship of permanent value.[2]

Of this interview Brooke wrote in his diary:

" *August 16th. Teheran 9½ hours. 2000 miles.* My pen has run out and I dare not wait till to-morrow, as events follow so fast on each other it is hard to remember them.[3] I was called at 3.15 a.m. and left hotel at 4.15; raining heavily. However, by the time we reached the aerodrome it was only a drizzling, but rather a dull drab grey dawn. A large crowd at the aerodrome, guard of honour, Press cameras, Press, officials, etc. P.M. was somewhat late and no wonder! He went to see Stalin for a final visit at 7 p.m. and remained with him till 3 a.m. He had no time for bed and after a bath came straight on to the aerodrome. He arrived with Molotov. The band played the ' International,' ' God Save the King,' and the ' Star Spangled Banner,' during which period we all stood to attention and saluted. Then a series of good-byes to Molotov, Shapo-

---

[1] *Churchill*, IV, 445-9.

[2] Colonel Jacob, however, though he admired the brilliant way the Prime Minister played his cards, doubted whether much had been achieved. " I don't believe that it is possible," he wrote in his diary, " to make friends with a man like Stalin in the sense that we understand friendship. The thing that impressed me most about Stalin was his complete self-possession and detachment. He was absolute master of the situation at all times and appeared to be cold and calculating. He had a gentle voice, which he never raised, and his eyes were shrewd and crafty. He has a well-developed sense of humour, though his smile gave one the impression that it would be chiefly exercised in a cruel way. All his life he has been a revolutionary fighting for his own position. He would have his closest associate shot without the smallest compunction if he calculated that it was necessary. . . . I should say that to make friends with Stalin would be equivalent to making friends with a python." Sir Ian Jacob, *MS. Diary*, 16th August, 1942.

[3] The diary is written in pencil for that day.

shnikov, Anders, etc., etc. Finally at 5.30 a.m. we took off in four Liberators and flew off in formation."

'Winston's final visit to Stalin had been a useful one judging by the interpreter's notes of the interview. During the course of the evening they became on very friendly terms and began to ask each other why they had done various things in the past. Winston asked Stalin how it was that he had double-crossed us at the beginning of the war when our mission was in Moscow apparently making good progress and suddenly he swung right over to sign an agreement with Ribbentrop? Stalin replied that he thought England must be bluffing; he knew we had only two divisions we could mobilise at once, and he thought we must know how bad the French Army was and what little reliance could be placed on it. He could not imagine we should enter the war with such weakness. On the other hand, he said he knew Germany was certain ultimately to attack Russia. He was not ready to withstand that attack; by attacking Poland with Germany he could make more ground, ground was equal to time, and he would consequently have a longer period to get ready. I should think that this was probably a fairly true statement of the reasons that led to his decision.'

'Stalin then asked Winston why he bombed his Molotov when he sent him to Berlin. Winston replied that in war no advantages can ever be neglected. Stalin then said that Molotov was engaged in conversation with Ribbentrop, who was saying that the British Empire was now finished and that the time had come to work out the partition of those lands between Germany and Russia. At this moment the bombers arrived, and Ribbentrop decided to continue the discussion in the dugout. When safely established underground Ribbentrop continued saying that, as he had already mentioned, the British Empire need no longer be taken account of. Molotov interrupted at this point with the awkward question: "Then why are we down here now?" This had pleased Stalin very much and he told Winston that his Molotov had a good sense of humour. Personally, I had never credited him with possessing any sense of humour.'

' The only tragedy concerning this last visit of Winston's to Stalin was connected with poor Anders. I had succeeded in getting him his interview, which was to have taken place at 8.30 p.m. that evening on Winston's return from Stalin. Anders waited till 3 a.m. for him and, when he returned, Churchill said: " Ah! my poor Anders. I have been detained by M. Stalin and now I must fly off, but you come along to Cairo and we shall have a talk there." Anders had already flown from Tashkent to Moscow to see him and now he was asked to come to Cairo as if it was in the next street. To give Anders credit, he got into his plane and followed laboriously in our wake, reaching Cairo before we had left there, and had his long-sought interview.'

' While we were flying away from Moscow I had established myself with Archie Wavell in the small cabin in the rear of the Liberator. We were lying on the floor as there were no seats. I was reading but Archie was busy writing notes in his corner. I wondered what he was writing about and wondered whether he was busy writing notes on our meetings in Moscow and wondered whether I was neglecting my duties not following his example. Suddenly he stopped and threw across to me the result of his labour. The paper was headed, "Ballad of the Second Front." It ran as follows:

"MOST PERSONAL AND VERY SECRET

BALLAD OF THE SECOND FRONT

P.M. Loquitur

1. I do not like the job I have to do. I cannot think my views will go down well.
   Can I convince them of our settled view; will Stalin use Caucasian oaths and yell?
   Or can I bind him with my midnight spell; I'm really feeling rather in a stew.
   It's not so hot a thing to have to sell; No Second Front in 1942.

2. I thought so, things are stickier than glue; they simply hate the tale I have to tell.
   Stalin and Molotov are looking blue; if I give in a inch they'll take an ell.
   I wonder if they'll put me in a cell and deal with me like Hitler with a Jew.
   It's not so hot a thing to have to sell; No Second Front in 1942.

3. Come, things are taking on a rosier hue; the whole affair has got a
    better smell.
   I think that after all we'll put it thru'; though not as merry as a wed-
    ding bell
   The sound is now less like a funeral knell; another vodka for? Here's
    Fortune—Phew !
   I've got away with what I came to sell; No Second Front in 1942.

ENVOI

4. Prince of the Kremlin, here's a fond farewell;
   I've had to deal with many worse than you.
   You took it though you hated it like hell;
   No Second Front in 1942."

" The Liberator was not as comfortable as the Russian
Douglas plane we had flown up in, but faster, being
capable of 200 miles per hour. We flew back over Kuibyshev, then on to the Ural River when I moved up into the
second Pilot's seat and had a grand view. We flew right
down the Ural through deserts and swamps to the Caspian.
Then we came down the east coast for a change which
was interesting. Finally we cut across the Southern Caspian
to Pahlevi, over the mountains to Kazvin and back to
Teheran where we landed after an excellent nine and a
half hours' non-stop flight."

" We all went up to the hill Legation where we had an
excellent dinner under the lovely Persian tent with the
blue pool with the gold-fish. Now off to bed for another
early start to-morrow morning."

" *August 17th. 5½ hours. 1300 miles.* Another 4.30 a.m.
rise and off by 6 a.m. We had a wonderful fly-back to
Cairo averaging well over 200 miles per hour. I went up
to the second Pilot's seat after we had taken off and
remained there till just before landing. We rose steadily
to 15,000 ft. . . . . to clear the hills on our path, and then
remained between fourteen and fifteen thousand feet up
to avoid the bumps owing to heat off desert hills. Glorious
wild mountain ranges which I was very interested in in
connection with the defence of Persian oil against invasion
from the Caucasus. After the mountains we passed over
the valley of the Tigris and the Euphrates. We were some

way north of Baghdad. We then had a very bleak stretch of desert before reaching Amman, the only interesting part in this section being the oil pipe-line which we flew along for some time."

" We struck the Dead Sea near its northern end, flying at 1400 ft. with beautiful visibility. I was able to see the whole Dead Sea from end to end, Jerusalem, Bethlehem and Hebron all at the same time. It was a thrilling sight. As I looked down on the Dead Sea from above, I thought of Our Lord walking on the Sea of Galilee, and from the height we were at it seemed quite a natural thing to do; the water looked like a solid sheet. We then flew over Beersheba and I could see Gaza and the sea in the distance. Finally we crossed the top of the Sinai Peninsula and struck the Canal at Ismailia from which we glided down to Heliopolis aerodrome in Cairo."

" We were met there by Miles Lampson and Casey. Adam and Alexander also turned up. After lunch P.M., Alexander and I had a long conference on his plans and on the re-organisation of his Army . . . Monty, I hear, is settling down well and going great guns. I pray to God that the new Alexander-Monty combination will be a success. I can think of nothing better. . . ."[1]

" *August 18th. Cairo.* Determined at last to have a good night's sleep. I slept solidly from midnight to 8.30 a.m. Whilst dressing the P.M. blew into my room in his dressing-gown and told me he had been thinking over the urgency of the attack against Rommel. He then started producing all the old arguments that I have so frequently battled against for speeding up the date. I had to point out that it was exactly two days ago that Alex had taken over and Monty arrived, that there was a mess to put right,

[1] The two men had started to collaborate as soon as Montgomery arrived in Egypt on the morning of August 12th. On reaching Eighth Army Headquarters on the 13th, two days before Auchinleck was to hand over the Middle East Command to Alexander, Montgomery had been so impressed by the dangers in the Army's situation that, ignoring the fact that he was not due to take over till the 15th and without consulting Cairo, he issued immediate orders that, if Rommel attacked, all units should fight on the ground where they stood and that there should be no withdrawal and no surrender. The effect on the Army was electric.

etc. I know that from now on I shall have a difficult time curbing his impatience."

" I then went round to G.H.Q. to meet Archie and explain to him my latest plan: namely, Iraq-Persia to be handed over at once to India from Middle East so as to free Alex of this responsibility; Archie Wavell to act as foster-parent and to prepare this Command for an independent existence at the earliest date. I feel convinced that we cannot leave the all-vital Abadan oil centre in a sector which represents the poor sister of either Middle East or India. It must have a life and entity of its own and be prepared by an energetic commander for the vital conflict which may have to take place in this area if the Caucasus breaks. Archie Wavell agrees with me. . . ."[1]

". . . At 5 p.m. a big conference attended by P.M., Miles Lampson, Iraq Ambassador, Wavell, Alexander, Tedder, Peirse, Admiral, Lindsell and Jacob to decide on future of Iraq-Persia Command. P.M. is taken with my scheme, and meeting took to it too. Very satisfactory. Committee appointed to go into details and report day after to-morrow."

" After the meeting I found P.M. was again toying with the idea of stopping on here till the 30th. This is because there is an indication of a possible attack on the 26th and he would like to be here for it. I had to be as firm as I could with him and told him he would put himself in an impossible situation if he stopped on and would be accused of taking control. (It would be far worse than his Antwerp visit in the last war, but I did not say so and only implied it.) I told him we must arrange to start next Saturday or Sunday at latest. I think I have brought him round, and hope he will not slip back."

' . . . The Iraq-Persian Command had given me great anxiety for some time. Whilst it remained as part of Middle

[1] At this time, according to the letter the Prime Minister wrote Roosevelt after the Moscow visit, Alanbrooke was not at all hopeful that the Russians would be able to withstand the Germans' drive. " My own feeling is that it is an even chance they will hold, but C.I.G.S. will not go so far as this." *Churchill*, IV, 445. A week after the British party left Moscow, the Germans broke through the Russian lines near Stalingrad and virtually surrounded the city. At the same time they drove deep into the Caucasus.

East Command, its importance was continually put in the shade by the more imminent dangers on the Desert front. I had for some time wanted to establish a separate Command coming directly under me at the War Office and which could be built up to meet the impending threat. That the threat did not materialise is no evidence that I had exaggerated its importance. It was due solely to the fact that Hitler missed one of the great opportunities of the war. Strategically an offensive directed against the oil area of Iraq and Persia far outweighed anything that might be gained through the capture of Stalingrad. Thank heaven he did make this mistake; had he not, the course of the war would have been seriously affected to our disadvantage. . . .'

" *August 19th. Desert.* Started with breakfast on terrace with P.M. Then over to G.H.Q. for final talk with Adam before his departure for home. From there on to see Wavell and had a long argument with him and Peirse as regards future of Iraq-Persian Command and the difficult problem of allotting the air to this theatre. Did not get much further with the problem."

" Back to the Embassy to read recent telegram about Dieppe Raid, and to pack for our departure for Desert after lunch. Alex came along with us. We left Embassy at 3.15 p.m. and motored the whole way out, only reaching Eighth Army H.Q. at about 7.30 p.m. Then Monty gave us an excellent appreciation of the situation and an outline plan of what he proposed to do if Rommel attacked before he was ready and also his plans in the event of his starting the offensive. He is in tremendous form, delighted at being out here, and gave me a wonderful feeling of relief at having got him out here."

" We dined in their Mess and I slept in an ambulance converted into a caravan for Alex. Very comfortable. Very lovely night with the sound of the waves only a few yards away. On the way to bed P.M. took me down to the beach where he was transformed into a small boy wishing to dip his fingers into the sea. In the process he became very wet indeed! "

' Monty's performance that evening was one of the high-
lights of his military career. He had only been at the head
of his Command for a few days, and in that short spell he
had toured the whole of his front, met all the senior Commanders, appreciated the tactical value of the various
features, and sized up admirably the value of all his subordinate Commanders. He knew that Rommel was expected
to attack by a certain date. He showed us the alternatives
open to Rommel and the measures he was taking to meet
these eventualities. He said he considered the first alternative
the most likely one, namely, a penetration of his southern
front with a turn northwards into the centre of his position.
He explained how he would break up this attack with his
artillery, and would reserve his armour to finish off the
attack after the artillery had rough-handled it. His armour
would then drive Rommel back to his present front and no
further. He would then continue with his preparations for
his own offensive which were already started. He would
attack on the northern part of his front. It would mean hard
fighting and would take him some seven days to break
through, and he would then launch his Armoured Corps (his
Corps de Chasse, as he called it) which he had already formed.
This statement remained rooted in my mind, and, although
many years have passed since then, the above statement
cannot be far adrift from his actual statement. I knew my
Monty pretty well by then, but I must confess that I was
dumbfounded by the rapidity with which he had grasped
the situation facing him, the ability with which he had
grasped the essentials, the clarity of his plans, and above all,
his unbounded self-confidence—a self-confidence with which
he inspired all those that he came into contact with. His
statement was made with such complete confidence that
everything would plan out just as he had settled, that Winston
took all this for granted, and we shall see later on that when
after seven days hard fighting Monty was not through the
enemy position as he had promised, a very serious flutter
resulted in the Cabinet dove-cot.'

' After having explained his dispositions he said that on

the following day he would take us out to see his preparations on the ground.'

'I went to bed that night with a wonderful feeling of contentment. It had not been an easy matter to get Winston to accept Monty in command of the Eighth Army, but now that at last he was there he was more than fulfilling the hopes I had placed in him. I did not dare let myself think too optimistically yet, but I had an inward happy feeling that at last we might begin to meet with some success, a feeling I had not yet experienced since I had taken over the duties of C.I.G.S.'

"*August 20th, 1942. Cairo. 40 minutes. 100 miles.* Called at 6 a.m. P.M. had a sea-bathe before breakfast. We then proceeded to the front where we visited 44th Division, 22nd Armoured Brigade, 4th Light Brigade, 7th Motor Brigade, and New Zealanders, finally, lunching with 13th Corps H.Q. with Horrocks. After lunch P.M. visited squadron of the 4th Hussars, his old Regiment. We then motored back to Eighth Army H.Q. where we had a sea-bathe and tea. Then on to Alexandria from where we flew back to Cairo, arriving there about 6.15 p.m."

" At 7 p.m. conference on Iraq-Persia. Committee had sat and produced report on transfer to India. Still impossible to obtain decision from P.M. Usual Air Force difficulties and he will not face up to them. I pointed out that while we are talking, the Germans are marching through the Caucasus. He nevertheless decided he would write a paper which we should discuss to-morrow."

" After dinner he suddenly said that he did not think we could get off before Monday. I had another long argument and brought him back to Sunday, but shall probably again have difficulties to-morrow."[1]

'The day had been a wonderful example of Winston's vitality. We had been called at 6 a.m. He had started the

[1] But on the morrow, yielding to advice, the Prime Minister wrote to Mr. Attlee, " Everything has been done and is being done that is possible, and it is now my duty to return home, as I have no part to play in the battle which must be left to those in whom we place our trust. . . . C.I.G.S. and I plan to start Sunday night." Prime Minister to Deputy Prime Minister, 21st August, 1942. *Churchill*, IV, 467.

day with a bathe in the sea; we had then spent a very strenuous day touring the front. This had entailed motoring in clouds of sand, long walks between troops, addressing groups of troops, talks with officers, in fact, a non-stop tour of inspection. Return to camp with another bathe, contrary to his doctor's orders. He was rolled over by the waves and came up upside down doing the " V " sign with his legs! Then followed a drive to aerodrome, and, as soon as we had emplaned, he said, " I am now going to sleep," and pulled out a bit of black velvet or cloth out of his pocket which he placed over his eyes. The effect was marvellous. He instantaneously went to sleep and never woke up till we had bumped half-way down the Heliopolis runway. Then followed a conference, dinner, after which he kept me up till 2 a.m. on the lawn outside the Embassy. On our way up to bed he said, " Breakfast on the verandah at 8.30 as usual," which I agreed to, and went off to bed dog-tired.'

' At 7.30 a.m. I woke with my bed shaking, and on opening my eyes saw him standing at the end of my bed shaking it! I thought I had overslept, and hurriedly looked at my watch. It was 7.30 a.m. " Come and have breakfast with me," he said, to which I replied, " It is only 7.30; you said breakfast at 8.30." That did not affect him in the least and he continued, " I know, but I am awake." I had one more attempt to gain a few more minutes sleep and said, " Yes, but I am not awake, I have not washed nor shaved." It was useless, he replied, " Never mind, neither have I. Come along, let's eat! " There he was at 7.30 a.m. after a long day in the desert, followed by a late night, far fresher than I was.'

' So up I got, cleaned up as best I could, and went to breakfast with him, where we were joined later by Gort.'

" *August 21st. Cairo.* Breakfast on the terrace with P.M. and Gort. During the night P.M. had produced a new paper on the organization of the Persia-Iraq front, which is nothing more than the original plan of making it an independent Command from the very start. He has not yet solved the main difficulty, namely, the control of the air forces. However, it is a possible start and one which can be built up on provided we make use of "Jumbo" Wilson for this purpose. . . ."

" Then went round to G.H.Q. to discuss with Wavell and McCreery the allocation of forces to the new Command. After this I went to see the Admiral, and had a long interview with Anders, who has returned from Moscow via Tashkent and who is very upset about the organisation of his force in Palestine. Apparently he and Sikorski are not seeing quite eye to eye."

" At lunch the Vice-President of the Greek Government was there. . . . After lunch had a long talk with Gort to put him into the picture of recent events. At 5 p.m. went out with the Ambassador and his wife to be taken round the shops to purchase presents. It was rather an interesting part of Cairo I had not been in before."

" Had to return to Embassy by 7 p.m., as P.M. was having a conference there to settle question of handing over the running of the Persian railway to the Americans to develop. Decided that P.M. should, on Harriman's recommendation, wire to the President asking him if he would be so kind as to take it over. I then remained on with P.M. to settle final details concerning formation of Iraq-Persian Command. Decided to hand it over to " Jumbo " Wilson to start it. I had sent for " Jumbo " and went out to probe him to find out whether he was prepared to take it on. He said he was delighted to do so. . . . It is imperative that something should be done quickly as the Germans are pushing on into the Caucasus rapidly. Our defences in Iraq-Persia are lamentably weak. " Jumbo " Wilson will have an uphill task. He and Dick McCreery came to dine. Dick has settled down to the Chief of General Staff job well, and should, I think, make a success of it."

" We have carried out some drastic changes while we have been out here. I feel convinced they are for the better, and do hope events will prove this to be the case."

" *August 22nd. 35 minutes. 100 miles.* I had breakfast at 6.15 a.m. and left at 6.45 with the P.M. to visit the Caves of Tura. They are caves that were created by the quarry-

ing of the Pyramid stones and are now being used as vas
workshops by the R.A.F. for repairs of aircraft engines an
for overhauls."

" From there we drove to Heliopolis aerodrome wher
we emplaned for Abu Suire where bomber squadrons ar
located. We had breakfast there and then motored on t
inspect the 51st Division at Quassassin.[1] They have onl
just arrived out here, and were recently in the Camberley
Aldershot-Hartley Wintney area. Men looking very fi
after their sea journey, but not yet tanned by the sur
We spent about one and a half hours with them and the:
motored back, arriving in time for a late lunch."

' That morning's visit with 51st Division has always re
mained rooted in my mind. I had seen them recently a
home, and there they were all pink and white, having nc
yet been absorbed by the desert. The officers were walkin;
about with long Scottish sticks that did not blend with th
flat sandy surroundings. The whole Division had an appear
ance of rawness, but of great promise. . . .'

" After lunch P.M. called Alex and me into his stud
for an hour's discussion on prospects of Rommel's possibl
attack on 25th. I suggested that petrol reserves at pump
'(ordinary refilling stations)' should be reduced in case c
temporary break-through with a thrust on Cairo. Mile
Lampson was called in and put in contact with Alex t
attend to this danger. I am surprised it was not looke
into sooner."

" From 5 p.m. to 6.15 p.m. long interview with "Jumbo"
Wilson to discuss further details concerning his ne
Command. He has been getting busy and has made goo
progress in the preliminary measures. I then went off t
look up Casey who has been ill, and to tell him of all th
recent developments. . . . Platt (C.-in-C. East Africa
turned up this evening, and Alex also came to dinner."

" This should be our last evening here, and I feel tha
during the last three weeks I have lived through a ver
full quota. . . . It has all been intensely interesting, bu

[1] The Highland Division under Maj.-Gen. Douglas Wimberley.

very hard work when the background of constant contact with Winston is taken into account. And yet nobody could have been kinder and more charming than he has been throughout the trip."

"*August 23rd. Cairo.* Breakfast on terrace with P.M. and Gort. Then long interview with Platt concerning operations in Madagascar and raising of East African Forces. We both then went on to see the P.M. and had a long discussion with him. Jumbo Wilson then came round to discuss further questions of the organisation of command in Iraq-Persia. . . . After him Alex and Dick McCreery came round to discuss their proposed organisation of the armoured and ordinary divisions. This conforms to home except for minor differences. . . ."

"All preparations now made for our secret departure. P.M. goes off as if visiting Casey and then slips off to aerodrome. Cadogan and I leave here at 5.15 p.m. I think plane is timed to take off at 7 p.m. I am glad to be off, as I want to pick up threads at home where there is a great deal to be done."

"However, I am delighted that we came out as I could never have put matters right here from a distance. It has also been very interesting meeting men like Smuts and Stalin. Such a contrast! Smuts I look upon as one of the biggest of nature's gentlemen that I have ever seen. A wonderful clear grasp of all things, coupled with the most exceptional charm. Interested in all matters, and gifted with the most marvellous judgment. Stalin, on the other hand, a crafty, brilliant, realistic mind, devoid of any sense of human pity or kindness. Gives one almost an uncanny feeling to be in his presence. But undoubtedly a big and shrewd brain with clear-cut views as to what he wants and expects to get."

"*Later.* At 5.15. Cadogan and I left the Embassy for the aerodrome. P.M. had gone on ahead, dropping in on Casey to simulate a proposed visit there. The aerodrome was in an unpleasant condition with continuous minor sand-storms. Finally, by 7.30 p.m. we took off, P.M. being fifteen minutes ahead in his plane. Twelve fighters overhead to cover us. We climbed steadily and headed S.W."

'The reasons for the secrecy concerning our departure was due to the fact that by now the Germans knew well that he was in Cairo and bound to return soon. They also knew that if he flew he would have to fly over territory held at that time by German and Italian troops. Any leakage of information, so easy in Cairo, might well have resulted in special fighters being despatched to endeavour to intercept his plane. By leaving at 7.30 p.m. we soon had the advantage of the cover of darkness.'

'It was a great relief to have succeeded in getting Winston away before Rommel's attack. I heaved a sigh of relief as I saw his plane take the air.'

Before leaving the Embassy for the airfield, Brooke sat down and wrote a letter of farewell to the general to whom at last he had been able to give his opportunity.

" My dear Monty,
Before leaving Egypt I must just send you a short line to tell you how happy I am to feel that the Eighth Army is in your care. I have had a difficult time out here trying to get things in better shape, and am leaving with a great feeling of satisfaction at the thought of Alex and you at the helm.

You have wonderful prospects out here and I have the fullest confidence that you will make the most of them. You can rest assured that, if there is anything I can do from my end to help, it will be done if it is possible.

Look after yourself, don't work too hard, and may God give you all the help and assistance you may require. God bless you, and the *best* of luck to you in your great enterprise.

Yours ever,
BROOKIE " [1]

" *August 24th. Gibraltar. 13¾ hours. 2500 miles.* Our party consisted of Cadogan, Jacob, Peter Dunphie (my personal assistant), Mr. Kinna (one of Winston's clerks) and our airmen. We headed S.W. and then turned west,

---

[1] *Communicated by Field Marshal Viscount Montgomery of Alamein.*

passing only 200 to 250 miles south of Benghazi; from there straight on over southern Tripoli, Algeria, and finally came out over Spanish Morocco into the western parts of the Gibraltar channel. Here we bore north for a bit and then turned east to approach the Rock as if we were coming from home, for security purposes. Low-lying clouds, through which the jagged top of the Rock stuck out. Not much of the runway to be seen through the clouds. However, pilot did a wonderful landing and put us down at 9.15 a.m. I was not feeling very fresh, having tried to sleep on a hard floor with a thin mattress (1 inch thick). I felt rather as if a steam roller had been over me! We had also done a good deal of the journey at 15,000 feet, and lying down at that height makes one very short of breath. After a bit the oxygen supply was turned on and we put on masks like the dentist produces to give one gas, not comfortable for sleeping in. . . ."

" We came straight up to Government House for a shave, bath and breakfast. P.M. had arrived in his plane with Harriman and Sir Charles Wilson just fifteen minutes before us. Weather reports over England are unfavourable, apparently foggy mornings likely to prevail for a bit. The possibility of going on again in a few hours and doing the journey by day, instead of by night, is being examined at present. . . ."

" P.M. is in any case to be confined to the house for security reasons. He discussed disguising himself as an Egyptian demi-mondaine or an Armenian suffering from toothache so as to be allowed out! I do not think that he will be allowed either of these alternatives."

" I feel that it is a great triumph having got him to start from Egypt last night. He had every intention of wriggling out of it if he could. He felt that the Cabinet had given him leave till the 30th and that he should be allowed to stop till then. . . . I knew that he would have given any-thing to stop on this week so as to be there if Rommel attacks on the 25th August."

" *Later.* At 1 p.m., just as we were going in to lunch, we were suddenly informed that London had approved doing journey by day and that we were to start at 1.30 p.m. This entailed desperate rush, as we had to change, pack, lunch and get down to aerodrome in thirty minutes."

" *London. 8 hours, 1600 miles*. By 1.45 p.m. we were off, skirting along the Spanish coast as far as Trafalgar Point, from there we lost sight of land and sailed out to sea. While we were in the Bay of Biscay I went up to the Second Pilot's seat, and remained there for most of the journey. There were nice cloud banks which we kept close to in case of attention of German planes operating from Brest. We saw none, and had a peaceful journey till we approached England. Here we ran into dirty weather, heavy clouds and electric storms. Wireless failed to function and we were thus deprived of directions or locations, and, after flying some seven hours over the sea, I think there were some doubts as to where we had got."

" However, as light was beginning to fail, we struck the coast of Wales north of Pembroke. Most of us thought we were over Cornwall and mistook the Welsh mountains for Dartmoor. Finally, with the light almost gone, the pilot made an excellent landing at Lyneham, near Swindon. There we found the P.M. had landed ten minutes before us. He had been met by Mrs. Churchill, Randolph and Chief of Air Staff, Harriman's daughter. We motored to special train where we dined on the way to London. Arrived at 11.15 p.m. to find large crowd, and to my great joy you were amongst them. . . ."

" I pray God that the decisions we arrived at may be correct, and that they may bear fruit."

Chapter Ten

ATTACK

*There are times when I wish I could wake up to find myself
in October next with the Germans held in Russia and Egypt
safe! It would be a great joy to start building instead of
repairing and patching.*

BROOKE TO WAVELL

5th July, 1942

FIVE DAYS before the Prime Minister and Brooke returned
to England, the landing in France for which the un-
informed had been clamouring was made at Dieppe.
Planned by Lord Louis Mountbatten's Combined Operations
Staff, and officially described as a reconnaissance in force, its
objectives were the capture of a Channel port, its retention for
a day in the face of attack and a successful re-embarkation with
data for a full-scale landing later. It had been authorised by
the Chiefs of Staff in the spring and fixed originally for July.
That it was purely experimental in scale and purpose was due
in part to Brooke's restraining hand. When owing to unfavourable weather it had to be postponed, the officer responsible
for the military side, Lieutenant-General Montgomery, had
recommended that it should be abandoned in view of the
security risks in remounting it. But because of American and
Russian feelings and the importance of obtaining data for later
landings, the Prime Minister had favoured proceeding with the
operation—the most important yet undertaken by Combined
Operations. To spare the French, the preliminary air bombardment was omitted from the final plan, while General Montgomery, appointed to overseas command, had ceased to have
any connection with it.

The operation took place on August 19th. The troops

attacking the port—a Canadian division of 5000 men with armour—never got farther than the water-front. The thousand Commandos detailed to storm the cliff defences on either flank suffered comparatively few casualties and captured a battery, but the Canadians lost three-quarters of their force, including nearly 3000 killed and prisoners. Even the R.A.F.'s fifty-six fighter squadrons—a force larger than the entire Command which had won the Battle of Britain—though successful in protecting the landing parties from air-attack and forcing the Luftwaffe to engage in an all-out battle of attrition, lost twice as many aircraft as they destroyed.[1] This bloody affair, though productive of many valuable lessons, ended the summer's attempt to draw off planes from Russia by trailing Fighter Command's coat over northern France—a gesture that had cost Britain nearly a thousand pilots and aircraft. Though the R.A.F.'s routine attacks on airfields and rolling stock in the Pas de Calais continued to prevent the despatch of enemy squadrons to the east, there seemed for the present no way in which Britain could relieve Russia save by sending supplies through Murmansk and Persia, bombing Germany's industrial cities, and striking at the Axis flank in Africa.

.   .   .   .

Of all Brooke's responsibilities that autumn, by far the most important were the two impending operations, separated from one another by two thousand miles of enemy and neutral territory, at either end of the Mediterranean. With the reinforcements and supplies he had been sending all summer pouring into Egypt and his two most trusted lieutenants in command, there was little to be done but await with patience the offensive they were preparing. On the last day of the month news arrived from Cairo that Rommel's expected attack had begun.[2]

Everything went as Montgomery had predicted. The enemy,

[1] At the time it was thought that at least 135 German aircraft had been brought down for the loss of 106 British, but after the war the number was ascertained to be only 48. *Royal Air Force 1939-45* (H.M.S.O.), II, 144.

[2] "If our blow succeeds," Rommel wrote to his wife, "it might go some way towards deciding the whole course of the war." "Either," he told a colleague, "the army in Russia succeeds in getting through to Grozny and we in Africa manage to reach the Suez Canal, or . . ." *Rommel Papers*, 274-5.

boasting he would be in Alexandria in three days, came on in a great sweep of armour round the British southern flank and made for the Alam Halfa ridge in its rear—the key, as Montgomery had seen, to the battlefield and the position where he had dug in his tanks and anti-tank guns to receive them.[1] Fighting like Moore at Corunna and Wellington at Busaco with a concealed reserve at the point where he had calculated the enemy's drive would tire, the British commander counter-attacked on the fourth day and pushed the attackers back into the minefields, using his armour to destroy their soft-skinned transport which, unlike their tanks, could neither be repaired nor, because of the attack from Malta on their supply ships, replaced. All the while he kept his army closely in hand, refusing to allow it to pursue the discomfited panzers too far. His object was to see them off with the maximum loss to themselves and the minimum to himself. He was not prepared to attempt more until he was sure he was strong enough to win, not a temporary victory, but a permanent and decisive one.

Given the chance for which he had so long been preparing himself, this great soldier in three weeks had galvanised his disillusioned and battle-weary troops with his own self-confidence. The post-Tobruk atmosphere of uncertainty had vanished; officers and men were no longer looking over their shoulders expecting retreat but shared their new commander's belief that they could destroy the enemy. Instead of its artillery and armour being dispersed and its fighting divisions split " into bits and pieces," the Eighth Army was now a closely-knit, integrated force. Much remained to be done before it could take the offensive—its new units trained for attack and its cavalry taught to use the Sherman tanks sent from America. But the Desert Army knew where it was going. It felt instinctively that there were to be no more failures. Auchinleck had kept it in being in the dark days of retreat; in the seven

[1] " You have been very much in my thoughts ever since Rommel started his attack," Brooke wrote to him on September 3rd. " I can so well imagine what all your preoccupations must be and, having seen the ground, almost feel that I am with you. I do wish I could drop in for a talk with you like we did in France. You have got a tough proposition in front of you, but I have the *greatest* confidence in you." Brooke to Montgomery, 3rd September, 1942. *Communicated by Field-Marshal Viscount Montgomery of Alamein.*

days' battle of Alam Halfa, Montgomery had made it a conscious instrument for victory.

.   .   .   .

Yet, if in Montgomery's and Alexander's hands matters seemed to be shaping well at one end of the Mediterranean, they were far from doing so at the other. Two days after his return to England Brooke spent a most difficult morning in the Chiefs of Staff Committee trying to sort out the confusion that had arisen over the impending expedition to French North Africa. The Americans, so confident a few weeks earlier of their ability to storm Hitler's Western Wall, were showing an unexpected reluctance to take risks inside the Mediterranean. Fearful lest the Spaniards, with their dominating position on both sides of the Straits of Gibraltar, should cut their communications with the Atlantic, their Chiefs of Staff were jibbing violently at the latest proposal of the British planners and of their own Commander-in-Chief, Eisenhower, to by-pass Morocco and commit the entire Allied force in a bid to seize the Mediterranean littoral of Algeria. Instead, they wished to confine the landings to the Atlantic coast of Morocco —the limited objective of the original and purely American " Gymnast "—and, since there seemed insufficient force available to attack from both seas, to concentrate on securing a safe base. Anything else, they argued, would be courting disaster. Nor were they prepared to accept the Churchillian contention that the advantages to be gained by surprise justified launching the operation before the landing parties and crews were properly trained. Far more conscious now than in the spring of their lack of battle experience, they feared a sudden switch of Rommel's armour from the east against their raw troops.[1] The farthest they were now prepared to chance their arm inside the Mediterranean was Oran, more than two hundred miles short of the Algerian capital and six hundred from Tunis. " A single line of communication through the Straits," wrote

---

[1] " The American troops were green. They had not been tried in battle. We expected to contend with strong German air-power after we landed. If General Rommel could get into French Africa before we did, it would be practically impossible for us to establish beachheads with the forces then available." Fleet Admiral William Leahy, *I Was There*, 136.

Roosevelt epitomising his advisers' views, " is far too hazardous in the light of our limited joint resources."

In the hope of winning their allies to bolder measures the British Chiefs of Staff had offered to postpone the operation until November. But the Prime Minister, who as usual was all agog to attack at once, had on his return from Cairo sent off an impulsive telegram to the President proposing October 14th as the date for the landings. The result was a complete *non possumus* from Washington. By the evening of August 26th— the day on which the American memorandum arrived proposing the elimination of all Algerian landings—tempers in London were distinctly strained. " We had to have a second C.O.S. meeting at 6.30," Brooke wrote that night, " at which I am afraid I was very rude to all members of the C.O.S. . . ."

During the last days of August and the first of September the British Prime Minister and Chiefs of Staff, stoutly supported by Eisenhower, wrestled with their Washington colleagues' fear of what they called putting " their heads in a noose." It stemmed partly from Marshall's deep-seated conviction that nothing decisive could be achieved by the British policy of re-opening the Mediterranean and tightening the ring round the Axis from the south and that to risk precious shipping and the flower of the American Army on such an object was unjustifi-able; partly from the fact that, following the abandonment of ' Sledgehammer,' Admiral King and the American Navy had embarked on costly operations in the South Pacific from which withdrawal was impossible. Deeply conscious of the strength of Japan and of the importance of depriving her of the initiative, King had secured the reluctant agreement of his Army colleagues to a landing on the beaches of Guadalcanal and Tulagi in the Solomons. His aim—a far-sighted as well as a bold one—was to forestall any further advance of the Japanese against Australia and its communications with Hawaii by breaking into their outer chain of island airfields. The landings were made on August 7th and precipitated a ferocious, ding-dong struggle, not only on the beaches of these remote Pacific islands, but in the waters around them. In its first few days alone four American cruisers were lost. For the next few months it constituted a drain on U.S. naval and merchant shipping comparable to that which might have faced Britain had the Chiefs of Staff yielded to the Prime Minister's plea for a landing in Norway. Early in September, with Australian troops and American airmen MacArthur launched a second counter-offensive in New Guinea to drive the Japanese back across the Owen Stanley range. This, too, though carried out by remark-ably small forces and brilliantly directed, made heavy demands on shipping and tended, like the more critical operations off Guadalcanal, to throw the maritime burden of " Torch " on Britain. Only with the utmost difficulty was Eisenhower even able to obtain from the Pacific-minded King a list of American warships available for North Africa.

To the British the primary object of " Torch " was to reach Tunis and Bizerta before the Germans and, by simultaneously driving back Rommel towards Benghazi and Tripoli, to win enough of both ends of the North African coast to provide continuous air-cover for their convoys to Malta. It was the one way to break the enemy's stranglehold on the Sicilian Narrows before the exhaustion of the supplies sent to the island in August and to preserve a base essential for opening the Mediterranean and threatening southern Europe. The only overland communi-cation from Morocco to Algeria was a single rickety railway, and to direct the bulk of the landing forces to the former, more than a thousand miles from Tunisia, seemed not only a waste of the mobility offered by sea-power but an invitation to the enemy to seize Tunis and Bizerta, and even Algiers, before the Allies could reach them. With its knowledge of the world's seas and shores and its experience of running convoys to Malta, the Admiralty regarded a landing among the Atlantic rollers of the Moroccan coast as a graver hazard than a five-hundred-mile run into the Mediterranean.[1] Even in the early autumn it was only possible to beach on that ocean shore one day in four, while the new French battleship, *Jean Bart*, with her great guns, lay at Casablanca and the *Richelieu*, at Dakar, only three days' cruise to the south. " It is by far the most difficult point of attack," the Prime Minister wrote to the President, " and the one most remote from the vital objectives in the Mediter-ranean. Casablanca might easily become an isolated failure

[1] *Churchill*, IV, 576.

and let loose upon us for a small reward all the perils which have anyway to be faced in this great design."

For a few days the American War Department's view was so strongly maintained that the Prime Minister had thoughts of another visit to Washington, and a plane was kept in permanent readiness to carry him and the C.I.G.S. there.

" *September 1st.* A short Chiefs of Staff meeting till 11 a.m. when we went to meet P.M. to discuss his proposed wire to the President. Before going there Sir Charles Wilson asked to see me. He told me that he had heard that P.M. was thinking of going over to America to try and straighten out the North African attack. He said that last time the P.M. was in Washington he had had trouble with his heart and that he thought it unwise for him to go. He asked whether I could not offer to go over instead of him. I should be only too delighted to do so, but, as the problem is mainly a political one, it is essential that some Cabinet Minister should come with me. We discussed P.M.'s reply from 11 a.m. to 12.45 p.m. and made several minor alterations. Attlee, Oliver Lyttelton and Eden were there. The P.M.'s reply conceded to the President the fact that they were at liberty to take full responsibility for the expedition and to base their hopes on a political re-entry without the necessity of force. He pointed out, however, all the dangers and pressed for the inclusion of Algiers at any rate. P.M. seemed dejected, tired and depressed."

" *September 3rd.* Arrived at C.O.S. to find that P.M. had just received President's reply to his wire. He ordered us to meet him at 10 Downing Street at 11 a.m. This was quite useless as the President's wire required examining with experts to arrive at the implications. He kept us waiting till 11.15 a.m., then talked round the subject till 11.45, when Attlee, Eden and Oliver Lyttelton turned up. ...At last I obtained leave to withdraw the C.O.S. to consider the matter and to report again at 5 p.m."

" We sent at once for Eisenhower and Clark and also for Ramsay. The new plan contemplated an assault of some 34,000 at Casablanca, where the surf will probably render a landing impossible, and only 10,000 at Algiers which is the key to the whole front. We concluded that the Casablanca landing must be cut by some ten to twelve thousand to render Algiers possible. P.M. and Ministers agreed; he then told me and Eisenhower to draft reply to the President suggesting this change."

" He is sending Eisenhower, Ramsay and Mountbatten to Washington, and asked me whether I thought I ought to go over. I said that, as the main difference rested on a matter of shipping, assault craft and naval cover, I did not feel I could assist much; especially in view of the fact that Dill is also going back and can deal with the major points."

" *September 4th.* We received rumours in the morning that the President would probably agree to our proposal, except that he would only reduce Casablanca by five thousand instead of the ten to twelve thousand. . . . President's wire was reported to be coming in late that evening. Finally escaped and went home feeling very weary."

Not till September 5th was the transatlantic essay competition, as Eisenhower called it, resolved. On that day the awaited cable arrived from the President—who for all his advisers' misgivings had never lost sight of the real objective—agreeing to transfer enough landing-craft from the Casablanca contingent to enable 10,000 British and American troops to land at Algiers. " Torch," wrote Brooke in his diary, " is now again in full swing." The compromise was the one which he himself had advocated a week earlier when, after a Sunday morning conference at Chequers, he had written:

" Agreed that we should examine possibility of doing Casablanca, Oran and Algiers, instead of Oran, Algiers and Bone. This is, I think, a much wiser plan and conforms much nearer to the U.S.A. outlook. The difficulty is that we shall require additional forces for it which can only be found by drawing on the Pacific. . . ."[1]

For Brooke neither believed that the expedition could be

[1] *Diary*, 29th August, 1942.

sustained without securing its rear nor that it could achieve its
object without taking risks.

· · · · · · · ·

It was not only the Americans who were anxious about the
proposal to send an amphibious expedition into the Mediterranean with nothing to protect its flank and rear but the Rock
of Gibraltar and its minute airstrip. On September 1st the
British Ambassador to Madrid had called on the C.I.G.S.
" He painted," Brooke wrote, " a gloomy picture. It is hard to
maintain one's determination to carry out an operation when
everybody keeps pouring into one's ear all the awful dangers
one is likely to meet. It takes far more trouble than anybody
would believe to stick to one's plan and refuse to be diverted."
' This conversation with Sam Hoare,' he recalled afterwards,
' had been an important one. . . . A great deal depended on
the attitude of Spain. . . . Gibraltar was bound to become a
hive of activity. . . . Masses of fighter aircraft would be unboxed
on the small airfield right under the Spanish noses, Eisenhower's
headquarters would be established there with consequent
danger of leakage of information. At any moment the use of
the naval base, port and airfield could be denied us by military
action on the part of the Spaniards without even necessitating
the capture of the Rock. There were risks, very serious risks
that had to be taken.'[1]

For, though less suicidal than an attempt to storm Hitler's
Channel defences, the venture on which the Western Allies
were staking their hopes was perilous in the extreme. They had
to convoy, in the face of submarine and air attack, more than
six hundred vessels, carrying an assault force of 90,000 men,
and 200,000 more to follow, with all their supplies and weapons,
across fifteen hundred miles of sea from Britain and three
thousand from America. They had to land them on neutral
territory in which they did not hold a single port or airfield
and which was guarded by 200,000 French troops, an air force
of five hundred planes and a powerful Navy whose officers
still bitterly resented the British attack of two years' before.
Once inside the Mediterranean, their sole air-cover would be

[1] *Notes on My Life*, VII, 521.

afforded by two, or at the outside three, British aircraft-carriers and by the solitary, overcrowded air strip at Gibraltar, itself five hundred miles from Algiers. And to obtain airfields from which to protect the expedition after landing, parachute troops would have to be flown from England more than 1200 miles across occupied France. For, whatever the attitude of the French, strong and immediate reaction was certain from the Luftwaffe and Regia Aeronautica, whose nearest air bases were closer to Algiers than Gibraltar and only a hundred miles from Tunis and Bizerta.

These vast and complex operations had to be planned in the utmost secrecy and haste and executed, within three months of the decision to stage them, before winter gales made landings on open beaches impossible. They had to be conducted on *terrain* with which no British or American officer was familiar and directed by an international staff, without previous experience of working together, under a Supreme Commander who had never taken part in active service operations or seen a shot fired in anger. The logistical difficulties were enormous. The runway at Gibraltar, the free world's sole remaining foothold in Europe and the hinge-pin of the whole operation, had to be extended for a quarter of a mile into the sea—the only way it could accommodate the fighters that were being sent there by ship. Fuel tanks had to be sunk into the solid rock, skilled technicians and mechanics flown from England to reassemble the crated aircraft on arrival. Everything had to be improvised at short notice and out of inadequate resources. " We were still existing," the Commander-in-Chief wrote, " in a state of scarcity; there was no such thing as plenty of anything. . . . The situation was vague, the amount of resources unknown, the final object indeterminate, and the only firm factor . . . our instructions to attack."[1] Hundreds of ships had to be withdrawn from the sea-lanes to refit and assemble for the largest amphibious expedition ever projected. The British part alone of the naval operations involved orders to more than two hundred warships and their routeing and exact timing of arrival at their Mediterranean landing stations. In the course of a few hurried weeks intensive training had to be

[1] *Eisenhower*, 86.

carried out for the assault troops, and, even more important, for the crews of the new landing-craft, which were beginning to arrive from America in western Britain, though still in far too small numbers. And all the while the Spaniards and French had to be watched, and constant air reconnaissance kept on Dakar, Casablanca, Toulon and the Italian ports, on the U-boat packs in the Atlantic, and on the German capital ships—that remote but very real menace—in the fiords of northern Norway.

For though Britain was still mistress of the Atlantic approaches to Europe and Africa, her control of them was anything but secure. When the decision to stage " Torch " was taken, Allied shipping losses since the beginning of the year had reached the appalling total of four million tons—a rate, as Churchill cabled Roosevelt, " unexampled in this war or the last." The number of U-boats was steadily growing; by that autumn there was more than a hundred operating in the Atlantic, including ocean-going vessels of over a thousand tons with a range that enabled them to attack in the deep central waters outside the reach of long-distance air patrols. Halted at Stalingrad and Alamein and faced by the need to prevent the immense resources of America from being deployed in Europe, Hitler had accepted his admirals' view that everything depended on strangling the West's sea communications while there was still time. On September 28th, as the first winter fog fell on London, and Brooke in the Chiefs of Staff Committee discussed with his colleagues the almost insuperable problems of running convoys to Malta and Murmansk, the Fuehrer summoned a special conference to consider how the U-boat war could be intensified. Despite new British measures against the " wolf-packs " in the Atlantic and Bay of Biscay and the institution at last of regular convoys along the eastern American coast, the under-sea campaign threatened to defeat every Allied attempt at the offensive. Again and again some ship allocated for " Torch " was sunk before it could reach the port where it was to load.

Yet, grave as were the perils facing the expedition, the man appointed to its command was equal to the occasion. Eisenhower might be without experience of war but he had precisely the qualities—of character, selflessness and good sense—to knit the staff officers of two nations into an integrated organisation in which national differences and jealousies were forgotten. His insistence that Anglo-American rivalry was the unforgivable sin created in his raw headquarters a new conception of inter-allied unity. " We proceeded," he wrote, " as though all its members belonged to a single nation." Though to create the impression that the liberation of French Africa was an American, not a British venture, both his Deputy and his Chief of Staff—Mark Clark and Bedell Smith—were Americans, the fighting commanders of his advance task forces in the Mediterranean were British. The leader of the eastern striking force, which, after disembarking under American command at Algiers, was to advance with all speed on the Tunisian frontier, was to have been Sir Harold Alexander. When in August, first Alexander, and then his successor, Montgomery, were appointed to command in Egypt, another Dunkirk veteran, Kenneth Anderson, took their place. And as Commander-in-Chief of his naval forces, Eisenhower was given, first, Bertram Ramsay who had directed the Dunkirk evacuation, and then Andrew Cunningham, the admiral who for two years had held the Eastern Mediterranean against the heaviest odds in British naval history.[1] Like their chief they and their team of British and American staff officers, through all their initial teething troubles and misunderstandings, consistently sought to eliminate national and Service rivalries and create a team that, in Eisenhower's words, " in its unity of purpose, devotion to duty and absence of friction could not have been excelled if all its members had come from the same nation and the same Service."[2]

.   .   .   .

" For the moment," Smuts cabled Churchill, " all depends on Alexander's success and on ' Torch ' being undertaken as soon as possible consistent with firm prospect of success. We dare not fail with this venture on which so much depends for our victory."[3] The war was at its most critical stage; the

[1] " He was the Nelsonian type of admiral. He believed that ships went to sea in order to find and destroy the enemy. He thought always in terms of attack, never of defence. . . ." *Eisenhower*, 99.

[2] *Idem*, 85.

[3] *Churchill*, IV, 453.

enemy, who had all but reached his goal—in Russia, in the
Pacific, in North Africa, in the Atlantic—was still massing for
the attack. At any moment he might break through at some
point in the straining Allied lines. In August the U-boats,
hunting in ever larger packs, moved southward down both
shores of the Atlantic, operating off West Africa and Brazil
against the convoys from Britain and America to the Middle
East, while Japanese submarines ranged far into the Indian
Ocean and Pacific. Two days after the President and Prime
Minister exchanged their jubilant signals over the agreement
about " Torch," four American cruisers were sunk off Guadalcanal and, as the Japanese made effort after effort to clear the
island, the U.S. Marines were left in almost as desperate a plight
as their comrades in the Philippines six months earlier. Meanwhile the German blows against the southern Russian armies
continued unceasing. Stalingrad was invested a week after the
British visit to Moscow, and by the end of August the panzers
had reached the fringes of the Grozny oilfield. In Washington
and London it seemed as if the Russians might break at any
moment, though the Prime Minister, remembering his final
conversation with Stalin, remained consistently optimistic. In
the middle of September the Black Sea naval port of Novorossisk
fell, and Field Marshal Paulus, obeying Hitler's impassioned
orders, began his all-out assault in the Stalingrad streets.

On October 5th, after a month of ominous silence, the
Russian dictator cabled the Prime Minister that the situation
had deteriorated so gravely that the Germans, by withdrawing
reserves from the West, had secured a two-to-one superiority
in the air. Two days later he appealed to Roosevelt for a
minimum monthly delivery of five hundred fighters and eight
thousand tanks, as well as for vast quantities of ammunition,
and this at the moment when, for the sake of mounting
"Torch" the Western leaders had decided to suspend the
sailing of the October convoy to Murmansk. For, with the
decision to stake everything on the Mediterranean, any
operation that made rival demands on shipping had to be
jettisoned. Even the reinforcement of the British forces in
Egypt, the next priority on the Allies' list, had to be carried
out in unescorted liners. Everything else had to take a sub-

ordinate place—the perilous naval operations in the South Pacific, where the American Marines had to hang on as best they could, the supply of the distant battle-fronts in Russia, China and Burma, the assembly in the United Kingdom of heavy aircraft for bombing Germany, and the build-up—till now the first of priorities—of men and supplies for the invasion of Europe.

Desperately the President and Prime Minister sought for ways to help their Russian ally, who they feared, feeling betrayed, might otherwise make peace. Yet, beyond pressing on with their plans for re-opening the Mediterranean and releasing the shipping to strike at Europe in 1943, there was little they could do. Apart from implementing Churchill's promises to pulverise Germany from the air, the only immediate aid they could offer Russia was to establish an Anglo-American air unit in the Caucasus. But until Rommel had been driven from Egypt, this was a mere aspiration—a sugar-coating to sweeten the non-delivery of urgently-needed aircraft at Murmansk—while the number of heavy bombers reaching Harris's squadrons from the factories was still barely enough to enable that most persistent of commanders to send two or three hundred planes over Germany on eight or nine nights a month. No more thousand-bomber raids had proved possible, and the elimination of the Reich's fifty largest cities—the Air Ministry's proclaimed target—was still far beyond Bomber Command's reach. The latter was being subjected to every kind of demand—from the Admiralty for raids on U-boat bases and mine-laying expeditions against the German coastal lanes, from the planners of " Torch " for attacks on Italian factories, for sacrificial attempts to destroy the German surface warships in the Norwegian fiords. For the present the most it could do —and at the cost of casualties that only the highest morale could sustain—was, by pressing home its attack on every possible occasion and experimenting with new devices for target-finding, to force the enemy to keep at home a growing number of fighters, guns, men and equipment that would otherwise be used on the Russian front.

As for the convoys to Murmansk, despite the insistence of President and Prime Minister on their overriding importance, the facts were too strong for them. Though the first convoy to sail in the autumn escaped the all-but complete annihilation of its predecessor, it lost, for all its formidable escort of seventy-eight warships, a third of its strength. To all demands from Downing Street and the White House for a successor, the Admiralty returned an unyielding *non possumus*.

" P.M. as usual," Brooke wrote on September 12th , " trying to get last ounce out of the naval forces and consequently wanting to run the convoy if possible."[1] When he was thwarted by the impossibility of making one ship perform the part of two, he tried to achieve his ends in a different way. Determined to succour Russia, he reverted to his plan for securing the Murmansk sea-route by seizing a base in northern Norway. On the 15th the Chiefs of Staff were summoned by him after their usual morning meeting to discuss the possibility of a landing there in January. " He has promised," Brooke wrote,

" something of the kind to Stalin in his last interview with him ' (when he went to say good-bye) ' and now he is trying to drive us into it. To my mind it is quite impossible at the same time as the North African expedition. Shipping alone will make it impossible. He would not agree, and we had a difficult hour with him till 1.30 p.m."

When the Joint Planners, to whom the Chiefs of Staff referred the matter, produced irrefutable evidence to prove that the adventure was incompatible with " Torch," the Prime Minister tried another device. ' It was about this time,' Brooke wrote,

' that McNaughton '—the Canadian Commander-in-Chief —' arrived one morning to inform me that he had been invited to Chequers for the following week-end to discuss something about Norway. I told him all the back history and the fact that the operation had already been examined twice for Churchill and turned down each time as impracticable. I warned him that he might well now try to have the attack done by Canadian troops. He assured me

[1] Not till September 28th did Brooke note in his diary, " P.M. . . . is at last taking a firmer attitude towards Maisky's unpleasant remarks and criticisms as to our handling of our naval forces."

that he would not dream of accepting such a task for his troops, and I asked him anyhow to see me on Monday after his visit to let me know the results of his talk.'

' On the following Monday a limp-looking McNaughton walked into my room and literally poured himself into my armchair. I asked him how he had got on. He informed me that he had had a ghastly week-end. He had been kept up till all hours of the morning until he did not know which way he was facing. Winston's control of the English language . . . had left him dumbfounded! '[1]

Two days later, on the 23rd—when Brooke had a long midnight " hammer and tongs argument " with his irrepressible master, ending " on friendly terms," about a proposal of his to offer tanks to Turkey—it transpired that he was planning to send the Canadian Commander-in-Chief to Moscow for immediate staff conversations with Stalin. By this time, however, the Canadian Government had considered the proposal and taken the same view of it as the Chiefs of Staff. When after lunch on the 24th Brooke was again summoned to his presence he found the Prime Minister greatly depressed by a telegram from Mackenzie King, the Canadian Premier. " I asked him," Brooke wrote, " if he had yet seen McNaughton's letter. He said he had not, and I told him the contents of it. He then became very worked up about the whole show and in the end was very pathetic. He said this machine of war with Russia at one end and America at the other was too cumbersome to run any war with. It was so much easier to do nothing! He could so easily sit and wait for work to come to him. Nothing was harder than doing things, and everybody did nothing but produce difficulties. He is a wonderful mixture and one never knows what mood he will be in next."[2]

Churchill's chagrin at being able to do nothing was only natural. ' It was very difficult on these occasions,' Brooke wrote, ' not to be filled with sympathy for him when one realized the colossal burden he was bearing and the weight of

[1] *Notes on My Life*, IV, 302-3.
[2] *Diary*, 24th September, 1942. ' Frequently in this oration he worked himself into such a state from the woeful picture he had painted that tears streamed down his face.' *Notes on My Life*, VII, 536.

the responsibility he shouldered.' Not having like his Service chiefs to direct the detailed planning of the impending counter-attack, he inevitably tried to expedite matters by forcing their hands. All through that autumn he was in a fever of impatience, urging Alexander and Montgomery to hasten their attack in Egypt and " talking our affairs over, back and forth," as he called it, with Eisenhower over the Irish stew at their regular Tuesday luncheons at 10 Downing Street and at repeated midnight sessions. Brooke was present at one of these at Chequers when the company, after a two-hour film, sat with their host from 1 a.m. to 3 a.m., " arguing on the prospects of the North African attack and the reception which the Americans are likely to receive."[1] The Prime Minister's view was that, unless a firm date was fixed for " Torch," the sense of urgency that the operation demanded would be lacking, and that, as administrative and logistical delays would be sure to retard it in any case, the only sure way of staging it before the winter gales began or the enemy discovered what was afoot, was to fix a day well in advance of the latest date possible.

The date finally chosen by Eisenhower, on September 22nd, was that which the American Navy had advocated from the start—November 7th. It was a month later than that originally proposed by the British and far too late for the Prime Minister's liking, but, out of deference to his allies' views, he felt bound to acquiesce. No such consideration deterred him from demanding an acceleration of Operation " Lightfoot," the name given to Alexander's and Montgomery's impending offensive in the Western Desert. " My next trouble," Brooke had written on the day he learnt that Rommel's attack on Alam Halfa had been defeated, " will now be to stop Winston from fussing Alex and Monty and egging them on to attack before they are ready. It is a regular disease that he suffers from, this frightful impatience to get an attack launched."[2]

Montgomery's refusal to launch his offensive before he was ready soon precipitated a crisis. In the middle of September Brooke asked his master if he might combine a visit to the School of Infantry at Barnard Castle with three days' grouse shooting on the Durham moors, his first and only leave of the

[1] *Diary*, 11th September, 1942.   [2] *Diary*, 8th September, 1942.

year. ' He said it was an excellent idea and that a change would do me good.' But on the evening of September 19th when Brooke returned to his host's house at the end of his first day's shoot, he was met by a summons to go at once to the nearest " scrambler " telephone—fifteen miles away at Catterick Bridge —for a conversation with the Prime Minister about a telegram he had just received from Alexander putting off the date of Montgomery's attack. ' When I finally got through to him on the telephone,' Brooke wrote,

' and he asked me what I thought of Alex's last message I replied, " I have not seen it." This met with grave dis-approval, and he replied, " You have not seen it! Do you mean to say you are out of touch with the strategic situation?" I replied, " I told you I was going grouse shooting to-day, and I have not yet solved how I am to remain in touch with the strategic situation whilst in a grouse-butt." " Well, what are you going to do about it now? " was his next question, to which I replied, " If you want to know what I think of Alex's wire, I shall have to have it sent up here to-night and shall let you know to-morrow." Back came, " How? How will you send a telegram? Have you got a Cypher Officer with you? " My temper was beginning to get worn and I replied, " No, I do not take a Cypher Officer to load for me when I go grouse shooting! I shall come back here to-morrow morning and continue this conversation with you on the ' scrambler ' when I have read Alex's wire." This finished the conversation, and I then had to get through to the War Office to arrange for an unfortunate Contact Officer to be sent up to Darlington with a copy of the wire on his motor bicycle. The annoying part of the whole thing was that there was nothing urgent in Alex's wire that could not easily have waited till I returned.'[1]

" *September 20th. Sunday.* Low mist and rain. Drove to Catterick aerodrome for another talk with P.M. I had by then received a copy of the telegram and Alexander's reasons which I thought were excellent. I told him so on telephone and thought he said that he agreed with me. As

[1] *Notes on My Life*, VII, 532-3.

a matter of fact he sent a wire to Alex, I discovered afterwards, trying to make him hurry up.'

'Thank heaven,' Brooke commented, 'Alex made no alterations.'

Three days later, on resuming work after his holiday, Brooke noted:

> " Many troublesome things on foot. . . . After lunch P.M. sent for me to discuss a wire he wanted to send to Alexander. I tried to stop him and told him that he was only letting Alex see that he was losing confidence in him, which was a most disconcerting thing before a battle. He then started all his worst arguments about generals only thinking about themselves and their reputations and never attacking until matters were a certainty; of never being prepared to take any risks, etc. He said this delay would result in Rommel fortifying a belt twenty miles deep by forty miles broad; that we should never get through owing to a series of Maginot defences. I had a very unpleasant three-quarters of an hour. However, I succeeded in getting a very definite tempering down of the message."[1]

Yet within a week the Prime Minister was at it again, trying to advance the date of the Middle East attack by a day or two on the ground that this would impress Spain and protect the flank of " Torch." ' His argument,' Brooke commented, ' was thoroughly unsound; by advancing the date we might seriously endanger the success of the attack, and failure might well affect the Spanish outlook and attitude. . . . On the other hand, the advantages of a few more days to appreciate the results of success were very theoretical and doubtful. . . . At the root of it all lay his everlasting desire to speed up the date of all attacks irrespective of the effect such measures might have on the preparations.'[2] Yet when Brooke told him so, he was " very reasonable and handed over his draft telegram for us to adjust."

.   .   .   .

[1] *Diary*, 23rd September, 1942. The telegram as sent is printed in *Churchill* IV, 527.
[2] *Notes on My Life*, VII, 540.

The pressure on the Prime Minister at this time was enormous and not only military. Still after three years the main director and inspiration of the war, he was bound to have fears that the victory he had striven for so long might be snatched from him by excessive caution and delays. His most formidable colleague, Sir Stafford Cripps, was at that moment threatening resignation out of disgust at mismanagement of the war, while his greatest ally, Roosevelt, whose support meant so much to him, was facing a critical Congressional election. An early victory was essential to re-establish confidence in both Britain and America. And the position of Malta was so grave that, unless either the Cyrenaican or Tunisian airfields could be won, the chance of saving it was negligible. At the end of September, at a long Chiefs of Staff meeting attended by the Permanent Secretary of the Colonial Office, the official responsible for the island's victualling presented a most alarming report. " The present supplies," Brooke wrote, " finish about the middle of October. Future supplies will depend on success of Middle East offensive or North African venture. If neither succeed God knows how we shall keep Malta alive."

Nor was the island, so vital to every Allied hope, threatened only by starvation. Angered by the use made by its aircraft and submarines of the supplies sent in the August convoy and their effect on the battle of Alam Halfa and on Rommel's dwindling petrol reserves, Hitler had resolved at last to finish Malta off. On September 14th he ordered as a preliminary a new all-out assault from the air. It began on October 10th, when the enemy started sending over two or three hundred planes a day. For ten days the attack never slackened. Park's fighters put up a magnificent defence, bringing down nearly a hundred German and Italian aircraft for the loss of only thirty Spitfires. But the problem of getting fuel to them and to the bombers which were blasting Rommel's sea communications could only be met by loading the Navy's fastest mine-layer with as much petrol as she could carry and letting her run the gauntlet of " Bomb Alley." ' A forlorn hope,' commented Brooke, ' calling for great gallantry considering the highly inflammable cargo they were carrying. I never feel that these acts received sufficient recognition.'[1]

.   .   .   .

It was not only the danger to Malta that worried the Allied leaders during this time of waiting. With the steadily mounting preparations for the two offensives was the risk that the enemy would learn their plans and forestall their attack. On the narrow front at Alamein strategical surprise was impossible, but tactical deception in timing and dispositions was essential. In North-West Africa the very existence of the landings had to be concealed if the enemy or the French, or even the Spaniards, were not to make them impossible. The Americans placed high hopes on French connivance; both their Agent-General in Algiers, Robert Murphy, and Admiral Leahy—former Ambassador to Vichy and now Roosevelt's personal Chief of Staff and Chairman of the American Joint Chiefs of Staff—banked heavily on the friendly relations which the United States had maintained with France since 1940. They believed that American troops, as distinct from British, would be hailed as liberators and were constantly trying to establish contacts, at considerable risk to security, with leading French colonial officers and officials. They also had high hopes that by enlisting the support of General Giraud, the hero of a recent spectacular escape from a German fortress, and smuggling him out of Vichy France to join their troops in North Africa, they would provide a figurehead round which all patriotic Frenchmen would rally. The British, on the other hand, with memories of Oran and Dakar and of recent experiences in Syria and Madagascar, had no illusions about their popularity with the Regular officers of the French Navy and Army. Their appeal, and that of their unaccommodating protégé, General de Gaulle, was to the non-possessing, non-official classes in France and her dependencies, not to the comfortable men in power who had compounded with Germany to save their property and were now more than ordinarily touchy about France's " honour " and their own. They naturally hoped that the magic of the Stars and Stripes and its historic association with the Tricolour

[1] *Notes on My Life*, 526. She got through but later was sunk.

would stay the hand of hurt national pride, but they knew that
the landing-parties would probably have to fight the French
for their footing and that the reaction of the Germans in Sicily
and Italian North Africa would be fierce and instantaneous.
The only certain insurance in their view against a hostile
French reaction was to strike with such strength that the
colonial authorities would treat the Western invaders with the
same respect as the men of Vichy had treated the Germans.
Speed and surprise seemed imperative.

As the day for " Torch " drew near, the fear grew that the
enemy would discover the destination of the vast armada
assembling in the Clyde and the eastern American ports and
the meaning of all the activity going on at Gibraltar under the
very noses of the Spaniards and German agents. On September
29th Brooke's diary mentioned " alarming information
of loss of a Catalina seaplane between Lisbon and Gibraltar,
and bodies being washed up at Cadiz with letters in their
pockets containing details of North African attack plans."

' This Catalina accident,' he recalled,

' was the first of the three serious scares that we had concerning secrecy. . . . One of the passengers was a naval officer
who had on him a letter from Bedell Smith, Ike's Chief of
Staff, to Mason MacFarlane, the Governor of Gibraltar,
arranging all details for establishing Ike's H.Q. at Gib. . . .
The capture of this letter by the Germans would at once have
disclosed the fact that operations in North Africa were
intended. The Spaniards informed us at once when this
naval officer's body was washed up on the beach and we sent
off a party to examine the corpse. They found the letter inside
his breast pocket, the envelope unsealed by action of the
water, but letter quite legible. The doubt at once arose as to
whether the German agents had arrived there first, copied
the letter and replaced it. It had, however, been noticed,
when unbuttoning the jacket to get at the letter, that sand
had fallen out of the buttonhole. This sand had evidently
been rubbed into the buttonhole as the waves washed the
corpse up on to the beach. It was agreed that if an agent had
unbuttoned the jacket he would not have thought, after

replacing the letter, to replace sand when buttoning up the jacket again. Our security in this case rested on a pinch of sand.'[1]

Next day a further scare occurred when M.I. 5 agents picked up a microphoned conversation between two unauthorised persons. " It went very near having discovered all about the North African attack and evidently had been obtained from someone in possession of plans." A third scare arose through one of the Air Ministry's confidential secretaries taking home with him—a thing strictly forbidden—a Minute from the Prime Minister to the Chief of Air Staff about " Torch." ' Next morning on his way to the Air Ministry, whilst boarding a bus and pulling out his season ticket, he dropped this important letter on the pavement and sailed off on his bus. A charwoman picked it up and handed it over to the young airman for whom she was working. Luckily he had his head well screwed on his shoulders. He appreciated the importance of the document, took it to the Air Ministry and refused to show it to anyone until he reached the Vice Chief of Air Staff to whom he handed it over.'[2]

On October 14th Brooke received from Egypt information whose secrecy was, if possible, even more vital than that of " Torch." It was the plan of Montgomery's attack and its date, with a special request from its author that it should be shown to no one. Brooke had to make up his mind whether to tell even the Prime Minister, whose anxiety at what he regarded as the unaccountable delay in launching the attack was becoming a major problem. ' I had,' he wrote, ' to judge between the relative importance of maintaining complete secrecy and, on the other hand, of stopping Winston from wiring to Alex and Monty and upsetting them and their plans with his impatience.' In the end, after lunching with him on the 16th and finding him in his best form, he revealed the secret. It was a measure of the strain of that time that even its com-

[1] ' This instance stimulated the fertile brains of our Cover Plan Branch and led to Operation " Mincemeat," when a dead gardener was converted into a marine officer and used by means of a submarine to convey false information to German agents in Spain. This latter operation inspired Duff Cooper, as he was then, to write " Operation Heartbreak." ' *Notes on My Life*, VII, 538-539.
[2] *Notes on My Life*, VII, 542.

munication a few days later to the Commander-in-Chief of
" Torch " caused the C.I.G.S. to reproach the Prime Minister
for taking risks. " I rubbed his iniquity into him," Brooke
wrote, " and he was very nice and repentant and said he would
send for Eisenhower at once to impress necessity for security
on him."[1]

On the night of October 23rd the long-awaited news from
Egypt arrived. It was a particularly anxious day for the Allied
cause, for in the course of it serious damage was inflicted on two
fleet-carriers attempting to reinforce the Marines on Guadalcanal, and, until new deliveries could be made from the shipyards, the Americans in the Pacific were left without a single
carrier. All day, following its four weeks' intensive battering
of Rommel's sea and land communications, the R.A.F. kept
up a non-stop bombardment of the German and Italian
batteries and airfields, until, as the full moon rose on the desert,
a thousand guns opened out on a 7000-yard front, and the
infantry and sappers, following the barrage, moved forward
into the enemy mine-fields.[2]

" This evening after dinner," ran Brooke's entry that night,
" received call from War Office to say that Middle East attack
had started. We are bound to have some desperately anxious
moments. . . . There are great possibilities and great dangers.
It may be the turning point of the war leading to further
success combined with the North African attacks, or it may mean
nothing. If it fails I don't quite know how I shall bear it. I
have pinned such hopes on these two offensives." ' I remember
that evening,' he wrote afterwards, ' as if it was yesterday, and
can see myself sitting at my writing-table in my Westminster
Gardens flat, finishing those last lines and remaining seated
staring into space.'

.   .   .   .

The next few days were not easy. ' Watching a battle from
a distance,' Brooke wrote, ' is far worse than being mixed up

[1] *Diary*, 22nd October, 1942.
[2] " Such drum-fire had never before been seen on the African front." *Rommel Papers*, 302. " I am glad that I succeeded in making a gunner of you," Brooke wrote to Montgomery after the battle, " and that you fully realise the value of this arm." Brooke to Montgomery, 11th November, 1942. Lord Alanbrooke, *Personal Files*.

in the middle of it and absorbed by running it. . . . Since our return from Cairo I had been inwardly eaten up with anxiety as to the results of this attack. The very fact that these feelings had to be kept entirely to myself had made them all the harder to bear.' With the fresh divisions and new drafts from England, the tanks, guns, aircraft and transport which he and his colleagues had been sending out in every available ship, his chosen general had been given the tools for the job. The Eighth Army had superiority in numbers, armour and air and, for the first time, something like equality in weapons and equipment. Yet unless its commander could do what others had failed to do and, not only drive the enemy from his immensely strong position threatening Egypt, but inflict such a defeat on him that his stranglehold on the African coastline would be broken for ever, Britain's hopes of winning the initiative would be defeated and with it Brooke's long-term strategic policy. " The first results are beginning to come in," he wrote to Montgomery on the second day of the battle, " and the suspense between messages is almost unbearable. . . . You are engaged in the biggest thing in your life and I am confident you will pull it off."[1]

For three days everything went according to Montgomery's plan: the attack in the north where the foe was strongest and least expecting it, the gaps punched through his front-line defences and minefields by the patient infantry and sappers, and the passage through them of armour, not to join in the all-out traditional cavalry charge that had led to disaster at Knightsbridge, but to engage, on carefully selected ground, the expectant panzers and, strongly supported from the air, wear them down in a long-range, hull-down shooting combat. But this preliminary " crumbling process " took longer than had been hoped, and after a week's hard slogging and ten thousand casualties—the figure Montgomery had predicted before the battle—the offensive seemed little nearer its goal than at the beginning. And rumours began to reach Whitehall and Downing Street—painfully reminiscent of the aftermath of earlier offensives—that the general was pulling divisions out of the line.

[1] Brooke to Montgomery, 25th October, 1942. *Communicated by Field Marshal Lord Montgomery of Alamein.*

The crisis for Brooke came on October 29th. " Before I got up this morning," he wrote in his diary, " I was presented with a telegram which P.M. wanted to send Alexander. Not a pleasant one!" Later, he was summoned to his presence and met by a storm of reproach.

' What, he asked, was *my* Monty doing now, allowing the battle to peter out. (Monty was always my Monty when he was out of favour.) He had done nothing now for the last three days, and now he was withdrawing troops from the front. Why had he told us he would be through in seven days if all he intended to do was to fight a half-hearted battle? Had we not got a single general who could even win one single battle? etc., etc. When he stopped to regain his breath I asked him what had suddenly influenced him to arrive at these conclusions. . . . The strain of the battle had had its effect on me, the anxiety was growing more and more intense every day and my temper was on edge. . . . He flared up and asked whether he was not entitled to consult whomever he wished. To which I replied he certainly could provided he did not let those who knew little about military matters upset his equilibrium. He continued by stating that he was dissatisfied with the course of the battle and would hold a Chiefs of Staff meeting under his chairmanship at 12.30 to be attended by some of his colleagues.'

At this meeting Brooke had to contend with the fear of his country's rulers that Montgomery and Alexander were failing to show true offensive spirit and had lost grip of the situation. To the Prime Minister and the other members of the Cabinet who argued that for the past three days the Eighth Army Commander had done nothing, he pointed out that he had withstood a series of fierce counter-attacks in which Rommel had suffered heavy casualties. The initial advance, only made possible by concentrated gunfire, had carried the attackers forward for several thousand yards; before the offensive could be resumed, the artillery had to be brought up and new stocks of ammunition established. As to the charge that Montgomery was withdrawing formations, had his critics forgotten, he asked, that the first principle of all offensive tactics lay in promptly creating new striking reserves for the next stage of attack. It was this, as those of his auditors with military experience must know, that the British commander was doing. ' I then went on to say that I was satisfied with the course of the battle up to the present and that everything I saw convinced me that Monty was preparing for his next blow.'

When Brooke had finished the Prime Minister turned to Smuts. " You are aware, Prime Minister," the latter replied, " that I have had no opportunity of discussing the matter with the C.I.G.S., but I am in entire agreement with all the opinions he has expressed." ' The flow of words from the mouth of that wonderful statesman was as if oil had been poured on troubled water. . . . Winston's wire was not to be sent, and Alex and Monty would not be disturbed by him at this tense moment when interference might have resulted in chaos.'[1]

Yet Brooke was far from feeling at peace. ' Personally . . . I had my own doubts and my own anxieties as to the course of events, but these had to be kept entirely to myself. On returning to my office I paced up and down, suffering from a desperate feeling of loneliness. I had during that morning's discussion tried to maintain an exterior of complete confidence. It had worked; confidence had been restored. I had told them what I thought Monty must be doing, and I knew him well, but there was just that possibility that I was wrong and that Monty was beat. The loneliness of those moments of anxiety, when there is no one one can turn to, have to be lived through to realise their intense bitterness. . . . It was fortunate that on that day I had not yet received a letter from Monty which arrived a few days later telling me what his feelings were at this juncture of the battle.'

That night, at 11.30 p.m., Brooke was again sent for by the Prime Minister.

" He . . . was specially nice. Referring to Middle East he said, ' Would you not like to have accepted the offer of Command I made to you and be out there now? ' I said, ' Yes,' and meant it. And he said, ' Smuts told me your reasons, and that you thought you could serve your

[1] *Notes on My Life*, VII, 560-2; *Diary*, 29th October, 1942. For the revised telegram sent to Alexander by the Defence Committee, see *Churchill*, IV, 534.

T.O.T.   R

country best by remaining with me, and I am very grateful
for this decision.' This forged one more link between him
and me. He is the most difficult man I have ever served
but thank God for having given me the opportunity of
trying to serve such a man in a crisis such as the one this
country is going through."[1]

.   .   .   .

While Brooke waited for news from Egypt, he was waiting
too, like the other members of the little inner circle in the
secret, for news of the last-minute attempts to pave the way for
the Algerian landings. A few days before Montgomery's
offensive began Eisenhower had received an urgent request
from Murphy, the Agent General, that a senior military representative should be sent to Algiers to make secret contacts with
leading French officers, including General Juin, the Commander-in-Chief. It had been decided to send the Deputy
Commander of the expedition, General Mark Clark, who had
accordingly flown to Gibraltar, continuing his journey by
submarine to a rendezvous on the Algerian coast. Nine days
later, on October 26th, Brooke lunched again with the Prime
Minister to hear Clark's account of his adventures.

"Apparently Clark flew to Gib; as no 'rendezvous'
had yet arrived, he went on by submarine and had
'rendezvous' wirelessed to him. Meeting-point was
signalled by lamp with white blanket behind it shining
through window. Went ashore in canvas boat and upset
by surf on landing. Met by Murphy, French staff-officers
and later by Commanding French General. All contact
most favourable and every chance of Giraud coming over.
Meeting interrupted by police; Clark and his companions
hid in wine cellar, where one of them, a British captain,
started a coughing fit. Clark asked him if chewing-gum
would help him and gave him a bit out of his mouth.
After a bit the captain asked for more; Clark said he
hoped he had not swallowed it. The captain said, 'No,
but the bit you gave me has not got much taste.' Clark
replied, 'That is not surprising as I have been chewing it

[1] *Diary*, 29th October, 1942.

for two hours!' The party then had a desperate time getting back again and were very nearly drowned, the boats being repeatedly swamped."[1]

'This journey of Clark's,' Brooke recalled,

'was a real epic and he displayed both bravery and efficiency in its execution. . . . The trouble started after the meeting was over when the party tried to board the canvas craft in a heavy swell. Clark was thrown into the sea and drenched; it was found impossible to launch the canvas boats and the decision was taken to wait till the sea abated. Meanwhile Clark stripped his wet clothes and decorated himself in an embroidered table cover used as a kilt, a tin hat and a carbine. It was only after repeated attempts that they finally embarked successfully, only to be confronted with further difficulties in establishing contact with the submarine.'

On November 2nd, six days before the North African landings were to take place and while the convoys and their escorts were still steaming through the submarine-infested waters of the Atlantic, Brooke lunched once more with the Prime Minister to bid farewell to Eisenhower and Clark before their flight to Gibraltar. That afternoon a telegram arrived from Montgomery that he had resumed his attack on the previous night. Before doing so he had sent a long personal letter to the C.I.G.S. "A real hard and very bloody fight has gone on now for eight days. It has been a terrific party and a complete slogging match, made all the more difficult in that the whole area is just one enormous minefield. . . . I have managed to keep the initiative throughout, and so far Rommel has had to dance entirely to my tune; his counter-attack and thrusts have been handled without difficulty up to date. I think he is now ripe for a real hard blow which may topple him off his perch. It is going in to-night and I am putting everything I can into it. . . . If we succeed it will be the end of Rommel's army."[2]

All next day, November 3rd, while Brooke was inspecting the new Airborne Division at Andover and making trial trips

---

[1] *Diary*, 26th October, 1942.
[2] Montgomery to Brooke, 1st November, 1942. Lord Alanbrooke, *Personal Files*.

in gliders and tug-planes, Montgomery's armour, pouring through the gap which the New Zealanders had made, grappled with the panzers on the Rahman track, while, beyond, the R.A.F. harried the enemy's transport along the coastal road to Libya. News of the battle reached Brooke at lunchtime, when he was called to the telephone and told that reports coming in showed that Rommel's situation was desperate. ' It can be imagined what the receipt of this message . . . meant to me. I dared not yet allow myself to attach too much importance to it, but even so felt as if I were treading on air the rest of that day.'

When next morning, after a foggy drive, the C.I.G.S. reached London, he was greeted by the Prime Minister with the news that Hitler had ordered his troops to choose between victory or death.

> " P.M. delighted. At 3.30 p.m. he sent for me again to discuss the project of ringing church bells. I implored him to wait a little longer till we were quite certain we should have no cause for repenting ringing them. More good reports from Alex during afternoon. At 11 p.m. sent for again by P.M. who was busy dictating messages to Roosevelt, Stalin, Dominions, Commanders, etc. He was in a great state of excitement. . . ."

> " The Middle East news has the making of the vast victory I have been praying for. A great deal depends on it as one of the main moves in this winter's campaign in North Africa. Success in Libya should put Spaniards and French in better frame of mind to make ' Torch ' a success. And, if ' Torch ' succeeds, we are beginning to stop losing this war and working towards winning it. However, after my visit to Cairo and the work I had done to put things straight, if we had failed again I should have had little else to suggest beyond my relief by someone with fresh ideas. It is very encouraging at last to begin to see results for a year's hard labour."

Throughout the 5th reports of victory continued to pour in:

> ". . . Monty has now got the whole of Rommel's army

on the move; as they are very short of both transport and petrol he has chances of a tremendous haul.   If only luck will be really kind to us!"

Nor was it only "Lightfoot" that was succeeding. Though the suspense was still intense, the parallel operations at the other end of the Mediterranean were promising equally well:

"The North African preparations are going well and so far have not created too much excitement amongst Spaniards, French and Germans. I had never hoped we should get off with it so quietly. Eisenhower left this morning, and to-night the submarine should pick up Giraud to convey him to Gibraltar. A great deal of history will be written either one way or another during the next week."

That night the vanguard of the armada began to steam in darkness through the Straits. Such had been the vigilance of the air patrols from England and Gibraltar and the watch kept on the French U-boat bases that, out of four hundred ships sailing in fourteen convoys not one had been sunk or even attacked. And though German agents sat with spy-glasses on every roof in La Linea watching the constant coming and going of aircraft on the crowded Gibraltar runway, the only result of their vigil to date was a concentration of sixty U-boats off Dakar and the Atlantic islands, which Hitler and his admirals supposed must be the goal of all this activity.[1]

By the evening of November 6th, 30,000 prisoners, 350 tanks and 400 guns had been taken in the Western Desert. Rommel and the remnants of the Afrika Korps were in full retreat, four German and eight Italian divisions had ceased to exist, and General Alexander was able to cable the Prime Minister, "Ring out the bells!" But that night rain started to fall and continued to fall all next day, turning the crowded desert tracks to the Libyan frontier into rivers of mud and making it im-

[1] Until the convoys in the Clyde sailed south, Hitler had been convinced that their destination was Norway. *Hinsley*, 210-11, 217.

possible for the British armoured divisions to outdistance and cut off the flying remnants of German armour.[1] By sundown on the 7th Rommel's rearguard was nearly two hundred miles from the battlefield and the main stream of his transport was starting to cross the Libyan frontier.

Yet, though the desert fox made good his escape, fifteen hundred miles in his rear the Allies were preparing to stop his earth. As the rain fell steadily in Egypt all that Saturday, the great armada in the western Mediterranean still steamed eastwards, while far ahead the battleships *Duke of York*, *Rodney* and *Renown* and the aircraft-carriers, *Victorious*, *Formidable* and *Furious*, trailed their coat to draw the enemy's fire. And as night fell, while the Germans and Italians scanned the sea approaches to Sardinia, Sicily and Malta,[2] the transports turned southwards on their true course, dividing into two streams, the one for Oran and the other for Algiers. Only a single American transport suffered any damage, being torpedoed a hundred miles from her destination by a stray U-boat.[3] The only other casualty was poor General Giraud—" King-pin "—who was nearly dropped into the sea while being transferred from the submarine to the aircraft which was to carry him to Gibraltar. 90,000 men, with their arms and equipment, had been brought over thousands of miles of U-boat-infested ocean without the loss of a life. " It is quite unbelievable," wrote Brooke that night, " that things should have gone so well up to date. It is

[1] " What saved him from complete annihilation was the rain; I had nearly reached Matruh and was getting in behind all his transport when torrential rain turned the desert into a bog, and I had two armoured divisions . . . bogged and unable to move. . . ." Montgomery to Brooke, 10th November, 1942. Lord Alanbrooke, *Personal Files*.

[2] The Italians seem to have formed a clearer idea of the expedition's destination than the Germans. " What will the various convoys do that have left Gibraltar and are eastward bound? " Ciano wrote in his diary on November 7th. "According to the Germans the provisioning of Malta or an attempt at landing in Tripolitania in order to fall upon Rommel's rear. According to our General Staff the occupation of French bases in North Africa. The Duce, too, is of this opinion; in fact, he believes that the landing will be accomplished by the Americans who will meet almost no resistance from the French." At the back of Ciano's mind and that of his father-in-law lay the conviction that the Allies' ultimate object was the destruction of Italy. " All the Anglo-Saxon preparations," he had written a week earlier, " lead one to believe that in a short while a powerful blow will be delivered in the Mediterranean to strike at Italy, which is judged to be the Achilles heel of the Axis." Ciano, *Diary*, 537, 540.

[3] The 1400 American troops aboard took to their landing-craft and reached their destination only twelve hours late. Lord Cunningham of Hyndhope, *Sailor's Odyssey*, 483.

a great gamble for a great stake, and I pray God that it may come off."

Despite the inexperience of the landing-craft crews, it came off next morning almost beyond expectation. At 1 a.m. on Sunday November 8th the troops began to go ashore on the Algiers beaches. By ten o'clock they had captured both local airfields and made them available to R.A.F. fighters flown in, with no hope of return, from Gibraltar. Apart from the surrender of a solitary fortress by a collaborating French general, little help was given by the military authorities or the local population, who remained sullenly inactive or openly hostile. The Commander-in-Chief, General Juin, upon whose known pro-Allied sympathies much hope had been built, was arrested by the police with the American Agent-General soon after the landings began. But the defenders had been taken completely by surprise and, despite fierce fighting in the harbour, where two British destroyers were sunk, their resistance was sporadic and confused. And by an uncovenanted benefit, which at first appeared as a piece of supreme ill-luck, the most influential of all Frenchmen after Pétain, Admiral Darlan—the Minister of Marine—happened to be in Algiers visiting a sick son. Impressed by the invaders' apparent strength this arch-opportunist, who had been the first to support the Marshal in his surrender to Germany in 1940, now temporised in face of the might of Germany's enemies and, without committing himself, authorised Juin to request a local armistice. At seven o'clock that evening the city surrendered.

Meanwhile to the west the situation remained obscure. At Oran, where, though the naval forces were British, the landing parties were American, the assault on the town was held up and fighting continued all that day and next. In Morocco, which Washington had considered the only safe part of the enterprise and where there were no British to antagonise French feelings, the invaders had some difficulty in getting ashore at all, and encountered fierce resistance when they did. On the day before the landings the surf was reported to be fifteen feet high, and only a bold decision by the American Admiral to take advantage of a brief lull in the weather saved the enterprise from being abandoned.[1] After three days' hard fighting General Patton's 34,000 troops had still failed to capture Casablanca, while a major naval engagement had to be fought to silence the guns of the French Fleet.

Yet six hundred miles to the east the trump card of the African pack was already in the Allies' hands. It had been secured by British insistence on attacking Algiers and by the luck of Darlan's visit. The American hopes of an official land-slide in favour of their two high-placed military contacts, Giraud and Juin, had proved as vain as had earlier British reliance on de Gaulle and the Free French. When, after a fantastic midnight interview with Eisenhower at Gibraltar, in which he demanded command of all the Allied forces in Africa and an immediate invasion of France, Giraud reached Algiers on the morning of the 9th, the French authorities completely ignored him. Apart from *force majeure* the only orders they were prepared to take were those of the head of their State, and, in his absence, his legally appointed lieutenant, Darlan. And when on the day after the landings they began to realise how much weaker the invaders were than they had supposed, an exceedingly awkward situation threatened. For the troops round the city outnumbered the invaders by two to one and the Germans had already begun to bomb the port and, with Vichy's connivance, to fly in men and aircraft to Tunisia.

The *impasse* was resolved by the moral courage and good sense of the American Commander-in-Chief and his Deputy, and the impatience of the Germans. On the 9th Mark Clark flew from Gibraltar to Algiers, and, realising Giraud's im-potence, at once opened negotiations for an armistice with Darlan. The latter tried to temporise, but when on the morning of the 10th—the day that Oran surrendered to the Americans—Clark threatened him with arrest, he agreed to a general cease-fire throughout North Africa " in the name of the Marshal." And when, under pressure from Laval, Pétain disowned his action and Darlan tried to rescind his order,

[1] When the Prime Minister stayed at Casablanca for ten days in the following January " there was not," he wrote, "one calm day." "Wonderful waves rolling in, enormous clouds of foam, made one marvel that anybody could have got ashore at the landing. . . . Waves fifteen feet high were roaring up terrible rocks. No wonder so many landing-craft and ships' boats were turned over with all their men." *Churchill*, IV, 605.

Clark's firmness in refusing to let him do so was quickly justified by secret news that the Germans had ordered the invasion of unoccupied France. This characteristic Hitlerian act, which followed with clockwork Teuton efficiency at dawn on the 11th, enabled the Admiral to follow the line of least resistance without any breach of legality or of his oaths to the Head of the French State. The Armistice had been broken, the Marshal was in the hands of the enemy, and his lieutenants were free to act in his name as they chose.

As, therefore, the panzers roared across the roads of southern France, the French generals and admirals in Morocco and Algeria, at Darlan's orders, ceased resistance. In little more than three days the great strategic prize of French North Africa had passed, with French assent, into the Allies' hands. Only in Tunisia, where the Germans had already taken possession, was the Resident-General unable to obey the Admiral's instructions. Two days later, on November 13th, Eisenhower flew to Algiers and, regardless of political repercussions in Britain and America, concluded a military agreement recognising Darlan as *de facto* head of the French State in North Africa with Giraud as his Commander-in-Chief. In no other way could the Allied communications have been secured in time for the race for Tunisia and the shore of the Sicilian Narrows.[1]

The effect of these events in London, which even Stalin hailed as the turn of the tide, is set out in Brooke's diary:

> " *November 11th.* . . . Events moving fast. Germany now invading unoccupied France. Fleet moved out from Toulon; Oran and Casablanca now captured. But Germans landing airborne forces in Tunisia. We have moved to Bougie

[1] " In view of all sorts of rumours about the attitude of the U.S.S.R. towards the use made of Darlan. . . ." Stalin wrote to Roosevelt in December, " it may not be unnecessary for me to tell you that in my opinion, as well as that of my colleagues, Eisenhower's policy . . . is perfectly correct. I think it a great achievement that you succeeded in bringing Darlan and others into the main stream of the Allies fighting Hitler." " Military diplomacy," he declared in a message to Churchill, " must be able to use for military purposes, not only Darlan but ' even the Devil himself and his grandma! ' " *Churchill*, IV, 598. *White House Papers*, II, 647. " Eisenhower took full responsibility. Roosevelt quoted him as having said later, when they met in Casablanca: ' I believe in a Theatre Commander doing these things without referring them back to his home Government and then waiting for approval. If a mere General makes a mistake, he can be repudiated and kicked out and disgraced. But a Government cannot repudiate and kick out and disgrace itself—not, at any rate, in wartime.' " *Idem*, II, 647.

and are making all preparations for an early push eastward by land, sea and air. Meanwhile political side in the balance; Giraud has not moved and Darlan remains an unknown factor."

" *November 12th.* The situation has not unfolded itself much during the day. Rommel is no doubt in a bad way, and retiring as fast as he can. Meanwhile Mussolini abuses him for abandoning Italian troops. On the other side, the Germans are occupying France and Corsica fast and endeavouring to build up a bridgehead in Tunisia. We are rushing troops over as fast as possible to evict them. . . ."

" *November 13th.* . . . We had General Bedell Smith in the C.O.S. meeting to discuss the problem of organising future offensive against Sardinia, and to estimate the repercussions on our very limited shipping. . . ."

" *November 15th.* Left . . . at 9 a.m. and motored over to Chequers where I attended Conference at 11 a.m. on future strategy in Mediterranean. P.M. presided, and attended by Smuts, Eden, Leathers, Chief of Naval Staff, Chief of Air Staff, Chief of Combined Operations, ' Pug ' and me. We lunched there and then had a second meeting with Bedell Smith and Humfrey Gale there. Most of the discussion centred on the advisability of letting Darlan take charge of the French in North Africa. . . . P.M. for it. . . . In any case no alternative at present. . . ."

" *November 16th.* Left usual early hour, and in War Office by 9.10 a.m. Lots to read before C.O.S. Then difficult C.O.S. till 1 p.m., correcting P.M.'s Directive on Strategy."

" Lunched at Dorchester alone with Sikorski, as usual quite charming and full of congratulations on our recent success. Walked back to War Office to put in crammed work from 3 to 6 p.m. Then Cabinet Meeting 6 to 8 p.m. at which I had to do much talking, explaining the military situation. After dinner C.O.S. meeting again from 9.30 to 10 p.m. followed by Defence Committee meeting from 10 p.m. to 12.15 a.m., still discussing Mediterranean strategy which is now fairly clear."

" *November 17th.* . . . Was told on the 7 a.m. news that I had been promoted to Knight Grand Cross of Order of Bath for work done in connection with North African campaigns."

.　　.　　.　　.　　.　　.　　.　　.

That month of November proved, as Brooke had prayed it would, the turning point of the war. It saw not only the rout of Rommel's army and the winning of fifteen hundred miles of Mediterranean coastline, but, as the by-product of these successes, the relief of Malta and, a few days later the capture of the great prize of Dakar and French West Africa, which its Governor, in obedience to Darlan's orders, brought into the Allied fold on November 23rd, with the battleship *Richelieu* and three cruisers. A German attempt to retaliate by seizing the Toulon fleet—the " Operation Attila " that for two years had been the Admiralty's nightmare—was thwarted by the French Admiral's scuttling, in the nick of time, seventy-three warships in the harbour. And far away, in the Pacific and on the south Russian plains, two great victories were won for the Allies, the one, though at a heavy cost, by the American Fleet off Guadalcanal, the other to the west of Stalingrad. Here on November 19th, aided by Luftwaffe withdrawals to defend Tunisia, the Russians launched their counterattack, taking the Germans completely by surprise and smashing two broad holes in the weak satellite forces on either flank of their huge salient before the city. Within a week 65,000 prisoners had been taken and von Paulus's army was encircled.

Three days after the North African landings, on November 10th, Brooke heard the Prime Minister speak at the Lord Mayor's Luncheon Banquet at the Mansion House.

" P.M. made very good speech, and, in referring to good war news, said: ' This must not be considered as the end; it may possibly be the beginning of the end, but it certainly is the end of the beginning.' "

The Prime Minister made no attempt to minimise the magnitude of the struggle; as always, he offered the British people blood, sweat and tears. Yet success—the more so for being unwonted—had whetted his appetite for more and, in his eagerness to engage the enemy more closely, he began once more to assume that more could be undertaken than the means available admitted. Before the African victories he was still, like his official advisers, thinking in terms of following up " Torch " in 1943 by an invasion of Sicily and Italy and a possible intervention by Turkey on the enemy's Balkan flank. But, having seen Libya conquered and French North Africa gained—Britain's objectives since the dark days of 1940—he turned instinctively to other and more remote goals: to the liberation of Burma and the reopening of the China road, a landing in Norway to ensure the uninterrupted flow of supplies to Russia, and, above all, the relief of the Red Army by a direct blow across the Channel. Though the Allied shipping losses had risen that month to the dreadful figure of 807,000 tons—the consequence, in part, of withdrawing escorts from the trade-lanes for " Torch "—to Churchill early offensive action on the largest possible scale seemed imperative. Tunis he expected to fall by the end of the month, after which a joint advance on Tripoli from east and west would, he believed, clear the southern shore of the Mediterranean in a few weeks.[1]

Thus it came about that, in the midst of his preoccupations over Darlan, Eisenhower received from his Chief of Staff in London a high-level suggestion that, in view of the initial successes and certain outcome of " Torch," the build-up of the Allied Forces in North Africa should be cut so that more important strategic ends could be pursued. To this the Commander-in-Chief replied with unwonted asperity:

" Unalterably opposed to reducing contemplated ' Torch ' strength. The situation is not crystallized. On the contrary, in Tunisia it is touch and go. Country is not pacified completely, communications are a problem of first magnitude .... Rather than talk of possible reduction we should be seeking ways and means of speeding up the build-up to clean out North Africa. We should plan ahead in orderly fashion on strategic matters, but for God's sake let's get one job done at a time."[2]

[1] See *Churchill*, IV, 586-7.   [2] *Eisenhower*, 118.

About the time of this unofficial exchange between Downing Street and Algiers the Prime Minister—on November 18th— dictated a Minute for the Chiefs of Staff pointing out that the African venture, which was employing only thirteen divisions, was no substitute for the invasion of France which had been promised for 1943 and for which, under the Marshall Plan of April, forty-eight divisions had been allocated. " My own position," he wrote, " is that I am still aiming at a ' Round-up ' retarded till August. I cannot give this up without a massive presentation of facts and figures which prove physical impossibility. . . . I never meant the Anglo-American Army to be stuck in North Africa. It is a springboard and not a sofa."[1] A week later he followed this up with a letter to Roosevelt protesting at the scaling-down by the American War Department of " Bolero." The Russian break-through at Stalingrad, he pointed out, showed that the chance for a cross-Channel attack might come far sooner than had appeared possible and that the Allies must be ready to seize it.

To Brooke all this seemed an attempt to take fences far too soon. He had never wavered in his belief that the only course that the shipping situation admitted was to exploit any success in North Africa to the full, reopen the Mediterranean and then, during 1943, strike across it at Italy, so engaging the enemy's forces at the weakest point of his Continental fortress until ships and landing-craft were available to strike at its strongest. As a practical soldier, he knew that his chief was being much too optimistic about the difficulties of capturing Tunis and Bizerta. The forces available for advancing four hundred miles through difficult country with poor communications in the teeth of growing attack from the excellent airfields the Germans had seized in Tunisia, consisted of only four British brigades. General Anderson's Eastern Task Force had begun its race for Tunisia as soon as Darlan issued his cease-fire. Two days later, on November 12th, a handful of British commandos and infantry, after being repeatedly dive-bombed, had been landed by the Navy at Bone, 250 miles east of Algiers. But owing to the lack of airfields in the wild hill-country they were entering, they and the troops behind them had had to continue their

[1] *Churchill*, IV, 583.

advance with inadequate air-cover against an enemy whose strength grew steadily as Hitler flew in men and supplies from Sicily. By the 17th the British advance-guard was in contact with the Germans twenty miles inside the Tunisian frontier and only fifty from Bizerta. Since passing Gibraltar ten days earlier it had covered eight hundred miles. But it had far outrun its supplies, whose build-up primitive roads, bad weather and the bombing of the Algerian ports were making increasingly difficult.

On the day that Churchill dictated his views on " Round-up," Brooke wrote in his diary:

" *November 18th*. Not much news from either front. Tunis advance progressing rather slowly and Monty delayed by administrative problems. On the other hand, . . . it is plain that Rommel is at present in a very bad state, lacking reinforcements, tanks, ammunition, transport and petrol. Unfortunately we are not in a position to take full advantage of this condition. By the time Monty has overcome his administrative difficulties the situation will no longer be so rosy."

" *November 19th*. Chiefs of Staff meeting mainly concerned with support Malta could be expected to give in operations directed against Tunis. All depended on convoy to Malta arriving safely and being unloaded. . . . News from Tunisia rather sticky; only hope Anderson is pushing on sufficiently fast. Benghazi looks like being captured within the next twenty-four hours."

" *November 20th*. Malta convoy of four ships arrived safely, thank God! This puts the island safe again for a bit. Benghazi was also evacuated by Rommel. Attacks against Tunis and Bizerta not going quite as fast as I should like, and reinforcements of Germans and Italians arriving fairly freely. Discussed with the chief administrative officers the gradual build-up of American forces in this country and the tendency to stop the build-up after completing the first five divisions."

" *November 21st*. Usual Chiefs of Staff meeting followed by a Cabinet meeting at 12 noon to discuss the proposed agreement between Eisenhower and Darlan. As far as I can see there is at present nothing to do but to accept the Darlan situation and get on with pushing the Germans out of Tunisia. . . ."

" *Monday. November 23rd.* Arrived back in War Office just after 8 a.m. following a very cold drive up. Masses of situations, wires, maps and briefs to look through before 10.30 a.m. Then C.O.S. till lunch. After lunch series of interviews to stop me preparing statement for Cabinet on week's fighting. 5.30 p.m. to 7.30 Cabinet at which I had to make a long statement. Then half-hour before dinner and one hour after dinner all-out trying to do day's files. Finally at 10 p.m. to 12.45 a.m. meeting with P.M. to ' discuss telegram about return of 9th Australian ' Division and New Zealand Division, convoys to Russia, sending aircraft-carriers to Pacific, etc."

" Operations in Tunisia not going as fast as they should, and on the other hand, Monty's pursuit of Rommel is badly delayed by weather. As a result Rommel given more time than I like to re-establish himself."

" *November 24th.* Am still very worried with slow rate of progress in Tunisia, in spite of long report from Eisenhower. . . ."

' I was beginning at that time to feel uneasy about the course of operations in North Africa. Eisenhower seemed to be unable to grasp urgency of pushing on to Tunis before Germans built up their resistance there. It was a moment when bold and resolute action might have gathered great prizes. Eisenhower . . . was far too much immersed in the political aspects of the situation. He should have left his Deputy, Clark, to handle these, and devoted himself to the tactical situation. . . . It must be remembered that Eisenhower had never even commanded a battalion in action when he found himself commanding a group of Armies in North Africa. No wonder he was at a loss as to what to do, and allowed himself to be absorbed in the political situation at the expense of the tactical. I had little confidence in his having the ability to handle the military situation confronting him, and he caused me great anxiety. . . . He learnt a lot during the war, but tactics, strategy and command were never his strong points.'[1]

It was this problem, and that of restraining his indomitable chief from embarking on new adventures for which resources were not available, that brought back into Brooke's diary, even in this month of victory, the old note of anxiety. By the last week of November Anderson's First Army was halted in the Tunisian mountains and the Eighth Army at the Agheila bend from which, in the past two years, it had twice been thrown back to Egypt.

" *November 25th.* A very difficult and long Chiefs of Staff at which we tried to clear up future operations in the Mediterranean. The first thing that requires deciding is the organisation of control of operations, namely the Higher Command. It is quite one of the most tricky problems I have met."

" *November 27th.* Again a long discussion at the C.O.S. concerning problems of Command in the Mediterranean. There is, I feel, no solution except an Allied Command in North Africa under a Supreme Commander (Eisenhower) and the present arrangements of a trinity in the Eastern Mediterranean, with a dividing line through Tripoli-Tunis frontier prolonged to Corfu so as to include Malta. . . ."

" *November 30th.* . . . C.O.S. at which we examined most recent ideas of P.M. for re-entry into Continent in 1943, and where he is again trying to commit us to a definite plan of action. After lunch interview with Secretary of State on new proposed man-power cuts of P.M. He never faces realities: at one moment we are reducing our forces, and the next we are invading the Continent

---

[1] *Notes on My Life,* VII, 572-3. 'Where he shone was his ability to handle Allied forces, to treat them all with strict impartiality, and to get the very best out of an inter-Allied force. In all the early times he was uncommonly well served by his Chief of Staff, Bedell Smith, who had far more flair for military matters than his master. In addition Ike was blest with a wonderful charm that carried him far; perhaps his great asset was a greater share of luck than most of us receive in life. However, if Ike had rather more than his share of luck we, as allies, were certainly extremely fortunate to have such an exceptionally charming individual. As Supreme Commander what he may have lacked in military ability he greatly made up for by the charm of his personality.' *Idem,* 589-90.

with vast armies for which there is no hope of ever finding the shipping. He is quite incorrigible and I am quite exhausted. . . ."

" Cabinet meeting from 5.30 to 8 p.m. and now we are off for another meeting with P.M. from 10.30 p.m. to God knows when, to discuss more ambitious and impossible plans for the re-conquest of Burma."

" It is now 1 a.m. and I am just back from our meeting. With to-day I complete my first year as C.I.G.S.; not that I think I shall complete a second one. Age or exhaustion will force me to relinquish the job before another year is finished. It has been quite the hardest year of my life, but a wonderful one in some ways to have lived through. . . . By the end of the third week I thought I was finished and that I could never compete with the job. . . . The P.M. was desperately trying at times, but with his wonderful qualities it is easy to forgive him all. A hard task-master, and the most difficult man to serve that I have ever met, but it is worth all the difficulties to have the privilege to work with such a man. . . ."

" And now, at last the tide has begun to turn a little, probably only a temporary lull, and many more troubles may be in store. But the recent successes have had a most heartening effect, and I start on a new year with great hopes for the future."[1]

" *December 3rd.* C.O.S. meeting at which we were faced with a new paper by the P.M. again swinging back towards a Western Front during 1943, after having repeatedly said that North Africa must act as a ' spring-board ' and not as a ' sofa ' to future action. After urging attacks on Sardinia and Sicily he is now swinging away from there for a possible invasion of France in 1943."

" Lunched with de Gaulle. He was on the whole in a

[1] *Diary*, 30th November, 1942. Ten days earlier Brooke had written to his old friend, Major Nigel Aitken, " Fortune was very kind to us throughout; we had to take great risks and gamble fairly recklessly. . . . There were moments when I felt worn and old, but the last few weeks have washed that away and rejuvenated me. . . . I have got another week to do to finish my first year of penal servitude! . . . They can't give me more than six months run as I become 60 in July. When I finish this job, war or no war, I shall fish continuously for three months without stopping if my body stands up to it. . . ."

good mood, but very bitter against Darlan. . . . In the evening 5.30 p.m. meeting of C.O.S. with P.M., Attlee, Eden and Leathers. Long harangue by P.M. that the Army must in 1943 fight the German Army. However, after pointing out to him the small forces that might be made available, he inclined to agree we might perhaps do more in the Mediterranean unless there were signs of great weakness in Germany."

' Matters at that time were taking a bad turn. I was quite clear in my own mind that the moment for the opening of a Western Front had not yet come and would not present itself during 1943. I felt that we must stick to my original policy for the conduct of the war, from which I had never departed, namely, to begin with the conquest of North Africa, so as to re-open the Mediterranean, restore a million tons of shipping by avoiding Cape route; then eliminate Italy, bring in Turkey, threaten southern Europe, and then liberate France. This plan, of course, depended on Russia holding on. Although in the early stages of the war I had the most serious doubts whether she would do so, by the end of 1942 I did not think such an eventuality likely. Russia had by now withstood the attacks against Moscow, Leningrad and Stalingrad; was getting stronger and better equipped every day. It seemed a safe bet that she would last out.'

' Up to now I had been able to carry Winston and the other two Chiefs of Staff with me, but now Winston was suddenly swinging away and wanting to establish a Western Front in 1943. At that afternoon meeting, after saying that the Army would have to fight the German Army in 1943, he said, " You must not think that you can get off with your ' Sardines ' (referring to Sicily and Sardinia) in 1943; no—we must establish a Western Front, and what is more, we promised Stalin we should do so when in Moscow." To which I replied: " No, *we* did not promise." He then stopped and stared at me for a few seconds, during which I think he remembered that, if any promise was made, it was on that last evening when he went to say good-bye to Stalin and when I was not there. He said no more and according to the diary gave me the impression that he was inclined to return to the Mediterranean strategy.'

' I knew him too well by then not to realize there was no certainty that he would not return to the Western Front conception. There were already too many pressing for a Western Front. Stalin, of course, Marshall, Stimson, Beaverbrook Press, Trafalgar Square and Albert Hall meetings, etc. If Winston was now to throw his lot in with the advocates of a Western Front in 1943, it would indeed become difficult to stick to my policy.'[1]

For though, since the Allies' successes and his own, Stalin's communications had become far more friendly, he was persisting in his demands that the Allies should strike across the Channel. And these demands continued to give rise to a strong belief in political circles that failure to do so might result in a compromise peace in the East. Brooke's diary for December contains several references to it:

" *December 9th.* Clark Kerr, Ambassador in Moscow, came to see me this evening and I had a long talk with him. He corroborates all my worst fears, namely, that we are going to have great difficulties in getting out of Winston's promise to Stalin, namely, the establishment of a Western front in 1943. Stalin seems to be banking on it, and Clark Kerr fears a possible peace between Hitler and Stalin if we disappoint the latter. Personally I cannot see such a settlement. Stalin is just beginning to get the better of the Boche and would only accept a settlement entailing restoration of old frontiers, plus Baltic States, plus share of the Balkans, plus many guarantees for the future which Germany cannot give. On the German side, Germany cannot carry on without grain from the Ukraine and oil from the Caucasus, plus oil from Rumania. I, therefore, feel that the danger of a peace between Russia and Germany is mainly useful propaganda from either side to secure their own ends."

Meanwhile beyond the Atlantic, encouraged by the news

[1] *Notes on My Life,* VII, 579-580.

that the Prime Minister was once more talking of " Round-up " and of transferring all landing-craft from North Africa to England by June, 1943, Marshall, who had little liking for Mediterranean adventures, warned the President of the immense logistical difficulties of further operations in that area and the danger of " dabbling wastefully." Instead, in a conference with him on December 10th, he urged a speedy liquidation of the remaining Axis forces in North Africa so that the entire Allied offensive effort could be concentrated in the United Kingdom for an emergency attack on the Brest peninsula or Pas de Calais by the spring of 1943. In a talk with Dill a few days later, he welcomed the identity of the British leader's view-point with his own and spoke of pouring American troops into England " instead of sending them to Africa for the exploitation of ' Torch.' "[1] Even the victor of Alamein added his voice at this time to those opposing a Mediterranean strategy, writing from Cyrenaica at the end of November to propose that, as the Germans could counter any attack on Italy or Sicily from the air, the best hope for 1943 was a cross-Channel attack:

> " This obviates all difficulties of shipping, air-support and so on; we should be developing the offensive from a firm base. It would be costly but it would bring off a fight with the Germans. I am quite certain that the way to deal with the German is to face up to him in battle and fight him; it is the only way to deal with him, because then you kill him. . . . Given a large number of Americans I believe the invasion of western Europe could be brought off successfully next summer, about June, when the weather is good."[2]

To this and a further letter on the same subject Brooke replied in his usual laconic epistolary style—for it was his habit to avoid written argument—

> " Paras. 2 and 6 of your letter are not quite in accordance

[1] *Strategic Planning for Coalition Warfare*, 363-4. For his earlier views see also, *White House Papers*, II, 654-5.
[2] Montgomery to Brooke, 27th November, 1942. Lord Alanbrooke, *Personal Files*.

with future possibilities owing to your not being in possession of full picture."

.   .   .   .

Yet events—and the Prime Minister's sturdy horse-sense, which usually in the end counteracted the promptings of his over-impulsive temperament—were working in Brooke's favour. Fearful of an assault on a restless Europe from the south and conscious of the declining morale of Italy, now panic stricken by R.A.F. raids on her northern cities, Hitler had decided to stake everything on defending the Tunisian peninsula. With its dominating strategic position, military airfields and great naval port of Bizerta, he saw in it the only means of denying the passage of the Mediterranean to the Allies and preventing an invasion of Europe from the south. According to a statement made by General Warlimont after the war, the German leader had been taken completely by surprise by the North African landings, which established " a spring-board for a thrust into the groin of Fortress Europe, the naturally weak and practically unprepared south flank," and so was " decisive for the whole conduct of the war."[1] While, therefore, he continued to order the encircled von Paulus to hold his ground in front of Stalingrad, he simultaneously refused to contemplate any abandonment of the new German foothold beyond the Sicilian Narrows. Instead, leaving Rommel, who withdrew under pressure from Agheila on December 13th, to retreat across the desert towards Tripoli, he continued to fly men and supplies across the narrow sea-channel to make Tunisia an impregnable outer bastion for Italy and a stronghold for all the Axis forces in Africa. His henchmen even spoke of reaching Morocco by the spring and driving the Americans into the sea.[2]

During the last weeks of the year the effect of this decision became increasingly apparent. On December 1st, the Germans

[1] *U.S. War Department Official History, European Theatre, Cross-Channel Attack,* 143. " If Tunisia should fall," Ciano wrote on November 17th, " we should lose our last defensive bastion. . . ." Ciano, *Diary,* 544. For Hitler's decision see *Hinsley,* 223.

[2] Ciano *Diary,* 550. According to the *Rommel Papers* Hitler and Kesselring, the commander of the Luftwaffe in the Mediterranean, still hoped to retain both Tripoli and Tunisia, though Rommel himself believed that neither could be held.

in Tunisia, already more than 20,000 strong, attacked the British advance posts, at that moment only twelve miles from the capital, and, despite American reinforcements hastily brought up from Algiers, forced them back. Since even the most ardent advocates of an early cross-Channel operation were agreed that Africa must be cleared first, this unexpected development had the effect of strengthening Brooke's hand. If " Round-up " was not going to be logistically possible in 1943 because the troops and landing-craft already committed to the Mediterranean campaign could not be released in time, some other form of attack would have to take its place. For no one, least of all the British Prime Minister, wished to allow the coming summer to pass without a major offensive somewhere. Brooke's diary reveals what happened as he and his colleagues persistently opposed to idealistic projects the logic of unfolding fact:

" *December 4th 1942.* Chiefs of Staff meeting at which we again examined P.M.'s recent swing-round to an invasion of France instead of Mediterranean operations. . . . News from Tunisia not too good and I do not like much the way things are going there."

" *December 7th.* A quieter Monday than usual. Situation in North Africa none too good. Eisenhower far too busy with political matters connected with Darlan and Boisson. Not paying enough attention to the Germans who are making far too much progress and will now take a great deal of dislodging out of Tunis and Bizerta. Cabinet at 5.30 p.m."

" *December 8th.* Finished C.O.S. meeting fairly early. We were discussing line of action to adopt in order to induce the P.M. to abandon the idea of invasion of France in 1943 for the more attractive prospects in the Mediterranean. . . ."

" *December 11th.* . . . This evening received a wire from Dill giving insight into Marshall's mind. Apparently he considers we should close down operations in the Mediterranean once we have pushed Germans out, and then concentrate on preparing for re-entry into France, combined with a move through Turkey. I think he is wrong and that the Mediterranean gives us far better facilities for wearing down German forces both land and air, and of withdrawing strength from Russia."

" *December 15th.* We finished off our paper refuting P.M.'s arguments for a Western Front in France (1943) and pressed for a Mediterranean policy aiming at pushing Italy out of the war and Turkey into it. By this means we aim at relieving the maximum possible pressure off Russia."

" Clark Kerr, the Ambassador in Moscow, gave us an hour on his views of Stalin's reactions if we do not start a Western Front in France. He urged that such a course might well lead to Stalin making a separate peace with Hitler. I refuse to believe such a thing possible and fail to see how any common agreement could ever be arrived at between them which would not irreparably lower the prestige of one or the other in the eyes of their own people. . . ."

" *December 16th.* . . . At 6 p.m. we had a C.O.S. meeting with P.M.; Anthony Eden also there. All about policy for 1943. As the paper we put in went straight against Winston, who was pressing for a Western Front whilst we pressed for amphibious operations in the Mediterranean, I feared the worst. However, the meeting went well from the start and I succeeded in swinging him round. I think he is now fairly safe, but I have still the Americans to convince first and then Stalin next."

' This,' wrote Brooke,

' was a great triumph for the present and we had avoided the grave danger of Winston siding with the Americans. There was of course always the chance that he might swing round again, but I felt fairly safe. I knew from what Dill had written to me that I was going to have a very tough time of it to swing Marshall away from his Western Front theories. As we shall see my apprehensions were not misplaced, and Casablanca turned out to be a very desperate struggle. The last few lines of the diary were evidently not written seriously. I had no illusions as to the possibility of convincing Stalin, as it would not suit *his* policy to be convinced.'[1]

Yet even Marshall did not advocate leaving the Germans in Tunisia. Three days before Christmas, with every road a quagmire of bottomless mud, and supplies repeatedly delayed by air-raids on the Algerian ports, the Allies resumed their attack on the Tunisian highlands. But 50,000 Axis troops were by now holding the peninsula, and with the R.A.F. partially grounded for lack of hard-surface airfields, and with only a single precarious line of communications, the weak and ill-co-ordinated British, American and French forces, for all their gallantry, could effect nothing. After three days of continuous rain, Eisenhower called off the offensive. A stalemate was now inevitable until either drier weather returned with the spring or Montgomery could capture Tripoli and, sustained from that port, attack Tunisia from the south-east.

A new strategic decision by the Western Allies was, therefore, essential. Since the end of November suggestions had been under consideration for a meeting in the New Year between the political and military leaders of the two democracies and, if possible, of the U.S.S.R. But Stalin, who was directing the Russian armies, declined to leave Moscow, and in the course of December Roosevelt, rejecting Churchill's suggestion of a rendezvous in Iceland, agreed to meet the British leader and his advisers at some carefully guarded spot in the French empire they had together liberated. On the 22nd, six days after the Prime Minister had reluctantly accepted the strategic plan of his persistent Chiefs of Staff, Brooke's diary records:

> " Roosevelt has sent message to Winston suggesting a meeting in North Africa somewhere near Casablanca about January 15th. We shall consequently soon be travelling again."

---

[1] *Notes on My Life*, VII, 585.

Chapter Eleven

CASABLANCA

The time was ripe for the emergence of the master plan, the blueprint for how to set about winning the war.

MARSHAL OF THE ROYAL AIR FORCE
SIR JOHN SLESSOR

DURING THE first week of January both the British and American Chiefs of Staff were perfecting the plans with which they intended to confront one another at Casablanca. The British were quite clear what they wanted and, under Brooke's chairmanship, presented to their political chiefs and allies an unshakable front. Behind them and the Defence Minister was a stream-lined professional organization, the result of years of evolution and experience. For every argument they advanced they were able to produce chapter and verse, with plans and statistics worked out to the last detail. The policy they advocated was that the successes won by Alamein and " Torch " should be swiftly followed up: that in the course of the summer, after the destruction of the remaining Axis forces in Africa and the re-opening of the Mediterranean to Allied shipping, the British and American land, sea and air forces should strike from the spring-board where they were already deployed at the exposed under-belly of Hitler's Europe—the point where the Axis was most vulnerable. It would break the crumbling morale of Italy, throw the Balkans into a ferment, and, possibly, bring Turkey into the war. No time should be allowed to the enemy forces in the Mediterranean basin to recover, and help should be afforded to Russia by keeping them continuously engaged.

Meanwhile the bombing of Germany's industrial centres and communications from Britain was to be intensified and, as the Axis resistance in Africa weakened, to be reinforced by the bombing of southern Europe from African and, later, Sicilian and Italian bases. And, while, apart from minor operations to reopen the Burma road into China, the Japanese were to be contained with the minimum of force, a great Anglo-American army and air force in Britain were to be built up for cross-Channel operations in 1944 as rapidly as was compatible with a 1943 victory in the Mediterranean. " We believe," the British Chiefs of Staff wrote, " that this policy will afford earlier and greater relief, both direct and indirect, to Russia than if we were to concentrate on " Bolero " to the exclusion of all other operations, observing that at the best we could not put a force of more than twenty-five divisions on the Continent in the late summer of 1943. . . ." " To make a fruitless assault before the time is ripe would be disastrous to ourselves, of no assistance to Russia and devastating to the morale of occupied Europe."[1]

This programme was based on a close and realistic appreciation of the Allied strength deployed in every theatre of war, and particularly of the ships and landing-craft available. The deciding factor in planning the coming offensive were the United Nations' resources in shipping and naval assault-forces. " The reason," Churchill wrote to Stalin, " why these performances have fallen so far short of the expectations of last year is not that the troops do not exist, but that the shipping at our disposal and the means of escorting it do not exist."[2] During the course of 1943, because the American shipbuilding programme had at last begun to overtake the rate of sinkings, it should become possible, it was estimated, to move, roughly, a million American troops overseas or about the same number as were already serving abroad. The reopening of the Mediterranean would add at least another million tons to the capacity of the British Merchant Marine, at present fully stretched in importing the bare minimum of foodstuffs and raw materials needed by the United Kingdom and in supplying and reinforcing the British fronts in the Middle

[1] *Churchill*, IV, 601-2; *Strategic Planning for Coalition Warfare*, 1941-42, 377-8; *U.S. War Department Official History, European Theatre of Operations—Cross-Channel Attack*, 37.

[2] Prime Minister to Stalin, March 11th, 1943. *Churchill*, IV, 671.

East, Tunisia and India. If a victory could be won by the summer over the U-boats, and the terrible monthly drain of over half a million tons could be reduced, the offensive mobility of the Western Powers would be correspondingly increased. But during the past year more than a thousand ships had been sunk and losses had exceeded new construction by a million tons, so that at the moment the Western Powers, though possessing more troops and greater resources, were even less mobile than they had been a year before. Because of this threat to their very existence the building of landing and assault craft—essential for any invasion—had had throughout 1942 to give way to the building of escort-vessels. This was the hard logistical reality on which all Brooke's calculations were based and which the Americans, in their desire to get to grips with the Germans, were still not facing.

As for Allied air power, the R.A.F.'s night bombing force in Britain still only numbered eight hundred first-line aircraft —a fifth of the number originally planned for the summer of 1943. But it was growing fast in bomb-bearing capacity, and, as new technical aids became available, increasingly successful at finding and attacking strongly-defended targets which, for the first time in the war, were beginning to suffer serious damage at its hands. Its striking-power was still very limited, but it was on the point of becoming far more formidable. It had been joined during 1942 by a force of five hundred large American day-bombers which, however, owing to their vulnerability to fighter attack, had been unable as yet to take part in major operations over Germany. For the present the main American striking-power in the air was concentrated in the Pacific and the Mediterranean, where it was already starting to rival the strong R.A.F. forces operating in that sea.

* * * * * * * *

The American Joint Chiefs of Staff approached the Conference without the clear-cut certainty of their British colleagues, though with a stubborn resolve not to give way to them. Despite their far greater potential resources and the boundless energy and optimism of the nation whose forces they directed, they lacked their ally's administrative machine. They were not even united, the Navy and Army being rivals, and often almost independent rivals, for resources and equipment. Admiral King, as the officer mainly responsible for the Pacific, was always trying to ear-mark shipping for it, and still enjoyed almost a monopoly of landing-craft, which the Army consequently had great difficulty in obtaining.[1] He and General Marshall were at one, however, in their belief that, so far as Germany and not Japan was the principal enemy, operations across the English Channel were the only decisive means of attack. General Arnold, Chief of the Army Air Force and the third member of the Joint Chiefs of Staff, while partly sharing this view, believed, on the other hand, that the Reich might be crippled, if not wholly destroyed, from the air. All three of them and their newly appointed Chairman, Admiral Leahy, felt that operations in the Mediterranean were logistically wasteful, could have no effect on the main Axis partner, Germany, and might, if the latter counter-attacked through Spain, prove dangerous. " They regarded the Mediterranean," wrote the Assistant Military Secretary of the War Cabinet, " as a kind of dark hole, into which one entered at one's peril. If large forces were committed . . . the door would suddenly and firmly be shut behind one."[2] They also suspected that the British wished to exploit operations in that sea, especially at its eastern end, to further their imperial ends. They, therefore proposed that the African campaign should be completed as soon as possible, and that thereafter the main effort for 1943 should be put into " Round-up," with subsidiary offensives by the British in Burma and by themselves against the Japanese communications in the South Pacific.

[1] In his diary of the Casablanca Conference, Brigadier (now Lt.-Gen. Sir Ian) Jacob wrote, "Apparently the operations in the Pacific are planned exclusively by the Navy Department, who in their turn leave the rest of the world to the War Department. There is little or no collusion, so that the allocation of resources as between the Pacific and the rest of the world is inevitably a hit and miss affair, or perhaps one could better describe it as a game of grab. The Navy have their ships and the Army have theirs. The Navy control the landing-craft, so that the Army finds it difficult to squeeze out what they want for their own projects. On the other hand, the Navy is apt to find itself in difficulty on the administrative or logistical side of their Pacific operations, as they often do not bring the Army into the picture early enough. This happened at Guadalcanal, where the U.S. Marines were thrown ashore and then it was found that there was no follow-up, no maintenance organisation, and no transport. The Army was then called in to help—very nearly too late." Sir Ian Jacob, *MS. Diary*, 13th January, 1943.

[2] Sir Ian Jacob, *MS. Diary*, 14th January, 1943.

Neither, however, the President nor all the officers of the Plans Division of the War Department at Washington any longer shared General Marshall's belief in the possibilities of an early invasion of Europe. Several of the less rigid military planners had been profoundly shaken by the Dieppe casualties, and in the light of the recent deflection of resources and, above all, of landing craft, to the Pacific and North Africa, considered that it would not now be logistically possible to stage any large-scale cross-Channel operation before the summer of 1944. They, therefore, either felt, like King, that greater efforts should be made to defeat Japan, or, alternatively—though without much enthusiasm—that it would be better, while maintaining a growing air-bombardment of Germany, to continue a limited pressure in the Mediterranean in pursuit of what they called " the psychological and tangible advantages promised by ' Torch.' " The President's instinct, as always, was to defer decision until events had unfolded sufficiently far to make it, if not inevitable, politically unanswerable. Unlike his Service mentors, he had no particular aversion to Mediterranean adventures, and, though he did not engage in military arguments with his Service advisers like the Prime Minister, he was not prepared to commit himself in advance to their views. He merely warned them that the British would come to the conference with a plan " and stick to it."[1]

In this he was right. Unlike their American colleagues, the British took to the Conference an elaborate staff, cipher and planning organisation, with the technical mechanism for presenting every quantitative calculation that might be called for.[2] They sent it out in advance to Casablanca in a 6,000-ton liner, equipped by Combined Operations Command as a headquarters and communications vessel, thus temporarily transferring Great George Street to Morocco. The principals—consisting of the Prime Minister, the three Chiefs of Staff,

[1] *Strategic Planning for Coalition Warfare*, 365-6; 379. *European Theatre of Operations—Cross-Channel Attack*, 38.
[2] " What was completely lacking in the American party was any kind of staff who could tackle the problems that were bound to arise in the course of the conversations, and to produce detailed solutions for the Chiefs of Staff. When the U.S. Chiefs saw how the land lay and the size of our party, they suddenly woke up to the fact that they had left most of their clubs behind." Sir Ian Jacob, *MS. Diary*, 13th January, 1943.

their respective Directors of Plans, the Chief of Combined Operations, the Military Secretary of the War Cabinet, and a number of other senior staff officers—followed by air on January 12th. It had been originally proposed that they should travel by cruiser, but in view of the violence of the U-boat campaign against " Torch's " Atlantic communications, the First Sea Lord opposed the suggestion. There was, therefore, some last-minute difficulty in assembling sufficient long-range aircraft to carry so large and distinguished a party over 1,400 miles of sea, and the great ones, except for the Prime Minister, were forced to travel in very close proximity. Brooke described their start in a new volume of his diary.

> " *January 12th 1943. 1,400 miles.* . . . I was then told that all plans were changed. We are not going by Clipper as sea was too rough at Gibraltar, but should go by Liberator instead. We were to go by car, leaving London at 7.30 p.m. and motor some ninety miles in the dark to an aerodrome near Swindon. We took off at 2 a.m. and had a very good journey. We had to wear flying kit to counteract the cold, but with the fur-lined clothes kept very nice and warm."

' Our departure,' he added afterwards, ' had been kept remarkably secret in London, and we did not even know what aerodrome we were going to. We were given a rendezvous when the cars met and were led to the aerodrome, which I think must have been Lyneham. There we had a long wait, being issued with flying kit and lectured as to what we did if we landed in the sea. Finally we embarked in one of the uncomfortable converted Liberators. I slept on the floor of the little cabin in the rear of the plane and had Dickie Mountbatten sleeping next to me. I did not find him a pleasant bed companion, as every time he turned round he overlay me, and I had to use my knees and elbows to establish my rights to my allotted floor space! '

> " *January 13th.* Arrived at Casablanca at 11 a.m. after quite an interesting flight down the coast. Here we are

stopping in a very comfortable modern hotel just outside the town, with two modern villas close by, one for Winston and one for Roosevelt.[1] The former arrived at the same time as we did and the latter should arrive to-morrow. We are a large party—P.M., Lord Leathers, three Chiefs of Staff, ' Pug ' Ismay, Mountbatten, Jacob, John Kennedy, Slessor, three Joint Planners and many others. On American side President, Marshall, King, Arnold, Cooke, Somervell, Clark, Eisenhower, Leahy, Dill, Harriman . . . In addition Alexander and Tedder arrive to-morrow."

" At 4.30 p.m. we had Chiefs of Staff meeting for Dill to give us the American outlook. At 6 p.m. a meeting with P.M. to discuss with him most recent conclusions as regards relative advantages of Sardinia versus Sicily. Then dinner with Marshall and had long talk with him after dinner. Am now tired and very sleepy, but must prepare my address to the Combined Chiefs of Staff meeting on the world situation and our proposed policy."

' In settling our future Mediterranean policy we had had long discussions as to whether we should invade Sicily or Sardinia once we had cleared North Africa. I could see very few advantages in selecting Sardinia, and had been a strong supporter of Sicily; distances were shorter, landings easier to support, and it was on the direct route to Italy. I had had some trouble with the Joint Planners, who were inclined to favour Sardinia, their argument being . . . that the opposition on beaches would be less and that aerodromes in Sardinia would be better placed for air action against Italy. I had finally got agreement to settle on Sicily, and it was the Sicily landing that I was to put forward to the Americans as our next objective. . . .'

[1] The site had been chosen by Ian Jacob, who had been sent out immediately after Christmas to prospect. It consisted of the Anfa Hotel, about five miles from Casablanca, on a knoll overlooking the sea with a number of comfortable villas surrounding it. " The peculiar shape of the building allowed for wide verandas all round, and the view out over the Atlantic, or overland to Casablanca, was truly magnificent. The dazzling blue of the water, the white of the buildings in Casablanca and the red soil dotted with green palms and bougainvillia and begonia made a beautiful picture in the sunlight." Sir Ian Jacob, *MS. Diary*, 28th December, 1942.

At that evening's meeting with the Chiefs of Staff the Prime Minister set out the line he wished them to follow with the Americans. They were not to hurry or try to force agreement, but to take plenty of time; there was to be full discussion and no impatience—" the dripping of water on a stone." In the meantime he himself would pursue the same tactics with the President. He added that he would like to see agreement reached, not only to clear the North African shore and capture Sicily in 1943, but to recapture Burma and launch a preliminary invasion of France. Nothing less, he felt, would be worthy of two great Powers and their obligations to Russia.

During the next five days the Combined Chiefs of Staff, meeting usually morning and afternoon, sought agreement. There was no set programme, and the Prime Minister's advice was followed of allowing the fullest possible expression of everyone's opinion. Dill, who during his year in Washington had won the complete trust of Marshall and his colleagues and understood their point of view, explained it before the Conference to the British Chiefs of Staff: their fear of Mediterranean commitments which would neither defeat the main enemy, Germany, nor check the very formidable subsidiary one, Japan, and the conviction, particularly of King and the American Navy, that the British underestimated the Pacific problem and the need to keep China in the War.

As British chairman Brooke at the start encouraged King to expound his views. " Our Chiefs," wrote Ian Jacob, who was acting as Secretary to the British C.O.S., in his diary of the Conference, " felt that they knew so little of what was really going on in the Pacific, of what the U.S. Navy planned to do, and of the amount of resources that these plans would absorb that some enlightenment would be valuable. They also felt that 'Uncle Ernie' would take a less jaundiced view of the rest of the world if he had been able to shoot his line about the Pacific and really get it off his chest. General Marshall, too, who has, and always has had, a strong feeling for China, was full of ideas about Burma, which it would be desirable to bring out into the light of day."[1] Brooke describes what followed:

[1] Sir Ian Jacob, *MS. Diary*, 14th January, 1943. Sir Ian described King as

" *January 14th* (2 a.m.). A very long and laborious day.
Breakfast at 8.30 a.m. followed by an hour and a half's
hard work preparing my opening statement for our first
meeting with the American Chiefs of Staff. At 10.30 a.m.
we met. I started off with a statement of about an hour
giving our outlook on the present war situation and our
opinion as to the future policy we should adopt. Marshall
then followed on with a statement showing where they
disagreed with our policy. We stopped for lunch and
met again at 2.30 p.m. I then asked them to explain their
views as to the running of the Pacific War. Admiral King
then did so, and it became clear at once that his idea
was an ' all out ' war against Japan instead of holding
operations. He then proposed that 30 per cent of the war
effort should be devoted to the Pacific and 70 per cent
to the rest. We pointed out that this was hardly a scientific
way of approaching war strategy. After considerable
argument got them to agree to our detailing the Combined
Planners to examine and report on the minimum holding
operations required in the Pacific and the forces necessary
for that action."[1]

" We broke up the meeting about 5 p.m., had tea, and
then had a meeting with our Joint Planners to instruct
them on the line of action to take. I then went for a
walk with John Kennedy to the beach to look at birds."

" Returned to find invitation to dine with the President

" well over sixty, but active, tall and spare, with an alert and self-confident
bearing. He seems to wear a protective covering of horn which it is hard to
penetrate. He gives the impression of being exceedingly narrow-minded and to
be always on the look-out for slights or attempts to put something over on him.
. . . His manners are good as a rule, but he is angular and stiff and finds it difficult,
if not impossible, really to unbend. I am convinced, however, that there is much
more to him than appears on the surface, and that if one could get beneath the
horn shell that one would be surprised at what one would find beneath." It was
a joke between King and Roosevelt, who had a great respect for him, that he
was so tough that he shaved with a blow-torch. *Whitehill,* 204.

[1] ' I am afraid that nothing we ever said had much effect in weaning King
away from the Pacific. This is where his heart was, and the bulk of his Naval
Forces. The European war was just a great nuisance that kept him from waging
his Pacific war undisturbed.' *Notes on My Life,* VIII, 599. Portal summed up
the problem by saying, " We are in the position of a testator who wishes to leave
the bulk of his fortune to his mistress. He must, however, leave something to his
wife, and his problem is to decide how little he can in decency set apart for her."
Sir Ian Jacob, *MS. Diary,* 14th January, 1943.

who had arrived that afternoon. Party consisted of P.M., President, Harry Hopkins, Harriman, Elliot Roosevelt, Marshall, King, Arnold, Dudley Pound, Portal, Mountbatten and self. King became nicely lit up towards the end of the evening. As a result he got more and more pompous and, with a thick voice and many gesticulations, he explained to the President the best way to set up the political French organization for control of North Africa. This led to many arguments with P.M. who failed to appreciate fully the condition King was in. Most amusing to watch. At about 1.30 a.m. an Alarm was received, lights put out, and we sat round the table with faces lit by six candles. The P.M. and President in that light and surroundings would have made a wonderful picture . . ."

" *January 15th (1.15 a.m.)*. . . . Got up fairly early and by 8.45 a.m. started off with Kennedy for a walk to look at birds. Delightful hour and a half, during which we saw goldfinch, stonechat, warblers of all sorts, white wagtail and several kinds of waders on the sea-shore, such as sanderlings, ring plover, grey plover and turnstones."

" Then C.O.S. conference till 12 noon, when P.M. came and I told him what we had done the previous day. After lunch Combined Chiefs of Staff meeting, first discussing security of communications and, secondly, relative advantages between Western Front in France and Mediterranean amphibious operations. I made long statement in favour of the latter which went down fairly well and remains to be argued further to-morrow. Eisenhower also came to give statement of operations in Tunisia. I had to criticise his operation against Sfax, which is in no way co-ordinated with either First Army or Eighth Army operations."

" At 5.30 p.m. Combined Staffs, Eisenhower, Alexander and Tedder met President and P.M., at which we did little except that President expressed views favouring operations in the Mediterranean. Both Eisenhower and Alexander made statements on their operations. Finally dined with P.M., Alexander, Tedder and Portal. After dinner Hopkins and Harriman came in, the former in a rather bitter mood I had not yet seen him in. There is no doubt that we are too closely related to the Americans to make co-operation easy."

' I cannot remember what these last lines were based on, as they do not represent my feelings on this matter. On the contrary, I feel that our close relationship made it possible to have the most heated professional discussion and even rows without affecting our personal relations to each other. On the evening of the 15th I was no doubt feeling the strain of the discussions.'

For some time Brooke had been disquieted by Eisenhower's proposal to make a dash at the end of January through southern Tunisia for the Mediterranean port of Sfax, so driving a wedge between the Germans and Italians at Tunis and Rommel's retreating army. The danger was that, planned without any form of co-operation with the Eighth Army, still five hundred miles away in the Sirte desert, it would lay the attackers open to a concerted assault by superior forces from both sides at the very moment when Montgomery's men, if successful in capturing Tripoli, would be immobilised after their long advance. Alexander, who had flown from Cairo to Casablanca for consultation and was charming everyone at the Conference by what Churchill called his " easy smiling grace " and " contagious confidence," felt with Brooke that no action should be taken until everything was prepared for a combined assault by all the Allied forces in Africa. Political issues, too, were bedevilling the Tunisian campaign. Giraud had refused to let French troops serve under British command, and to overcome the difficulty it had been decided by Head-quarters at Algiers, while leaving Anderson in charge of the British First Army, to put the American and French troops under a separate American Command, with a small command-post under Eisenhower's nominal direction to co-ordinate their joint activities. Though in his wish to further the cause of Allied unity Anderson had loyally accepted the situation, he and his men had been left to hold the main German army in northern Tunisia with very little knowledge of what was happening on their right.

Brooke referred to this problem on the 16th:

" . . . At 9.30 a.m. conference till 10.30 with Eisenhower and Alexander to co-ordinate the attacks on Tunisia. Eisenhower's previous plan was a real bad one, which could only result in the various attacks being defeated in detail. As a result of our talks a better plan was drawn up."

" From 10.30 to 1 p.m. Combined Chiefs of Staff meeting at which I had again to put forward all the advantages of our proposed Mediterranean policy and counter arguments in favour of a French Front plan. It is a slow and tiring business which requires a lot of patience. They can't be pushed and hurried, and must be made gradually to assimilate our proposed policy."

" After lunch went for a walk with Alexander and had a long discussion with him about the Middle East, commanders, his hopes and proposed operations, etc. From 3.30 to 5.15 p.m. another Combined Chiefs of Staff meeting. I think we are beginning to make some progress, and that they are getting interested in our proposals."

" At 5.30 p.m. we had to go to the P.M. for me to report progress of our work. He was in a very good mood, and had spent most of the day planning a conciliation between de Gaulle and Giraud.[1] Back home and off to dine with General Patton, the American general who carried out the landing on the Morocco Front. A real fire-eater and definitely a character. . . ."

" Now I am off to bed early for once and feeling dog-tired as a result of the last few days' work. It is a slow and tedious process as all matters have to be carefully explained and re-explained before they can be absorbed. And finally the counter-arguments put forward often show that even then the true conception has not been grasped, and the process has to be started again."

" *January 17th.* A desperate day. We are further from

[1] Rendered necessary by the assassination on Christmas Eve of Darlan, which had left French North Africa without a political head.

obtaining agreement than we ever were. Started Combined Chiefs of Staff meeting to be told by Marshall that there was disagreement between the Joint Planners on the question of Burma. Then a long harangue again on the question of the Pacific from Marshall, and finally questions about Iceland! Decided that it was useless going on conferring until the Joint Planners had made more headway."

" Had a meeting between Chiefs of Staff and our Joint Planners when we found that main difficulty rested in the fact that the U.S.A. Joint Planners did not agree with Germany being the primary enemy and were wishing to defeat Japan first. We have therefore prepared a new paper for discussion to-morrow at which we must get this basic principle settled. . . . After dinner another meeting with Joint Planning Staff which took us up to 11 p.m."

" *January 18th.* . . . From 10.30 to 1 p.m. a very heated Combined Chiefs of Staff meeting at which we seemed to be making no progress. King still evidently wrapped up in the war of the Pacific at the expense of everything else. However, immediately after lunch I sat down with Dill, I must confess without much hope, trying to define the line of our general agreement. In the middle Portal came in with a better paper. I therefore decided on the spur of the moment, and without a chance of seeing the First Sea Lord, to try and use this proposed policy as a bridge over our difficulties."

" We met again at 3 p.m. and I produced our paper which was accepted with few alterations. I could hardly believe our luck."

" Shortly afterwards we were informed that the President would hold a full meeting with the P.M. and all Combined Chiefs of Staff to hear results we had reached. We met at his villa at 5.30 p.m. I was asked to sit next to him, and he asked me who had been acting as our Chairman and I informed him that Marshall had been invited by us to perform that function. He then called on Marshall, who at once asked me to expound the results of our meetings. It was a difficult moment. We had only just succeeded in getting the American Chiefs of Staff to agree with us. However, the statement went all right, was approved by the Americans and the President and P.M., and received a full blessing. So we have reached some results after all."

' The fact that we had finally secured an agreement with the Americans on this memorable day,' Brooke wrote,

' was for the greater part due to Dill. . . . That morning as we had left the Combined C.O.S. meeting I was in despair. . . . Whilst walking upstairs I said to Dill: " It is no use, we shall never get agreement with them." To which he replied: " On the contrary, you have already got agreement to most of the points, and it only remains to settle the rest. Let's come to your room after lunch and discuss it." '

' We sat on my bed after lunch and he went through all the points on which we had agreement and then passed to those where we were stuck, asking me how far I would go to get agreement. When I replied that I would not move an inch, he said, " Oh yes, you will. You know that you must come to some agreement with the Americans and that you cannot bring the unsolved problem up to the Prime Minister and the President. You know as well as I do what a mess they would make of it." He then put up a few suggestions for agreement and asked me if I would agree to his discussing these with Marshall. I had such implicit trust in his ability and integrity that I agreed.'

' At this juncture Portal arrived with his proposed plan for seeking agreement, which was somewhat similar to some of Dill's suggestions, and we decided to adopt it.[1] Thereupon Dill proceeded to see Marshall before the

[1] It had been drafted by Air Marshal (now Marshal of the Royal Air Force Sir John) Slessor, Commander-in-Chief elect of Coastal Command, who had accompanied Portal to the Conference. It read: " Operations in the Pacific and Far East shall continue with the forces allocated, with the object of maintaining pressure on Japan, retaining the initiative and attaining a position of readiness for the full-scale offensive against Japan . . . as soon as Germany is defeated. These operations must be kept within such limits as will not, in the opinion of the Combined Chiefs of Staff, prejudice the capacity of the United Nations to take any opportunity that may present itself for the decisive defeat of Germany in 1943." J. Slessor, *The Central Blue*, 446.

meeting to discuss these suggestions. I am certain that the final agreement being reached was due more to Dill than anybody else. . . . I owe him an unbounded debt of gratitude for his help on that occasion and in many other similar ones.'

.   .   .   .

According to Ian Jacob, the C.I.G.S. handled this crucial part of the Conference with the greatest skill, putting all he had into it and exhausting himself by the finish. His summary of the war situation on January 16th was a masterpiece—a counterpart to the talks on global strategy, given without a note and holding his audiences enthralled, that he used to give at the Staff College and G.H.Q. Home Forces. The case he had presented was unanswerable: that until the U-boat menace could be overcome shortage of shipping must remain " a stranglehold on all offensive operations," and that with only twenty-one divisions—all that could be assembled in England and carried across the Channel by August, 1943, in the ships and assault-craft available—any invasion of northern France could be easily held or repelled by the far more numerous German divisions already in Western Europe without making any call on the Russian front. On the other hand, he had shown how, by striking across the Mediterranean a victory in Europe could be won in 1943 which would fatally strain the enemy's inadequate north-to-south communications, whose capacity, because of the Alpine ranges, was only about a seventh of those from east-to-west, and compel him to deploy and keep deployed large forces to defend an immense additional stretch of coastline and hold down the restless peoples of southern and south-eastern Europe. By doing so and knocking Italy out of the war, the Allies would leave Germany by the end of the year some fifty-four divisions and 2,200 aircraft short of her minimum requirements for holding her present Russian front and garrisoning the West against the major cross-Channel attack which the Allies would be able to launch by 1944.[1] They would force her to

[1] Answering an American question on January 18th, Brooke stated that the Allies could definitely count on invading France on a large scale in 1944. *U.S. War Department Official History, European Theatre of Operations Cross-Channel Attack*, 44.

extend her commitments on the one front where her advantage of interior lines would be lost and where, in the long mountainous peninsulas of the Mediterranean, her supply-lines would be most stretched. She would have to make permanent withdrawals both from the existing Russian front and the incipient Channel one. Without these she would still be strong enough to repel any attack from the West until 1945 or even 1946.

But the Americans, though compelled to admit the force of Brooke's logic, were still suspicious of him. His swift, abrupt speech, his downright categorical expression of his views and occasional impatience, that shrewd observer, Jacob, noted, made them afraid he was putting something over on them and that they were being outsmarted. During the Conference, when the subordinate officers relaxed in private together, Jacob's colleague, Brigadier Vivian Dykes—British Secretary of the Combined Chiefs of Staff—would sometimes mimic the C.I.G.S.'s " birdlike aspect and fast clipped speech. . . . his constant habit when talking of shooting his tongue out and round his lips with the speed of a chameleon." " I have never met," Jacob wrote, " a man who so tumbles over himself in speaking. He cannot make his brain move slowly enough to fit his speech or his reading, especially when his interest is strongly engaged."[1] Born to command in action, an Irishman with an Irishman's quickness, Brooke found it hard to communicate what he saw so clearly to those of slower mind. With his habitual efficiency he had adapted himself to the rôle of international committee man he was called upon to play, but, unlike Eisenhower and Alexander—men with a genial gift for accommodating and reconciling divergent views—he found it an unnatural one, involving, as his diary shows, continual strain. Reading his accounts of the interminable conferences and committees he attended, one is sometimes, for all his modesty and simplicity, left with the impression of an eagle trying to walk in a hen-run. At this stage, before he and the Americans had learnt to understand one another, it was

[1] Sir Ian Jacob, *MS. Diary*, 14th-18th January, 1943. " Dumbie " Dykes, a brilliant soldier with a great future, was killed, together with the Army Director of Plans, Colonel Guy Stewart, in a flying accident while returning from the Casablanca Conference.

fortunate that he should have had two such brilliant and sympathetic interpreters as Dill and Portal. The Chief of Air Staff proved himself a tower of strength at Casablanca. The accord he had established with his American *vis-à-vis*, Arnold, constituted a bridgehead, like Dill's friendship with Marshall, between the two Chiefs of Staff. It was he who more often than anyone found the key in argument acceptable to all.[1]

Having agreed, as a first priority for 1943, on offensive operations which, by menacing the entire coastline of southern Europe and of Sicily, Sardinia, Crete and the Dodecanese, would compel Germany to withdraw forces from Russia and the Channel shore, the Combined Chiefs turned in the second half of the Conference to the detailed means of implementing their policy. This involved several new hurdles, including a reorganisation in the command of the Anglo-American Forces in French North Africa and their co-ordination with the more powerful British Army approaching under Alexander and Montgomery from the east. As soon as the latter could reach the Tunisian frontier, as soon, that is, as Montgomery had taken Tripoli and repaired the port to supply his further advance, the British forces in the fighting-line, already four divisions to the American three, would be increased to eleven or twelve—a preponderance which, added to the fact that all the naval forces in the Mediterranean were British, would make the American command of what would by then be a single campaign, not only disproportionate, but rather dangerous. For though, thanks to Eisenhower, there was remarkably little friction at his headquarters between the staff officers of the two nations, it was still proving very difficult for them, trained as they were under entirely different systems, to work together efficiently. With their more elaborate staff training and greater experience of war, the British tended to regard American methods of co-ordination as unprofessional and slap-dash. The Assistant Military Secretary of the War Cabinet, when he visited Algiers at the end of December, noted

[1] " The Americans put their money on Portal. They would accept him as Commander-in-Chief over everything. They would put all the Allied Air Forces from Iceland to Bombay under his control. His great asset is his unshakable honesty of thought and deed. They knew he knew his stuff and they trusted him one hundred per cent." Sir Ian Jacob, *MS. Diary.*

" a general air of restless confusion, with everyone trying their best in unnatural conditions . . ." Sudden and frequent changes of plan increased the general chaos. " There is lack of dignity about the H.Q., an air of aimless bustle, a constant cluttering of hangers-on and visitors, and at the same time an amateur flavour that makes one wonder how anything ever gets done."[1]

To these administrative problems Brooke and his colleagues now addressed themselves:

> " *January 19th*. . . . From 10 a.m. to 12 a Combined meeting settling details required by our main policy. From 2 to 3 p.m. a C.O.S. meeting in anticipation of a Combined meeting from 3 to 5 p.m. At 5 p.m. Giraud came round to see the Combined Chiefs of Staff and made a series of statements concerning French Forces he considered could be raised in North Africa provided equipment was found for them. The force amounted to three armoured and ten motorised divisions . . . ."

> " Just before dinner P.M. came round to the hotel and told me he proposed to go to Marrakesh on Saturday. That I was to accompany him there, and that from there we should go on to Cairo. Whilst there he hoped to go on to Cyprus to meet Turks and prepare for their entry into the war. We should then go on to Tripoli, which he hoped would be captured by then, and from there home. A very interesting trip and I hope it comes off all right."

' In discussing this trip he told me that he proposed to see the President fly off from the Marrakesh aerodrome and that he would subsequently spend two days in Marrakesh to rest and to paint. He told me that it was seven years since he had painted in Marrakesh, that he had brought his paints on purpose, and was very much looking forward to this opportunity. I thought the plan was excellent. I was feeling a bit tired after all the recent work, and at once made plans for one day's tour in the Atlas mountains and one day's partridge shooting with a local sheik.'

[1] Sir Ian Jacob, *MS. Diary*, 30th December, 1942.

" *January 20th.* . . . At 10 a.m. we had a Combined Chiefs of Staff meeting at which we started with a shipping discussion for which we brought Lord Leathers in. We then thrashed out the system of command in Tunisia after arrival of the Eighth Army, deciding that it must then be transferred to Eisenhower's command. In order to assist in the control and co-ordination of the First and Eighth Armies and French and Americans in Tunisia, Alexander to become Eisenhower's Deputy. The Air Command, with Tedder as Supreme Commander of Mediterranean, was also settled at the same time."

" American Chiefs then withdrew to see the President and we carried on with a Chiefs of Staff meeting which lasted till 12.45 and at which we discussed the Sicilian operation. . . . At 2 p.m. we again met as Combined Chiefs and thrashed out plans for the capture of Sicily. The meeting went far better than I had hoped for and finished about 4 p.m., when I went round to the P.M.'s house to discuss details of my journey with him to Cairo. Finally another walk with Kennedy, during which we added three new specimens to our finds in the shape of a wimbrel, sandpiper and yellow wagtail."

" The back of the work here is broken and thank God for it! It has been one of the most difficult tasks I have had to do, and at one time I began to despair of our arriving at any sort of agreement. Now we have got practically all we hoped to get when we came here."

" They are difficult, though charming people to work with. Marshall's . . . thoughts revolve round the creation of forces and not on their employment. . . . King's . . . vision is mainly limited to the Pacific; . . . although he pays lip service to the fundamental policy that we must first defeat Germany and then turn on Japan, he fails to apply it in any problems connected with the war. Arnold limits his outlook to the air and seldom mixes himself with other matters. But as a team . . . they are friendliness itself, and, although our discussions have become some- what heated at times, yet our relations have never been strained. I hope we shall leave here with a more closely united outlook on the war."

' On this date we had achieved another marked success. We had got agreement on the organisation of Higher Command in North Africa. . . . It was clear that centralized command was essential to co-ordinate the actions of the First and Eighth Armies and the American and French forces; but who was to be placed in this responsible position? From many points of view it was desirable to hand this Command over to the Americans, but unfortunately up to now Eisenhower . . . had neither the tactical or strategical experience required for such a task. By bringing Alexander over from the Middle East and appointing him as Deputy to Eisenhower, we were carrying out a move which could not help flattering and pleasing the Americans in so far as we were placing our senior and experienced commander to function under their commander who had no war experience. . . . We were pushing Eisenhower up into the stratosphere and rarified atmosphere of a Supreme Commander, where he would be free to devote his time to the political and inter-allied problems, whilst we inserted under him one of our own commanders to deal with the military situations and to restore the necessary drive and co-ordination which had been so seriously lacking.'

" *January 21st.* Started the day with a C.O.S. meeting from 9.30 a.m. to 10 a.m. We then carried on with a Combined C.O.S. meeting till 12 noon, during which we discussed the building up of American Forces in England during 1943 and their employment. At 12 noon we met the P.M. and remained with him till 1.15 discussing the possibilities of expediting operations in the Mediterranean."

" At 2 p.m. we again met the Combined Staffs and carried on till 4 p.m., when we went down to Casablanca to inspect a Headquarters ship which Mountbatten had got ready for us. Whilst there we also saw the French battleship, the *Jean Bart*, which had been hit by three 1,000-lb. bombs during the American bombardment of the harbour. The bow and stern were almost completely blown off. Came back and spent rest of evening preparing for a British Chiefs of Staff meeting after dinner, which lasted from 9 p.m. to 12 midnight. There we had long and protracted arguments as to the relative advantages of Sardinia as opposed to Sicily as an objective. There are a thousand different factors connected with the problem. In my own mind there is not the least doubt that Sicily should be selected, but on the whole the majority of opinion is hardening against me."

" When an operation has finally been completed it all looks so easy, but so few people ever realise the infinite difficulties of maintaining an object or a plan and refusing to be driven off it by other people for thousands of good reasons. A good plan pressed through is better than many ideal ones which are continually changing. Advice without responsibility is easy to give. This is the most exhausting job, trying to keep the ship of war on a straight course in spite of all the contrary winds that blow . . . ."

' I have the most vivid recollection of that exhausting evening. I had already had a long day when we started, and had a very heavy encounter with the bulk of the C.O.S. against me. We had had many debates on the relative advantages of Sardinia and Sicily before leaving England, and it was only at the end of much hard work that I had obtained general agreement on Sicily. All my arguments with Marshall had been based on the invasion of Sicily and I had obtained his agreement. And now suddenly the Joint Planning Staff reappeared on the scene with a strong preference for Sardinia and expressing most serious doubts as to our ability to take on the Sicilian operation. They had carried with them Mountbatten; . . . Peter Portal and " Pug " Ismay were beginning to waver, and dear old Dudley Pound was, as usual, asleep and with no views either way.'

' I had a three hours hammer and tongs battle to keep the team together and to stop it from wavering. I told them that I flatly refused to go back to the American Chiefs of Staff and tell them that we did not know our own minds and that, instead of Sicily, we now wanted to invade Sardinia. I told them such a step would irrevocably shake their confidence in our judgment. What is more, I told them frankly that I disagreed with them entirely and adhered to our original decision to invade Sicily and would not go back on it.'[1]

" *January 22nd.* I went in to our Combined Chiefs of Staff meeting at 10 a.m. with some misgivings. . . . The Americans, I knew, would not look at Sardinia, and might well accuse us of not knowing our own minds, and wish to close down operations in the Mediterranean. . . . The meeting, however, went off far better than I had hoped, and the determination to proceed with our plans for Sicily were confirmed subject to a revision at a later date as regards resources and training. This was really the culmination of all my efforts. . . ."

" After lunch, which I had with the P.M., Randolph and Ismay, we met again at 2.30 in a Combined meeting which lasted till about 4.30 p.m. After tea I went for a walk with John Kennedy. We found five of the small owls and a marsh harrier. It is an untold relief that this meeting is drawing to a close. It has done a great deal, and I feel certain that we now understand each other and our respective difficulties far better."

" Am just back from seeing the P.M., who wanted to get Alexander back to Marrakesh on Sunday to see him. As he has already been away from his Command for a week, at this critical moment I did not think it desirable and told him so. He had been seeing de Gaulle after his

---

[1] *Notes on My Life*, VIII, 611. " The decisive factor in the Committee was the view of the C.I.G.S. He had carefully studied the plans for the two operations, and he had come to the conclusion that Sicily would be the better of the two. He was convinced in his mind that, as fast as we went into the south of Sardinia, enemy reinforcements would pour into the north. He foresaw a long and difficult campaign to master the island, by which time the chance of taking Corsica easily would have gone. On the other hand, he reckoned that the plan for taking Sicily would ensure the quick fall of the island. Reinforcements could only come through Messina, out of which only two coast roads led, and these could easily be blocked. These ideas fixed themselves firmly in his mind, and nothing would shake him. Being a very obstinate man, further argument only annoyed him, and he became more and more rabidly against Sardinia and in favour of Sicily." Sir Ian Jacob, *MS. Diary.*

historic meeting with Giraud.[1] Apparently this interview did not go too smoothly, and I doubt whether such opposed characters can possibly pull together."

"*January 23rd.* We met again at 10 a.m. to thrash out the final points and to discuss our report to the President and Prime Minister on the work of our meetings. After lunch we motored out to Fedala, the site of one of the American landings. We collected an American, Colonel Ratlye, to come with us, who had actually taken part in this landing. It was most interesting, and quite evident that, if the French had put up any real resistance, the landing could never have been carried out. . . ."

" At 5.30 p.m. we attended meeting with President and P.M. in the chair.[2] Lasted till 7.30 p.m. We were congratulated by both of them on the results of our work and informed that we had produced the most complete strategic plan for a world-wide war that had ever been conceived, and far exceeding the accomplishments of the last war."

" They then discussed details, tried to push forward the Sicilian date, insisted on more stress as to the assistance to China, and a few other minor points. Finally we had our last meeting at 9.30 p.m. to bring this final document into line with the remarks of the President and P.M. . . ."

The strategic plan which so pleased the President and Prime Minister and which Brooke had first outlined to them, at Marshall's request, at the plenary meeting of the Combined Chiefs of Staff on January 18th, laid it down that, since all offensive measures must depend on sea-communications, the defeat of the U-boat must be the first charge on the resources of the Western Powers. Their objective was to defeat Germany in the shortest possible time with the maximum forces they

[1] The " shot-gun marriage," as the Americans called it. *Whitehill*, 216.
[2] ANFA 3rd Meeting—Attended by:

U.S. President	*British* Prime Minister
General G. Marshall	Admiral of the Fleet Sir D. Pound
Admiral E. King	Field-Marshal Sir John Dill
Lt.-Gen. H. Arnold	Gen. Sir Alan Brooke
Lt.-Gen. B. Somervell	Air Chief Marshal Sir C. Portal
Mr. Harry Hopkins	Vice-Admiral Lord Louis Mountbatten
Comd. R. E. Libby	Lt.-Gen. Sir Hastings Ismay

could bring to bear. The immediate target for 1943, after the liquidation of the Axis forces in Africa, was to be Sicily and, by its capture, the creation of such a position of Allied strength in the Mediterranean as would undermine the shaky Axis empire in the Balkans and bring Turkey into the war. Simultaneously the heaviest possible air-attack on Germany was to be maintained from the United Kingdom, at night by the R.A.F. and by day, when they were ready to undertake it, by American Flying Fortresses. Subject to the prior need to capture Sicily, powerful American forces were to be assembled in Britain as fast as shipping became available in order to be able to land in France in the autumn should any signs of a German crack in the east occur. Though the British, apart from the Prime Minister, did not regard it as logistically possible until 1944, this last was a concession to General Marshall who throughout the Conference had fought a stubborn rearguard action for a 1943 " Round-up." Pressure was also to be maintained against Japan, by a British autumn campaign to re-capture Burma and, if resources admitted, by American operations against the Marshall and Caroline Islands, but only if these could be undertaken without jeopardizing the chance of defeating Germany in 1943. To this the President and Prime Minister added a general rider, in the form of a letter to their respective Chiefs of Staff, that the Sicilian operation ought to be conducted, if possible, in the June moon, that Russian convoys should somehow be run even while it was being staged, that air reinforcements should be sent to China, and that U.S. forces in Britain should be built up fast enough to undertake " Sledgehammer " in August. The President also added an unexpected postscript at a Press Conference next day when he announced to an assemblage of reporters that the Allies were going to insist on " unconditional surrender."

The final Report was not everything Brooke had hoped for, since, in its attempt to satisfy everyone, it proposed too much. And it made no mention of the invasion of the Italian mainland which he was convinced should follow the occupation of Sicily. But it at least provided for a hundred per cent Anglo-American co-operation in carrying out the next two essential steps of his Mediterranean strategy. Under the supreme command of Eisenhower it placed the active direction of the land, sea and air operations to clear the African coast—that day brought a stage nearer by Montgomery's capture of Tripoli—and to invade Sicily, in the hands of three British officers, Alexander, Cunningham and Tedder. It thus went far beyond what had seemed possible in the early stages of the Conference. Brigadier Jacob, whose business it was to draft the final agreement, wrote that if before the Conference he had had to write down what he hoped its decisions would be, he could never have written anything so sweeping, comprehensive and favourable to British ideas as in the end he found himself writing. " Our ideas had prevailed almost throughout."[1]

On Sunday the 24th, the process of inter-Allied agreement being completed, the captains and kings departed. Churchill, who wanted to introduce Roosevelt to the Moorish city of Marrakesh before his return to America, was hoping, after his sketching holiday, to fly to Cairo with the C.I.G.S. in order to meet the Turkish President and Commander-in-Chief. His and Brooke's idea was, by offering them modern arms and building up their strength, to induce them to enter the war as soon as the Axis position in the eastern Mediterranean started to crumble. With his instinct for bold measures, he felt that a meeting between himself and the Turkish President, coming on the morrow of the Allied victories in Africa and Russia, would have a profound effect on the morale of the Axis satellites and the subject peoples of Europe. He had, therefore, started to bombard a reluctant Cabinet, who wished him to return to London, with telegrams demanding their agreement to what seemed in their eyes and that of the Foreign Office a highly speculative and rather dangerous journey, and one likely to be followed by a humiliating rebuff from Angora. At the time the Conference broke up they were still resisting stoutly.[2]

"*January 24th. Marrakesh (150 miles).* Finished packing up, everybody dispersing in different directions.

[1] Sir Ian Jacob, *MS. Diary*, 23rd January, 1943. The writers of the American War Department's admirably lucid *Strategic Planning for Coalition Warfare*, 382, take the same view of what happened.
[2] The exchange of telegrams is amusingly set out in *Churchill*, IV, 626-9.

Marshall for Algiers and back to America, Dill to Algiers and on to Delhi, Arnold also for Delhi and on to Chungking from there. Portal to Algiers, Malta and home. Dudley Pound Algiers and home. I came on here with Jacob, Stirling and Boyle by Liberator, and had a lovely fly with excellent view of the country. It is an amazing sight as one approaches the Atlas Mountains to see miles upon miles of snow peaks in front of one."

" President and P.M. were to come on by road. We arrived in time for lunch and were taken by . . . the American Vice-Consul in Morocco to a house owned by a Mrs. Taylor for lunch. It is the house the President and P.M. are to stop in. Built in complete Moroccan architecture in the middle of what used to be an olive plantation. Very ornate with a wonderful garden round it. After lunch we climbed up the tower to see the view. An astonishing mixture with palm trees and an Arab-Moroccan town in the foreground and lovely snow-covered peaks in the background."

" From my hotel ' (Mamounia Hotel) ' window I have a wonderful view right over an orange tree plantation, covered with oranges, and through a fringe of palm trees the glistening snow peaks in rear. I spent a real peaceful afternoon looking for birds in the lovely garden of the hotel and found several very interesting specimens. It is great fun identifying the European specimens in the form of some sub-species with minor variations. It is also very interesting seeing what a great difference there is between the bird life in Casablanca and that at Marrakesh, although the distance between them is only some 130 miles."

" *January 25th.* We had made a plan for two quiet days here, with a day's partridge shooting. P.M. sent for me this morning and said he wanted to start to-night for Cairo. We sent for pilot, who said weather conditions were excellent. Telegrams were therefore sent to Miles Lampson that we were coming and to 'Jumbo' Wilson to come to Cairo. Our plan now is to arrive at Cairo to-morrow early, and go to Cyprus if Cabinet removes objection to P.M. meeting Turks, which they don't seem to like. Then to Tripoli to meet Montgomery and Anderson and from there home."

"After lunch drove off into the Atlas Mountains and had a lovely drive. We went well up into the hills and stopped to hunt for birds. Saw an eagle in the distance, but too far to make out what he was. Meanwhile Winston had climbed up the tower of Mrs. Taylor's villa with his easel and oil paints and was busy painting. . . ."

'The events of this day have not been done full justice in the diary, and luckily they remain very vividly recorded in my memory. Life seemed specially attractive that morning. The heavy work of the Casablanca Conference was over, and I had two clear days in front of me to forget the war momentarily. It was therefore with a light heart that I walked out of the Mamounia Hotel to get into the car for a day's trip in the Atlas Mountains and a day's partridge shooting to look forward to. Fate had however decided otherwise.'

'Before I reached the door of the car I was stopped by a shout informing me that I was wanted on the telephone. This turned out to be a call from Winston requesting me to come round to Mrs. Taylor's villa at once. I went there and was shown into his room where he was in bed. I had frequently seen him in bed, but never anything to touch the present setting. It was all I could do to remain serious. The room must have been Mrs. Taylor's bedroom and was done up in Moorish style, the ceiling was a marvellous fresco of green, blue and gold. The head of the bed rested in an alcove of Moorish design with a religious light shining on either side; the bed was covered with a light blue silk covering with 6-in. wide lace *entre-deux* and the rest of the room in harmony with the Arabic ceiling. And there in the bed was Winston in his green, red and gold dragon dressing-gown, his hair, or what there is of it, standing on end, the religious lights shining on his cheeks, and a large cigar in his face! I would have given anything to have been able to take a coloured photograph of him.'

'He greeted me by telling me that we were off at 6 p.m. I replied that I was under the impression that we had come here for him to paint the scenery he had been longing to get at for the last six years. He said he would paint two hours in the afternoon and that we should start at 6 p.m. I drew his attention to the fact that even he could not hope to do justice to the wonderful effects of palm trees and snow peaks in two hours. He replied again, " I am off at 6 p.m.," by way of clinching the argument. I then said, " All right, if we are off at 6 p.m., where are we going? " His reply was typical. " I have not decided yet." On being asked as to what the alternatives might be, he replied, " I am either going to answer questions in the House to-morrow or I am going to Cairo." On being further questioned as to what would decide him, I was informed that he was awaiting a telegram from Anthony Eden concerning his proposed visit to the Turks. If the Cabinet agreed, we should go to Cairo.'

'I had one final attempt to save my partridge shoot and drew his attention to the fact that there was little time in which to warn Cairo. The telegram would have to be encoded here, decoded in London, re-encoded and finally decoded in Cairo. Miles Lampson would only receive it late in the evening. This met with no success, and I was told that there would be ample time. I then reminded him that the last time he was in Cairo he took Lady Lampson's bedroom and he also possessed himself of Miles Lampson's study, which was also the only downstairs air-conditioned room. He was therefore not leaving them much time to alter all the rooms in the Embassy, snatch some sleep and motor out twenty miles to the aerodrome. It was useless; he considered they had ample time, reiterated the fact that he was off at 6 p.m., and crashed all hopes of my partridge shoot.'

'My two days' plan was now ruined, and all that was left to me was to salvage out of the wreck a few hours in the Atlas Mountains that afternoon. The wire from Anthony Eden arrived shortly afterwards. . . .'

" At 5.30 p.m., after having tea with the Danish Consul and his wife, we left the Mamounia Hotel for the aerodrome. We had two Liberators, one for the P.M., Randolph, doctor, secretary, Flag-Lieutenant, detective and valet, the other for me, Jacob, Rowan, the other secretary, the chief clerk, another detective, and Boyle." (' my Military Assistant.')

" We took off at 6.30 p.m. and, after climbing round in rings, gradually struck out to cross the snowy peaks of the Atlas Mountains. We climbed to 14,500 feet before crossing. It became bitterly cold, but the view was glorious. The sun was setting, there was not a cloud in the sky, and the horizon all round was lit with a pink glow which was reflected on the snowy peaks. As we passed over the mountains the sun set, and the whole scenery gradually disappeared into darkness till we were left alone in the dark driving into the unknown with 2,300 miles of desert in front of us."

" We then had a dinner of boiled eggs and sandwiches. After that rolled up for the night, and packed stacks of blankets on top to keep warm. We had dropped down to 9,000 feet, which was more comfortable, but still very cold."

' That flight over the Atlas Mountains made a vivid impression on me. I have seldom seen any scenery to touch it. The red glow in the western sky and its reflection on those snowy peaks was thrown into special relief by the darkness of the sky behind the mountains. A darkness representing thousands of miles of desert, with the additional spice of excitement that to the ordinary dangers of a forced landing was added that of falling into enemy hands.'

" *January 26th. Cairo (2,300 miles)*. After a somewhat uncomfortable night looked out to see dawn breaking over the desert. We had been flying for about eleven hours. Shortly afterwards we landed, having arrived a few minutes before the P.M. . . . We drove straight to the Embasy, where we were met by Miles Lampson and

Jacqueline. We were given a good breakfast, after which I had a bath and a shave."

' We had one amusing little episode which I did not record in the diary, probably due to sleepiness, but which I remember well. Just after arriving in the Embassy and being greeted by the Miles Lampsons, Winston turned to me and said, " Shall we have breakfast now? " I felt that he should have addressed this question to Jacqueline, so replied, " I think we had better first of all get washed and have a shave." This did not suit him, and he went on with, " No! we shall have breakfast now," and then turned to Jacqueline and asked her if breakfast was ready. She assured him that it was and led him to the dining-room where she offered him a cup of tea. This offer was not at all acceptable and he asked for a glass of white wine. A tumbler was brought which he drained in one go, then licked his lips, turned to Jacqueline and said, " Ah! that is good, but you know I have already had two whiskies and soda and two cigars this morning." It was then only shortly after 7.30 a.m. We had travelled all night in poor comfort, covering some 2,300 miles in a flight of over eleven hours, a proportion of which at over 14,000 feet, and there he was as fresh as paint drinking white wine on top of two previous whiskies and two cigars! '

" I got Alexander to come round at 10.30 a.m. and had a long talk with him on the clearing of Tunisia and on the Sicilian operation. It is very strange being back here after little more than five months, and so much has happened in that time. When I was here last I kept wondering if the day would come when Germans would be firing across the Nile into the Embassy gardens, and now they are on the point of being driven out of Tripoli."

" After lunch I went round with Alexander to his map-room to examine the situation in Tripoli and the prospects of opening the port. Whilst there the P.M. turned up and became involved in a long discussion on the situation of the French naval forces under Godfroy in Alexandria with Admiral Harwood. P.M. all for firmer attitude with these forces to induce them to join the French movement to free France, either under Giraud or under de Gaulle."

" Did not succeed in getting off to bed till near 1 a.m. Very sleepy after poor previous night in the plane."

"*January 27th.* Had a grand sleep to make up for previous night. At 10.30 a.m. attended Alexander's Staff Conference at which all intelligence was reviewed. After Conference had an interview with Morshead to say good-bye to him before his departure with his division for Australia. Then 'Jumbo' Wilson turned up from Baghdad, and I put him into the picture and settled details as to his taking over from Alexander, what his tasks would be in the administration of the Eighth Army, training formations for the Sicilian operation and preparing troops for Turkey."

" Reply had come from Turkey, stating they were delighted with proposed visit, but suggesting we should come to Angora. However, for security decided that meeting had better take place near frontier. Plans being worked out on that basis."[1]

" . . . Being back here reminds me the whole time of that nightmare of a first week last August with all the unpleasantness of . . . relieving Auchinleck and of re-constituting the Command and Staff. Thank heaven that is all over now and this visit is consequently much more pleasant. Slipped out before dinner to collect some Turkish Delight for the young. . . ."

"Just before dinner I received a letter from Montgomery reporting that the clearing of Tripoli harbour was not proceeding quickly enough. After dinner I told the P.M. we ought to do something about it. He telephoned for Admiral Harwood to come at once. We have just had an interview with him and his Staff Officer. . . . 1.30 a.m. and I am very sleepy."

"*January 28th* (*800 miles*). Left the Embassy at 9.30 a.m. and took off by air from Heliopolis for Siwa Oasis

---

[1] " The Prime Minister was delighted. ' This is big stuff! ' he kept saying. He read and re-read the telegrams and was obviously not unhappy at the thought of how right he had been and how wrong the Cabinet and their advisers had proved." Sir Ian Jacob, *MS. Diary*, 27th January, 1943.

at 10 a.m. Strong head wind and the four hundred miles took us two and three-quarter hours. A most interesting spot, surrounded by sandy crags and small sandy hills of queer terraced shapes due to erosion of wind and rain. Most of the water of the oasis is salty in varying degrees, but two or three springs are of the most lovely clear water welling straight up from the bottom of a deep hole."

" We had lunch alongside one of the biggest of those holes, and two of the main sheiks came with offerings of dates and sweet lemons in the most attractive baskets made of palm leaves. After lunch we examined one of the two main villages which had had to be vacated in recent times owing to a cloudburst which washed most of the structure of the houses away. However, in washing away the houses the remnants of a well-built stone temple appeared which is considered to be that of the famous Oracle of Siwa whom even Alexander the Great came to consult. The total population of the oasis is about 4,000 and they exist through the cultivation of dates and olives, plus a limited amount of grain which they grow."

" We then went on to the next village where we were given an official reception by the sheiks all in their best clothes and with their swords of office on. The local band also turned out for our benefit, and a small choir of women who produced their 'Welcome Song.' It was something between a Red Indian call and an owl hooting! We sat under a covering of palm tree trunks covered with palm leaf mats, and ate dates and drank small glasses of very highly flavoured tea. We were also presented with the top of a palm tree to take away and eat ! "

" They seemed a thoroughly cheerful and happy little community in spite of alternative occupation of Italian, British and German forces according to the swaying backwards and forwards of the fighting in Libya. Their opinion of the Italians was not very high, as owing to shortage of rations the Italians had stolen and eaten some of their donkeys. However, there are still some supporters of the Italians amongst the population. . . ."[1]

" We left at 3.20 p.m. and had a strong following wind; made the journey in two hours. Both going and coming we had an opportunity of seeing the famous Qattara Depression from the air. It was a most interesting day that I would not have missed for a great deal."

" I had hoped to see some bird life of interest, but the resident types are few, and it is only during the migration that bird life is plentiful. I did see a white-rumped chat which I had not seen before, and otherwise only two ravens and one hooded crow. . . ."

' Winston was originally to have come with Alexander and me to the Siwa Oasis, but suddenly the evening before he decided he would not come. He said that he would always fly when duty demanded it, but would not take the unnecessary risk just for pleasure. It was a surprising decision, as he had been looking forward to the trip and wanted to see the Oasis. So Alexander and I went by ourselves with our personal staff.'

" *January 29th.* Attended Intelligence meeting at G.H.Q. at 9.15 a.m., and I then gave the Commanders-in-Chief (Navy, Army and Air) half an hour's talk on proposed plans in the Mediterranean. Then discussed with Alexander the organisation of his planning staff for Sicily."

" Back to Embassy to try and raise some clothes to proceed to Turkey in, as we are not supposed to wear uniform while we are there. . . . It is settled now that we start to-morrow."

" *Later:* I have now succeeded in raising the different outfits. Some are too tight in the waist, some too long in the legs, some too thin in the material, but I hope out of the lot to produce something in which I can appear without shame in front of the President of Turkey! . . ."

' I have often wondered what the Turks must have

[1] The Arab population had given Rommel an equally enthusiastic reception when he visited the Siwa Oasis on September 21st, 1942. *Rommel Papers*, 292-3.

thought of us when they saw us arrive in our strange clothes. "Jumbo" Wilson had borrowed a suit from Miles Lampson which even he could not fill adequately, and the jacket on him had the appearance of a maternity garment. I had borrowed Lampson's A.D.C.'s clothes, and, as he was quite eight inches taller and very long in the leg, I had serious trouble with the trousers. I braced them up till they caught in my arm-pits and would go no further, and then found that the top fly button appeared above the waistcoat-opening and half concealed my tie. We looked more like a third-rate theatrical travelling company than anything else.'

" *January 30th, 1943. Adana (700 miles)*. We left the Embassy at 9 a.m. for the aerodrome from which we departed at 10 a.m. for Adana in Turkey. We skirted up the coast of Palestine and Syria, and saw Haifa, Beirut, Gaza, Tripoli, etc., on the way up. Weather bad and trip very bumpy. We saw two waterspouts from the air, which was interesting. Finally arrived Adana at 1 p.m. after three hours' flying. There we were met by the Prime Minister, Sükrü Saracoglu, and the Foreign Minister. . . . Country all round soaking wet from recent rains."

" A certain delay then occurred as our train had not yet arrived. Finally we boarded the train and lunched as we pushed out some twenty miles west where we joined the President's train. There we met the President, General Ismet Inönü (Ismet Pasha of old) and Field-Marshal Çakmak. We had first of all a very awkward phase of meetings and polite speeches which were very protracted. However, finally we started our conference with an opening speech in French by the P.M. The political heads then withdrew and the military heads got busy, Çakmak presiding on one side of the table and I on the other."

" I soon found that Çakmak had no conception of the administrative aspects of handling modern armies. He had not prepared his case, consequently was continually involved in discussions with his advisers which made it hard to keep one's temper. We went on till about 6 p.m. and covered a great deal of ground, and have, I think, got them definitely working towards fulfilling my hopes of ultimately coming to our assistance.[1] But they have got a long way to go before they can be considered a really efficient force, and how we are to provide them with the necessary equipment in spite of their poor communications is a mystery."

"Finally we finished up with a dinner with the President at which the P.M. was a great success, and the day ended on the whole most successfully. . . . We are living and feeding and sleeping in the train on a siding in a wilderness of cotton cultivation—a sea of mud at present."

' There were a few additional incidents on that day that are worth recording. On our arrival in Adana the Turkish Foreign Minister after greeting me told me how delighted the whole of Turkey was at this visit by the P.M. I asked him how this could be, since the visit was being kept as a matter of first-class secrecy and nobody could know that he had arrived. To this he replied: " How could you keep an event of that kind secret? Of course everybody knows about it!" This was disconcerting as the necessity for secrecy had been strongly impressed on them. The situation was far from safe; there was a German company working in the vicinity of Adana reclaiming marshland. They were certain to become aware of the visit, and the Turkish security arrangements were not likely to be of a very efficient nature. Our two trains were drawn up tail to tail in the middle of an open plain and were supposed to be surrounded by Turkish sentries. I thought it advisable to have a look round these sentries and found just what I expected. As it was raining each sentry had sat down on his hunkers and put his blanket on his head. Their primary concern was to keep dry, and the security of the P.M. ranked as a very bad second. . . .'

'. . . During our discussion with Çakmak I was facing him seated at a long table running down the centre of the

[1] " The C.I.G.S. fortunately speaks perfect French at his usual lightning speed. . . ." Sir Ian Jacob, *MS. Diary*, 30th January, 1943.

railway carriage. Whilst talking to him I could see out of
the window behind him, and suddenly spotted what I
thought was a pallid harrier busy quartering over the plain.
I had never seen a pallid harrier and was not certain
whether what I was looking at was one or a hen harrier.
I was consequently very intent in looking out of that
window much to Çakmak's discomfiture, who kept looking round and possibly thought I had spotted someone
getting ready to have a shot at him. It was not possible for
me to explain through the interpreter that I was only
bird-watching.'

' The dinner party was a screaming success. Winston
was quite at his best and had the whole party convulsed
with laughter. In his astounding French, consisting of a
combination of the most high-flown French words mixed
with English words pronounced in French, he embarked on
the most complicated stories which would have even been
difficult to put across adequately in English.'[1]

' On leaving the dinner table for his cabin he asked me
to come along with him. He then informed me that he
proposed to stop on for an additional day, that he had a
great deal more to discuss with Inönü and would require
at least another day. He also said that he felt certain I
required much more time. I told him that it was highly
undesirable that he should stop on and that all arrangements had been made for our departure for Cyprus by
12 noon the next day. I told him how inadequate the
security arrangements were, and pointing to his berth told
him it would be quite easy for anybody to blow him sky
high in his bed. He gave the berth one slightly perturbed
look and said, " Oh! do you think so." I assured him that
I had instructed his detectives to take every precaution
against such a regrettable contingency, so considered he
would probably have a good night.'

' Once more I impressed on him the fact that we must

[1] The Prime Minister's speech in French, Sir Ian Jacob wrote, was a real
tour de force. He " waded resolutely on and came out at the far end bloody but
unbowed. . . . Peculiar though it all was, I do not think anyone felt like laugh-
ing. They couldn't help admiring his determination and self-possession. The
Turks were much too polite to express any amusement." Sir Ian Jacob, *MS
Diary*, 30th January, 1943.

stick to our plan and be ready to depart on the morrow. Once more he repeated all the arguments that made it necessary to stop on. I bade him good-night and left him, hoping for the best.'

" *January 31st. Cyprus (150 miles).* Moderately comfortable night in a very dirty sleeping car, with continual hammering of the hot-water system. At 11 a.m. we were by way of having another Military Conference with Çakmak. However, owing to some hitch Çakmak had not been warned, and they were not ready. . . . We met again at 11.45 and went over a draft of the conclusions arrived at during previous meeting. . . . On the whole the visit was a tremendous success. P.M. is delighted. Turkey's neutrality will, from now on, assume a more biased nature in favour of the Allies, I hope somewhat similar to that of the Americans prior to their entry into the war."

" Finally we all had lunch again with the President as the train moved off for Adana. On arrival we had a great rush for the plane as at that moment plans were to return direct to Cairo. . . . We had already got into the plane . . . when P.M. discovered that the pilot was still under the impression he was still going to Cyprus. This was enough for a new change of plans! The P.M. now decided that we should adhere to our original plan and go to Cyprus."

" Off we started down the runway, but in turning one of the corners a wheel got off the runway and sank up to the axle. So we all got out again and for nearly an hour a crowd of jabbering Turks endeavoured to pull the wheel out of the mud.[1] As they were making no progress we decided to change to the second Liberator, so out came all the luggage out of both machines and ours was transhipped. We then all packed in, warmed up the engines, and were moving down the runway when

[1] " It was not long before the P.M. himself was to be seen with a rather rakish Homburg hat and his cigar, looking quite pleased with the whole affair, and presumably giving his views on the situation in the middle of the crowd round the wheel." Sir Ian Jacob, *MS. Diary,* 31st January, 1943.

we were told that our plane had now been pulled out of the mud. However, we decided to stick where we were, and took off for Cyprus."

' The changes of plans in the morning had been very typical of Winston. After we had swung him away from his plan to remain on for an extra night in Turkey he swung right round and was in a great hurry to get back to Cairo; he had many telegrams he must send, he must not be delayed, it was now quite impossible to spare the time for Cyprus, etc., etc. Then, after telegrams had been sent to Cairo and Cyprus to change plans, and we were seated in the plane, the pilot walked past between us, and Winston said he hoped the weather was good and that the pilot knew we were going to Cairo. This stopped the pilot short who said he had not yet been told we were not going to Cyprus, but that he would at once get ready to fly to Cairo. He took two steps forward when Winston stopped him and said, " Stop—no, I shall not go to Cairo, I shall go to Cyprus after all! " '

' He loved these sudden changes of plans. Unfortunately he often wished to carry out similar sudden changes in strategy. I had the greatest difficulty in making him realise that strategy was a long-term process in which you could not frequently change your mind.'

" As we rose and left Adana we had a wonderful view of the whole of the Taurus range of mountains, from one end to the other, all covered with snow glittering in the sun. After about half an hour's flying we struck the east end of the island . . . with good visibility and lovely evening lights. The Governor met us, and we are now very comfortably installed in Government House. . . ."

" *February 1st. Cairo (600 miles).* Had a grand sleep and comfortable morning with breakfast at 9 a.m. After breakfast talked to a large gathering of representative magnates of Cyprus who had come to see P.M. Finally he appeared on the scene and made a very nice little speech to them."

" I then went off with Hughes . . . who commands the

troops in Cyprus. We went to his H.Q., and then climbed
on to the roof from which we had an excellent view of
the whole island. He explained to me the defensive
organisation and plans to meet attacks. We then drove
up to the passes on the road from Nicosia to Kyrenia on
the north coast and a possible point of landing and attack
on the capital. We then drove back to lunch with Hughes
at his Mess and from there down to the aerodrome.
Meanwhile P.M. had been inspecting 4th Hussars. We
all met and took off at about 2 p.m."

" Lovely clear weather and we had a beautiful fly back
to Cairo. . . . From Cyprus we went straight to Haifa and
then down the coast to the boundary between Egypt and
Palestine. From there we struck up for Ismailia where
we crossed the canal and on to pass just north of Cairo
and came down at our usual aerodrome. It has been a
most satisfactory trip, and I never thought that we
should make such headway with the Turks. Some of
my wild dreams of bringing Turkey along with us no
longer look quite so wild."

" After tea Alexander and Dick McCreery came to
see me to discuss the organization of the planning staff
for the Sicilian operation. . . ."

' Our own Joint Planners had worked out a basic plan
for the invasion of the island. This plan now wanted breaking down in detail by a Planning Staff of the commander
of the operation. It was the organization of this staff that
I discussed with Alexander.'

" *February 2nd, 1943.* Started the day by attending
G.H.Q. 9.15 a.m. conference to hear the latest about the
general situation. Then spent an hour with 'Jumbo' Wilson
running through his task with him, and settling details
as to how he is to look after the administration of the
Eighth Army, attend to equipping of Turks, and at the
same time ensure that formations required for amphibious
operations receive their full training."

" Came back to Embassy and was given telegram from
P.M. to Roosevelt to check over. It was rather too

optimistic as to what we are likely to be able to do during 1943, and I had to go to him to tone it down. . . . "

" All plans are now made for our departure to Tripoli to-morrow morning early, weather permitting. I only hope he will not suggest any more changes of plans at the last moment. It is high time we started turning homewards, and I shudder at the work to catch up again with events when I get home."

" *February 3rd. Tripoli (1,200 miles).* We said good-bye to the Embassy at 8.30 and left for the aerodrome, where we took off at 9.45 a.m. We had a lovely calm fly and most interesting. After lunch I went forward to the second Pilot's seat. We were just over El Alamein at that time and from there on I was able to look down on the various battle scenes, Buerat and then Misurata where we picked up an escort of fighters to accompany us."

" Up to then we had flown over continuous and never-ending desert. Now we came into the beginning of some elementary farming: Mussolini's colonising settlements consisting of little white cottages, a well and a few palm trees. Finally at 4.30 p.m. we landed at Castel Benito aerodrome outside Tripoli and were met by Monty and Alex. We drove off to Monty's camp where he gave the P.M. and me a long talk on his situation. He then paraded the whole of his H.Q., which was addressed by the P.M. on a loud-speaker. Then we had further talks with Monty and dined in his Mess—the same tent we had dined in with him before the battle of El Alamein. Now I have retired to my caravan. It is infernally cold, so shall get into bed quickly so as to get warm."

" It is a wonderful feeling finding myself back with the Eighth Army H.Q. and Monty after the last few months and to feel that during that short space the whole aspect of the war in North Africa has been changed."

" *February 4th. Tripoli.* P.M. and I have been stopping in Montgomery's camp whilst the rest of the party were with Alexander. At 9.30 a.m. we all assembled and started off by car for Tripoli. It was most interesting seeing the place for the first time. The streets and house-tops were lined with sentries who held back the local inhabitants. When we arrived on the main square and sea front we found there the bulk of the 51st Division formed up. . . . The last time we had seen them was near Ismailia just after their arrival in the Middle East. Then they are still pink and white; now they are bronzed warriors of many battles and of a victorious advance. I have seldom seen a finer body of men or one that looked prouder of being soldiers. We drove slowly round the line and then came back with the men cheering him all the way. We then took up a position on a prepared stand, and the whole division marched past with a bag-pipe band playing. It was quite one of the most impressive sights I have ever seen. The whole division was most beautifully turned out, and might have been in barracks for the last three months instead of having marched some 1,200 miles and fought many battles. . . ."

" After the review we drove out into the country to see some of the Corps troops, Medium Artillery, Field Artillery, Anti-Tanks, Engineers, etc. In many places the native population cheered and clapped their hands as we went by. Oliver Leese, the Corps Commander, gave us a most excellent open-air lunch, after which we examined the various types of mines used by the enemy and the ways of defeating them. From there we drove to the New Zealand Division which was formed up complete on parade with Bernard Freyberg at its head. He gave a ' General Salute ' by microphone and loud-speaker, which was admirably carried out. We then drove round the parade, and finally the whole division marched past."

" We then had tea and drove off to Castel Benito aerodrome for the P.M. to visit the Air Force. From there down to the harbour, where we did a complete tour of the harbour in a launch and visited the blockships which they are busy clearing. They had just succeeded in bringing in a 2,900 ton ship, the first to be got through. We finished up . . . by seeing the destruction of the wharfs and quays carried out by the Germans, and the

work we were doing to put it right. The Germans did a
very thorough job of it, and a great deal of work i
required."

"Returned to camp to find a telegram from hom
trying to stop P.M. from going to Algiers, owing to a
message . . . pointing towards attempts on his life. . .
He decided to carry on with his original plan. W
therefore start at 5 a.m. to-morrow for Algiers, and ther
are not many hours left for sleep. While I write a heav
air-raid on Tripoli is going on and we have been watchin
the A.A. shells bursting."

' This had been a memorable day and one I shall neve
forget, but what stands out clearest . . . was the march-pas
of the 51st Division. As I stood by Winston watching th
division march past, with the wild music of the pipes in m
ears, I felt a lump rise in my throat and a tear run dow
my face. I looked round at Winston and saw several tear
on his face. . . . For the first time I was beginning to liv
through the thrill of those first successes that were no
rendering ultimate victory possible. The depth of thes
feelings can only be gauged in relation to the utter darknes
of those early days of calamities, when no single ray of hop
could pierce the depth of gloom. . . . I felt no shame tha
tears should have betrayed my feelings, only a deep relief.'

"*February 5th. Algiers (900 miles).* I was called a
3 a.m., had a 3.30 breakfast and by 4 a.m. started off fo
Castel Benito aerodrome. We arrived there about 5 a.m
and by 5.30 sailed off into the dark. We had to hea
south-west first, to avoid Tunisia, and finally north fo
Algiers. This deviation resulted in some 900 miles
I slept for the first three hours of it and then spent th
last hour looking at southern Algeria."

"We finally arrived at 10 a.m. on Maison Blanch
aerodrome. There I found Eisenhower to meet me. H
told me P.M. had landed some ten minutes previousl
and that he had sent him on in his half-armoured ca
with windows smeared with oil and mud. He was to g
by a circuitous route. I could see Eisenhower was som

what worried with the responsibility of having him on his hands. I then got into Eisenhower's car, and we drove back by the direct route with a man armed with a Tommy-gun beside the driver, and Eisenhower with a revolver. We saw no suspicious characters."

" On arriving here ' (Ike's house),' I had breakfast, bath and shave. . . . Anderson then turned up from First Army and I had a long talk with him on questions affecting his front. It was a useful meeting as it became clear to me at once that he required more infantry. On the strength of this I got Eisenhower to send a telegram on my behalf to the War Office to order an additional infantry division."

" Anderson and I then had to go to the P.M. We found him in bed. He started by saying he proposed to stop another day! I told him that if the weather was good we should decide to go to-night. After some difficulty I got him to agree."

" I then attended a large lunch given by Eisenhower and attended by P.M., Giraud, Nogues, Boisson, Peyrouton, Alex Cadogan and Cunningham. . . . After lunch I had a long talk with Cunningham and then had a walk round looking for birds in the garden. Discovered the same African blue-tit that I saw in Marrakesh. Had tea with Eisenhower and a long talk with him before dinner which we had in Admiral Cunningham's villa. P.M., Cunningham, Randolph, doctor, Bedell Smith, etc., were there."

" After dinner we formed a convoy and departed for the aerodrome. I got into the plane, put on pyjamas and a flying suit on top and fur-lined boots, and prepared to take off. Engines warmed up and went on turning round, and yet we never took off. At last pilot sent word to get out again. . . . We discovered that one of the two magnetos of Engine No. 1 of the P.M.'s plane had refused to function just before starting and would have to be changed. We soon found that the delay would make it impossible for us to start, so there was nothing for it but to dress again and return to Eisenhower's house for the night. Finally rolled into bed at 2 a.m. dog tired."

' It was most unfortunate that we had to delay another night in Algiers, as according to Intelligence a notorious agent was supposed to have been sent there for the specific purpose of bumping Winston off. We had gone to Algiers contrary to the Cabinet's wishes, and it was certainly not desirable to stop a moment longer than necessary.'

" *February 6th. Gibraltar (500 miles).* I had a grand sleep till 9 a.m., a good breakfast, and then went round to see the P.M. about the journey on. I had discovered from my pilot that he did not at all like the idea of going direct from Algiers to England as his plane was not so well fitted out with radio directional gear as the P.M's. . . . We therefore decided that I should go to Gibraltar and on, whilst P.M. went direct, and that we should time to arrive about the same hour."

" I consequently had an early lunch with Eisenhower, and was at the Maison Blanche aerodrome by 2 p.m. Just as we were moving off to get into position to take off, two fighter planes came in simultaneously, apparently not seeing each other. They both crashed on the runway, one of them turning over on to the pilot and bursting into flames at once. The other luckily did not catch fire, and I do not know whether the pilot was damaged or not. We had to move right up to within thirty yards of the crash in order to get sufficient of the runway to take off."

" We had an excellent journey, leaving at 2.30 p.m. and reaching Gibraltar at 5 p.m. We skirted along the African coast, passing Oran and Melilla. Arrived here with lovely lights over the Rock. Mason-MacFarlane met us on the aerodrome and took us up to Government House where we had tea. After tea I had a walk in the garden looking for birds. Saw a peregrine falcon high up in the sky."

" Mason-MacFarlane staged a defensive-fire demonstration after dinner. We were motored up to the top of the Rock at about 11 p.m. and from there had a wonderful view of the tracer-bullets of machine-guns firing out to sea in a zone illuminated by searchlights. At the same time searchlights and all A.A. guns engaged imaginary targets in the air. It was a most impressive sight."

" At 1.15 a.m. we went down to the aerodrome and at 2.15 a.m. started into the darkness on the last stage of the journey."

" *February 7th. Ferney Close (1,500 miles).* A cold and uncomfortable night. At 9 a.m. we were over the Scilly Isles and ten minutes later came to Land's End. Clouds were low and the going very bumpy. However by 10 a.m. we reached Lyneham aerodrome and made a safe landing. We found that we were about thirty minutes ahead of the P.M.'s plane which had flown direct from Algiers. Cadogan and I went on direct to the train, where we had breakfast and a wash and greeted the P.M. a few minutes later.[1] By 1 p.m. we arrived in London where to my great joy you met me."

" I have finished a journey of some 10,200 miles which has been full of interest and resulted in agreements with Americans and Turks far above anything I had hoped for. . . . I now foresee some hard work ahead to convert the paper work of the last three weeks into facts and actions."

---

[1] Soon after this flight the Prime Minister's plane, *Commando*, " perished with all hands, though with a different pilot and crew." *Churchill*, IV, 648.

Chapter Twelve

TRIDENT

It will take the rest of this year to finish the show in North Africa and give Italy a proper bang. Then next year, 1944, we had better land in Western Europe and I would like to come home and take part in that. I look forward to leading the Eighth Army into Rome. By Jove, what a party!

LT.-GEN. MONTGOMERY TO GEN. BROOKE

16th February, 1943

DURING THE first days of February 1943, while the Prime Minister and Brooke were on their way home from Turkey and immediately afterwards, three events of great significance occurred. On February 2nd the last remnants of Field-Marshal Paulus's twenty-two beleaguered divisions before Stalingrad laid down their arms. On the same day the first British supply-ship entered Tripoli and began to serve the Eighth Army through the re-opened port. Two days later, after advancing 1,600 miles in three months and completing the conquest of the Italian Empire, Montgomery's advance-guard reached the south-eastern frontiers of Tunisia, thus bringing into effect the Casablanca Conference's directive for the fighting forces of Britain and the United States in North Africa to pass under a single command. And on February 9th, following six costly naval battles and the despatch to the South Pacific of ever-growing reinforcements and supplies, the six months' struggle for Guadalcanal, authorised by the American Chiefs of Staff in July, ended in the withdrawal of the Japanese from the island.

By that day the Chief of Imperial General Staff was back at his desk in Whitehall. After a night at his Hampshire home on Sunday the 8th, he returned to harness on the 9th to attend the usual Monday evening meeting of the War Cabinet, with Attlee taking the chair in the Prime Minister's absence. " Since dinner," he wrote that night, " I have been digging into old files and trying to get level with the work again. It is funny how quickly one settles back into the old groove. I hardly feel as if I had been away."

The old familiar problems recurred. Almost at once Brooke had to record attempts by the Prime Minister and his brother in great-hearted optimism, the President, to force the pace of the Sicilian landings. The difficulty of fixing a date for the operation was made all the harder because those who were to command the invading forces were engaged in Tunisia and could only give their attention to planning when they had finished with the enemy there.

> "*February 10th.* At this morning's C.O.S. we struggled with attempts to put a day for the attack on Sicily earlier and into June. Both President and P.M. are hankering after this. Personally I feel we are running grave risks of wrecking the whole show by trying to rush it. . . ."
>
> "*February 15th.* Spent most of the C.O.S. meeting in examining possibility of shifting forward date of Sicily attack to June instead of July, on the assumption that Tunis can be cleared by May 1st. As both the American and British considerations have to be taken into account, it is not easy to arrive at a conclusion. . . ."
>
> "*February 18th.* Bertie Ramsay just back from North Africa came to our C.O.S. meeting, and gave us the most recent information about the planning side of the Sicilian operations. Evidently Eisenhower does not think he can possibly undertake the operation before the July moon in spite of the pressure that is being applied on him to do it in June. In any case, after the recent defeat he has suffered in Tunisia, I doubt very much whether he can clear Tunisia of Germans before May at the very earliest, if even then."

For a few weeks, however, Brooke enjoyed a respite, though an anxious and unwelcome one, from the daily pressure of his old chief and friend. Both Churchill and Roosevelt—the one

68, and the other 61 and a victim of infantile paralysis—came back from their travels with impaired health. Five days after the Prime Minister's return Brooke found him in bed with fever and was so worried by his condition that he went away with a number of urgent questions undiscussed. Three days later the indomitable statesman presided over the Cabinet but with a bad sore throat and cold. By the 16th he was down with pneumonia, and, when he protested at the reduced number of papers reaching his bedside, the consultant who had been called in by his doctor told him that pneumonia was known as the old man's friend, " because," he explained, " it takes them off so quietly."

For the next week the familiar flow of minutes, " prayers " and queries from the Prime Minister's desk ceased. Brooke did not see him again till February 22nd, when, summoned to help him compose a letter to the King about the North African campaign, he found him " still looking very ill, although he said that he was much better with a temperature of only 100 degrees and was quite ready to joke." In his absence, he noted, the War Cabinet that night was " peevish and full of questions about Tunisia." But by the beginning of March Churchill had turned the corner and was on the mend. Brooke, spending an hour with him on the night of the 1st, trying to settle some belated military appointments, was delighted to find him in his old form, ranging the globe and remarking cheerfully of the Turks, " We must start by treating them purry-purry, puss-puss, then later we shall harden! "[1]

By that time Brooke himself was under the weather. February had proved an anxious month, with U-boat sinkings rising again, the Russians checked and turning sour, the Americans embarking on new Pacific ventures, the Prime Minister ill, and the African campaign going badly. Though the port of Tripoli was working, it could still supply only two of Montgomery's divisions on the Tunisian frontier, and, until larger forces could be brought up, the Eighth Army was cut off from the First and barred from further advance by the Mareth Line which, built by the French to keep out the Italians, was now manned by Germans and Italians to keep

[1] *Diary*, 1st March, 1943.

ut the British. The distances involved were enormous; as
Montgomery put it in a memorandum to Brooke, the distance
rom Cairo to Tripoli alone—and his advance-guard was now
wo hundred miles beyond Tripoli—was as far as from White-
all to the Kremlin, while to have to supply his army in
Tripoli from Benghazi, which he had to do until the former
ort was in full operation, was like having to maintain one
n Vienna along a single road from London. For a time the
orward corps on the Tunisian frontier was separated from
he reserve corps at Tobruk by more than a thousand miles—
a position calling for the utmost vigilance in the presence of
o formidable a commander as Rommel. The latter, now
appointed to command all the Axis' troops in Africa
—some fourteen divisions operating on interior lines—was for
he moment free to concentrate against the Anglo-American
orces threatening Tunisia from the west. This he did on
February 14th, striking suddenly with his new tanks at the
till unfledged 1st U.S. Armoured Division and capturing
nearly half its tanks and guns. For a few days, with the
Kasserine Pass in his hands, it looked as if his panzers might
ut Anderson's communications with Algiers. Then, with
Alexander taking personal command of the battle, the Americans
allied strongly, while the head of the attack was blunted by
he stubborn British infantry in the hill defiles to the north.
By the end of the month most of the ground lost had been
regained and the enemy was back where he had started. It had
been an anxious fortnight, and Brooke, now within a few
months of his sixtieth birthday, was feeling the strain. On
he 18th, four days after Rommel's attack, the tone of his diary
became unwontedly querulous:

" Attended dull Cabinet at 6 p.m. . . . This evening
heated argument with Secretary of State trying to prevent a most awful broadcast by Commanders-in-Chief
during a B.B.C. Army Week. He is adopting a peevish
childish attitude which makes him impossible to deal
with."

' It cannot,' Brooke commented afterwards,

' have been a very heated argument as I remember nothing about it. It must have been a very exceptional occasion for P.J. to adopt a peevish or childish attitude, as I cannot recall his ever being in that frame of mind. It seems more probable that I was in a peevish and childish mood myself! '

He certainly wrote at this time with some asperity of several colleagues for whom he had the highest regard, lashing out on February 19th at Mountbatten over a proposed attack on the Channel Islands, which he regarded as " not in its proper strategic setting and tactically quite adrift," and adding a few days later:

> " Very heated argument at C.O.S. with Mountbatten who was again putting up wild proposals disconnected with his direct duties. He will insist on doing the work of Force Commanders. . . . Both Portal and I were driven to distraction."

Even one of his favourite divisional commanders, " Boy " Browning—trainer of the new Airborne Forces—received a dressing down for " causing trouble by writing letters to politicians."[1]

Between March 14th and the 24th Brooke was in bed with long staved-off influenza. When he returned to work on the 24th the Prime Minister sent for him and was " very nice," telling him not to overwork and to take it easy for a few days. Two days later, on Friday the 26th, there is a charming entry in the diary:

> " During the meeting the P.M. sent for me. By the time I . . . reached him in the Annexe he was in his bath. However, he received me as soon as he came out, looking like a Roman Centurion with nothing on except a large bath-towel draped round him. He shook me warmly by

---

[1] " He took it very well." *Diary*, 26th February, 1950. Brooke had the highest opinion of Maj.-Gen. (now Lt.-Gen. Sir Frederick) Browning. ' If it had not been for this difficult pioneer work of Browning' he wrote, 'we should certainly not have had our Airborne Division ready in time. . . . " Boy " Browning's drive and energy had been generating considerable heat in many quarters in the War Office. He knew he had my support and I had instructed him to stand no delays or prevarications in any quarter.' *Notes on My Life* V, 340-1.

the hand in this get-up and told me to sit down while he dressed. A most interesting procedure. First he stepped into a white silk vest, then white silk drawers, and walked up and down the room in this kit looking rather like 'Humpty-Dumpty,' with a large body and small thin legs. Then a white shirt which refused to join comfortably round his neck and so was left open with a bow-tie to keep it together. Then the hair (what there was of it) took much attention, a handkerchief was sprayed with scent and then rubbed on his head. The few hairs were then brushed and finally sprayed direct. Finally trousers, waistcoat and coat, and meanwhile he rippled on the whole time about Monty's battle and our proposed visit to North Africa. However, the main thing he wanted to say was that he thought I looked tired last night at the meeting we had, and that I was to take a long week-end."[1]

On the Monday, when Brooke returned after his two days in Hampshire, the two convalescents, sitting in arm-chairs in the Prime Minister's drawing-room, dined *tête-à-tête* on " plover's eggs, chicken broth, chicken pie, chocolate soufflé and, with it a bottle of champagne, followed by port and brandy."[2]

. . . .

The strategic triumvirate over which Brooke presided had to ride three horses that spring. There was the two-sided attack on Tunisia, the preparations for the Sicilian invasion, and the cross-Channel assault on Hitler's Western Wall, which the Chiefs of Staff did not believe could be stormed until 1944 but which the Prime Minister and the Americans were still hoping to attempt in the autumn. There was also the Burmese campaign which the latter were urging the British to launch in the belief that Chiang Kai-shek's China was an indispensable base for the defeat of Japan and that it would collapse unless the Burma Road was re-opened. At the back of all lay the shortage of landing-craft and the never-

[1] *Diary*, 26th March, 1943.
[2] *Diary*, 29th March, 1943.

ceasing U-boat attack on the Atlantic sea-lanes. In March the Allied shipping losses, which had risen again from 260,000 to 400,000 tons in February, reached nearly half a million tons. Despite the growing pace of American shipbuilding no sustained assault on Hitler's European fortress was possible until this wasting disease had been halted.

When Brooke returned to work on March 24th, he was met with new anxieties. At the end of February Alexander, after regrouping the American and French forces in the south, had warned the Prime Minister that victory in Tunisia was not just round the corner. Despite immense shipping and air losses, Hitler was still flying men and supplies in from Sicily, and the Axis had by now a quarter of a million troops there, half of them Germans. On March 6th, having given the Americans and British a taste of his metal, Rommel turned south and struck at Montgomery at Medenine, sixty miles from the Tripolitanian frontier, hoping to smash his advance-guard before the rest of the Eighth Army could be brought up for the assault on the Mareth Line.

But Montgomery was expecting him. A week earlier he had told the Prime Minister in a letter that he proposed to fight Rommel in his present position and " see him off should he attempt any dirty work." It was the kind of waiting battle on chosen ground in which he excelled. " Rommel attacked me at dawn," he wrote to Brooke that night. " It was very foolish of him. I have five hundred 6-pdr. anti-tank guns dug in on the ground; I have four hundred tanks, and I have good infantry holding strong pivots, and a great weight of artillery. It is an absolute gift, and the man must be mad."[1] As at Alam Halfa, the Eighth Army beat off every attack and, with only 130 casualties and without even engaging its carefully husbanded armour, destroyed more than fifty tanks. A few days later Rommel, a sick and discomfited man, left North Africa for ever and was succeeded by von Arnim.

Yet the Mareth Line had still to be stormed, and, until it had been, there could be no junction between the two halves of the Allied forces, no hope of clearing Tunisia, and no re-opening of the Mediterranean and invasion of Sicily. And

[1] Montgomery to Brooke, 6th March, 1943. Lord Alanbrooke, *Personal Files.*

the Kremlin was growing restive again. By the end of February its own offensive had been halted, and the Germans, counter-attacking, had regained Kharkov and stabilised their lines in the south. " It is evident from your message," Stalin wrote to Churchill on the 16th, " that, contrary to your previous calculations, the end of operations in Tunis is expected in April instead of February. I hardly need to tell you how disappointing is such a delay. . . . It is just because the military operations in Tunis slackened that Hitler was able to throw in some additional troops against the Russians[1]. . . . In order not to give the enemy any respite it is extremely important to deliver the blow from the West in the spring or in the early summer and not to postpone it until the second half of the year." To make matters worse, though this had still to be broken to the Russian dictator, the British and American Chiefs of Staff had decided to cancel the sailing of the March convoy to Murmansk and run no more until after the capture of Sicily. On March 4th the C.I.G.S. and his colleagues were prevented at the last minute from attending a " Wings for Victory " lunch at the Guildhall by the need to redraft a long telegram of the Prime Minister's to Stalin on this painful subject.[2]

While Brooke was still convalescing from influenza Montgomery opened his attack on the Mareth Line. Before his main body struck on the 22nd at the seaward flank of the narrow defences between the Mediterranean and mountains in order to draw the enemy's reserves, a carefully-concealed force of 27,000 men and two hundred tanks, consisting of Freyberg's New Zealand Division, the 8th Armoured Brigade and Leclerc's Free French, set out on a two-hundred-mile desert march round the mountains—a route till now regarded as impassable for military vehicles. But the frontal attack— the wearing-down dog-fight on which Montgomery had reckoned—stuck in the enemy minefields, and by the night of March 23rd the British infantry were back where they had

[1] *Churchill*, IV, 667-8. This was untrue. But, in accordance with their normal winter routine, the Germans had merely used their excellent west-to-east communications to rest tired divisions from Russia by exchanging them with fresh ones from France and the Low Countries.

[2] It was not sent until March 30th. *Churchill*, IV, 675-6.

started. When next day Brooke returned from his sick-bed to his London desk he was greeted by the news that Montgomery's attack had failed.

Montgomery took the blow on his right only to strike out the more fiercely with his left. Instantly cutting his losses, he despatched the 1st Armoured Division and part of the X Corps to join Freyberg's thrust beyond the mountains against the defenders' rear. By the late afternoon of the 26th, aided by a tremendous bombardment by the Desert Air Force, they were pounding at the defile to El Hamma and the Gabes plain. That night they broke through and, after a day's further fighting, forced the enemy to withdraw from the Mareth Line to avoid encirclement, leaving 7,000 prisoners in their hands. Ten days later, on April 6th, the Eighth Army, having taken Gabes, stormed the Wadi Akarit after one of Montgomery's sudden artillery barrages and debouched on to the central Tunisian plain. By the 7th its advance-guard was in contact with the U.S. II Corps, and the junction of the two Allied armies in Africa had been achieved. The port of Sfax fell on the 10th and Sousse on the 12th. Von Arnim's quarter of a million men were hemmed into the mountain massif in the north-east between Enfidaville and Beja.

.   .   .   .

With the coming of spring the justification for Britain's Mediterranean strategy became far clearer than during the frustrations, rains and set-backs of the winter. Even Stalin started once more to praise it. At the end of March he wrote to Churchill of the pleasure with which he had watched the Alamein picture, *Desert Victory*. " The film depicts magnificently how Britain is fighting and stigmatises those scoundrels (there are such people also in our country) who are asserting that Britain is not fighting at all but is merely an onlooker." A fortnight later he wrote again, " The speedy development of the Anglo-American advance in Tunis constitutes an important success. . . . I wish you to kill the enemy and capture as many prisoners and trophies as possible."[1] Goebbels himself testified to the success of Brooke's strategy,

[1] *Churchill*, IV, 675, 677.

writing in his diary: " They are certainly sitting on a high horse in London and congratulating themselves ". . . . " Their triumphant cries really get on one's nerves, and unfortunately they are not entirely without ground and reason."[1]

Even more worrying for the Germans was the manifestation of the R.A.F.'s growing power. " Your primary object," ran the directive of the Combined Chiefs of Staff at Casablanca to the Commander-in-Chief, Bomber Command, " will be the progressive destruction and dislocation of the German military, industrial, and economic system, and the undermining of the morale of the German people to a point where their capacity for armed resistance is fatally weakened." With nearly a thousand first-line heavy bombers, a new technique of Radar target-finding and a specialised " Pathfinder " force, Air-Marshal Harris was now ready to start making the directive effective. At the beginning of March he turned from the bombing of U-boat bases, to which Bomber Command had temporarily been deflected, to a major assault on the most important industrial target in Germany. On the 5th, four hundred of his aircraft fell on Essen, the capital of the Ruhr, dropping more than a thousand tons of high explosives and incendiaries in just over half an hour and inflicting tremendous damage. In the course of two further raids six hundred acres of the Krupps armament works were laid waste. " Things simply cannot go on like this," Goebbels wrote, " the damage . . . is colossal and indeed ghastly. . . . Nobody can tell how Krupps is to go on." Other cities of the Reich were similarly visited; "it drives one mad," the Doctor added a few days later after a comparatively minor raid on Berlin, "to think that some Canadian boor, who probably can't even find Europe on the globe, flies here from a country glutted with natural resources which his people don't know how to exploit, to bombard a continent with a crowded population."[2] What enraged him and his master most was that, owing to the dispersal of the Luftwaffe over a 1,500-mile front in Russia and a 2,000-mile one in

---

[1] Goebbels, *Diary*, 9th April, 1943.

[2] Goebbels, *Diary*, 3rd March, 1943. " The English Minister for Air delivered a speech that puts into the shade anything ever said. He proclaimed the British intention of causing a German migration . . . from the big cities. The cynicism under-lying such a statement simply cannot be beaten." *Idem*, 13th March, 1943.

the Mediterranean, it was impossible to muster enough bombers to retaliate, while the entire German aircraft industry had to be concentrated on the production of fighters, not to destroy the Russian air force, but to keep off Harris's raids. " We are completely at the mercy of the English," he lamented. " One need only think six months ahead to see us facing ruin in many cities ". . . . " Until then the English can lay a large part of the Reich in ruins if they go about it in the right way."[1] With large-scale raids on no less than thirteen nights in March there seemed every indication that they meant to. By the end of the month the American day-bombers had joined in, bravely disregarding the lack of long-range fighter escort. On the 20th they swept in from the sea over Bremen and, bombing from three miles high, inflicted major damage on the port and city. " I hope the air offensive against Germany," wrote Stalin, " will go on inexorably increasing. I will be very grateful if you will send me your photographs of the destructions in Essen."[2]

. . . .

While Harris was softening up the Ruhr—the first round of a long, mounting battle waged over the cities of the Reich to stop the supply of Germany's eastern armies and drive the heart of her war-industry away from the invasion beaches—his masters in the Chiefs of Staff Committee were preparing to assault Europe, first from the south and then from the west. For 1943 their objectives were Sicily and, if they could carry the Prime Minister and Americans with them, southern Italy. From this they hoped would follow the downfall of Mussolini, the capture of the Fascist fleet, the bombing of Fortress Europe from the south, and, with the control of the Adriatic and the entry of Turkey into the war, the crumbling of the Axis empire in its most restless and unsettled part, the Balkans. " Tunisian news continues to be excellent," Brooke wrote on April 13th, " C.O.S. meeting at which we discussed future moves after capture of Sicily. This evening meeting with P.M., which started by being stormy

---

[1] Goebbels, *Diary*, 6th, 9th March; 9th April, 1943.
[2] Stalin to Prime Minister, 27th March, 1943. *Churchill*, IV, 674.

and then improved. Discussing advisability of removing all landing-craft from this country to the Mediterranean for 1943 and devoting the whole of our energies to the Mediterranean. Luckily P.M. finally agreed, but we are to put paper up to Defence Committee to prove our case."[1] Next day he continued, " We were busy again with future operations in the Mediterranean and elaborate deception plans."

What form Italy's collapse would take, when it would come and what plans the enemy would make to forestall it, it was not yet possible to say. But Brooke was no longer seriously worried about the enemy's plans. In Europe and the Pacific those who a year earlier had been carrying all before them had lost the initiative and were standing on the defensive. The British Chiefs of Staff meant to keep them there. If the maritime Powers, by defeating the U-boat, could regain mobility at sea and use it to make the enemy fight where it was hardest for him to do so, the game was in their hands. Britain's problem, and Brooke's, was to induce those who held the winning cards to play them right:

> " *April 21st.* Remarkably quiet day. A short C.O.S., no interviews and not much office work. Spent most of the afternoon appreciating probable course of action by the Germans during 1943. Not a very easy problem. I think, however, that their policy will aim at maximum offensive against our shipping at sea and defensive on land and air on all other fronts."

Had the C.I.G.S. been able to look over the shoulders of those two other diary-keepers, Goebbels and Count Ciano, he would have found confirmation of his belief. The enemy assurance of the past three summers that the war was won had changed into a melancholy and dubious, " We cannot lose," and a conviction that at best it was bound to be a disastrously drawn-out affair. Since Alamein and Stalingrad the Germans had stopped thinking in terms of 1940 and had begun to recall 1918. Even that *sanctum sanctorum* of the Prussian spirit, the Army, Ciano wrote, was weakened by the " doubting mind." It made no difference to its valour, for the Germans

[1] *Diary*, 13th April, 1943.

were a brave and tough people. Nor, because they knew
that for them at least there could be no going back, did
it weaken their rulers' resolution to fight on; indeed, it
made them only the more ruthless in their cruelties, since these,
by arousing universal hatred, burnt not only their own
boats but those of the German people. That spring orders
were given for the progressive incineration of the entire
Jewish population of Europe; in the Warsaw ghetto, which
was appointed the chief clearing-house for the massacres,
the victims procured arms from unreliable elements in the
satellite armies and turned them in despair against their
destroyers.

By their capture of the initiative the Allies had taken the
pounce and fire out of Axis strategy. Even the Fuehrer had
lost his old resilience, and, brooding, pallid and twitching in
his gloomy underground headquarters in the East Prussian
forest, relaxed only when, in the company of old Party comrades, he speculated on the fine things he would do after the
war. In March he had still been peddling dreams and talking
of sending Rommel back to Africa to capture Casablanca,[1]
but before April was out he knew that the troops and supplies
he had flown into Tunisia during the past six months had
been wasted. He talked now only of a limited offensive on
the Eastern Front, was pessimistic, though indignant, about
the air-war, and saw no present means of victory but to hold
on stubbornly to every inch of conquered ground and use the
submarine " to cut the arteries of the enemy's war of movement."[2] So defensive-minded had he become that in January
he resolved to lay up his fleet of powerful surface-raiders and
rely solely on submarines. Only with the utmost difficulty
had he been persuaded by his new naval chief, Doenitz, to
retain the *Tirpitz*, *Scharnhorst* and *Lützow* for use against the
Murmansk convoys and the defence of Norway. As for his
fellow dictator, Mussolini, he was now a mere shadow of his
old bombastic self; when he visited Hitler at the beginning
of April, the latter found him a broken man, sick, frail and
tired.

---

[1] *Rommel Papers*, 419.
[2] Goebbels, *Diary*, 7th, 8th May, 1943.

Yet the Axis still possessed immense strength. It controlled all Europe and everything in it on wheels, from Biscay to the Donetz and from the North Cape to Sicily, the whole eastern littoral of Asia and every Pacific island from the Kuriles to the Central Solomons. Its hold on this vast territory could only be broken by fierce, concentrated, sustained attack by the sea Powers. Because of this the hopes of mankind in the spring of 1943 turned, apart from Russian resistance, on two factors: the training and equipment of invasion armies and their supporting air-arms and the provision of shipping and assault-craft to deploy and maintain them. Where and when they should be deployed and how that shipping, still desperately restricted by the U-boats, should be used, was the responsibility of the President and Prime Minister and of half a dozen British and American professional soldiers, sailors and airmen. And in the last resort it was the two soldiers, Brooke and Marshall, who had to shoulder the responsibility of solving the hardest problem of all. For, though securing the passage of the seas and winning control of the air were the responsibility of their naval and air colleagues, the direction and supply of the invading armies were theirs. Though neither before nor during the invasion could the soldier operate without the aid of the sailor and airman, once on shore the soldier would have to decide the issue. ' We are, after all,' Brooke wrote, ' land animals and cannot live indefinitely at sea or in the air.' It was this that caused him to write once in a moment of exasperation: " We had the Joint Planners in and discussed future Mediterranean policy after the capture of Sicily. I had difficulties with Portal and Pound, who wandered about on their fluid elements and seldom touched the ground with their feet."[1]

At that moment the Chiefs of Staff were having to plan four invasions and their supply and reinforcement. Three of these—Sicily, Italy and Burma—had to be launched before the winter; the fourth, the most ambitious amphibious

---

[1] *Diary*, 8th April, 1943. Yet Brooke believed that in future wars air-planning would play a much greater part than land-planning. ' With the ever-increasing importance of the air rôle in modern war I am certain that in future the airman will occupy this central position in planning, and that Supreme Commanders will best be found from amongst airmen.' *Notes on My Life*, VIII, 671.

'expedition ever attempted, within little more than a year. Some professional soldiers at this time looked on a major cross-Channel assault as something that would never happen—a logistical and military impossibility that existed only in the imaginings of politicians. But, though he challenged the assumption of his American colleagues that it could be achieved easily or prematurely, Brooke from the start was convinced that it would be essential. "Harry Crerar[1] to dinner," he wrote on February 10th, "and a long harangue from him as to the necessity of getting some Canadians fighting soon for imperial and political reasons. I fully see his point and his difficulties, but wish he could see mine in all their complexity." ' This last,' he added,

> ' was connected with the growing uneasiness amongst Canadians lest the war should finish without their having been engaged in any active operations. Crerar was full of the fact that the present situation would strain Commonwealth relations and that something must be done at once. I had to remind him that the main factor that had up to date militated against their use in Africa was the stipulation made by the Canadian Government that the Canadian Army must not be split up and must only be used as a whole—a conception that McNaughton had always upheld with the greatest tenacity. Crerar realised this concept must be broken down, but I could not get him to realise that there would still be opportunities in operations connected with the re-entry into France. He looked upon such conceptions as castles in the air.'[2]

How far they were from being castles in the air for Brooke is shown by his diary. "Had fairly long C.O.S. meeting," he wrote on March 25th, "at which we discussed organization for planning re-entry into Europe and the appointment of a Chief of Staff until such time as we are able to appoint a Supreme Commander." A week later there was a further discussion on this officer's staff; "then after lunch interview with Ludlow-Hewitt[3] on organisation of Air Force destined

[1] Lt.-Gen., now Gen., H. D. Crerar, Commander 1st Canadian Corps.
[2] *Notes on My Life*, VIII, 641.
[3] Air Chief Marshal Sir Edgar Ludlow-Hewitt, Inspector General of R.A.F.

to co-operate with Army; then Hobart on questions of organization of his division which was to handle various specialized forms of armoured vehicles such as amphibious tanks, searchlight tanks, mine-destroying tanks, flame-throwers, etc." This was the experimental 79th Armoured Division whose work was to provide such a sensation on the D-Day beaches and to whose command Brooke, in conjunction with Combined Operations, had just appointed that ingenious retired officer, Major-General Hobart, General Montgomery's brother-in-law. ' It was a very happy brain-wave,' he recalled, ' to have selected Hobo to control and command all the supplementary tank equipment. With his fertile brain and untiring drive all these various forms of tank made unbounded strides and contributed greatly to the successes in Normandy. . . . He had found a job completely to his heart's liking and he put everything he had into it.'

.   .   .   .

That spring the tide turned at last in the battle Brooke had always known must be won before Europe could be invaded. A fortnight before the " Torch " landings and in the month that saw the worst shipping losses of the war, the most famous of all British submarine officers, Max Horton, had been appointed to the chief naval command against the U-boat. From the headquarters of Western Approaches at Liverpool, acting in the closest co-operation with R.A.F. Coastal Command, this great seaman, during the long stormy winter of 1942-3, prepared his plans for taking the offensive. Applying to undersea warfare the Nelsonian adage that the best defence of the country was to lay his ships alongside the enemy, he assembled, in the teeth of acute shortages, enough escort-vessels and converted escort-carriers to form six roving " Support " Groups, whose crews and pilots had been trained as teams with one object—the hunting and destruction of U-boats. By the end of March the Admiral was ready. Concentrating them in the mid-ocean gap—the " black pit," as the Germans called it—where long-range aircraft from Britain and Canada were still unable to shadow Doenitz's submarines, he loosed them on the wolf-packs as they dogged the convoys of slow-moving merchantmen. The hunters suddenly became the hunted.

Horton's dramatic switch from the defensive to the offensive was only made possible by the substitution of a unified North Atlantic authority for the divided control that had hitherto kept that ocean in separate British and American zones. With the British and Canadian Admiralties now solely responsible for the North Atlantic convoys and the American Admiralty for the U.S. convoys to the Mediterranean and North Africa, a great change came over the U-boat battle. Shortly afterwards the gap of unpatrolled ocean in the centre of the Atlantic was closed by very long-range aircraft operating from Newfoundland and Iceland and able to afford daylight air-cover for the convoys in the area where the U-boats were not only most dangerous but also, by reason of their concentration, most vulnerable.

The effect on the overall strategic situation was as spectacular as it was on the morale of the till now triumphant U-boat crews. During April the Allied losses in the North Atlantic fell by fifty per cent while those of the U-boats rose more than fivefold. In May Horton decided to press home his advantage and ordered the convoys to steam straight through waters where the enemy's concentration was known to be greatest. The effect was a knock-out blow. One support group, aided by long-range R.A.F. Liberators, sank half a dozen U-boats without losing a ship from the convoy they were shadowing. With forty submarines lost in two months —or nearly half his normal operational strength in the Atlantic —Doenitz withdrew his hunted packs to less dangerous waters. As he did so the new Commander-in-Chief of Coastal Command, Air Marshal Sir John Slessor—a man as strongly imbued with the offensive spirit as his naval colleague— intensified his attack with the submarine's deadliest enemy, shore-based aircraft, on the transit lanes in the Bay of Biscay through which the submarines had to pass on their way from their French bases to their Atlantic killing grounds. In June Slessor's aircraft sank seven U-boats in the Bay alone, and the Allied losses in the Atlantic dropped to a twentieth of the March figure. For the moment, until new methods could be found to outwit their attackers, the U-boats had ceased to be a menace. Just as Trafalgar created the conditions for an invasion of Napoleon's Europe, so the victory of the British and Canadian Navies and of R.A.F. Coastal Command in the battles of " the Gap " and Bay of Biscay created conditions for an invasion of Hitler's.[1] The Fuehrer had lost his first-line of defence.

Yet though the chief obstacle to a rapid build-up of American strength against Germany had been suddenly removed, everything depended on whole-hearted Anglo-American co-operation to exploit it. And, despite the agreement reached at Casablanca, there were signs that, though such co-operation was being achieved under Eisenhower's leadership in the field in North Africa, it was still lacking in the wider sphere of global strategy. The American Chiefs of Staff had never wholly accepted the Casablanca decisions. Their feeling was summarised by their chairman, Admiral Leahy, who, prevented from attending the Conference by illness, wrote of his colleagues' report on it:

" Their comments led me to believe that little of value toward ending the war was accomplished. It appeared that our British Allies had been forced to accept the necessity for some aggressive action against Japan in the South-West Pacific and in Burma. The American plan to invade France by way of the Channel in 1943 was not accepted by the British, and in its place was substituted a decision for combined action against the Mediterranean islands, principally Sicily."[2]

The War Department planners naturally followed their seniors' lead. Since what they regarded as their defeat by the British at Casablanca, they had been engaged in what their

[1] " The failure of our submarines to win victories is having regrettable consequences." Goebbels, <i>Diary</i>, 14th May, 1943. " Developments in submarine warfare are very disagreeable. . . . If this continues we have to accustom ourselves to the thought that submarine warfare, at least for the present, has taken an unfavourable turn." <i>Idem</i>, 16th May, 1943.

[2] <i>Leahy</i>, 174.

official historian called regrouping for " a counter-offensive."[1] Impressed by the thoroughness with which the British had presented their case at the Conference, they had set themselves to prepare a more elaborate analysis of the " American position," that is, of General Marshall's and Secretary Stimson's passionately held belief that everything should give way to the build-up of a Western Front in France. And since, for lack of shipping and landing-craft such a front was not immediately possible, this had had the effect in practice of playing into the hands of Admiral King and those who thought the Pacific war more important than the European and of releasing for it resources that were urgently needed in Europe if the Germans and Italians were to be fully engaged in 1943.[2]

Nor was it only the preoccupation of King and his admirals with Japan's ocean power that was drawing American resources westwards instead of eastwards. For all his conviction that Germany was the chief enemy and must be defeated first, General Marshall, like many other Americans, had a romantic belief in the potential power of China. Until France could be invaded, a campaign to re-open the Burma Road and supply the Chinese armies seemed to him a more useful operation than an extension of the war in the Mediterranean. In February that attractive and compelling lady, Madame Chiang Kai-shek, stayed at the White House and made an eloquent plea for China before a joint session of Congress. There was talk in Washington of ambitious schemes for capturing naval and air bases in the South-west Pacific and even of a drive across the Central Pacific to the Philippines to establish a direct link with the Chinese mainland.

[1] *Strategic Planning for Coalition Warfare*, 382.

[2] At a naval conference on February 23rd King told Admiral Nimitz that " he would continue pressing the Army to fulfil their Pacific air commitments and would allocate as large a proportion as possible of new construction Navy aircraft to the Pacific. Since, however, it had been agreed at Casablanca that the submarine menace was the first charge upon the resources of the Allies, it would be necessary to allocate certain planes . . . to the Atlantic for anti-submarine work. As a matter of principle, however, the great majority of naval planes would be allocated to the Pacific. . . . The Combined Chiefs of Staff had agreed that sufficient forces be allocated to the Pacific so that it would be unnecessary to prejudice operations elsewhere by withdrawing forces from them to relieve a desperate situation in the Pacific. King said that the Combined Chiefs' Casablanca paper on the Pacific could be taken as the basis on which to plan future operations there." *Whitehill*, 222-3.

All this affected the preparations which Brooke and his colleagues were making in London. It undermined not only the possibilities of decisive action in the Mediterranean in 1943 but of action in France in 1944. By the Casablanca agreement 80,000 more American troops were to have reached England in the first quarter of 1943, but owing to the deflection of cargo and troop-carrying shipping to the Pacific, it had only proved possible to send 15,000 and in British ships. The entries in Brooke's diary tell the story of his growing concern:

"*February 17th, 1943.* At this morning's C.O.S. meeting we had Andrews, the new American General, and also the principal administrative officers, to discuss the flow of American reinforcements into this country to build up the American Force. Something has gone wrong with our Casablanca agreements and the flow here not started at all . . ."

"*February 25th.* . . . Am very worried by the way the Americans are failing to live up to our Casablanca agreements. They are entirely breaking down over promises of American divisions to arrive in this country . . ."

"*March 1st.* C.O.S. mainly concerned with shipping situation and the fact that the American C.O.S. are not living up to our Casablanca agreements. Marshall . . . now proposes to waste shipping equipping French forces which can play no part in the strategy of 1943 . . ."

"*March 2nd.* . . . A long and difficult C.O.S. on shipping, attended by Lord Leathers and Lord Cherwell. The Americans are letting us down, and we cannot find the shipping for all our enterprises. Some centralized shipping Control Board handling global shipping is essential. . . ."

"*April 15th.* . . . A depressing C.O.S. meeting, as recent telegrams from America show that we are just about back where we were before Casablanca. Their hearts are really in the Pacific and we are trying to run two wars at once, which is quite impossible with our limited resources of shipping. All we can hope for is to go all out to defeat Italy, and thus produce the greatest dispersal of

German forces and make the going easier for the Russians. If we even knew what the Russians hope to do. But we have no inkling."

By the time this last entry was made the American tendency to pursue an independent line in the Pacific was threatening to destroy all Brooke's plans for forcing the Germans to disperse their reserves in the defence of southern Europe. King's sole idea seemed to be to defeat Japan, and Marshall's to liquidate the Mediterranean war as quickly as possible. To neither did the latter appear to offer any long-term prospects. On the evening of Saturday April 17th, just after Brooke had reached his home, he was rung up by the Prime Minister about a wire just received from Marshall, proposing that, to end the campaign quickly, the Sicilian landings should be attempted while the Tunisian campaign was still in progress. " Quite mad and quite impossible," Brooke commented, " but P.M. delighted with this idea, which showed according to him a high strategic conception. I had half an hour's row with him on the telephone." And, though with his usual magnanimity, the Prime Minister had forgiven and forgotten the C.I.G.S.'s anger by the Monday, when they drove back together in perfect amiability from a demonstration of jet aircraft at Hatfield,[1] the threat involved in Marshall's ill-considered suggestion remained.

Yet by now, six months after the first landings in North Africa, the scene was set at last for the second act of the Mediterranean drama. By the end of the third week in April the British-American army in Tunisia was ready for the final assault. After an unsuccessful attempt by the Eighth Army to carry the almost impregnable Enfidaville hill-position from the south, Alexander and his very able Chief of Staff, General McCreery, on Montgomery's advice transferred three of its divisions to the First Army in the north. On the day before St. George's Day the Allies began to fight their way eastwards through the mountains, the Americans aiming at Bizerta and

---

[1] " We were . . . shown latest aircraft without propellers driven by air sucked in in front and squirted out behind. Apparently likely to be the fighter of the future. Drove back to London with P.M., who had forgiven my frankness on telephone on Saturday." *Diary*, 19th April, 1943.

the British at Tunis. Despite ceaseless bombardment from the air the enemy resisted fiercely, and a week later the attackers, though gaining ground everywhere, were still held up in the hill defiles. But with the Luftwaffe driven from the skies, and the Royal Navy blockading the coast, any reinforcement or supply of von Arnim's men was by now impossible, and the end was certain. As Brooke had cabled Montgomery after his capture of Sfax, the time had come to settle the Dunkirk debt at last.[1]

An immediate decision on the next steps in the Mediterranean was, therefore, essential. With thirteen British divisions alone in North-West Africa and at least seven more in the Middle East, it was vital as soon as possible after the fall of Sicily to direct the Anglo-American Mediterranean Army against some point on the European circumference where it could relieve the pressure on Russia and deny the enemy the respite he so sorely needed. Both Brooke and Churchill strongly felt the urgency of this, particularly the former who wanted to see every available landing-craft, soldier and aircraft concentrated against Italy to knock her out of the War and so force the Germans to fill the vacuum in southern Europe with their strategic reserve. The Prime Minister also wished, regardless of the lack of landing-craft, to substitute an amphibious operation against the tip of Sumatra for the American project of re-conquering Burma by land. The latter, he told the C.I.G.S., seemed to him like " munching a porcupine quill by quill! "[2]

On April 29th, therefore, a week after the Tunisian offensive began, Churchill telegraphed to President Roosevelt: " It seems to me most necessary that we should all settle together now, first, Sicily and then exploitation thereof, and, secondly, the future of the Burma campaign in the light of our experiences

---

[1] C.I.G.S. to Montgomery, 12th April, 1943. Lord Alanbrooke, *Personal Files.* " If we play our cards properly," Montgomery had written to Brooke two months earlier, " we cannot fail. I look forward to a first-class Dunkirk on the beaches of Tunis. I have a few old scores to pay off myself in respect of that other Dunkirk! " Montgomery to Brooke, 16th February, 1943, *Idem.*

[2] " He considered," Brooke wrote, " we should wait till we got Russia against Japan. We should then establish air-bases near Vladivostok from which Japan could be bombed, and according to him, we should then sing the ' Ladybird Song ' to the Japs, namely, ' Ladybird, Ladybird, fly away home, your house is on fire and your children at home! ' " *Diary,* 22nd April, 1943.

and the shipping stringency. There are also a number of other burning questions which you and I could with advantage bring up to date. I think I could manage to be with you by Tuesday May 11th. Please say whether you would like this?"[1] Then, without awaiting an answer, he started to pack.

.   .   .   .

As the doctors were opposed to the Prime Minister travelling by air so soon after his bout of pneumonia, it was decided that the journey should be made in the *Queen Mary*, one of the two giant liners being used on account of their speed to ferry American troops across the Pacific and Atlantic without the delays involved in sailing in escorted convoy. At that moment she was about to make a return-journey to New York with a load of German prisoners. Brooke's diary tells the story:

"*Thursday April 29th, 1943.* A troublesome day. Whilst at C.O.S. meeting Portal first of all informed me that P.M. last night decided to start with Chiefs of Staff for Washington on Wednesday next. Then Dudley Pound said he had just been with him and we were to start on Sunday. . . . At 5 p.m. meeting with P.M. to try and postpone date of departure. I told him we were not ready to discuss plans on far side yet. He said we should have time in the *Queen Mary*. Luckily Transportation said *Queen Mary* was full of vermin. The vermin became our allies and our departure is now postponed till next Wednesday. . . ."

'Our 5 p.m. meeting was an amusing one. First we discussed the security aspect of the journey. The main danger rested in the German Embassy in Dublin. They would soon be aware of the journey and might use their wireless to inform Germany who would then be in a position to station submarines to try and intercept the *Queen Mary*. However . . . the risk did not appear to be much. We were then told about the vermin which had resulted from troop

[1] *Churchill*, IV, 700.

movements.[1] It was impossible to clear this entirely without
going into dry-dock and a long process, but by a system of
gassing the live insects would be killed but not their eggs.
We should consequently have the period of incubation, about
six days, of relative immunity. P.M. accepted the risk.'

' The last blow however was a heavier one. The ship
was " dry "! At this Winston pulled a very long face, but
was reassured that the suite occupied by him need not be
dry. That satisfied him.'

" *April 30th.* More preparations for our departure,
but no reply yet from U.S.A. A meeting convened at
4 p.m. by P.M. to discuss security of the trip. Apparently
impossible to conceal nature of preparations on the
Queen Mary, and quite possibly news might get over to
Dublin. . . . Pound explained that a carrier had been
detailed to act as escort in area where Focke-Wulf
aircraft might operate. Also cruisers detailed to provide
protection on sections of the journey. As a result of conference decided to carry on with the original plan and to
prepare for departure on Wednesday. Quite possible,
however, that we may not be welcomed on far side. . . ."

". . . *May 1st.* Still no decision as to whether we are
to start for America on Wednesday or not! Anyhow all
preparations continue . . ."

". . . *May 3rd.* We heard definitely this morning that
we are to go to Washington, and that we start to-morrow
evening by train."

" *May 4th.* A very artificial day during which I have
lived an ordinary day feeling anything but ' ordinary '
owing to impending departure. We had our usual Chiefs
of Staff meeting at which we made final preparations for
all the work on the journey. . . . Then back to War Office
for a Selection Board and a series of interviews."

" Finally back to flat at 8 p.m. for dinner and packing.
I am now just off to the station to start on my journey to
Washington. A busy time ahead, and am feeling uncom-

[1] According to Sir Ian Jacob, the origin of the bugs was Suez. The " Queens "
had been used on the run from Australia to Suez, and the coolies who had come
on board to unload at that port had put down their outer clothing on the ship.

monly tired and weary before starting, but sea-journey should freshen me up before the hard work of the Conference starts. I do not feel very hopeful as to results. Casablanca has taught me too much. Agreement after agreement may be secured on paper, but, if their hearts are not in it, they soon drift away."

" *May 5th—Queen Mary.* Last night after dinner, at 11.15 p.m. I started for the station outside Olympia (Addison Road) where our special train was waiting for us. . . . Our party consists of P.M., Averell Harriman, Beaverbrook, Leathers, Charles Wilson, Cherwell, Wavell, Peirse, Somerville, three Chiefs of Staff, all Joint Planners, and in addition Shipping, Movement, Administrative, Intelligence, etc., staff officers from the Admiralty, War Office and Air Ministry, and finally many clerks, detectives, etc."

" We arrived at Greenock at 3.40 p.m. and then transferred to a launch which took us to the *Queen Mary*. The height of her was most impressive as we drew alongside, and when we got on board it was a job to find one's way about. She had been completely stripped and turned into a troop carrier, and it has entailed considerable work restoring her into a suitable condition to take the P.M. and us. They have done marvels in the short time and the cabin I am in must be almost up to pre-war standard. A very large double room very well fitted with sitting-room, two bathrooms and masses of cupboards and arm-chairs, etc.[1] There are about 3,000 troops on board with us, but she can carry 15,000. This leaves her almost empty."

" We started at 5.30 p.m. and Dudley Pound took Portal and me up on to the bridge where he introduced us to the Captain. We remained there for a couple of hours till we had sailed down the coast of Ayrshire, which brought back many memories of our visits there with

[1] " The whole delegation was accommodated on the main deck, which was sealed off from the rest of the ship. Offices, conference rooms, and, of course, the Map Room, stood ready for immediate use. From the moment we got on board our work went forward ceaselessly. . . . About five thousand German prisoners were already on board." *Churchill*, IV, 700.

you. . . . I have just had dinner and a talk with Wavell and am now preparing to go off to bed. Just before dark we saw the northern coast of Ireland and the Giant's Causeway. To-morrow we have an escort of an aircraft-carrier and a cruiser to look after us."

" *May 6th. Queen Mary.* We started the day with a boat-drill parade, during which we were shown the life-boat we should use in the event of being torpedoed. At 10.30 we had a C.O.S. meeting attended by the Indian Commanders-in-Chief. We also had Leathers (Minister of Transport) and Holmes (Director-General of Trans-portation) and discussed the shipping situation at some length. There is no doubt that, unless the Americans are prepared to withdraw more shipping from the Pacific, our strategy in Europe will be drastically affected. Up to the present the bulk of the American Navy is in the Pacific and larger land and air forces have gone to this theatre than to Europe in spite of all we have said about the necessity of defeating Germany first."

" Before lunch I went up on to the bridge with Pound and Portal. We watched our accompanying cruiser ploughing through the fairly heavy seas. In the sky we were accompanied by a Sunderland flying-boat, whilst ahead we had an aircraft-carrier. . . . After lunch I went for a good walk on the deck where I met Cher-well and listened to him for about an hour. After tea I got down to work again, preparing for our coming meetings."

" In the evening dined with P.M. He had Beaver-brook, Leathers, Harriman, Wavell, "Pug" Ismay and self. He was in great form and thoroughly enjoying the trip. To-night we go through the worst part of the run and there are several submarines spread out on our course, but they are mainly on their way to and from the ports of Biscay and Northern Convoy routes. Escaped reasonably early, and in bed by midnight."

' We had taken a southerly course towards Cape Finisterre so as to cross the " Submarine Piccadilly "—the route linking their operating areas with their reporting bases—at right angles.'

"*May 7th. Queen Mary.* We got through the submarine belt safely and by morning we were about 500 miles west of Cape Finisterre and altered course about 12 noon for our bearing fairly directly on New York. We received news of thirteen ships having been sunk out of one of our convoys between Newfoundland and Greenland but at the cost of five German submarines."

"At 10.30 we had a C.O.S. meeting at which we discussed line of action to take at our impending meeting with Doctor Evatt of Australia who will be in Washington when we get there endeavouring to extract additional forces for the security of Australia. After lunch I had more papers to go through followed by a walk on deck, and after tea another C.O.S. meeting to discuss lines on which we are to approach our American friends to inform them that the reconquest of Burma in 1943-44 is not possible."

"Just before dinner good news came in of operations in Tunisia, where Alexander's last offensive is making good progress. We have again altered course a little further south and temperature is much milder. . . ."

"*May 8th. Queen Mary.* Another day mainly devoted to Conferences. We started the day with a discussion over my opening statement at the Conference in Washington. We then had another discussion on shipping attended by Lord Leathers and Cherwell, a good conference which has gone a long way towards clearing the air. The afternoon I spent reading up papers on our action in the event of a collapse of the Italian nation, which we then discussed at 5.30 p.m."

"Meanwhile P.M. had been writing a long paper on our future actions against Japan in which he forgot to take into account the basic limitation of our strategy, namely shipping![1] He also offended Archie Wavell badly

---

[1] "The Chiefs of Staff met daily, and sometimes twice a day. I adhered to my usual practice of giving them my thoughts each morning in the shape of minutes and directives, and I generally had a discussion with them each afternoon

by adversely criticising the operations in Burma which have just been completed. So much so that Archie was indignant and I had to pacify him. Running a war seems to consist in making plans and then ensuring that all those destined to carry them out don't quarrel with each other instead of with the enemy! "

" Capture of Tunis and Bizerta seem to be confirmed. We altered course even further south to-day. . . ."

" *May 9th, Queen Mary.* More troubles! Archie Wavell's Personal Assistant arrived while I was shaving with a note from Archie in which he said that he had been unable to sleep and was so upset by Winston's references to the Burma operation that he proposed to send him the letter which he enclosed. In that letter he said that, since Winston had lost confidence in him, it was better for him to send in his resignation. I went round and saw him and advised him not to send the letter. Later he saw Winston, had a talk to him, and now all is quiet and I may shave in peace to-morrow."

' I remember that when I was discussing the matter with Wavell and trying to stop him from sending in his resignation, I told him that if I were to take offence when abused by Winston and given to understand that he had no confidence in me, I should have to resign at least once every day. But that I never felt that any such resignations were likely to have the least effect in reforming Winston's wicked ways! I think this argument fortunately convinced him.'

" Our British escort left us to-day and we picked up two American cruisers and four of their destroyers. C.O.S. again from 10.30 a.m. to lunch and from 5 p.m. to dinner, and much reading in between."

" *May 10th.* *Queen Mary.* This should be our last day at sea, as we are due to arrive to-morrow morning if we go on defeating submarines as we have up to the present. There are about a hundred of them operating in the North Atlantic, but most of them are concentrated further

---

r evening. These processes of probing, sifting and arguing continued throughout
e voyage." *Churchill*, IV, 701. For the Prime Minister's paper, see *Idem*, 702-5.

north. There are only two reported in front of us on the
approaches to New York. But, as we have now also
picked up a Catalina flying-boat in addition to our two
cruisers and four destroyers, we should be well protected.'

" News from Tunisia continues to be excellent. This
morning from 10.30 to 11.30 we had our final C.O.S
meeting on our proposed Mediterranean strategy. We
then went on to the P.M. at 11.30 a.m. and discussed the
Far East strategy till 1.30 p.m. A thoroughly unsatisfactory meeting at which he again showed that he cannot
grasp the relation of various theatres of war to each other
He always gets carried away by the one he is examining
and, in prosecuting it, is prepared to sacrifice most of
the others. I have never in the year and a half I have
worked with him succeeded in making him . . . relate
the importance of the various fronts to each other."

" At 5.30 p.m. we had another meeting with the P.M
that lasted till close on 7 p.m. We were intending to
discuss Mediterranean strategy, but it was not long before
we were drawn off again to his pet of the moment in the
shape of an attack on Northern Sumatra or Penang
A different theatre, but not only that—a theatre entirely
secondary to the European one which must remain our
primary consideration."

" After this meeting Pound ran a small sherry party
for the naval officers in charge of this ship which we
were invited to attend. Now I am off to bed, and if we
do not meet a submarine we should be in New York
fairly early to-morrow morning. It has been a very
comfortable trip, with plenty of work to fill in the time
and we should by now be ready for our Conferences with
the American Chiefs of Staff."

" I do not look forward to these meetings; in fact I
hate the thought of them. They will entail hours of
argument and hard work trying to convince them that
Germany must be defeated first. . . . It is all so maddening
as it is not difficult in this case to see that, unless our
united efforts are directed to defeat Germany and hold
Japan, the war may go on indefinitely. However, it is

not sufficient to see something clearly. You have got to convince countless people as to where the truth lies when they do not want to be. . . . It is an exhausting process, and I am very *very* tired and shudder at the useless struggles that lie ahead."

' On reading over these pages of my diary I think that I must have been still suffering from the after effects of . . . flu. . . . It is, however, interesting as exemplifying the fits of depression which occasionally get the better of one when subjected to heavy stresses and strains,—a depression which may well undermine one's own confidence in oneself.'

' The American departure from our basic strategy was mainly due to Admiral King. . . . For him the main theatre lay in the Pacific where the bulk of the American Naval Forces were . . . employed. As a result precious shipping, landing-craft and equipment were finding their way to the Pacific instead of being allotted to the main front in Europe. It was easy enough to lay down, and to accept, the concept that Germany must be defeated first. Where the difficulty rested, however, was to decide how much effort should be devoted to hold Japan. The holding of Japan provided all the excuse necessary for a continual diversion of effort not truly required for a holding rôle. I still feel that, if at that stage . . . our basic strategy had been more strictly adhered to, we should have finished the war a few months sooner.'

. . . .

During the voyage, though Brooke, intent on his mission, only referred to them in two laconic sentences, the fruits of the victory in North Africa for which he had waited so long were garnered. On May 6th, the morning after the *Queen Mary* sailed from the Clyde, and while the air above the Tunisian hills was black with British and American aircraft, Alexander launched his final attack. The Americans in the north drove towards Bizerta and the British along the Medjez-Tunis highway. By the afternoon three British armoured divisions had passed through the infantry. Tunis and Bizerta fell next day, and six Italian and five German divisions, three of them armoured, were at the victors' mercy. By his decision to defend southern Europe from the far side of the Mediterranean Hitler had delayed the reopening of that sea to Allied shipping for nearly six months and had multiplied doubts in American minds about the wisdom of Brooke's strategy. Yet by this act he had given hostages to the sea-gods whom Brooke and his colleagues served, and marooned in a blockaded peninsula the army—the flower of the German forces in the South—which should have guarded the Italian shore. Operating from airfields in Central Tunisia which Montgomery's earlier victories had won, Tedder's aircraft had established unchallenged ascendancy in the skies between Tunis and Sicily while in the waters below, so long dominated by the Luftwaffe, Cunningham's ships kept an unceasing watch—" Operation Retribution "—on Bizerta and the beaches of the Cape Bon peninsula. On the morning after Tunis fell the admiral, who two years before had evacuated the British Army from Greece and Crete, signalled, " Sink, burn and destroy. Let nothing pass! " Of the quarter of a million German and Italian soldiers remaining in North Africa a bare seven hundred, mostly by air and at night, made good their escape. The remainder, with more than a thousand guns and several hundred tanks, laid down their arms. Two days after the *Queen Mary* docked at New York the bells of every English church started to peal. A victory had been won that rivalled Stalingrad,[1] and the soft underbelly of Fortress Europe lay open to invasion.

" *May 11th.   Queen Mary.*   I rose earlier so as not to miss any of the sights on the way to New York.   But Fate was unkind, and I was again destined to see nothing of New York.   There was a heavy mist and then heavy rain which made it difficult to even see the shore or the approaches.   We stopped a long way short for security reasons, and were taken ashore in small craft to a station in some docks.   We had lunch in the train and . . . reached Washington at 6.30 p.m., where we were met by President,

[1] " All London is drunk with victory . . . Our losses there are enormous. We are indeed experiencing a sort of second Stalingrad. . . . It is understandable that the English speak of a first-class victory. They have so far never won any decisive victories." Goebbels, *Diary*, 9th May, 1943.

Marshall, King, Dill, etc. We had to go straight to a cocktail party given in our honour in a large hotel. From there we did not escape till 8.15 p.m. We then returned to Dill's house where Archie Wavell and I are being very kindly put up. Dill is only just recovering from his operation for hernia, and not looking at all well."

" Rather hot sticky night. I must now prepare my opening remarks for to-morrow's Combined Chiefs of Staff Conference, and must muster all our arguments. We have a very heavy week's work in front of us."

" *May 12th. Washington.* Started the day with a Conference at 9.30 with the Joint Staff Mission and Dill to find out what the probable reactions would be to our proposals. We then lunched with Leahy, Marshall, King, etc. At 2.30 p.m. we went on to the White House to attend meeting with the President at which they laid down their conception of future strategy."

" I could not help wandering back to eleven months ago when P.M. and I were alone with the President in that room and Marshall came in with the news of the surrender of Tobruk. I could see us standing there, and the effect it had on us. And then I wandered through the last eleven months with all their anxieties, hopes, disappointments and worries. And now! At last the first stage of my proposed strategy accomplished in spite of all the various factors that have been trying to prevent it. I felt as if in a dream, to be there planning two stages ahead, with the first stage finished and accomplished."

" P.M. gave a very good opening address, followed by the President, who showed less grasp of strategy. At 5 p.m. another meeting with Dill and Mission officers to put them into the picture as far as is possible."

In his opening speech the Prime Minister stressed that the British had come to the meeting adhering to the decisions reached four months earlier at Casablanca, though the recent victories might make minor adjustments necessary. " *Torch* was over, Sicily was near; what should come next? "[1] If the

---

[1] " We had been able by taking thought together to produce a succession of brilliant events which had altered the whole course of the war. . . . It was our

Allies could seize the great prize now waiting in the Mediterranean, the Italian Fleet and the twenty-six divisions with which Italy was garrisoning the Balkans would be lost to Germany, Turkey might be brought into the war to open the Dardanelles to supplies for Russia, and the British Mediterranean Fleet would be released for amphibious operations in the Bay of Bengal in support of Wavell's Eastern Army. In his reply the President admitted the urgent need to consider where to go from Sicily and how to keep employed the score or more of battle-trained Anglo-American divisions in the Mediterranean. But the continuing drain involved in any attempt to occupy Italy might prejudice the build-up of forces for a cross-Channel invasion, and, though there now seemed no chance of the latter in 1943, it would have to be launched on the largest scale in the spring of 1944. The only certain way to force Germany to fight and aid Russia was by striking at once through France.

The President's speech stressed, too, the importance of attacking Japan's overstretched supply-lines in the Pacific before she had time to consolidate and of keeping China in the war. Behind his words lay the American people's hatred of Japan, the American Navy's absorption in the Pacific and the American Chiefs of Staff's decision that a firm commitment must be obtained from the British for a cross-Channel attack early in 1944 so that the full force of the Grand Alliance could be speedily turned against Japan. Officers of Eisenhower's staff who visited America that spring were amazed to find how much more interested everyone was in the Pacific war than the Mediterranean. Public opinion, they reported, was " veering . . . to lick the Japs first and let Hitler wait."[1]

This was the emotional background against which Brooke and his colleagues had to contend. Its spokesman was the tough and stubborn King—the old crustacean, as one of his countrymen called him—the ablest strategist on the American Chiefs of Staff, though overshadowed in statesmanship and

---

duty to redouble our efforts and to grasp the fruits of our success." *Churchill*, IV, 707.
[1] Butcher, 241, 246.

grandeur of character by the great Virginian, Marshall. It was supported by the prestige, the immense man-power—three times larger than that of Britain—and the productive capacity of the most vigorous and self-confident nation on earth.

" *May 13th. Washington.* We started our first Combined Meeting at 10.30 this morning. Leahy began by restating the American conception of Global Strategy, which differs considerably from ours in two respects: firstly in allowing too much latitude for the diversion of force to the Pacific; secondly by imagining that the war could be more quickly finished by starting a Western Front in France."

" It is quite clear from our discussion that they do not begin to realize the requirements of the European strategy and the part that Russia must play. I am afraid that we shall have a very difficult time, and that we shall leave here having accomplished little towards altering the conception which is deeply rooted in their hearts. I am thoroughly depressed with the prospects of our visit."

" We lunched with the American Chiefs of Staff after which Marshall took me round to see the new War Department Buildings (the Pentagon), the American War Office. A vast building which has only just been completed. At 5.30 p.m. we had a British C.O.S. meeting attended by Dill to discuss line of action to take to-morrow. Dined quietly with Dill."

" *May 14th. Washington.* Started our Combined Chiefs of Staff meeting at 10.30 a.m. when we stated that we did not agree with their paper on Global Strategy. I then had to make a statement on the ' Anakim ' Operation (i.e. Burma). This was followed by Wavell, who explained fully the situation in Burma and various alternatives. Stilwell (Vinegar Joe) followed and disagreed with most of what Wavell had said, and we left the problem even more confused than when we had started."

" We then lunched with American Chiefs of Staff and went on to the White House at 2 p.m., where we met President and P.M. and again discussed the whole of Burma. First the President, then P.M. made statements.

Then Wavell was called upon, followed by Somervell (U.S. Chief Administrative Officer), who contradicted him. Then Stilwell, who disagreed with both of them and with himself as far as I could see! . . . The whole problem seemed to hinge on the necessity of keeping Chiang Kai-shek in the war. Chennault was then called upon, followed by more Stilwell and more confusion. President and P.M. had some more to say about it. In the end, and by the time we left, what is not a very simple problem had become a tangled mass of confusion."

" At 5.30 p.m. one of our own C.O.S. meetings to discuss the general trend of the Conference which is most unfavourable and unpromising at present. Dill gave dinner-party in the evening."

" The President's writing-table always interests me owing to the congestion on it. I tried to memorize the queer collection: blue vase lamp, two frames, bronze bust of Mrs. R., bronze ship's steering-wheel clock, four cloth toy donkeys, one tin toy motor-car, one small donkey made of two hazel nuts, jug of iced water, pile of books, large circular match-stand and ink-pot, plus many other articles that I cannot remember. Most of the donkeys have been there since I was in Washington last July."

' It may be argued that I would have been better employed trying to reduce the confusion that the Conference had got into than to memorize the articles on the President's table. I remember feeling the absolute hopelessness of it. The Americans were trying to make us undertake an advance from Assam into Burma without adequate resources—in fact, an advance which was only ultimately made possible by the provision of air-transport for supply purposes. Except for Wavell those arguing certainly did nothing to clarify the situation. Somervell had never seen the country and had no conception of the administrative problems. Stilwell was a strange character known as " Vinegar Joe," a name that suited him admirably. One of Marshall's selections, and he had a high opinion of him. Except for the fact that he was a stout-hearted fighter suitable to lead a brigade of Chinese scally-wags I could see no qualities in him. He was a Chinese linguist, but had little military knowledge and no strategic ability of any kind. His worst failing was, however, his deep-rooted hatred of anybody or anything British. It was practically impossible to establish friendly relations with either him or the troops under his command. He did a vast amount of harm by vitiating the relations between Americans and British both in India and Burma.'[1]

' Chennault, a very gallant airman, had originally commanded a volunteer American Air Force supporting the Chinese. A fine fighting man, but of limited ability who added little of use to our discussions that day.'

" *May 15th. Williamsburg.* Started the day with a Combined Chiefs of Staff meeting which on the whole was most unsatisfactory. We are a long way apart in our strategy in the European theatre, and I feel great doubts whether the end of next week will see us much closer."

" After lunch drove to the aerodrome and flew down to an aerodrome some twenty miles from Williamsburg, to which we went by car. On arrival there we visited the Capitol first and then went to the main inn, all restored exactly as in the original colonial days. Apparently Rockefeller spent a fortune in restoring the whole village to its original condition as the heart of Virginia. It has been marvellously done."

" We dined in an hotel nearby and after dinner visited the Governor's house, all lit by candlelight. It was the most impressive sight. I kept on feeling that I had been transported back to the old days, and expected the Governor to appear at any moment. The flowers in the various rooms were one of the most impressive sights,

[1] Field-Marshal Slim, who saw much more of Stilwell than Brooke, liked him. " He was not a great soldier in the highest sense," he wrote, " but he is a real leader in the field. No one else I know could have made his Chinese do what they did." Sir W. Slim, *Defeat into Victory*, 51. General Stilwell's own summary of the Conference was: " Churchill has Roosevelt in his hip pocket. . . . The Limeys are not interested in the war in the Pacific, and, with the President hypnotised, they are sitting pretty." *White House Papers*, II, 726.

and had been done by one of the ladies of the University who had made a study of floral decorations of that period. They were quite lovely and gave the final touch to the whole scene. In addition, odd bits of garments, etc., were lying about as if the house was inhabited. In the sitting-room the chessmen were out on a board, in the Governor's wife's room her dress was thrown across the sofa and a collar across the back of a chair. Gloves were lying on a table, and books pulled out from a book-case for reference, etc."[1]

" *May 16th. Washington.* Got up leisurely and break-fasted on the terrace outside the hotel. We then went to the old Colonial Church for morning service. The church was crammed and the singing very good. The congregation impressed me by their high standard. All women beautifully turned out; no poverty, and all well educated. Dudley Pound read the second lesson. We were then given a large lunch attended by the Mayor of Williamsburg. After that we flew back (160 miles) to Washington and at 5.30 p.m. had a C.O.S. meeting to prepare for to-morrow's work. Then on to the Embassy to dine. . . ."

" I wish the next week was over. . . ."

" *May 17th. Washington.* Another very disappointing day. We had a long meeting of Combined Chiefs of Staff from 10.30 a.m. onwards, again discussion of Global Strategy which led us nowhere. The trouble is that the American mind likes proceeding from the general to the particular, whilst in the problems we have to solve we cannot evolve any form of general doctrine until we have carefully examined the particular details of each problem. The background really rests on King's desire to find every loophole he possibly can to divert strength to the Pacific."

[1] There is a charming account of this visit in a letter written by General Marshall to Mrs. M. C. Long about Lord Alanbrooke. " I was most impressed by him as a guest of mine when I was entertaining the British Chiefs of Staff with Lord Wavell at . . . Williamsburg. Some swam (the Sea Lord, Dudley Pound), some occupied themselves in photography (Lord Wavell) but Alanbrooke, with his field-glasses, devoted his time to a study of the Virginia birds. His persistence and his pleasure in the task were very appealing. We had been having a very hard time in Washington reaching agreement, but the week-end in Williamsburg with no business discussion cleared the air entirely."

" Lunched with the American Chiefs, and then at 2.30 p.m. went to see Winston about command of formations at home. He was in a bad mood. . . ."

" *May 18th. Washington.* Met American Chiefs at 10.30 a.m., but their paper on the European Theatre was not yet ready . . . and they had not yet properly digested ours. We therefore accomplished nothing."

" It is quite apparent now that we are a long way apart. What is more, the Americans are taking up the attitude that we led them down the garden path by taking them to North Africa. That at Casablanca we again misled them by inducing them to attack Sicily. And now they do not intend to be led astray again. Added to that the swing towards the Pacific is stronger than ever, and before long they will be urging that we should defeat Japan first! "

" We have now at last received their paper and are to discuss it to-morrow. I shudder at the results. Had a talk with Bedell Smith off the record this evening. He thinks a solution may be put forward which will limit the European theatre, both cross-Channel and Mediterranean, for the benefit of the Pacific. Dined with Admiral King, who received us on his ship and produced films after dinner."

' It is evident from the diary that at this period I went through a phase of deep depression. I think this was due to the fact that, in spite of all my hard work at Casablanca and in spite of the rich fruits we had gathered up to date as a result of our strategy, the Americans still failed to grasp how we were preparing for a re-entry into France through our actions in the Mediterranean. We had now opened the Mediterranean and in doing so had regained the equivalent of about a million tons of shipping, thus regaining a great deal of the strategic mobility which we had lost. We had taken a quarter of a million prisoners and inflicted very heavy losses on the enemy both at sea and in the air. We had now opened the way for an attack on Sicily and Italy and we were forcing the enemy to expend forces for the defence of Southern Europe, a region of bad intercommunication and likely to absorb more than its share. We were, in fact, taking the best road to prepare the ground for the liberation of France and final defeat of Germany, which was being subjected to ceaseless bombardment.'

' And yet in spite of all these advantages it was, I think, about this time that, as I was walking with Marshall and Dill to one of our meetings, Marshall said to me: " I find it hard even now not to look on your North African strategy with a jaundiced eye." I replied: " What strategy would you have preferred? " To which he answered " Cross-Channel operations for the liberation of France and advance on Germany; we should finish the war quicker." I remember replying " Yes, probably, but not the way we hope to finish it! " . . .'

' On top of it all, King had been gaining ground recently and was diverting more and more strength to the Pacific. Any attempts to unduly push our strategy on Marshall had a distinct tendency to drive him into King's Pacific camp. He even stated once or twice that, if our strategy was to be one of wasting our time in the Mediterranean, the American Forces might well be better employed in the Pacific. To me the strategy which I had advocated from the very start, and which was at last shaping so successfully, stood out clearer and clearer every day. . . . My temporary inability to bring the Americans along with us filled me with depression, and at times almost with despair.'

" *May 19th. Washington.* Started the most difficult day of the Conference. Up in the office by 8.30 a.m. to study again the American Paper. Then C.O.S. Conference at 9 a.m. when we decided the line of action I was to take up."

" At 10.30 a.m. we met American Chiefs of Staff and started by criticising each others' papers on the proposed European Strategy. Then Marshall suggested the meeting should be cleared for an ' Off the Record ' discussion between the Chiefs of Staff alone. We then had a heart to heart talk, and as a result of it at last formed a bridge across which we could meet. Not altogether a satisfactory one, but far better than a break-up of the Conference."

" We met again at 4 p.m. in a C.O.S. meeting to consider the draft of our conclusions. At 4.30 p.m. we returned to a Combined Chiefs of Staff meeting to pass our resolutions, and at 6 p.m. we went round to the White House to report to the President and the P.M. the result of our work."

" Our conclusions are that we are to prepare some twenty-nine divisions for entry into France early in 1944, and at the same time maintain a continuance of pressure against Italy in the Mediterranean. The latter is a triumph, as Americans wanted to close down all operations in Mediterranean after capture of Sicily."

" Dined with Admiral Noble, Archie Wavell coming with me. Heavy thunderstorms at present cooling the air a little, and thank heaven for it as evening was very oppressive."

' I think that this must have been the first of our " Off the Record Meetings," a procedure we had to adopt on several occasions when we had arrived at loggerheads. It always helped to clear the air. The trouble was often due to the fact that the number of attendants during our Conferences had grown far too large. The Americans had gone on adding more and more staff officers and we had followed suit. This had resulted in some twenty to thirty odd people coming in besides the Chiefs of Staff. We sat facing each other, and behind us on each side, seated on chairs, was a row of some fifteen staff officers. I felt that frequently Marshall did not like shifting from some policy he had been briefed in by his staff lest they should think he was lacking in determination.'

' The " Off the Record Meetings " consisted only of the Chiefs of Staff and a secretary. Leahy remained of course as chairman of the American C.O.S., and Dill also remained with us as Head of the British Staff in Washington. For our Combined Meetings the chair was taken by either the American chairman of their C.O.S. or by me in the capacity of chairman of the British C.O.S. When we met on American soil they took the chair; on British soil I did.'

" *May 20th. Washington.* A very full day: 8.30 to 9 a.m. Office, trying to read through masses of papers produced during the night for to-day's Conference. 9.00 to 10.30 a.m. C.O.S. meeting during which we had to decide the attitude we would take to resist American pressure to do impossible operations in Burma in order to satisfy the Chinese and public opinion."

" 10.30 a.m. to 1.30 p.m. Combined C.O.S. at which we reached a complete impasse with a suggestion by Leahy that we should have to send in separate reports. They were still pressing for a full-scale advance from Assam into Burma contrary to all administrative possibilities. However, we finally decided to have an ' Off the Record Meeting ' in the afternoon to try and reconcile our differences. . . ."

" 2.30 to 3.30 p.m. Another C.O.S. meeting at which we decided line of action to adopt, and drew up a proposed agreement. 3.30 to 5 p.m. ' Off the Record Combined C.O.S. Meeting ' at which we finally reached agreement and obtained practically exactly what we had originally put forward as a result of our work on board ship."

" 5 to 5.45 p.m. Garden Party at White House with the Marine Band. 5.45 to 7.30 p.m. meeting of Dominion Representatives under P.M., including Mackenzie King and Dr. Evatt. . . . P.M. reviewed world situation. 7.30 to 8 p.m. Dashed back through office to Dill's house to meet Secretary Stimson. 8 to 11.30 p.m. dinner at the hotel (The Statler) which we gave for American Chiefs of Staff. And now at last bed and rest."

" *May 21st. Washington.* . . . Started again with a C.O.S. Meeting at 9 a.m. and followed up with a Combined Meeting at 10.30 a.m. The work was easier and there was less controversy. We dealt with the Pacific and accepted what was put forward."[1]

" In the evening at 5 p.m. we had another White House Conference with P.M. and President, when we put up the results of our work. It was all accepted and we received congratulations on our work, but I do not think either of them realised how near we were to a failure to reach agreement. We spent about one and a half hours listening to P.M. and President holding forth on strategy and shivering lest either of them should suddenly put their foot right into it and reopen some of the differences which we had reconciled with such difficulty. It would not have taken much to start some of our troubles again. Thank heaven we got through it safely."

" After the meeting P.M. called us all in and started discussing whether Archie Wavell still had enough drive and energy to carry on with his job, and to discuss his proposed plans for changes. He wishes to restrict the Commander-in-Chief in India to pure command of India alone, and to divorce him from the operations outside India. The problem is complicated by the desirability of appointing a Supreme Commander to co-ordinate the activities of American and British in this theatre. . . ."

' A short while before we left London Amery had sent for me to discuss this question of Command of India. While the operations in Burma and Assam were connected with the immediate defence of India it was right that the Commander-in-Chief India should be in command of these operations. The problem had now changed and we were engaged in operations for the liberation of Burma, support of Chinese and defeat of Japanese. It was therefore now necessary to look upon India as the base of these operations under its own Commander-in-Chief, and to appoint a new Commander-in-Chief.'

[1] " King gave an extensive exposition of the projected operations in the Pacific and Far East in 1943 and 1944 . . . King felt that all operations in the Pacific should be directed towards severing Japanese lines of communication. . . . The immediate objectives . . . appeared to be Rabaul, Truk and then the Marianas. . . . The Marianas, in King's opinion, were the key to the situation because of their location on the Japanese lines of communication. . . ." *Whitehill*. 228-29.

'The problem bristled with difficulties, mainly due to Chiang Kai-shek and to Stilwell and his Chinese Forces. Marshall with his high opinion of Stilwell wished him to perform a multitude of jobs simultaneously, such as liaison officer with Chiang Kai-shek, command of Chinese Forces, and command of American Forces in India. To perform these duties he required to be in three different places at the same time, and later on, when South-east Asia Command was formed, he wished him, on top of it all, to act as Deputy-Commander to Mountbatten.'

'It was growing very evident at this stage that Winston had again lost confidence in Wavell. He had never been able to appreciate his sterling qualities or his strategic ability. His quiet manner and his long silences Winston considered an indication of lack of drive and energy. He was anxious to replace him in the command of operations in Burma, and, as far as I can remember, it was this same day when he began to consider Wavell as a possible candidate for the Indian Viceroyalty which he was having serious difficulties in filling.'

"*May 22nd. Washington.* A very much easier day. We cut out the early C.O.S. meeting and went straight to the Combined Meeting at 10.30 a.m. Then we discussed the submarine warfare, which led to a small altercation between King and Pound. Otherwise we did not do much business beyond being photographed in session."

"Closed at 12 noon, and I went to get my hair cut before lunch and after lunch fell down fourteen stone stairs with serious bruising all over my body, but no real harm done. In the evening went to the Mellon Picture Gallery and was dumb-struck by the pictures and their wonderful setting. Mr. Finlay, the Curator, took us round and was quite charming. . . ."

"*May 23rd. Washington. Sunday.* We started with a C.O.S. meeting to which we invited Lord Leathers and Cherwell, and discussed the whole of the shipping situation in relation to the plans we had been making. Luckily the shipping worked out all right and covered all our plans.[1] At 2 p.m. we had a combined C.O.S. meeting and did not meet with very much difficulty in making the American Chiefs agree to the arguments put up. It was a very satisfactory ending to a difficult period. I then went for a short walk with Dill and in the evening dined out with the Rex Bensons."

' Any agreement and progress we may have made at this conference was again very greatly due to Dill and his help. He was a sick man suffering from an infection which had followed his operation for hernia. He ran low temperatures, suffered from heavy perspiration at night, and looked very run down. Yet in spite of it all he was always ready to act as an intermediary between Marshall and me.'

" *May 24th. Washington.* To-day we reached the final stages of the Conference, the ' Global Statement of our Strategy.' We started with a C.O.S. at 9 a.m. to look over our proposals and followed up with a long Combined Meeting at which we still had many different opinions which were only resolved with difficulty."

" Our difficulties still depended on our different outlook as regards the Pacific. I still feel that we may write a lot on paper, but that it all has little influence on our basic outlooks which might be classified as under:

(*a*) King thinks the war can only be won by action in the Pacific at the expense of all other fronts.

(*b*) Marshall considers that our solution lies in a cross-Channel operation with some twenty or thirty divisions, irrespective of the situation on the Russian front, with which he proposes to clear Europe and win the war.

(*c*) Portal considers that success lies in accumulating the largest Air Forces possible in England and that then, and then only, success lies assured. . . .

(*d*) Dudley Pound on the other hand is obsessed with the anti-' U 'boat warfare and considers that

[1] Resolved at 6.45 a.m. that morning, after a titanic struggle between the American and British shipping authorities. *Merchant Shipping and the Demands of War* (H.M.S.O.), 369-73.

success can only be secured by the defeat of this menace.

(e) Alan Brooke considers that success can only be secured by pressing operations in the Mediterranean to force a dispersal of German forces, help Russia, and thus eventually produce a situation where cross-Channel operations are possible.

(f) And Winston? Thinks one thing at one moment and another the next moment. At times the war may be won by bombing, and all must be sacrificed to it. At others it becomes necessary for us to bleed ourselves dry on the Continent because Russia is doing the same. At others our main effort must be in the Mediterranean directed against Italy or the Balkans alternately, with sporadic desires to invade Norway and 'roll up the map in the opposite direction Hitler did.' But more often than all he wants to carry out all operations simultaneously, irrespective of shortage of shipping."

". . . At 4.45 p.m. we went to the White House, first to be photographed and then to attend Conference with President and P.M. Then the P.M. entirely repudiated the paper we had passed, agreed to, and been congratulated on at our last meeting. He wished to alter all the Mediterranean divisions. He had no idea of the difficulties we had been through, and just crashed in 'where angels fear to tread.' As a result he created a situation of suspicion in the American Chiefs that we had been behind their backs, and has made matters far more difficult for us in the future."

" There are times when he drives me to desperation. Now we are threatened by a redraft by him, and more difficulties to-morrow. . . ."

' Winston's attitude at the White House Conference was tragic. He had originally agreed entirely to the paper we were discussing and with Roosevelt had congratulated us on it. Now at the eleventh hour he wished to repudiate half of it. Some of the alterations he wished to make were on points we had been forced to concede to the Americans in order to secure more important ones. From the attitude he took up the American Chiefs might well have believed that we had gone behind their backs in an attempt to obtain those points through Winston. On their side they knew that Roosevelt would not take such action unless briefed to do so by his Chiefs of Staff, and it was not possible for us to explain to them how independent Winston was in his actions.'

'. . . In later Conferences he always feared that we should " frame up " (he actually accused me in those terms one day) with the American Chiefs of Staff against him. He knew the Americans could carry the President with them and he feared being opposed by a combined Anglo-American block of Chiefs of Staff plus President. As a matter of fact on those occasions I was far from " framing up " with Marshall, and on the contrary was more liable to be at loggerheads with him over Pacific and cross-Channel strategy. Under such circumstances it may be imagined how complicated matters became.'

" *May 25th. Washington.* I went over to the office early to find out result of P.M.'s attempts to alter wording of our agreement. I discovered from Ismay that the P.M. had produced an impossible addition to our agreement which would have crashed the whole discussion, as we could never have got the American Chiefs of Staff to agree. Luckily, however, Harry Hopkins succeeded in getting him to withdraw it at the last moment, and he finally only put up a matter of wording, which only altered details and none of the principles. We were therefore exactly as we started so far as the paper we had submitted to the President and P.M. was concerned, but the P.M. had done untold harm by rousing all the suspicions, as regards ventures in the Balkans, which we had been endeavouring to suppress."

" He had, however, succeeded in getting the President to agree to Marshall coming with us to North Africa on our impending visit. This has now become essential, as otherwise, after the P.M.'s statements, I feel certain that a visit by the P.M. and myself to North Africa would be looked upon with grave suspicion as an attempt to swing Eisenhower in our direction at the expense of decisions arrived at in Washington."

" We met at 8.45 a.m. at a C.O.S. meeting to consider the P.M.'s amendments. At 10.30 a.m. we met for the last time as a Combined C.O.S. meeting of 'Trident' (name given to present meeting). The meeting was short and we went on to the White House where we again reported to the President and P.M. at 11.30 a.m. The meeting lasted till 1 p.m. without any startling developments and finished up with cocktails."

" Before lunch I had an opportunity to thank Harry Hopkins for all his help. We then assembled for a vast lunch in the White House given to Chiefs of Staff, Planners, Shipping experts, etc., etc. I sat between Secretary Stimson and one of the U.S. Admirals. Cordell Hull, Knox, etc., were there. President and P.M. made speeches at the end."[1]

" I then went to do final shopping before starting back, feeling very flat after all the exertions of the last two weeks. Came home and dined quietly with Dill and finished arrangements for early departure to-morrow. Another Combined Conference over. I have now attended four, two small ones in London with Marshall and King, and two large ones at Casablanca and here. They are the most exhausting entertainments imaginable. I am convinced they do a lot of good in securing greater understanding between us, and yet—they fall short in so far as our basic convictions remain unaltered. . . . Compromises emerge and the war is prolonged, whilst we age and get more and more weary."

' Looking back on the Conference in the light of the

[1] The list of the forty-eight guests is given in *White House Papers*, II, 725. They, included, in addition to the above, Averell Harriman, Hopkins, Stettinius, Wavell and Admiral Somerville from India, and Generals Stilwell and Chennault from China.

.results that ensued, the " compromise " that emerged was almost exactly what I wanted. We continued with the war in Italy with the object of eliminating Italy. We forced dispersement of German forces in Southern Europe under conditions strategically bad for them. On the other hand, the concessions to Marshall were that we should go on building up forces for the liberation of France at some later date, and not quite so early as he wanted. King, however, was the unconvertible one, and I knew well that shipping and landing-craft would continue to be sucked into the Pacific, irrespective of requirements for the war in Europe.'

In the closing stages of the discussion of the Allies' agreed statement—" Overall Strategic Concept for the Prosecution of the War "—King had tried to get his way over the Pacific by a phrase in the first two paragraphs of the U.S. draft:

" (a) In co-operation with Russia and other allies to force an unconditional surrender of the Axis in Europe;
(b) *Simultaneously . . . to maintain and extend unremitting pressure against Japan with the purpose of continually reducing her military power and attaining positions from which her ultimate unconditional surrender can be forced . . .*"

The British objected to (b) as giving a blank cheque for Pacific operations, and Marshall, Arnold and Leahy agreed with them. This, the Admiral's biographer, has written, left " King *contra mundum*. That did not affect him in the least. . . . It was pointed out to him that everyone else was in agreement against him, but he did not consider that relevant when a matter of principle was involved. A way out of the impasse was found when Pound proposed the addition to section (b) of a final sentence, ' The effect of any such extension of the overall objective to be given consideration by the Combined Chiefs of Staff before action is taken.' This amendment saved the day by its face-saving implication. . . . It placated King, for even with its addition the approved strategic concept made possible a vigorous prosecution of the Pacific war."[1]

[1] *Whitehill*, 232-3.

The slight alteration in wording which the Prime Minister made in the Allies' main objectives is shown in his history.[1] Other objectives were that, after defeating the Axis in Europe, both Great Britain and the United States should concentrate their entire force against Japan, and that the security of the British Isles, the defeat of the U-boats, the intensification of the air offensive against Germany and the build-up of forces for " a decisive invasion of the Axis citadel " were to be treated as a first charge against the two nations' joint resources. No specific agreement, however, was made for an invasion of Italy after the capture of Sicily, and the British were only able to obtain a resolution,

> " that the Allied Commander-in-Chief North Africa will be instructed, as a matter of urgency, to plan such operations in exploitation of Husky "—the code-name for the attack on the island—" as are best calculated to eliminate Italy from the war and to contain the maximum number of German forces. Which of the various specific operations should be adopted and thereafter mounted is a decision which will be reserved to the Combined Chiefs of Staff."[2]

As a result, however, of a last moment appeal by the Prime Minister to the President, it was decided that General Marshall, who was about to visit the South-west Pacific, should first accompany Churchill and Brooke on a fact-finding mission to Algiers to take counsel with Eisenhower and Alexander as to the next move after Sicily.

.   .   .   .

" *May 26th, 1943. Botwood (2,300 miles)*. At 7.30 a.m. a security car came to pick me up at Dill's house and took me to the moorings of the clipper ' Bristol ' on the Potomac just below Washington. The President came down himself with the P.M., who told me to go and sit with him for a few minutes in his car. He was as usual charming and said that next time I came over I must come to Hyde Park to see where my father and Douglas had looked for birds. The Halifaxes also came down to see

---

[1] *Churchill*, IV, 722.
[2] *Churchill*, IV, 724.

us off, and Dill had come with me. Harriman and Harry Hopkins were also there."

" At 8.30 a.m. we took off in fairly heavy rain and were soon in the mist. We saw a little bit of Nova Scotia, but the weather cleared well as we struck the south coast of Newfoundland. I was surprised to see a lot of snow still lying, especially along the southern coast. The southern part of the island is practically uninhabited, at any rate along the route we took. At about 5 p.m. (Washington time) we made a very good landing and went up to the Air Force Mess for dinner, as by their time it was about 7.30 p.m. The P.M. was kept very busy signing up ' Short Snorters.' "

' Short Snorters . . . were at that time very popular. Originally you could only become one if you had flown the Atlantic. It cost you 5s. and you were initiated by someone who already belonged to this sect. Your name was entered on a bank note, and you then collected signatures of all other " Short Snorters " till you had to gum several notes together. Mine consisted of a Russian note, a Turkish note and an American one, and was covered with signatures including President, P.M., Hopkins, Harriman, Anthony Eden, Attlee, Inönü, etc., etc.'

" At 9 p.m. we started off again and only just in time as the weather was clouding up fast and clouds lowering. P.M. sat talking for some time, but luckily we succeeded in getting him off to bed at a reasonable time."

" *May 27th. Mid-Atlantic (3,260 miles).* I had quite a fair night and got up at 8 a.m. which according to Washington time was 3 or 4 a.m. We are now somewhere north of the Azores heading for Gibraltar, and according to the estimates should arrive there about 4 p.m. We now have a tail wind which has put our speed up a bit. The total distance from Botwood to Gibraltar is about 3,260 miles. It is rather difficult to compete with the changes of temperature. Washington very hot and stuffy, Botwood bitterly cold, and the outside temperature zero at 7,000 feet, the height we were flying at. I had rather a job to keep warm enough at night. Beautiful calm sea below now and patches of fleecy clouds."

Later. Gibraltar. " During last night I heard two bangs followed by a flash as if something had hit the hull of the flying ship. I was informed in the morning that this was the result of two electric discharges, like lightning flashes, that had hit the bows of the machine.[1] At 3.30 p.m. we made a perfect land-fall just off Cape St. Vincent and then skirted the southern Portuguese coast, and, cutting across the bay of Cadiz, struck Cape Trafalgar, round the point of which we saw the top of the Rock emerging from a blanket of clouds. It looked at first as if the bay was covered with mist, but this turned out to be only a strip outside the harbour."

" The boat made a perfect landing and we were towed in to a buoy where Mason MacFarlane with his launch picked us up. We had been seventeen hours flying. Unfortunately it was now too late to go on to Algiers, and we were forced to spend the night in Gib. After dinner Mason MacFarlane produced a display of defensive fire for the P.M. which we watched from the top of the Rock."

" *May 28th. Algiers (450 miles).* Had a comfortable and good night's sleep. At breakfast General Catroux and Macmillan turned up from England on their way to Algiers where they are preparing for de Gaulle's arrival to-morrow. I had a talk with Catroux at breakfast. He seemed very relieved that his negotiations between Giraud and de Gaulle were at last coming to a conclusion of some kind. Personally I have serious doubts whether there can ever be any form of permanency in any Giraud-de Gaulle agreement. Their characters are not calculated to blend. . . . Weather in Gib. cooler than I had expected. At 11.30 a.m. P.M., Marshall and I went with Mason-MacFarlane for a tour of the Rock.

---

[1] " All at once there was a sudden shock and bump. I awoke. Something had happened . . . After a while I asked the pilot what caused the bump. ' We were struck by lightning,' he said, ' but there's nothing wrong.' This was good news. We had not caught fire or broken up in the air; there was no need to make a forced landing a thousand miles from anywhere." *Churchill*, IV, 727.

We did not have time to do much as we were due to emplane at 1.30 p.m."

" It was our first trip in the P.M.'s new plane, a Lancaster converted for him and called a York. Very comfortable, with special cabin for P.M., dining-room, berths for four besides P.M., and lavatory. We took off at 1.40 p.m. and had a lovely trip. We crossed the African coastline east of Melilla and travelled some ten to fifteen miles south of the coastline. Lovely clear day, and a very good view of all the country. We arrived Algiers at 4.30 p.m. Eisenhower, Cunningham, Alexander and Coningham were all on Maison Blanche aerodrome. Drove up to Eisenhower's house where I am in same room as I had last time. To-night Marshall and I dined with Cunningham where the P.M. is stopping. The dinner consisted of P.M., Cunningham, Marshall, Eisenhower, Tedder, Bedell Smith, Ismay, Alexander and some of Cunningham's staff."

" After dinner we had a long discussion as to what our future action in the Mediterranean should be. P.M. and I were busy trying to impress on Eisenhower what is to be gained by knocking Italy out of the war. I still do not think that Marshall realizes this, and I am quite certain that Eisenhower does not begin to realize the possibilities that lie ahead of us in this theatre. . . ."

" *May 29th. Algiers.* Had a very good night's sleep and woke up to a very warm day. After breakfast Eisenhower came into my bedroom, hung round with the ribbon of a Grand Commander of the Legion of Honour which Giraud had hung round his neck at a ceremony this morning. Giraud had said that no one could say that he was not entitled to do so as it was his own one, which had been put round his neck on the field of battle. Eisenhower said he accepted it as a token of the strength of Allied friendship, but that he would on his part refrain from wearing it until they met in Metz."

" *Later.* I now hear that de Gaulle is indignant that Giraud should have done this without consulting him."

" Alexander came to see me in the morning, and I had

a long talk with him until sent for by the P.M. I lunched
with Cunningham to meet Giraud and Georges, who
were lunching there to meet the P.M. Georges has just
been extracted out of France by us. I had not seen him
since that memorable meeting with him and Weygand,
when I was instructed to ' hold Britanny ' after returning
to France for the final days subsequent to Dunkirk. He
has aged a great deal, but was very interesting on the
question of conditions in France, German morale and
Italian morale."

" After lunch Humfrey Gale came to see me. He is
the British Chief Administrative Officer with Eisenhower.
I discussed all his difficulties with him from 3 to 4
p.m., when Alexander came back for another talk which
lasted till 5 p.m. We then had a conference with the
P.M. to discuss conclusions of Washington Conference
and to find out what Eisenhower's reactions were. The
meeting was of good value, and I think went a long
way towards securing the action after Sicily that we
look for."

" I then had another talk with P.M. at which I recommended that Wavell should be made Governor of Australia.
P.M. liked the idea and wired home about it. Dined
with Eisenhower and Marshall."

At that evening's meeting in Eisenhower's villa, with the
Supreme Commander, Marshall and Bedell Smith facing the
Prime Minister, Brooke, Alexander, Cunningham, Tedder and
Ismay across the table, Eisenhower explained his and his
commanders' plans for invading Sicily. " We then came,"
Churchill has written, " to the crucial issue. General Eisenhower told us he had had a long talk with Sir Alan Brooke,
who had emphasised that the Russian Army was the only land
force that could produce decisive results in 1943. The efforts
of our armies should therefore be directed towards diverting
the Germans from the Russian front in order to enable the
Russian armies to inflict decisive defeat upon them. . . . If we
were going to knock out Italy we ought to do so immediately
after Sicily and with all the means at our disposal. . . . If

capturing Sicily proved to be easy we ought to go directly into Italy. This would yield far greater prizes than any attack on islands. . . ."

" The C.I.G.S. then made his general statement. A hard struggle between the Russians and the Germans was imminent, and we should do all in our power to help the former and disperse the latter. . . . The Germans were faced with operations in Russia, with possible trouble in the Balkans, and with dangers in Italy, France and Norway. Their forces were already widely stretched, and they could not further reduce them either in Russia or in France. . . . If Italy were knocked out of the war Germany would have to replace the twenty-six Italian divisions in the Balkans. They would also have to reinforce the Brenner Pass, along the Riviera, and on the Spanish and Italian frontiers. This dispersal was just what we needed for a cross-Channel operation, and we should do everything in our power to increase it. The defences on the coast of France would present no difficulty unless they were held by determined men and the Germans had mobile reserves with which to counter-attack."

" Eisenhower then declared that the discussion had seemed to simplify his problem. If Sicily were to succeed, say within a week, he would at once cross the straits and establish a bridgehead. . . . I expressed a personal view that Sicily would be finished by August 15th. General Marshall thought we ought to have a good idea of this by the end of July. . . . Brooke raised the possibility of a crack-up in Italy during the Sicily fighting. In that case we ought to have a scheme of action and he felt that General Eisenhower should give some thought to the consideration of armistice terms and how far up into Italy we should go."[1]

In his book, *Crusade in Europe*, Eisenhower, writing from memory, referred to a private conversation with Brooke during his visit to Algiers—apparently on this day—in which he reported him as saying that " he favoured a policy of applying our naval and air strength towards the blockading of Germany and the destruction of its industry but avoiding great land battles on the main fronts. He held the belief that in ground

---

[1] " This was getting on very fast." *Churchill*, IV, 731-3.

conflict in a large theatre we should be at a great disadvantage
and would suffer tremendous and useless losses. He wanted to
open no larger front than one we could sustain in Italy."[1]
Either, as Lord Alanbrooke states, Eisenhower must have
misunderstood him or, as seems more likely, his memory after
the war must have been at fault. For, as both Churchill's
account of this meeting and the C.I.G.S.'s own contemporary
diary show, the latter's insistence on an invasion of Europe
from the south was based on the belief that such action in
1943 was an indispensable preliminary to a successful cross-
Channel attack in 1944. That Eisenhower should have been
suspicious of British intentions and slow to commit himself,
especially in Marshall's presence, to any firm promise to attack
southern Italy, was only natural, for, as the latter's chief
planning officer in the spring of 1942, he had been the author
of the American project for invading France that year or at
latest in 1943, which Churchill and the British Chiefs of Staff
had provisionally accepted as a desirable target and later
turned down as impracticable. At this time he still believed,
like Marshall, that the Mediterranean campaign, successful
though it had proved, was a regrettable diversion from the
more worthwhile objective of striking directly at Germany's
heart,[2] and that the British, in seeking, however plausibly, to
postpone the date of the latter, were trying to avoid the
necessity for it altogether in favour of imperial adventures in
the eastern Mediterranean.

[1] *Eisenhower*, 185. " Impulsive by nature, as became his Irish ancestry, Brooke
was highly intelligent and earnestly devoted to the single purpose of winning the
war. When I first met him in November, 1941, he seemed to me adroit rather
than deep, and shrewd rather than wise. But gradually I came to realize that his
mannerisms, which seemed strange to me, were merely accidental, that he was
sincere and, though he lacked that ability so characteristic of General Marshall
to weigh calmly the conflicting factors in a problem and so reach a rock-like
decision, I soon found it easy to work with him. He did not hesitate to differ
sharply and vehemently, but he did forthrightly and honestly, and heated
official discussion never affected the friendliness of his personal contacts or the
unqualified character of his support. He must be classed as a brilliant soldier.
So I listened carefully to the expression of his ideas at that moment."

[2] After the war Eisenhower acknowledged that the limited range of fighter
aircraft in 1942 " could not have provided sufficiently effective air-cover over the
Cotentin or Britanny peninsulas against the German air strength as it then
existed ", and " that out of the North-west African operation flowed benefits to
the Allied Nations that were felt all through the war and materially helped to
achieve the great victory when the invasion actually took place in 1944."
Eisenhower, 79.

After their conference at Algiers the visitors proceeded with their hosts to inspect the victorious armies:

" *May 30th. Algiers.* At 10.30 a.m. Humfrey Gale sent a car to pick me up and to bring me down to his Head-quarters Office where I spent about an hour going round the offices and being introduced to various officers. Most of the rooms are occupied by Combined Staffs of American and British, and it is a wonderful example of what can be done in the way of close-co-operation between allies."

" At 11.30 a.m. a car from Alexander collected me and brought me out through his H.Q. to his Camp in the woods some 10 miles west of Algiers. A most delightful spot right in the middle of pine trees and looking down on to the sea. We had lunch there and then went to look at the beaches west of Algiers where the Americans landed originally. Then we had a walk along the beach and a very pleasant bathe. We came back to have tea and then drove back home when I spent an hour in the garden looking for birds before going to dine in the Senior Staff Mess with Humfrey Gale."

" Returning back here to find a very sleepy Eisenhower waiting for the P.M., who had telephoned through saying he wanted to see him on his return from dining with Alex. I smiled at his distress, having suffered from this type of treatment repeatedly."

" *May 31st. Algiers (400 miles).* Alex came to pick me up at about 9.30 and we drove to Maison Blanche aero-drome to pick up his aeroplane to go on to inspect the 51st Division. We flew to Setif but landed on a wrong aerodrome and had to take off again to find the right one. When we did find it, it was so late that it was not possible to motor from there to Jijeili, which we had intended to do to see the lovely country. We therefore emplaned again and flew to Jijeili and from there on to see 51st Division. We found them . . . just east of Bougie. I had no conception that North Africa could be so beautiful. Cork tree forests with carpets of spring flowers, golden fields of calendulas, hedges covered with convolvulus, and green fields leading to tree-covered hills on one side and to blue Mediterranean on the other. A lovely place to rest a war-weary division."

" At 3.15 p.m. we flew back and arrived at 5.30 p.m., half an hour late for a Conference of the P.M. on the same subject as we discussed the other day. Anthony Eden turned up, having been wired for by the P.M. so that he might become familiar with the de Gaulle aspect in this country. We did not get very much further at the meeting, and the situation is on the whole much as we settled it in Washington, which is as it should be."

" After the Conference, Cunningham suddenly informed me that the P.M.'s latest idea is to go to Moscow from here! Later Eisenhower gave a large dinner to which the following came: P.M., Anthony Eden, Macmillan, Murphy, the U.S. Under-Secretary for Air, Marshall, Tedder, Cunningham, U.S. Admiral, Ismay, etc. Before dinner Anthony Eden drew me aside to ask me about the Moscow plan. I told him I considered we should stop the P.M. at all costs owing to the strain on his health. I said that it was very necessary that I should get home soon, but that, if my going with Eden might stop the P.M. from going, then I should be only too ready to do so. I just hate the thought and am longing to get home where there is masses for me to do."

" Eden was very nice in congratulating me on the results of Washington. He said he had read the Minutes and considered I could not have handled the affairs better, which is satisfactory."

" *June 1st. Algiers.* We left at 8.30 a.m. for Maison Blanche aerodrome where we emplaned in the P.M.'s York and flew to Château d'Un aerodrome. There we attended the briefing parade of an American squadron starting off to bomb Pantelleria defences. We then watched the bombers take off on their mission. At 11.30 a.m. we left for El Anerin aerodrome just outside Tunis. From there we motored to Carthage where a large party of men had been assembled in the old Roman amphitheatre. It was a most wonderful setting for the P.M.'s address to the men, and the acoustics were so perfect that no loudspeakers were necessary. . . ."

" After lunch we motored through Tunis and on towards Tebourba examining the main line of the attack on Tunis. . . . It was a most interesting trip and I was much impressed by the wonderful tank country over which the attack was made."

" Finished up by going to Eisenhower's ' Fairfield Camp,' where we were made very comfortable for the night. We had a very amusing dinner party consisting of P.M., Anthony Eden, Alex, ' Pug ' Ismay, Randolph, Tommy (P.M.'s Flag Officer) and self. We had tremendous arguments as to how the de Gaulle-Giraud difficulties should be settled. P.M. was in remarkable form, delighted at having had the chance of speaking from the Carthage amphitheatre! ' Yes, I was speaking from where the cries of Christian virgins rent the air whilst roaring lions devoured them—and yet—I am no lion and certainly not a virgin! ' "

" We slept in very comfortable tents with a lovely breeze blowing through."

" *June 2nd. Algiers (900 miles).* Left camp at 9 a.m. and proceeded to see 34th U.S. Division gunners. From there to Tunis where we examined a Mark VI (Tiger) German tank. Most interesting. From there to see more of 46th Division, then 4th Division and finally 6th Armoured Division, and 20th Guards Brigade. Keightley (Commander of 6th Armoured Division) gave us an explanation of the action of his division at Hamman Lif, most interesting with actual details of the positions held by the enemy and method by which they were defeated."

" We then went on to lunch with Coningham in a wonderful villa owned by a M. Germain, a Spaniard. . . . Here we had an excellent lunch and then went on to Grombalia aerodrome where we took off for Algiers. P.M. took the controls and gave us somewhat of a swaying passage for a bit. Returned here by 8 p.m. and dined with Eisenhower, followed by an early bed. The last two days have been intensely interesting. It is a great joy at last to see the real ground after looking at the maps for weeks and weeks trying to imagine what it is like."

" After seeing the ground and discussing the recent fighting with most of the commanders, I feel fairly certain that our future plans are on the right lines. We have definitely got the Germans in a difficult position. They must do something in Russia, and yet have not got the resources to do anything on a large scale. At the same time the Italian situation cannot fail to cause them the gravest of anxiety. We can at present help Russia best by hitting at Italy. I have since the start, and, in spite of many tribulations, aimed at three main points: (*a*) Secure the whole of North Africa (which we have now done). (*b*) Eliminate Italy (which we may hope to do before long). (*c*) Bring Turkey in (which must remain dependent on situation in Russia). If once we succeed in attaining these three points, a re-entry into France and a conclusion of the war should not be long delayed, all dependent on the situation in Russia. In any case the horizon is far brighter than it has been for some time."

" *June 3rd. Algiers.* P.M. sent for me during breakfast and told me that he was now considering starting to-morrow. It is only yesterday that we had settled that Alexander and I should start back with Anthony Eden on Friday 4th, whilst the P.M. stopped on to greet the next visitor (H.M. The King) here. However, whilst we were discussing the question he began to swing towards leaving on Saturday instead. He also discussed various questions of Command and showed me a wire to Curtin (P.M. of Australia) suggesting Wavell as future Governor of Australia. I failed, however, to get any definite decisions as regards commanders in any theatre."

" Montgomery arrived last night (from leave in England) and I had a long talk with him until P.M. sent for him. He requires a lot of educating to make him see the whole situation and the war as a whole outside the Eighth Army orbit. A difficult mixture to handle, brilliant commander in action and trainer of men, but liable to commit untold errors, due to lack of tact, lack of appreciation of other people's outlook. It is most distressing that the Americans do not like him, and it will always be a difficult matter to have him fighting in close proximity to them. He wants guiding and watching continually and I do not think that Alex is sufficiently strong and rough with him. After the P.M. had finished he came back and we had another long talk till 12.30 p.m."

" I then drove out to Alexander's H.Q. and had lunch with him in his camp, after which I went for a short walk in the pine woods round his camp to look for birds. I found a cross-bill, several green finches and some doves, but not much else."

" Then picked up Alex and drove back here where I had told Monty to meet me at 4 p.m. We had tea in my bedroom and discussed commanders. Then at 5 p.m. we had another conference with P.M. which did not get us much further, but we reviewed all the agreements we had arrived at during the last few days. On the whole, I think the visit has been a success in ensuring that the decisions arrived at in Washington were correctly interpreted here."

" In the evening I dined at the Admiral's villa at request of the P.M. The party consisted of P.M., Cunningham, Marshall, Eisenhower, Tedder, and Montgomery. After dinner Anthony Eden and Macmillan dropped in with latest information concerning Giraud-de Gaulle negotiations which have made great strides during the last twenty-four hours. As a result there is to be a great lunch party to-morrow to celebrate the fusion of the parties, just prior to our departure."

' My morning interview with Monty was another of those instances when I had to haul him over the coals for the trouble he was creating. . . . When we arrived in Algiers he was in England having a very well-earned period of rest after the fighting from El Alamein to Tunis. I was reluctant to call him back but found it was essential that I should see him before leaving North Africa and this only entailed curtailing his leave by a few days.'

' In my first interview with Eisenhower I discovered that he was boiling over internally with anger over Monty's insistence in extracting a Fortress aircraft out of him for Monty's personal services. The matter had originated from a remark which Bedell Smith had made jokingly whilst visiting Monty. He had said to him that, if he cleared Sousse of the enemy by a certain date, he would earn a Fortress aircraft. This statement had been light-heartedly made and far more as a joke than a real promise. However, Monty reached Sousse by the date mentioned and promptly wired to Bedell Smith for his Fortress aircraft. Bedell Smith still looked upon the matter as a joke and tried to laugh it off in his reply. This apparently did not satisfy Monty, who wired back stating that he was still expecting delivery of his aircraft. Bedell Smith was then forced to take the matter to Eisenhower, who was infuriated that he should be bounced in this way by Monty. However, being the past-master at cementing inter-allied relations, Eisenhower ordered that Monty should be given the Fortress aircraft, together with the American crew to fly it. Monty had thus gained his aircraft, but in doing so he had annoyed Eisenhower intensely. . . .

' The above details are based on the story given to me by Ike and Bedell Smith. I did my best to smooth over the harm that had been done, but realized that my efforts were falling short of what I hoped to achieve. When I accused Monty of stupidity for impairing his relations with Eisenhower for the sake of an aircraft which might have been provided from our resources, he told me that he was under the impression that Eisenhower had considered the whole transaction as an excellent joke. I told him that if he had heard Ike express his views to me he would certainly have had no such illusions. He was as usual most grateful for having his failings pointed out to him. This gratitude was genuine and not assumed, that I am certain. I am also convinced that . . . he was genuinely under the impression that his insistence in obtaining his aircraft was looked on as a joke by Ike.'

" *June 4th. Gibraltar (500 miles).* In the air between Oran and Gib. Packed up my kit in the morning and had long talk with Eisenhower. Later Monty came and we had a final talk about impending operations ('Sicily'). At 12.45 I went to the Admiral's house for a lunch party to celebrate the drawing together of Giraud and de Gaulle. Lunch consisted of P.M., Anthony Eden, Admiral Cunningham, Giraud, de Gaulle, Catroux, Georges, Phillip, Monnet, Margerie and Macmillan. I sat between de Gaulle and Margerie. De Gaulle very sticky and stiff, Giraud very pleasant, old Georges quite delightful. I had several interesting talks with Georges, who described to me what his feelings were at the beginning of the war and how well he realised the deficiencies of the French Army. At the end of lunch P.M. made an excellent speech in French, followed by Giraud and de Gaulle. Anthony Eden then spoke and finally old Georges said a few words. Photos were taken and then they departed."

" We then left for Maison Blanche aerodrome at once, and shortly afterwards at 3.30 p.m. took off for Gibraltar in the P.M.'s York. Party on board comprising P.M., Anthony Eden, Alexander, Rowan (secretary), Tommy (Flag Officer) and self."

" 6 p.m. we are just approaching Gib."

" *Later.* Arrived in Gib. to be told that we could not go on owing to weather. P.M. in depth of gloom. However, at end of dinner we were suddenly informed that we might go, starting at 10 p.m. This meant a mad rush, but by 10.30 we were off in the ' York,' not the Boeing Clipper we had intended to use."[1]

---

[1] " As my presence in North Africa had been fully reported, the Germans were exceptionally vigilant, and this led to a tragedy that much distressed me. The regular commercial aircraft was about to start from the Lisbon airfield when a thick-set man smoking a cigar walked up and down and was thought to be a passenger on it. The German agents therefore signalled that I was on board. . . . A German war plane was instantly ordered out and the defenceless aircraft was

"*June 5th. London (1,400 miles).* Arrived at Northolt at 6 a.m. after an excellent trip back. Bath, shave, and then collected you at Goring Hotel and went home to Ferney Close for a quiet week-end."

"*June 6th.* Long sleep and lovely peaceful day."

ruthlessly shot down. Thirteen passengers perished, among them the well-known British actor, Leslie Howard." *Churchill*, IV, 742. The hapless traveller who was mistaken for the Prime Minister was a brilliant accountant and amateur musician twenty-five years his junior named Alfred Chenhalls and a close friend of the writer of this book.

Chapter Thirteen

RETURN TO EUROPE

We are about to embark on the most momentous enterprise of the war—striking for the first time at the enemy in his own land.

ADMIRAL SIR ANDREW CUNNINGHAM
Message to all ships, 9th July, 1943

O N THE day on which the Prime Minister and Brooke left Washington, after six hundred miles of channel had been swept by the Royal Navy, the first British convoy to pass through the Mediterranean since 1941 reached Alexandria without loss. The attempt of the Italians and Germans to make that sea an Axis lake and break across the Nile Valley into Asia, so nearly successful, had cost them nearly a million casualties, 8000 aircraft, 6000 guns, 2500 tanks, 70,000 trucks, and 2,400,000 tons of shipping. Its defeat was as momentous as Stalingrad and achieved at a far lower cost. From Alamein and the first " Torch " landings in November to the final surrender in May, the Allies had lost little more than two per cent of the ships they had sent into the Mediterranean and only 70,000 men including wounded. By its re-opening they reduced the length of the passage from Britain to the Middle East from 13,000 to 3000 miles—a saving of forty-five days on the average time of every convoy—and gained the equivalent of at least a million tons of shipping.

It was this and the sudden defeat of the U-boat campaign that aroused Hitler's fears. The capture of the Tunisian bastion, he had estimated at Christmas, would save the Allies from four to five million gross tons of shipping and compel the U-boat fleet, even at its then high rate of sinkings, to work for four or five additional months to make good the deficiency.[1]

[1] *Hinsley*, 223-4.

Now, at the very moment that the enemy had re-opened the Mediterranean the U-boats had suffered a disastrous defeat, their Atlantic sinkings falling from ninety-two in March to forty-one in May and only six in June, while their own losses were such that they had had to withdraw from the trans-oceanic sea-lanes. The Atlantic, which Hitler had described as his first-line of defence in the West, had ceased to be a defence line at all. And as the threat from the West grew, the ring of sea-power round Hitler's Europe simultaneously tightened from the south, and the whole Mediterranean littoral lay exposed to attack as Alexander's victory in Tunisia gave the Royal Navy and the British and American air forces control of that sea.

That June—in eastern Europe and the Mediterranean, in the skies over western Europe and Germany, along the Burmese mountain border and in the immense spaces and jungle islands of the Pacific and South-East Asia—the em-battled armies, fleets and air forces of the world were struggling for position in the fifth summer of a war in which for the first time the enemies of the Axis enjoyed the initiative. In Russia the Germans, having halted the Red Army's great winter counter-attack, had been making preparations for their usual summer offensive. But the scale of these was far smaller than in the previous year, and, though they still felt confident of their ability to defeat the Russians in a war of manœuvre, they were no longer the assured masters of the field they had been before Stalingrad. It was not only Russia's distances and apparently inexhaustible reserves of man-power that worried them, but the fact that, equipped from their new Ural and Siberian factories, the half-mechanized peasant levies that had so nearly succumbed in 1941 and 1942 were becoming a modernized, mechanized army, capable not only of sustaining hard knocks but of giving them. And behind their lines, harrying the German communications as Malta's submarines and aircraft had done in the Mediterranean, was a guerilla army which struck by night, dynamiting bridges and trains, sabotaging machinery and attacking every isolated patrol and garrison.

Nor were the Russians fighting any longer unaided. For

though, as the Germans concentrated for their summer offensive, Stalin intensified his reproaches against his allies, the threat of an Anglo-American attack from the south was already presenting Hitler with a major problem. A third of his Army and two-thirds of his air force were now tied down garrisoning and guarding the European coastline, whose assailable length had been doubled by the re-opening of the Mediterranean. With their increased defence commitments in Sicily, Italy, southern France and the Balkans, and their losses at Tunis and Stalingrad, the Germans could not, for all their 320 nominal divisions, create the mobile reserve they needed to recover the initiative in the east. At the moment when their chief tank expert, Guderian, was urging the withdrawal and regrouping of their armour to form a central strategic reserve for employment against either east or west, the Wermacht was so extended that Hitler could not meet his request without abandoning the summer offensive on which he had based all his hopes of avenging Stalingrad and advancing again on the coveted Caucasian oilfields. To Guderian's fury it had even proved necessary to send a crack panzer division to Greece to guard against British landings in the Ægean, where Admiral Cunningham's battleships were cruising to keep Hitler and Mussolini guessing where the assault on southern Europe would fall. "Our strongest reserve," Guderian wrote, ". . . was to be wasted in this extraordinary fashion. When I protested irritably, I became involved in an utterly grotesque argument with General Keitel. I maintained that a mountain division would be far more suitable for Greece; he replied that it would be impossible to supply such a division with the necessary amount of fodder, as this would require too much transport. Against such arguments there was nothing more that I could say."[1] It was a demonstration of the prescience of Brooke's strategy and of the logistical and military difficulties in which it was beginning to involve the Axis.

Moreover, as Hitler reminded those of his generals who advocated withdrawal to shorten the vast circumference they were now defending, it would be perilous to yield any part of

---

[1] *Guderian*, 310. "We were soon bitterly to miss the 1st Panzer Division in Russia."

the space that was needed to cushion the Reich against invasion and air bombardment. Though the first might seem far away, the second was already a terrible reality. The vulnerability of Germany's western factories to the growing might of the British and American air forces showed the danger of allowing any approach from south or east that might bring the Allies' bombers within range of the war industries of Silesia, Austria, Bohemia and of the Rumanian oilfields. For, despite heavy casualties, the R.A.F.'s offensive battle with the German night-fighters and anti-aircraft defences was being doggedly maintained.[1] At the end of May the manufacturing city of Dortmund suffered the worst raid so far of the war, nearly a hundred thousand people being rendered homeless. In June more than half Düsseldorf, the Manchester of the Ruhr, was burnt to the ground. In the second quarter of the year 35,000 tons of bombs, nearly three times the total dropped on London in the blitz-autumn of 1940, fell on Germany's greatest armament-producing district, while a raid in May by a squadron of low-flying precision bombers—a feat rivalling in daring the historic exploits of Drake—destroyed the Möhne dam. All the while, the Reich was kept in a state of constant alarm by nuisance-raids by small, fast, high-flying aircraft. " The Fuehrer," reported Goebbels, " is exceedingly impatient and angry about the lack of preparedness on the part of our Luftwaffe. . . . We must try to develop counter-measures as fast as possible, especially reprisal attacks. Otherwise, sooner or later, the war in the air will become unbearable for us. . . . The London public fears that a German air *blitzkrieg* will suddenly break out again overnight. Would to God that we were in a position to do it! "[2]

Yet now that Nemesis for the evil they had done had begun to overtake them, the reaction of the German people to misfortune was more stoic than either the British Air Ministry or their own propaganda chief expected. The destruction of their cities might seem unendurable, but they endured it. They were controlled by a ruthless, highly-organised despotism whose leaders, having risen to power by makeshifts, were accustomed

[1] During the attacks on the Ruhr in the spring and summer of 1943, 628 British bombers and nearly 6000 highly-trained airmen were lost.

[2] *Goebbels*, 21st, 22nd May, 1943.

to extemporising. The normality of Germany's civil life in the triumphant epoch that followed her conquest of Europe was succeeded in her stricken industrial towns by a sudden state of national emergency. Factories vital to war production were rapidly rebuilt, often underground or in eastern and southern districts outside the reach of Bomber Command, and their workers rehoused in the surrounding countryside or in temporary, mass-produced huts.[1] Owing to the ease with which Germany had overrun the Continent in 1940, her war economy had never been stretched like that of Britain, and there was still plenty of slack. With more than six million foreign and slave workers to draw on, she had ample industrial, as distinct from military, man-power. Her weakness lay rather in over-extended defence lines and communications and shortages of raw materials. Bomber Command's offensive gravely aggravated these, but its effect on Germany's labour force was not what its authors had hoped.

Moreover, the rising tide of American war-production and the loss of Germany's superiority in arms and equipment caused Hitler to react vigorously. A month after the Casablanca Conference, as the implications of the Allies' Mediterranean campaign became clear, he had called to the total direction of his war industry a thirty-six-year-old architect named Albert Speer whom a year earlier he had made Minister of Munitions. To Speer, an organiser of genius, was given the task of overcoming the crisis by rapidly multiplying German and European arms production, by building a new U-boat fleet of revolutionary design and by the development of secret aerial weapons of shattering power. With these, and the measures he was taking to strengthen the Channel defences and build a central reserve, Hitler believed he would be able to throw the Allies into the sea as soon as they landed and inflict on them a defeat so calamitous that all further danger of invasion from the West would be at an end.[2] With the advantage of interior lines, he

---

[1] " Those who are not needed in the cities must get out. . . . Small houses will be built in very large numbers. They are to have a bedroom for the parents, another one for the children with double-decker bunks, and a place for cooking." Hitler's Instructions of 11th August, 1943, quoted *Hinsley*, 229-30.

[2] " The West," Rommel remarked that July, " is the place that matters. If we once manage to throw the British and Americans back into the sea, it will be a long time before they return." *Rommel Papers*, 453.

would then be able to concentrate the whole, instead of only two-thirds of his army, against Russia and achieve in the east the decisive result he had been vainly seeking for the past two years.

As a result the summer and autumn of 1943 saw an immense increase in German arms production. Despite the mounting weight of Harris's air offensive against the Ruhr and Rhineland, the output of field, anti-tank and anti-aircraft guns rose during the year from 12,000 to 27,000, of tanks and self-propelled guns from 6000 to 12,000, and of aircraft from 13,000 to 22,000. Had it not been for Bomber Command's sacrificial efforts these increases would have been even greater and their deployment far more rapid. A particularly serious threat to the Allies' coming offensive was the building of giant submarines able to travel at high speeds underwater and to attack convoys without exposing themselves to watching aircraft. Just as six months earlier the Combined Chiefs of Staff had accepted Brooke's thesis that no decisive attack on Europe was possible until the submarine threat had been mastered, so Hitler had resolved to stake everything on breaking the conveyor-belt between America and Europe. On July 8th, after a conference with Admiral Doenitz, he ordered production of the new U-boats to be given absolute priority.

Two days later the Fuehrer gave Speer a more momentous order. Following successful experimental flights in Poland of pilotless, guided, jet-propelled flying-bombs and of long-range rockets projected through the stratosphere, instructions were given for the immediate large-scale production of both these weapons for launching against London and the southern English ports. On June 10th, following an ecstatic visit to the secret rocket-research station on the Baltic island of Peenemünde, Hitler informed his generals that they had only to hold out till Christmas for the British capital to be razed to the ground. Rumours of these developments had reached London through the Polish underground movement during the spring, and R.A.F. reconnaissance planes had brought back photographs from Peenemünde of large mysterious cigar-shaped objects. The Chiefs of Staff had first considered the matter in April, and at their request a committee had been set up under the chairmanship of the Prime Minister's son-in-law, Duncan Sandys, to investigate the facts. " Dinner at the flat with you," ran Brooke's diary entry for June 29th,

> " followed by a meeting with the P.M. attended by Eden, Lyttelton, Morrison, Cripps, Chiefs of Staff, Sandys, Crow (rocket expert), Professor (Lindemann), etc. We met to discuss the new rocket weapon which the Germans are supposed to be developing and which Sandys has been enquiring into. Arrived at conclusion that a definite threat exists and that we should bomb Peenemünde experimental station at earliest possible date."

Thus, by the beginning of 1944, Hitler reckoned, London and the embarkation ports would be under a continuous bombardment from thousands of flying-bombs and rockets—both impossible to stop—the convoys bringing American reinforcements and supplies to Europe would be at the mercy of his new submarines, and a striking reserve of twenty mobile divisions, in addition to the forty or fifty already stationed behind the Atlantic Wall, would be waiting to throw the western invaders into the sea. Yet at this moment, impervious to the fact that the Fuehrer, with his three hundred million subjects and serfs and magnificent east-to-west communications, was certain to be planning counter-measures against their impending blow at his heart, the Americans—to whom all things now seemed possible—were allocating ever more men, ships, planes and assault-craft to Pacific campaigns whose logistics necessitated ocean supply lines far longer even than those with which the Germans were struggling in Russia. And, once launched, these were bound to absorb men and resources needed to ensure success in Europe. Already, despite the decision that Germany should be attacked first, there were thirteen American divisions in the Pacific to ten in the United Kingdom and Mediterranean, while only three or, at the outside, four of these could be deployed against Italy owing to shortages of assault-craft and shipping. Claiming that the United States was alone responsible for the Pacific War and relying on the permissive mandate he had wrung from the Casablanca and Trident Conferences, Admiral King and his military colleague and rival, General MacArthur, embarked that summer on offensives whose conception showed a strategic grasp of the highest order,[1] marred only by their incompatibility with the thesis that, if the war was not to be indefinitely prolonged or lost, Hitler's European fortress must be stormed at the earliest possible moment. Nimitz and MacArthur did not fall, like their compatriots who were planning the liberation of Europe, into the error of wishing to attack only a single point of the vast sea-littoral before them. Their strategy was to strike, first at one point and then at another, and so deprive the enemy of his advantage of interior lines. Based on America's rapidly growing fleet of aircraft-carriers and the opportunities they offered for concentrating overwhelming air-strength at any given point, it consisted of a carefully planned game of leap-frog from island to island, aimed at by-passing and isolating an ever-growing number of Japanese garrisons and carrying the attackers to within air-striking distance, first of the Philippines—the key to the China seas—and then to Japan itself. In place of the laborious process of capturing every outpost in turn, the Americans would be able, long before the Co-prosperity Sphere was consolidated, to open direct sea-communications with China and bomb the Japanese mainland.

Yet the fanaticism and tenacity of the Japanese soldier still made it necessary to storm a succession of island fortresses held by troops prepared to die to the last man. The plan required ships, carriers, aircraft, assault-vessels of every kind, specialised weapons for landing operations and ample supplies and reinforcements—in fact, everything that was needed in the Mediterranean and Atlantic if Europe was to be stormed from the sea and advantage taken of the vast sea circumference Germany and Italy were now forced to man. Without sufficient sea-borne air-power, shipping and landing-craft to strike at any point they chose, the Allies could only in reality threaten a few hundred miles of the six thousand miles of Axis-held European coastline. Without this all the rest, being out of reach of land-based fighters, was immune from serious invasion. To keep the Germans dispersed and unable to concentrate against the point

[1] Brooke regarded MacArthur as the greatest strategist of the War and his campaign in the South-West Pacific as a masterpiece.

where the real attack at their heart was to be made, it was essential to use at the moment all available surplus naval and air strength, not in the Pacific, but in the seas round Europe, especially the Mediterranean.

It was thus impossible for Brooke not to view with misgiving the succession of amphibious operations being launched on the other side of the world. The very rapidity and brilliance with which they followed one another constituted a growing threat to the coming assault on Europe. On May 11th, by-passing Japanese-held Kiska, the Americans landed on Attu in the Aleutians—the thousand-mile chain of rocky, fog-bound islands that linked the extreme north of America to the extreme north of Asia. In June, after a victory in March in the Bismarck Sea, in which an entire division sailing to reinforce the Japanese on New Guinea was sent to the bottom for the loss of four American aircraft, MacArthur occupied Woodlark and Kiriwina islands in the Tobrian group and established an air-link between New Guinea and the Solomons. Simultaneously the conquerors of Guadalcanal occupied Rendova island, two hundred miles to the west. A few days later, leap-frogging a hundred miles along the shores of New Guinea, MacArthur's Australians and Americans landed behind the Japanese in Nassau Bay. On July 2nd and 3rd the Americans in the Solomons established bridgeheads in New Georgia to capture the great airbase of Munda. Fierce naval battles followed, at Kula Gulf on the 6th and 7th, and at Kolombangara on the 12th and 13th. And while this was happening in the South-West Pacific, three thousand miles away in the Hawaiians, Nimitz and his brilliant Chief of Staff, Spruance, were creating a vast, self-contained, mobile naval and air base to accompany their fleets and marine armies. With its floating dockyards, foundries, repair shops, labour battalions for building wharves, roads and airfields, it was designed to enable an amphibious force of carriers, battleships, transports and landing-craft to operate thousands of miles from its nearest shore base and pounce at will on any Japanese island, however strongly defended. Surprising and isolating it by dominating the sea and air around it, and storming it with specially trained assault troops, the attackers, with their immense technical resources, could then establish new bases for operations in the heart of the enemy's position. By the summer of 1944, it was reckoned, all the island groups in Japan's outer defence line—Gilberts, Marshalls, Marianas, Carolines—would lie at their mercy.

Nor did the Americans content themselves with this tremendous programme against Japan. They had insisted, at Casablanca and Washington, that the British should start offensive operations in Burma to re-open the road to China. By this they had presented Brooke and his colleagues with additional problems and a call for arms and equipment which at that moment were urgently needed elsewhere. With Ceylon and India now held in sufficient strength and with growing British and American air power,[1] Brooke did not consider that the Japanese, with their inadequate shipping and over-strained communications, were likely to succeed in making much farther advance westwards. Nor did he believe that any advantage could come from pouring resources into that bottomless pit of Oriental inefficiency and corruption, Chiang Kai-Shek's China, or from consuming them in offensive operations in Burma until the progress of the war in the West made it possible to do so on a decisive scale. But he was the servant as well as a member of the Combined Chiefs of Staff, and the decision having been taken to stage an offensive in Burma with such force as was available, it had had to be attempted. Before the rains brought operations to a close in May two small-scale expeditions were launched by Wavell, the first in the Arakan mountains, which ended in failure; the other, smaller in scope but daring and original in character, in which a young brigadier, who had won fame as a guerilla leader in Abyssinia, penetrated hundreds of miles behind the Japanese lines in the northern Burmese jungle with a group of raiding columns supplied entirely from the air. Though effecting little of material consequence—for only a few thousand men were engaged—the first Chindit campaign proved two things: that

[1] Between March and June, 1942, the Air Force in India had grown from five to twenty-six squadrons. By June, 1943, there were fifty-three, thirty-eight of them operational. In the same period over two hundred airfields were built. The Japanese, on the other hand, facing growing American air power in the Pacific, were becoming weaker in the air. *Royal Air Force 1939-1945* (H.M.S.O.), III 299, 305-6.

air transport was the key to jungle warfare and that British infantry, given proper training and leadership, were more than a match for the supposedly invincible Japanese.

. . . .

The problem facing Brooke and his fellow Chiefs of Staff was to make all this compatible with the two successive invasions of Europe from the sea—the one in 1943 and the other in 1944 —on whose success he believed victory to depend. Having at last got his American colleagues to recognise that a preliminary attack across the Mediterranean might have some part in the overall strategy of the war, he had now to leave its implementation to others. It rested with those planning " Husky "— as the Sicilian operation was christened—with the British and American forces concentrated in North Africa and the Mediterranean; with Alexander and Montgomery; above all, with the American Supreme Commander whose recommendation to the Combined Chiefs of Staff was to determine whether the Sicilian landings were to be followed up by an invasion of the Italian mainland. Though still engaged in discussions with the Prime Minister in the Cabinet and Chiefs of Staff Committee about the expedition's build-up and the various deception and security measures for keeping the enemy guessing its destination,[1] Brooke and his British colleagues, planning as always for events several months ahead, were more occupied that summer with preparations for the still greater operation to which they were committed for 1944. For this, as he and the Chief of Combined Operations were continually stressing, the overriding need were landing-craft. On the number and type of these available depended both the size of the assault forces and the width, and, therefore, security, of the bridgehead, as well as the speed with which strength could be built up inside it to withstand German counter-attack. Here the chief obstacle was the slowness of the Americans—the arch-protagonists of

---

[1] " Our morning C.O.S. meeting was greatly taken up with an interview with the deputy of the Minister of Information in order to try and regulate the Press, which as usual is discussing the fact that it is inevitable that we should carry out exactly what we propose to do. So far it has worked quite well as a ' double cross', as the Germans cannot imagine that we should be such fools as to give the Press such liberty. But we cannot hope to go on fooling them in this way." *Diary*, 18th June, 1943.

cross-Channel invasion—in appreciating that landing-craft were an overriding priority, and the stranglehold of King and the Pacific admirals on their allocation. Even in the President's " Must " programme of production-priorities at the beginning of the year there had been no mention of the specialized landing-ships and assault-craft which Mountbatten and his Combined Operations staff were insisting must be made before any invasion of Europe was possible. Because, in view of the U-boat menace, the Casablanca Conference had made the construction of escort vessels the first call on all shipyards, a British request in March that more tank-landing ships should be built in the United States for use in the Channel had been flatly turned down by King.[1] Even during the Trident Conference in May the Washington planners had continued to question the British estimate of the number of landing-craft required, forgetting that it had been drawn up by an Anglo-American planning staff in London. Of the nineteen thousand assault vessels built in American shipyards in 1943, only a thousand had so far been allocated for " Round-up." With those that could be built in Britain—a mere three or four hundred a month—only enough would be ready by the spring of 1944 to lift three divisions in the first wave instead of the minimum of five demanded by the Planners. It was this that had caused Brooke to remark at the outset to General Morgan—the head of the Anglo-American planning staff responsible for drawing up preliminary plans for the invasion: " Well, there it is. It won't work, but you must bloody well make it! "[2]

Much else besides landing-craft had to be made ready in the next ten months if the Allies were to breach Hitler's Western Wall from the sea. As a result of the experience gained in the Dieppe raid, two essentials had been laid down for any opposed landing. Because Dieppe had shown that no pre-liminary bombardment from the sea was ever likely wholly to neutralise the enemy's defences, covering fire must be given before and during the landing from guns, mortars and rockets mounted in the assault-craft and special support-craft. And

[1] *U.S. War Department Official History, European Theatre of Operations—Cross-Channel Attack*, 63-70.
[2] *Struggle for Europe*, 169, also *Idem* 174-8; *British War Production* (H.M.S.O.), 293; *U.S. War Department Official History*, 63-70, *Cross-Channel Attack*.

because the infantry could not hope to survive without, tanks must go ashore with the first wave of attackers to drench the defenders with fire during the landing. Within three days of his return from Africa Brooke flew to Northumberland to inspect the new invasion tanks which that pioneer of armour, General Hobart, was developing, in conjunction with Combined Operations Headquarters, in his experimental armoured division. Far in advance even of the ingenious weapons American industry was making to enable King's Marines to storm Japanese islands, Hobart and Mountbatten's scientists were devising tanks that swam under their own power, tanks that scaled sea-walls, tanks that pounded concrete fortifications with explosives or spanned ditches with bridges, tanks with searchlights, tanks that emitted flames or acted as ramps for other tanks. When in July the C.I.G.S. visited the Norfolk Broads in Hobart's company, he enjoyed his first trip in an amphibious tank. " Most interesting and inspiring," he found it; he was delighted, he wrote, " to see old Hobo so happy and so well employed." A few days later he gave orders for the conversion of nine hundred Sherman tanks, despite the view of the Admiralty and Ministry of Supply that such unnatural hybrids could never be made seaworthy.

In the same month Brooke formed the British troops who were to invade France—fifteen picked divisions, five of them armoured—into a new Command named 21 Army Group under his former Chief of Staff and successor at Home Forces, General Sir Bernard Paget. A trainer of troops in the classic Light Infantry tradition of John Moore, Paget's ideal was Moore's " thinking fighting man "—the self-reliant, resourceful soldier who knew what he was doing because its reason had been made plain to him. Like all who had experienced the massacres of the first war and twenty years later led the British Army through the fiery ordeals of Norway, Dunkirk and Greece, Paget had set himself to solve the problem—unresolved on the Somme and at Passchendaele—of bridging, in the face of modern automatic weapons, " the gap between the barrage and the bayonet." He sought, by closely co-ordinating fire-power and movement, to restore the infantry to its old pre-eminence as " the cutting-edge " and arbiter of the battlefield.

He was confronted with the task of training it and its supporting arms, not merely to storm Hitler's coastal fortifications, but, supplied from open beaches, to fight its way forward through ideal defensive country against an army of veterans who enjoyed the initial advantage of possessing everything that ran on wheels on the Continent. At the great School of Infantry which he and Brooke had created on the Durham moors,[1] and in the divisional battle-schools which based themselves on its teaching, the conditions which the fighting man would have to encounter in Europe were reproduced in training more realistic and imaginative than any yet devised for preparing troops for the shock of war. The force that was to cross the Channel in 1944 was to be a very different one to that with which Brooke had sailed for Cherbourg in the autumn of 1939.

It was to fight beside allies of, at first equal, and later preponderant strength. In the summer of 1943 there was still only one American field division in the United Kingdom, with about 150,000 ground, base and air personnel. But by the spring of 1944, it was expected that at least a million American troops would be based there, including fifteen fighting divisions. Thereafter, the American build-up would rapidly outstrip the British. For after four years of war, with an Air Force that was now as large as the Luftwaffe, the world's second largest Navy and nearly five million men in arms, Britain, with her comparatively small population, was more highly mobilised for war than any other belligerent. Preparations for a cross-Channel operation, the chief initial burden of which principally fell on the United Kingdom, were gravely aggravating the growing shortage of man-power and making any further increase in the overall size of the Armed Forces impossible—a fact that the Prime Minister, with his desire to uphold the prestige of the country, was most reluctant to admit. More men were needed to man the landing-craft than the entire pre-war personnel of the Royal Navy, while the building of wharves and " hards," railways, roads and aerodromes, training and transit camps, and specialized invasion equipment, like the two pre-fabricated harbours or " Mulberries," were making immense inroads on

[1] Brooke had first urged the establishment of a School of Infantry before the War when Director of Military Training, but the proposal had been turned down by the then C.I.G.S.

Britain's limited labour force. Her normal export and import trade had been pared to the bone and even grandmothers conscripted into the factories. Brooke's diary that summer contained repeated references to this problem.

"*July 9th*..... Speeded up Chiefs of Staffs' meeting, as at 10.45 we had to attend a Cabinet meeting on man-power. We have now reached a stage when all three Services, and industry supplying them, are living above their means. . . . Cuts must be made; unfortunately, whilst recognising that cuts must be made, Winston won't face up to reducing formations. It is useless retaining emaciated formations which we cannot maintain, and I refuse to do so, and that leads to differences of opinion of the severest nature with Winston."

' His desire,' Brooke wrote, ' was to retain formations long after it had been made clear that the man-power conditions no longer admitted of their retention. It was almost a childish dislike to having his battalions and divisions reduced. This failing increased as the U.S. formations outnumbered ours. I could not make him realize that it was a matter of living in a fool's paradise to maintain emaciated divisions. I tried repeatedly to explain that the efficiency of formations rapidly deteriorated when unable to maintain their numbers. It was all of no use. He became more and more obstinate, and it was only with the greatest difficulty that I obtained my way in this matter.'[1]

. . . .

Because in 1943 Britain was still militarily the predominant Power and because the Supreme Command in the Mediterranean had been given to an American, many, including the Prime Minister, expected that command of the armies that were to liberate Western Europe would be entrusted to a British soldier. An understanding to this effect had been reached by Roosevelt and Churchill when the latter had agreed

[1] *Notes on My Life*, IX, 735. In the end the Army's planned strength was reduced by the equivalent of four divisions and that of the R.A.F. by fifty-seven squadrons in 1943 and eighty-nine squadrons in 1944. *British War Production* (H.M.S.O.), 226.

to Eisenhower's appointment as Supreme Commander in Africa despite the fact that Britain had at least a dozen divisions there to America's seven. The obvious choice was Brooke.[1] A British Chief of Staff, Lieutenant-General F. E. Morgan, had already been appointed to plan the operation by the Combined Chiefs of Staff with an Anglo-American planning staff under him. Much of Brooke's time that summer, both in private conference and in the Chiefs of Staff's Committee, was spent in discussing invasion problems with this officer, whose headquarters was known by the initial letters of his title, COSSAC—" Chief of Staff to the Supreme Allied Commander (Designate)." The question of who was to be designated, however, still remained undecided.

But ten days after their return from Africa, on Whit Monday, Brooke was sent for by the Prime Minister before the evening meeting of the War Cabinet. " P.M. called me in," he wrote, " to tell me that he had been wanting to let me know during the last few days that he wanted me to take Supreme Command of operations from this country across the Channel when the time was suitable. He said many nice things about being full of confidence in me, etc."[2] It was only as yet an expression of the Prime Minister's personal wish—a hint at a possibility rather than an offer. But it naturally thrilled Brooke. ' It would be the perfect climax,' he wrote, ' to all my struggles to guide the strategy of the war into channels which would ultimately make a re-entry into France possible, to find myself in command of all the Allied Forces destined for this liberation.'[3] As he had been sworn to secrecy, he did not even tell his wife, but set down the fact in his diary when he returned to his flat after leaving the Prime Minister. " Am now off," he continued, " to one of his evening meetings at 10 p.m. on tank armament." In his final entry that night, he recorded only the routine discussion that followed. " We had

[1] " Prior to the Quebec Conference it had been generally assumed that the Supreme Command for " Overlord " would be British: for one thing the huge operation was to be mounted in the United Kingdom and, for another, it was Britain's turn to take top rank. . . . Churchill had promised the new post to Sir Alan Brooke." *White House Papers*, II, 755. " In the earlier stages of planning this operation it had been generally assumed that the Supreme Commander would be British." *Whitehill*, 294.

[2] *Diary*, 15th June, 1943.

[3] *Notes on My Life*, IX, 723.

a desperate meeting with P.M. up till 1.30 a.m. and never arrived at a single decision."[1]

Four days later, however, the C.I.G.S. had a further indication of the dazzling opportunity that might come to him, when his friend, the Adjutant-General, lunched with him on his return from North Africa. " He surprised me by telling me that Eisenhower had said . . . that he considered there were only two men to take on the Supreme Command in this country, and that one was Marshall and the other myself. That astonished me as I did not believe that he had much of an opinion of me."[2] But in the rush of problems pouring in on him from every corner of the globe—the allocation of troops from the Middle East for operations against Italy, the separation of Burma Command from India and the replacement of Wavell by Auchinleck, impending changes at Canadian Headquarters, the complications caused by General de Gaulle's unaccommodating patriotism—Brooke made no further reference in his diary until July 7th to the possibility that was haunting his mind. But that night, after a dinner party at 10 Downing Street for the King, the Prime Minister again raised the matter:

" After the King had left, the P.M. kept us on till 1.30 a.m. Finally when we were saying good-bye he took me off into the garden of 10 Downing Street in the dark, and again told me that he wanted me to take over the Supreme Command of operations out of this country. But that I was to stop on as C.I.G.S. till January or February, and that I should only take over if it looked pretty certain that the operation was possible. He could not have been nicer, and said that I was the only man he had sufficient confidence in to take over the job."

' This time he was actually mentioning a suggested date for my take-over, a date only just over half a year ahead. I was too excited to go to sleep when I returned home, and kept on turning the thought over and over in my mind. Was Fate going to allow me to command the force destined to play

[1] *Diary*, 15th June, 1943.
[2] *Diary*, 19th June, 1943.

the final part in the strategy I had been struggling for? It seemed too much to hope for that the strategy should plan out as I had wanted and that, in addition, I should command the forces destined for the final blow. Fortunately, I realized well all the factors that might yet influence the final decision and did not let my optimism carry me off my feet.'[1]

For the ultimate decision, Brooke knew, would not rest with the Prime Minister only, but with the President of the United States and the Combined Chiefs of Staff.

Even now, when his chief's proposal had become an offer, Brooke did not tell his wife. It was left to Churchill to do so a week later at a Downing Street sherry party:

" P.M. then asked you how you liked the idea of my becoming Supreme Commander of the invasion of France. And I had not yet told you anything about it, as it was still all so distant and indecisive."[2]

Accustomed, for all the hopes and anxieties he confided to his diary, to hide every thought under a mask, this most reticent of men concealed the offer and what it meant to him from everyone, and never even mentioned it to his British, or later, his American colleagues.[3] Nor would he allow his hopes to disturb his inner calm. During his hours of relaxation he continued to put the war out of his mind and to seek peace in his family and love of nature. A few days after the Prime Minister had first suggested that he should command the Liberation Armies, he took a step he had been contemplating for some time and called at a second-hand bookshop to invest a proportion of his modest capital in a magnificent set of Gould's bird-books. " It remains to be seen," he noted that night, " whether my forecast of the set going up in value comes true." ' My purchase of Gould's " Birds," ' he wrote afterwards, ' was a big venture. There were forty-five volumes for

---

[1] *Notes on My Life*, IX, 733.
[2] *Diary*, 14th July, 1943.
[3] " There were reports that Churchill had promised this choice assignment to his own Staff Chief, Sir Alan Brooke, although Brooke never told any of us about it. He undoubtedly would have been a good commander." *Leahy*, 212.

which I gave just over £1500, but my forecast was correct and at the end of the war I sold these books for twice their cost. Meanwhile I had had wonderful value from them as an antidote to the war. . . . Whilst looking at Gould's wonderful pictures I was able to forget everything connected with the war.' When that July on his sixtieth birthday—the day on which he should have passed from the Active Army List—he was given a birthday cake with sixty candles by his American friend, Admiral Stark, he bore it home on the following Saturday for a grand birthday tea with his children.

·   ·   ·   ·   ·   ·   ·   ·

It was not only from his personal hopes and fears that Brooke sought escape that summer. When he returned to England only five weeks remained before the day fixed for the greatest amphibious operation ever undertaken in the history of war— one for which he was primarily responsible, for which he had struggled, first with his political chief, then with his British colleagues and lastly with the Americans, and on whose success he believed the whole future of the war depended. If it triumphed and was followed up, victory would be in sight; if it aborted and the Allies failed to establish their southern continental bridgehead, the prospects of the far more difficult operation in the West planned for 1944 would be bleak indeed. It was a venture of extreme complexity, more so even than " Torch " which had preceded it by eight months. It involved transporting in more than two thousand ships, under an escort of twelve hundred naval vessels, including eight battleships and two aircraft-carriers, a force of 160,000 men with 1800 guns, 600 tanks and 14,000 other vehicles. These had to be carried through waters heavily mined, guarded by U-boats, a powerful battle-fleet and German and Italian air forces operating from shore airfields, to storm open beaches and conquer an island defended by more than twice as many troops, a substantial part of them German. Everything depended on the most meticulous planning, on complete control of the sea approaches and on mastery of the air, not only over the invasion beaches and Sicily itself but over the straits dividing it from the mainland, across which additional German and Italian divisions could be ferried to reinforce those already on the island.

The early days of planning " Husky " had been attended by grave difficulties, partly owing to the fact that the senior officers most responsible for its execution—Eisenhower, Alexander, Montgomery, Andrew Cunningham, and Tedder—were all fully engaged until May in liquidating the quarter of a million Axis troops still defending the island's outer approaches in Africa. The first plans put forward by the Allied planners had aroused the scathing criticism of that outspoken realist, General Montgomery—the man who, under Alexander's command, was to lead the British half of the landing forces. " A dog's breakfast," he had described one of these in a private letter to Alan Brooke; " it breaks every commonsense rule of practical fighting and would have no chance of success. . . . Unless someone will face up to this problem and give a decision there will be a first-class disaster." " My remarks on the plan," he wrote again at the end of April, " have caused a most frightful tornado and it is clear to me that I am regarded as a most unpleasant person. . . . They want me to operate in little brigade-groups all over the place, and I refuse. . . . We cannot go on this way. Unless we get a good plan and a firm plan at once on which we can all work there will be no ' Husky ' in July."[1]

After the fall of Tunis these difficulties had been resolved. Thanks to the statesmanship of Eisenhower and Alexander—the overall operational commander of the expedition—synthesis had been reached between the military requirements of Montgomery and those of the Anglo-American naval and air commanders. Though the final plan adopted was not wholly to Montgomery's satisfaction—for owing to American doubts about the future of the Mediterranean campaign it failed to define the objectives of the two Armies sufficiently clearly—it embodied three principles which he had laid down for any disputed landing in territory held by German troops, and on which he, Cunningham and Tedder, though each approaching it from the angle of his own Arm, were agreed: that it must be made by a well-concentrated and integrated

[1] Montgomery to Brooke, 30th April, 1943. Lord Alanbrooke, *Personal Files.*

force on a coast where sufficient fighters, shore-based or carrier-borne, could protect the transports and landing-parties from air interference; that it must enable the invaders to capture, within a few hours of landing, airfields from which to maintain air ascendancy; and that it must secure, within reasonable time, at least one deep-water port through which to build up strength before the enemy could counter-attack.[1] Instead, therefore, of attempting, as had been first proposed, two widely separated landings at either end of the island, it was agreed that the British Eighth Army should go ashore in the Gulf of Noto and astride the Pachino peninsula in the extreme south-eastern corner close to the port of Syracuse, while the American Seventh Army under General Patton should storm the beaches immediately to the west to secure the all-important airfields of the Gulf of Gela. Then, with their inner flanks mutually protected and with air-cover assured over the battlefield, the two armies were to strike northwards from their adjacent beach-heads, the British along the eastern coastal plain to capture the ports of Syracuse, Augusta and Catania, the Americans through the hilly interior to cut the Palermo-Messina road on the north coast and then having secured Palermo as a base, to turn eastwards towards the Messina Straits—the gateway to the Italian mainland.

Apart from the ever-present problem of the enemy guessing the destination of the armada assembling in the ports of North Africa, Brooke's main anxiety during the waiting weeks between his return to England and the Sicilian landing was lest his master and American colleagues would involve the United Nations in some new operation which, by deflecting shipping and resources, should prevent them from seizing the almost boundless opportunities that would follow the capture of Sicily. In addition to America's Pacific ventures and Marshall's demands for early action in Burma, a new distraction had arisen in June from a proposal of Admiral King's at the Trident Conference that Britain should seize the Azores as an air and anti-submarine base to safeguard transatlantic communications for the invasion of France. At the Cabinet's instance

[1] Field-Marshal Montgomery, *El Alamein to the River Sangro*, 87-8.

it had been agreed that a diplomatic approach to Portugal should precede such high-handed action, but this had introduced a new complication, since the Portuguese, though sympathetic, were naturally anxious to know what help the Allies could send them in the event of the Germans retaliating by invading the Peninsula. At a time when every available vessel and landing-craft was going to be mortgaged for months ahead both for the build-up of the Sicilian invasion and for the assault on Italy which Brooke hoped would follow, this proved a serious embarrassment, for, with their love of expeditions, both the Prime Minister and President responded warmly to the idea. The latter even went so far as to discuss with the American Chiefs of Staff the substitution of a full-scale Peninsular campaign for a cross-Channel attack.[1] Several times that June and July this particular hare crossed the pages of Brooke's diary, with the Chiefs of Staff Committee in anxious pursuit.

> " *June 21st.* Now I have to go off for a P.M.'s meeting of C.O.S. at 10.30 p.m. to discuss implications of protective measures for Portugal in the event of occupying the Azores. I feel that we are not in a position to guarantee the security of Portugal."
>
> " *July 1st.* We were worried this morning with the repercussions on Portugal by proposed operations in the Azores and on attempts to get Portugal to hand over these islands to help us to overcome submarines. . . . This evening received two troublesome telegrams from the President to P.M. . . . "
>
> " *July 2nd.* . . . A long Chiefs of Staff meeting to consider a long telegram from the President. The first suggested sending a whole division, plus four hundred A.A. guns and some fourteen squadrons of fighters, to support Portugal in the event of Salazar granting us facilities in the Azores for submarine-hunting aircraft. Such action, to my mind, inevitably endangers our relations with Spain. . . . The whole situation is very dangerous and we may well find ourselves driven into a Peninsular war against our

[1] *Leahy,* 197-8.

wishes. . . . At 3 p.m. I went round to 10 Downing Street
for a two-hour meeting with the P.M. We warded off all
the immediate dangers, but I am not certain that he
realises yet all the dangers that lie ahead of us in connection
with our Azores policy."

.　　.　　.　　.　　.　　.　　.　　.

As, owing to shortage of shipping and landing-craft, it proved
impossible to launch the invasion in June, the Sicilian landing
had been fixed for the earliest favourable moon period in July.
While the ships were being mustered and loaded in the ports
of North Africa and Egypt and even in distant Britain and
America, the Allied Mediterranean air forces—267 squadrons
strong, 146 of them American and 121 British—maintained a
continuous bombardment of military installations, airfields and
communications, not only in Sicily and Italy, but, in order to
deceive the enemy, on every Axis-held coast and island in the
Mediterranean. Carried out from Malta and North Africa, it
was the most extensive air attack that had ever preceded a
land campaign. During June the island fortresses of Pantellaria
and Lampedusa between the North African coast and Sicily
were pounded into surrender with their Italian garrisons of
15,000 men, and the little rock island of Gozo off Malta was
miraculously turned into an air base by American engineers
working at unheard-of speed after the more hidebound British
had declared the feat impossible. By the end of the first week of
July ten of the twelve Axis airfields in southern Sicily had been
put out of action, four of the five train-ferries across the Straits
of Messina sunk, and the Luftwaffe and Regia Aeronautica all
but driven from the skies.

.　　.　　.　　.　　.　　.　　.　　.

On July 5th the Germans opened their long-awaited Eastern
offensive. Throwing more than thirty divisions, seventeen of
them armoured, against either side of the Russian salient near
Kursk, they applied, for the fifth summer running, the familiar
and formerly irresistible tactics of the *blitzkrieg*. Two days
after their attack commenced two thousand British and
American ships, supported by a vast fleet and over four

thousand aircraft, began to converge on Sicily from every port in North Africa. By daylight on July 9th the vast, slow-moving convoys, guided by a single hand, were converging on either side of Malta—those carrying the American Seventh Army to the west of the island and those carrying the British Eighth Army to the east. During the day the wind freshened steadily, reaching gale force by evening and heaping huge breakers on the southern Sicilian beaches where the Americans were to land. Operational direction of the expedition had been vested in Alexander, Cunningham and Tedder, and] the Supreme Commander, awaiting the issue in Malta, had at this critical stage of the proceedings only the power to call them off. Yet with the moral courage he had shown before " Torch " and was to show on a still greater occasion, Eisenhower never flinched and supported Cunningham's bold decision to allow the armada to proceed. His firmness was rewarded in the night by a sudden drop in the wind which left nothing worse at daybreak than a heavy swell. A few of the smaller craft were late at their landing stations but, as the enemy had been thrown off his guard by the weather, resistance on the beaches was far slighter than had been expected and casualties comparatively few. The new American swimming load-carrier or " D.U.K.W." was an enormous success and made the build-up on the beaches far quicker than anyone a short while before could have conceived possible. Only the British airborne brigade, making its first landing in enemy territory, met with disaster.[1] Nearly half its gliders were lost at sea, many of the crews being drowned, and only twelve out of a hundred and thirty-seven landed anywhere near the vital bridge on the road to Syracuse which was their objective. Yet eight officers and sixty-five men held the bridge for twelve hours and, when the last nineteen survivors had been driven from it, the advance-guard from the nearest beachhead was close enough to recapture it before it could be destroyed. Meanwhile their comrades of the American parachute brigade, who had also been blown far from their objectives, caused such

---

[1] As a result partly of the gale, partly of a mistaken decision—taken against General Browning's advice—to use gliders instead of parachutes, and partly of inadequate training of the American tug-pilots, who had only a few days in which to practise the operation with the pilots of the gliders, R. Seth, *Lion with Blue Wings*, 25-9, 36-9, 70-81; *The Royal Air Force 1939-1945* (H.M.S.O.), II, 308-9.

confusion throughout the area in which they descended that they contributed almost as much to victory as if they had dropped directly on to the airfields and key-points they had been sent to capture.

.   .   .   .

Far away in England the man who had been primarily responsible for bringing all this to pass set down in his diary what it meant to him:

> " *July 9th, 1943.* . . . To-night the attack on Sicily starts and thank heaven the suspense will be over. It has been getting more and more trying waiting for operations to start. . . ."

> " *July 10th.* A thrilling day with reports of Sicily coming in. Few people, if any, realize what the weight of responsibility of this attack is like. . . . Now it remains to prove that I was right or wrong. Anyhow the start has been good."

By the evening it was known that the initial assault had succeeded and that both British and Americans, having achieved tactical surprise, were pushing ahead fast. Syracuse, the first port, was captured intact that night. Brooke was able to spend Sunday the 11th

> " peacefully at home moving bookcases and working hard at repairing the Pook's goat-cart to keep my mind occupied and my thoughts away from Sicily. Reports all good, thank heaven."

" Back to work as usual," he wrote next day. " Reports from Sicily continue to be good. Cabinet at 6 p.m. when I had to give full account of operations." By then the whole south-eastern corner of the island, including the port of Augusta, had been captured by the British, while the Americans, after taking the airfields and repelling a German armoured attack on the beachhead, had started their drive towards the centre and west, so isolating the large Italian force which had been expecting a landing in the neighbourhood of Palermo.

During the next four days, while the build-up of reserves

and supplies—the most difficult part of the operation—proceeded with little interruption, the Eighth Army fought its way northwards through the closely cultivated Catanian plain, where the Hermann Goering division was resisting fiercely. By now twelve airfields were in Allied hands, with more than a thousand enemy aircraft lying destroyed or damaged on them. Opposition in the air had become negligible, and by the 16th Brooke was able to write:

> " News from Sicily continues to be good, and thank heaven for it. I do not know what I should have done if things had gone badly."

Only four days before the landing, with the implementation of his concentric-strategy still in the balance, he had noted in his diary:

> " U.S.A. look at present like trying to close Mediterranean theatre if they can after Sicily. We must wait and see how Sicily operations go and what I can do at next Combined Chiefs of Staff meeting."[1]

Now, with the invasion's success following hard on the triumphs of Tunis, " Torch " and Alamein, the significance of the attack from the south was becoming obvious to all, and on Sunday the 18th, just over a week after the landing, to Brooke's intense relief Eisenhower cabled his recommendation to the Combined Chiefs of Staff that, as soon as they had taken Messina, they should follow up their victory by crossing the straits and carrying the war to the mainland. He also proposed that an attack on the toe and heel of Italy should be accompanied by a landing in Salerno Bay, nearly two hundred miles up the coast, in order to cut off the defenders of Calabria and seize the port of Naples.

All next day, Monday the 19th, while their transatlantic colleagues debated the issue in Washington, the British Chiefs

---

[1] *Diary*, 5th July, 1943. Three days earlier, Churchill had written in a minute for the C.O.S. Committee, " We cannot allow the Americans to prevent our powerful armies from having full employment. Their Staffs seem now to be wriggling away to the idea of Sardinia. We must stiffen them all up and allow no weakness. I trust the Chiefs of Staff will once again prevent through the Combined Chiefs of Staff this weak shuffling away from the issue." *Churchill*, V, 570.

of Staff and Prime Minister were considering the form the attack should take.

" A long C.O.S. trying to decide what our next best plan should be after Sicily. We were examining attempting attack direct on Naples. Air cover bad and dependent on carriers; also put forward by Joint Planners with only three divisions, quite inadequate. Rate of build-up also slower than that of the Germans. Unfortunately Intelligence Branch are not good at deciding probable enemy moves."

" Busy afternoon in office followed by Cabinet at 6 p.m. when luckily news of Sicily was good and cheerful. At 8.30 p.m. received new appreciation of attack on Naples which I studied till 9.30 p.m. A bad paper again. We then met as Chiefs of Staff till 10.30 p.m., when P.M., Eden, Attlee and Oliver Lyttelton came along to discuss prospects. . . . Winston on the whole very open to reason, and on the right lines. We shall have a busy time to knock it into some shape to wire out to Eisenhower, and to bring Marshall along with us without frightening him out of the Mediterranean."

Though he had always been opposed to Britain's concentric strategy, the American Chief of Army Staff had given his word that, if the Sicilian campaign ended quickly enough to allow of further operations without prejudicing the build-up of "Round-up," an attack should be made on Italy. He was a man of the strictest honour, and on Tuesday he and his colleagues gave their consent. To the surprise of London, both he and King opted for the bolder course of a landing in Salerno Bay, King because as a sailor a leap across sea seemed the right way to attack a long, narrow peninsula, Marshall because it afforded a hope of terminating the Mediterranean campaign quickly and releasing the forces there for an all-out cross-Channel attack. The Prime Minister, who favoured all bold courses, was naturally delighted. " Why," he asked, " crawl up the leg like a harvest bug from the ankle upwards? Let us rather strike at the knee."

The difficulty, however, of such an operation, which was only just within range of shore-based fighter-cover, was that it would require more carriers than the Allies possessed in the Mediterranean and far more assault-craft. Most of the landing-vessels assembled for the invasion of Sicily were either fully engaged in supplying the forces on the island or were refitting in North African ports after the damage they had suffered during the initial landings. Others, as a result of decisions taken at the " Trident " Conference in May, were scheduled for early return to the United Kingdom or for despatch to Burma. While welcoming the proposal for an attack on Naples, the British Chiefs of Staff, therefore, urged their American colleagues to agree to a standstill of all forces already in that sea and the immediate allocation of additional carriers and assault-craft to enable Eisenhower to strike before the Italians could recover from the confusion into which the Sicilian victories had thrown them. " Our C.O.S. meeting," Brooke wrote on the 20th, " was mainly concerned with adjusting future planning in accordance with last night's meeting with the P.M. We drafted a telegram for Washington supporting Marshall's aspirations for Naples, but pointing out that this must entail certain changes and retentions in the Mediterranean at the expense of operations in Burma and across the Channel. This will not be greeted with great joy."[1]

Two days later Brooke was still hoping for an agreement that would exploit the success won.

> " A strenuous day. Started with a usual meeting with Joint Planners at the C.O.S. when we discussed the Naples attack and its prospects of success. Came to the conclusion that it was a gamble, but probably one worth taking."

On that day the great Sicilian port of Palermo was captured by General Patton's Seventh Army, and all Italy was in a state of the wildest alarm following a daylight raid on the 19th on the marshalling yards and principal airfield at Rome by more than five hundred Flying Fortresses and Liberators. Meanwhile the German summer offensive, launched at the precise point where the Russians were expecting it, had dwindled and failed, and the Russians themselves had taken the offensive

[1] *Diary*, 20th July, 1943.

near Orel. All the auspices were, therefore, favourable to
striking hard, and with everything available, in the one
theatre where American and British forces were at present
deployed.

But in their *idée fixe* that the British were trying to use the
Mediterranean campaign as an alternative to a cross-Channel
invasion, the Americans had insisted during the " Trident "
Conference on a schedule of firm logistical commitments and of
troop and ship movements that should make it impossible for
their allies to evade their obligations. To these they now
insisted on adhering. The British request was met by a rigid
refusal to modify the timetable of two months before. Eisenhower and Alexander, London was told, must make do with
what they had. Three American heavy-bomber groups, four
American and three British divisions, and the bulk of the
landing-craft were to return, as arranged, to England so as to
make sure they would be available for an operation that was
not to take place for nearly a year and whose success was
dependent on the extent to which the Allies exploited their
present opportunity of drawing the German reserves into the
South. On the 24th, Brooke noted sadly,

> " A very disappointing wire from American Chiefs of
> Staff. Marshall absolutely fails to realize the strategic
> treasures that lie at our feet in the Mediterranean and
> hankers after cross-Channel operations. He admits
> that our object must be to eliminate Italy and yet is always
> afraid of facing the consequences of doing so. . . ."

.   .   .   .

The reason for this refusal would have seemed clearer to
Brooke and his colleagues if they could have seen the report
which the American Secretary of State for War, then in London,
was preparing for the President. This high-minded but dog-
matic septuagenarian was a staunch admirer of Marshall and
had never wavered in his belief, so correct in 1918 when they
had served together under Pershing in France, that everything
ought to be concentrated on a single Western Front. He
regarded the invasion of Sicily as an unfortunate diversion like

the Salonica expedition in the first war and, though he greatly admired, was deeply suspicious of the Prime Minister, seeing him, in the light of his own undeviating faith in the Second Front, as a dangerous heretic and Brooke as his mere loyal echo. How completely he failed to understand the latter's strategy of weakening the enemy at every point of his over-extended circumference before striking at the most vulnerable, is revealed by a sentence in his autobiography about the President's attitude at the " Trident " Conference: that " he insisted that the first problem was to plan the landing in northern France; when that had been done it would be possible to see what supplies and troops were available for other operations."[1] For to Stimson the only effect of such entangle-ments, as he called them, was to deflect resources from " Round-up." They seemed merely indications that the British were " stalling " on their promises.

While he was in England that July inspecting American troops, Stimson had called on General Morgan or COSSAC— the Chief cross-Channel planner. From him and his American Deputy, General Barker, he had secured, or at any rate supposed he had secured, an admission that grave delays in the invasion programme might be caused by " getting too deep into commit-ments in the Mediterranean." With this confirmation of his fears in his pocket he had several conversations with the Prime Minister whom he found delighted with Marshall's readiness to back a landing at Salerno. " He took this," Stimson reported, " as an endorsement by Marshall of his whole Italian policy." The American Secretary for War pointed out that Marshall had only proposed it as a short-cut " to hasten the completion of the Italian adventure so that there would be no danger of clashing with the preparations for ' Round-hammer ' "—Stimson's slightly confused name for the Second Front. He even telephoned Marshall to obtain a confirmation of this view, subsequently repeating his conversation with him to Churchill.

The effect was disastrous. Argument on strategic matters was meat and drink to the Prime Minister, and he embarked on an impassioned disquisition that confirmed Stimson's worst

[1] *Stimson*, 225.

fears. " He at once," the latter wrote, " broke out into a new attack upon ' Roundhammer.' The check received by the British attack at Catania, Sicily, during the past few days had evidently alarmed him. He referred to it and praised the superlative fighting ability of the Germans. He said that if he had fifty thousand men ashore on the French Channel coast, he would not have an easy moment because he would feel that the Germans could rush up sufficient forces to drive them back into the sea. He repeated assertions he had made to me in previous conversations as to the disastrous effect of having the Channel full of corpses of defeated allies. This stirred me up and for a few minutes we had it hammer and tongs. I directly charged him that he was not in favour of the ' Roundhammer ' operation and that such statements as he made were ' like hitting us in the eye ' in respect to a project which we had all deliberately adopted and in which we were comrades. . . . On this he said that, while he admitted that if he was Commander-in-Chief he would not set up the ' Roundhammer ' operation, yet having made his pledge he would go through with it loyally. I then told him that, while I did not at all question the sincerity of his promise to go with us, I was afraid he did not make sufficient allowance for the necessary long-distance planning and I feared that fatal curtailments might be made impulsively in the vain hope that those curtailments could be later repaid. . . . When I parted with him, I felt that, if pressed by us, he would sincerely go ahead with the ' Roundhammer ' commitment but that he was looking so constantly and vigorously for an easy way of ending the war without a trans-Channel assault that, if we expected to be ready for a ' Roundhammer ' which would be early enough in 1944 to avoid the dangers of bad weather, we must be constantly on the lookout against Mediterranean diversions."[1]

Having thus fortified his innate suspicions of the British leader's intentions, the old statesman—now close on his 76th birthday—flew to Africa where, according to his own account, he obtained Eisenhower's confirmation of his view that the only worthwhile objective in Italy was the Foggia airfields for bombing Austria and the Ploesti oil-wells. In his diary, how-

[1] *Stimson*, 225-6.

ever, the Supreme Commander's naval aide-de-camp, Captain Butcher, presented a rather different view of the visit, in which it seems that Stimson subjected Eisenhower to much the same kind of "high-pressure inquisition against the exploitation of the Sicilian victory as Churchill had done a few weeks before in favour of it." "He felt," Butcher wrote, "that the Prime Minister was obsessed with the idea of proving to history that invasion of the Continent by way of the Balkans was wise strategy and would repair whatever damage history now records for Churchill's misfortune at the Dardanelles in the last war. The Secretary seemed apprehensive lest the P.M. would seek to avoid the commitment of the British and American Governments to invade France next spring. The P.M. had repeatedly referred to corpses floating in the Channel. What the Secretary wanted from Ike was his opinion, because he had to hurry home to express, not only Ike's, but his own views to General Marshall and the President before the next meeting of the Combined Chiefs at Quebec." "Ike," continued Butcher, "was confronted with a difficult situation. If he fails to exploit what now appears to be a rapidly approaching victory over Italy, history will say that he "missed the boat," yet our own Government seems to want to slam on the brake just when the going gets good."[1]

By the time, however, that Stimson reached Algiers, the Italian situation had taken the course that Brooke had predicted to Marshall and Eisenhower in May. On the morning of July 26th, before the Supreme Commander sat down to his breakfast, he received dramatic news. A week earlier, on the day on which Rome had been bombed by the Americans, a meeting had taken place near Rimini between Mussolini and Hitler, in the course of which the latter had exhorted his fellow-dictator to turn Sicily into a second Stalingrad. But when that night Mussolini returned to the capital, he had been greeted by clouds of smoke from the bombed railway yards and by a sullen Court and populace. Five days later, on July 24th, the Grand Council of the Fascist Party met. During the meeting the Duce was violently attacked by several of his leading supporters and a resolution was carried calling on

[1] *Butcher*, 317.

the King to assume greater powers. On the evening of Sunday 25th, the latter received Mussolini in audience. He told him that the country had gone to bits, that Army morale had reached rock bottom and that the soldiers did not want to fight. As the protesting Dictator left, he was arrested by Carabinieri acting under secret orders from the High Command. That night Rome radio broadcast to the world the news that the King had entrusted the task of forming a new Government to the 71-year-old Marshal Badoglio, a known critic of the Fascist régime.

Meanwhile, after a quiet Sunday morning at home, Brooke had left Hartley Wintney with his wife to spend the night at Chequers. " We found," he wrote,

> " Winston, Clemmie, Mary, Sarah, Cherwell, Martin, etc. . . . Before dinner Winston took me off to a seat in the orchard where . . . he discussed future Mediterranean strategy. We are both in complete agreement but fully realize the trouble we shall have with the Americans. After dinner we had a film, ' *Sous les toits de Paris*.' In the middle came news of Mussolini's abdication. Winston dashed off to talk with Eden. A memorable moment and at least a change-over from ' the end of the beginning' to ' the beginning of the end.' Escaped to bed by 1.30 a.m."[1]

. . . .

The British Prime Minister and Chief of Imperial General Staff were not the only people who sat up late that night discussing Mussolini's fall. The Fuehrer, who had bidden his fellow-dictator farewell only six days before, was in conference at his East Prussian Headquarters when the news came. His first thought was to order a panzer division to " drive without any ado into Rome and arrest the Government, the King—the whole bag of them—especially the Crown Prince and Badoglio."[2] Then, remembering that for the moment he had immobilized his entire available armour in the abortive Kursk offensive and that the Russians were now attacking on the centre front, he

[1] *Diary*, 25th July, 1943. [2] *Struggle for Europe*, 133.

decided to hold his hand and temporize with the new Italian Government until he had reorganized his eastern front and could spare a dozen of his best divisions to deal with the situation. In the meantime, he announced, he would withdraw the 70,000 Germans defending Sicily, abandon the toe of Italy and so avoid the danger of having them cut off by a British-American landing, while Rommel, whom he had recently sent to that country to organise its defence, should form a line across the Apennines from Pisa to Rimini. Yet within twenty-four hours his views had changed again. Fearful of exposing the Balkans, where the guerillas were growing increasingly active, to an Allied invasion across the Adriatic, he decided to postpone the evacuation of Sicily and hold the island and southern Italy with the German troops already there until he could reinforce them from Russia. " We must act at once," he declared, " or the Anglo-Saxons will steal a march on us by occupying the airfields."[1]

It was an alarming moment for the Axis. That week-end Goebbels' diary became a litany of woes. " It is simply shocking," he wrote, " to think that a revolutionary movement that has been in power for twenty-one years could be liquidated in such a way." The Pope, he reported, was intriguing against Germany, Stalin had issued an order of the day claiming the Wehrmacht's summer offensive had failed, reprisals against England had been delayed by the beating the Luftwaffe had taken in Sicily, a former Prime Minister of Bulgaria had criticised the German alliance in that satellite's parliament. There was even criticism in Germany itself; " the letters addressed to me . . . keep asking why the Fuehrer does not visit the bombed areas, why Goering is nowhere to be seen, and especially why the Fuehrer doesn't talk to the German people and explain the present situation." " One worry after another piles up on us," the Doctor complained, " and we hardly know how to meet them."[2]

As for the air-raids from Britain, they now reached a new climax of horror. At the end of June Brooke had attended a conference to consider a new technical means to counter the German air defences. " A debatable point," he wrote, " as the

[1] *Hinsley*, 228-9. [2] Goebbels, 25th, 27th July, 1943.

weapon is two-edged and can be turned on us. However, in view of heavy losses by Bomber Command we decided to make use of it. I hope that we may have been right."[1] This device called " Window," which consisted of dropping strips of tinfoil to confuse the enemy's Radar readings, was again discussed at a Chiefs of Staff meeting on July 15th attended by the Prime Minister, his scientific adviser, Lord Cherwell, and the Home Secretary, Herbert Morrison, who was deeply concerned by the reports of Germany's new secret weapons. In view of their menace and the urgency of striking at her war industry while the Allies held the initiative, it was felt that Air Marshal Harris's plea to be allowed to employ "Window" could no longer be refused.

The result was sensational. On the night of Saturday July 24th, Hamburg—the second city and largest port in the Reich —was attacked by more than seven hundred aircraft dropping showers of metallic strips to jam the Radar stations controlling the night-fighters. It was completely successful. Only twelve bombers were lost or less than two per cent of the force despatched. 2,396 tons of high explosive and incendiary bombs were dropped, the dockyards were gravely damaged, and fires started which burnt for twenty-four hours. Next morning— it was the Sunday of Mussolini's fall—sixty-eight American Flying Fortresses again bombed the port. That night more than six hundred aircraft of Bomber Command dropped over 2000 tons of bombs on Essen, rendering 35,000 people homeless and doing such damage to the Krupps works that when Gustav Krupp saw the devastation in the morning he had a fit.

Two nights later a further raid on Hamburg took place in which the city suffered a disaster, in the words of the German official report, " beyond all human imagination." Freed from the enemy fighters, whose control stations were completely unable to locate the invaders, Harris's bombers saturated the defences with a storm of high explosive and incendiary bombs that turned the air in the burning streets into "a fire typhoon such as was never before witnessed, against which every human resistance was quite useless."[2] A third raid followed on the night of the 29th. In all more than 7000 tons of bombs

[1] *Diary*, 23rd June, 1943.
[2] From a German secret document quoted by Marshal of the R.A.F. Sir Arthur Harris in his *Bomber Offensive*, 174. " Trees three feet thick were broken

were dropped, twelve square miles of the city were burnt out, and three quarters of its inhabitants driven from their homes. Albert Speer reported to the Fuehrer that a continuation of attacks on such a scale would cripple the will of the populace to sustain armament production and bring about a rapid end of the war.[1]

.   .   .   .

Throughout the last week of July, while Hamburg was blazing in the north and in the south the invaders of Sicily prepared to storm the German defences around Mount Etna, the political and military leaders of Britain and the United States were debating across the Atlantic the steps necessary to exploit Mussolini's fall. Hopes that the conquest of the island would be completed by the end of the month had been dashed by stubborn German resistance before Catania and by a certain lack of co-ordination between the Seventh and Eighth Armies, due to Washington's refusal to agree to any plan of operations against Italy before the Sicilian landings. While the British were halted in the rocky hill country before Mount Etna by four German divisions in ideal defensive positions, Patton's Americans, instead of wheeling right to outflank the volcano from the north, had swung left to overrun the rest of the island, capturing with splendid élan the ports of Palermo and Marsala and nearly a hundred thousand Italians. But the latter had by now little heart for the fight and were ready to surrender in any case, and the expedition's strategic objective—the strait dividing the island from the mainland—had been temporarily forgotten. It was not till the end of the month that the victorious Seventh Army turned eastwards to start to fight its

---

off or uprooted, human beings were thrown to the ground or flung alive into the flames by winds which exceeded 150 miles an hour. The panic-stricken citizens knew not where to turn. Flames drove them from the shelters, but high-explosive bombs sent them scurrying back again. Once inside, they were suffocated by carbon-monoxide poisoning and their bodies reduced to ashes as though they had been placed in a crematorium, which was indeed what each shelter proved to be. The fortunate were those who jumped into the canals and waterways and remained swimming or standing up to their necks in water for hours until the heat should die down." *The Royal Air Force 1939-1945* (H.M.S.O.), III, 9. "It must," Harris wrote, "have been even more cataclysmic than the bursting of the two atom bombs over Japanese cities."

[1] *Bomber Offensive*, 176.

way towards Messina through the hills between Mount Etna and the sea.

Because they lacked the landing-craft and carriers to strike at the enemy's exposed communications, not only along the rocky coasts of north-east Sicily but along the whole length of western Italy, the Allies could not seize the immense opportunity presented to them. They had nearly a million fighting men in the Mediterranean, but were unable at that crucial moment to deploy them. The tactics which MacArthur was pursuing with such brilliant success against the Japanese in New Guinea could not be used against the isolated Germans in Italy because the additional assault-vessels which would have made the six-hundred-mile-long peninsula a death trap for them were on the far side of the globe executing King's Pacific strategy. Most of the craft used in the original invasion of Sicily were now refitting for the descent on Salerno Bay, while others, in accordance with decisions reached two months before at Washington, were scheduled for early despatch to England and India. Except for a few small-scale landings of battalion strength behind the enemy's lines on the Sicilian coast, nothing could be done to exploit the command of the sea-approaches to southern Europe which the Allies had won. Brooke's trump card against the Axis's over-extended and almost defenceless Mediterranean littoral could not be played.

Thus, at the very moment that the new Italian Government, trembling between the German devil and the British deep sea, was seeking a way to escape the former by yielding to the latter, the pressure on Italy relaxed. Eisenhower wanted to offer the Italians an easy and honourable way out—a " white alley," as he called it—in return for immediate use of their airfields and strategic strong-points. Roosevelt, and to a lesser degree, Churchill, stuck to the former's formula of "unconditional surrender." In the end, after the Chiefs of Staff in London had discussed the matter on five successive days and the Prime Minister had called the War Cabinet out of bed at half-past one in the morning of July 30th and kept them up till four, the two Governments decided that, while the Supreme Commander must await the first overture from the Badoglio Government, he should be allowed to issue a radio appeal over its head to the Italian people. He was also given instructions as to the terms on which an armistice, if sought, could be granted. He was to insist on the immediate return of all Allied prisoners—a point that particularly concerned the British who had 74,000 men in Italian prison camps—the surrender of the Italian Fleet and Air Force, the withdrawal of all garrisons from Greece and the Balkans, and the occupation of Corsica, the Dodecanese and the chief strategic points on the mainland.

But the one indispensable condition for surrender was lacking —the ability of the Allies to land their forces in the heart of Italy. Without this the Italians, anxious though they were for peace, dared not make it, for to do so would be to expose themselves to the vengeance of the Germans. The bulk of their Army had either been captured in Africa or was garrisoning the Balkans, and there were only twelve weak divisions in the entire peninsula, armed with obsolescent tanks and guns. The Germans had already eight divisions there, four of them armoured.

What the Badoglio Government needed to enable it to yield was an Allied landing in the north of the peninsula to cut the German communications. Yet when two days after Mussolini's fall, Eisenhower, hoping to rush a division to Naples, tried to expedite the attack on Salerno bay, he was told by his planners that it would be logistically impossible for lack of assault-craft and carriers to land there before the second week in September. Even a crossing to the mainland across the narrow Messina strait would not be practicable for another four or five weeks. The great prize the Allies had fought so hard to win was still beyond their reach. And though the British Chiefs of Staff on their own initiative had ordered the whole of their disposable force in the Mediterranean basin to stand by in readiness for immediate operations against Italy, their American colleagues still refused to commit more than the scheduled proportion of resources to that sea. The most they would agree to was the temporary loan of three groups of heavy bombers from England to bomb the Rumanian oilfields.

To Brooke all this seemed tragic. The opportunity for which he had worked so long had come; everything had happened as he had predicted; the fruit was ripe for picking. ' We had left far behind,' he wrote,

' the period of stopping Marshall and the Americans from going across the Channel under entirely unsuitable conditions. We were beyond the days of coaxing them into North Africa and from there on into Sicily. We had made one million tons of shipping by opening up the Mediterranean; we had achieved a partial agreement for the elimination of Italy. . . . During this period Russia had held and was now beginning to show some offensive power. Bombing . . . . was gradually ripening up Germany for the final stages, whilst at sea the German submarines were being checked. In fact, all had gone admirably in our preliminary stages of preparations for the liberation of France.'

' We had now arrived in the orchard and our next step should be to shake the fruit trees and gather the apples. Southern Europe was now threatened on all sides. Italy was tottering and seeking for a way out of the war; all partisans in the Balkan States had been inspired by our successes and stirred to new activities; Turkey, which had for some time been sitting on the fence, was showing signs of leaning towards our side. Success breeds success in these cases, and the ball was at our feet. . . . What was wanted was to knock all the props from under the Germans in the defence of the Mediterranean; let them alone to bear the full burden. . . . Europe was just one large strategic front with German forces distributed round the perimeter in accordance with the existing threats in each respective theatre. Forces in France watched the Channel approaches, those in Norway and Denmark held down these countries; from there eastwards and southwards vast armies contained the Russians; in the south further detachments threatened Turkey and kept peace in the Balkans; whilst finally considerable force was employed in holding on to Italy and guarding southern France.'

' All these forces were handled centrally and served by the most perfect east and west railway system in existence—a system which had been built up in the first World War and reinforced by the *autobahn* system of roads. It was easier and quicker for the Germans to convey divisions from the Russian front to the French front than it was for us to convey similar formations from the Italian front by sea to the French front. The German north and south communications were, however, nothing like as efficient, comprising only one double line of railway through the leg of Italy and one through the Balkans to Greece.'

' Our strategy had now become a delicate matter of balancing. Our aim must be to draw as many divisions as possible from the French Channel and to retain them in southern Europe as long as possible. Any failure to take full advantage of our present position must also fail in drawing reserves away from the Channel. On the other hand, any tendency to weaken our forces in the Mediterranean would at once lead to the move of German forces to the Channel.'

' When arguing with Marshall I could never get him fully to appreciate the very close connection that existed between the various German fronts. For him they might have been separate wars, a Russian war on the one side, a Mediterranean war on another and a cross-Channel one to be started as soon as possible. I have often wondered since the war how different matters might have been if I had had MacArthur instead of Marshall to deal with. From everything I saw of him I put him down as the greatest general of the last war. He certainly showed a far greater strategic grasp than Marshall. I must, however, confess that Winston was no great help in the handling of Marshall, in fact the reverse. Marshall had a holy fear of Winston's Balkan and Dardanelles ventures, and was always guarding against these dangers even when they did not exist.'[1]

. . . .

Brooke was not well that summer. Since his influenza in the spring he had been increasingly feeling the strain of working under the unceasing pressure of a man of inexhaustible vitality invested with supreme political power, while having simul-

[1] *Notes on My Life*, X, 828-30.

taneously to direct a vast and complex military machine. " It has been very interesting," he wrote to a friend, a fortnight after his return from North Africa, " but travelling and working for Winston is not a rest cure; it is like living on the lip of a volcano and never knowing when it is going to erupt next. It is the night work after dinner till 1 a.m. with him that kills me."[1]

How long and crowded the C.I.G.S.'s days were can be seen by an extract from his diary at this time made a week before his sixtieth birthday. It was the day of the funeral of the Polish leader, General Sikorski, who had been killed in an air accident at Gibraltar while flying home from the Middle East.

> " *July 15th, 1943.* Commenced earlier, as Chiefs of Staff meeting was at 10 a.m. From 9 to 10 I dealt with a mass of wires on general situation, and the briefing for the C.O.S. Then meeting of C.O.S. with Joint Planners at which we discussed the future of the Mediterranean campaign. At 11.10 a.m. we all left for poor Sikorski's funeral at Westminster Cathedral. The service was too theatrical and fussy to stir up my feelings till the very end. But when I saw the empty stand where the coffin had been with six ' cierges ' burning round it, and on either flank representative ' colours ' of Regiments borne by officer parties, it struck me as a sad picture of Poland's plight; both its State and Army left without a leader when a change of the tide seems in sight. I was very fond of Sikorski personally and shall miss him badly."[2]

> " Went straight from Cathedral to Hendon to fly to Norfolk. Attending funerals in war of victims of air accidents is not a sustaining process to one's flying nerves, and should be avoided. Had a bumpy flight. Met by Hobart and taken to see his amphibious tanks . . . I finished with a sail in one of them. . . ."

> " Flew back to Hendon and put in very busy hour at

---

[1] To Major Nigel Aitken, 22nd June, 1943.

[2] ' I did not realise at that time what a loss Sikorski's death was going to be to the Poles in the future. He might not have saved the situation entirely in the end, but he had established a valuable contact with Stalin and might have done something to prevent the ghastly massacres of the Warsaw underground army.' *Notes on My Life,* IX, 732.

War Office. . . . Then at 10.30 had to go to 10 Downing Street for meeting of Chiefs of Staff with P.M., Herbert Morrison and Lord Cherwell . . . to discuss Morrison's claims for additional shelters to meet threat of German rocket. We then discussed next meeting with Americans in Quebec in early August, and finally again attacked East Asia Supreme Command. . . ."

" As I walked out feeling very weary, P.M. said, ' You look tired, C.I.G.S., are you doing too much? Don't go flying about too much.' Coming from him a remark like that means a lot and more than compensates for any extra strain."

" At last at 1.30 a.m. I am off to bed."

A few days later Brooke wrote again to Aitken: " I am feeling very cooked and have to pull out the whip to keep myself going round the course. However, the results of the work have been so encouraging lately that they have put new life into me. But you have no idea of the ' agony and bloody " sweat " ' that these offensives entail in their preparations. It is difficult enough at times to make up your mind as to what ought to be done, but it is infinitely more difficult to get that thing done once you have decided to go for it! Everyone seems to have an excellent reason why it should not be done, or for some mad scheme instead of it. I am getting very impatient in my old age and shall probably be sacked before long for insubordination! "[1]

Now once more, less than two months after his return from his six weeks' trip to Washington and North Africa, Brooke had to face the prospect of another 6,000-mile journey and a further prolonged Conference with his American colleagues to decide issues on which the whole future of the war depended. It had been agreed after " Trident " that the next meeting of the Combined Chiefs of Staff should be in London, and as late as July 18th Eisenhower had been expecting to fly to the British capital for it at the end of the month. But three days earlier the C.I.G.S. and his colleagues had been summoned by the Prime Minister to discuss a proposal of Roosevelt's for

[1] Gen. Brooke to Major Nigel Aitken. 29th July, 1943.

changing the venue to Quebec, so that the latter could attend it without leaving the Western Hemisphere. For the divergence in strategy between Great George Street and the Pentagon, brought to a head by the success of the Sicilian landings, could only be resolved at the highest level, and the Washington planners were determined not to be outwitted in London as they felt they had been a year before. They meant now to play their trump card. The time had come to discipline the British and their formidable, unaccountable leader by the growing numerical power and superior wealth of the United States and the immense prestige of the President.

Chapter Fourteen

QUEBEC

The power of Germany must be broken on the battlefields of Europe.

PRESIDENT ROOSEVELT

O N THE morning of Monday August 2nd, the British and American armies in Sicily resumed their offensive to capture the ports of Catania and Messina and clear the rest of the island. About the same time—it was August Bank Holiday—Brooke, after spending Sunday at Hartley Wintney, drove to London for three days of business before sailing from the Clyde to attend the " Quadrant " Conference at Quebec.

" *August 2nd, 1943.* Early rise. Found table crammed with messages about Italians prepared to surrender in Dodecanese, Crete, Balkans, etc.[1] Very long C.O.S. trying to decide how to deal with the Azores. We are again coming very near committing ourselves to come to the assistance of the Portuguese. C.O.S. lasted till 1.30 p.m."

". . . Long interview with Director of Military Operations, Deputy Chief of Imperial General Staff and Quartermaster-General, discussing what we could do in Italy. At 6 p.m. Cabinet that lasted till 8.20 p.m., and I then had to rush to the Dorchester to dine with Devers[2] and some Congressmen. From there I just escaped in time for a

---

[1] These much excited the Prime Minister, who minuted the C.O.S. that day. " Here is a business of great consequence to be thrust forward by every means. . . . This is no time for conventional establishments, but rather for using whatever fighting elements there are. Can anything be done to find at least a modicum of assault shipping without compromising the main operation against Italy? . . . Surely caiques and ships' boats can be used between ship and shore? " *Churchill,* V, 181.

[2] Gen. J. L. Devers, Commander-in-Chief, American Troops in United Kingdom.

Defence Committee meeting at 10.30 p.m. which lasted till 1.30 a.m. . . . Selborne there pleading for more aircraft for subversive operations. He asked the P.M. to approach the President with a view to securing more Liberators. P.M. replied: ' What you are after is for me to pull the teats off the cow! ' "

" Then discussed Portugal again with the Azores. . . . Finally telegram from America stating President was considering agreeing to Rome being an ' open town.' This was the climax of an unpleasant evening."

" *August 3rd.* . . . Long Chiefs of Staff meeting with difficult man-power problem, trying to arrive at proportional cut between land and air forces. As usual in such a case impossible to arrive at a decision. Then Doctor Soong came to see us to enquire on behalf of Chiang Kai-shek as to how we were getting on with preparations for operations in Burma. A delicate problem, as Doctor Soong was very inquisitive and there was a good deal to conceal from him. He remained for over an hour with us till close on 1.45 p.m."

" At 3 p.m. Ralston, Canadian Defence Minister, came to see me and remained nearly two hours. . . . Then Browning just back from Sicily and full of details of Airborne Forces and their landings, and work in the attack. After much hard work in the past they promise quite well for the future. Then Military Secretary for half an hour, and finally Weeks and Nye for discussions on many points. By then 8 p.m. and none of my trays empty of files. Consequently a long evening's work in front of me now."

" Preparations for departure to Quebec are moving on. . . . I hate going and dread the conferences in front of us; the work will be never-ending and very trying."

" *August 4th.* Another hard day continually on the rush. F. E. Morgan came to the C.O.S. meeting to discuss his plans for cross-Channel invasion, very over-optimistic in places. Had another heated argument with Chief of Air Staff on the question of finding the deficient man-power from either the Army or Air Force. We got no further."

" At 1 p.m. Cabinet meeting to discuss the President's
wires insisting on declaring Rome an ' open town.' Chiefs
of Staff and Cabinet all strongly opposed. Afternoon long
and interesting talk with Ramsay who gave me many side-
lights on various personalities connected with the Sicily
operations. Then a visit from Wingate back from Burma
to discuss his mobile column tactics."

Far removed from the battlefronts and longing to return to
active command, Brooke was always quick to respond to any
personal contact with the fighting men on whom, in the last
resort, all his plans depended. A few days earlier, between a
C.O.S. discussion on Italian truce terms and a long session
with his deputy on the military organisation of the proposed
South East Asia Command, he recorded an interview with

" a Quartermaster-Sergeant Cook of the Airborne Division
who put up a very fine fight against the Boche in Tunisia,
was captured, taken to Italy, dug tunnel for escape, was
caught, put into solitary confinement, beaten up, transferred to hospital, escaped, got into Vatican and was
finally repatriated home."[1]

He had been similarly thrilled a few weeks earlier by a talk
with two of Wingate's officers, who had just returned from the
Burmese jungle and whose account of the courage and endurance of British soldiers beyond the Chindwin had formed a
heartening contrast to the usual lugubrious tales from the
Japanese front about Army morale. Now he was able to talk
with their leader himself. ' I was very interested,' he wrote,

' in meeting Wingate. . . . He had originally been operating
in Abyssinia, after which he had a nervous breakdown. . . .
Amery had then asked me whether I would consider sending
him out to Burma where he might prove useful. I wired to
Wavell asking him whether he wanted him, and he replied
he could make use of him. He turned out a great success and
originated the Long-Range Penetration Forces which worked
right in Japanese-held territory. In the discussion I had with
him he explained that he considered that what he had done

[1] *Diary*, 29th July, 1943.

on a small scale could be run with much larger forces. He required, however, for these forces the cream of everything, the best men, the best N.C.O.s, the best officers, the best equipment and a large air-lift. I considered that the results of his form of attacks were certainly worth backing within reason. I provided him with all the contacts in England to obtain what he wanted, and told him that on my return from Canada I would go into the whole matter with him to see that he had obtained what he wanted.'[1]

After leaving Brooke that afternoon, Wingate reported at 10 Downing Street. In his history Churchill has described how he made the young brigadier dine with him, still wearing the clothes in which he had flown home from the front, how he had felt himself " in the presence of a man of the highest quality," and how, after deciding to take him with him to America, he had given orders, with impulsive and characteristic generosity, for Wingate's wife—still unaware of her husband's arrival—to be roused from her bed in Scotland and brought to Edinburgh to join the special train that was to take him and his entourage to the Clyde.

Meanwhile the C.I.G.S. had been completing his business before travelling overnight to the north.

> " Long talk with Secretary of State on man-power and many appointments. Finally series of talks with Director of Military Operations, Director of Military Intelligence, and Deputy and Vice Chiefs of Imperial General Staff on all sorts of pending matters. Then dined at 7 p.m. and proceeded at 8.20 p.m. to catch train for the north to embark in *Queen Mary* for Canada. . . . On arrival at Addison Road station to my astonishment I was informed that Winston was taking Wingate and his wife with him to Canada."

An A.T.S. captain, who was travelling with the Combined Operations Staff to Quebec, remembered seeing Brooke for the first time that evening. She had been intrigued by the fact that her chief, Mountbatten, who ordinarily stood in awe of no

[1] *Notes on My Life*, IX, 751.

man but the King, before going to a Chiefs of Staff meeting would say, ' It's no good putting that paper up—the C.I.G.S. will never accept it,' or ' It's all right, I've got the C.I.G.S.'s backing so the Chiefs of Staff are bound to approve.' " Mountbatten," she wrote, " would if necessary fight the Admiralty and the First Sea Lord to the last ditch but not the C.I.G.S. . . . So that evening as we gathered in the gloom of Addison Road station I made a special point of watching for the C.I.G.S. I saw him arrive with what looked to me like a steel map-case in his hand and stride rapidly to the waiting train. A brief nod to officers who saluted him and he was gone."[1]

Brooke resumed his diary on the *Queen Mary*, starting, as usual, a new volume for the journey.

" *August 5th, 1943*. *Queen Mary*. Left London last night after dinner from Addison Road station shortly after 9 p.m. In the morning found ourselves on the banks of the Clyde. After breakfast we embarked in one of the old Calais-Dover steamers and were taken to the *Queen Mary*. She had been painted lately and looked much smarter than last time."

" We arrived on board before lunch and P.M.'s train arrived shortly after lunch. Party consists of P.M., Mrs. Churchill, Mary, Averell Harriman and his daughter, all living with P.M. The whole of the C.O.S., Lord Leathers, Lord Moran, Riddell Webster (Quartermaster-General), Wingate . . . with his wife, and all the various Planners, Intelligence, Transportation, etc., Staff."

" We had a Chiefs of Staff meeting after ten, and Winston asked me to dine. Dinner consisted of Winston, Clemmie, Mary, Harriman, his daughter, Leathers and self. After dinner Winston started a game of Rubicon Bezique with Harriman and Leathers, and I slipped off. Dirty windy weather, very overcast, and forecast of weather bad for next thirty-six hours. Fortunately so far *Queen Mary* is not wobbling about much. . . . At dinner this evening the steward was filling tumblers with water before

[1] Communicated by Mrs. M. C. Long.

going round with the champagne. Winston stopped him by saying: ' Stop pouring all that water out, it is too depressing a sight! ' "

" *August 6th.* . . . Started with a C.O.S. meeting at 10.30 at which we discussed how best to tackle the Mediterranean situation with American Chiefs of Staff. Decided to relate the action in this theatre to the requirements in Northern France . . . to admit of an invasion. In my mind it is all so clear and palpable that the policy we must pursue is to complete the elimination of Italy, profit from the situation by occupying as much of Italy as we require to improve bombing facilities of southern Germany, and to force a withdrawal of German forces from Russia, Balkans and France in order to face Italian threat. If we pin Germany in Italy, she cannot find enough force to meet all her commitments."

" I spent rest of day reading F. E. Morgan's plan for cross-Channel operations. A good plan, but too optimistic as to rate of advance to be expected."

" After tea sent for by P.M. to discuss man-power cuts in the Army, and also South-East Asia Command. Got him to agree to Giffard commanding the Land Forces, and Wingate to have the Long-Range Jungle Groups. He also informed me that he now contemplated giving Dickie Mountbatten the Supreme Command of South-East Asia. He will require a very efficient Chief of Staff to pull him through. . . ."

' This was the first that I had heard of Mountbatten's suggested appointment to the Supreme Command of South East Asia. He had never commanded anything more than destroyers. . . . What he lacked in experience he made up in self-confidence. He had boundless energy and drive, but would require a steadying influence in the nature of a very carefully selected Chief of Staff.'

" *August 7th. Queen Mary.* Spent whole morning with C.O.S. discussing the cross-Channel operations, examining the possibility of such an operation, and estimating the reduction of German forces in France necessary to render such an operation possible. After lunch had interview with Wingate to discuss what he could do in Burma. . . .

" At 6.30 p.m. a meeting with Winston when I had a hammer and tongs argument with him on the set-up of Command in South-East Asia. He was upholding the theory that no Army Commander was necessary in Assam; that the Commander of Land Forces of South-East Asia working with Supreme Commander, and also responsible for any operations in Malaya, should be capable of doing both jobs from Delhi! After an hour's bitter arguing I partially convinced him, but may well have to start it all over again to-morrow."

" Dirty weather again to-day."

" *August 8th. Queen Mary.* News from Sicily good. The Etna position is being rapidly turned on the north."

" A difficult C.O.S. at which we discussed the line to take concerning Burma campaign. . . . We got Wingate to come in and discussed what could be done with the Long-Range Penetration Group organisation, and finally arrived at a line of action with which to take on the American Chiefs of Staff and to prove to them that we are in no way neglecting the operations in Burma."

" After lunch P.M. sent for me and I had about an hour with him. In the first place he argued with me as regards organisation of command in South-East Asia and agreed to all he had argued so hard against yesterday. Then he informed me as to his views concerning Sumatra and his wish to localise an offensive in the north of the island, and not to carry it across on to the mainland at Penang. . . ."

' This was, I think, the first day on which Winston began to develop his affection for the northern tip of Sumatra. It became an obsession with him somewhat similar to Trondheim in the early days.'

Events in Europe were now moving rapidly; on the day the *Queen Mary* left the Clyde Montgomery's men entered the Sicilian town of Catania and the Americans captured a key hill point north of Etna, while on the day before the Russians had taken Orel. As a result of the threat to their position in southern Europe and of the failure of their Kursk offensive, the Germans, seeking to release troops for Italy, had now started to withdraw along the whole of their south Russian front towards the Dnieper. A German summer retreat in the east was something new. Yet at the moment that this proof was being afforded of the success of Brooke's Mediterranean strategy, the Americans were proposing to abandon operations in that sea altogether. " Received message from our Staff Mission at Washington," Brooke's diary entry for the 8th concluded,

> " that we are to have a very difficult time of it at this Conference. Americans determined to carry on with pre-parations for re-entry into France and for Burma campaign at expense of elimination of Italy. They do not seem to realise the truth of the motto that, ' A bird in the hand is worth two in the bush.' "
>
> " *August 9th. Queen Mary.* We had our usual C.O.S. meeting at 10.30 to deal with various small points, including the scheme for making aircraft-carriers out of ice. One of Dickie Mountbatten's bright ideas."

This project was based on a substance compounded of ice and wood-pulp called pykrete after its inventor, a scientist on Mountbatten's Combined Operations Staff. Its code name, " Habbakuk," had been chosen by the Prime Minister, from the text,

> ' Behold ye among the heathen, and regard, and wonder marvellously: for I will work a work in your days which ye will not believe, though it be told you.'

A 1000-ton model, 60 feet long, was to be made at Patricia Lake, Jasper, in Canada, and it was expected that a full size Habbakuk, 200 feet long by 300 feet wide and propelled by numerous electric engines, would weigh 2,000,000 tons.[1] It was first mentioned in Brooke's diary in December, 1942, and made a strong appeal to his sense of humour.

> ' It originated, during the small hours of the morning, at Chequers during a week-end between Winston and Dickie.

---

[1] *Whitehill,* 277.

Dickie returned to the C.O.S. meeting on Monday and informed us that we were now going to cut an aircraft-carrier out of an iceberg. I thought he was pulling our leg, but discovered that he was in earnest about this project. Not only in earnest, but most enthusiastic about it. According to him a brilliant idea, and almost ready-made. All that was required was to shape it into a carrier, smooth off a landing-deck, insert engines, hangars, etc. If bombed, it was easy to repair. You just filled the bomb-craters on the deck with water and, on freezing, the surface was restored. I suggested that the propeller shafts would probably generate some heat and work loose, but was told that this was provided for by a refrigerating plant which would counteract any unrequired heat.'

' It was soon found that the iceberg was not so handy, and it was decided instead to build a carrier out of ice. As ordinary ice was found to be too brittle, experiments were carried out to make more suitable ice. Finally an establishment was set up in Canada to build a section of a carrier in ice. Heaven knows how much money went down the sink over this project! '[1]

" During afternoon land loomed up in sight and we gradually approached Halifax. From the bridge, where I joined P.M., Mrs. Churchill, Mary, Pound, Portal and Mountbatten, we had a wonderful view of the harbour and of the pilot carrying out the difficult task of bringing the vast *Queen Mary* into port."

" We were given a very comfortable train with the most wonderful compartments. . . ."

" *August 10th. Quebec.* After a very comfortable night I woke to look out on a country that reminded me most of Scotland. Very attractive rivers and lakes that I should have loved to fish in. We had an interesting journey which I thoroughly enjoyed, with opportunities of looking at a new country. Just before crossing the St. Lawrence River the train stopped, and the P.M. and family were collected by Mackenzie King and taken on by road."

[1] *Notes on My Life*, IX, 757-8.

" We went on by train arriving at Quebec station about 5.30 p.m. There we were met by the Washington Joint Staff Mission and taken up to the Château Frontenac Hotel. . . . We have taken the whole hotel for our Conference. The Americans do not arrive till Friday, which is a pity and means wasting a few days."

"*August 11th. Quebec.* We started the day at 10.30 a.m. with a meeting with Joint Staff Mission to discuss the background to our coming meeting and to gather from them what lies at the back of all the opposition we have been meeting lately. As far as I can gather King is at the back of most of the trouble and with his Pacific outlook is always opposed to most operations in Europe. In addition Marshall still feels injured that we turned down his plans for cross-Channel operations last year."

". . . After lunch we had a meeting with the Canadian Chiefs of Staff to explain to them the general trend of operations. After that I was kept at it till 8 p.m. reading appreciations of the situation carried out by the Americans, and also examining Wingate's proposals for the Burma campaign."

" Pouring rain and strong wind most of the day. Winston left for Hyde Park to spend a few days with Roosevelt."

" *August 12th. Quebec.* We took a day off. Pound, Portal, Riddell-Webster, Mountbatten and self all started at 9 a.m., motored forty miles due north, then on foot for three-quarters of an hour on a bush-trail till we came to a lake. There we took to a motor-launch and crossed the lake to a small fishing-lodge owned by a French Canadian. The country was lovely; pine-tree covered hills leading down to the lake, and wild enough for moose to come down to the lake, whilst bears lived in the woods, and beavers had one of their dwellings on the upper of the two lakes that we fished. The fishing was poor, only small trout and not many of them, but that did not matter or detract from our enjoyment. Everything was provided; rods, lines, flies and a vast lunch. . . . The lakes we went to are, I believe, called St. Vincent and St. Guillaume."

" On the way home I passed a chipmunk within a couple

of yards and was fascinated by it; a most delicious creature. Finally . . . a skunk crossed the road in the beam of the headlights. We got out to look for it, but it was gone."

" By the time we returned to the hotel it was close on 10 p.m. and we had had a good full twelve-hour day away from work. . . ."

' This was the first day on which we noticed signs of failing on the part of Dudley Pound. On the way out he had lost his balance and nearly fallen into a small ravine, only just caught in time by Dickie Mountbatten. On the way back we had great difficulty in getting him back to the car. He seemed completely exhausted.'

. . . .

Meanwhile the Pentagon planners had been carefully preparing the ground. According to their official historian, they had " analysed at length the technique of previous conferences, the debating techniques of the British and even the precise number of planners required to cope on equal terms with the British staffs. . . . They went to Quebec determined to make their ideas prevail by all means at their disposal."[1] In this they were aided by their country's growing strength and martial achievements. Though Britain was still deploying much larger forces in the European and Mediterranean theatres, the Americans were in a far stronger position than at the beginning of the year. Their production of war materials was by now prodigious; in June their shipbuilding programme, far exceeding the total German sinkings, reached its peak. Their Navy and Marines had wrested the initiative from the enemy in the Pacific, while their Army's set-back at Kasserine—and the temporary deflation that had followed—had been gloriously avenged by Patton's exploits in Sicily, which were having the same tonic effect as Montgomery's victories on the British in the previous winter. Patton now spoke of the Seventh Army as " the best group of fighting men in the world." Nor was it only Americans who felt pride in its achievements. One of the

[1] *U.S. War Department Official History, European Theatre of Operations—Cross-Channel Attack*, 90.

British planners on Eisenhower's staff, where Britons and Americans vied in singing one another's praises, commented, as Patton's men swept towards Messina, " He's got the Eighth Army bloody well surrounded! "[1]

" We must go into this argument in the spirit of winning," Marshall told his colleagues.[2] Though he and King were still seeking divergent aims—the one to make sure that the cross-Channel attack was launched at the earliest possible moment, the other to step up the percentage of Allied resources in the Pacific for the coming offensive against Japan—they were at one in their intense dislike of a concentric strategy involving the use of additional resources against the crumbling Axis position in the Mediterranean. When, a few days before the British delegation sailed for America, King had held a naval conference with his Pacific admirals at San Francisco to settle the final details of the attack on the Gilberts in November, his plans met with no opposition from Marshall. For though they ran counter to the principle of Germany first, they made little demand on purely military man-power. The capture of ocean coral islands, unlike that of Mediterranean peninsulas, called for picked assault troops rather than large masses, while the concentration of aircraft-carriers needed for such operations, far from competing with Marshall's chosen project, would make it almost impossible for the British to stage an invasion of Europe anywhere except in the Channel. Apart from King's concentration of nine-tenths of America's landing-craft in the eastern hemisphere, the arch-protagonists of Second Front and Pacific War for the moment were on common ground.

Until now—at least in the eyes of his professional advisers—the chief obstacle to the triumph of American strategic ideas had been the President's readiness to yield to Churchill's diversionist beguilements and sell the pass to the British. And no sooner had he arrived at Quebec with his lieutenants than to their alarm the old tempter set off to spend a couple of days with Roosevelt at Hyde Park. Little more than a year before a similar visit had led to the abandonment of " Sledgehammer" and the adoption of " Torch " and a Mediterranean strategy.

[1] *Butcher*, 332.
[2] *U.S. War Department Official History, European Theatre of Operations—Cross-Channel Attack*, 95.

This time Roosevelt's lieutenants were resolved there should be no betrayal. On the day the Prime Minister reached Quebec, that staunch champion of cross-Channel attack, Secretary Stimson, submitted to his chief a memorandum crystallizing, in the most forceful terms, the conclusions he had reached during his recent visit to England. These, he stressed, had become increasingly clear " through the fog of successive conferences with the British."

" First: We cannot now rationally hope to be able to cross the Channel and come to grips with our German enemy under a British commander. His Prime Minister and his Chief of the Imperial Staff are frankly at variance with such a proposal. The shadows of Passchendaele and Dunquerque still hang too heavily over the imagination of these leaders of his Government. Though they have rendered lip-service to the operation, their hearts are not in it and it will require more independence, more faith, and more vigour than it is reasonable to expect we can find in any British commander. . . ."

" Second: The difference between us is a vital difference of faith. The American staff believes that only by massing the immense vigour and power of the American and British nations under the overwhelming mastery of the air which they already exercise far into the north of France . . . can Germany be really defeated and the war brought to a real victory. On the other side, the British theory (which cropped out again and again in unguarded sentences of the British leaders with whom I have just been talking) is that Germany can be beaten by a series of attritions in northern Italy, in the eastern Mediterranean, in Greece, in the Balkans, in Rumania and other satellite countries. . . . To me, in the light of the post-war problems we shall face, that attitude . . . seems terribly dangerous. We are pledged quite as clearly as Great Britain to the opening of a real Second Front. None of these methods of pinprick warfare can be counted on by us to fool Stalin into the belief that we have kept that pledge."

" Third: I believe, therefore, that the time has come for

you to decide that your Government must assume the responsibility of leadership in this great final movement of the European war which is now confronting us. We cannot afford to confer again and close with a lip-tribute to " Bolero "[1] which we have tried twice and failed to carry out. We cannot afford to begin the most dangerous operation of the war under half-hearted leadership which will invite failure or at least disappointing results. Nearly two years ago the British offered us this command. I think that now it should be accepted—if necessary, insisted on. . . ."

" Finally, I believe that the time has come when we must put our most commanding soldier in charge of this critical operation at this critical time. . . . General Marshall already has a towering eminence of reputation as a tried soldier and as a broad-minded and skilful administrator . . . I believe that he is the man who most surely can now by his character and skill furnish the military leadership which is necessary to bring our two nations together in confident joint action in this great operation."[2]

Armed with this document, the old War Secretary, who was deeply convinced of the need to bring a weakening ally up to scratch, had what he described as a most satisfactory conference with his chief. It was also attended by the U.S. Chiefs of Staff. " The President," he reported, " went the whole hog on the subject of ' Roundhammer.' He was more clear and definite than I have ever seen him since we have been in this war, and he took the policy that the American Staff have been fighting for fully. He was for going no farther into Italy than Rome and then for the purpose of establishing bases. He was for setting up as rapidly as possible a larger force in Great Britain for the purpose of ' Roundhammer ' so that, as soon as possible and before the actual time of landing, we should have more soldiers in Britain dedicated to that purpose than the British. . . . He said he wanted to have an American commander and he thought that would make it easier if we had more

[1] American statesmen never seemed able to distinguish between " Bolero "— the code name for the Anglo-American build-up in Britain preparatory to the invasion—and " Round-up," until now the name of the invasion itself.
[2] *Stimson*, 228-230.

men in the expedition at the beginning. I could see that the military and naval conferees were astonished and delighted at his definiteness."[1]

When the Prime Minister arrived at Hyde Park on the 12th, armed with the usual copious memoranda, his host's mind was made up. Roosevelt's resolve—and, when resolved, no man could be more stubborn—was to concentrate every available soldier in Britain for a cross-Channel attack in 1944 and eschew all further Mediterranean diversions. He had also decided that Marshall, not Brooke, should command the expedition, so reversing the earlier understanding that, in return for Supreme Command in the Mediterranean being entrusted to an American, " Round-up " should be given to a British commander. His guest proved surprisingly amenable. The Prime Minister's mind, always a move or two ahead of the immediate game, was at the moment obsessed with projects for capturing Ægean islands and for seizing the northern tip of Sumatra to cut the Japanese sea-communications between Singapore and Rangoon. He was, therefore, quite willing to exchange British command of the cross-Channel invasion for Supreme Command in the Mediterranean and South-East Asia. He was naturally delighted at the President's new-found wish to build up an overwhelming American force in Britain and Europe. His earlier offer to Brooke seemed irrelevant beside such considerations. Indeed, according to his own account, it was he himself who, " impressed with the very great preponderance of American troops that would be employed after the original landing . . . took the initiative in proposing to the President that an American commander should be appointed for the expedition to France."[2]

---

[1] *Idem*, 230.

[2] " He was gratified at this suggestion, and I dare say his mind had been moving that way." *Churchill*, V, 76. The President told Stimson afterwards that " Churchill had voluntarily come to him and offered to accept Marshall for the Overlord Operation," thus making it unnecessary to move more troops to England in order to force the issue. Churchill, according to Stimson, also told the President that " he had done this in spite of the fact that he had previously promised the position to Brooke and that this would embarrass him somewhat." Stimson, " Diary Notes on Vacation Trip, August 1943," quoted in *Stimson*, 231. In his history Churchill states that he had informed Brooke of his intention to give him the Command *early in 1943*—italicising the words—but, as Brooke's diary shows, he did not mention the matter until June 15th and only formally offered it to him on July 7th, less than a month before they sailed together for Quebec.

While Roosevelt and Churchill were conferring in the August heats above the Hudson river, four hundred miles away at Quebec the Combined Chiefs of Staff were meeting for their conference in the Frontenac Hotel. Here, against a background provided by the scarlet uniforms of the " Mounties " and the view of the St. Lawrence, they debated the triple issues of the invasion of France, the war against Japan, and the existing campaign in the Mediterranean. The American Chiefs of Staff arrived on the afternoon of August 13th and their first discussion with their allies opened next morning. Their mood, though friendly, was even more than usually unyielding. " General Marshall," wrote their chairman, Leahy, " was very positive in his attitude against a Mediterranean commitment. Admiral King was determined not to have a single additional warship, so badly needed in the Pacific, diverted to any extra operations in that area so favoured by our British allies. British insistence on expanding the Italian operations provoked King to very undiplomatic language, to use a mild term."[1]

In one respect, however, the Conference was far less of a head-on collision than the Americans had expected. For, instead of the British being opposed to a cross-Channel attack as in 1943, their only concern now seemed to be, not to prevent or postpone one, but to ensure that it was carried out with sufficient force. They had spent the voyage over discussing with the Prime Minister the conclusions the London planners had reached as to its locale and the means of overcoming its technical difficulties, about both of which they had thought far more deeply than the Americans. Far from trying to discourage a more rapid transatlantic build-up, Brooke and his colleagues welcomed it wholeheartedly and urged that, in order to widen the initial assault, for which the planners had been allowed smaller naval assault-forces even than for Sicily, 25 per cent more landing-craft should be allocated. Only when the Americans declared that their Pacific commitments made this impossible, did the British Chiefs stress the unpalatable conclusion of the COSSAC planners that, in that case, in order to reduce the weight of the inevitable German counter-attack, the enemy mobile reserve in France and the Low Countries must

[1] Leahy, 208.

first be reduced by diversionary operations elsewhere to not more than twelve divisions.

It was over this proviso that dispute arose. King was insistent that the United States was far too deeply committed in the Pacific to be able to deflect assault-craft from it without disaster. When Brooke asked whether, to retain the initiative against Japan, it was necessary to attack simultaneously both in New Guinea and the mandated Japanese islands, King replied that any resources released from one of these theatres would have to be allocated to the other. What was more, he reported that on that very next day an attack was about to be launched on Kiska in the Aleutians to open up a third line of advance across the Pacific. As for the British proposal to use command of the Mediterranean to force the deflection of further German reserves from France to Italy and the Balkans, neither Marshall nor King would hear of it. The latter even revived the old bugbear of a German attack through Spain to trap the Allied forces in that dangerous inland sea and strongly urged that all resources not required for the invasion of France should be immediately transferred to the Pacific to increase the inadequate forces deployed against Japan.[1]

Brooke's diary tells the story of how he and his colleagues wrestled with this inflexible attitude.

> " *August 13th, 1943. Quebec.* . . . Met Dill after breakfast and had to tell him how we stood. Then a rush trying to read correspondence of two days in thirty minutes. Then C.O.S. meeting from 10.30 to 1 p.m. with the Joint Staff Mission from Washington with us. Followed by photograph with Canadian Chiefs of Staff before lunch. After lunch three hours hard reading till 5.30 p.m. when we had a second C.O.S. meeting which lasted till 7.30 p.m. Dinner with Marshall, Arnold and Somervell followed by a reception by Mackenzie King and the Prime Minister of Quebec, which lasted till midnight."
>
> " Now I must get down to preparing my remarks on

[1] " He pointed out that if some 15 per cent of the resources of the Allies were then deployed against Japan, an increase of only 5 per cent would add one-third to our strength in the Pacific while decreasing the forces employed against the Axis in Europe by only 6 per cent." *Whitehill*, 275.

the American papers on European strategy which we received to-day. I am delighted with the papers and feel that at last they are beginning to see some daylight in the problems confronting us. But we still have several difficult points to settle."

' As our Combined C.O.S. Conference was being held on British soil, according to our rule I should have to take the chair for the meeting. This entailed a good deal more work, for not only had one to prepare to deal with all the aspects of the strategic problems and to marshall the arguments in support of our policy, but in addition one had to clear one's mind as regards the best lines on which to steer the Conference. These meetings in any case meant working at hard pressure, first rendering oneself thoroughly familiar with the matter to be discussed, which entailed a great deal of reading, secondly, running our own C.O.S. meeting to ensure we were speaking with one voice, then meetings with our American colleagues, and finally meetings with Winston to keep him acquainted with what we were settling or failing to get agreement on.'

" *August 14th. Quebec.* At 10.30 a.m. we started our first Combined meeting; not a difficult one. Our first task being to settle the Agenda for the Conference, and secondly to run through a general outline of the war as we saw it. Before lunch we finished the European theatre in complete accord. After lunch we went on with the Pacific theatre till 4 p.m., but meanwhile we had received a telegram from Auchinleck giving a full account of the floods west of Calcutta. These floods look like affecting the Burma campaign drastically and put us in a difficult position in view of the pressure put on us by our American friends to carry out a Burma campaign. . . ."

" *August 15th.* The end of a gloomy and unpleasant day. Started with C.O.S. meeting. . . . Then Winston sent for me, asking to see me a quarter of an hour before lunch. He had just returned from being with the President and Harry Hopkins at Hyde Park. Apparently the latter pressed hard for the appointment of Marshall as Supreme Commander for the cross-Channel operations and, as far as I can gather, Winston gave in, in spite of having previously promised me the job. He asked me how I felt about it, and I told him that I could not feel otherwise than disappointed.[1] He then said that Eisenhower would replace Marshall and that Alexander was to replace Eisenhower, whilst Monty would be required at home to take Paget's command."

" The whole C.O.S. lunched with P.M. and then went hurriedly back for our 2.30 p.m. Conference with the American Chiefs of Staff. It was a most painful meeting and we settled nothing. I entirely failed to get Marshall to realize the relation between cross-Channel and Italian operations and the repercussions which the one exercises on the other. It is quite impossible to argue with him as he does not begin to understand a strategic problem. He had not even read the plans worked out by Morgan for the cross-Channel operation and consequently was not even in a position to begin to appreciate its difficulties and requirements. The only real argument he produced was a threat to the effect that, if we pressed our point, the build-up in England would be reduced to that of a small corps and the whole war re-oriented towards Japan. We parted at 5.30 p.m., having sat for three very unpleasant hours."

" I did more office work and then went for a short walk for a breath of fresh air. Dined by myself as I wanted to be with myself. After dinner discussed with Dill till midnight what our best plan of action was. Dill had been for a private talk with Marshall and had found him most unmanageable and irreconcilable. Even threatening to resign if we pressed our point."

' This had indeed been a black day. First my interview with Winston before lunch. I remember it as if it was yesterday as we walked up and down on the terrace outside the drawing-room of the Citadel, looking down on to that

[1] " I informed General Brooke, who had my entire confidence, of this change and of the reasons for it. He bore the great disappointment with soldierly dignity." *Churchill*, V, 76.

wonderful view of the St. Lawrence River and the fateful
scene of Wolfe's battle for the Heights of Quebec. As
Winston spoke all that scenery was swamped by a dark
cloud of despair. I had voluntarily given up the opportunity
of taking over the North African Command before El
Alamein and recommended that Alexander should be
appointed instead. I had done so . . . because I felt at that
time I could probably serve a more useful purpose by
remaining with Winston. But now when the strategy of
the war had been guided to the final stage—the stage when
the real triumph of victory was to be gathered—I felt no
longer necessarily tied to Winston and free to assume this
Supreme Command which he had already promised me
on three separate occasions. It was a crushing blow to hear
from him that he was now handing over this appointment to the Americans, and had in exchange received the
agreement of the President to Mountbatten's appointment
as Supreme Commander for South-East Asia. Not for
one moment did he realize what this meant to me. He
offered no sympathy, no regrets at having had to change his
mind, and dealt with the matter as if it were one of minor
importance. . . .'

" *August 16th.* Just as we had settled down at our
morning C.O.S. meeting to decide our plan of action
for the Combined C.O.S. meeting Winston sent for us.
He wanted to discuss a telegram from Anthony Eden
forwarded on from Sam Hoare.[1] In it he gave an account
of an interview with a general sent by Badoglio to settle
peace-terms with us on the basis of proposed co-operation
of Italian troops with us in assisting in clearing the Germans
out of Italy. The whole matter wants going into carefully
to decide how to make best use of their offer. We had our
conference with Winston in his bed and he read to us the
telegram he was sending to Roosevelt. . . ."

" We then came back (from the Citadel) and had the
difficult task of finding a bridge to span our differences with
the Americans. This took us till 1.30 p.m. At 2.30 p.m.

[1] British Ambassador in Madrid.

we met them in a small session with all secretaries and planners removed. Our talk was pretty frank. I opened by telling them that the root of the matter was that we were not trusting each other. They doubted our real intentions to put our full hearts into the cross-Channel operation next spring, and we had not full confidence that they would not in future insist on our carrying out previous agreements irrespective of changed strategic conditions."

" I then had to go over our whole Mediterranean strategy to prove its objects which they have never fully realised, and finally I had to produce countless arguments to prove the close relation that exists between cross-Channel and Italian operations. In the end I think our arguments did have some effect on Marshall. . . . We finished our Conference about 5.30 p.m., having been three hours at it. . . ."

.   .   .   .

The news about the Italian peace-feelers had arrived at a most dramatic moment. It came just in time to prevent the abandonment, when its first-fruits were waiting to be gathered, of Brooke's Mediterranean strategy. During the day Patton's Seventh Army captured Messina, and in the course of the night the Germans began to stream back across the straits. By the evening of the 17th the Allies were in possession of all Sicily. The conquest of the island had taken only thirty-eight days with a loss to the enemy of nearly a quarter of a million troops, a quarter of them German. The British and Americans had only lost 31,000 men, most of them wounded and therefore able to fight again. It was a brilliant illustration of what the strategic use of sea-power could effect.

On the same day, Tuesday, August 17th, President Roosevelt arrived at Quebec, together with the Foreign Ministers of Great Britain and the United States. During it confirmation of the Italian peace-proffers came from the British Minister in Lisbon where General Castellano had arrived from Rome, ostensibly to welcome home the returning Italian ambassador to Chile, in reality to ask for a secret

and immediate meeting with Allied plenipotentiaries. Nor,
it appeared was he only asking for peace; he was seeking
leave for his country to change sides and join the Allies.
Seven weeks had passed since the Italians had cast out their
pro-German dictator. The political leaders of the United
States and Great Britain had demanded unconditional
surrender, and so weary was Italy of war that even this might
not have deterred its Government from making peace if the
British and Americans had been able to land an army and
expel the Germans. But though at that time the latter were in
no great force in the peninsula and the whole of its long exposed coastline and coastal communications lay open to attack
from the sea, the Allies lacked the assault-craft for a landing
and were unable to follow up their victory. As a result,
though they had started to prepare for an attack in September,
Italy remained at war and allied to Germany. Momentarily
caught off his balance by Mussolini's fall, Hitler was thus able
to take advantage of the breathing-space allowed him to secure
every strategic vantage-point on the mainland.

Yet so alarmed were the Germans by the threat of the Allies'
Mediterranean offensive that they poured into Italy during the
early part of August so many troops and technicians that the
Italians became only the more desperate for peace and eager
for the arrival of their so-called enemies to save them from their
so-called friends. Their rulers' difficulty, closely watched as
they were by their suspicious Teuton masters, was to establish
contact with the Allies—a thing they were unable to do through
the Vatican because the British and American Ministers to
the Holy See had not been provided with a cipher which the
Germans could not break. Hence General Castellano's
mission to Lisbon and the almost desperate appeal to the heads
of the Western Democracies to send troops without delay to
liberate the country.

But though the Supreme Commander in the Mediterranean
was now authorised to open negotiations for simultaneous
surrender and invasion, his troops could not strike for at least
another fortnight. Even then they could only cross the Straits
of Messina and land in the extreme southern toe of the peninsula
—two hundred miles from Naples and more than three hundred

from the capital. The proposed landing in Salerno Bay to capture Naples could not be made until the second week in September. With thirteen German divisions now in the country the Italians were powerless to move. Immediate orders were given for two divisions of Montgomery's Eighth Army to cross the Straits of Messina—" Operation Baytown "—at the beginning of the month and for two American and two British divisions under General Mark Clark to land at Salerno a week later, while other forces were to stand by to seize Corsica and Sardinia. There was talk, too, of dropping an airborne division on Rome with Italian connivance. But until then nothing could be done.

Brooke's diary continues:

" *August 17th. Quebec.* Most of the morning C.O.S. meeting was taken up with preparations to meet the situation created by the most recent peace offers from Badoglio. We prepared a message to Eisenhower instructing him to send a staff officer to Lisbon to meet the Italian general. The matter is a difficult one to handle since, if Badoglio does too much to help us before our arrival in strength, he will be replaced by some Quisling by the Germans. At 2.30 we had our meeting with the Americans and started with a closed session with only Chiefs of Staff attending. To my great relief they accepted our proposals for the European theatre, so that all our arguing has borne fruit and we have obtained quite fair results. We then went on to discuss the Pacific and the Burma campaigns. Quite a good meeting at which I produced Wingate who gave a first-class talk on his ideas and his views on the running of the Burma campaign. Unfortunately the heavy floods west of Calcutta have seriously affected all our plans and schemes.

" At 6 p.m. I went with Dill and Somerville to the Citadel to attend a cocktail party given by the Governor General (Lord Athlone) to celebrate the President's arrival. As soon as I arrived I was roped in by the P.M. to discuss with him, the President and Admiral Leahy the wire to be sent to Eisenhower connected with Badoglio's proposals. The President altered one sentence concerning bombing, otherwise was in full agreement and we sent it off."

" *August 18th*. A fairly easy C.O.S. meeting at which our main difficulty was connected with landing-craft. We then proceeded to the Citadel for lunch with the Athlones; a large lunch to meet the President. After lunch a series of photographs were taken of groups."

" We had to rush back to get on with our afternoon Combined meeting. There we had a considerable discussion on the question of Stilwell and how he was to perform the multitude of duties assigned to him. . . . The meeting, however, remained on friendly terms and went fairly fast."

" We then went to the Heights of Abraham to study Wolfe's attack on the French during the battle of Quebec. In the evening we all went to a large dinner given by Mackenzie King. We finished up with short speeches by him, answered by the President and the P.M. The evening finished with some dull films."

' These continual lunches, dinners and cocktail parties in Quebec were a serious interruption to our work. When occupied with continuous conferences, time is required to collect one's thoughts, read papers and write notes.'

There is an account of the Combined Chiefs of Staff's visit to the Heights of Abraham in Admiral King's *Life*. The battlefield was poorly marked and the guide was unable to answer all the searching questions asked by these formidable visitors. As they " were wandering about the field, trying to locate the salient points, they chanced to meet an old French priest who knew the area thoroughly. He spoke no English, but Brooke's French was fluent, and so for some time the heads of the land, naval and air forces of Great Britain and the United States grouped themselves closely around a country priest in shabby cassock, who instructed them in military history, with the Chief of the Imperial General Staff acting as interpreter."[1]

[1] *Whitehill*, 281.

" *August 19th*. . . . I had a rushed time going through papers from 9 to 10.30 a.m. Then a difficult C.O.S. meeting till 12 noon when we went to the Citadel to see the P.M. to discuss South-East Asia operations. I had another row with him. He is insisting on capturing the tip of Sumatra island irrespective of what our general plan for the war against Japan may be. He refused to accept that any general plan was necessary, recommended a purely opportunist policy. . . . Got nowhere with him and settled nothing. This makes my arguments with the Americans practically impossible."

" Back to the hotel for a rushed lunch followed by a meeting with the Americans at 2 p.m. and followed by another with President and P.M. at 5.30 p.m. We gave them results of our work up to date and got our agreements accepted by them fairly easily."

" Back to hotel in time for dinner with Quartermaster-General to discuss the Burma administration aspect. From dinner straight to Marshall's room for an hour's talk on the Burma and Japan war. Then to my room where Mallaby, Director of Military Operations India, was awaiting me to go on discussing India and its power to conduct operations in Burma and in Sumatra simultaneously. Dill joined us and remained till midnight. I then had to settle down to it and read for an hour to get ready for to-morrow. I feel cooked and unable to face another day of conferences. It is quite impossible to run a Conference such as the present one with the P.M. chasing hares in the background."

' Winston was by now revolving round the northern end of Sumatra as he had done over Trondheim in the past. He had found with a pair of dividers that we could bomb Singapore from this point and he had set his heart on going there. It was not a suitable base for further operations against Malaya, but I could not get any definite reply from him as to what he hoped to accomplish from there. When I drew his attention to the fact that when he put his left foot down he should know where the right foot was going to, he shook his fist in my face, saying, " I do not want any of your long-term projects, they cripple initiative! " I agreed that they did hamper initiative, but told him that I could not look upon knowing where our next step was going as constituting a long-term project. I told him he must know where he was going, to which he replied that he did not want to know.'

There was an interlude of comedy at the end of that afternoon's session, provided by Lord Louis Mountbatten's scientific advisers' scheme for making aircraft-carriers of ice. ' Dickie,' Brooke wrote,

' had come up to me just before our Combined C.O.S. meeting, at which I knew I was going to have difficulties with Marshall, and asked me if he might explain to the Americans at the end of the meeting the progress that had been made with " Habbakuk." I am afraid that I replied, " To hell with Habbakuk! We are about to have the most difficult time with our American friends and shall not have time for your ice-carriers." However, he went on begging that I should remember if there was time.'

' The meeting was as I expected a heated one, and halfway through I suggested to Marshall that we should clear the room of the sixty-odd officers that attended these meetings, and that we should have an " off the record " meeting to try and solve our differences. He agreed, and after further heated arguments in our closed session we ultimately arrived at an agreement and were just breaking up the meeting when Dickie rushed up to remind me of " Habbakuk." '

' I therefore asked Marshall if he and the American Chiefs would allow Dickie to give an account of recent developments in " Habbakuk." He kindly agreed and we all sat down again.'

' Dickie, having now been let loose, gave a signal, whereupon a string of attendants brought in large cubes of ice which were established at the end of the room. Dickie then proceeded to explain that the cube on the left was ordinary pure ice, whilst that on the right contained many ingredients which made it far more resilient, less liable to splinter, and consequently a far more suitable material for the construction of aircraft carriers.

' He then informed us that in order to prove his statements he had brought a revolver with him and intended to fire shots at the cubes to prove their properties. As he now pulled a revolver out of his pocket, we all rose and discreetly moved behind him. He then told us that he would fire at the ordinary block of ice to show how it splintered and warned us to watch the splinters. He proceeded to fire and we were subjected to a hail of ice splinters. " There," said Dickie, " that is just what I had told you; now I shall fire at the block on the right to show you the difference." He fired and there certainly was a difference; the bullet rebounded out of the block and buzzed round our legs like an angry bee. . . .

' It will be remembered that, when our original meeting had become too heated, we had cleared the room of all the attending staff. They were waiting in an adjoining room, and, when the revolver shots were heard, the wag of the party shouted: " Good Heavens, they have started shooting now! " [1]

" *August 20th.* We struggled with the war with Japan till after 1 p.m. in our morning C.O.S. meeting without arriving at any very definite conclusions. . . . At 2.30 p.m. we met the American Chiefs and had a difficult time keeping the conference away from any definite conclusions until such time as we had held a final discussion with the P.M. I then went for a walk which was badly needed, as I was in a foul temper from continuous work and no exercise."

" After dinner Planners came to my room and were joined later by Dill and Portal. With their aid we finally arrived at a suitable document to continue with to-morrow. I proposed first of all to get it through the C.O.S., then to

[1] *Notes on My Life*, IX, 771-2. According to Admiral King's *Life* the bullet nicked the leg of the Admiral's trousers. *Whitehill*, 278. Churchill, in his account, says it narrowly missed Portal and that it was preceded by an attempt by General Arnold, the strong man of the party, to break the block of pykrete with a chopper —an attempt which was not only unsuccessful but wrung a cry of pain from the general. *Churchill*, V, 80-1.

take it to Winston and finally get it approved by our American friends."

"*August 21st.* . . . We started our C.O.S. meeting by considering the paper Portal, Dill and I, aided by Planners, had produced yesterday evening. We altered it slightly and accepted it. We then had to meet Winston at 12 noon to discuss it with him. He was more reasonable, and did accept the fact that an over-all plan for the defeat of Japan was required, but still shouted for the Sumatra operation. . . . However he accepted our paper."

" At 2.30 p.m. we met the Americans and presented the paper to them, suggesting we should withdraw to let them discuss it between themselves. For this they took a full hour, and when we returned we found that they wished to amend those points which would have made the paper entirely unacceptable to Winston. More discussion ensued in getting them to agree to a form which should be acceptable to Winston and to ourselves. This was a relief as it broke the final difficulties of this Conference and practically completed our work."

" We then embarked on a ship provided by the Canadian Government for a trip up the Saguenay River. Our party consisted of some three hundred Americans, Canadians, and British who had been taking part in the Conference. We spent the whole night sailing down the St. Lawrence River and then up the Saguenay River. At dawn we turned round and sailed back. The scenery was quite beautiful and the ship very comfortable. A great rest after the strenuous week we had just finished. . . ."

" *August 23rd.* Last day but one of our Conference— and thank God for it! . . . We have struggled all day with a series of C.O.S., Combined C.O.S., and Plenipotentiary meetings with P.M. and President. As a result we have practically broken the back of all the work and have had our proposals accepted and approved by the almighty."

" I am not really satisfied with the results. We have not really arrived at the best strategy, but I suppose that when working with allies, compromises, with all their evils, become inevitable."

The final decisions of the Combined Chiefs of Staff were approved that afternoon. They gave the invasion of northern France priority for 1944. The target date was fixed for May 1st, and the operation—rechristened " Overlord "—was in general principle to have first call on all American and British ground and air forces. The COSSAC plan prepared in London during the summer was approved and detailed planning was now to proceed with all speed. The landing was to be made on open beaches in western Normandy, where the Cotentin peninsula afforded some slight shelter from Atlantic gales and where an early German counter-attack would be more difficult to mount than east of the Seine. Two artificial harbours were to be built in England and towed in sections to Normandy after the landing, and the port of Cherbourg was to be captured as soon as possible. The enemy's counter-attack was to be delayed by massive air attack on his communications, particularly on the bridges over the Seine and Loire—the rivers on either flanks of the Allied bridgehead within which during the first five weeks after landing it was hoped to build up a force of between thirty and forty divisions. A strong rider was added by Brooke and the Prime Minister for a 25 per cent increase in landing-craft so as to raise the initial assault force from three to five divisions.

Brooke's project for deflecting further German reserves to southern Europe by exploiting to the full the Allied power deployed in the Mediterranean was only adopted in part. Because of the Italian offer to surrender as soon as the Allies landed in Italy, certain concessions were made by the Americans, and it was agreed that Rome as well as Naples should be captured; that Sardinia, Corsica and, if possible, the Dodecanese should be occupied; that air bases for bombing central Europe should be established at Foggia and in the Campagna; and that the Balkan guerillas should be helped with supplies across the Adriatic. The difficulty of carrying all this out, however, lay in the extreme shortage of landing-craft and the continued refusal of the American Naval Department to allocate more. Apart from this the principle governing all operations was that, wherever there was a shortage of resources, they were to be distributed with the primary object of ensuring the success of " Overlord." Those in the Mediterranean were to be carried out with the forces allocated at the " Trident " Conference except so far—an important proviso to which Brooke had obtained American agreement—as these might be varied by decision of the Combined Chiefs of Staff. A proposal was also made, at American instance, for a supplementary landing in southern France to utilise such of the Allied ground forces as were not needed for containing the Germans in Italy and could not be employed in " Overlord." It was hoped that this operation, which was given the name of " Anvil," would help to speed up the liberation of France, but though strongly advocated by the Americans, who saw in it a means both of utilising the French North African Army and of discouraging the Prime Minister from Eastern Mediterranean adventures, it was opposed by the British, who doubted whether it could serve any useful purpose and would have much preferred to use the troops and assault-craft employed on it either for a landing behind the German lines in northern Italy or an operation in aid of the Balkan guerillas beyond the Adriatic.

As for the war against Japan, which was already engaging the overwhelming bulk of the United States' battle and carrier Fleet, eleven-twelfths of its landing-craft and thirteen of its assault divisions, it was agreed that maximum attrition should be applied in 1944 to the enemy's dwindling naval, air and shipping resources, and that operations should be conducted against Wake, the Gilbert, Marshall, Paulu and Caroline Islands and the eastern half of New Guinea. It was also agreed that Britain and the United States should seek to bring about the unconditional surrender of Japan within twelve months of the defeat of Germany. Meanwhile, under the supreme command of Mountbatten, an attempt was to be made to re-open land communications with China and to harass the Japanese in Burma by a limited British and Chinese offensive assisted by a new long-range penetration, supplied by air, by Wingate's " Chindits." Churchill's plan for a landing in northern Sumatra—Operation " Culverin "—found no more acceptance with the Americans than it had done with Brooke and was abandoned, despite the Premier's eloquent plea for it as " the *Torch* of the Indian Ocean," and a " great strategic blow that should be struck in 1944."

With this the C.I.G.S. and his colleagues had to be content. It was not all he had hoped for, but it was a great deal better than he had at one time feared, and it at least ensured that the reserves the Germans had poured into Italy would be kept there and away from the Normandy beaches. Yet so much remained undone that might have broken the German hold on southern Europe that he was left dispirited and disappointed. " The Conference," he wrote on the 24th, " is finished and I am feeling the inevitable flatness and depression which swamps me after a spell of continuous work and of battling against difficulties, differences of opinion, stubbornness, stupidity, pettiness and pig-headedness. When suddenly the whole struggle stops abruptly and all the participants of the Conference disperse in all directions, a feeling of emptiness, depression, loneliness and dissatisfaction over results attacks one and swamps one. After Casablanca, wandering alone in the garden of the Mamounia Hotel in Marrakesh, if it had not been for the birds and the company they provided, I could have almost sobbed with the loneliness. To-night the same feelings overwhelm me, and there are no birds."

. . . .

The rest of Brooke's diary entry for August 24th dealt with the usual daily routine.

" We had an early C.O.S. at 9.45 a.m. followed by a C.O.S. at 10.30 to clear up the few remaining points requiring discussion. During this meeting Doctor Soong came to visit us and asked indiscreet questions which could not be answered, mainly owing to the fact that the Japanese have broken into Doctor Soong's cipher and intercept all his messages."

" At 1 p.m. we joined with the American Chiefs to lunch the Canadian Chiefs of Staff. After lunch we broke up and all went their respective ways. The Americans started back for Washington. Dill accompanied Marshall, and the hotel rapidly emptied. Portal and I are stopping on till Saturday when we fly back. Meanwhile we propose to go fishing for two days. We therefore proceeded to purchase casts, flies, trousers and socks to go fishing with."

" I also had a final interview with Mallaby and Wingate to settle details of the Long-Range Penetration Groups to be raised to fight the Japs."

" Just before dinner Winston requested to talk to me from the Citadel on the scrambler. He was in a . . . highly-strung condition. Notes from a lecture given to C.C.S. had set him off. In it one of Alexander's staff officers had stated that six divisions would not be installed in Naples until about 1st of December. The lateness of this forecast sent him quite mad, and during a twenty minutes' talk I failed to calm him. I must now go to see him at 10 a.m. to discuss this situation further."

" *August 25th. Quebec.* Reading over what I wrote last night I feel that I must have been very liverish. I should like to remove these pages, and should do so if it did not mean having to write them again in a less despondent strain."

" The morning started with a conference with Winston, postponed from 10 a.m. to 11 a.m. He was still in a very peevish and difficult mood about the rate of build-up of our divisions in Italy, and had already prepared a wire to Alex."

" After the conference I rushed back, lunched early, changed into plain clothes, and started off with Portal and a Mr. Campbell for Lac des Neiges to fish for two days. Campbell was there to look after us and we were to go to a camp owned by a Colonel Clarke who was also coming out with the P.M. and family. They were to stop at a lower camp and join us on the lake. After sixty-odd miles of road, mostly through the bush, we arrived at the lake and embarked in motor boats for the camp some two miles up the lake. There we found a delightful camp (log-hut) with sitting-room, dining-room, dormitory, guides, canoes, etc."

" Portal and I started fishing at once. I was getting on very well in an excellent spot when to my horror up turned Winston with Clarke and I had to turn out. . . ."

" However, before dinner I had caught ten lovely trout averaging $1\frac{1}{2}$ lbs."

It was on this occasion that the A.T.S. officer who had noticed the steel map-case in the C.I.G.S.'s hand at Addison Road station discovered what it was. As she saw him leaving the hotel for his fishing trip with it still firmly grasped in his hand, she turned to his Military Assistant, Colonel Boyle, and said, " Good Lord! Does the C.I.G.S. always take his secret maps about with him on these sort of jaunts?" At which Boyle replied: " That is a ' Top Most Secret ' specially-built fishing-rod, suitable for practically any type of fish or fishing which might present itself anywhere in the world. He wouldn't dream of letting anyone else look after it—it's much too precious."[1]

" *August 26th. Lac des Neiges.* Portal and I got up at 6 a.m. Pouring rain and damned cold. We fished practically all day, and finished up with forty trout again averaging about $1\frac{1}{2}$ lbs. and best about 3 lbs. Also was an osprey at close quarters as he sat about fifty yards from me, a Great Northern diver, a spruce partridge and a black duck and a falcon which I thought was a ' duck hawk,' but am not certain."

" The lake is a grand wild spot with virgin woods running down to it on all sides, which they are cutting for pulp-wood. Bears frequent them, and one frightened Louise the cook when she walked out to empty slops behind the camp some time ago."

" *August 27th. Quebec.* Another 6 a.m. rise to find a glorious morning but the lake shrouded in mist. It did not last long, however. Portal and I had tossed the previous evening as to who should go up and who should go down the lake. He won the toss and had a wonderful morning with fifty-five trout whilst I caught nine. However, we changed over at lunch and I followed him in the spots where he had been and caught forty-five. So I finished the day with fifty-four trout over $1\frac{1}{4}$ lb. average, including

[1] *Communicated by Mrs. M. C. Long.* "Brooke," said Andrew Cunningham, "would always travel with a long tubular metal map-case which he would let no one else touch."

several of about 2¼ to 3 lbs. . . . I have never had such lake fishing."

" We left at 7 p.m. and motored to the P.M.'s camp which we reached about 8.30 p.m. and dined with Clemmie, Mary, Anthony Eden, Cadogan, Moran, Martin and Thompson, plus our two hosts, Clarke and Campbell. After dinner we motored on here where we arrived at midnight, and I am feeling dog-tired but very much the better for my two days."

. . . .

" *August 28th. In the air on return from Quebec.* The morning was spent in packing, visiting old Dudley Pound and running round to a book shop to collect a book I had ordered on Canadian birds."

' Little did I realise on saying good-bye to old Dudley Pound that I should never see him again. He was sitting in an armchair with his feet up and looked far from well. It was very shortly after this that he had his first stroke on arrival in Washington. He travelled back as a sick man, was met by an ambulance on arrival in London, and died shortly afterwards. A very gallant man who literally went on working till he dropped. . . . He was a grand colleague to work with, and now that I realise how sick a man he was lately I withdraw any unkind criticism I may have made in my diary concerning his slowness and lack of drive.'

" At 11 a.m. we left the hotel and dropped down to the landing-stage where we embarked in a launch to take us to the Clipper which was lying out in the St. Lawrence just below Quebec Citadel. Our party consisted of Anthony Eden, Portal, Mountbatten, Jacob, Boyle, Barney and three others. At 11.45 a.m. we made a perfect take-off up the river and then swung round over Quebec and on down the St. Lawrence. Lovely scenery most of the way. We lunched shortly after starting and arrived at Botwood for dinner, having to put clock on a couple of hours. After dinner we made a lovely take-off just as the sun was setting and sailed off into the darkness."

" We are now over the eastern edges of Newfoundland and shall soon be heading off into the Atlantic. It is now my third trip over this direction, but it still has the same thrill as the first crossing—a thrill which present generations will never have, as the background of the difficulties of early flights across the Atlantic can never mean the same to them, not having lived through those days."

" *August 29th. In the air returning from Quebec.* A very cold, but calm night. I got up at 9 a.m. British time, about equivalent to 4 a.m. Canadian time, and after a good breakfast hoped to see our land-fall off the coast of Ireland. Unfortunately the whole of Ireland and England were covered by clouds. We flew right over Lough Erne and Belfast, but never saw a thing. We had one glimpse of the Irish Channel, a bit of Wales near Shrewsbury, some of Salisbury Plain, what I think may have been Salisbury Cathedral through a hole in the clouds, and finally reached Poole Harbour when we descended through the clouds and made a perfect landing at 2 p.m. after an eighteen to nineteen hours' journey from Quebec. There we were met by a coach and taken to a special train which reached London about 5 p.m. I came straight on home to you by car, and a great joy and relief to be peacefully home."

" *August 30th.* Went up to the War Office at usual time, and spent a busy time with a series of interviews— Secretary of State, Director of Military Intelligence, Director of Military Operations, Mallaby, Vice Chief of Imperial General Staff, Deputy Chief of Imperial General Staff, and Military Secretary. All of them had to be informed of latest decisions from Quebec, and then I had to hear from them the latest news from the War Office. . . ."

" Soon I shall be back at the usual grinding work, but feel badly in want of a let-up just at present. The Quebec Conference has left me absolutely cooked. Winston made matters almost impossible. . . . He has an unfortunate trick of picking up some isolated operation, and, without ever really having it looked into, setting his heart on it. When he once gets into one of those moods he feels everybody is trying to thwart him and to produce difficulties. He becomes more and more set on the operation, brushing everything aside, and, when Planners prove the operation to be impossible, he then appoints new Planners in the hope that they will prove that the operation is possible...."

" I wonder whether any historian of the future will ever be able to paint Winston in his true colours. It is a wonderful character, the most marvellous qualities and superhuman genius mixed with an astonishing lack of vision at times, and an impetuosity which, if not guided, must inevitably bring him into trouble again and again."

" Perhaps the most remarkable failing of his is that he can never see a whole strategical problem at once. His gaze always settles on some definite part of the canvas and the rest of the picture is lost. It is difficult to make him realise the influence of one theatre against another. The general handling of German reserves in Europe is never fully grasped by him. This failing is accentuated by the fact that often he does not want to see the whole picture, especially if the wider vision should in any way interfere with the operation he may have temporarily set his heart on."

" He is quite the most difficult man to work with that I have ever struck, but I would not have missed the chance of working with him for anything on earth."

. . . .

Only a few days now remained before the invasion of Italy and the surrender that was to precede the landing at Salerno. Events were everywhere moving at speed. In Russia the Germans, to shorten their lines and release troops for Italy and the Balkans, were still withdrawing along the entire southern front; on the 23rd the great city of Kharkov was retaken by the Russians and Taganrog on the 30th. Freed by the sudden weakening of German pressure from the nightmare of another autumn *blitzkrieg* and impressed by the victories of those whom he affected to regard as defaulting allies, Stalin had so far relented towards them as to agree to a three-Power meeting of Foreign Secretaries in Moscow—a move foreshadowing an early Conference between the heads and Service chiefs of the three nations. " Your Majesty will have noticed," Churchill wrote to the King from Quebec, " that I have heard from the Great Bear and that we are on speaking or at least growling terms again."[1] Meanwhile the Portuguese, to everyone's surprise, announced their readiness to grant Great Britain air and naval bases in the Azores against the U-boats—a significant sign of the decline in Axis prestige.

It was Hitler's growing realization of this decline and of the danger of invasion from the south that was causing him to rush troops across the Alps and Balkans into an area where it would be hard to supply them and from which it would be even harder to extricate them. Everything, he believed, depended on his ability to hold the Allies at bay at the farthest possible distance from the German frontiers and keep southern Europe in subjection until his new air weapons were ready. On August 17th a raid on Peenemünde by six hundred of Harris's bombers had thrown back his plans for destroying London and the invasion ports for many months; there was now no possibility of using his rockets and flying-bombs till well into 1944. He dared not yield ground in Italy, the Balkans or even in the islands of the Ægean and Eastern Mediterranean for fear of precipitating a rising of the warlike races of South-East Europe and of exposing his aircraft and war factories in the former Austrian Empire to Allied bombing. At the beginning of August, American Liberators and Flying Fortresses, operating from North Africa, had attacked the Ploesti oilfields in Rumania, and, though only 120 of the 171 that set out reached the target and many failed to return, five out of the seven refineries were hit. Raids on Vienna and other industrial centres in Austria followed, foreshadowing what would happen if the heavy bombers of the U.S.A.A.F. and the R.A.F. were allowed to establish themselves on the Italian airfields. For this reason everywhere except in the extreme toe of Italy, where they were withdrawn for fear of an Allied landing in their rear, the German defenders of southern Europe were ordered to stand fast and disarm their defaulting allies on the least sign of surrender. Other Germans were still being

---

[1] *Churchill*, V, 73.

hurried south, not only into Italy, where by the beginning of September they had eighteen divisions, but into Jugoslavia, Albania, Greece and the East Mediterranean islands to take the place of the suspect Italian garrisons.

By then, as the crowded Allied transports and assault-vessels from Africa and Sicily steamed on the last stage of their journey across the Tyrrhenian Sea, Montgomery's men who had crossed the Straits of Messina on September 3rd, had covered fifty of the two hundred miles of mined and bridge-blown mountain-road that separated them from the Salerno beaches. Here, before dawn on Thursday, September 9th and nine hours after the announcement of the Italian surrender, General Mark Clark's two American and two British divisions began to put ashore in the face of German resistance. Owing to the strength which the Germans had built up in Italy during the wasted weeks of opportunity and the distance at which the land-based fighters covering the landing had to operate, Brooke had doubts whether the expedition could master the odds against it and make good its foothold before the inevitable counter-attack. Yet, though the chance of striking earlier had been lost, there seemed nothing for it now but to be bold. Everything depended on the endurance of the landing-parties, the striking-power of the Allied bombers, and the speed with which Montgomery's two divisions from Calabria could fight their way to their comrades' aid. " We are gambling and taking risks, . . ." Brooke wrote, " but I feel we are justified in doing so."[1]

While Mark Clark's men were struggling ashore on the hill-encircled, fire-ringed beaches south of Naples, a hundred and fifty miles to the east the Royal Navy was carrying out an operation of extreme hazard and daring. It was executed at the orders of Sir Andrew Cunningham, who, finding there were no transports to carry troops to the Italian naval base of Taranto, embarked the British 1st Airborne Division in six cruisers on the evening of September 8th and sent it, under escort of two battleships, through mined and battery-defended channels into the harbour's mouth. For the loss of one cruiser he secured the greatest strategic prize in Italy and a port in

[1] *Diary*, 8th September, 1943.

full working order for future operations in the Adriatic. Beyond, a hundred and twenty miles to the north, lay the airfield of Foggia and the key to the bombing of southern Europe.

Two days later the same staunch and cheerful seaman set the seal on Brooke's 1942-43 Mediterranean strategy. In accordance with the terms of the Armistice, the Italian Fleet put to sea in two divisions on the evening of September 8th in order to avoid capture by the Germans. The Spezia division was intercepted next day off the Sardinian coast by German bombers which sank the flagship *Roma* with one of their new radio-controlled gliding bombs. But the rest of the Italian Navy, including four battleships and eight cruisers, reached the appointed rendezvous at Valetta. Here in the Grand Harbour, on Saturday, September 11th, amid the devastation wrought by three years of bombing, the victor of Matapan received its formal surrender. " Be pleased to inform their Lordships," he signalled the Admiralty, " that the Italian Battle fleet now lies at anchor under the guns of the fortress of Malta."

. . . .

Twenty-one months earlier—on December 3rd, 1942, and two days after taking up his duties as C.I.G.S.—Alan Brooke had written: " I am positive that our policy for the conduct of the war should be to direct both military and political effort towards the early conquest of North Africa. From there we shall be able to stage offensive operations against Italy." Now with all her armed forces that country had been forced to surrender, the Mediterranean and its central islands were in Allied hands, and the British battle fleet had been freed for operations against Japan. In the ten months since Alamein the Germans had lost a million men—in Africa, Russia and Sicily. Already forced to keep a third of their Army and two-thirds of their Air Force to guard Western Europe's three thousand miles of coastline against an attack from the West, they had now been compelled by the Allied victories and the collapse of their principal ally to man in haste a further three thousand miles of coast in the south. Instead, as they had hoped, of throwing a premature Allied assault against

their Western Wall back into the sea and then transferring
their victorious legions to the east to smash Russia, they were
now having to employ, in addition to fifty waiting divisions in
France and the Low Countries, twenty-two more in Italy to
hold back seven British and four American divisions—and a
possible new Allied landing in the north of that country—and
a further twenty-four divisions in the Balkans. In the face of
every obstacle Brooke had achieved his consistently pursued aim
of drawing Germany's reserves into the mountainous peninsulas
of southern Europe, where they could no longer be transferred
at will along her fine east-to-west communications to repel an
attack from the Channel or subject the Russians to a second
Tannenburg. Meanwhile, increasingly relieved from the full
weight of German attack, the Russians after their victory at
Stalingrad had recovered vast areas of their country, ended
the threat to Moscow and the Caucasian oil wells, and advanced
from the Volga to the Dnieper, while the Germans, in order
to shorten their lines to release troops for Italy and the Balkans,
had been prevented from preparing new defences in time to
halt the Red Army's growing momentum.

With Germany short of men in the east, with her reserves
committed to the Mediterranean shores and the wild Apen-
nine and Balkan hills, and with the plans for the liberation
of France in the coming year approved by the Western
Allies' supreme strategic council, the scene was set for the
final stage of the drama. Between the advancing Russians
and the Anglo-American armies, fleets and air forces in Italy
and the Mediterranean lay the insurgent Jugoslavs, Greeks and
Albanians, the war-weary and wavering Rumanian, Bulgarian
and Hungarian satellites and, on their southern flank, the
expectant Turks. And in the west, in the island that Hitler
had failed to destroy in 1940, great offensive projects were
on foot and new forces gathering. The Axis attack had been
defeated, the initiative won and the road to victory built.

MAPS

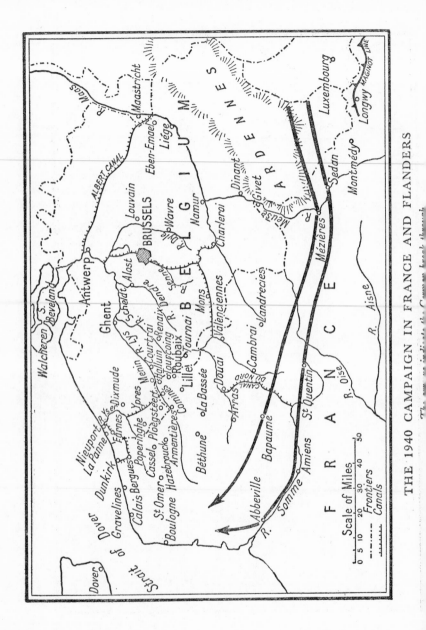

THE 1940 CAMPAIGN IN FRANCE AND FLANDERS

The arrows indicate the German break through

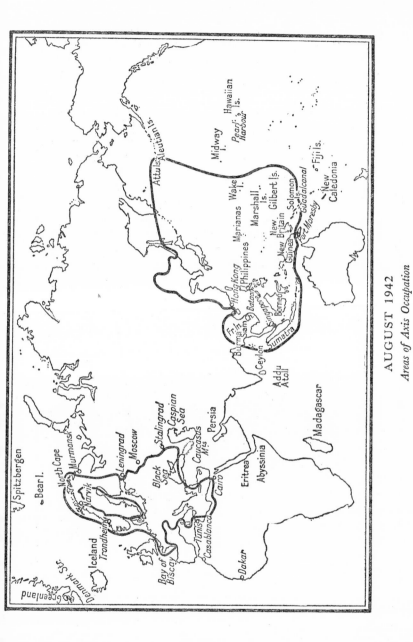

AUGUST 1942

Areas of Axis Occupation

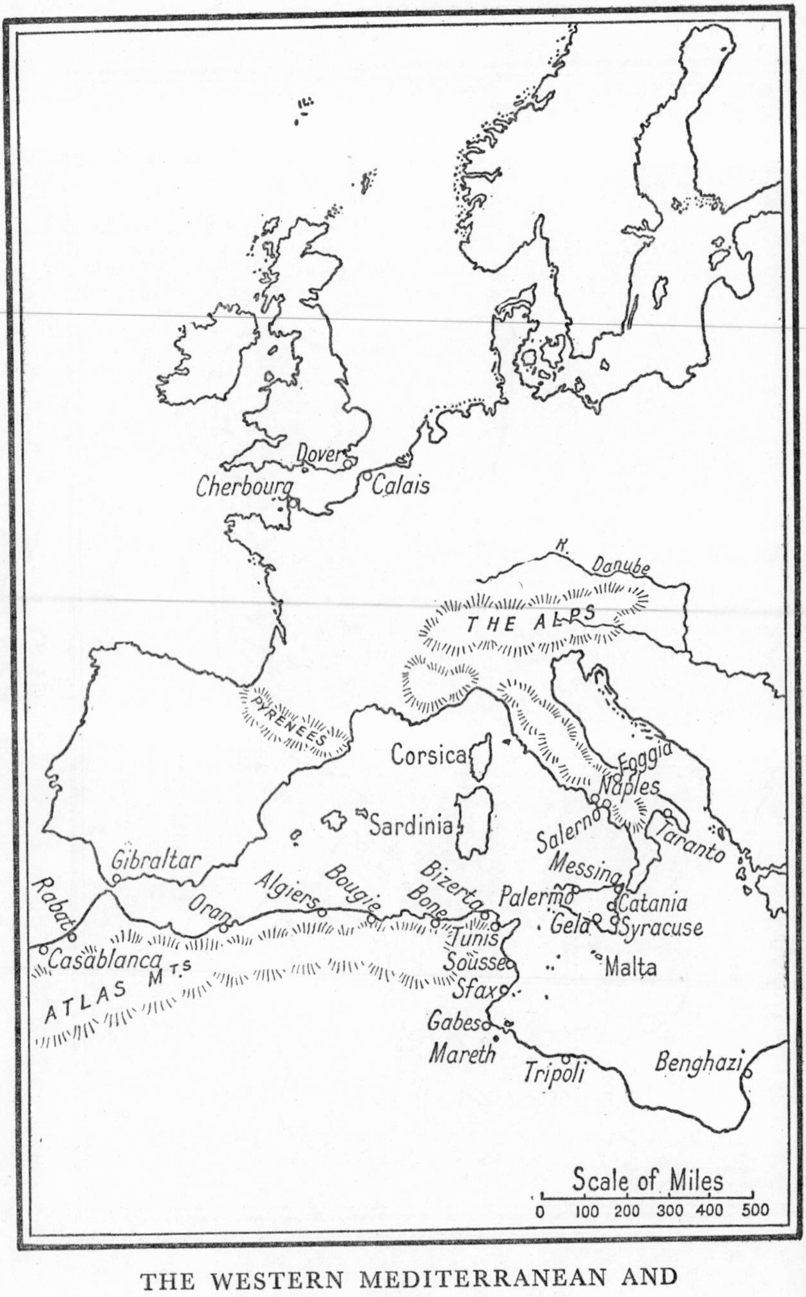

THE WESTERN MEDITERRANEAN AND
EASTERN ATLANTIC AREA

THE EASTERN MEDITERRANEAN AND
RUSSIAN AREA

ACKNOWLEDGMENTS

In ADDITION to the obligations mentioned in the Prelude which I am under to Lieutenant-General Sir Ian Jacob, Field Marshal Viscount Montgomery and Lady Dill for their generous permission to make use of valuable unpublished material, I am indebted to the Countess Wavell for leave to quote the delightful verses written by her husband, the late Field Marshal Earl Wavell, on the floor of the Liberator after his and Lord Alanbrooke's visit to Moscow in August 1942. Others who have kindly allowed me to quote from letters or statements given in interviews or personal conversations about Lord Alanbrooke's war services are General of the Army George Marshall, Admiral of the Fleet Lord Cunningham of Hyndhope, Marshal of the Royal Air Force Lord Portal of Hungerford, Field Marshal Lord Montgomery, Admiral of the Fleet Earl Mountbatten of Burma, General Sir Bernard Paget, General Sir Harold Franklyn, General Sir Miles Dempsey, Lieutenant-General Sir Archibald Nye, Lieutenant-General Lord Weeks, the Rt. Hon. Sir James Grigg—who, as Permanent Under-Secretary of State at the War Office and later Secretary of State for War, was respectively the Field Marshal's colleague and official chief for the greater part of the War—and Colonel R. Stanyforth, who was his Military Assistant. Major Nigel Aitken has also kindly given me and Lord Alanbrooke leave to quote from personal letters written to him by the latter.

Of more personal services I must acknowledge first and foremost the assistance of Mrs. M. C. Long. Appointed six years ago by the Royal Regiment of Artillery to collect and prepare material for the official Life of Lord Alanbrooke which I had been invited by the Regiment to write in the event of my outliving him, during the first three years of her task she worked single-handed, amassing and arranging a

735

vast mass of information drawn from many sources, both written and verbal, about the Field Marshal's life and work. Much of this material, collected for the purposes of the biography, is outside the scope of this volume and much, too, cannot yet be used, but to her and to the Colonel Commandant and officers of the Royal Regiment of Artillery, as well as, and above all, to Lord Alanbrooke himself, I owe a great debt for the foundations they helped to lay. Mrs. Long, as a wartime member of the Staff of Combined Operations, attended most of the inter-Allied Conferences, and her experience and many wartime contacts have much facilitated her task and mine.

Other friends who have read and criticised the whole or part of my manuscript and helped me to correct its errors and omissions are Mr. Milton Waldman—at once the most severe and constructive of critics—General Sir Bernard Paget, who with his habitual generosity read the book at each successive stage of its repeated rewritings, Lieutenant-General Sir Ian Jacob, The Rt. Hon. Sir James Grigg, General Sir Richard O'Connor, General Sir William Morgan, Major-General Viscount Bridgeman, Mr. C. D. Hamilton, Mr. Bernard Knowles, Mrs. Astley—who, as Miss Joan Bright, was General Lord Ismay's secretary during the war years—my publisher, Mr. W. A. R. Collins, and Mr. Mark Bonham Carter, Mr. Adrian House, Mr. Ronald Politzer and Miss Patsy Cohen of the House of Collins. I should like also to record my debt to the late General Sir Otto Lund, former Colonel Commandant of the Royal Regiment of Artillery, but for whose inspiration this book would never have been written and whose sudden death deprived me, like so many others, of that selfless wisdom which he placed at the service of all his friends, and to Mr. H. V. Hodson, whose advice I sought when my undertaking this task was first mooted. I should like, too, to acknowledge the courtesy and kindness of the War Office Librarian and his staff. Above all, I am indebted to my secretary, Miss Elizabeth Black, to my wife and to Miss Violet Thayre for the typing and constant re-typing which the preparation of this book has entailed.

I would like to thank Miss D. E. Collins and the publishers for the lines " I tell you naught for your comfort . . ." from *The Ballad of the White Horse* by G. K. Chesterton (Methuen). I am also grateful to the authors and publishers for permission to quote important extracts from the following works:

The Second World War by Sir Winston Churchill, Cassell, and Houghton Mifflin; *Crusade in Europe* by D. Eisenhower, Wm. Heinemann and Doubleday & Co.; *On Active Service in Peace and War* by Henry Stimson and George Bundy, Hutchinson, and Harper & Bros.; *The War in France and Flanders* 1939-40 by Major L. F. Ellis, Her Majesty's Stationery Office; *U.S. Army in World War II, European Theatre of Operations* and *Cross Channel Attack*, State Department, Washington; *Goebbels's Diaries*, Hamish Hamilton, and Doubleday & Co.

A list of abbreviated titles of books used in the footnotes is appended.

ARTHUR BRYANT

LIST OF ABBREVIATIONS USED IN
FOOTNOTES

ARMY QUARTERLY.—*Army Quarterly.*

ARNOLD.—H. H. Arnold, *Global Mission*, 1951.

BLACKWOOD'S.—*Blackwood's Magazine.*

BOMBER OFFENSIVE.—Sir Arthur Harris, *Bomber Offensive*, 1947.

BRITISH WAR PRODUCTION.—M. M. Postan *British War Production* (H.M.S.O.), Official History of the Second World War, 1952.

BULLOCK.—A. Bullock, *Hitler*, 1952.

BUTCHER.—H. C. Butcher, *Three Years with Eisenhower*, 1946.

CHURCHILL.—W. S. Churchill, *The Second World War*, Vols. I to V, 1948-52.

CIANO.—*The Ciano Diaries* (ed. H. Gibson), 1946.

CROSS-CHANNEL ATTACK.—*United States Army in World War II: European Theater of Operations—Cross-Channel Attack*, U.S. Official War History.

DIARY.—Field Marshal Lord Alanbrooke, *MS. Diaries, 1939-45.*

EISENHOWER.—D. Eisenhower, *Crusade in Europe*, 1948.

EL ALAMEIN TO THE SANGRO.—Field Marshal Montgomery, *El Alamein to the River Sangro*, 1946.

GOEBBELS.—*The Goebbels Diaries* (ed. L. P. Lochner), 1948.

GUDERIAN.—H. Guderian, *Panzer Leader*, 1952.

HINSLEY.—F. H. Hinsley, *Hitler's Strategy*, 1951.

JACOB.—Lt.-Gen. Sir Ian Jacob, *MS. Diaries.*

LEAHY.—Fleet Admiral W. D. Leahy, *I Was There*, 1950.

LYET.—P. Lyet, *La Bataille de France*, 1947.

MERCHANT SHIPPING.—C. B. A. Behrens, *Merchant Shipping and the Demands of War* (H.M.S.O.) Official History of the Second World War, 1955.

NEMESIS OF POWER.—John Wheeler-Bennett, *The Nemesis of Power*, 1953.

NOTES ON MY LIFE.—Field Marshal Lord Alanbrooke, *MS. Autobiographical Notes.*

NUREMBERG DOCUMENTS.—*The Trial of Major War Criminals before the International Military Tribunal.*

PERSONAL FILES.—Field Marshal Lord Alanbrooke, *MS. Files of Personal Correspondence.*

PRELUDE TO DUNKIRK.—E. Spears, *Prelude to Dunkirk*, 1954.

ROMMEL PAPERS.—*The Rommel Papers* (ed. B. H. Liddell Hart), 1953.

ROYAL AIR FORCE, 1939-45.—D. Richards and H. St. G. Saunders, *Royal Air Force, 1939-45.* (H.M.S.O.) 1954.

SAILOR'S ODYSSEY.—Lord Cunningham of Hyndhope, *A Sailor's Odyssey*, 1951.

SHULMAN.—M. Shulman, *Defeat in the West*, 1947.

SLESSOR.—J. Slessor, *The Central Blue*, 1956.

STETTINIUS.—E. R. Stettinius, *Lend-Lease*, 1944.

STIMSON.—H. L. Stimson and McG.Bundy, *On Active Service in War and Peace.*

STRATEGIC PLANNING FOR COALITION WARFARE.—*United States Army in World War II: Strategic Planning for Coalition Warfare.* War Department Official History, 1953.

STRUGGLE FOR EUROPE.—Chester Wilmot, *Struggle for Europe*, 1952.

WAR AT SEA.—S. W. Roskill, *The War at Sea*, 1939-45. (H.M.S.O.) Vol. I (Official History of the Second World War), 1954.

WAR IN FRANCE AND FLANDERS.—L. F. Ellis, *The War in France and Flanders, 1939-1940.* (H.M.S.O.) (Official History of the Second World War,) 1953.

WEEKS.—R. Weeks, *Organisation and Equipment for World War II*, 1950.

WEYGAND.—M. and J. Weygand, *The Role of General Weygand*, 1948.

WHITEHILL.—E. J. King and W. M. Whitehill, *Fleet Admiral King*, 1953.

WHITE HOUSE PAPERS.—Robert E. Sherwood, *The White House Papers of Harry L. Hopkins*, 1949.

INDEX

INDEX